ĀGAMA AURA TRIPIṬAKA
(A Comparative Study of Lord Mahāvīra and Lord Buddha)

Also available

Agama and Tripiṭaka : A Comparative Study of Lord Mahāvīra and Lord Buddha Vol. II : Language and Literature

Agama and Tripiṭaka : A Comparative Study of Lord Mahāvīra and Lord Buddha Vol. III : (in Press)

आगम और त्रिपिटकः एक अनुशीलन

खण्ड : १ इतिहास और परम्परा

खण्ड : २ भाषा और साहित्य *(In Press)*

खण्ड : ३ तत्व, आचार व कथानुयोग

ĀGAMA AURA TRIPIṬAKA

A Comparative Study of Lord Mahāvīra and Lord Buddha

Volume 1

History and Tradition

By

Rashtrasant Muni Shri Nagrajji

D. Litt.

A Review by

Dr. Pt. Sukhalalji

English Version by

Muni Shri Mahendra Kumarji

and

K.C. Lalvani

Edited by

Bhupendra Swarup Jain

and

Raghunath Sarma

CONCEPT PUBLISHING COMPANY, NEW DELHI-110059

Cataloging in Publication Data—DK
Courtesy: D.K. Agencies (P) Ltd. <docinfo@dkagencies.com>

Nagraj, *Muni,* 1917-
[Āgama aura Tripiṭaka : eka anuśīlana. English]
Āgama aura Tripitaka : a comparative study of Lord Mahāvīra and Lord Buddha Acharya / Nagraj ; a review by Pt. Sukhalalji ; English version by Mahendra Kumarji and K.C. Lalvani ; edited by Bhupendra Swarup Jain and Raghunath Sarma.
v. cm.
Translated from Hindi.
Critical study of the Jaina and the Buddhist canonical literature.
Includes bibliographical references.
Includes indexes.
Contents: v. 1. History and tradition — v. 2. Language and literature
ISBN 8170227305 (set)

1. Āgamas.—Criticism, interpretation, etc. 2. Tipi-taka.—Criticism, interpretation,etc. I. Mahendra Kumar, Muni, 1937- II. Lalvani, K. C. (Kastur Chand), 1921- III. Jain, Bhupendra Swarup. IV. Sarma, Raghunath. V. Title.

DDC 181.043 82 21

ISBN : 81-8069-140-3 (Vol. I)
ISBN : 81-7022-730-5 (Set)

First Published 2005

Published and Printed by
Ashok Kumar Mittal
Concept Publishing Company
A/15-16, Commercial Block, Mohan Garden
New Delhi-110059 (India)

Phones: 25351460, 25351794
Fax : 091-11-25357103
Email: publishing@conceptpub.com

PREFACE

I have never favoured a language on the basis of a region or a state. Rather, on account of its all-pervasiveness, I had always been a protege of the English language. Though English is not the only language of the world, yet it is the most prominent one. When I term it as most prominent, I mean that it has more readers as compared to all the other languages.

Late Dr. S. Radhakrishnan once said to me, "You people write books in Hindi alone without calculating as to how many people in the world can read and write Hindi. Non-Hindi-speaking states outnumber the Hindi-speaking ones". He further remarked, "I am not the only scholar of Indian philosophy in the country. But I am more popular in the world than any other Indian scholar because all my works have been in English only."

It gives me great pleasure to note that the English edition of my work '*Āgama aura Tripiṭaka,* Vol. I' is with its learned readers. Though its Hindi edition was published long ago, I am confident that in the realms of English language it is bound to evince same degree of novelty and freshness as it once did in the field of English language.

A long chain of events have intervened between the translation and publication of this work which can be summed up as follows. Some of the chapters of the work were translated into English by Muni Mahendra Kumarjī (II). These chapters were about to be published as separate books. Late Upādhaya Muni Mahendra Kumarjī (I) of Calcutta got rest of the chapters translated into English by Prof. K.C. Lālvānī. Thus, both Muni Mahendra Kumāra Jī (I) and (II) are associated with the work from the editing of the Hindi edition to the translation of the English edition.

During the Delhi Caturmāsya of Ācārya Tulasī, task of publication of the book began with the consent of Ācārya Jī under the over all guidance of Muni Mahendra Kumārjī (II) through Śrī Rajendra Kumāra, Director of the 'Today and Tomorrow's Publications. As far as editing and making improvements is concerned Muni Mahendra Kumāra Jī (II) shouldered all the responsibility then. When the project was almost near its completion the events took a fateful turn. A situation of separation came in. The apple-cart was upset. The publication came to a standstill. The situation forced me a separation from my work. At about this time some chapters translated and duly corrected were misplaced and lost.

I have absolutely no doubt about the personal interest in the project of the publisher Śrī Rajendra Kumāra Jain, but he is too busy with the current scientific publications, therefore it was necessary to find someone who could inspire him in completing a oriental, religious and technical book (with diacritical marks).

We found such direction from Dr. B.S. Jain of University of Delhi. By nature Dr. Jain is a man of sobre personality and he generously offered to undertake all the responsibilities relating to the project. The English manuscript like the prodigal son of the Testament was lost or almost dead but brought back to light and life by Dr. Jain. One fine morning he came all the way from Delhi to meet me at my Calcutta Camp along with the manuscript for putting a life into the project, and since then he has become an important link in the chain of events leading to the publication of the work. He has been very successfully removing all the obstacles and has all along been an instrument of putting the publisher Śrī Rajendra Kumāra Jain back to the saddle. In a nutshell the major portion of the credit of the publication of this English edition goes to Dr. Jain.

In this project Dr. Jain received great help from his esteemed colleague Dr. Raghu Nātha Sarma—a scholar of Sanskrit and English language in Delhi University. Dr. Sarma, inspite of his very heavy schedule, took pains to go through the English manuscript, made numerous valuable suggestions and improvements and also put diacritical markings in most of the chapters. Dr. Sarma had long sittings with Dr. Jain and discussed various aspects of the work. The completion of this work has been possible only because of the selfless services of Dr. Jain and Dr. Sarma.

There was a big question mark whether, in the changed situation, to give or not to give the name of Muni Mahendra Kumāra Jī (II) as translator. However, for the sake of personal differences distorting of literary and historic realities or even detracting from their importance sounds shallow. It was, therefore, thought proper to suitably associate his name in the present venture. How Muni Mahendra Kumāra Jī (II) or other responsible personalities react, is a matter for their personal judgement.

In conclusion, I highly appreciate the interest shown both by the publisher as well as editors, and I am confident that like the Hindi edition this English edition will also interest and attract the scholars here in India as well as abroad. To my mind this will be greatly rewarding to researchers working in the realms of Bhagavān Mahāvīra and Buddha.

May 6, 1985

MUNI SHRI NAGRAJJI
Vira-Nagara, Jain Colony,
Delhi (India)

A REVIEW

I have been much impressed on hearing the text of Āgama aura Tripiṭaka : Eka Anuśīlana written by Muni Śrī Nagrājajī. The pain undertaken by Muni Śrī in looking into and utilizing some of the texts of the Tripiṭakas in the present volume is indeed laborious and unprecedented. This makes his work important and useful. I have told Muni Śrī that many topics discussed in this book may be good enough for independent papers. I think, even earlier, some writers have proceeded in this direction and produced valuable results. Muni Śrī's plan is to produce three volumes on the topic is in itself a first of its kind. The text was read to me for about three weeks. During this period, there was also a threadbare discussion on interconnected topics with Muni Nagrājajī and Muni Mahendrakumārajī (Dvitīya). I was delighted at the depth of the study by Muni Śrī and the profundity of his thinking on the subject. Having heard the volume entitled 'History and Tradition', whatever considerations came upper-most in my mind and whatever ideas took shape in me are, in brief, as follows :

Between the two streams of the Indian culture, *viz.*, Brāhmaṇa and Śramaṇa, a casual observer will discover differences in many respects. Whereas the Brāhmaṇa cult lays emphasis on sacrifices leading to animal slaughter, on the purification of diction, purification of the enchanted words (*mantras*), these items are just secondary in the Śramaṇa cult. But in contrast, between the two streams of Śramaṇa cult, *viz.*, Jaina and Bauddha, there is much common ground in these matters. Both have questioned the divine origin of the Vedas and denied recognition to the erstwhile caste system. Herein, the major emphasis is on restraint, meditation, etc. Even the lay followers in these two have been required to turn their gaze mainly to restraint. There are many other items which are common in the two.

Mahāvīra (Nigaṇṭha Nātaputta) and Gautama Buddha apart, other leaders in the Śramaṇa cult who have been noticed in the text are Pūraṇa Kāśyapa, Ajita Keśakambala, Sañjaya Velaṭṭhiputta, Makkhalī Gośālaka and Prakuddha Kaccāyana. In the Buddhist Tripiṭakas written in Pāli, one comes across more details about these leaders and their teachings. But unfortunately, besides Mahāvīra and Buddha we do not find other leaders' organisation or literature. The information that we get in the Buddhist literature about Nigaṇṭha Nātaputta and his disciples leaves no room for doubt about Mahāvīra being recognised a Tīrthaṅkara of that age and about his organisation being fairly vast and active.

In the Buddhist texts, the number of such references is 51[1] distributed as follows : main Tripiṭakas having 32, Majjhima Nikāya 10, Dīgha Nikāya 4, Aṅguttara Nikāya and Saṁyukta Nikāya 7 each, Sutta Nipāta 2 and Vinaya Piṭaka 2. These refer to discussions between the Buddha and the Nirgrantha monks and various contemporary events of the period.

Certain portions of the work discuss topics relating to conduct, wherein the fourfold restraints of the Nirgranthas have been brought to lighted. The fourfold restraints have been stated as desisting from killing, from falsehood from theft and from sex-behaviour,[2] and elsewhere they have been stated to be desisting from unboiled water and sins.[3] In a context discussion turns to restraint in speech—the point at issue being whether the Buddha could or could not utter words which were unpalatable to others.[4] In another context on meat eating, this as prescribed by the Nirgranthas, has been decried.[5] Another instance discusses the behaviour and garments of a monk.[6] Still another rejects as unworthy of a monk the display of his occult powers, which further throws light on the conduct of the monk.[7] The discussion on *uposatha* in the context of the conduct and thinking of the lay followers is another important item.[8]

Some topics throw light on the fundamentals. The penances by the monks,[9] and *karma* theory[10] have come in for discussion at a number of places wherein the notion of uprooting of the *karma* or the end of misery as a consequence of penance been reviewed. There is a dialogue between the Buddha on the one hand and a Nirgrantha monk Dīrgha Tapasvī and householder Upālī, on the other, on restraint of mind, speech and body.[11] The conclusion regarding the eradication of *karma* through penance justly corroborates with the Jaina terminology. Even the words *'daṇḍa'* and *'vedanīya karma'* are widely used in the Jaina texts. *Āśrava*[12] *Abhijāti (Keśyā),*[13] limit and non-limit of the *Loka*[14] *avitarkavicāra-samādhi (dhyāna-*contemplation),[15] *Kriyāvāda-Akriyāvāda,*[16] offer to a right and wrong person,[17] etc. are to be found in their texts which justifies the views on the fundamentals of the Jainas. A distinct reference and review of the Jaina view of omniscience has to be come accross at many places.[18] There are some paragraphs on the 'personality of Nirgrantha Nātaputta' wherein he has been depicted to be inferior to the Buddha.[19]

At some places, there is a discussion about Mahāvīra's order of monks and of his followers. It appears from one description that at the time when there occured a famine in Nālandā, Mahāvīra and his monks were staying at that place.[20] Given at several places is the description about the schism or rift in the order of monks shortly after Mahāvīra's entered into liberation.[21] Even effort has been made to impress that compared to the followers of Mahāvīra those of the Buddha were much more loyal, devoted to their spiritual master.[22]

In this manner, in the Buddhist Tripiṭakas, there exists a huge material on the Jaina practices, fundamentals, personality of Mahāvīra, his church, etc., which is of great value not only to the historians but also to the researchers.

From the standpoint of historical material, the Jaina Āgamas are as much elaborate as the Buddhist Tripiṭakas about the contemporary political scene and the royal households. The two sources have presented monarchs like Śreṇika Bimbisāra, Ajātaśatru Kūṇika, Caṇḍa Pradyota, Vatsarāja Udayana, Udrāyaṇa of Sindhu Sauvīra and many others in their distinctive way. Some of these were the followers of the Buddha as some others were the followers of Mahāvīra, and there were some others who had sympathy and support for both. Muni Śrī Nagrājajī has also thrown light on this.

When both the Jaina and the Bauddha texts have given a general description of the political and social conditions of the time and when the latter have presented a free description about the Nirgrantha monks, it becomes a natural curriosity to enquire if the Jaina texts too contain a comparable account of the Buddha and his followers. The fact that Mahāvīra and Buddha were contemporary makers of history has no scope for debate or dispute and yet it is surprising that the Jaina texts are wholly silent about the Buddha and his followers. There are however a few couplets in the *Sūtra-kṛtāṅga* which may be considered to be an indication or hint of the existence of some such faith. In one of these, the followers of the Buddha have been called *'khaṇajoiṇo* and the same couplet states five *skandhas* as discovered and propounded by them.[23] The following couplet has a mention of four materials *(dhātus)* of the Bauddhas.[24] Elsewhere in the same Jaina text, there are a few more couplets which lend further support to this.[25] While saying so, it must, however, be admitted that so far as the Jaina texts are concerned, at least the portions of these which are considered very old, the Buddhist order finds no mention whatsover, whereas there are copious items and events of the Jaina interest including Mahāvīra and his followers which have been widely recorded in the Buddhist Tripiṭakas,—all directed to the same purpose which is to establish the inferiority of Mahāvīra and his order in order to highlight the superiority of the Buddha and his order. Comparing the texts from the two sources, one cannot but be struck by this wide divergence between these two. One explanation for this may be that Mahāvīra and his followers were much more interested in self and turned inward that they did not bother as to what was going on to others or elsewhere; but this cannot be the whole explanation since at places, even the Jaina texts have taken interest in others, for instance, in Gośālaka, Mahāvīra's opponent, who has been depicted as a villian of the worst type, or in Jamālī, who left the organisation of Mahāvīra, and in innumerble Tāpasa monks who practised spirituality in a wrong way. Why then this complete blackout on the Buddha and his followers.

The only reason for this which may appeal to the intellect may be that Mahāvīra was senior to the Buddha in age. He was initiated earlier, attained the supreme knowledge earlier and was earlier to deliver his first sermon. In fact, he was already established when the Buddha entered into the stage. Buddha being younger, he had yet to win acceptance. Among his rivals, the most important was Mahāvīra; so he and his followers tried again and again to come up by decrying from time to time Mahāvīra.[26] At a later period, even Śaṅkarācārya in his commentary on the Brahma Sūtra has followed the suit. Assuming the Sāṅkhya view as his principal adversary, he has discussed it at length and in trying to demolish it, he has assumed the demolition of the rest.[27] The influence of Mahāvīra was so well secured in Society that he felt no danger to himself or his order from the newly emerging Buddha. So he preferred to overlook him. Gośālaka was a fellow monk who had practised penance with Mahāvīra. Even two years prior to Mahāvīra's omniscience he had announced himself to be a Jina and a Kevalin, knowing and seeing everything. It is further accepted that Gośālaka's following was larger than that of Mahāvīra. It was for this reason that Gośālaka was real adversary and it had become necessary to write at length about this man in the Jaina texts. Taking a full view, it appears convincing that Gośālaka was an obstruction on the way of Mahāvīra's rise; so he had to discuss again and again about this man. Likewise, Mahāvīra was an obstacle to the growth of the Buddhist order and this easily explains why Mahāvīra has figured so often in the Buddhist texts.

It may be necessary to state that Jamālī separated from Mahāvīra's church and this somewhat weakened it. It might have been still weaker. So he has been discussed by Mahāvīra. In contemporary life, even the Tāpasa monks enjoyed a great influence. They used to give much weight to penances, which Mahāvīra rejected. Likewise had the Buddha been elder than Mahāvīra and equal in strength, in that case, Mahāvīra would have to face similar issues as, being junior and less powerful, Buddha did. In another sense, however, Mahāvīra and Buddha were very near to each other, since both were leaders within the fold of Śramaṇa cult. It is but natural that enmity or hostility is at its highest among like-minded sects within the fold of the same cult rather than when they belong to diverse sects among different cults. The total blackout about Gautama Buddha in the Jaina texts only supports the seniority and superior edge of Jainism over Buddhism.

Even some of the passages in the Tripiṭakas quoted at Chapter 17 of the present text clearly indicate that Buddha was junior and Mahāvīra senior. For instance, according to Sutta Nipāta, Bhikṣu Sabhiya is said to be thinking as follows :

"Even Pūraṇa Kāśyapa, Makkhāli Gośāla, Ajita Keśakambala, Prakrudha Kāccāyāyana, Sañjaya Belaṭṭhiputta and Nigganṭha Nātaputta who are worn out, old, aged, who are at the fag end of life whose life is nearing its close, senior, experienced, ever-initiated, master of the Order, master of Gaṇa, head of Gaṇa, widely known, famous, creator of the Tīrtha, respected by many, even such Śramaṇas and Brāhmaṇas have failed to give answer to my questions, and having failed, they expressed anger, malice, displeasure, and asked me in return, to provide the answer. When such is their position, how can Śramaṇa Gautama give reply to these questions? He is younger in age and fresh in initiation. But though young, he is powerful and brilliant. So let me try these questions with him."

Again, as per Dahara Sutta of Saṁyutta Nikāya, king Prasenajit is said to have told the Buddha as follows : "Even Pūraṇa Kāśyapa, till Nigaṇṭṭha Nātaputta cannot speak with authority about right and unprecedented enlightenment; then how can you who are much younger in age and just initiated make a claim like this?"

Likewise, according to Sāmaññjaphala Sutta of Dīgha Nikāya, the ministers of Ajātaśatru described the six spiritual leaders aforesaid to be ever initiated, advanced and aged.

In the same manner, at three places in the Tripiṭakas, Mahāvīra is said to have entered into liberation prior to Buddha. These are additional proofs about Mahāvīra's seniority in age. According to Pāsādika Sutta of Dīgha Nikāya and Samāgama Sutta of Majjhima Nikāya Bhikṣu Cuṇḍa Samaṇuddeśa spent four months of the rainy season at Pāvā and returned and gave the following report to Buddha and Ānanda : "Only recently, Nigaṇṭha Nātaputta has passed away at Pāvā.[28] The Nigaṇṭṭhas are fightings fiercely on the question of succession." According to the Saṅgīri Paryāya Sutta of Dīgha Nikāya, Sāriputta drew the attention of his monks to his monks to this unfortunate episode at Pāvā and advised them to remain united.

When three references in the Tripiṭakas state the prior liberation of Mahāvīra and when neither in the Tripiṭakas nor in the Āgamas, there is any contradictory statement, the aforesaid three references remain undisputed. It may even be possible that these three references are a later interpolation in the Tripiṭaka literature. Everything is indeed possible, but so long as there is no solid basis for the surmise, there is hardly any ground to doubt its authenticity.

In the later Buddhist lateraturе, Aṭṭhakathā and others, there are references to the Nigaṇṭha monks and Nigaṇṭha Nātaputta. Apart from being a sordid endeavour to establish the superiority of Buddha and inferiority of Mahāvīra, this is full of many references which are in bad taste and fictitious description of events. In contrast, in later Jaina literature, Niryukti, Bhāṣya, Cūrṇi, etc., there is no effort whatsover at decrying Buddha. This indicates the difference in the mental plane of the Jaina savants and their Buddhist counterparts. The Jaina savants always and invariably gave a precedence to the true well-being of the self over that of their order.

From the beginning of the Christian era, however, when the age of discussion (controversy) started, even the Jaina savants descended to the same plane where their earlier Buddhist counterparts had been. This receives further support from the posterior ṭīkā (commentary), literature and kathā (story) literature.

Muni Śrī Nagrājajī has highlighted these various aspects as indicated above in this volume. These will be of immense value to the inquisitive as well as the enquirer.

Pt. Sukhalāla Saṅghavī

REFERENCES

1. Vide the present text, Chap. 17.
2. (a) Saṁyuta Nikāya, Nānā Titthiya Sutta. (Reference No. 31).
   (b) Saṁyuta Nikāya, Kula Sutta (R. No. 6).
   (c) Aṅguttara Nikāya Pañcaka Nipāta (R. No. 39).
   (d) Majjhima Nikāya, Upālī Sutta (R. No. 2).
3. Dīgha Nikāya, Sāmañjaphala Sutta (R. No. 22).
4. Majjhima Nikāya, Abhaya Rājakumāra Sutta (R. No. 3).
5. Vinaya Piṭaka, Mahāvagga, Bhaiṣajjya khandhaka (R. No. 1).
6. Sañjuta Nikāya, Jaṭila Sutta (R. No. 33).
7. Vinaya Piṭaka, Cūlavagga, Khuddaka vathukhandhaka (R. No. 18).
8. Aṅguttara Nikāya, Tika Nipāta (R. No. 27).
9. (a) Majjhima Nikāya, Cūla Dukkhakhanda Sutta (R. No. 5).
   (b) Aṅguttara Nikāya, Tika Nipāta (R. No. 10).
   (c) Majjhima Nikāya, Devadaha Sutta (R. No. 4).
   (d) Aṅguttara Nikāya, Catuvak Nipāta (R. No. 12).
   (e) Aṅguttara Nikāya, Catuvakka Nipāta (R. No. 38).
10. (a) Majjhima Nikāya, Devadaha Sutta (R. No. 4).
    (b) Aṅguttara Nikāya, Catukka Nipāta (R. No. 12).
11. Majjhima Nikāya, Upālī Sutta (R. No. 2).
12. Aṅguttara Nikāya, Vappa Sutta (R. No. 12).
13. Aṅguttara Nikāya, Chakka Nipāta (R. No. 28).
14. Aṅguttara Nikāya, Navaka Nipāta (R. No. 11).
15. Saṁjuta Nikāya, Gāmaṇī Saṁyuta (R. No 8).
16. Vinaya Piṭaka, Mahāvagga (R. No. 1).
17. Majjhima Nikāya, Cūla Saccaka Sutta (R. No. 29).
18. (a) Majjhima Nikāya, Sandaka Sutta (R. No. 30).
    (b) Majjhima Nikāya, Cūla Sakuludāyī Sutta (R. No. 13).
    (c) Aṅguttara Nikāya, Tika Nipāta (R. No. 10).
19. (a) Sutta Nipāta, Dhammika Sutta (R. No. 34).
    (b) Dīgha Nikāya, Mahāparinirvāṇa Sutta (R. No. 25).
    (c) Saṁyuta Nikāya, Dahara Sutta (R. No. 24).
    (d) Sutta Nipāta, Sabhiya Sutta (R. No. 23).
20. Saṁyuta Nikāya, Gāmaṇī Saṁyutta (R. No. 7).
21. (a) Majjhima Nikāya, Sāmagāma Sutta (R. No. 14).
    (b) Dīgha Nikāya, Pāsādik Sutta (R. No. 15).
    (c) Dīgha Nikāya, Saṅgītipatyāya Sutta (R. No. 16).
22. Majjhima Nikāya, Mahāsakuludāyi Sutta (R. No. 26).
23. Pañcakhandhe vayaṁtege bālā u khanajoiṇo.
    aṇṇo aṇṇaṇṇo ṇevāhu heuyaṁ ca aheuyaṁ.
    –Sūtrakṛtāṅga, Śrutaskandha 1, Adhyayana 1, Śloka 17

24. Pūḍhavī āyu teu ya tahā vāū ya egao.
cattāri dhauṇo ruvam evamāhaṁsu āvare.
–Sūtrakṛtāṅga, Śrutaskandha 1, Adhyayana 1, Śloka 18
25. Sūtrakṛtāṅga Sūtra, Śrutaskandha 2, Adhyayana 6, Ślokas 26-30. Vide the present text.
26. In the beginning Buddha himself practised the Jaina austerities. But he was not successful. Vide the present text.
27. Sarvavyākhyānādhikaraṇaṃ, 28.
Etena sarve vyākhyātā vyākhyātāḥ, 28/1.4.28.
Ikṣaternā śabdaṁ (1.1.5) ityārabhya pradhānakāraṇavāda sūtrai-reva punaḥ punarāsaṅkhya nirākṛtaḥ.... devalaprabhṛtibhiśca kaiściddharmasūtrakāraiḥ svagrantheśvāśritaḥ tena tatpratiṣedhe eva yatno'tīva kṛto nāṇvādikāraṇavādapratiṣedhe/ te'pi tu brahmakāraṇavādapakṣasya pratipakṣatvātpratiṣeddhvyāḥ/... ataḥ pradhānamalla nibarhaṇanyāyenātidiśati—etena pradhānakāraṇa-vādapratiṣedhanyāyakalāpena sarve'nvādikāraṇavadā api pratiddhatayā vyākhyātā veditavyāḥ/
—Brahmasūtra, Śāṅkara Bhāṣya, Pub. Motilal Banarasidass, 1964, p. 139
28. Pāvā in Jain tradition was to the south of the Gaṅgā near Rājagṛha. But from the study of Tripiṭakas and other historical materials it has been now discarded. The real site of the nirvāṇa of Mahāvīra (Pāvā) was that Pāvā as noticed in the Buddhist literature. It was on the northern side of the Gaṅgā near Kuśīnara.

INTRODUCTION TO THE FIRST HINDI EDITION

Difference and non-difference both are the Dharma (characteristic) of vision or the outlook. Wherever you look for them, you will find them. The Jain and Buddhist traditions abound both in differences and non-differences. Because of the two-sided nature of the vision, we are able to arrive at the Real. The aim and object of the present venture is to attain this Real. It has been my endeavour to keep apart from the prejudice of one or the other in order to arrive at the Real.

Life has been accustomed to think in terms of the alphabet of synthesis and to traverse the path of unity. How then can I write otherwise? The Present work 'Āgama and Tripiṭaka. Eka Anuśīlana is one more link in the chain of my other work Ācārya Bhikṣu aura Mahātmā Gāndhī, Jaina Darśana aura Ādhunika Vijñāna, 'Ahiṁsā-Paryāvekṣaṇa'. To be frank, I had never had a plan to write anything comparative, but it has come in the most natural way. A good thing that emerges automatically is superior to a good thing which is the outcome of concious endeavour.

A literary creation that establishes some fact is not bad, but it cannot be said to be of very high order. There are already many works in different languages on Jaina as well as Buddhist tradition. When we represent them in our own language or order it does not make a new creation. For generations, this work of representation goes on. But in a comparative or analytical research work, there emerges a new outlook, a new outcome. A reader finds in it many things not known to him, never ready by him. The flow of knowledge shoots out in many currents and moves ahead. This has been one of the basic inspirations which has especially taken me in this direction.

From the days when I was engaged in my studies, a notion got established in my heart that it would be really worthwhile, enjoyable and unprecedented to enter upon a comparative study of Mahāvīra and Buddha. Occasionally, to give vent to it, I wrote even short papers. But during the past five or six years I took total leave of everything else and devoted myself wholely to this assignment.

As my structure started coming up, I could perceive, many of my predecessors having tread the same path. Some had gone a bare two steps and some about ten. Their goal was different from that of mine and so was heir way, but at some moments of proximity of contact, our ways have become one. For me, their obscure and scattered footprints have become a guide, a source of inspiration. In this connection, I recall a booklet entitled Mahāvīra and Buddha by Dr. Lauman. Dr. Hermann Jacobi in his learned introduction to his translation of the Ācārāṅga and Uttarādhyayana, etc. has touched on different facets of comparison. Dr. Cerpentier too has made a similar endeavour in his edited version of Uttarādhyayana Sūtra and in several other articles. Dr. Hoernle has touched this in Upāsakadaśāṅga Sūtra, edited and translated by him. Dr. Schubring has, in his masterly work on Jainism, at innumerble places hinted openly at this. In his research work on Ājīvakas Dr. Basham has in his own way thrown light on Mahāvīra, Buddha and Gośālaka and their tradition.

Among the indigenous scholars, Pt. Sukhalālajī has in his articles unfolded many aspects of comparison. Pt. Becaradāsa Dośī in his edition of the Bhagavatī Sūtra and Pt. Dalasukha Mālvaṇiā in his translation of Sthānāṅga-Samavāyāṅga have further unfolded the matter. Similarly Pt. Rāhula Sāṁkṛtyāyana, Dharmānanda Kauśāmbī, Dr. B.C. Law, Dr. Nathamala Tāṇṭiyā, Dr. Jagadīśa Candra Jaina, Dr. Govinda Candra Pāṇḍe, Dr. Gulāba Candra Caudharī, Bharata Siṅgha Upādhyāya and many other have enriched the process of comparison through their learned contributions. Most of them have said that this kind of research is important and useful and should be undertaken independently and in a wholesome manner.

From an acquaintance with these, I had a feeling, as it, I had unknowingly entered into a terrible forest which has no highway no track, no rest house. But soon I realised that the direction in which I was moving had at its end a citadel, and my path, apart from being an untrodden one, was the known and well understood path of many, before me.

I have divided the entire work into three volumes—Volume One : History and Tradition; Volume Two : Literature and Teaching; Volume Three : Philosophy and Ethics. Volume one on History and Tradition is just ready. I intend to write the three volumes before the 2500th Nirvāṇa Anniversary of Bhagavān Mahāvīra.

I have tried to safeguard the diction of this volume from the niceties of a pure literary work on the one hand and of dull philosophy on the other. Historical research is concerned with the establishment of truth. It has its own style which has no scope for ornamentation. Its yardstick is appropriateness of words and clarity of thought.

A research work has of necessity to be precise and terse. But I have been very elaborate. The former type can be used by scholars, especially those who are in that particular field only but my aim has been to reach simultaneously a wide spectrum of lay readers.

Each chapter in this volume is self sufficient and complete so that it may serve as an independent paper. This is why it has been possible for me to use them in research journals, commemoration volumes and Oriental conferences. Chapter Four on Chronology is being printed as separate book.

Compared to earlier chapters, I am afraid, the richness of presentation may have somewhat run down in later chapters. But this is not unnatural in the case of a work which is spread over a wide canvas.

Simultaneous with the completion of this book, there has happened an event which is of great personal value to me. It is this that the whole text has been read to that great savant and doyen of Jainology, Pt. Sukhalālajī. Despite his age and other pre-occupations, I must say, Paṇḍitajī has taken a deep interest and immensely enjoyed hearing the reading. He himself suggested many parallel discussions and crucial points which are of immense value. As a result of these three weeks of intensive reading of the text, thinking over it and taking a closer-view of the whole, I have the greatest pleasure to say that there has emerged a strong support from him about the seniority of Mahāvīra which has taken the form of "A Review" by him printed at the beginning of this volume. This has really tied me in a debt of gratitude to him, particularly when I recollect that he is already 88.

While considering the present text, the keen-sighted scholar, Pt. Becaradāsajī pointed out that '*puttam piyā samārabbha...*' of Sūtrakṛtāṅga[1] appeared to him to be a reference to Buddha's having taken the pork and so it might not be correct to suggest that the Jaina Āgamas made no mention of any event in Buddha's life.[2] His contention has been that for lack of proper understanding, at some age, the word '*puttiṁ*' must have changed into '*puttaṁ*'. In Sanskrit, the word '*potrin*' stand for a pig.[3] In Prākṛta, in second case-ending singular number, the form of the word is '*puttiṁ*'.

To a certain extent, the above contention is supported by the Cūrṇī of Sūtrakṛtāṅga. In elaborating it, the writer of the Cūrṇī states, *śūkaraṁ vā cchāgalaṁ vā* (a pig or a goat);[4] but there is no hint in this of the Buddha's having taken the pork. This Gāthā is illustrated with the example of a bird (*Lāvaka*) which was killed and served in the bowl of a bhikṣu.

In the Padaccheda of the Cūrṇī of the aforesaid Gāthā, the reading of Jinadāsa Gaṇi is '*putraṁ api tāvat samārabhya*'. In his commentary, Śīlaṅkācārya reads it as '*putraṁ pitā samārabhya*'. Some scholars regard the padaccheda of the Cūrṇī as correct. According to them, it is not uncommon if in certain situations, the father slaughters his son. So the word '*putraṁ api*' in the padaccheda of the Cūrṇī. Hence, the meaning of the padaccheda of the Cūrṇī and Ṭīkā in the sense of the slaughter of the son stands. The word father here may be interpreted to include mother also. In modern age, the slaughter of the son by father is very uncommon, ghastly and a crime, but in ancient literature such events are found recorded at many places.

According to Telovāda Jātaka (Bālovāda Jātaka, No. 246),[5] 'Bhikṣu taking Uddiṣṭa meat specially prepared for him is involved in the sin. In giving reply to this statement, Boddhisattva said,

puttadāraṁ'pi ce hantvā deti dānaṁ asaññato,
bhuñjmāno'pi sappaññjona pāpamupalimpati.

Here clearly the wife and the son have been butchered to feed a bhikṣu. This has affinity of thought and expression with the aforesaid Gāthā of Sūtrakṛtāṅga.

According to Culla Pauma Jātaka,[6] in one of his earlier lives, Bodhisattva and his six brothers with their seven wives were crossing through a forest. On the way, they killed one wife per day and gratified their hunger.[7]

We have the following from the Jaina Āgama named Jñātādharmakathāṅga : Trader Dhannā and his sons discussed among themselves the idea of killing one per day in order to feed the rest and save their life. In the end, they gratified their hunger and quenched their thirst by taking the flesh and drinking the blood of their deceased daughter and sister Suṣamā and thereafter passing through a forest, they reached Rājagṛha.[8] In this ghastly act, they were not bothered about taste of the shaff. Their sole motive was to cross through the forest and reach Rājagṛha. Citing the example of this story, Mahāvīra said, 'In the same manner, a monk takes food not to improve the colour, appearance, strength or earthly objects, but only to attain the state of liberation.'[9]

According to the Puttamansasutta of Saṁyutta Nikāya[10] a couple killed their only son, ate his flesh and crossed through a forest. They used this flesh not for pride, intoxication, adoration or decoration, but simply to pass through the forest. In reviewing the story, Buddha said 'O bhikṣus! In the same manner a noble follower does not take food for pride, intoxication, etc. but simply to pass through this world which is a wilderness.'[11]

We have the following couplets in Manusmṛti[12] :

Jīvitātyayamāpanno yo'nnamatti yatastataḥ
ākāśamiva paṅkena na sa pāpena lipyate.
ajirgataḥ sutam hantumupāsarpadbubhukṣitaḥ
na cālipyata pāpena kṣutpratīkāramācaran.

Here we have an account of sage Ajīrgata[13] who killed his son and yet did not incur any sin.

From these accounts cited above from different sources, it should be clear that there must have been an age when the killing of the son by the father under exceptional circumstances been recorded and this had been freely repeated in the Jaina, Buddhist and Vedic traditions to establish or demolish a point. Under the circumstances, '*puttaṁ piyā samārabbha*' appears to be the correct reading. Sūtrakṛtāṅga only cites this to indicate a Buddhist practice. This has been met and demolished in the Gāthās that follows.

The renouned scholar Dr. A.N. Upadhye read the book from cover to cover and I have the pleasure to say that he is in agreement with the dates of my chronology.

In the preparation of this volume, at least 300 books have been directly used. An even larger number of books it has been necessary to consult. I express my deep gratitude to their writers. I have tried to meet the findings of many of them. In doing so, I have always been objective and analytical, and never communal or parachial. I hope, the scholars will take them in that light.

This volume has been edited by Muni Mahendrakumārajī Pratham and Muni Mahendrakumārajī Dvitīya. The amount of labour and erudition they have mobilised and applied in this arduous job is clear from the Index of Jaina and Buddhist Technical terms given in the Appendix. The work of these fellow monks was not restricted to this but has extended from the preparation of the outline of the work till its completion in connection with thinking, consideration, reading, search and other ways.

Indirect help in the preparation of the volume has been received from Muni Mānmalajī of Bīdāsara. He has been available to me in other respects also which are in no way inferior or less necessary than the main object.

The concluding lines of the present volume I am writing seated at the confluence of the ocean and the earth (in Bombay) in the expectation that my work Āgama and Tripiṭaka : A study, may be the meeting point of the Jaina and the Buddhist cultures.

MUNI SHRI NAGRĀJJĪ

REFERENCES

1. Puttaṁ piyā samārabbha āhārejja asamae.
   bhuñjamāṇo ya mehāvī kammuṇā no vilappai.
   –Sūtrakṛtāṅga, Śru. 1, A. 1, U. 2, S. 28
2. Present work.
3. Varāhaḥ śūkaro ghṛṣṭiḥ kolaḥ potrī kiṭiḥ.
   –Amarkoṣa, Part II, Siṅghādivarga, S. 2.
   Varāhaḥ kroḍa-potriṇau.
   –Abhidhāna Cintāmaṇi, Part III, S. 180.
4. Sūtrakṛtāṅga Cūrṇī, Pub. Ṛṣabhadevajī Keśarīmalajī Śve. Saṁsthā, Ratlama, p. 50.
5. Vide the present text.
6. Jātaka No. 193.

7. The first part of this story is similar to that of the well-known Jaina story 'King Jitaśatru and Queen Sukumālā'.
8. For full details see Śrutaskandha 1, A. 18.
9. Dhāṇeṇaṁ satthavāheṇam no vannaheum vā no rūvaheum vā no balaheum vā no Visayaheum vā sumsumāe dāriyāe mansasoṇie āhārie nannatha egāe rāyagihaṁ saṁpāvaṇaṭṭhāyae evāmeva samaṇauso jo amhaṁ nigganthо vā nigganthī vā imassa orāliyasarīrassa vantāsavassa pittāsavassa sukkāsavassa soṇiyāsavassa jāva avassavippajahiyavvassa no vaṇṇaheum vā no ruvaheum vā no balaheum vā no visayahem vā āhāram āhārei nannattha egāe siddhigamaṇa-saṁpāvaṇaṭṭhayāe.

— Nāyadhammakahāo, ed. N.B. Vaidya, p. 214

10. Nidāna Vagga, Nidāna Saṁyutta, 2/12/63.
11. Tam kim maññjatha bhikkhave api nu te devāya vā āhāraṁ āhāreyyuṁ, madāya vā āhāraṁ āhāreyyuṁ, maṇḍanāya vā āhāreyyum vibhūsanāya vā āhāraṁ āhāreyyum ti?
no hetam, ante
nanu te bhikhve yāvadeva kantārassa nittharaṇatthāya āhāraṁ āhāreyyum ti?
evaṁ bhante
evameva khvāhaṁ bhikkhave kabalīkāro āhāro daṭṭhabbo ti vadāmi kabalikāre bhikkhave āhāre pariññjāte pañcakāmaguṇiko rāgo pariññjāto hoti. parijcakamaguṇika rāge pariññjāte jatthi taṁ samyojanaṁ yena saṁyojanena saṁyutte ariyasāvako puna imaṁ lokaṁ āgacheryya.

–Saṁyukta Nikāya Pāli ed. Bhikṣu Jagadīśakassapo, p. 84

12. A 10, S. 104, 105.
13. This story is fully available in the story of Ajīrgata in Bahavṛc Brāhmaṇa.

CONTENTS

1

MAHĀVĪRA AND BUDDHA

One or Two

Bhagavān Mahāvīra and Gautama Buddha were born in about the same time and in the same country.[1] Both of the were *Kṣatriya* princes. Both were married, both had a child each and both discarded their home and hearth, in youth. Accordingly to the Jaina and the Buddhist text, both attained enlightenment after a fairly long penance, and, thereafter, according to the some sources, both of them propounded their respective tenets. The followers of both of them came to be known as *śramaṇa, bhikṣu* and *śrīvaka*. On the occasion of their final liberation (*nirvāṇa)* their followers, in the monarchies of the Mallaki and Licchavi clans, were present. And hence, these are some of the striking very unusual similarities in the lives of Bhagavān Mahāvīra and Gautama Buddha that suddenly make a thinker to ponder. Is it that known by two different names of Mahāvīra and Buddha, it is the only one great personality intended? On account of this reason and the manifold similarities of the Jaina and Buddha traditions the western scholarship misconstrued Buddha and Mahāvīra as one individual.

The field of history was over-shadowed by mist and fog for quite some time. But it has been variously confirmed on account of the multifarious evidences available that known by the two names of Mahāvīra and Buddha, there are two great personalities. Still, the aforesaid similarities are so striking that scholars dwelling upon them, from time to time, repeat the contention that Mahāvīra Buddha are infact, One and not two. In the year 1962, the well known Buddhist scholar from Śrī Laṅkā, Dr. Jayasūrya, had come on the pilgrimage of Rājagṛha. There, while giving an account of the similarities in the life of Mahāvīra and Buddha, 'he thus spoke to the Press correspondents :

> "In my opinion, Bhagavān Mahāvīra and Buddha could hardly be two persons. It is possible that historians in this regard failed to make a thorough investigation."[2]

Certain individuals may continue to harp on the same chord, from time to time, but history is very clear in this regard. This is no longer a subject for fresh investigation, though some people are still in the habit of repeating a past confusion. When I started a comparative study of Jainism and Buddhism, the same illusion flashed to me for a moment; but as I plunged head along and dived deep into the subject, it vanished automatically.

Nirgranṭha Influences on the Penances of the Buddha

Bhagavān Mahāvīra was senior to Gautama Buddha. When Bhagavān Buddha had just started preaching his religion, Mahāvīra had already securely established his mission. From a recorded event in the life of the Buddha, we come to know that he must have been in some way connected with the tradition of Pārśva or even of Mahāvīra at the time when he was undergoing his penances. He thus spoke to his leading disciple Sāriputta, "Sāriputta! Before my enlightenment I used to tonsure hairs from my moustache and beard, practised penances in a standing posture and used to remain nude. I did not observe the popular customs. I used to receive food on my palm. I would not accept the food offered to me on my seat, nor one cooked for me, nor would I accept an invitation for a feast. I did not accept any food from a pregnant woman, or a woman engaged in breast feeding."[3] Well, what Gautama practised were the normal penances of the Jaina monks—some fulfilled by the *Sthāvirkalpis* and some by the *Jinakalpis*. From this account, it is evident that he was initiated in the *śramaṇa* order in the tradition of Pārśva and derived many a Truth therefrom.

In the Jaina canonical and other old texts, we do not especially get the life-story of Gautama Buddha. In a text entitled *Darśanasāra* by one Devasenācārya of the *Digambara* sect (8th century A.D.), there is a mention of Gautama Buddha's Jaina initiation. So runs the account : "A Jaina monk named Pihitāśrava initiated him in the order of Pārśva in a village named Palāśa on the bank of the river Sarayū and the new monk was named Buddhakīrti. After sometime, he began to take fish and meat, and by donning scarlet robes, he began to preach his new religion."[4] A mention like this cannot be said to be a very important historical record in itself, but it may still have some value which one may be prepared to attribute to it.

Paṇḍita Sukhalāl Jī in his *Cāra Tīrthaṅkara* and the Buddhist scholar Dharmānanda Kośāmbī in his *Pārśvanātha kā Caturyām Dharma* have expressed their belief that Bhagavān Buddha must have joined the order of Pārśva, even though it might have been for a short while. While in that order, he practised penances like tonsure of hairs and got to the heart of the four Great Vows (*caturyām*).

According to well known historian Dr. Radhakumud Mukherjee, "In reality, it appears that the Buddha followed both the existing practices of penance for some time in the interest of acquiring complete self-discipline. For some time, he took guidance about the *Brāhmaṇa* way from one Udraka and then about the Jaina way before he developed his own independent way."[5] He also agrees with the view that "he (the Buddha) went to the cantonment area of the Magadhan Republic, called Uruvela, and began to strive for higher knowledge at a place near a river and hamlet which would be convenient for him to beg his food. His penances became increasingly harder, of which the direction is given in Jainism and because of which he was reduced to bones and skin. He established strict control on his respirations as well as on food and lived on a handful of lintels and pulses like *moong, kulthi, maṭar* and *harenuka*."[6]

Mrs. Rhys Davids says, "Buddha started his spiritual investigation in the company of five *Parivrājakas*, who were also called *Pañca Vargīya Bhikṣu*. They were Ajñakauṇḍinya, Aśvajit, Vaspa, Mahānāma and Bhadrika. In his moral and psychological advancement, the Buddha was immensely helped by them. He started a penance which was widely in vogue among the Jaina inhabitants, of Vaiśālī. He took part in discussions in contemporary philosophical doctrines. He derived his idea of nature and *karma* from the *nirgranthas*, of meditation from Alara and Udraka and of the later Brāhmanical thought from the *Sāṅkhya* text which was propounded for the first time by Ācārya Kapila either at Mathura or Taxila. These apart, he participated in discussions about many more things. By a process of synthesis of this vast material, he discovered and propounded his own path."[7] Elsewhere too, Mrs. Davids has noticed the Buddha having practised the Jaina method of penance in the following words, "In search of a *guru* he first reached Vaiśālī where he met Alara and Udraka and afterwards he practised the Jaina method of penance."[8]

REFERENCES

1. According to the *Digambara* tradition, Bhagavān Mahāvīra was initiated into monkhood at an early age before his marriage.
2. Hindustan, New Delhi, March 31, 1962.
3. *Majjhima Nikāya*, Mahāsimhanad Sutta, 1/1/2; also Dharmānanda Kośāmbī, Bhagavan Buddha, pp. 68-69.
4. Devasenacharya, *Darašanasāra*, Ed. Paṇḍit Nathuram Premi, Jain Grantha Ratnākar Kāryālaya, Bombay, 1920, śloka 6-8.
5. Dr. Radhakumud Mukerjee, *Hindu Civilisation*, revised by Dr. Vāsudevaśaraṇa Agarwal, Rajkamal Prakashan, Delhi, 1955, p. 239.
6. *Ibid.*, pp. 239-40.
7. Rhys Davids, *Śākya*, p. 123.
8. Rhys Davids, *Gautama the Man*, pp. 22-25.

2

CONTEMPORARY RELIGIOUS TEACHERS

During the days of Bhagavān Mahāvīra and Gautama Buddha, clashes between the *śramaṇas* and the *brāhmaṇas* had become a glaring feature. Even the *śramaṇas* were divided into many groups. We have it on the authority of the *Āgamas* as well as the *Tripiṭakas* that the *śramaṇas* not only fought with the *brāhmaṇas,* they also fought among themselves.

IN THE TRIPITAKAS

At several places in the Tripiṭakas, there are mentions about seven Jinas who were Pūraṇa Kassapa, Makkhalī Gośāla, Ajita Keśakambalī, Pakudha Kāccāyana, Sañjaya Veltthiputta, Nigantha Nāthaputta and Gautama Buddha. We have an account of these seven in the Sāmānaphala Sutta of *Dīgha Nikāya*. Dharmānanda Kośāmbī has summarised these accounts as follows[1]:

1. Pūraṇa Kāśyapa : *akriyā-vādī*

Pūraṇa Kassapa was the supporter of *akriyavāda* (which implied that no activity was a sin). Said he,

> "If someone does something or gets it done, cuts something or gets its cut, tortures himself or induces others to cause grief, causes pain himself or induces others to cause pain, himself generates fear and makes others to generate fear, kills living beings, steals, breaks into a house, robs, attacks the same house again and again, indulges in sinful acts, rapes another's wife, speaks untruth, even then he commits no sin. There is nothing wrong in these. If someone beats others on the south bank of the Gaṅgā, cuts himself or induces others to cut, causes pain himself or induces others to cause pain, he absolutely commits no sin. If, on the north bank of the Gaṅgā, somebody distributes alms or induces others to distribute alms, performs sacrifices or helps others to do the same, even then, he acquires no virtue. One does not acquire virtue by giving alms, by pious deeds, by practising restraints, and speaking the truth."

2. Makkhalī Gośālaka : *niyati-vādī*

Makkhalī Gośāla was a fatalist. Said he,

> "There is no reason, no cause, to make living being impure. They become impure without a reason, without a cause. There is no reason, no cause, to make living beings pure. They become pure without a reason, without a cause. Nothing can be attained by one's own capacity; nothing can be attained by another's capacity; nothing can be attained by man's own capacity. No one is endowed with any strength, power, capacity and exertion. All the static beings (*sattva*), all the two- to four-organ beings (*prāṇa*), all the flora-bodies (*bhūta*) and all the five-organ beings (*jīva*) are surely weak and without capacity. If still they transform, they do so because of luck, association and nature, and they experience pleasure and pain by remaining in one or the other of the six forms of existences."

3. Ajita Keśakambalī : *uccheda-vādī*

Ajita Keśakambalī was an *ucchedāvādī* (who believed that everyone was uprooted). Said he,

> "Offers, sacrifices, oblations are all useless. Good or bad deeds yield no result, they have no outcome. There are no such things as this life, next life, parents, or celestial and infernal beings. There are no philosophers who can acquire a correct knowledge about the world and transmit it to others, and there are no *śramaṇas* or *brāhmaṇas* in the world who are moving on the right track. Man is made of four elements. When he dies, the earth element goes into the earth, the water element into water, the heat element into fire and the air element into the air, and the organs of senses are absorbed in the sky. The corpse is placed in the coffin and carried by four persons to the cremation ground. They talk about his merits and demerits. His bones become white. The offerings poured on his body turn into ashes. It is the fools who have suggested that offerings should be placed on dead-bodies. Those who believe in the *āstikavāda* are false; they are wholly in the wrong. After the body is dead, the learned persons as well as the fools are equally uprooted, both get lost. After their death, nothing remains of them."

4. Pakudha Kāccāyana : *annyonya-vādī*

Pakudha Kāccāyana was an *annyonyavādī* (who believed in the indestructibility of elements). Said he,

> "The seven elements nobody makes, nobody causes them to be made; nobody creates them, nobody causes them to be created. They are fixed, indestructible and permanent. They neither move nor change. They do not torture one another, and they are unable to cause pleasure and plain to one another. These, elements are : earth, water, fire, air, pleasure, pain and soul. There is none to kill them, nor cause them to be killed; none to listen to them, nor make them listen, none to know them, none to describe them. If someone cuts one's throat, he does not kill his soul. It needs be understood that the weapon only penetrates into the gap between these seven elements."

5. Sañjaya Velaṭṭhiputra : *vikṣepa-vādī*

Sañjaya Velaṭṭhiputra was a *vikṣepa-vādī (*who had no set idea on anything). To quote him,

> "If someone asks me if there is another life, and if it appears to me that there is one, then, I shall say, 'Yes, there is another life'. But, to me, this does not seem to be so. And it does not appear to me either that there is no life hereafter. I have no fixed idea as to whether there are celestial and infernal beings or not, whether good and bad deeds have their outcome and whether the soul exists after death."

6. Nirgrantha Jñātaputra : *cāturyāma-saṁvara-vādī*

Nirgrantha Jñātaputra (Mahāvīra) was a *cāturyāma-saṁvara-vādi* (who believed in four checks on the influx of fresh *karma*-fetters). These four checks were as follows :

(1) a *nirgrantha* prohibits the use of water so that living beings (water-bodies) in it do not die;
(2) a *nirgrantha* prohibits all sinful activities;
(3) a *nirgrantha* is absolved of sins for having prohibited all sinful activities; and
(4) a *nirgrantha* is engaged in prohibiting all sinful activities.

In this manner, a *nirgrantha* is protected by four checks on the influx of fresh *karma*-fetters because of which they become uncovetous (*gatātmā*), restrained (*yatātmā*) and contented (*sthitātmā*).[2]

* * * * *

The above account of the six religious teachers has been given by the Buddhist canonists in a half-hearted and casual manner so that the account cannot be accepted as fully authentic and adequate. A perusal of the account of *Nirgrantha* Jñātaputra should convince one that the Buddhist writers did not exercise adequate caution or mobilise full knowledge to prepare it. The reaction about other accounts also will not be very much different. But, on the whole, it will not be wrong to say that these accounts contain at the most a very incomplete and indistinct shadow about the place of these spiritual leaders in contemporary society. This, however, is not to discount the importance of these accounts, howsoever cursory, in throwing some light on what might have happened at the dawn of history.

The main purpose of this account in the *Sāmaññaphala Sutta* seems to be to magnify, in contrast, the achievements of Gautama Buddha and belittle those of other spiritual leaders of the age. The occasion is provided by the visit paid by Ajātaśatru (Kūnika), the king of Magadha, to the Buddha. He came to the Buddha and raised a question about the visible effect of *śramaṇa*-hood. Said the Buddha,

> "Oh King! Did you raise the same question about the visible effect of *śramaṇa*-hood with other spiritual leaders?"
>
> To this, Ajātaśatru replied,
>
> "Yes, *bhante*, I did. I asked the same question to six of them. They expressed their views, but these did not appear to me to be right answers. So, *bhante,* their answers did not satisfy me."

From his own angle, Bhagavān Buddha elaborated the visible effect of *śramaṇa*-hood in the following words :

> "Oh King ! A valet of yours who acts according to your wishes, who is always ready to carry out your orders, who is sweet in his speech, and who is ready for everything, thinks that the way of virtuous activities, the outcome of virtuous activities, is highly strange and wonderful. He thinks that Ajātaśatru, the king of Magadha, is a human being, and he is also a human being. But the king moves about like a god enjoying all the five objects of desire, whereas he is a mere valet of the king, and so

he serves him. He thinks that he should do pious deeds, tonsure his head and chins, put on red robes and renounce his home. And he does as he had thought. Restrained in body, words and mind, he starts wandering (like a monk). Satisfied with simple food and clothes, he leads a lonely life. Now, King, if someone reports this to you, will you then desire that this man be brought back from his seclusion, made to resume his duties and to live on like that (for the rest of his life) ?"

— "No, *bhante*, I would surely not desire like that. I shall take my hat off him, I shall honour him, I shall serve him, I shall give him a seat, I shall invite him to accept food, clothes, bed, seat, medicine, sickman's food, etc., from me, and I shall take care of him in every respect."

— "Oh King! If this be so, then, don't you think that this is the most visible effect of *śramaṇa*-hood?"

— "To be sure, *bhante*, I do. I fully agree that this is the visible effect of *śramaṇa*-hood."

* * * * *

IN THE ĀGAMAS

An in the *Sāmaññaphala Sutta*, so in the *Suyagaḍāṅga* we get a glimpse of many contemporary philosophical schools. The *Suyagaḍāṅga*, however, makes no attribution by name, but merely states, 'some are of opinion, etc., etc...' In this *Āgama*, (*Śrutaskandha* I, *Adhyayana* I, *Uddeśaka* I), in *gāthā* 13, we have a succinct indication of *akriyāvāda* of Pūraṇa Kāśyapa,[3] in *gāthās* 15-16, of *anyonyavāda* of Pakudha Kāccāyana,[4] and in *gāthā* 11-12, of *ucchedavāda* of Ajita Keśakambalī.[5] In the discussion on *ajñānavāda* contained in the same *Āgama*, we have a glimpse of *vikṣepavāda* of Sañjaya Velaṭṭhiputra. Also contained in the same *Āgama* are clear views on the Buddhists and the Ājīvikas. Commentator Śrī Sīlaṅkācārya has identified these philosophical schools as the Buddhistic, the Bārhaspatya, the Cārvāka, the Vedānta, the Sāṅkhya, the Adṛṣṭavāda, the Ājīvaka, the Trairāśikas, the Śaivas, etc.

The canonists have identified the then philosophical schools as *Kriyāvāda, Akriyāvāda, Ajñānavāda* and *Vainaytkavāda.*

Like *Sāmaññaphala Sutta*, the Chapter entitled *Addaijjanāma* (*Ādrakīyākhya*) in *Sūyagaḍāṅga* gives an elaborate account of diverse philosophical schools of that period. Ārdrakakumāra was a prince from Ārdrakapura.[6] Once his father sent a costly gift for his friend King Śreṇika of Magadha. At the same time, Prince Ārdrakakumāra had sent a gift for Prince

Abhayakumāra. In return, the King and the Prince of Ārdrakapura received gifts from Rājagṛha. Abhayakumāra had sent an image of an arhat-jina as his gift for Ārdrakakumāra. On receiving this, Ārdrakakumāra became very happy. Soon his memory of his previous birth came back to him, and on the basis of that memory, he got initiated and started to see Bhagavān Mahāvīra. On the way, he met, one after another, the leaders of diverse philosophical schools. When the latter saw Ārdrakakumāra, they entered into philosophical discussions with him. Ārdrakakumāra refuted them all and established the superiority of the philosophy of Bhagavān Mahāvīra. This interesting discussion is recorded as follows :

Monk Ārdrakakumāra and Gośālaka

Gośālaka—Ārdraka ! I shall narrate for you the early life of Mahāvīra. In the beginning, he was a *śramaṇa* monk wandering alone. Now, he moves with a band of monks and preaches his religion. In this manner, this restless soul has built up a profession for earning his subsistence. Thus, there is a clear contradiction between his present behaviour and his past behaviour.

Monk Ārdraka—Bhagavān Mahāvīra's solitude is the same in the present as it has been in the past, and I assure you, it will remain the same in the future. Freed from attachment and malice, though he lives in the midst of thousands of men, still he practises his penances in solitude. A monk who has conquered his senses preaches keeping in view the merits and shortcomings of his speech, and I think, there is not even an iota of fault in it. One who understands well such tenets of the *śramaṇa* order as the great vows, lesser vows, influx of fresh *karma*-fetters, is, in my view, a *śramaṇa.*

Gośālaka—In my considered view, a solitary monk incurs no sin whatsoever in drinking fresh (unboiled) water, in eating grains (seeds), in accepting purposive food and in enjoying women.

Monk Ārdraka—If this be so, then (it should follow that) all householders are *śramaṇas*; for, in fact, they do all these things. Those monks who take fresh water, eat grains, etc., have turned monkhood into a mockery in order to earn a living. I do not agree that they make themselves fit for. liberation by mere renunciation.

Gośālaka—But, my dear sir, in expressing such a view, you are, in fact, decrying all other views.

Monk Ārdraka—The heretics extol their own views and decry those of others. They claim, 'we alone are in possession of truths, none else'. But I decry wrong principles, not personalities. How can those monks who do not even desire as much as to inconvenience immobile beings decry others?

Gośālaka—Your monks do not stay in garden-house or charitable guest house because they do not want to come into contact with scholars and learned monks. They are afraid that the latter may ask them questions about which they may not be able to provide an answer.

Monk Ārdaka—Bhagavān Mahāvīra does not do anything unless necessary, nor does he act like a fool without calculation. He does not preach out of fear for the governmental power even; then, pray, what else is afraid of? Sometimes he gives reply to questions and sometimes he does not give a reply. He preaches for his own perfection, as also for the liberation of the *Āryans*. This omniscient personality preaches either by going or without going to competent listners. But the non-Āryans have no faith; so the Bhagavān does not go to them.

Gośālaka—Your Mahāvīra is a profit-seeking merchant who like his brother-in-profession (*i.e.*, other merchants) established contact with other merchants for buying and selling wares.

Monk Ārdraka—Mahāvīra, you should know, acquires no new *karma;* he destroys the old ones. I agree with you that he desires the attainment of liberation, and in this sense alone he is profit-seeking. But he is unlike other merchants who indulge in killing, falsehood, sex behaviour and many other sinful deeds, and what do they earn therefrom? repeated transmigration in four forms of existence. The profit earned by Bhagavān Mahāvīra has a beginning but no end. He is fully abstained from killing, he is always ready to help others on the spiritual path and he himself is fixed in piety. You should not compare him with other merchants who act contrary to their larger spiritual interest. In doing so, you expose your own ignorance of him.

Monk Ārdraka and a Buddhist Bhikṣu

Bhikṣu—If someone cooks a lump of oil-cake considering to be a human being, or cooks a gourd by considering it to be a boy, then, in my view, he incurs the sin of killing a man or a boy. If, on the other hand, someone pierces and cooks a man or a boy by considering them to be a lump of oil-cake or a gourd, then he does not incur the sin of killing a man or a boy. And I would go further to add that the cooked meat is wholesome and is good enough for the breakfast by the enlightened *(buddhas).*

Continuing in the same strain, the *bhikṣu* added,

Ārdrakakumāra! My philosophy lays down that if someone entertains with food 2000 *snātaka*[7] *(bodhisattva)* monks everyday, he acquires a place in the celestical existence, and is born as *Āropya,* the best among the gods.[8]

Monk Ārdraka — It is not fit for a monk to kill two- to four-organ beings and flora-bodies (etc.) and to extol it to be no-sin. Those who preach like this, and those who listen such discourses—both are ignoramous, and both are condemned to ill-fare. Can anyone who practises restraint and non-injury to life, who is free from delusion, and who understands the real nature of mobile and immobile beings, indulge in such talks? Is it practicable to cook a boy by considering it to be a gourd, or a gourd by considering it to be a boy? Those who speak like this indulge in falsehood and are non-Āryans.

(Continued he :)

Is it the sign of a restrained person that in his mind he understands a boy to be a boy and still he calls him a gourd? Suppose some people kill a thick and fat ram, carefully cut and separate its meat, pour salt on it, fry it in oil, dress it with spices and prepare it for your sake; and you eat that meat and brag that you have committed no sin. This indicates your wickedness and your greedy tongue. If someone inadvertently eats this meat, still he commits a sin. If this be correct, then, if somebody ways that he ate the meat without knowing it to be meat, and that he is not telling a flat lie?

(Ārdrakakumāra went on :)

The monks in the order of Nātaputta avoid purposive food out of fear of sin because they cherish compassion for all living beings and they avoid all conscious lapses. Those who so scrupulously avoid causing even the slightest pain to mobile and immobile beings cannot allow themselves to be a victim of delusion. You should realise how very minute is the way of a restrained person.

(He said in conclusion :)

He who feeds 2000 *bhikṣus* everyday is wholly an unrestrained person. A man who has dipped his hand in blood is fit to be chastised in this life; how can he improve his existence in the next life? Even such words that incite sin should never be uttered. Such empty words are devoid of merit. An initiated monk should never use such words.

(He addressed these final words to the monks of his own order :)

Oh monks! You have acquired knowledge about objects and you have understood pious and impious results of *karma.* Perhaps it is because of this superior knowledge that your fame has spread as far as the seas in the east as well as in the west, and you have thoroughly seen the entire world, as if it is in your own hands.

Monk Ārdraka and a Vedic Brāhmaṇa

Brāhmaṇa—It is revealed in our *Vedas* that he who entertains 2000 *snātaka Brāhmaṇas* by offering food acquires a great merit and is born in the celestial existence.

Monk Ārdraka—He who feeds 2000 *snātaka* Brāhmanas who move from door to door like a cat goes to hell which is full of great pain and is peopled by meat-eating birds. A man who decries religion based in compassion and extols another based on injury to life, and who feeds even a single Brāhmaṇa fallen from discipline moves to and fro in a dark hell. How does he attain the celestial life?

Monk Ārdraka and Ātmadvaitavādī [9]

Advaitavādī—Monk Ārdraka! Our religions are alike. Both existed in the past and both will continue to exist in the future. In both our religions, emphasis is on knowledge and on conduct based upon practices. There is no difference either in our view on rebirth. But I believe in a Supreme Soul (*Ātman*) who is indescribable, all-pervading, indestructible and permanent. Like the moon in the midst of the stars. He resides in all living beings,

Monk Ārdraka—If what you say is true, then there will be no distinction between a Brāhmana, a Kṣatriya, a Vaiśya and a Śūdra : or between insects, birds, reptiles, men and gods. And, pray, who should they glide back and forth in this world experiencing pleasures and pains ?

(Continued he :)

Those who preach to others without knowing and seeing the universe with the help of their supreme and unobstructed, (*kevala*) knowledge, they cause harm to self and to others. Those who preach to others after having known and seen the nature of the universe with the help of their supreme and unobstructed knowledge, and those who have concentration in full knowledge, not only themselves cross through the world, but also help others to do so.

(Concluded Monk Ārdrakakumāra :)

Therefore, oh long-lived, one by describing the Advaitavādins who are in possession of a condemnable knowledge and the Jinas who are perfect masters of faith, knowledge and conduct to be at par, you are only making a contradictory statement.

Monk Ārdraka and Hastī Tāpasa

Hastī Tāpasa—I kill one elephant and live on its flesh for full one year. I do so for practising compassion and non-injury to living beings.

Monk Ārdraka—During a year, you say, you kill only one animal and kill no more; but in this manner, you cannot absolve yourself of sin. There is not much of a difference between you who kill only one animal and other householders (who may kill more animals). A man like you who acts contrary to his self can never acquire omniscience.

(Concluded Monk Ārdraka :)

Instead of pursuing one's own preconceived notions, one who has fixed oneself on the road to liberation by mind, words and deeds as per the prescription of the seers, who has protected one's own self against lapses, and acquired the means of crossing through the wordly ocean, is the only fit person to preach to others.

Chapter entitled Addaijjanama in the *Sūyagaḍaṅga,* like the *Sāmaññaphala Sutta,* meets the views of the various schools of heretics, though these schools have not been mentioned by name in the chapter. On the basis of the ideas expressed therein, the commentators have tried to identify these schools. Thus in *gāthā* 28, we have : *buddhāṇa taṁ kappati pāraṇāe* (is good enough for the breakfast of the enlightened). The commentators have taken the word *'buddha'* in plural. If we agree with them (*i.e.*, if we accept that the word makes no personal reference. to Gautama Buddha), then we may safely say that at no place in the Jaina *Āgamas*, Gautama Buddha has been subjected to any, reflection. We have the word *'Siṇayagāṇaṁ' (snātakas)* in *gāthā* 29, and according to the commentators, the word means '*bodhisattva*'. This meaning is based on inference. Elsewhere, the commentators, have explained the word as *nityaṁ snāyino brahmacārinaḥ snātakāḥ* (*i.e.*, *snātakas* are celibates who indulge not in sexual relationship).

Just as the word *'buddha'* has been used to refer to the Buddhists in general, so Ārdrakakumāra has used the word '*buddha*' also to signify the Jaina monks[10] who are planted in good conduct *(sīla-guṇopapeta).*

INTRODUCTION TO LIFE-HISTORY

The life-stories of Mahāvīra and the Buddha are recorded at many places; but about the life-history of the remaining five spiritual leaders, we do not have either an authentic or an adequate account. The reason for this is that their lines have become extinct. We only occasional mentions about them in the *Āgamas* and the *Tripiṭakas.*

1. Pūraṇa Kassapa

He was called 'Pūraṇa' because people took him to be full of experience. He was a *Brāhmaṇa,* hence named Kāśyapa. He remained unclad and had a following of 80,000. According to a Buddhist fable, he was born in a well-to-do family. One day, his master assigned him the duty of a gate-keeper. Kāśyapa took it as an insult. Out of sheer disgust, he gave up the job and turned his steps towards the forest. In the way, the thieves took away his clothes. Since then, he remained unclad. When once he did not accept them saying,

> "Clothes are necessary to cover one's bashfulness, and the root of bashfulness are our sinful inclinations. I am fully secured against such inclinations. So what do I need clothes for?"

People were very much impressed at his detachment and solitary living, and became his followers.[11]

The *Viyāha Paṇṇatti (Bhagavatī Sūtra)* of the Jainas (S. 3, U. 2) gives a detailed account of one *Pūraṇa* Tāpasa who was also a contemporary of Bhagavān Mahāvīra. But it does not seem that this *Pūraṇa* Tāpasa was in any way the same person as Pūraṇa Kassapa.

In the *Dhammapada-aṭṭhakathā,* we have a strange and somewhat unusual account of the death of *Pūraṇa* Kassapa. It is stated therein, in part, as follows :

Once there was a competition at Rājagṛha between the heretics and the Buddhists about the display of their respective occult powers. The Buddha announced in the presence of King Bimbisāra : 'I shall display my occult powers at Śrāvastī on the forthcoming full-moon day in the month of *Āṣāḍha.'* The heretics heard this announcement and followed the Buddha (to Śrāvastī) in order to demonstrate the efficacy of their own occult powers and the failure of those of the Buddha. The Buddha started for Śrāvastī, and so did the heretics. The latter collected their followers in the largest number. They raised one lakh *kārṣāpaṇas* (a standard coin of that name) to meet the costs. The *paṇḍāla* was erected with posts made from *khaira* trees. All the people sat down in the *paṇḍāla* to display or witness their occult powers.

King Prasenajit of Kośala came to the Great Leader (*i.e.*, the Buddha) and submitted,

> "*Bhante!* The heretics have put up a *paṇḍala* for their own use. (if you kindly permit me,) I would like to erect one for thy use."
> —"No, King, I have another person who will erect the *paṇḍāla* for me."

—"*Bhante!* Who else other than me can erect a *paṇḍāla* for thee here?"
— "Oh Kingt (Don't you worry.) This will be done for me by Śakra, the King of the gods."
—"Then, *bhante,* where will ye display thy occult power?"
—"Why? Beneath the mango tree of Gaṇda."

This news soon spread. The heretics heard this and managed to remove all mango trees upto a distance of one *yojana*. (What to speak of full grown trees,) not even a fresh sprout was allowed to remain on earth.

The Great Leader entered Śrāvastī on the full-moon day of *Āṣāḍha*. Gaṇḍa, the keeper of the king's garden saw a big-sized ripe mango behind a shrub. He drove away the crows that were attracted to it by its smell and juice. Then he took the mango in his hand and started to present it to the king. In the way, he saw, the Great Leader. Suddenly a thought sprouted in his mind, 'If I give this mango to the king, he will given me at the most eight or sixteen *kārṣāpaṇas*. That will not be enough for my livelihood. But if I offer the mango to the Great Leader, then that will do me good for an unlimited time.' Having thought thus, he brought the mango to the Great Leader. The Leader suck the juice of that mango and said to Gaṇḍa,

"You dig the soil here and sow this seed."

Gaṇḍa did accordingly. The Leader washed his hands on the spot. In a moment, there grew out a giant mango tree fifty cubits long. Its trunk produced four big branches which spread forth in four directions, each being fifty cubits long, and these, along with the central trunk, looked like five great summits. Just then the tree took forth flowers and fruits. Each branch bent low under the weight of ripe mangoes. The *bhikṣus* who followed the Buddha ate the ripe-fruits to their heart's content. The king (Prasenajit) heard the full account and was very much surprised. The king at once sent guards for the protection of the tree so that no one would be able to fell it.

This mango-tree was sown by the garden-keeper Gaṇḍa because of which it became known as Gaṇḍa's mango tree *(gaṇḍamb-rūkkha)*. Even the heretics ate the fruits of this tree. While throwing the seeds, they said, '*Śramaṇa* Gautama is to display his occult powers, under Gaṇḍa's mango tree. It is for this that even fresh sprouts have been removed. Wherefrom has this tree come then?"

Indra had become furious with the heretics. To belittle them, he said to the God of Wind,

'Blow away the *paṇḍāla* of the heretics and deposit it on the heap of rubbish.'

He said to the Sun,

> 'You concentrate your energy on the heretics and burn them.'

The two gods carried out the orders of their king. Indra said again to the Wind,

> 'Start a terrific cyclone.'

There started a terrific cyclone, and the heretics who were already burnt by the blazing sun were now buried under the dust. The skin of all the people turned grey under the dust cover. Then Indra commanded the God of Rain,

> 'Hurl a heavy shower on them.'

This was done. There was a heavy down-pour, and all the heretics now looked like so many cows lacking lustre. The, *nirgranthas* took to their heels out of shame.

A peasant who happened to be the disciple of Pūraṇa Kassapa, had heard about this competition, and desired to witness it. He unyoked his bulls, took his food packet (containing rice and pulses boiled together) and the rope (that, was tied to the bulls' neck) in his hands and took the road to Śrāvastī. On the way, he saw Pūraṇa Kassapa fleeing. Said he to him,

> "*Bhante!* I am going to see the display of occult powers by the Āryans. Whither bound you are at such a rapid pace?"

Pūraṇa Kassapa who was still running said,

> "What have you got to do with the display of this occult power? Give that food-packet and rope to me."

So saying, he extended his hand at once. The peasant gave both the things to him. Pūraṇa Kassapa took them and came to the bank of the river. With the rope, he tied the food packet round his neck. Then without speaking a single word, out of profound shame, he jumped into the river and lost his life. He was born (thereafter) in the hell.

About the above record of Pūraṇa Kassapa's death, it is very difficult to say if the account comes in any way near to facts; but such is the Buddhist chronicle. Needless to add, the record is far from convincing. The impropriety of the account is further indicated by the fact that while the life-story of Pūraṇa

Kassapa is the main theme under consideration, the chronicle did not fail in the end to introduce the *nirgranthas* as 'fleeing out of shame' (This was wholly uncalled for). The same source *(Aṭṭhakathā)* reveals that Pūraṇa Kassapa was a slave in a richman's family. This is also not very convincing. A man who was rich in experiences (*Pūrṇa*) and who was a *Brāhmaṇa* (Kāśyapa) by caste could not surely have been a born slave.[12]

2. Pakudha Kaccāyana

Pakudha Kaccāyana had discarded the use of cold water : only hot water was acceptable to him.[13] He was born beneath a *kakuddha* tree because of which he took the prefix *kakuddha* to his name.[14] According to the *Praśnopaniṣad* (1. 1), he was a contemporary of Ṛsi Pippalāda and a *Brāhmaṇa* by caste. In that *Upaniṣad,* he has been called Kabandhi Kātyāyana. Now, the two words *'Pakudha'* and *'Kabandhi'* signify the same, *viz.* a hunchback.[15] According to the Buddhist Commentators, Pakudha was his line, *(gotra)*[16] but Ācārya Buddhaghoṣa is of opinion that the word 'Pakudha' was a proper name, the surname being Kāccāyana.[17] Dr. Fear has substituted 'Kakudha' in place of 'Pakudha'.[18]

3. Ajita Keśakambalī

Ajita Keśakambalī used a blanket made of hairs. Because of this the was called Keśakambalī. F.L.Woodward opines that the blanket was made from human hairs.[19] His philosophy did not rise very much above common life (i.e., akin to *cārvākism.* Accordingly, some scholars are of the view that Ajita Keśakambalī was the founder of atheism in India. It seems that at a later period, it was *Bṛhaspati* who had elaborated his philosophy.[20]

4. Sañjaya Velaṭṭhiputta

We have no authentic material about the life-story of this man. About his name, there is no room for any controversy. Like Maṅkhaliputta Gośālaka, Sañjaya Velaṭṭhiputta was a proper name. In those days, it was a common practice to call one as the son of so and so (either parent). We come across many such names as Miyāputta .[21] Thāvacacāputta[22] in the Jaina texts. According to Ācārya Bhuddhaghoṣa, too, Velaṭṭhiputra was the son of one Velaṭṭhi. Some scholars are of the view that Sañjaya Velaṭṭhiputta was the same person as Sañjaya Parivrājaka who was an *ācārya* before Sāriputta and Moggalāna.[23] But this view does not appear to be correct. Had it been so, there would have been a clear record of this in the *Tripiṭaka*. Rather, the *Tripiṭakas* state that Sāriputta and Moggalāna gave up their own preceptor Sañjaya Parivrājaka and joined the holy order of the Buddha but they go no further.[24] The title Parivrājaka further suggests that this man was in the Vedic line, and hence that he should be distinguished from other spiritual stalwarts like Pūraṇa who took refuge in the *śramaṇa* brotherhood. Dr. Kāmtāprasad is of the view that Sañjaya Velaṭṭhiputta was the preceptor of Sāriputta and was himself a Jaina *ācārya*[25], but this view is far from acceptable. It is equally improper to confuse this Sañjaya with another in the *Uttarājjayaṇaṇi*[26] or with a lowly carana who was named *Ṛddhidhara* Sañjaya. Dr. G.P. Malalasekera has described him as the preceptor of Sāriputta and Moggalāna, but he has produced no evidence in support of his view.[27]

Some people have viewed Sañjaya's *Vikṣepavāda* as the forerunner of *syādvāda;* but the view that *syādvāda* developed from *vikṣepavāda* has no basis and is no better than a flight of imagination.[28]

Such is the account we have about the leading spiritual teachers and their schools of philosophy of that phase of history; but the account is by no means exhaustive. These leading schools of philosophy apart, there were many other views current at that time. According to the Jaina tradition, there were a total of 363 such views,[29] while according to the Buddhist tradition, the number was only 62.[30] The *Āgamas* and the *Tripiṭakas* contain copious references to monks of many sects.

REFERENCES

1. Dharmānand Kauśāmbī, *op. cit.*, pp. 181-83.
2. *Dīghanikāya* (Hindi), summary of p. 21.
3. *Cf.* Sūyagaḍāṅga (1. 1. 1. 13)
   kuvvaṁ ca kārayaṁ ceva savvaṁ kuvvaṁ na vijjai evaṁ akārao appā evaṁ te upagabbhiā.
4. *Cf. Ibid.*, (1. 1. 1. 15-16)
   śānti pañca mahabbhūyā ihamegesi āhiyā
   ayachattho puno āhu āyā loge ya sāsae
   duhao ṇa vinassaṁti no ya uppajjae ase
   savvevi savvahā bhāvā niyattī bhāvā magayā.
5. *Cf. Ibid.* (1.1.1.11-12)
   patteaṁ kasine āyā je bālāje ya padiyā
   sānti piccā na te sānti natthi sttovavāyiyā
   natthi punne va pāve va nathhi loe ito vare
   śarīrassa vināsenaṁ vināso hoi dehino.
6. According to Dr. Jyotiprasād Jain, Ārdrakakumāra was the son of the Iranian Emperor Cyrus (*circa* 558-530 B. C.) *Bhāratīya Itihāsa : Ek Dṛṣṭi*, Bhāratīya Jñāmpīṭh, Kasi, 1961, pp. 67-68.
7. Śrī Sīlaṅkācārya, *Sūtrakṛtāṅgavṛtti*, Śrī Godījī Pārśvanāth Jain Derāsarpedhi, Bombay, 1950, Sru. 2, adhyāya 6, gāthā 29.
8. In *Dīghanikāya Mahānidāna Sutta*, three types of existences have been distinguished. They

are : kāma bhāva, rūpa bhāva, arūpa bhāva. In arūpa bhāva, there is no form. The last species has been stated to be the best. *Cf. Sūyagaḍāṅga*, Rajkot, 1938, Sru. 2, Adhyayana 6.

pinnāgapiṇḍīmavi viddha sūle,
kei paejjā purise immetti.
alāuyaṁ vāvi kumaraga tti,
sa lippai pānivahena amhaṁ.
ahavāvi viddhuṇa milakkhu sūle,
pinnāgabuddhīe naraṁ paejjā.
kumāragaṁ vāvi alāue tti,
na lippai pānivahena amhām.
purisaṁ ca viddhuna kumāragaṁ va,
sūlammi keī pae jāyatee.
pinnāyapiṇḍim sāimarūhettā,
buddhāna taṁ kappatti pāranāe.
sināyagānaṁ tu duve sahasse,
je bhoyne niṭae bhikhāyanaṁ.
te punnakhamdham sumahajjanītta,
bhavanti acoppa mahaṁtasattā.

9. Commentator Sīlāṅkācāryā (2. 6. 49) has called him ekadaṇḍi. According to Jacobi, he was a vedantist (S.B.E., vol. XV, p. 417n). The latter view seems more appropriate.
10. *Cf.* nigganṭha-dhammaṁmi imaṁ samāhiṁ
assim suṭhiccā aṇihe carejjā
buddhe munī sīla-gunovave-e
accathataṁ (o) pāunatī silogaṁ.
11. Bauddha-parva (in Marathi) Pra. 10, p. 127; Also *Bhagavatī Sūtra*, ed. by Paṇḍit Becardās, Vol. II, p. 56.
12. *Cf.* G.P. Malalasekera, *Dictonary of Pali Proper Names*, Vol. II, p. 242.
13. *Dhammapada-aṭṭhakathā*, 1. 144.
14. Dr. Radhakumud Mukerjee, *op. cit.*, p. 216 (Hindi).
15. Barua, *Pre-Buddhistic Indian Philolsophy*, p. 281.
16. *The Book of the Kindred Sayings*, Part I, p. 94n.
17. *Dhammapada-aṭṭhakathā*, 1. 144.
Also *Saṁyuttanikāya-aṭṭhakathā*, 1. 102.
18. *The Book of the Kindred Sayings*, Part I, p. 94n.
19. *The Book of the Gradual Sayings* (translated by F.L. Woodward), Vol. I, p. 265n.
20. Barua, *op. cit.*, p. 288.
21. *Uttarajjayaṇāṇi*, Adhyayana 19.
22. *Jñātā-dharma-kathāṅga Sūtra,* Adhayana 5.
23. Gopaldas Patel, *Mahāvīra Svāmino Saṁyama dharma*, (Gujarati), Navajivan, Ahmedabad, 1935, p. 35.
24. *Vinayapiṭaka*, Mahāvagga, Mahāskandhaka.
25. Mulchand Kisandas Kapadia, *Bhagāvan Mahāvīra aura Mahātmā Buddha*, Surat, 1926, pp. 22-24.
26. *Uttarajjayanāni*, Adhyayana 18.
27. *Dictionary of Pali Proper Names*, Vol. II, p. 1000.
28. Dharmānand Kauśāmbī, *op. cit.* p. 187. For a contradiction of this erroneous view, read Dr. Kāmtaprasād's article entitled "*Syādvād Siddhānta kī Moulikatā aura Upayogitā*" in Ācārya Śrī Tulsī Abhinandana Grantha, Chapter 4, pp. 54-56.
29. *Cf. Bhārata-mukti,* pp. 246-249.
30. *Dīghanikāya,* Brahmajāla Sutta, 1.1.

3

GOŚĀLAKA

In the Āgamas (Scriptures)

The sect founded by Gośālaka, son of Maṅkhali, was known as *Ājīvaka*. In the rock inscriptions of Emperor Asoka, there is mention of grants of caves to Ājīvaka monks.[1] It is difficult to say accurately how long that sect continued to function, but its existence till the second century B.C. is proved from inscriptions, etc.[2] According to *Āgamas,* Gośālaka was connected with Lord Mahāvīra more in the form of a rival than anything else. A detailed account of the life and the beliefs of Gośālaka is found in Jaina scriptures. A number of topics is thus easily available from this source. In *Bhagavatī, Śataka* XV, we find a detailed biography of Gośālaka in a horripilating and eventful form. There it is told :

"Koṣṭhaka Chaitya was situated in the north-eastern corner of the city of Śrāvastī. In this city lived a lady potter named Hālāhalā who was a devotee of the Ājīvaka sect. She was immensely rich and influential. No one could defeat her in argument. She knew by heart the Ājīvaka principles. Her whole being was immersed in attachment to them. She used to say, 'Ājīvaka faith alone is the truth and the highest spiritual knowledge. All the others are in vain.'

"Once Maṅkhali's son, Gośālaka, who had been initiated twentyfour years earlier, was staying in the pottery mart of Hālāhalā, who was an ardent follower of *Ājīvaka Saṅgha*. Six *Disacharas*,[3] namely, Śāna, Kalanda, Karnikāra Acohidra, Agniveśyāyana, and Arjuna, son of Gomayu, came there to meet him. They were well versed in eight types of *Nimitta* (knowledge of good and bad omens, astrology, music and dance. They became disciples of Gośālaka.

"Gośālaka had some knowledge of the eight branches of *Nimitta* and could, therefore, give truthful answers to everybody about gain and loss, happiness and misery, and life and death. On the strength of this knowledge of *Nimitta* alone, he began proclaiming himself *Jina* (who has suppressed enemies in the form of attachment and aversion, *Tīrthaṅkara*, Arahanta), without being one, *Kevali* without being *Kevali* (knower of *Kevala* knowledge, the liberated), and *Sarvajña* (Omniscient) without being such. He used to say : 'I am *Jina*, *Kevali* and *Sarvajña*.' As a result of such announcement, he became the topic of constant discussion an three-road junctions, cross-roads and the royal highways of Śrāvastī.

"One day Bhagavān Mahāvīra visited Śrāvastī. People assembled for His religious discourse. The meeting ended. The eminent disciple of Mahāvīra, Indrabhūti Aṇagāra of the clan of Gautama, went to the city for alms. On the way he heard from many persons about the proclamation of Gośālaka. He came to Lord Mahāvīra, asked Him about it and requested Him to relate the story of Gośālaka from beginning to end.

Early Life of Gośālaka

Said Mahāvīra : "Gautama, the claim of Gośālaka is false. He is neither *Jina*, nor *Kevali*, nor *Sarvajña*. His father was Maṅkhali of Maṅkha caste. Maṅkhali's wife was Bhadrā who was gentle and beautiful. Once she was with child. A *brāhmin* by the name of Gobahula lived in the village Śaravaṇa. He was rich and also knew well the *brāhmaṇa śāstras* like *Ṛgveda.* He had a Gośālā (cow-house).

"Once, Maṅkhali, accompanied by Bhadrā, who was pregnant, came to Śaravaṇa after roaming about from village to village. He carried with him a *chitrapaṭa* (cloth or board with portraits painted on it). He kept his belongings in the Gośālā of Gobahula and went into the village for alms. He searched for a place where he could find shelter, but without success. Therefore, he decided to spend the *Chāturmāsa* (four months of the rainy season) in a portion of the *Gośālā*. At the end of nine months and seven and a half days, Maṅkhali's wife, Bhadrā, gave birth to a lovely and gentle child. On the twelfth day, the parents named the child Gośālaka as he was born in the *Gośālā* of Gobahula. By and by, Gośālaka grew up and, after studies, became of ripened intellect. In course of time, Gośālaka also started earning his livelihood independently with *Chitrapaṭa* in hand.

Gośālaka's First Contact with the Lord

"I lived at home for thirty years. On the demise of my parents, I gave up wordly riches like gold, etc., and, putting on the robe of the mendicant, got myself initiated in ascetic life. I spent my first *Chāturmāsa* in Aṣthigrāma, doing *Pākṣika* (fortnightly) penances. Next year, *Chāturmāsa* was observed by me, after taking the required special vows, with *Masika* outside Rājagṛha. At that time, Gośālaka, who was going about from village to village with *Chitrapaṭa* in hand, thus maintaining himself by alms, also came to the same weaver's shed. While collecting alms, he tried to find some other suitable lodging for himself but did not get any. So he too decided to spend *Chāturmāsa* in the same weaving shed. It was the day for me to break my fast after the first *Masika* austerities. Making round of the house of upper, middle and low class families of Rājagṛha for alms, I arrived at the home of Vijaya Gāthāpati (prosperous house-holder who does farming as well as business), who was overjoyed at seeing me there. He got up from his seat and came forward seven or eight paces to receive me. Adjusting the outer garment and with folded hands, he saluted me by walking round me thrice. He entertained me with food as prescribed for ascetics, drinks, dry fruits and cardamom etc. Vijaya Gāthāpati gave charities with the three-fold, purity of receiver, giver and what is given, and with the purity of means, and thus reduced his worldly possessions. This resulted in a rain at his house of five heavenly gifts of gold etc. In a short while, this news spread all over the city. People began praising Vijaya and his human birth and saluting his virtuous actions.

"Gośālaka, the son of Maṅkhali, also heard the news, which made him inquisitive and curious. He went to the house of Vijaya Gāthāpati. He noticed the objects that had rained, and also saw me and the house-holder Vijaya coming out of the house. He felt happy in his hearts and came over to me. He offered me salutation by walking round me three times and said : *'Bhagavān,* you are my *Dharmācārya* (religious preceptor or *Guru)* and I am your disciple'. At that time I did not pay attention to what he said and kept quiet. The fast was broken for the second month's penance at the house of Ānanda, for the third month's penance at Sunanda's, and for the fourth month's penance at the house of Bahula brāhmin in Kollaka village near Nālandā. At all these three places the same blessing of austerities was evident.

"Not finding me in the weaving house, Gośālaka started looking for me in Rājagṛha but got no trace of me. He returned to the weaving house. He gave away to brāhmins his clothes, utensils, shoes and the Chitrapaṭa and shaved his beard and moustache. He left for Kollaka where he heard from people about the rain of gold etc. at the house of Bahula. The thought came to his mind : 'No other sage or brāhmin can possibly have the radiance, effulgence, glory, strength, splendour, prowess and prosperity as possessed by my preceptor and preacher Bhagavān Mahāvīra.' He alone must be my *Guru* and *Ācārya.* Searching for me, he came to the beautiful outskirts of Kollaka. He greeted me in the usual respectful manner and made the submission : *'Bhagavān,* you are my *Dharmācārya* and I am your disciple'. I accepted the request of Gośālaka, son of Maṅkhalī, and did *Vihāra* (stayed) with him at that consecreted ground for six years, experiencing the opposites : loss and gain, pleasure and pain, and honour and dishonour.

"Once, during the autumn, there was no rain. Accompanied by Gośālaka, I was going from Siddhārtha village to Kūrmagrāma. On the way, we noticed a sesamum plant with leaves and flowers. Gośālaka asked : 'Bhagavān, will this plant bear fruit?' I replied 'Gośālaka, this plant will bear fruit, and these seven living things in its flowers will die and become seven grains in a pod of this plant.'

Vaiśyāyana, a Bāla Tapasvī (performing penances in ignorance and without the right knowledge)

"We arrived at Kūrmagrāma. Outside the village, Vaiśyāyana was constantly exposing himself to heat facing the Sun with arms outstretched upwards, and observing the *Chaṭṭha* (two day fast) austerity. Due to the Sun's heat, lice were failing from his head to the ground. With compassion in his heart for every *Prāṇa* (lower forms of life like insects, etc.), *Bhūta* (living things like plants etc.), *Jīva* (higher forms of life like human beings), and *Sattva* (living beings of land, water, fire and air–synonymous with *Jīva),* he was picking up the fallen lice and placing them in his hair again. Gośālaka saw the *Bāla Tapasvī.* Leaving me aside, he we went to him and said, 'Are you a *Tapasvī* or the shelterer of lice?' Vaiśyāyana did not mind what Gośālaka had said and remained silent. Gośālaka repeated his question again and again. This made Vaiśyāyana angry. He came down from the spot of penance and walked seven or eight paces backwards. Charged with emotion, he directed at Gośālaka to burn him down, a *Tejoleśya* (bolt of intense heat) which he had acquired by his penances. I took pity on Gośālaka, the son of Maṅkhali, and ordered my cool and serene *Tejoleśya* to counteract the effect of Vaiśyāyana's bolt, which it accomplished. The experiment of the ascetic failed. Seeing Gośālaka standing unharmed, the Tapasvī understood the entire mystery. He drew back his *Tejoleśya* and kept repeating for some moments, *'Bhagavān,* I have known you now, I have known you'.

"Gośālaka had not followed the entire chain of events. He came to me and said, *'Bhagavān,* what was this harbourer of lice doing to you?' I narrated the whole account to him. Gośālaka was afraid, and at the same time happy that he had narrowly escaped death. He saluted me and asked, *'Bhagavān,* how can concise and profound *Tejoleśya* be attained'? I replied, 'With handful (hand closed with nails inside) of *urad* beans and palmful of water, if a person observes the *Chaṭṭha* austerity continuously and exposes himself to the heat of the Sun, facing it with hands outstretched upwards on holy ground, he can acquire both the concise and the profound *Tejoleśyas* after a period of six months'. Gośālaka accepted what I said with humility.

Attainment of Tejoleśya

"One day I travelled with Gośālaka from Kūrmagrāma to Siddhārthagrāma. We arrived at the spot where the sesamum plant grew. Gośālaka remarked about sesamum seeds, '*Bhagavān,* whatever you had told me about 'the sesamum plant turned out to be wrong. Neither the plant has borne fruit nor have the seven souls in its flowers died and become seven seeds'. I narrated to him all that had happened and said, 'Gośālaka, to prove me wrong, you had uprooted the plant. By accidental rain, however, it took root again and the seven souls have also taken the shape of seeds in its pod. What I had predicted is not even slightly wrong'. Gośālaka did not believe me. He went to the plant and plucked the pod. It contained just seven seeds. Gośālaka thought : 'Just as living things in the vegetable domain die and are reborn there, so also can other beings be reborn after death in the same spheres'. Thus, Gosālaka propounded his new doctrine of *Parivṛtya Parihāra* (fated change of mortal forms). Gośālaka's attention was diverted towards attainment of mystical powers. He, therefore, separated from me. After the prescribed penance of six months, he attained both the concise and the profound '*Tejoleśyās*'.

"After a few days, the six *Diśācaras* also joined him. Since then, he proclaims himself as *Jina* without being so, *Kevali* without being a *Kevali,* and *Sarvajña* without being such.

"This news spread round in Śrāvastī. Everywhere people started commenting : 'Gośālaka is not *Jina.* His talk of being *Jina* is senseless. *Bhagavān* Mahāvīra says so'.

Gośālaka also heard the comment from several persons, which made him very angry. Burning with wrath, he came from the penance ground to the pottery bazar of Hālāhalā and sat with members of his Ājīvaka *Saṅgha* in great rage."

Gośālaka and Ānanda

At that time, Lord Mahāvīra's *Sthavira* (reclaimer of fallen *Sādhus)* disciple Ānanda had gone into the city to get alms. He was simple and humble. He used to perform the *Chaṭṭha* penance regularly. Making rounds of the households of different strata of society he passed by the pottery mart of Hālāhalā. Gośālaka saw him and spoke to him thus : 'Ānanda, come here and listen to an example'. Ānanda complied with the request and Gośālaka began to say :

"It in an old story. Some greedy businessmen started on a business trip loading carts with groceries and other goods, and taking with them provisions for the journey. On the way, they entered a large forest, which was devoid of sources of water or any habitation or communication. By the time they had crossed a part of the jungle, their stores of water was exhausted. Suffering from, thirst, they started discussing their plight. A difficult problem faced them. Lastly, they started searching for water on all sides. In doing so, they came to a thick forest which had a large mole-hill in it. It had four high peaks. They broke open one of them. They found in it clean, digestive and crystal-clear water. They drank the water, gave it to bullocks and other animals and filled jars with it for the journey. Feeling greedy, they broke open another peak. They got from it a large quantity of gold. Their greediness increased and they opened up the third peak hoping to find in it precious stones. They found in it such wealth. Then they considered breaking open the last peak in the hope of finding in it the best and the most precious diamonds of great import and fit to be worn by great men. Among the businessmen there was one wise person who felt compassion for all and who wished everybody happiness and welfare. He said, 'We should not break the fourth peak. It might bring us misery and difficulty.' His companions did not heed his advice and opened up the fourth peak. From it came out a most terrible and extremely dark snake which could inflict poison simply by sight. No sooner had its angry look fallen on the businessmen than they all turned to ashes together with all their goods. The sole survivor was the person who had advised against the breaking of the fourth peak. The snake reached him to his house with his goods. Ānanda, likewise has your *Ācārya* and *Guru* Jñātaputra (a name of Lord Mahāvīra) attained the highest state. He enjoys glory and honour among gods, men and others. But if he says anything against me, like those businessmen, I will destroy him with divine powers achieved by me. Like that well-wishing businessman, I will save you only. Now go to your *Dharmācārya* and tell him what I have said".

Ānanda was terrified after listening to Gośālaka. He went to *Bhagavān* Mahāvīra and told him about it. He also enquired if Gośālaka had the power to burn Lord Mahāvīra.

Said Mahāvīra : "With the powers achieved by him, Gośālaka can no doubt destroy any person in one blow, but he can do no harm to Arahanta Bhagavān. *Anagāra's* who has taken strict and blameless vows) divine powers are far superior to those of Gośālaka, as the former can overcome anger with mercy. Similarly, the virtue of compassion makes the powers of *Sthavira* several times higher than those of *Anagāra*. And the powers of Arahanta, on account of His Pure Compassion, are infinitely superior to those of *Sthavira*. Therefore, none can consume Him by fire although one might cause Him some trouble. Therefore, go and tell the *Nirgranthas* (ascetics who have renounced all worldly possessions and wander naked) like Gautama, "O *Āryas*, do not instigate Gośālaka by entering into any religious argument with him, nor contradict him and say aught against his doctrine. Give him no offence by speaking, against his belief, as he has adopted mean tendencies, not behoving an Ārya."

Prāvṛta-Parihāra (the doctrine of migration of soul from one body to another)

As Ānanda Anagāra was passing on this information to the sage Gautama and others, Gośālaka arrived at Koṣṭhaka Chaitya after leaving his followers behind. Standing at a distance from Bhagavān Mahāvīra, he said : "Longlived Kāśyapa, when you say that Gośālaka, the son of Maṅkhali, was your religious disciple, you are right. That disciple of yours, after a noble and virtuous death, has been reborn as a god in the heavens. I am Udāyi of the Kauṇḍinyāyana *Gotra* (clan). Leaving the body of Arjuna, son of Gautama, in the seventh *Pravṛtta Parihāra,* I entered the body of Gośālaka, son of Maṅkhali. According to our theory, those who attained salvation in the past, are now attaining it, or will do so thereafter—all have, to go through 84 lakh *Mahākalpas,* seven *Deva Bhāva,* seven *Saṁyutha Nikāya* and seven *Sanjñigarbha* (human embryo) births. Then come seven migrations from body to body and, last of all, exhausting of 5,60,603 *Karmas*. That is the only way to achieve liberation, knowledge and salvation. That is how it has happened in the past; that is how it will take place henceforth."

"...... During boyhood, I developed a desire for renunciation and for taking the vow of *brahmacarya* (continence). I renounced the world. I changed bodies seven times. The following were my names during these migrations : Aiṇeyaka, Mallarāma, Maṇḍika, Roha, Bhāradvāja, Arjuna, son of Gautama, and Gośālaka, son of Maṅkhali. In the first transmigra-tion, leaving the body of Udayana, descendeant of Kauṇḍinyāyana, I entered the body of Aiṇeyaka at Maṇḍikukṣi Caitya outside Rājagṛha. I resided in that body for twenty two years. From the body of Aiṇeyaka, I transmigrated to that of Mallarāma at Chandrāvataraṇa Caitya outside Uddaṇḍapura, and in that body I stayed for twentyone years. At Angamandira Caitya outside Champanagarī, I passed on from the bodily abode of Mallarāma to that of Maṇḍika, and live there for a period of twenty years. In the fourth change of bodies, I entered into the body of Roha leaving that of Maṇḍika at Kāma-mahāvana Caitya outside the city of Vārāṇasī where I remained for nineteen years. For the fifth change, I went over to the body of Bhāradvāja from that of Roha at Prāptakāla Caitya outside the city of Ālabhika. There I spent eighteen years. In the sixth transmigration, at Kauṇḍiyāyana Caitya on the precincts of Vaiśālī, I entered the body of Arjuna, son of Gautama, leaving that of Bhāradvāja and stayed therein for seventeen years. The seventh transmigration took place when I left the body of Arjuna, son of Gautama, and entered that of Gośālaka, son of Maṅkhali, at the pottery mart of Hālāhalā in this very city of Śrāvastī, since I considered the body of Gośālaka capable, stable, adequate, healthy, fit for adoption as my abode, and strong enough to bear cold etc. Therefore, Kāśyapa, Gośālaka, son of Maṅkhali, may be considered your disciple only in this context."

Replied Mahāvīra : "Gośālaka, you are trying to conceal yourself like the thief who, running from fear of the villagers and not finding any place like pit, cave, fort, moat or any other inaccessible hiding spot, tries to cover himself with the frontal point of wool, hemp, cotton or straw. Such a cover does not hide him but he considers himself hidden. You are trying to cover yourself in similar manner and you consider yourself concealed. Without being somebody else, you are calling yourself such. Do not do this. It does not suit you."

"The above remarks of *Bhagavāna* Mahāvīra greatly angered Gośālaka and he started abusing the Lord in impolite language. He shouted loudly and descended to a very low stratum of discussion. He said, "It seems to me that you are going to fall and be utterly destroyed today itself. Perhaps you shall not survive this day. You shall have no peace from me."

Use of Tejoleśya

"Sarvāṇubhūti Aṇagāra from the east could not contain himself on hearing Gośālaka. By nature he was polite, humble and simple. Out of love for his Dharmācārya and caring little for the threat of Gośālaka, he rose and told him : "Gośālaka, on hearing any monk-brāhmin, an Ārya salutes him, revers him as an abode of *Deva* and a harbinger of welfare, and worships him. What to speak of you? Bhagavān initiated you, educated you and made you well informed. Even then, you are treating your preceptor in such *an-āryan* manner. There is no doubt that you are the same Gośālaka. This type of behaviour does not befit you." Gośālaka's face flushed with anger on hearing this. He burnt up Sarvāṇubhūti Aṇagāra with one stroke of his *Tejoleśya,* and continued his tirade as before.

"Sunakṣatra Aṇagāra could not bear this. Like Sarvāṇubhūti Aṇagāra, he too went near Gośālaka and started reasoning with him. Gośālaka became angrier still, and struck Sunakṣatra also with *Tejoleśya* Sunakṣatra Aṇagāra came at once to Bhagavān Mahāvīra and did obeisance to Him by going round Him thrice. He recited the five *Mahāvratas,* begged pardon of monks of both sexes and left his mortal body.

"Bhagavān Mahāvīra also reasoned with Gośālaka as Sarvāṇubhūti Aṇagāra had done. It was natural for Gośālaka to be angry. He retraced seven or eight paces and hit *Bhagavān* Mahāvīra with *Tejoleśya* to kill Him. Just as intermittent breeze cannot harm mountain, tope or wall, so also that *Tejoleśya* was not effective. It moved forwards and backwards, and after going round Mahāvīra, it jumped up into the sky. Thence it came down and entered the body of Gośālaka, consuming him.

Being defeated by his own *Tejoleśya,* Gośālaka addressed Bhagavān Mahāvīra thus: "Kāśapa, after being afflicted and conquered by this *Tejoleśya,* which I achieved as fruit of my *tapa,* you will meet your death within a period of six months in a *Chaḍmaṣṭha* state (till soul attains *Kevala Jñāna,* its state is called *Chaḍmaṣṭha).*"

The Lord replied : "Gośālaka, being vanquished by your own *Leśya* and suffering from bilious fever, you will die in a *Chaḍmaṣṭha* state after seven nights. As far as I am concerned, I shall move about as *Jina-Tīrthaṅkara* for sixteen years more."

The news of this incident spread in Śrāvastī in a short while. It became the sole topic of discussion on the streets and cross-roads of the city. People were saying : "Outside the city, in Koṣṭhaka *Caitya,* two *Jinas* are censuring and vilifying each other. One says the other will die first, and vice versa. Who is right and who wrong"? The wise and the respected persons would say : "Bhagavān Mahāvīra speaks the truth and Gośālaka utters falsehood."

Bhagavān Mahāvīra sent for the *Nirgranthas* and addressed them thus : "Just as a heap of straw, wood, leaves, etc. is destroyed after being burnt by fire, in the same manner, Gośālaka has lost his mystical force by using *Tejoleśya* to kill me. You may now gladly refute his doctrine to his face, ask him to give detailed explanations for it, have religious confrontation with him, and silence him by question, reasoning, analysis and explanation."

Gośālaka was silenced by the *Nirgranthas* by questions and answers of different types. He became infuriated but could not cause the slightest harm to the *Nirgranthas.* Many Ājīvaka *Sthaviras* felt dissatisfied and left the *Saṅgha* of Gośālaka. They came to the *Saṅgha* of *Bhagavān* Mahāvīra and engaged themselves in devotion.

The Eight Ultimates

Having failed in his objectives, Gośālaka came out of Koṣṭhaka Caitya. Like an insane person, he was looking into all the four directions. Heaving deep sighs, pulling out hair from his beard, scratching the neck, waving both arms and making sounds with them, stamping feet and shouting 'Oh, I am dying, I am dying', he arrived at the pottery market of Hālāhalā. There to mitigate the feverish heat felt by him, he would suck raw mango, drink wine, again and again sing, dance and greet Hālāhalā with folded hands, and pour over his body cold water stored in clay jars.

"Śramaṇa Bhagavān Mahāvīra told the *Nirgranthas :* "O *Āryans,* the *Tejoleśya* used by Gośālaka to kill me was capable of hitting, destroying and burning sixteen countries, namely, 1. Aṅga, 2. Baṅga, 3. Magadha, 4. Malaya, 5. Mālava, 6. Accha, 7. Vatsa, 8. Kautsa, 9. Pāṭha, 10. Lāṭa, 11. Vajra, 12. Mauli, 13. Kāśī, 14. Kauśala,15. Abadha, 16. Saṁbhuktara. Now, in the pottery mart, he is sucking raw mango, drinking alcohol, dancing, and, folding hands again and again, pouring cold water over his body. To hide his sins, he is propounding the Eight Ultimates, that is, Ultimate drinking, Ultimate singing, Ultimate *drama,* Ultimate *Añjali Karma,* Ultimate Mahāmegha, Ultimate Sechanaka *Gandhahasti,* Ultimate *Mahāśīla Kaṇṭaka Saṅgrāma*, and, in this *Avasarpiṇi Kāla* (period of decay), the manifestation of the Ultimate *Tīrthaṅkara* in his person. To hide fact of having to pour cold water over his body, he is talking of four types of drinkable and four types of non-drinkable water. The drinkable types are : 1. What falls from the hind portion of a cow, 2. Water poured by hand, 3. What is warmed up by the rays of the Sun, and 4. What comes out of the rocks. The other four types are non-drinkable, but may be used to mitigate burning or heat. They are : 1. Stored water: Water stored in cold earthen jars. They may be touched by hand, but their water is not to be drink. 2. Skin water: Chewing of raw fruits like mango, its stone and berries, but not swallowing the juice. 3. Pod Water : Chewing raw pods of *urad, mūṅg*, green peas etc., but not swallowing the liquid. 4. Pure drinking : A person eats pure dried fruits and sweets for six months. For two months, he sleeps on the ground, for two months on a plank of wood, and for the last two months on straw. On the last night of the sixth month, he will be visited by two gods of prosperity, namely, Maṇibhadra and Pūrṇabhadra. They touch him with their cool and moist hand. If he responds to the cool touch, serpent's poison appears. If he does not, then flames arise from his body and turn it to ashes. Thereupon, that person attains liberation, knowledge and salvation."

"In the same city lived Ayaṁpula who was a follower of the 'Ājīvaka' sect. One night, while worrying about family affairs, he wondered what was the form of *Halla* (a kind of insect). To get an answer to this, he went to the pottery mart of Hālāhalā to meet his preceptor Gośālaka. He felt ashamed when he saw Gośālaka dancing, singing and drinking wine, and retraced his steps. The other Ājīvaka *Sthaviras* noticed him and called him. They acquainted him with the aforesaid eight Ultimate things and said : "Now you go and have an answer to your question."

"On an indication from the *Sthaviras,* Gośālaka kept aside the stone of mango and spoke to Ayaṁpula : "Ayaṁpula in the middle of night, you wished to know the form of *Halla,* but you could not satisfy your curiosity. You came to me for the right answer. Seeing me in this state, you felt ashamed and wished to go back, but you are mistaken. What I have in my hand is not a raw mango but its skin. To drink this at the time of attainment of *nirvāṇa* is essential. Dance, song etc. are also ultimate things at the time of *Nirvāṇa.* Therefore, you also play on the *Vīṇā* (lute).

Gośālaka's Repentence

"Ayaṁpula got the answer to his question and returned. Feeling that his last moments were near, Gośālaka sent for the Ājīvaka *Sthavira.* He said : "After I am dead, bathe my body with scented water, wipe it with scented ochre cloth, apply on it paste of sandal from Gośirsa mountain, put on it precious white clothes and adorn it with ornaments. Then put my body on a palanquin, which a thousand persons only can lift, and carry it through Śrāvastī announcing thus : 'The twenty-fourth and ultimate *Tīrthaṅkara* Gośālaka son of Maṅkhali became *Jina*, *Siddha* (free from birth and death) and *Mukta* (liberated), free of all sorrows'. Thus, with great celebration perform my last rites."

"At the end of the seventh night, Gośālaka's false notions left him. A thought came to his mind : "I am proclaiming myself *Jina* without being one. I killed *śramaṇas* and bore animus towards my *Ācārya. Śramaṇa Bhagavān* Mahāvīra alone is true *Jina.*" He called the *Sthaviras* again and told them : "*Sthaviras,* I have been proclaiming myself *Jina* without being one. I am a killer of Śramaṇas and was hostile to my *Ācārya*. Only *śramaṇa Bhagavān* Mahāvīra is true *Jina*. Therefore, after my death, tie a cord to my left leg, spit on my face thrice, and drag my body through the royal highways of Śrāvastī announcing : 'Gośālaka is not *Jina.* Mahāvīra alone is *Jina.*' He put the *Sthaviras* on oath for doing so."

Gośālaka's Death

"Gośālaka died. The *Sthaviras* closed the doors of the pottery mart. In its compound, they drew up a map of Śrāvastī. Everything was done according to Gośālaka's wishes. They spat on his face thrice, and, in a low tone, said : "Gośālaka is not *Jina*. Only *Śramaṇa Bhagavān* Mahāvīra is *Jina.*" The *Sthaviras* had fulfilled their promise. Now, according to the earlier instructions of Gośālaka they worshipped his corpse and performed the last rites with respect and pomp and ceremony."

Gautama Svāmī one day asked *Bhagavān* Mahāvīra : "*Bhagavān*, what has been the fate of Sarvānubhūti *Aṇagāra* who was burnt up by Gośālaka?" 'Bhagavān' Mahāvīra said : "Guatama, Sarvānubhūti *Aṇagāra* has been born as a *Deva* in the life-span of eighteen *Sāgaropamas* in *Sahasrāra Kalpa* (eighth heaven). After leaving it, he will take birth in the region of *Mahāvideha* (in Jambudvīpa) and attain freedom from birth and death, knowledge and salvation. Similarly, Sunakṣatra Aṇagāra has taken birth as a *Deva* in *Acyuta Kalpa* (twelfth heaven) with a life-span of twentytwo *Sāgaropamas*. From there he will also be born in *Mahāvideha* and become liberated after exhausting all his *Karmas*.

Gautama Swāmī asked again : "*Bhagavān*, where is your unworthy disciple, Gośālaka, born after death?"

Replied *Bhagavān* Mahāvīra : "He is born as a *Deva* in *Acyuta Kalpa* with the life-span of twentytwo *Sāgaropamas*. From there, he will go round many a world. In the last, he shall attain *Samyak Dṛṣṭi*. Right Perception of the Reality. When he will be a *Muni* of strong will and vows, he will become *Kevali* and thus end all his miseries."[4]

Kuṇḍakolika and Ājīvaka Deva

On Gośālaka's belief in *Niyativāda* (fatalism), the incident of Kuṇḍakolika *Śramaṇopāsaka* (Venerator of *Śramaṇas)* is both interesting and enlightening. Kuṇḍakolika was a rich house-holder of the city of Kaṃpilapura. He was a follower of *Bhagavān* Mahāvīra. At noontime one day he came to his Asoka *Vāṭikā* (Garden of Asoka trees which relieve one of anxiety or unhappiness) and sat on a stone seat. He took off his outer garment and put it aside. He removed his ring with his name engraved on it and put it near the garment. He began practice *Dharma Prajñapti* (religious teachings) as laid down by Lord Mahāvīra. All of a sudden, a *Deva* came there who, after removing the ring and garment, manifested himself in the sky with tinkling of small bells. Remaining in the a sky, he started conversation with Kuṇḍakolika.

Deva : "Kuṇḍakolika, the *Dharma Prajñapti* of Gośālaka son of Maṅkhali, is praiseworthy because there is no awakening, action, strength, prowess etc. These are all regulated by nature. The *Dharma Prajñapti* of Mahāvīra is not good as it accepts all the said qualities and they are not regulated automatically by tendency."

Kuṇḍakolika : *"Deva,* if that be so, please tell me how you became a *Deva.* Was it due to your efforts and awakening, or you got it as ordained? "

Deva : "Kuṇḍakolika, I believe that I attained the state of *Deva* as ordained. There was no prowess or effort behind it."

Kuṇḍakolika : *"Deva,* if that be so, then why did others not become *Devas?* Why did you alone become one? In other words, attainments come only from action, prowess and awakening. You are not right in saying that Gośālaka's *Dharma Prajñapti* is good and that of Mahāvīra not good".

On hearing all this, the *Deva* got confused about his faith and, after putting the ring and the garment at the spot he had picked them from, went to his own destination. On a suitable occasion, Bhagavān Mahāvīra praised this talk of Kuṇḍakolika before his *sādhus.*[5]

Śakadālaputra

Śakadālaputra was one of the ten prominent *śrāvakas* of *Bhagavān* Mahāvīra. He was in the beginning a follower of the *Ājīvaka* sect and later on became a worshipper of Mahāvīra. The entire account of this fact is found in *Upāsaka-daśāṅga Sūtra.* It is also an authentic account to understand the faith of Gośālaka.

There lived in Polāsapura a potter named Śakadālaputra. He possessed three crore gold coins and ten thousand cows. His wife's name was Agnimitrā. He had a vast industry for manufacture of pots etc. He was a follower of Gośālaka who was the leader of the Ājīvaka sect. One day in *Asoka Vāṭikā* he was fasting in the Ājīvaka way. A *deva* appeared before him and said : "Beloved of Gods, *Mahāmahana* is to come here tomorrow. He is *Jina* and worshipped by all the three *lokas* (worlds). Salute Him and serve Him."

Śakadālaputra started thinking : "Only my *Dharmācārya,* Gośālaka, son of Maṅkhali, is *Mahāmahana* and worthy of being worshipped by all the three *lokas.* He must be coming here tomorrow. I will serve Him."

Next day *Bhagavān* Mahāvīra arrived there with a group of *Śramaṇas.* Thousands of persons gathered to have His *darśana* and to listen to His discourse. Śakadālaputra became curious and inquisitive. He too went to pay his respects to Lord Mahāvīra. *Bhagavān* Mahāvīra told him : "The information given to you by some *Deva* yesterday about the visit of a *Mahāmahana* did not refer to Gośālaka." Sakadālaputra was deeply impressed with the unravelling of this mystery and he invited *Bhagavān* Mahāvīra to stay in his shops. *Bhagavān* started living there. Sakadālaputra was a confirmed fatalist. One day when earthenware were being dried, *Bhagavān* Mahāvīra told Śakadālaputra : "Beloved of the gods, have all these pots been prepared without any effort?"

Śakadālaputra : "These have not been produced by action. Whatever is ordained takes place."

Bhagavān : "If someone breaks the pots, or has intimacy with Agnimitra, what will you do?"

Śakadālaputra : "I will curse him, strike him and kill him."

Bhagavān : "Why should you be prepared to take such action if whatever has been ordained must happen?"

Samyaka Jñāna (right knowledge) now dawned on Śakadālaputra and he accepted the householder's *dharma* observing the *Anuvrata* Vows (adjuring as far as possible violence, untruth, stealing, incontinence and covetousness). *Bhagavān* Mahāvīra thereafter left the place.

To bring him back to his fold, Gośālaka one day visited the house of Śakadālaputra. The latter did not show him any respect. Finding no way out, Gośālaka eulogized fervently *Bhagavān* Mahāvīra. Śakadālaputra said : "Gośālaka, you have eulogized my *Dharmācārya.* Therefore, I invite you to stay in my shops and accept my lodging and hospitality." Gośālaka stayed there. He tried his best to bring Śakadālaputra back to his faith, but, not succeeding in his efforts, left the place.[6]

Other Contexts

Gośālaka stayed with *Bhagavān* Mahāvīra for a long time. Detailed account of this is available in scriptures like *Bhagavatī*. In later texts also there are several references to support it. The importance of those references may not be as great as that of references in the *Āgamas,* but they are worth reading and reflecting upon as they are interesting, stimulate knowledge and are good research material.

Once *Bhagavān* Mahāvīra travelled from Kollāga to Suvarṇakhala. Gośālaka was also with Him. On the way, some villagers were cooking *Khīra* (a dish made of rice, milk and sugar). On seeing *Khīra,* Gośālaka's mouth watered. He told *Bhagavān* Mahāvīra : "Let us stay here for a while. *Khīra* will be ready soon. We will also benefit from it." *Bhagavān* Mahāvīra replied : "What to speak of us, even those who are cooking it will not benefit from it. It will get destroyed before it is cooked." *Bhagavān* proceeded further on his way. To see what happened, Gośālaka stayed on there. Gośālaka also warned the villagers about the impending ill luck. The villagers became alert lest the earthen pot turned over or cracked. In the end, what *Bhagavān* Mahāvīra had predicted took place. The pot contained milk and rice beyond its capacity. The pot cracked as the rice swelled. The entire quantity of *Khīra* started flowing into the ashes and the ground. From this incident, Gośālaka leaned towards fatalism.[7]

Bhagavān Mahāvīra once went to a village named *Brāhmaṇa.* Gośālaka was also with Him. There were two parts of that village: 1. Nandapāṭaka, and 2. Upanandapāṭaka. Nanda and Upananda were two brothers. Each part of the village was named after the brother who owned it. *Bhagawān* Mahāvīra went to the house of Nanda in Nandapāṭaka to get alms. Nanda offered to *Bhagavān* rice mixed with curds : Gośālaka went to the house of Upananda in Upanandapāṭaka for the same purpose. The maid servant lifted some stale rice in a ladle for giving it to Gośālaka. Gośālaka felt insulted and started quarrelling with her. Upananda, who was sitting close by, noticed it all. He too felt angry at the behaviour of Gośālaka. He told the servant : "If he accepts stale rice, give it; if not, throw it on his head." The servant acted accordingly. Gośālaka's anger knew no bounds. He cursed : "If my *Guru* has any powers attained by penances, may your palace be on fire and turn to ashes. "The *Vyantara devas* (beings like *Yakṣas* etc.) destroyed that palace by fire to add to the prestige of Mahāvīra.[8]

On another occasion *Bhagavān* Mahāvīra went to Kālaya. There was a house in ruins outside the village. *Bhagavān* Mahāvīra sat in that house in the evening in meditation. Gośālaka stayed near the door. Sinha, the son of the owner of the village, by chance, came to the same house in the company of the slave girl Vidyunmatī for immoral purposes. He shouted : "Is anyone here?" *Bhagavān* Mahāvīra was in deep meditation. Gośālaka kept quiet. Thinking that the place was uninhabited, Sinha fulfilled his evil purpose there. When the couple were returning, Gośālaka, being struck with passion, caught hold of the hand of Vidyunmatī. Sinha was enraged at this and he thrashed Gośālaka soundly.[9]

Once *Bhagavān* Mahāvīra visited Kumārāka. He sat in meditation in a garden full of *campā* trees. At noon-time, Gośālaka told *Bhagavān* Mahāvīra : "*Bhagavān,* let us go for alms to the neighbourhood." *Bhagavān* replied : "I am fasting today and will not, therefore, go for alms."

Gośālaka went into the village. At the house of a rich potter named Kūpnaya, Ācārya Municandra of the Pārśvanātha tradition was staying with his disciples. Gośālaka was surprised to meet them. He said to himself : What sort of *sādhus* are these who put on clothes of different colours and keep materials like pots etc.? Gośālaka asked them : "Which *sādhus* are you?"

The reply was : "We are *Nirgranthas* and followers of Pāraśvanātha.

Gośālaka asked again : "What sort of *Nirgranthas* are you? You have all these possessions. My *Guru* and I only are true *Nirgranthas.* All of you have adopted this style as means of livelihood."

In counter reply the *sādhus* said: "Your *Dharmācārya* must also be like you."

Angry Gośālaka said : "You are insulting my *Dharmācārya.* I curse that, by the grace of the supernatural powers of my *Guru,* this habitation may be burnt down. Although *Gośālaka* repeated the curse several times, nothing happened. The followers of Pārśvanātha said, "Why are you wasting your time? Nothing will be set on fire, and you are going to get nothing." Somewhat confused, Gośālaka came to '*Bhagavān*' Mahāvīra and said : "I had an argument today with *sādhus* who keep material possessions. I cursed them but their place was not set on fire. *Bhagavān,* why was that so?" '*Bhagavān*' Mahāvīra replied : "Gośālaka, your contention is not correct. What they are doing is right. Your curse will not be effective on them."[10]

At one time *Bhagavān* Mahāvīra went to Chauraka. He was accompanied by Gośālaka. In that place, people were very much afraid of thieves. Guards were posted at different places. As soon as they entered the village, they were surrounded by the villagers who started asking them all sorts of questions. Mahāvīra remained silent. Seeing this, Gośālaka also kept quiet. The guards started harassing them, taking them to be spies. In that village lived Sona and Jayantī, sisters of Utpala *Naimittika.* They had earlier been initiated in *Śramaṇa dharma.* For circumstances beyond their control, they bad become ascetics. They came to the guards and pacified them. On knowing the facts, the guards apologised to *Bhagavān* Mahāvīra.[11]

On one occasion *Bhagavān* Mahāvīra visited the city of Kayaṅgalā. He stayed in a garden temple. In the night, in a corner of the temple, he became immersed in meditation. Gośālaka also took his seat at a place in the temple. It was the month of *Māgha.* The sky was overcast with clouds. There was a light drizzle. The wind was strong and very cold. The same night there was a religious celebration in the temple. To the accompaniment of musical instruments and songs, men and women were dancing together. Gośālaka, who was feeling very cold, did not like it. He started murmuring : What sort of religion is this? Men and women are dancing together. The people present did not like the comments of Gośālaka. They caught hold of him and turned him out of the temple.

Sitting in the open, Gośālaka was shivering with cold. He was saying : 'What a *Kaliyuga*! One who tells the truth is beaten.' Some people took pity on him again and called him inside the temple. He again started decrying their religion. The youth felt enraged. They wanted to beat him. The elders stopped them and said : "Let us play the musical instruments so loudly that his jabbering may not reach our ears." Thus the night passed, and in the morning *Bhagavān* Mahāvīra left for Śrāvastī.[12]

Once *Bhagavān* Mahāvīra left Kūpiya for Vaiśālī. Gośālaka had become tired of the strict rules of conduct of *Bhagavān* Mahāvīra. He told the Lord : "I shall accompany you no more. You do not look after me at all. I am reprehended by people from time to time. You keep standing with eyes closed and do nothing. Except facing privation and starvation, what do I get by remaining with you?"

Mahāvīra proceeded to Vaiśālī and Gośālaka to Rājagṛha. Gośālaka stayed away from Mahāvīra for six months. He had gone to Rājagṛha in pursuit of happiness, but only misery came his way. No one respected him. Nobody would give him alms with reverence. Being perplexed with difficulties, he began searching for *Bhagavān* Mahāvīra again. He found Him in Śāliśirsa. From there onwards he accompanied Him again.[13]

In Digambara Tradition

The aforesaid accounts of Gośālaka are taken from Śvetāmbara *Āgamas.* In *Digambara* texts, we get them in somewhat different form. According to them, Gośālaka was a *Muni* in the Pārśvanātha tradition. After joining the Mahāvīra fold, he wanted to be appointed as *Gaṇadhara* (main disciple who composes the sayings of a *Tīrthaṅkara* in the form of *Sūtras).* When this wish was not fulfilled, he separated from that fold. Coming to Śrāvastī, he became leader of the *Ājīvaka* sect and started calling himself a *Tīrthaṅkara.* He used to preach like this : "Knowledge does not lead to liberation. Absence of knowledge does so. There in no *Īśvara* (almighty) or *Deva.* Therefore, one should meditate according to one's will on a void."[14]

IN THE TRIPIṬAKAS

The Worst

Among contemporary faiths and their founders, Lord Buddha considered *Ājīvaka Saṅgha* and Gośālaka as the worst forms. Describing good and evil persons, he says : "Some person exists only for the disadvantage of a large number of people. He causes loss and pain to a great many. He causes harm and difficulty even to the *Devas,* e.g., Makkhalī Gośālā. I cannot think of a person worse than Gośālā. Just as a fisherman entraps fish in his net, Gośālā entraps human beings."[15] In a different context, Buddha also says : "In *Śramaṇa dharmas,* the worst and the most detestable belief is that of Gośālā like a hair blanket among clothes. Such a blanket is cold in winter and hot in summer. It is ugly to look at, unpleasant to touch and gives offensive smell.[16] In life, Gośālā's *Niyativāda* is equally useless."[17]

The followers of Buddha also used to look upon *Ājīvakas* with contempt. Living in Jaitavana, once Buddha permitted the monks to have bath in the rains. After removing clothes they started bathing. The maid servant of the prominent *Śravikā* Visākhā came to the retreat to inform the monks about dinner time. When she saw the naked monks, she thought they were *Ājīvakas.* She went back and told Visākhā that not *Śākya Bhikṣus* but *Ājīvaka Bhikṣus* were having bath there.[18] Visākhā understood the situation. When Buddha came to her house with the monks, she narrated the incident and submitted: "*Bhante,* nudity is scandalous and hateful."[19]

Like *Niyativāda,* the name of another belief of Gośālaka is *Śamasra-Suddhivāda.* According to it, there are fourteen lac six thousand six hundred main classes of life. There are five *Karmas* of five sense organs. Three *Karmas* are body, speech and mind. There is a *Pūrṇa* (complete) *Karma* (by comparison with body and speech). And there is an *Ardha* (half) *Karma* (compared to mind). There are sixty-two *mārgas* (paths) and sixty-two *Antarakalpas* (manner, conduct). The number of *Abhijātis* psychological classification is six. There are eight *Puruṣa Bhumis* four thousand nine hundred *Vyavasāyas,* four thousand nine hundred *Parivrājakas,* four thousand nine hundred *Nāga Avasas,* two thousand *Indriyas,* three thousand *Narakas* (hells), thirtysix *Rajodhātus,* seven *Sañjñī Garbhas,* seven *Devas,* seven *Manuṣyas* (human beings), seven *Piśācas* (demons), seven *Sāras,* seven hundred seven *Granthas* (knots), seven hundred seven *Prapatas* and seven hundred seven *Svapnas* (dreams). There are fortyeight lakh *Mahākalpas* (the longest measure of time). Both the learned and the foolish will exhaust their miseries after roaming about in them. If someone says that by a certain code of conduct, fast, penance or continence, he can ripen an unripe

Karma, or destory a ripe *Karma* by enjoying or bearing its fruits, it shall not be so. Happiness and pain are so fixed that they can be measured. They cannot be increased or decreased. Just as when a ball of thread is thrown, it will go on rolling till it is fully unwound, so also the end of miseries of both the wise and the foolish will come only after they have completed their rounds of universal existence."[20]

REVIEW

Veneration and its Reasons

Whatever might have been the philosophy or ideas of Gośālaka, it goes without saying that he was a popular and famous religious leader of those times. Jain tradition also accepts that his *Dharma Saṅgha* was larger than even the *Dharma Saṅgha* of *Bhagavān* Mahāvīra.[21] Like the ten *Śrāvakas* of Mahāvīra, Gośālaka also had twelve main *Śrāvakas.*[22] The statement of Buddha that "he entraps people in his net like fish" also speaks of the influence of Gośālaka. The question that arises is : if Gośālaka was not as great as Buddha or Mahāvīra in character, restraint and religious practices, how could *Ājīvaka Saṅgha.* become so wide-spread? The possible reasons are : Prophecy and hard perances. In the *Saṅghas* of Mahāvīra[23] and Buddha,[24] foretelling or interpreting of omens was prohibited. Gośālaka and his co-workers made use of it freely. The *Pārśvaṣtha* (putting on *Sādhu's* dress but not observing rules) *Bhikṣus* of Pārśvanāth depended mainly on it.[25] Some of them imparted this knowledge to Gośālaka and were his principal companions. Penances in the *Ājīvaka Saṅgha* were also very rigid. Jaina texts support this freely.[26] So also Buddhist texts refer to Gośālaka being steadfast in penance.[27] Research scholars also generally support this view. According to Ācārya Narendra Deva, *Ājīvakas* used to do penance with five types of fire. They used to dangle in the air like bats. This penance and suffering was probably the reason for the honour they enjoyed in society. People used to refer to them for the outcome of *Nimitta,* omen, dream, etc.[28]

Since both *Tapa* and *Nimitta* have always been the principal attractions in Indian society, Gośālaka enjoying so much respect in spite of his faults is not unnatural.

Name and Profession

Different accounts are available about the name and profession of Gośālaka. The Jaina canonical texts are decidedly and definitely of the view that Gośālaka was the son of Maṅkhali, who was a *Maṅkha.* In texts like *Bhagavatī* and

Upāsakdasaṅga, the name appears as "*Gośālā Mamkhaliputte*", that is, Gośālaka, son of Maṅkhali. The word *Maṅkha* is used for painter[29] at some places and for seller of paintings[30] at others. The meaning given by commentator Abhayadevasūri appears to be near reality. "*Citraphalakaṁ haste gataṁ yasya sa tathā*"—that is one who makes a living by keeping in hand a cloth or board with painting on it. *Maṅkha* was a caste whose members used to earn their livelihood by keeping a picture of Śiva or some other *Deva* in hand. Members of the *Dakota* caste even today make a living by keeping an image or picture of Śani (Saturn) *Deva* with them.

In the *Tripiṭaka* (Buddhist canonical book) tradition this *Ājīvaka* leader has been called Makkhali-Gośālā. A slightly strange story is found in Buddhist literature about the origin of the name Makkhali. According to it, Gośālaka was a slave. Once he was going ahead with an earthen pitcher full of oil, followed by his master. Slippery ground was ahead of them. The master said, "*Tata, Mā Khali, Tata Mā Khali*" (Do not slip, do not slip). But Gośālaka slipped and the oil flowed on the ground. Afraid of the master, he started running. The master caught hold of his garment. Leaving the garment, Gośālaka ran away naked. Thus he became a nude *Sādhu* and people started calling him Makkhali.[31]

This narration appears in Buddhist texts of a later period. Therefore, it can be taken only as a legend or hearsay.

Pāṇini, the grammarian, takes the word as "*Maskari*". The simple meaning of *Maskari* is given. as religious wanderer or monk.[32] Exegetist Patañjali says : "*Maskari* is not that *Sādhu* who goes about with *Maskara* or bamboo stick in 'hand. Then what is he? *Maskari* is that *Sādhu* who preaches : 'Do not indulge in action. The path of peace alone leads to welfare'.[33] Here Gośālaka may not have been referred to by name, but the indication of Pāṇini and Patañjali is clearly for him. It seems that the interpretation of "Do not indulge in action" started when Gośālaka had already become famous in the society as a *Dharmācārya.* May be they gave a new interpretation of the prevalent name. The idea of Jaina texts in this respect seems to be original. Side by side with calling him the son of Maṅkhali, they also describe him as one who was born in a *Gośālā* (cow-house). Pāṇini supports it etymologically thus : "*Gośālāyaṁ Jataḥ Gośalaḥ*" (4/3/35). Ācārya Buddhaghoṣa also accepts Gośālaka's birth in Gośālā in his commentary of Samaññaphala Sutta.[34]

Pāṇini's period is regarded as 480 to 410 B.C.[35] Even if he compiled grammar during the middle of his life its time will be near about 445 B.C. Mahāvīra attained *Nirvāṇa* during 527 B.C. and Gośālaka died sixteen years earlier, that is, in 543 B.C. In other words, there is a difference of nearly 100 years between the period of Gośālaka's death and the period of the compilation of grammar by Pāṇini. It is very natural that new and weighty interpretations are attributed to simple words or derivations during the period of rise of any religion or sect. We come across many such examples in the history of sects.

The *Śramaṇa*-tradition of Gośālaka is called *Ājīvaka* in *Tripiṭakas* and *Ājīvika* in *Āgmas*. Both the words have the same meaning. It appears that this name was coined only by opponents. The meaning of *Ājīvaka* or *Ājīvika* is—one who performs *Tapa* (religious austerity or penance) only for the sake of livelihood.[36] What meaning the *Ājīvakas* themselves gave to this word is not found in any text. May be they accepted it taking a lofty view of the fact that they were living by observing the rigid rules of monkhood. Like Jaina texts, Buddhist *Piṭakas* also mention about their strict rules of monkhood. According to *Majjhima Nikāya,* most of their rules are like those of *Nirgranthas* and some even stricter than theirs.[37]

As has been mentioned earlier, there is similarity of references to Gośālaka's *Saṁsāra-śuddhivāda* in *Āgamas* and *Tripiṭakas.* The measure of eightyfour *Mahākalpas* is found in the clear commentaries of *Āgamas.* Dr. Basham has written on all these subjects in detail.[38]

Proximity of Jains and Ājīvakas

While most of the topics of Jainas and Ājīvakas are indicative of mutual vituperation, some accounts of their proximity also exist. The reason may be the similarity of a few of their rules of conduct. Nudity has been respected in both traditions. And, in view of these characteristics, both the traditions have considered Jaina and Ājīvaka and any of them better than followers of other religions. Jaina *Āgamas* tell us that *Tāpasas* go up to *Jyotiṣka, Kandarpikas* up to *Saudharma, Caraka Parivrājakas* up to *Brahmaloka, Kilviṣikas* up to *Lantaka Kalpa, Tiryañcas* up to *Sahasrāra Kalpa, Ājīvakas* and *Abhiyogikas* up to *Acyuta Kalpa,* and *Darśanabhrașța Veśadhāris* up to ninth *Graiveyaka.*[39] Here *Ājīvakas* are said to go up to the twelfth heaven after death, whereas others do not go beyond the fifth.

Under another topic, giving a praiseworhty account of the monastic order of *Ājīvakas,* it is said : "In villages and cities live *Ājīvaka sādhus.* Some of them collect alms at an interval of two houses and others at an interval of three to seven."[40]

In *Bhagavatī*[41] *Āgama,* an account in high terms is given of the rules and code of conduct of *Ājīvaka* followers. It is said there : "They lock upon Gośālaka as *Arihanta* (the Worthy) *Deva,* show respect and render service unto parents, do no eat five types of fruits, namely, wild fig, banyan fruit, berry, fig and *Pilaṅkhu,* and tubers like onion and garlic, do not have bulls castrated or their noses and ears pierced, and who do not do business in which may kill *Trasa* (mobile) beings."

Gośālaka[42] determined six classes[43] and more or less divided among them different types of people and *Bhikṣus.*[44] They are as follows :

Kṛṣṇa (black) *Abhijāti* :	Butcher, hunter, trapper, fisherman, thief, robber, jailor and others who perform cruel acts.
Nīla (blue) *Abhijāti* :	Mendicants begging by sleeping on thorns and others believing in the Doctrines of *karma* and *kriyā* (action).
Lohita (red) *Abhijāti* :	*Nirgrantha* who puts on only one garment.
Haridra (yellow) *Abhijāti* :	Householder who puts on white garments and *Nirgrantha Śrāvaka.*
*Śukla (*white*) Abhijāti :*	*Ājīvakas* and their followers.
Mahāśukla (extra white) *Abhijāti* :	Nanda Vatsa, Kṛsa Sāṅkṛtya and Makkhali Gośālā.

Although the classification is not clear, but it clearly indicates that even *Ājīvakas* gave the place next to themselves to *Nigaṇṭhas,* just as *Nigaṇṭhas* put *Ājīvakas* in identical place.

Who the Guru?

Impartiality is absolutely necessary in history and research. Sectarian prejudice must also be kept out. But neutrality and new conclusions can also be disastrous if they take the form of predilections. The tendency for research with regard to Gośālaka has increased during the last few years. About *Ājīvaka* order and Gośālaka, occidental and oriental scholars have brought out a lot of new material. But it is sad to note that, for the sake of new conclusions, some scholars are turning history upside down as far as Gośālaka is concerned. Dr. Benimadhav Barua writes : "It can be said that on the basis of information available from Jaina and Buddhist literature it cannot be proved that Gośālaka was one of the two deceitful disciples proved that of Mahāvīra as made out by Jainas. On the contrary, it disproves that theory. In other words, I wish to say that if historians make some efforts in respect of this disputed question, they will have to admit that if, out of the two, one is indebted, it is the *Guru* and not, as held by Jainas, his fraudulent disciple."[45] In the background of this conclusion, Dr. Barua also says : "Mahāvīra was, in the beginning, in the sect of Pārśvanātha. After a year, when he became *Acelaka* (naked), he joined the *Ājīvaka* order."[46] At the same time, Dr. Barua supports his theory by saying that Gośālaka had attained the state of *Jina* two years before Mahāvīra did so.[47] Although Dr. Barua concedes that these are great experiments in imagination,[48] his assumptions have definitely effected some people. The conclusions are being drawn accordingly, and that too with double insistence. Gopaldas Jivabhai Patel writes : "Mahāvīra and Gośālaka had lived together for six years. Therefore, in Jaina *sūtras,* there must be particular introduction of Gośālaka. In *sūtras* like *Bhagavatī, Sūtrakṛtāṅga, Upāsakadaśāṅga,* etc. some brief and detailed accounts about Gośālaka are available. But in all those accounts so much effort appears to have been made to prove Gośālaka as characterless and as a disciple of Mahāvīra that generally it is difficult to accept those accounts as having any base. Benimadhav Barua has, to the best of his ability, made an attempt in his treatise[49] to put forward the philosophy of Gośālaka in proper perspective."[50]

Dharmānanda Kośāmbī and others has also expressed similar views. Dr. Hermann Jacobi[51] appears to have been the principal supporter of this idea. Thereafter, many authors went on writing on the subject. Dr. Basham in his great treatise, The History and Doctrines of the *Ājīvakas* has written on this subject in still greater detail. All this is indicative of the tendency that if a western scholar has written something, it must be of great value. It is well known that whatever facts are available about Gośālaka are connected with Jaina and Buddhist literature. We establish the life account of Gośālaka only on that basis. If we look for facts outside these traditions, perhaps we shall not even come across a person like Gośālaka. In the circumstances, we have to give credence to the facts as found in Jaina and Buddhist texts on the subject. To accept some of the facts as correct and the others as false will not be a historical method of dealing with them. They cannot be called baseless also on account of the fact that the accounts of two different traditions, that is, Jaina and Buddhist, support each other in this respect. Even Dr. Jacobi has advised : "In the absence of other proofs, we have to be vigilant about these narratives."[52]

Similar baseless conclusions also get currency because modern researchers tend to look more at branches than at roots. Not being conversant with Prākṛta and Pāli, they are unable to take an overall view of *Āgamas* and *Tripiṭakas* and the one-sided essays in Hindi and English become their mainstay. It is all the more surprising that even for material that can be easily had from the scriptures foreign scholars and their books are quoted for proof. It is a mistake to consider narratives on the subject found in Jaina *Āgamas* as offensive. Even though Jaina *Āgamas* belittle Gośālaka and his *Ājīvaka* faith, by sending him upto *Acyuta Kalpa* and by prophesying him as completely liberated, and by saying that his follower *Bhikṣus* have the capacity to reach that stage, they have also alluded him with glory. It will be very grotesque if, while discussing Gośālaka, we accept from Jaina *Āgamas* facts like he was born in a *Gośālā,* was a *Maṅkha* and the leader of *Ājīvakas*; and, as a retort to Jaina *Āgamas* saying that he was a disciple of Mahāvīra, we say, without any basis, that he was His *Guru.* This question would arise if the Jaina *Āgamas* had called him the disciple and the

Buddhist and *Ājīvaka* scriptures the *Guru.* On the contrary, the position is that before Mahāvīra, Gośālaka himself states : "Gośālaka was your disciple, but I am not that. I entered into the corpse of Gośālaka. This body is of that Gośālaka. but the soul is different." Thus, in the absence of any proof to the contrary, these experiments in imagination become meaningless. It is a happy augury that soon after this baseless conclusion came up, research scholars have also started refuting it.[53]

Incontinence in Ājīvakas

The account of *Ājīvaka 'Bhikṣus'* being devoted to non-observance of continence and religious discipline is found in the context of Ārdraka Kumāra. This is also considered as vilification.[54] It would require reconsideration if only Jaina *Āgamas* had said, so but the Buddhist scriptures also freely support it.[55] *Niganṭhas* were classified as observing continence and *Ājīvakas* as observing incontinence.[56] Gośālaka used to talk of three states : Bound, Liberated, and Neither Bound-Nor Liberated. He used to consider himself even beyond the state where man is free from the bondage of action. He was of the opinion that a liberated man need have no fear even of cohabitation.[57] All these topics may have come from the sects that are critical of *Ājīvakas*, but they do make the sexual activities of *Ājīvakas* a subject requiring research and investigation. As these references support one another, they do not by themselves become baseless. According to the historian, Dr. Satyaketu, sexual intercourse was one of the three items of differences, between Mahāvīra and Gośālaka.[58] Taking everything into consideration, it can be said that the comment of Jaina *Āgamas* about *Ājīvakas* indulging in sexual activity is not just a scandal. It is also not unusual if a particular sect does not emphasize continence as a matter of principle. There have been many religious orders in India the principles of which have accepted all possible options in renunciation and enjoyment. Why do we feel surprised only at the acceptance of incontinence or enjoyment? Among those religious leaders were also people like Ajita Keśakambalī who did not recognise even the existence of soul. It is a moot point why such people indulged in austerity and penance. Therefore, utmost care and seriousness are called for in giving currency to new conclusions and refuting the prevalent ones.

REFERENCES

1. Janardhan Bhatt, *Asoka Ke Dharmalekha*, Publication Division, Delhi, 1957, pp. 401-403.
2. Chimanlal Jaichand Shah, *Uttara Hindustān meṁ Jaina Dharma*, Longmans & Green Co., London, 1903, p. 64.

3. These Diśācaras were the fallen disciples of Mahāvīra according to the author of the ṭīkā, and followers of the Pārśvanātha tradition according to the author of the Chūrṇī.
4. Based on *Bhagawatī Sūtra* (Hindi translation) Translated by Madankumar Mehta, Publishers Shrut-Prakashan Mandir, Calcutta, pp. 629 to 652.
5. Based on *Upāsakadaśāṅga Sūtra*, Chapter VI.
6. *Upāsakadaśāṅga Sūtra*, based on Chapter VII.
7. *Śrī Āvaśyak Sūtra Niryukti*, Malaygirivṛtti Pūrva Bhāga, Gāthā 474, Patra No. 277-1; *Śrī Āvaśyak Chūrṇī*, Part I, Patra 283.
8. *Āvaśyaka Sūtra Niryukti*, Malaygiri's Vṛtti, Pūrva Bhāga, Gāthā 475, Patra No. 277-1-2; *Āvaśyaka Chūrṇī*, Part I.
9. *Āvaśyaka Sūtra Niryukti*, Malaygiri's Vṛtti, Pūrva Bhāga, Gāthā 476, Patra No. 278-1; *Āvaśyaka Chūrṇī*, Pūrva Bhāga, Patra No. 284.
10. *Āvaśyaka Sūtra Niryukti*, Malaygiri's Vṛtti, Pūrva Bhāga, Gāthā 477, Patra No.279-1; *Āvaśyaka Chūrṇī*, Pūrva Bhāga, Patra No. 285.
11. *Āvaśyaka Sūtra Niryukti*, Malaygiri's Vṛtti, Pūrva Bhāga, Gāthā 477, Patra No. 278-2, 279-1; *Āvaśyaka Chūrṇī*, Pūrva Bhāga, Patra No. 286.
12. *Āvaśyaka Sūtra Niryukti*, Malaygiri's Vṛtti, Pūrva Bhāga, Gāthā 478, Patra No. 279, *Āvaśyaka Chūrṇī*, Pūrva Bhāga, Patra No. 287.
13. *Āvaśyaka Chrūni*, Pūrva Bhāga, Patra No. 292.
14. Masayari pūrṇarisiṇo uppanno pāsanāhatitthammi, sirivīra samavasaraṇe agahiyajhunina niyatteṇa ṇiggai jhuṇīna aruho, ṇiggaya vissāsa sīsassa ṇa muṇai jiṇakahiya suyaṁ sampai dikkhāya gahiya goyamao,
vippo veyabbhāsi tamhā mokkhaṁ ṇa nāṇāo.
aṇṇāṇāo mokkhaṁ evaṁ loyāna payaḍmāṇo hu,
devo a ṇatthi koyi suṇṇaṁ jhāeha icchāye.
—Bhāvasaṅgraha, Gāthā 176-179.
15. *Aṅguttara Nikāya*, 1-18-4:5.
16. According to commentaries, this blanket is made of hurnan hair.
17. *The Book of Gradual Sayings*, Vol. I, p. 286.
18. The Siamere text roads ājīvika in the place of ājīva.
19. *Aṅguttara Nikāya Aṭṭhakathā*, 1-7-2.
20. Rhys Davids, *Dialogues of Buddha*, pp.72-73; cf. G.P. Malalasekara, *Dictionary of Pālī Proper Names*, Vol. II, pp. 398-99; *Dīghanikāya*, 1-53, *Majjhimanikāya*, 1-231, 238, 438, 516; *Saṁyutta Nikāya*, 1-66, 68, 3-211, 4-398; *Aṅguttara Nikāya*, 1-33, 286, 3-276, 384, *Jātaka*, 1-439, 509.
21. According to hearsay, the number of Gośālaka's followers was 11,61,000, whereas the number of Mahāvīra's followers was 1,59,000.
(*Kalpasūtra*, Sūtra 136)
22. *Bhagavatī Sūtra*, Śataka 8, Uddeśaka 5.
23. *Niśīth Sūtra*, U. 13-66; *Dasavaikālika Sūtra*, Chapter 8, Gāthā 50.
24. *Vinayapiṭaka*, Chullavagga 5-6-2.
25. *Āvaśyaka Chūrṇī*, Patra 273; *Trisaṣṭiśalakāpuruṣacaritraṁ*, Parva 10, Sarga 4, Śloka 134-35; *Tīrthaṅkara* Mahāvīra, Part 2, p. 103.
26. Ājiviyanaṁ chauvvihe tave p.t. ugga tave ghor tave rasanijjuhanata jibbhidiyapadi samlenatathāṅga Sūtra, Tha. 4, U. 2, S. 309.
27. *Saṁyuttanikāya* 10, Nana Titthiya Sutta.
28. *Bauddha Dharma-darśana*, p. 4.
29. *Indological Studies*, Vol. II, p. 254.
30. *Dictionary of Pālī Proper Names*, Vol. II, p. 400.
31. Ācārya Buddhaghoṣa, *Dhammapada-Aṭṭhakathā*; 1-43, *Majjhimanikāya*, Aṭṭha-Kathā; 1-422.
32. Maskaraṁ maskarinau venuparivrājakayoho—*Pāṇini Vyākarṇa*, 6-1-154.
33. Na vai maskaroasyatīti maskari parivrājkaḥ. kiṁ tarhi? Mākṛt karmāṇi mākṛt karmāṇi sāntirvaḥ śreyasityāhato maskari parivrājakaḥ-Pātañajala, Mahābhāṣya, 6-1-154.

34. *Sumaṅgala Vilāsini (Dīghnikāya Aṭṭhakathā)*, pp. 143-44.
35. Vasudevasharan Agarwal, Pāṇinikālīn Bhārat-Varṣa, p. 476.
36. See *Bhagavatī Sūtra Vṛtti*, S. 1, U. 2; *Jaināgama Śabda Saṅgraha*, p. 134. Hoernle, *Ājīvikas* in *Encyclopaedia of Religion and Ethics*; E.J. Thomas, *Life of Buddha*, p. 130.
37. *Mahāsaccak Sutta*, 1-4-6.
38. *The History and Doctrine of Ājīvakas*.
39. *Tapas : Sādhus* who eat fallen leaves.
    Kandarpika : Sādhus who indulge in levity and mean endeavour.
    Charakarivrājaka : *Tridaṇḍī Sādhus* who collect alms by looting.
    Kilviṣika : Sādhus who perform evil deeds by *vidyā*, *mantra* and betwichment.
    Darśana-bharaṣṭa : Nihnavac.
    —*Bhagavatī Sūtra*, S. 1, U. 2.
40. *Abhidhānā Rājendraḥ*, Part II, p. 116.
41. Śataka 8, Uddeśaka 5.
42. Some people consider Pūraṇa Kāśyapa as the aughor but in reality it should be Gośālaka. For details, see '*Nirgrantha in the Six Abhijātis*' in Chapter XVII.
43. Based on *Aṅguttaranikāya*, 6-6-57; *Saṁyuttanikāya*, 24-7-8.
44. Jaina Āgamas divide *Prāṇīs* in six Leśyas according to *Pariṇāma* and *Varṇa*. For comparative study, see '*Nirgrantha in the Six Abhijātās*' in Chapter XVII.
45. The *Ājīvikas*, J.D.L. Vol. II, 1920, pp. 17-18.
46. *Ibid.*, p. 18.
47. *Ibid.*, p. 18.
48. *Ibid.*, p. 21.
49. *Pre-Buddhistic Indian Philosophy*, pp. 297-318.
50. *Mahāvīra Swāmi No Saṁyama Dharma* (Gujarati translation of Sūtrakṛtāṅga), p. 34.
51. S.B.E. Vol. XLV, Introduction, pp. XXIX to XXXII.
52. *Ibid.*, p. XXXIII.
53. Dr. Kamtaprasad, Vīra, Vol. III, Nos. 12-13; Chimanlal Jaychand Shah, *Uttara Hindustān Meṁ Jaina Dharma*, pp.58-61, Dr. A.S. Gopani, *Ājīvika Sect—A New Interpretation*, Bhāratīya Vidyā, Vol. II, pp. 201-10; Vol. III, pp. 47-59.
54. *Mahāvīra Swāmī No Saṁyama Dharma*, p. 34.
55. *Ājīvakas*, Vol. I, *Majjhimanikāya*, (Part I, p. 524; *Encyclopaedia of Religion and Ethics*, Dr. Hoernle, p. 261.
56. *Majjhimanikāya*, Sandaka Sutta, 2-3-6.
57. Gopaldas Patel, *Mahāvīra Kathā*, p. 177; Śrīchand Rāmapuriā, *Tīrthaṅkara* Vardhamāna, p. 83.
58. *Bhāratīya Saṁskṛti Aura Usakā Itihāsa*, p. 163.

4

CHRONOLOGY

Introduction

Man is inquisitive by nature. Inquisitiveness adds to his knowledge that increases curiosity. There is an unending chain of knowledge and curiosity wherein lies the exhuberance of sublime bliss, rightly regarded as summum bonum of all life of worship, devotion, renunciation and penance. In this cycle of knowledge and curiosity lies the boundless joy of life. It is these two that lead unfailingly to divine citadel of truth or supreme abode of bliss.[1] When history initially peeped into the socio-philosophical exploits of both Mahāvīra and Buddha, the two stalwarts were misconstrued as identical by certain critics of Indian Philosophy and Indology. Still others had a miserable downfall when they ventured to establish an identity of Buddha with Gautam Svāmī, the chief disciple of Mahāvīra.[2] But a little analysis confirmed very soon that Mahāvīra and Buddha, though belonging to the same generation and country, were two distinct personalities, the former having lived on this earth for 72 years[3] and latter for 80 years.[4]

This analytical approach propelled the masses to pose a basic query : How long did Mahāvīra and Buddha live as contemporaries and who was older of the two? This question has drawn the attention of many a thinker and till now numerous efforts have been made to solve it. A good deal of new light has been thrown on it, but the findings arrived at are not indisputable. The various accounts described in the *Jain Āgamas,* the Buddhist *Tripiṭakas* and the historical works, which appear to be inconsistent with one another have led the scholars to diverse conclusions. The classification of the efforts made so far, their critical examination and a humble effort to push the subject to an indubitable stage on the basis of independent thinking, form the subject matter of the present critique.

VIEWS OF FOREIGN SCHOLARS

For a proper assessment of the subject at hand, it is worthwhile to look into observations of foreign scholars in the present context. We shall first take up the views of Dr. H. Jacobi.

Dr. Jacobi's First Approach

It was late, Dr. Hermann Jacobi, who first took the lead in making a significant effort[5] in this direction. Dr. Jacobi had added greatly to his credit by having translated four of the Jain canons viz. The *Ācārаṅga Sūtra,* the *Kalpa Sūtra*, the *Sūtrakṛtāṅga Sūtra* and *Uttaradhyayana Sūtra*. These translations were published in two volumes in the Sacred Books of the East Series,[6] edited by Max Müller, an outstanding scholar of oriental learning. Besides this, Dr. Jacobi has also rendered other valuable services to Jainism. We owe the credit to him for having brought Lord Pārśva Nātha, the 23rd *Tīrthaṅkara* in the category of historical personalities.[7] The fallacy prevalent in the field of history that Jainism was nothing but a branch of Buddhism, was also disembroiled mainly by Dr. Jacobi.[8] He also visited India twice in order to be able to get firsthand knowledge of the Jain traditions in vogue. He established direct contact with many Jain *Ācāryas* during his visits.[9]

Dr. Jacobi has referred to the controversy about the dates of the *Nirvāṇa* of Mahāvīra and Buddha at two different places and both the descriptions contradict each other. In one review he depicts Māhāvīra as having predeceased Buddha and vice versa in the other.

The First Review

His first review appeared in his Introduction to the *Ācārаṅga Sūtra* in 1884. Describing the events associated with the lives of Mahāvīra and Buddha he writes[10] : "We shall now put side by side the principal events of Buddha's and Mahāvīra's lives in order to demonstrate their difference. Buddha was born in Kapilavastu, Mahāvīra, in a village near Vaiśālī; Buddha's mother died after his birth, Mahāvīra's parents lived to see him a grown up man; Buddha turned ascetic during the life time and against the will of his father, Mahāvīra did so after the death of his parents and with the consent of those in power; Buddha led a life of austerties for 6 years, Mahāvīra for 12; Buddha thought these years wasted time, and that all his penances were useless for attaining his end, Mahāvīra was convinced of the necessity of his penances and persevered some of them even after becoming a *Tīrthaṅkara.*

Amongst Buddha's opponents Gośāla Maṅkhaliputta is by no means so prominent as amongst Mahāvīra's nor among the former's do we meet "Gamalī, who caused the first Schism in Jain Church. All the disciples of Buddha bear different names to those of Mahāvīra. To finish this enumeration of differences,

Buddha died in Kuśīnagar, whereas Mahāvīra died in 'Pāvā', avowedly before the former".

Dr. Jacobi has absolutely omitted the mention of evidences supporting his belief nor has he reviewed the dates of the birth and death of both. Hence, it is difficult to infer his view about the contemporaniety of Mahāvīra and Buddha.

The Date of Mahāvīra's *Nirvāṇa*

The allusions occurring in both the volumes of the *Jain Sūtras* edited by Dr. Jacobi bear testimony to the fact that he ragarded 526 B.C. as the date of Mahāvīra's *Nirvāṇa.* He writes,[11] "The recordation of the Jains canon or the *Siddhānta* took place, according to the unanimous tradition in the council of 'Vallabhī' under the presidency of Devardhi. The date of this event 980 (or 467 A.D.) is incorporated in the *Kalpa Sūtra"*.[12] This extract brings home the fact that Dr. Jacobi has accepted 526 B.C. as the date of Mahāvīra's *Nirvāṇa,* for we get 980 and 993 respectively only after adding 454 and 467 to 526. He has repeated the same fact, incidentally, in his introduction to the second volume of the *Jaina Sūtra* edited by him.[13] It was written in 1894 A. D., *i.e.* ten years after the introduction, he wrote the first volume. We come across one more allusion in that introduction which indisputably confirms 526 B.C. as the date of Mahāvīra's *Nirvaṇa.* Dr. Jacobi writes: "Khaluya Rohagutta of the Kauśika Gotra with whom Matam in 544 A.V. (18 A.D.)". Here too, we get 18 A.D. only after substracting 526 from 544.

The Date of Buddha's *Nirvāṇa*

Similarly, Dr. Jacobi has not referred to any specific date about the birth or death of Buddha in these Introductions, but whatever he has written there, even though in different allusions, reflect's his idea about the date of Buddha's *Nirvāṇa.* For instance, he writes quoting Max Müllar's extract.[14] "The lastest date of Buddhist cannon being composed at the time of the Second Council was 377 B.C." It is an unanimously accepted fact that this Council was held at Vaiśālī, 100 years after the *Nirvāṇa* of Buddha.[15] It follows that 477 B.C. is the date of Buddha- *Nirvāṇa.* In the opinion of Dr. Jacobi on the basis of his concept at that time, if these were the dates of the *Nirvāṇa* of Mahāvīra and Buddha, Mahāvīra was 41 years older than Buddha.

Dr. Jacobi's Second Approach

Dr. Jacobi had made another approach to the problem in his paper entitled as "The *Nirvāṇa* of Mahāvīra and Buddha published in the 26th issue of a German research magazine in the year 1930. Its Gujarati rendering was published in *Bhāratīya Vidyā*—a research journal[16] and subsequently is Hindi translation, as collected by Shri Kastura Chand Banthia, appeared in *Śramaṇa*[17] a monthly Hindi Magazine.

The conclusion of this article is[18] that Buddha died in 484 B.C. and Mahāvīra in 477 B.C. It means that Mahāvīra died 7 years after the death of Buddha and the former was fifteen years younger than the latter.

The Concluding Article

According to Śrī Kastura Chand Banthia[19], it was the last paper written by Dr. Jacobi and he has expressed therein an altogether different opinion. What astounds us is Dr. Jacobi's complete silence, in this comprehensive, about his earlier view and the view he propounded later on, and the reasons that led him to change his opinion. The only thing he says while introducing the essay is[20]: "One school of thought says that, in accordance with the historical view passed on to us by tradition and stabilized by evidences, Gautama Buddha had died many years before Mahāvīra. Another school of thought holds that, on the basis of the allusion found in the Buddhist scriptures, Mahāvīra died perhaps only a little earlier than Buddha. This critique is being written to discover the extent of the truth underlying this obviously discernible contradiction."

It is worth noting that Dr. Jacobi had already expressed his earlier view in the introductions to the volumes edited by him and they were published also during his life time. Nevertheless, why does not he again say his earlier statement in the last article? It might have happened under some circumstances and we have not go deep with its complicacies now. Here, we have only to see on what grounds he has based his novel theory and how far they are true. It is beyond doubt that Dr. Jacobi was a profound critic, and re-examine, any fact on various touch-stones, before accepting it.

The Gist of Dr. Jacobi's Paper

After studying this paper thoroughly one comes to know that this article was not written only with reference to the date of *Nirvāṇa* of Mahāvīra and Buddha, but one of the principal objects behind the writing of this essay was to bring to light the contemporary, political and regal conditions. The actual title of this essay, the *Nirvāṇa* of Mahāvīra and Buddha and the contemporary Political Condition of Magadha also signifies the same fact. Also whatever he has written about the dates of the *Nirvāṇa* is not only insufficient to lead the present controversy to a decisive phase, but it is a little unnatural too. The principal evidence, which Dr. Jacobi has advanced in support of his changed opinion that Buddha was older than Mahāvīra and that Mahāvīra survived Buddha by a few years, can be stated as follows :

> "The Jain scriptures furnish us with a further detailed account of the later events connected with the wars fought between Ajātaśatru (Konika), the king of Magadha and the Vajjis (or Cetaka, the king of Vaiśālī), etc. than what is found in Buddhist scriptures.
>
> In the Buddhist scriptures, Vassakara, the Prime Minister of Ajātaśatru only lays down a plan of the victory over Vajjis before Buddha, whereas the Jain scriptures bear a picturesque description not only of the *Mahā-Śīla-Kantaka* war and, *Rath-Mūsala* war that took place between Cetaka and Konika, but also of the demolition of the rampart of Vaiśālī and finally of the victory of the king of Magadha over the Vajjis."

On the basis of this evidence, Dr. Jacobi concludes.[21] "It confirms, that Mahāvīra survived Buddha by several years (probably seven years)".

The extent to which the compilers of the scriptures collected contemporary events in the scriptures, depended upon the nature of their selection and needs. Even if we accept that the compilation made by the Jains is more extensive and exhaustive in comparison to that made by the Buddhists, it does not prove that Mahāvīra lived for some years even after the death of Buddha.

Ajātaśatru in the Buddhist *Piṭakas*

It is a fact that the Jain scriptures have shed more light on detailed accounts related to Konika. This is just and natural because of Konika's intimate association with the Jain/religion. According to Dr. Rhys Davids, a distinguish scholar, who carried out a first rate research on the Buddhist literature, however extensive the delineation of Ajātaśatru in the Buddhist *Piṭakas* may be, it only proves that he was a mere sympathizer of Buddha, and not a follower. Ajātaśatru had once called on Buddha and asked him what the fruits of monkhood were[22]? With reference to that even Rays Davids writes.[23] At the close of the discourse the king is stated to have openly taken the Buddha as his guide in future, and to have given expression to the remorse he felt at the murder of his father. But it is also distinctively stated that he was not converted. There is no evidence that he really, after the moment when his heart was touched, continued to follow Buddha's teaching. He never, so far as we know, waited again either upon the Buddha, or upon any member of the order, to discuss ethical matters. And we hear of no material support given by him to the order during the Buddha's lifetime.

"We are told however, that, after the Buddha's death, he asked (on the ground that he, like the Buddha, was a *Kṣatriya*) for a portion of the relics; that he obtained them, and built a *Stūpa* over them. And though the oldest authority says nothing about it, younger works state that on the convocation of the First Council at Rajagṛha, shortly after the decease, it was the King who provided and prepared the hall at the entrance to the *Saptaparṇī* cave, where the rehearsal of the doctrine took place. He may well have thus showed favour to the Buddhists without at all belonging to their party. He would only, in so doing, be following the usual habit so characteristic of India monarchs, of patronage towards all schools."

Dr. Radha Kumud Mukherjee, the renowned historian, has also proved on the basis of the *Sāmānya-phala Sutta* that Ajātaśatru was a mere sympathizer, and not a follower of Buddha.[24]

Konika in the Jain Tradition

According to the Jain tradition, Konika was a staunch and devoted follower of Mahāvīra. He went so far as to establish a separate department headed by a special officer exclusively for the purpose of keeping himself informed of the activities of Mahāvīra's daily life. The officer was called Pravṛttivādūka, one who speaks of the activities. He was assisted by a number of subordinates, who used to communicate the news to him. The Pravṛttivādūka after editing the news, finally convey it to king Konika".[25] No sooner[26] did king Konika receive the news of Mahāvīra's arrival in the suburb of Campā, capital of his state, while sitting in his court assembly, than he stood up and came seven or eight steps ahead of the throne, in a blissful state; in the *uttarasaṅga* position[27] he masked his mouth by a scarf; and chanting *'Namotthunam'* [28], he said[29], 'To thee, O Mahāvīra, who first sowed the seeds of religion in my soul, my religious preceptor, I bow down in reverence from this move place, for thou art yet staying away (in the garden)'. After this, when Mahāvīra had arrived at Campā, Konika also presented himself in the religious assembly of Mahāvīra.[30] Not only Konika had visited Mahāvīra more than once, but also, after Mahāvīra's *Nirvāṇa,* he attended a meeting arranged by Suddharma Svāmī, the immediate successor of Mahāvīra, and put serious question to him.[31] In addition to these, we find a number of such conclusions in the Jain scriptures, which make it crystal clear that Konika was a staunch follower of Mahāvīra and Jain religion.

While, on the other hand, as Rhys Davids writes[32], "When the king of Magadha, the famous (and infamous) Ajātaśatru, made his only call upon the Buddha, he is said to have put a puzzle to the teacher to test him.........," and as we have already quoted Rhys Davids[33], "he (Ajātaśatru) never, so far as we know, waited again either upon Buddha or upon any member of the order to discuss ethical matters....," Ajātaśatru had little inclination towards Buddhism.

What opinion, Buddha had for Ajātaśatru becomes clear from his own words, he uttered[34] : "O *Bhikṣus !* the king of Magadha Ajātaśatru a friend to, an intimate of, mixed up with, whatever is evil". According to the Buddhist texts, Ajātaśatru was, interalia, a parricide, and a supporter of Devadatta, the great schismatic[35]. Again it was Ajātaśatru according to the Buddhist canons, who incited by Devadatta, ordered his men to deprive Buddha of his life.[36]

A similar is the case of Cetaka, the king of Vaiśālī. He was not only a maternal uncle of Mahāvīra[37], but also a staunch follower of Mahāvīra.[38] The Buddhist *Tripiṭakas* do not even mention the name of Cetaka, though they bear a long description of the Vajjis.[39] Dr. Jacobi, himself, has observed[40] that the reason of taciturnity of the Buddhist canonical texts about Cetaka is that Buddha's rival (*i. e.*, Mahāvīra) was benefited by the great influence of Cetaka and that the Jains give respect to Cetaka, the maternal uncle of Mahāvīra, because Vaiśālī became a strong supporter of Jainism on account of Cetaka, whereas the Buddhists call it (Vaiśālī) a monastery of heretics. Hence, if, according to Dr. Jacobi, the Jain *Āgamas* bear more extensive account of the events concerning Konika and Cetaka than the Buddhist *Tripiṭakas,* its natural and consistent reason is that they (Konika and Cetaka) were eminent disciples of Mahāvīra and Jain religion and 'heretics' in the view of Buddha and not, as Dr. Jacobi has inferred, that Mahāvīra survived Buddha. Dr. Jacobi's inference is based only on misunderstanding and misinterreplete with many such brilliant and candid descriptions, which show that Mahāvīra predeceased Buddha, while the Jain *Āgamas* say nothing about Buddha's *Nirvāṇa.*

In the light of the aforesaid discussion, the true inference should have been that Mahāvīra attained the *Nirvāṇa* before Buddha and Buddha attained the same later than Mahāvīra, for the Jain scriptures maintain no record of Buddha's *Nirvāṇa* and the Buddhist scriptures distinctly state that Mahāvīra died earlier than Buddha. The greatest flaw in Dr. Jacobi's article is that he has striven to prove the three allusions of the Buddhist *Tripiṭakas,* which refer to Mahāvīra's *Nirvāṇa*[41], false and fictitious with a view to stabilize his own farfetched interpretation. He says that[42] as these allusions occur in varying forms at different places, they are not credible. On the other hand, he also says that[43] despite the variance in these allusions, they have one and the same objective in common, *viz.,* giving the order of monks a message of love and unity by referring to Mahāvīra's *Nirvāṇa* indirectly. It is worth noting that in spite of these three allusions being slightly variant from one another, the reference to Mahāvīra's *Nirvāṇa* in all of them remains absolutely the same. The compilers of the scriptures might have embellished the prefaces with whatever style they choose, but it would be entirely unreasonable to think that they might have gone so far as to commit a blunder of calling, living Mahāvīra dead one.

Pāvā, the Place of Mahāvīra's *Nirvāṇa*

Another argument placed forth by Dr. Jacobi in this context is that the city Pāvā depicted as the place of Mahāvīra's *Nirvāṇa* in the Buddhist scriptures lay in the land of Mallas, where Buddha sojourned in his last days, whereas in accordance with the traditional belief of the Jains, Mahāvīra attained the *Nirvāṇa* in another Pāvā situated near Rājagṛha in Patna district. Hence, like the fictitious Pāvā, according to Dr. Jacobi, the whole story of Mahāvīra's *Nirvāṇa* seems to be nothing but a mere fabrication. Dr. Jacobi also holds that[44] it is not justifiable to doubt the Jain traditions about the sacred place of Mahāvīra's *Nirvāṇa*. Even if we may assume that the Buddhists had made this mistake on account of the identical name of Pāvā allotted by them, for such mistakes are liable to be committed, it cannot be interpreted that the whole story about Mahāvīra's *Nirvāṇa* is completely forged. As a matter of fact, Dr. Jacobi's caution against our expressing even the slightest possible doubt regarding the Pāvā accepted in the Jain tradition, has not only been rendered dubious on historical grounds, but it has also become baseless.

Often there happens to be a striking contrast between history and tradition. The traditional Kṣatriyakuṇḍa situated near Lichchhuada is supposed to be the birth-place of Mahāvīra but the research carried into it by modern history has proved it wholly un-authentic. According to the historical concept, the village Basadh situated in Mujjaffarpur District, 27 miles away to the North of Patna is no other than the Kṣatriyakuṇḍa, the birth-place of Mahāvīra. Thus, the traditional birth-place lies far off to South of the Ganges, while the historically accepted place is situated to the North of the Ganges.

So is the case of Pāvā. Traditionally accepted Pāvā lies in the South Bihar and the splendid temples standing there have made it to be the place of pilgrimage for the Jains. But history does not share the belief that it is the true place of Mahāvīra's *Nirvāṇa.* According to the modern view, the Pāvā of Mahāvīra's *Nirvāṇa* should be in the North of the Ganges, for the 18 kings of the republics of Mallas and Licchavis were present in Pāvā at the time of Mahāvīra's *Nirvāṇa*[45], and this can be more true only with regard to the Pāvā, situated in the North of the Ganges, since their kingdom lay stretched towards the North side, while the Pāvā situated in the South of the Ganges (near Rājagṛha) lay entirely in the land of their sworn enemy? Many thinkers and historians such as Pt. Rahul Sankrityayana[46], Dr. Rajbali Pandey[47], M.A. D. Litt., Nathuram Premi,[48] Dr. Nalinaksa Dutt[49], Shri Ranjan Suri Deo[50], Shri Shrichand Rampuri[51], Ācārya Vijyendra Suri[52], etc. have confirmed this fact. All of them agreed to the fact that Mahāvīra had died in the Pāvā of Mallas, that this Pāvā should be on the North of the Ganges[53] and that the Pāvā situated in the South of the Ganges (near Rājagṛha in Patna district) and traditionally believed to be the place of Mahāvīra's Nirvāṇa has erroneously been adopted by the Jains, being oblivious of the true Pāvā.

Thus, it becomes clear that the Pāvā, on the basis of which Dr. Jacobi rejects the Buddhist allusion about Mahāvīra's *Nirvāṇa* by ascertaining them as false and unreal, happens to be the historically accepted Pāvā and confirms the authenticity of those allusions.

Āgamas and Tripiṭakas in Relation to the Contemporary Conditions

Dr. Jacobi's view that the Jain *Āgamas* give a more comprehensive account of the contemporary conditions than what the Buddhist *Tripiṭakas* do, is also not trustworthy for, the events cited by Dr. Jacobi are not all contained in the original *Āgamas*. The whole event of "The victory over Vaiśālī which ensued after the *Mahāśīla-Kāṇṭaka* war and the *Ratha-Mūsala* war and where in the monk Kulavalaya became the cause of the demolition on the ramparts of Vaiśālī, has been quoted by Dr. Jacobi himself from a later Jain work, *Avaśyaka Kathā*. The *Āgamas* and the *Tripiṭakas,* which are the original canonicals*(iii)* texts of the Jains and the Buddhists respectively, in fact, do not differ much regarding the description of the contemporary political conditions. Now, if we consider the later works of both traditions, the work of the Buddhist traditions like *Mahāvaṁsa* contains as much vivid descriptions as we find in those of the Jain traditions. *Mahavāṁsa* contains even the chronology of the kings up to Asoka.[54] This by no means testifies to the fact that Buddha died later than Mahāvīra.

The Date of Mahāvīra's *Nirvāṇa*

Dr. Jacobi regards 477 B.C. as the date of Mahāvīra's *Nirvāṇa* and 484 B.C. as that of Buddha's *Nirvāṇa.* But he refrains from giving any specific indication throughout his essay why it became inevitable for him to accept these dates. He simply says[55], "Though according to the unanimous traditions of the Jains, Candragupta's accession took place 215 years A.V. (after the death of Mahāvīra), in accordance with the view propounded by Hemacandra, (Pariśiṣṭa Parva, 8-339) Chandragupta acceded to the throne 155 A.V." Dr. Jacobi has supported his view by citing another Jain work, *Kahavali* of Bhadreśvara.

Now, the fact is that, as stated by Dr. Jacobi, it is unanimously accepted in all the Jain traditions that Candragupta's, accession took place only 215 years after the *Nirvāṇa* of Mahāvīra[56] and not 155 years, as accepted by Ācārya Hemacandra.[57] The view of Ācārya Hemacandra would prove baseless, if tested on the touchstone of history. Also, the scholars have regarded it as a great blunder, omitted by Ācārya Hemacandra. The most substantiated opinion in this regard is that,[58] a king named Palaka was enthroned at Ujjain the very day on which Mahāvīra attained the *Nirvāṇa*. He (or his dynasty) reigned for 60 years.

Then ensued the Mauryan rule, that is to say Chandragupta Maurya was enthroned 215 years after the death of Mahāvīra. This allusion has been extracted from, *Titthogali Painnaiw* which is supposed to be much older than both the books *viz. Kahavali* of Bhadreśavara and *Pariśiṣṭa Parva* of Hemarandra.

It seems, that the period of 60 years of the reign of Palaka has completely been omitted in the calculation of Hemacandra's *Pariśiṣṭa Parva.* Mr. Purna Chandra Nahar, M.A., B.L., M.S., *and* Mr. Krishna Chandra Gosh, Vedāntacintāmaṇī write, "Hemcandrācārya must have omitted by oversight to count the period of 60 years of King Palaka after Mahāvīra's *Nirvāṇa.*"[59]

Dr. Jacobi has edited *Pariśiṣṭa Parva.*[60] He has observed in the preface to it that Hemacandrācārya had composed that work in haste, as a consequence of which the work is studied with errors. Elaborating the subject in the preface itself, Dr. Jacobi has illustrated several compositional and grammatical errors comitted by Hemacandra with concrete evidences. It is quite probable that the verse on the basis of which Dr. Jacobi has inferred the date of Mahāvīra's *Nirvāṇa,* might have also been composed with the same carelessness. The date of Mahāvīra's *Nirvāṇa*, accepted by Hemacandrācārya himself, while stating the period of his own contemporary king Kumārapāla is 527 B.C., and not 477 B.C. Hemacandrācārya writes in *Triśaṣṭiśalākapurscaritra*[61] : "When 1669 years will have been completed after the death of Mahāvīra, there will flourish a king named Kumārapāla who will shine like a moon of Cālukya dynasty". Now it is unanimously accepted that Kumārapāla's accession took place in 1142 A.D.[62] But according to Hemacandrācārya, the interval between this event and the date of Mahāvīra's *Nirvāṇa* is 1669 years. In this way, Hemacandrācārya himself has also accepted 1669–1142 = 527 B.C., as the date of Mahāvīra's *Nirvāṇa.*

The Date of Buddha's *Nirvāṇa*

Dr. Jacobi regards 484 B.C. as the date of Buddha's *Nirvāṇa,* for according to him,[63] "The southern Buddhists hold that Candragupta's accession took place 162 years after the death of Buddha. And the uncontroversial date of Candragupta's enthronement is 322 B.C. Hence 322 + 162) = 484 B.C. is the date of Buddha's *Nirvāṇa*". The fact regarding Candragupta's accession gleaned by Dr. Jacobi referring to the tradition of Southern Buddhists is taken from the Ceylonese chronicle—*Mahāvaṁsa.*[64] But on one hand the *Mahāvaṁsa* state that Candragupta's accession took place 162 years after Buddha's death, while on the other hand it shows 543 B.C. as the date of Buddha's *Nirvāṇa,.*[65] Dr. Jacobi, too has hold it as the most popular date of Buddha's *Nirvāṇa,* accepted by the traditions.[66] Now if *Mahāvaṁsa* considering 543 B.C. as the date of Buddha's *Nirvāṇa*, place Candragupta's enthronement 162 years after the death of Buddha, we get 381 B.C. as the date of Candragupta's accession. But it does not agree with the uncontroversial historical data of Candragupta's accession viz. 322 B.C. Hence, it is obvious that the date of Buddha's *Nirvāṇa* fixed by

Dr. Jacobi on the basis of the suspicious evidence of *Mahāvaṁsa*[67] is not compatible.

Inconsistencies

The acceptances of the date of the *Nirvāṇa* of Mahāvīra and Buddha inferred by Dr. Jacobi also gives rise to many inconsistencies. In the *Bhagavatī Sūtra,* Gośālaka speaks of eight finalities in his last days and *Mahāśīla-Kaṇṭaka* war was also one of them.[68] We deduce from it that Goíālaka died after the *Mahasila-Kaṇṭaka* war had taken place. Again seven days before the death of Gośālaka, Mahāvīra had announced.[69] "I shall remain alive yet 16 years from today without any hinderance like a supremely puissant elephant." In other words, even if we assume that *Mahāśīla-Kaṇṭika* war broke out immediately after Konika's accession to the throne, there elapsed at least 17 years between Konika's accession and Mahāvīra's death. But this, by no means, goes beyond 15 years, according to the date fixed by Dr. Jacobi.[70] Another inconsistency arising from Jacobi's findings becomes clear from the following event described in Jain literature :

Once[71] upon a time, the king Śreṇika asked Mahāvīra : "Who will be the last *Kevalin* (omniscent)"? Mahāvīra, answering the king's question, said to him : "On the seventh day from today, this good named Vidyunmālī, will be conceived in the womb of the wife of Ṛṣabhadatta, a businessman in your city Rājagṛha. That child will be named as Jambu-Kumāra, and he will be the last *Kevalin.*"

Now, all the Jain traditions unanimously accept the fact that when Jambu-Kumāra was 16 years old, he was initiated into monkhood by Sudharma Svāmī[72] the successor of Mahāvīra, in the same year in which Mahāvīra died.[73] This means that Jambu-Kumāra was conceived in the womb of his mother nearly 17 years before the *Nirvāṇa* of Mahāvīra. At the time, king 'Śreṇika' was alive. But as we have seen, the reign of Konika began more than 16 years before the *Nirvāṇa* of Mahāvīra. Therefore, we infer that the end of 'Śreṇika's rule and the beginning of Konika's rule took place nearly 17 years before the *Nirvāṇa* of Mahāvīra. But, the chronology proposed by Dr. Jacobi, allow a maximum interval of 15 years between these events. In this way the acceptance of these dates involves many objections.

Conclusion

The opinion that Mahāvīra attained the *Nirvāṇa* in 527 B.C. has remained almost uncontroversial and unique. No date of Buddha's *Nirvāṇa* has been taken to be so indubitable. A number of opinions about the date of Buddha's *Nirvāṇa* were in vogue in ancient time and they continue to exist even now.[74] Nevertheless, in this essay, Dr. Jacobi has gone so far as to ascertain (48 B.C.) the date of Budda's *Nirvāṇa* as almost unique and has tried to reconcile the events of Mahāvīra's life with it through far-fetched interpretations. By doing so, Dr. Jacobi has stirred up a new polemic with regard to the contemporaneity of Mahāvīra and Buddha. The view expressed by Dr. Jacobi has also been rendered obsolete for more than 33 years have elapsed since what he wrote.[75] In the mean time history has also renovated and modified to a very great extent. Hence it will not at all be reasonable to accept Dr. Jacobi's findings as final.

Paṇḍita Sukh Lal Ji and Other Scholars

Some critics of our present era have accepted Dr. Jacobi's view regarding the chronology of Mahāvīra and Buddha. The famous Jain scholar Paṇḍita Sukh Lal ji writes :[76] "Prof. Jacobi has found out on the basis of a comparative study of the Jain and the Buddhist texts in the light of history that Mahāvīra attained the *Nirvāṇa* decidedly certain years later than Buddha. Jacobi has made it clear by his deep research work that the war or the Licchavis and the Vajjis with Konika took place only after Buddha's *Nirvāṇa* and during the life-time of Mahāvīra. For, the description of the war is found only in the Jain Scriptures, though the Licchavis and the Vajjis are mentioned in both the Jain and the Buddhist texts."

The above quotation shows that Pt. Sukh Lal ji has accepted Dr. Jacobi's view as it is. He has not deliberated over the subject independently. Often we all do so, when a particular subjects is not ours or when we do not get an occasion to go deep into it, we generally accept the view of some scholar in that regard. It is also quite natural that many scholars are required to solve many problems. There is, then always a mutual exchange of views between the different scholars of different subjects.

Pt. Sukh Lal ji has given importance to two things—one is that while the Buddhist scriptures do not bear any description of the war of the Vajjis with Konika, the Jain Scriptures do. But, as we have already discussed, this is not at all important in deciding the present issue.

The other thing is that the above war was precedent to the *Nirvāṇa* of Buddha and antecedent to that of Mahāvīra. This view is based on the general belief that the *Mahā-Parinirvāṇa Sutta* contains only those events of Buddha's life that happened in his last days. The first event referred to by this *Sutta,* is the meeting of Vassakara, the chief minister of the king Ajātaśatru (Konika) with Buddha. The Vassakara lays forth a plan of victory over the Vajjis before

Buddha. This event, therefore, is believed to have been associated with the last days of Buddha.

That most of the events described in the *Mahā-Parinirvāṇa Sutta,* are connected with the last days of Buddha's life is understandable, but that all the events contained in above *Sutta* are so, cannot be accepted as a fact. It is to be noted that Sāriputta's conversation with Buddha is also one of the subject of the *Mahā-Parinirvāṇa Sutta,*[77] whereas it is unanimously believed that Sāriputta, had died long before Buddha's *Nirvāṇa.*

The fact appears to be that Vassakara had called on Buddha, when, after *Mahāśīla-Kaṇṭaka* and the *Ratha-Mūsala* wars, Konika had besieged the city of Vaiśālī, and he and his minister had been further devising the various plans to devastate the walls of Vaiśālī. This belief is also substantiated by the fact that according to the Jain sources, Konika was advised to employ the insidious strategies to enable him to enter into the city of Vaiśālī and also according to the Buddhist Scriptures, Vassakara, the chief minister of Ajātaśatru, after having talked with Buddha and having known about the invincibility of the Vajjis, decided to play the croocked trick of bribing the Vajjis, and thus creating a rupture in their unity.

In the same way, both the traditions consider the honour paid by the Vajjis to the *stūpas* and temples standing inside the walled city, to be the chief cause of their impregnability.

In the Jain source,[78] it has been said that as long as the *stūpa* of Mallinātha remained standing, Konika would not be able to win Vaiśālī. According to the Buddhist text,[79] Buddha says to Ānanda "......... so long as the Vajjis honour and esteem and revere and support the Vajjin shrines in town and country and allow not the proper offerings and rites, as formerly given and performed, to fall into destitude................may the Vajjins be expected not to decline, but to prosper." Then he addressed Vassakara, the *Brāhmaṇa,* and said, "So long as those conditions shall continue to exist among the Vajjins, ... so long may we expect them not to decline but to prosper."

There are many more such points wich make it crystal clear that the opinion of Dr. Jacobi that Buddha's *Nirvāṇa* was antecedent to the Vaiśālī war, is not correct.

We find that like Pt. Sukh Lal ji the scholars such as Śrī Gopalactase Patel and Kisturmalji Banthia have accepted Dr. Jacobi's view firmly, but this has happened only on account of their partial consideration.

Dr. Charpentier

Another independent effort to slove to the present enigma was made by Dr. Jorl

Charpentier in 1914[80] (*i.e.* in between the first and the second approaches of Dr. Jacobi), Dr. Charpentier's conclusion is that Mahāvīra attained the *Nirvāṇa* after Buddha's *Nirvāṇa.* According to him, the dates of the *Nirvāṇa* after Buddha's and Mahāvīra are 477 B.C. and 467 B.C. respectively. Dr. Charpentier's finding is mainly based on the following two assumptions : 1. Buddha died in 477 B.C. 2. Pāvā, the place of Mahāvīra's *Nirvāṇa,* is different from Pāvā recorded in the Buddhist *Piṭakas.* Now we find that these two fundamental notions have totally changed in the course of historical investigations. In past, at some time, 477 B.C. was considered by the historians to be the exact date of Buddha's decease. But in the modern history, the above date has no place at all. Secondly, Dr. Charpentier has tried to falsify the Buddhist account of the predecease of Mahāvīra on the basis that Mahāvīra died at Pāvā in South Bihar, whereas the Buddhist texts speak of Mahāvīra's *Nirvāṇa* at Pāvā in North Bihar, is the true place of Mahāvīra's *Nirvāṇa*[81]. Dr. Jacobi has quoted in his second approach, the above belief of Dr. Charpentier in support of his own viewpoint, but it is remarkable that Dr. Jacobi has not accepted by Dr. Charpentier. Actually it seems that the date of Buddha's *Nirvāṇa* which was popularly accepted in the history at the time of Dr. Charpentier's writing was made by Charpentier the basis of his research work. Sixteen years after this, when Dr. Jacobi made his second approach, the historical view regarding the date of Buddha's *Nirvāṇa* had undergone a change, and hence, Dr. Jacobi accepted the new date of Buddha's *Nirvāṇa.* But we should not forget that Dr. Jacobi's second approach has become nearly thirty-two years old, and that during this long period new views about the chronology of Mahāvīra and Buddha, have come to light in the field of history. It is, therefore, necessary to reconsider the whole issue in the light of the new facts.

DR. K.P. JAYASWAL

A renowned historian and editor of the Journal of Bihar and Orissa Research Society, Dr. K.P. Jayaswal has made a remarkable effort to solve this problem.[82] Dr. Jayaswal's view on the present subject, in short, can be summarised thus : The allusions about Mahāvīra's death found in the Buddhist texts should not be neglected. According to the *Samāgama Sutta,* Buddha had heard about Mahāvīra's death in his life-time and the popular belief is that Buddha died two years after this event. According to the Southern Buddhists, Buddha died in 544 B.C. Therefore, Mahāvīra should have attained the *Nirvāṇa* in 546 B.C.

Mahāvīra's *Nirvāṇa* and Vikramāditya

In order to reconcile this date (546 B.C.) of Mahāvīra's *Nirvāṇa* Dr. Jayaswal has tried to give a new interpretation to the traditional belief that Vikramāditya flourished 470 years after Mahāvāra's *Nirvāṇa*. Dr. Jayaswal's argument is[83] : "The view of the Jain-traditional chronology that the interval between Mahāvīra's *Nirvāṇa* and the Vikram era is 470 years, is, in reality the one, which is given in the *Pattavali of Śrāvastī Gaccha,* and which states the above period to be the interval between Mahāvīra's *Nirvāṇa* and the birth of Vikrama. Vikrama's enthronement is stated to have taken place when he was 18 years old, and the event was marked by the beginning of the Vikrama era. Thus (470 + 18 = 488 years) after Mahāvīra's *Nirvāṇa* commenced the Vikrama era (58 B.C.). But the above 18 years were left out in the Jain Chronology. Thus, it was clearly a mistake to count a lapse of 470 years between Mahāvīra's *Nirvāṇa* and the commencement of Vikrama era."

In this way, according to Dr. Jayaswal : Mahāvīra attained the *Nirvāṇa* in 488 + 58 = 546 B.C.

A Critique

Dr. Jayaswal's view that the Buddhist allusions about Mahāvīra's predecease should not be neglected, is really justifiable. But his assuming an interval of two years between the deaths of Mahāvīra and Buddha on the basis of the popular belief about the *Samāgama Suttānta,* and his computing the interval between Mahāvīra's *Nirvāṇa* and the Vikrama era by adding 18 years to the traditional number 470, are not based at all on confirmed sources. The famous historians,[84] commenting on the view, write : "The suggestion can hardly be said to rest on any reliable tradition—Merutunga[85] places the death of the last *Jina* or *Tīrthaṅkara* 470 years before the end of Śaka rule and the victory and not birth of the traditional Vikrama". Also the belief that Buddha had heard about Mahāvīra's *Nirvāṇa* in *Samāgama* exactly two years before his own death, is a mere speculation.

Dr. Radha Kumud Mukherjee

A prominent historian Dr. Radha Kumud Mukherjee, M.A., Ph.D., D. Litt., has treated the problem in a similar way. He, in his famous work, Hindu Civilization,[86] has clearly accepted the seniority and the predecease of Mahāvīra with respect to Buddha on the basis of the Buddhist *Tripiṭakas.* According to Dr. Mukherjee, these two facts are quite unequivocal. It is remarkable that he has approved his view of Mahāvīra's seniority to Buddha by citing several authoritative Buddhist work.[87]

As far as the dates of Mahāvīra and Buddha are concerned, he has wholly accepted the view of Dr. Jayaswal, according to which Mahāvīra died in 546 B.C. and Buddha in 544 B.C. But it should be noted that by accepting these dates for the *Nirvāṇa* of Mahāvīra and Buddha, Dr. Mukherjee has created self-contradiction in his view of Mahāvīra's seniority to Buddha. For the total age of Mahāvīra's was 72, and that of Buddha was 80, so that, if the above chronology is accepted, Buddha would become six years older than Mahāvīra.

Thus, we can conclude that though Dr. Mukherjee has succeeded in proving Mahāvīra's seniority and predecease with respect to Buddha, he has failed to reconcile his chronology with these facts.

Dr. Kamta Prasad Jain

Dr. Kamta Prasad Jain, a Jain Digambara scholar and the editor of *Ahiṁsā Vāṇī*, has also accepted the above date of Mahāvīra and Buddha. Though he is of the view that Mahāvīra predeceased Buddha, he clearly denies the belief that Mahāvīra was older than Buddha.[88] In order to support his view, Dr. K.P. Jain has tried to falsify a Buddhist allusion that Buddha was younger than Mahāvīra, by interpreting it as an 'irony'.[89] But his effort is a good example of far-fetched and unnatural interpretation. Also he has taken no account of other explicit references,[90] found in the Buddhist texts, showing Buddha's juniority to Mahāvīra.

Dharmananda Kausambi

A well-known Buddhist scholar, Dharmananda Kausambi has discussed the contemporaneity of Mahāvīra and Buddha in some of his books. It is his belief that Buddha was definitely the youngest amongst the seven religious teachers of his time,[91] and, that his order *(Saṅgha)* was the smallest of all. Śrī Kausambi has, however, neglected the chronological aspect of the problem. His argument is[92] : "Even if Buddha's birth-date is taken back or forth by few years, it would not deteriorate his character. The importance should be given not to the date of his birth, but to the circumstances existing before his birth, and to how he found out a new path in them".

The main reason of his neglecting the chronology seems to be that it is too equivocal to be determined.

Dr. Hoernle and Muni Jina Vijayaji

Dr. Hoernle has also discussed this problem in the same way.[93] According to him, Buddha died five years after Mahāvīra's *Nirvāṇa* (484 B.C.). This makes

Buddha three years senior to Mahāvīra. The main bases of Dr. Hoernle's view are almost the same as those which are already discussed in the present chapter in context of other scholars and hence need no further discussion.

A well-known archaeologist Muni Jina Vijayji has accepted Mahāvīra to have predeceased Buddha on the basis of Dr. Jayaswal's view.[94]

MUNI KALYĀṆA VIJAYAJĪ

An extensive effort has been made by a famous Jain historian, Muni Kalyāṇa Vijayajī to solve the present problem. His work on the subject, titled, *Vīra Nirvāṇa Saṁvat Aura Jaina Kalaganana* is really a treasure book for the research-workers. He has presented an independent solution to the problem of chronology of Mahāvīra and Buddha. His conclusion is that Buddha predeceased Mahāvīra by 14 years 5 months and 15 days. In other words, Buddha was 22 years older than Mahāvīra. The dates of the *Nirvāṇa* given by Muni Kalyāṇa Vijayajī is as follows :

Buddha's *Nirvāṇa* .... 542 B.C. (May)
Mahāvīra's *Nirvāṇa* .... 528 B.C. (November)

The date of Mahāvīra's *Nirvāṇa*—527 B.C.,[95] which is accepted by Muni Kalyāṇa Vijayajī, is based on a reliable tradition as well as direct evidences. Muṇijī has proved this date by citing various authorities and giving many reasons.

Muni Kalyāṇa Vijayajī has tried to prove that Buddha attained the *Nirvāṇa* nearly fifteen years before Mahāvīra's *Nirvāṇa*. He has argued that the story related in the *Samāgama Suttānta,* that Buddha had heard about the Mahāvīra's death, is not correct. According to Munijī, the event should have happened thus : When Mahāvīra was seriously injured by the *Tejo-leśya* of his Ājīvaka rival, Gośālaka, there prevailed a rumour that Mahāvīra would die within six months, as foretold by Gośālaka.[96] This rumour would have reached Buddha, and consequently the story about Mahāvīra's *Nirvāṇa* would have become prevalent.

Developing his line of argument, Muni Kalyāṇa Vijayajī writes.[97] "The belief of the Buddhist that Budha died just one year after he had heard about Mahāvīra's death (precisely speaking, the rumour of the Mahāvīra's death) gives us a clue to find out the exact interval between the death of Mahāvīra and Buddha". Further, he states that according to the *Bhagavatī Sūtra,*[98] Mahāvīra died 16 years after having been injured by *Tejo-leśya* of Gośālaka. On this basis, he has fixed the date of Buddha's *Nirvāṇa.* Muni Kalyāṇa Vijayajī also claims that[99] the date of Buddha's *Nirvāṇa* inferred by him is coincident with the Ceylonese date of Buddha's death.

A Critique

As far as the date of Mahāvīra's *Nirvāṇa* is concerned, Muni Kalyāṇa Vijayajī's view seems to be quite correct. But it appears that in deciding Buddha's date, he has nearly depended on guesswork. The allusions of the Buddhist scriptures, which relate the event of Mahāvīra's death, have been much distorted by him. Such far-fetched interpretations can never be regarded as historical facts. To call the date of Buddha's *Nirvāṇa* decided by him (542 B.C.), to be coincident with the Ceylonese date of the Buddha's *Nirvāṇa* (544 B.C.)[100] is a good example of far-fetching technique used cannot be regarded negligible, as he has asked us to do so.[101]

One of the evidence, adduced by him to show Buddha's seniority to Mahāvīra, is[102] : "In the Buddhist texts, wherever the rival teachers of Buddha are enumerated, the name of *Nigganṭha Nātaputta* (*i.e.* Mahāvīra) appears in the end of the lists. This has also happened, perhaps in the end of the lists. It is so, most probably because Mahāvīra was the youngest amongst the rivals of Buddha." The weakness of argument is obvious. Even Mahāvīra's name appears in the end of the list of Buddha's rivals, it does not at all means that Mahāvīra was younger than Buddha. On the contrary, such references clearly indicate that all the six rivals (including Mahāvīra) of Buddha had already earned fame and influence long before Buddha appeared on the scence. As a matter of fact, it is also not true, that Mahāvīra's name appears in the end everywhere in such lists, as argued by Muni Kalyāṇa Vijayajī. We find several such references in the Buddhist texts where *Nigaṇṭha Nātaputta* is not the last.[103]

Mahāvīra Middle-aged, Buddha—Young

In order to support his view, Muni Kalyāṇa Vijayajī has tried to misinterpret the *Sammaññyaphala Sutta* of the *Dīgha Nikāya.* Presenting his argument, he writes[104] : "The minister of the king Ajātaśatru tells[105] him 'O king! This *Nigganṭha Nātaputta* is having an assembly (of *Bhikkhus*) and a crowd (of followers), and is the pontiff of the order, a well known teacher, a famous leader and considered excellent by the multitude. He is long-ordained and middle-aged.[106] This shows that Mahāvīra was middle-aged (*i.e.* fifty years old), while Buddha was old." Now, if we study the above chapter with its fullest context, we find that it clearly describes Mahāvīra as middle-aged, and Buddha as young. For, the minister, here, intends to narrate the merits of Mahāvīra, and the word 'middle-aged', when used to exhibit a merit, should imply seniority. Secondly, in the above chapter of the *Dīgha Nikāya*, all the other rival teachers of Buddha, viz. Gośālaka, Sañjya Balaṭṭhiputta, etc. are also described as "long ordained" and, 'middle-aged' while in the context of Buddha, no such adjectives are used. This also proves that Buddha was younger than all the six rivals of him.

In connection with the above *Sammaññyaphala-Sutta* of the *Dīgha Nikāya* further states that the king Ajātaśatru, after having heard from his ministers about the merits of all the teachers went to Buddha for passing his time in religious discussion. There he asked Buddha what the direct fruit of monkhood was, and also informed Buddha that he had asked the same question to the six religious teachers before. This was the first contact of Ajātaśatru with Buddha. Are not all these facts enough to show that Mahāvīra and other five religious teachers were older than Buddha?

Testimony of the Later Works

One of the testimonies advocated by Muni Kalyāṇa Vijayajī to defend his view is[107] : "The Jain traditional record of Śreṇika and his queen Cellanā shows that Śreṇika was first a follower of Buddha and afterwards was converted to Jain faith." But, as a matter of fact, this account is based only on later Jain stories and hence it has no historical importance. Moreover, Muni Kalyāṇa Vijayajī has not mentioned, in which authoritative work, the said account is recorded. In a similar way, he has choosen five statements from the later Buddhist work to show the seniority of Buddha, and that too without mentioning the original references.[108] Most of those beliefs seems to have no connection with the Buddhist *Piṭakas*. Some of them even contradict the facts of the Buddhist *Piṭakas*.

Contradictions

The argument advanced by Muni Kalyāṇa Vijayajī are not at all sufficient to prove the seniority of Buddha to Mahāvīra. In his effort to reconcile his view, he has contradicted some fundamental and well-established facts. For example, the Buddhist *Tripiṭakas* state Mahāvīra to have died earlier than Buddha. They also elucidate that Buddha himself had accepted his juniority to all the six religious teachers of his time. In addition to this, at several places Buddha's juniority is clearly indicated in them.[109] Muni Kalyāṇa Vijayajī has not been able to reconcile his view with all these facts. He has called everywhere such events as fabrication and falsifying. His trend regarding the Buddhist *Tripiṭakas* cannot be called proper and justifying. It is to be noted that the historians eastern as well as Western, have recognised these scriptural evidences as fundamental facts in deciding the contemporaneity of Mahāvīra and Buddha. At some places Muni Kalyāṇa Vijayajī has contradicted his own arguments. For example, in the beginning of his book, he has accepted the belief of the later Buddhist works that Buddha died in the 8th year of Ajātaśatru's reign, as the basis of his view. Later on, he, on the basis of the fact that Gośāla's enumeration of the eight finilaties (Caramas) at the time of his death, was made sixteen years before the Mahāvīra's *Nirvāṇa*, concludes.[110] "Mahāvīra lived for more than sixteen years after the accession of Ajātaśatru while Buddha died in the eighth year of Ajātaśatru's reign.

Now, as we have already seen, the belief that Buddha's *Nirvāṇa* took place in the eighth year of the Ajātaśatru's reign, is quite legendary and only based on later works.[111] Even if we assume it to be correct for the sake of argument, it could not be reconciled with the fact that Śreṇika had died seventeen years before Mahāvīra's *Nirvāṇa*.[112] For if we assume Buddha's *Nirvāṇa*'s to have taken place in the eighth year of Ajātaśatru's reign, the interval between Buddha's and Mahāvīra's *Nirvāṇa* could not exceed nine years. But we have seen that Muni Kalyāṇa Vijayajī himself states this interval to be forteen and half years. Thus, there is a self-contradiction in his views. If there are such inconsistencies, how the solution put forward by Muni Kalyāṇa Vijayajī can be considered acceptable? In the field of history, one has always to think from a historian's point of view.

Śrī Vijayendra Sūri

Recently, a valuable effort was made by Śrī Vijayendra Suri to simplify the problem of contemporaneity and chronology of Mahāvīra and Buddha. His novel treatise,[113] dealing with the life of Mahāvīra, is really a treasure of historical facts. Śrī Vijayendra Suri has proved in this book by adducing a lot of authoritative references that the date of Mahāvīra's *Nirvāṇa* is 527 B.C.[114] Without making any critical remarks, he has accepted 544 B.C. as the date of Buddha's *Nirvāṇa*. Thus, it can be said that Śrī Vijayendra Suri has almost wholly supported the view of Muni Kalyāṇa Vijayajī except the following modification. Regarding the allusion of Mahāvīra's death in the Buddhist texts, Śrī Vijayendra Suri has accepted the view of Dr. A.L. Basham[115] that it was really the death of Gośālaka, and by mistake the Buddhist texts described it as Mahāvīra's death.[116] This assumption of Śri Vijayendra Suri and Dr. Basham, is more speculative rather than logical. For, it is possible that for a while such misunderstanding could have prevailed, but how is it possible that it was retained by the Buddhists, in spite of the fact that Mahāvīra had lived for 16 years even after the death of Gośālaka? Again, as Śrī Vijayendra Suri indicated,[117] the scholars believe that the Buddhist *Piṭakas* were compiled two or three centuries after Buddha's *Nirvāṇa*. Then, how could the above misunderstanding could have continued to exist for such a long time, even though both Mahāvīra and Buddha had lived contemporarily, preaching in the same limited area and both were the leaders of the same *śramaṇic* tradition?

Arguments ought to have been taken one by one and refuted authentically.

There is also a self-contradiction in the view of Śrī Vijayendra Suri. On the one hand he writes[118] "Buddha, in fact, should have received the news of Gośāla's death in the form of Mahāvīra's death". While on the other hand he states,[119] both Buddha and Gośālaka had died sixteen years before Mahāvīra's *Nirvāṇa*. But the Buddhist texts indicate that Buddha had heard about Mahāvīra's death long before he (Buddha) died, then how is it possible that he would have really received the news of Gośāla's death? If one accepts the veracity of the *Piṭakas'* evidence that the above event had really taken place, it is not reasonable to believe another testimony of the *Piṭakas* that the event had happened years before Buddha's death?

Dr. Shanti Lal Shah

A valuable work, title 'Chronological Problems', written by Dr. Shanti Lal Shah, has been published in 1934 from Bonn (Germany).[120] The object of this book, in the words of the author himself, is[121] : "Not alone to fix the death-years of Buddha or Mahāvīra or the coronation date of Candragupta and Asoka, nor to authenticate the Jain traditional account, but also to reconstruct the chronology of the whole history of Northern India from Ajātaśatru to Kaniṣka is the aim of the book."[122] The author has strived much to reconstruct the chronology of the kings from Ajātaśatru to Kaniṣka to fulfil his object. He has also succeeded in giving historical form to some beliefs, but his effort to authenticate the Jain traditional belief here and there, shows rather his opinionated tendencies.

Also, he has accepted some beliefs of the later Buddhist works, without having considered their veracity. Consequently, many a unanimous historical facts have been contradicted in his new chronology. As for example, it is now almost undisputable that Candragupta's accession took place in 322 B.C. and also this date serves as a 'light-house' in that dark period of Indian history. But, according to Dr. Shah's chronology the date of Candragupta's accession is 316 B.C.[123] Regarding the date of Mahāvīra's *Nirvāṇa*, it should be noted that 527 B.C. is traditionally as well as historically accepted date. But, the date of

Buddha's *Nirvāṇa* 543 B.C. is only based on the Ceylonese tradition and is found to be unauthentic in the historical investigations.[124]

Śri Śrīcand Rāmapuriā

Śri Śrīcand Rāmapuriā, a well-known literator, has collected a good deal of data on the present problem, in his article titled 'A Discussion on the age of Mahāvīra and Buddha.[125] He has elucidated both the sides of the controversy and criticized the prevalent views on the issue, but he has not reached a definite conclusion. However he seems to be more inclined to the view that Mahāvīra was older than Buddha. He has successfully refuted the arguments of Dr. Jacodi as well as Muni Kalyāṇa Vijayajī, which they advocated to prove Buddha's seniority to Mahāvīra.

Another remarkable point in the above article is that according to Śrī Rāmapuriā, there are only two allusions found in the Buddhist *Piṭakas,* which make the seniority of Mahāvīra a little dubious. Citing the first allusion, he writes[127] : "The Buddhist scriptures clearly show that Mahāvīra was alive when Ajātaśatru acceeded to the throne of Magadha.

"Again, they also state that once Mahāvīra had asked Abhaya Kumara (The minister of Magadha) to see Buddha and to have a discussion with him.[126] The subject of discussion was connected with the following event.[127]

"Then Devadatta, rising from his seat, having arranged his upper robe over one shoulder, having saluted the Lord with joined palms, spoke to the Lord : "Lord, the Lord is now old, worn, stricken in years, he has lived his span and is at the close of his life; Lord, let the Lord now be content to live devoted to abiding in ease here and now, let him hand over the order of monks to me. It is who will lead the order of monks."

"Enough, Devadatta, please do not lead the order of monks. And a second time...... And a third time Devadatta spoke thus to the Lord : "Lord the Lord is now old, worn, stricken in years.......... It is I who will lead the order of monks.

"I, Devadatta, would not hand over the order of monks even to Sāriputta and Moggallāna. How then could I to you, a wretched one to be vomited like spittle?

Then Devadatta, thinking : 'The Lord in an assembly which included a king disparaged me by (using) the term, 'one to be vomited like spittle', while he extolled Sāriputta and Moggallāna, angry, displeased, having greeted the Lord, departed keeping his right side towards him."

"And this was the first time that Devadatta felt malice towards the Lord."

Then Devadatta approached Prince Ajātaśatru; having approached, he spoke thus to prince, Ajātaśatru "Formerly prince, people were long-lived, now-a-days they are shortlived, and it is possible that you, while still a prince, might pass away. Well now, do you, prince, having slain your father, become king. I having slain the Lord, will become the Awakened One." And Prince Ajātaśatru, thinking : Now, master Devadatta is of great psychic power, of great majesty; master Devadatta must know (what is right), having fastened a dagger against his thigh, at an entered the (King's) private quarters forcibly. But the chief ministers in attendance in the private quarters saw him. Seeing him, they caught hold of him. They examined him and having seen the dagger bound against his thigh, spoke thus to Prince Ajātaśatru : "What is it that you, prince, want to do?"

> "I want to slay my father."
> "By whom are you being incited?"
> "By master Devadatta."

Then King Seniya Bimbisāra of Magadha spoke thus to Prince Ajātaśatru :

> "Why do you, prince, want to slay me?"
> "Sir, I have need of a kingdom."

"If it be that you, prince, have need of a kingdom this kingdom is yours and handed over the kingdom to prince Ajātaśatru."

Then Devadatta approached prince Ajātaśatru; having approached, he spoke thus to prince Ajātaśatru :

> "Your Majesty, command your men so that they deprive the recluse Gotama of life." Then prince Ajātaśatru commanded his men saying : "My good men, do whatever master Devadatta says". Then Devadatta enjoined the men, saying : "Go along, friend, the recluse Gotama is staying at a certain road", and he set two men on that road, saying : "Whatever man comes alone along this road, having deprived him of life, come back by this road."

"Then that one man approached Devadatta; having approached, he spoke thus to Devadatta : Honoured sir, I am not able to deprive that Lord of life, that Lord of great psychic power, of great might."

"All right, friend, do not you deprive the recluse Gotama of life. I myself will deprive the recluse Gotama of life."

"Now at that time the Lord was pacing up and down in the shade of Mount Vulture Peak. Then Devadatta, having climbed Mount Vulture Peak, hurled down a great stone, thinking : 'With this I will deprive the recluse Gotama of Life'. But two mountain peaks, having met, crushed that stone, and (only) a fragment of it, having fallen down, drew blood on the Lord's foot. Then the Lord, having looked upwards, spoke thus to Devadatta : "You have produced great demerit, foolish man, in that you, with your mind malignant, your mind on murder, drew the Truth finder's blood." Then the Lord addresssed the monks, saying : "This, monks, is the first deed whose fruit comes with no delay accumulated by Devadatta since he, with his mind malignant, his mind on murder, drew the Truth-finder's blood."

"Now at that time there was a fierce elephant in Rājagṛha, man-slayer, called Nalagiri. Then Devadatta, having entered Rājagṛha, having gone to the elephant stable, spoke thus to the *mahout* : "We, my good fellows, are relations of the kings. We are competent to put in a high position one occupying a lowly position and to bring about an increase in food and wages. Well now, good fellows, when the recluse Gotama is coming along this carriage road, then, having let loose this elephant, Nalagiri, bring him down this carriage road."

"Then the elephant Nalagiri, suffused by the Lord with loving-kindness of mind, having put down his trunk, approached the Lord; having approached, he stood in front of the Lord.

"The elephant Nalagiri, having taken the dust of the Lord's feet with his trunk, having scattered it over his head, moved back bowing while he gazed upon the Lord.

"People looked down upon, criticised, spread it about, saying : How evil is this Devadatta, how inauspicious, in that he tried to murder the recluse Gotama who is of such great psychic power, of such great might, and Devadatta's gains and honours declined; the Lord's gains and honours increased.

"Then Devadatta approached Kokalika, Katamorakatissaka, the son of the lady Khanda, and Samuddadatta; having approached, he spoke thus to Kokalika : "Come, we, your reverences, will make a schism in the recluse Gotama's Order a breaking of the concord."

"Then Devadatta together with his friends approached the Lord; having approached, having greeted the Lord, he set down at a respectful distance, Devadatta spoke thus to the Lord : Lord the 'Lord in many a figure speaks in praise of desiring little.... whoever should eat fish and flesh, sin would besmirch him."

"Enough, Devadatta," He said. 'Whoever wishes, let him be a forest dweller; whoever wishes; let him stay in the neighbourhood of a village whoever wishes, let him be a beggar for alms; whoever wishes, let him accept an invitation; whoever wishes, let him be a reg-robe wearer; whoever wishes, let him accept a householder's robes. For eight months Devadatta, loding at the root of a tree is permitted by me. Fish and flesh are pure in respect of three points : if they are not seen, heard or suspected (to have been killed on purpose for him)."

Then Devadatta, thinking "The Lord does not permit these five items joyful, elated, rising from his seat with his friends, having greeted the Lord, departed keeping his right side towards him. Then Devadatta having entered Rājagrha with his friends, taught the people by means of the five items, saying : 'We, friends, having approached the recluse Gotama, asked for five items, saying : 'Lord, the Lord in many a figure speaks in praise of desiring little."

"Monks heard these people who....... spread it about. Those who were modest monks........ spread it about, saying :

How can thus Devadatta go forward with a schism in the Order, a breaking of the concord? Then these monks told this matter to the Lord. He said : 'is it true, as is said, that you, Devadatta, went forward with a schism in the Order, a breaking of the concord?'

"It is true, Lord."

"Enough, Devadatta, do not let there be a schims in the Order, for a schism in the Order is a serious matter, Devadatta. Whoever, Devadatta, splits an Order that is united, he sets up demerit that endures for an aeon; he is boiled in hell for an aeon.

"Devadatta saw the venerable Ānanda walking in Rājagṛha for alms-food; seeing him, he approached the venerable Ānanda; having approached, he spoke thus to the venerable Ānanda : 'Now from this day forth will I, reverend Ānanda, carry out observance both in contradistinction to the Lord and in contradistinction to the Order of monks and will (so) carry out (formal) acts of the Order."

"As he was sitting down at a respectful distance, the venerable Ānanda spoke thus to the O Lord :

"Just now, Lord, I, having dressed in the morning, taking my bowl and robe, entered Rājagṛha for almsfood. Devadatta, Lord, saw me walking in Rājagṛha for alms-food; seeing me, he came up; having came up, he spoke thus to me : 'Nowfrom this day forth will I......(so) carry out (formal) acts of the Order. To-day, Lord, Devadatta will split the Order. Then the Lord having understood this matter, at that time uttered this utterance :

"Easy is good for the good, good for the evil is hard, evil for the eil is easy, evil for the noble ones is hard."

Now at that time as many as five hundred monks, Vijjis of Vaiśālī, were newly ordained and were not properly versed; and these thinking : This is the rule, this is discipline, this is the Teacher's instruction, took voting tickets. Then Devadatta, having split the Order, set out for Gayā Head taking as many as the five hundred monks. Then Sāriputta and Moggallāna approached the Lord; ......

"Can there not be for you, Sāriputta and Moggallāna compassion for these newly ordained monks? Go you along, Sāriputta and Moggallāna, before these monks fall into trouble and distress."

"Very well, Lord", and Sāriputta and Moggallāna having answered the Lord in assent, rising from their seats, having greeted the Lord, keeping their right sides towards him, approached Gayā Head.

Then Sāriputta and Moggallāna, taking those five hundred monks approached the Bamboo Grove.

"Then the Lord addressed the monks, saying : ..... Monks because he is possessed of these eight qualities, Sāriputta is fit to give a message.

"Monks! Devadatta, overcome and his mind controlled by eight wrong conditions, is doomed to the Downfall, to Niraya Hell, staying there for an aeon, incurable.

Mahāvīra had asked Abhaya Kumāra to question Buddha regarding the propriety of the harsh words spoken by Buddha to Devadatta. The question to be asked by Abhaya Kumāra was framed thus : 'Can the Blessed One (Buddha) utter the words which are unpleasant to other?' If Buddha would have answered in negative, the cross-question was going to be : 'Then, why did the Blessed One utter harsh words to Devadatta?' On the other hand, if Buddha would have replied to the above question in affirmative, the cross question would have been : 'Then, what is the difference between a layman and the Blessed One?'

"Now, all these fragments of truth, supplied by the Buddhist texts, when joined together, at once manifest that the event of Mahāvīra's *Nirvāṇa* must have taken place in between the event of utterance of harsh words by Buddha and that of the death of Sāriputta. Again, it is believed that Buddha died in the eighth year of Ajātaśatru's reign. If this is true, Mahāvīra's death should have taken place not later than this period of Ajātaśatru's reign, and not earlier than the commencement of his reign.

"Let us see, what conclusion we reach if we assume that Mahāvīra attained the *Nirvāṇa* in the first year of Ajātaśatru's reign. This would mean that when Mahāvīra died at the age of 72, Buddha was 73 years old. Secondly, when Mahāvīra attained omniscence at the age of 42, Buddha was 43, and when Mahāvīra was initiated into the ascetic life at 30, Buddha was 31. Lastly, when Mahāvīra was born, Buddha was one year old."

The conclusion drawn by Śrī Rāmapuriā in the above passage holds good only if the belief that Buddha died in the eighth year of Ajātaśatru reign, is true. But Śrī Rāmapuriā has himself based his calculation on the dubious, statement 'If this is true'. As already shown before, the above belief of Buddha's *Nirvāṇa* in the 8th year of Ajātaśatru's reign is based on the erroneous chronology[128] adopted in the Ceylonese Chronicle, *Mahāvaṁsa.*[129] Thus, the whole mention of the above conclusion that Mahāvīra was younger than Buddha, shatters down.

The second allusion giving rise to ambiguity with respect to Mahāvīra's seniority to Buddha, is described by Śrī Rāmapuriā as follows[130] : When Buddha was lying on the death-bed, the following event took place[131] : "Now at that time, a mendicant named Subhadda, who was not a believer, was dwelling at Kuśīnagara. And the mendicant Subhadda heard the news : 'This is very day, they say, in the third watch of the night, will take place the final passing away of the *Samana* Gotama."

Then thought the mendicant Subhadda.... Now a certain feeling of uncertainity has sprung up in my mind and this faith have I in the *Samana* Gotama, that he, me thinks, is able so to present the truth that I may get rid of this feeling of uncertainity.'

"Then the mendicant Subhadda went to the Sāla Grove of the Mallas, to the Upavattana of Kuśīnara, to the place where the venerable Ānanda was."

"And when he had come there he said to the venerable Ānanda : ......

"Now the Blessed one overheard this conversation of the venerable Ānanda with the mendicant Subhadda. And the Blessed One called the venerable Ānanda, and said 'It is enough, Ānanda : Do not keep out, Subhadda, Subhadda, Ānanda, may be allowed to see the *Tathāgata.* Whatever Subhadda may ask of me, he will ask from a desire for knowledge, and not to annoy me. And whatever I may say in answer to this question, that he will quickly understand."

"Then Subhadda, the mendicant, went into the place where the Blessed One was ...... And, when he was thus seated, Subhadda, the mendicant, said the Blessed One : 'The *Śramaṇas* and the *Brāhmaṇas* by saintliness of life. Gotama, who are heads of companies of disciplies and students, teachers of students, well-known, renowned, founders of schools of doctrine, esteemed as good men by the multitude to wit, Purāṇa Kassapa, Makkhali of the cattle-pen, Ajita of the garment of hair, Kakkayana of the Pakhuda tree, Sanaya the son of the Belatth slave girl, Nigaṇṭha of the Natha clan—have they all according to their own assertion, thoroughly understood things? Or have they not? or are there some of them who have understood, and some have not?"

"Enough Subhadda : Let this matter rest whether they, according to their own assertion have thoroughly understood things, or whether they have not, or whether some of them have understood and some have not! The truth, Ānanda will I teach you. Listen well to that and give ear attentively, and I will speak."

"Even so, Lord!" said the mendicant Subhadda in assent, to the Blessed One.

"The above event raises a question in our mind whether Mahāvīra was alive up to the last day of Buddha's life. But again we may ask whether the question of Subhadda was about the living *Tīrthaṅkaras* or merely a discussion of the views of deceased *Tīrthaṅkaras*?"

The above question shows that Śrī Rāmapuriā has vigilantly reflected upon the situation. It often happens that such questions are put up only in the form a 'wont'. The above question of Subhadda definitely seems to be a customary usage of speaking together the names of all the six *Tīrthaṅkaras*. This is also proved by the fact that the names of Makkhali Gośālaka and Purāṇa Kassapa also appear in the above list of Subhadda, whereas it is unanimously believed and definitely known that both of them had died long before Buddha's *Nirvāṇa.*[132]

HISTORIANS' VIEW

Much has been written on the present issue by the Western as well as the Eastern historians. A detailed discussion of all the different views would be too lengthy a task to be discussed in the present treatise. We quote, here a view, which can be regarded as a theme of the present-day historians' approach. In An Advanced History of India, written by the top-most historians of India, Dr. R.C. Majumdar, Dr. H.C. Raychawdhri, and Dr. K.K. Dutta, the subject has been elucidated to a great extent. It is to be noted that this work consisting of more than 1100 pages, has been prescribed as a text-book of history for the post graduate studies in almost all the Universities of India. In the first part Ancient India of the above treatise, in the context of *Nirvāṇa* the authors observe[133] : The event is said to have happened 215 years before the Mauryas, and 470 years before Vikrama. This is usually taken to refer to 528 B.C. But 468 B.C. is preferred by some modern scholars, who rely on a tradition recorded by the Jain monk Hemacandra that the interval between Mahāvīra's death and the accession of Candragupta Maurya was 155, and not 215 years. The latter date does not accord with the explicit statement found in some of the earlier Buddhist texts that Mahāvīra predeceased Buddha. The earlier date is also beset with difficulties. In the first place it is at variance with the testimony of Hemacandra, who place Mahāvīra's *Nirvāṇa* only 155 years before Candragupta Maurya. Again some Jain texts place the *Nirvāṇa* 470 years before the brith of Vikrama and not his accession and as this event, according to the Jains, does not coincide with the foundation of era of 58 B.C. attributed to Vikrama the date 528 B.C. for Mahāvīra's death can hardly be accepted as representing unanimous tradition. Certain Jain writers assume an interval of 18 years between the birth of Vikrama and the foundation of the era attributed to him and thereby seek to reconcile the Jain tradition about the date of Mahāvīra's *Nirvāṇa* (58+18+470=546 B.C.) with the Ceylonese date of the great disease of Buddha (544 B.C.). But the suggestion can hardly be said to rest on any reliable tradition. Merutuṅga places the death of the last *Jina* or *Tīrthaṅkara* 470 years before the end of Śaka rule and the victory, and not the birth of the traditional Vikrama. The date 528 B.C. for the *Nirvāṇa* of the Jñātrika teacher can to a certain extent be reconciled with the Cantonese date of the death of Buddha 486 B.C. But then we shall have to assume that Mahāvīra died shortly after Buddha's enlightenment, forty-five years before the *Parinirvāṇa,* when the latter could hardly have become a renowned religious teacher of long standing as the Buddhist (canonical) texts would lead us to belief. Certain Jaina Sūtras seem to suggest that Mahāvīra died about sixteen years after the accession of Ajātaśatru and the commencement of this war with his hostile neighbours. This would place the *Nirvāṇa* of the Jain teacher eight years after Buddha's death, as according to the Ceylonese chronicles, Buddha died 8 years after the enthronment of Ajātaśatru. The *Nirvāṇa* of the *Tīrthaṅkara* would, according to this view, fall in 478 B.C., if we accept the Cantonese reckoning (486 B.C.) as our basis, and in 538 B.C., if we prefer the Ceylonese epoch. The date 478 B.C. would almost coincide with that to which the testimony of Hemacandra leads us and place the accession of Candragupta Maurya in 323 B.C. which cannot be far from truth. But the result in respect of Mahāvīra himself is at variance with the clear evidence of the Buddhist canonical texts, which make the Buddha survive his Jñātrika rival. The Jain statement that their *Tīrthaṅkara* dies some sixteen years after the accession of Konika (Ajātaśatru) can be reconciled with the Buddhist tradition about the death of the same teacher before the eighth year of Ajātaśatru, if we assume that the Jain, who refer to Konika as the rule of Campā, begun their reckoning from the accession of the prince to the Viceregal throne of Campā while the Buddhist make the accession of Ajātaśatru to the royal throne of Rājagṛha the basis of their calculation.

Expressing their views on the date of Buddha's *Nirvāṇa*; the learned historians observe :[134] "The date of his great decease (*Parinirvāṇa)* is a subject of keen controversy." If, the Ceylonese tradition, that "218 years intervened between the *Parinirvāṇa* and the consecration of *Priyadarśana* (Asoka) has any value, the day cannot be far removed from 486 B.C., the starting point of the famous 'dotted record' at Canton."

A Critique

The most remarkable thing in the above view of the renowned historians is that they have given no place to the date of Buddha's *Nirvāṇa* proposed by Dr. Jacobi, and Dr. Charpentier. As pointed out before, the main reason behind this is that during the long period that has passed since the publication of the view of Dr. Jacobi and Dr. Charpentier, new conceptions have emerged in the field of history, concerning the pre-Christian period. With regard to the date of Mahāvīra's *Nirvāṇa,* these historians have given importance to two fundamental facts and have insisted on their complete inviolation, while unravelling the present problem. The first is that out of the three dates, which are in vogue, 528 B.C. is the most veracious one. The second fact concerns the allusion of the Buddhist *Piṭakas* regarding the death of Mahāvīra. Dr. R.C. Majumdar and his colleagues have definitely accepted the veracity of the *Piṭakas'* statement that Mahāvīra predeceased Buddha. They have also expressed a need of such a chronology that can be reconciled with the above facts.

The only limitation of the above view of the famous historians is that though they have tried to make the life-events of Mahāvīra and Buddha consistent with each other, they have failed to present a completely consistent chronology. For they have adopted 528 B.C. as the date of Mahāvīra's *Nirvāṇa* and the Cantonese reckoning 486 B.C. as the date of Buddha's *Nirvāṇas.* With such a long interval in between the deaths of Mahāvīra and Buddha, we cannot reconcile their life-events with each other. Thus, we have to discover such a chronology which is compatible with the true life-events of Mahāvīra and Buddha.

RESEARCH AND CONCLUSION

Need of an Exhaustive Research

An unprejudiced survey of the efforts made up to now by the various scholars shows that the problem of contemporaneity of Mahāvīra and Buddha, was, first of all, tried to be unravelled on the basis of general historical facts, then available. At a later stage, some scholars carried on research into it in the light of the Buddhist scriptures, while others arrived at their conclusions of the problem with the help of the Jain scriptures. The result was that on the one hand, the research based on general historical facts was in itself incomplete without bearing the imprint of the scriptural evidences, while on the other hand, the one-sided approach solely based on either the Jain scriptures or the Buddhist scriptures coloured the whole issue with sectarian tint. Some scholars regarded each and every word of the Jain scripture as a principle evidence and attached little significance to the Buddhist scriptures, whereas other did the vice versa. This cannot be the method of historical research. To arrive at the perfect solution, we have to think over the issue giving proportionate value to the general historical facts, the evidences of the Buddhist *Tripiṭakas* as well as the testimonies of the Jain *Āgamas.* We shall also have to pay heed to the fact that the *Āgamas* and the *Tripiṭakas* are taken to be the original and genuine evidences of the Jain and the Buddhist traditions respectively, while the evidences of the other traditional works are valid only so far as they conform to the original canons.

The Evidences of the Buddhist *Tripiṭakas*

The testimonies of the Buddhist *Tripiṭakas* are the most evident, obvious and direct ones out of the various evidences, which come across while considering the contemporaneity of Mahāvīra and Buddha. Hence, it necessitates a through and systematic analysis of these evidences of the Buddhist *Tripiṭakas.* We consider them here one by one.

The Event of Mahāvīra's *Nirvāṇa* in *Tripiṭakas*

The allusions of the *Tripiṭakas* in which the event of Mahāvīra's *Nirvāṇa* is discussed, are as follows :

1. "[135] The Exalted One (*i.e.* Buddha) was once dwelling among the Sakkas, at Samāgama. Now at that time, *Nigaṇṭha Nātaputta* (*i.e.,* Mahāvīra) had just departed from life in Pāvā. After his death the Nigaṇṭhas (*i.e.* the Jains) were divided into two groups. They making quarrels, making strife, falling into disputes, were wounding each other with the weapons of the tongue, and were saying to each other.... 'You do not know this law of discipline' : 'I know this law of discipline'; 'You cannot know this law of discipline you are having false beliefs, I am having true beliefs'; 'My statement is meaningful, your's is not'; You uttered the matter to be spoken first; last'; 'Your doctrine is lacking thoughtfulness, and hence, it is wrong'; 'You started the quarrel; you are unfit to be argued with'; 'Off with you'. Stray you to be free from quarrel'; 'If you can, end it'. Thus the Nigaṇṭhas of the Nātaputta were as if warring with each other.

   "The disciples of the Nigaṇṭhas who were wearing white robes and were householders were as much disinterested in, disgusted with and indifferent to those Nigaṇṭhas (monks) of the Nātaputta (Mahāvīra) as they were with respect to the religion of Nātaputta, which is not well-meaning, not well-founded, unable to carry one to the *Nirvāṇa,* unable to bring peace of mind, not expounded by an enlightened. One baseless, (supported) on broken pillars, and unfit to be strayed in.

   "At that time, Cuṇḍa Samānuddeśa, after having passed his rainy-season at Pāvā, went to Samāgama and approached the venerable Ānanda. Having approached, having greeted the venerable Ānanda he sat down on one side. So seated, he said to the venerable Ānanda. 'Reverend Sir, Nigaṇṭha Nātaputta has just departed from the in Pāvā. After his death, the Nigaṇṭhas were divided into two groups. They are making quarrels

.... which is unfit to be stayed in. 'There upon, the venerable Ānanda said to Cuṇḍa Samānuddeśa : 'Reverend Cuṇḍa, this news is worthy to be presented to the blessed one. Come reverend Cuṇḍa, let us go to the Lord. Having gone there, let us, tell this matter to the Lord'.

"Yes, reverend Sir!"

"Then, the venerable Ānanda and Cuṇḍa Samānuddeśa approached the Exalted One, saluted and sat down at one side. So seated, the venerable Ānanda said to the Exalted One : 'Lord! This Cuṇḍa Samānuddeśa says so, 'Nagaṇṭha Nātaputta has just departed .... unfit to be stayed in. Now, Lord! it seems to me that after *(the Nirvāṇa of)* the Blessed One, such a dispute may not occur in the order. If it occurs, it will be for the disadvantage of the many, for the unhappiness of the many, for the unwelfare of the many, for the disadvantage and unhappiness of gods and men.'

"Do you, then believe, Ānanda, that even two monks have different opinions regarding the truths, such as ..... preached by me, after having directly experienced them.

"Lord! I do not see difference of opinions of even two monks regarding the truth, such as ...... preached by the Lord. After having directly experienced them. But Lord! when the body, which is sustained by the— Lord, will exist after the Lord's *Nirvāṇa*, there may occur a dispute in the Order, regarding the livelihood and the rules of discipline. That dispute will be for the disadvantage....... of gods and men."

2. "[136] Thus have I heard :

"The Exalted One was once staying among the Sakkas, in the palace of the Sakkas in the Mango Grove called Vedhanna.

"At that time, Nigaṇṭha Nātaputta had just departed from life in Pāvā. After his death, the Nigaṇṭhas (*i.e.* the Jains) were divided into two groups. They making quarrels, making strifes, were wounding each other with the weapons of the tongue and were saying to each other : 'You do not know this law....... unfit to be stayed in'.

'At that time Cuṇḍa Samānuddeśa, after having passed ...... unfit to be stayed in'.

"Thereupon the venerable Ānanda .... to the Lord!"

"Yes, reverend, sir!"

"Then, the venerable Ānanda .... unfit to be stayed in".

"Then the Lord said to Cuṇḍa : 'Cuṇḍa, the religion (*i.e.* doctrines) of the order in which the master is not perfectly enlightened one is not well-meaning........

"Therefore, Cuṇḍa, the religion which has been preached by me after having attained the enlightenment, should be understood well by all of you unitedly and undisputedly."

3. "[137] Thus have I heard :

"The Exalted One while making a tour among the Mallas together with the large order of monks, numbering five hundred, arrived at Pāvā, a town of Mallas. He was staying there (at Pāvā in Mango Grove of Cuṇḍa, the son of the silversmith.

"At that time, the new and lofty assembly-house (*Saṁsthāgāra)* of the Mallas the natives of Pāvā, was just built and no recluse *(Śramaṇa)* or Brāhmaṇa or man had so far lived in it. The Mallas, the natives of Pāvā, heard–'The Lord has arrived at Pāvā, while making tour among the Mallas, and the Lord is now staying in the Mango Grove of Cuṇḍa, the son of the silversmith. Then the Mallas, the natives of Pāvā, approached the Lord. They having approached and having greeted the Lord–'Lord! A new and lofty assembly house ...... so far lived in it, Lord! the Lord is requested to use it as a dwelling place for the first time. The Mallas, the natives of Pāvā will use it as a dwelling place after the Lord has used it as a dwelling place. This will be for the advantage and happiness of the Mallas, the natives of Pāvā, for a long time.'

"The Lord accepted the invitation by keeping silence.

"Then, the Lord, having dressed of taking his bowl and robe, together with the Order of monks, went to the assembly-house. Having gone .... sat down.

"Then the Lord, having addressed the Mallas, the natives of Pāvā, by a talk on *dhamma* ...... said. *Vasiṣtas!* 'The night of yours is over. Now do what seem good to you!'

"Well Lord! .... the Mallas after standing up from their seats and greeting, went away.

"Then, in a little while after Mallas had gone away, the Lord, having seen the Order of monks completely soundless, addressed Sāriputta .... 'Sāriputta, the Order of monks is completely soundless. Sāriputta, address the monks with a talk on *dhamma;* my back aches and I will stretch it.'

"The venerable Sāriputta addressing the monks........ said : 'Nigaṇṭha Nātaputta, your reverences, has just departed from life in Pāvā. After his death the Nigaṇṭhas (*i.e.* the Jains) were divided in two groups. They making quarrels....... to be stayed in. But your reverences the

> dhamma (Doctrines) of our Lord is well-meaning, well-meaning, well-founded, able to carry to the *Nirvāṇa* (final emanicipation)" able to bring peace of mind, and expounded by the Enlighted One. Here, all should stay without controversy and dispute, so that this Order may endure for a long time, and this will be for the advantage and happiness of many....... '
>
> "......... Then, the Lord, having awoke, addressed Sāriputta........... 'Excellent Sāriputta! Excellent Sāriputta! Sāriputta, you have given a good talk to the monks on the way of unity'.
>
> "The venerable Sāriputta said this; the master (Buddha) agreed with him (on this point). The monks also, having satisfied with the speech of Sāriputta, greeted it."

A Critical Examination

The three allusions quoted above, though they differ slightly in their outer forms, contain essentially the same idea. In this first allusion, Buddha, after having received the news of Mahāvīra's *Nirvāṇa* preaches Ānanda; and in the second one, he preaches Cuṇḍa. In both the allusions, the exhortations are worded differently, yet, they have the same intention. In the first and the second allusions, Buddha receives the report from Cuṇḍa in Samāgama (a village among the Śākayas) and also admonishes Ānanda and Cuṇḍa in Samāgama. In the third allusion, Sāriputta preaches the monks the way of unity in Pāvā by referring to Mahāvīra's *Nirvāṇa* and the quarrels in his order after that event.

Now, some scholars have not accepted the validity of these allusions, because in their view they contradict one another. But the reality is as follows : History may not accept each and every word of any scriptural evidence as true. If the fundamental point of any such allusion is unequivocal, history adopts it as a valid proof. As far as the above allusions are concerned, the actuality is that their essences are not at all contradictory. If in the first allusion, Ānanda is admonished by Buddha and in the second one Cuṇḍa is given injuction, many an intelligible reason are possible for it. It is plausible that both of them might have heard the sermons simultaneously, but later on, the compilers of the first allusion by their own discernment, have deemed one of them more significant than the other and those of the second one by their own discernment might have deemed the vice versa. Another plausibility is that Buddha might have preached Ānanda and Cuṇḍa one by one intermittently. The third allusion is already independent in itself and also confirms the first two allusions. For, the whole incident of Mahāvīra's *Nirvāṇa* referred to above had happened in Pāvā, and hence, it is quite natural that on arriving at Pāvā, Sāriputta must have referred to it.

All the three allusions bear the description of the ideological split among the disciples of Mahāvīra after his *Nirvāṇa.* Though the Jain tradition itself does not give any direct clue to such an event, the possibility of some mutual discussion over the issue of Mahāvīra's successorship, cannot be ruled out. For, *Indrabhūti* Gautama Svāmī was the first Gaṇadhara, *i.e.* chief disciple in the charge of the suborder (Gaṇa) and hence, in normal state of affairs, he should have been ordained as Mahāvīra's successor, but as the traditional history informs us, Sudharma Svāmī, the fifth Gaṇadhāra was ordained as the successor of Mahāvīra and that too, under the rule that *Kevalin* (*i.e.* omniscent) cannot succeed to the *Tīrthaṅkara* and Gautama Svāmī was a *Kevalin* while, Sudharma Svāmī was not *Kevalin.* Now, it is plausible that this rule might have come into existence as a result of the above discussion. The possibility of a sort of dispute between the monks who were the disciples of Gautama Svāmī and the monks who were the disciples of Sudharma Svāmī, can also not be wholly ruled out. The fact that the Śvetāmbara a tradition of the Jains regards Sudharma Svāmī as the first successor of Mahāvīra, while, the Digambara tradition of the Jains regards Gautama Svāmī as the first successor, also affords a slight hint towards the above possibility. Moreover, the wordings....... 'The disciples of the Nigaṇṭhas who were wearing white robes' used in the Buddhist allusions quoted above, also points out to the dispute between 'the white clothed' (*i.e.* Śvetāmbaras) and the unclothed (*i.e.* Digambaras) *Nirgranthas.*[138] It is also probable that the Buddhists might have presented it in an exaggerated from in the above three allusions. It generally happens that the persons belonging to one sect often express even a triffling event of the rival sect in an exaggerated form. Dharmānanda Kauśāmbī, the renowned Buddhist scholar has, accordingly, regarded the undermining delineation of Gośālaka in the Jain *Āgamas* as an exaggeration.[139]

One of the arguments given by Dr. Jacobi against the authenticity of the above allusions is that the *Mahāparinirvāṇa Sutta,* which affords us the account of the events of Buddha's last days, says nothing about this event. But this argument of Dr. Jacobi does not prove at all that the aforesaid allusions are inconsistent. At the most it only proves that the event described in the above allusions had not happened in the last days of Buddha's life.

Muni Kalyāṇa Vijayajī has regarded the whole event alluded in the Buddhist *Piṭakas* to be a mere consequence of a misunderstanding of the Buddhist compilers. Muni Kalyāṇa Vijayajī, in his interpretation of the above allusions of the Buddhist *Tripiṭakas,* has observed[140] that the event of Mahāvīra's *Nirvāṇa,* which is described in the Buddhist canons, is merely the result of the rumour prevalent at the time of Mahāvīra's serious illness due to the injury caused by the *Tejoleśya* of Gośālaka. He has also traced the origin of the post-*Nirvāṇa* dispute among the *Nirgranthas* (Jain monks), referred to in the Buddhist allusions, to the schism in the Jain order caused by Jamāli during the life time of Mahāvīra. He writes[141] : "The Buddhist delineation of the dispute and quarrel among the Nigaṇṭhas after the *Nirvāṇa* of Mahāvīra, is, in fact, the grotesque form of the dispute between Jamāli and Indrabhūti narrated in the Jain canon *Bhagvatī Sūtra."*

As already pointed out, such efforts of 'reconciliations' can, in no way, be regarded as historical. It is in fact, a misuse of the word 'reconciliation'. For, the whole event of Gośālaka's dispute with Mahāvīra had happened at 'Śrāvastī',[142] whereas the disputation between Jamāli and Indrabhūti had taken place at Campā.[143] Both the events have no concurrence of the place and time, nor, the subject of these events are related to each other. Hence, the argument of Muni Kalyāṇa Vijayajī is not at all competent to prove the aforesaid three allusions as fallacious.

Again, it should be noted that all the three allusions explicitly mention Pāvā to be place of the event of the *Nirvāṇa,* and the event of post-*Nirvāṇa* dispute. How is it reasonable to relate with them the events having taken place at 'Śrāvastī' and Campā? Moreover, how can it be plausible that a rumour about the death of distinguished man of the age like Mahāvīra, might be connected and might continue to have its sway over the people for so long a time? In addition to this, the whole event was narrated again by Sāriputta during his speech, and that too in Pāvā itself. If Mahāvīra had not really died by that time, Sāriputta must have been informed of the reality by the people of Pāvā.

If there had been even a single reference in the Jain *Āgamas* contradicting the fact stated in the above three allusions *viz.* Mahāvīra predeceased Buddha, it could have created a doubt over the credibility of these allusions. But, because we do not get any such contradictory description in the Jain *Āgamas,* we should not doubt the veracity of these allusions. Secondly, had there been a fourth allusion in the Buddhist *Tripiṭakas,* stating something about Buddha's predeceasing Mahāvīra, it would have been necessary for us to ponder over the above there allusions seriously. But in absence of any such contradictions, it would not in the least be inequitable to accept these allusions, which are unequivocal in themselves, as the valid testimonies for the discovery of truth.

The Events of Mahāvīra's Seniority in Buddhist *Tripiṭakas*

Besides the above quoted three allusions, the Buddhist cannos are replete with numerous allusions which show that Mahāvīra was older than Buddha. Most of the scholars, so far, have mainly discussed the aforesaid three allusions only. Only God knows why they have lost sight of other relevant allusions wherein it is explicitly stated and even Buddha himself accepts that he is the youngest of all the religious leaders of his time. We quote here three such allusions[144] : "Thus have I heard :

The Exalted one was once staying near Savatthi, at the Jeta Grove, in *Anathapiṇḍika's* Park. Now the king, Kosalana Pasenadi, came into the presence of the Exalted One, and after exchanging greetings with him and compliments of friendship and courtesy, sat down at one side. So seated he said to the Exalted One.

'Does master Gotama also make no claim to be perfectly and supremely enlightened?'

'If there be anyone, sire, to whom such enlightenment might rightly be attributed, it is I. I verily, sire, am perfectly and supremely enlightened.'

'But, master Gotama, there are recluses and *brahmins* who also (like yourself) have each their order of disciples, their attendant followers, who are teachers of disciples, well-known and reputed theorizers, highly esteemed by the people—I mean Purāṇa-Kassapa, Makkhali Gośāla of the Cowstall, the Nigaṇṭha Nātaputta Nata's son, *i.e.* Mahāvīra Sañjaya Belaṭṭhi's son, Kāccāyana of the Pakudhas Ajita Keśakamblī of the Hairblanket. Now they, when I have asked this same question of them, have not laid claim to perfect and supreme enlightenment. How can this be? For (as compared with them) master/Gotama is young in years, and is a novice in the life of religion.'

"There are for young creatures, sire, who are not to be disregarded or despised, because they are youthful. What are the four? A noble prince, a snake, a fire, an almsman *(Bhikkhu)*. Yes, sire, these for young creatures are not to be disregarded or despised because they are youthful".

"Thus spoke the Exalted One. And the Blessed One so saying the Master spoke again on this wise :—

"A princely youth, by birth with fortune best,
Offspring of well-born families, let none
Disdain for being youthful nor despise.
The time may come when he, as lord of mean,
Comes to his heritage, and in his wrath
May with a despot's weapons seek revenge
With heavy hand. Hence from such attitude
Let everyone who guards his life refrain.

"Or if a man do walk within the woods
And see a snake glide by, let him not say
Disdainful : 'Tie young one,' and despise.
"In diverse shapes and with an ardent force

Fareth the snake. Should be attacking strike,
He bites the heedless, be it man or maid,
No matter when. Hence from such attitude
Let everyone who guards his life refrain.

"A fire ablaze with appretite immense
And *(svārthī)* trail let none despite as young
Since it was lit, nor hold of no account.
If it but win to fuel, growing great,
It may attack the heedless, man or maid,
And burn no matter when. From this therefore
Let everyone who guards his life refrain.

"The forest burnt by fire, the swarthy trailed,
After the lapse of many nights and days,
In shoots and seedlings springs once more to life.
But he whom almsman, strong in righteousness,
Burneth with ardent flame, may look in vain
For child, or offspring 'among his stock'. No wealth
His heire may find; childless and without heirs,
Like to a plam-tree stump such men become.

"Hence with these four—the seprent and the fire,
The prince of high estate, the saintly friar—
Let the wise man, his own goodwill in sight,
Conduct himself as seemly is and right."

When these things had been said, King Pasenadi, the Kośalan, spoke thus to the Exalted One :

" 'Most excellent, Lord, most excellent'. Just as if a man were to set up that which has been thrown down, or were to reveal that which is hidden away, or were to point out the right road to him who has gone astray, or were to bring a lamp into the darkness so that those who have eyes could see external forms—just even so, Lord, has the truth been made known to me, in many a figure by the Exalted One. I, even I, Lord, betake myself to the Exalted One as my refuge, to the Norms and to the Order. May the Exalted One accept me as a follower, as one who from this day forth as long as life endures has taken his refuge therein."

At one time *Bhagāvan, i.e.* Buddha was dwelling at Rājagṛha in Veṇuvana, in Kalandakanivapa. At and that time some questions were recited to Sabhiya, the Paribbajaka (a wandering mender mendicant), by an old benevolent diety (who had in a former birth been a relation of his) : 'He who, O Sabhiya, be it a

Śramaṇa or a *Brāhmaṇa,* explains these questions to thee when asked, near him you should live a religious life.'

"Then Sabhiya the Pribbajaka having learnt the questions from the deity, went to whatever *Śramaṇas* and *Brāhmaṇas* there were, who had an assembly (of *Bhikkhus),* and a crowd (of followers), and were well-known teachers famous leaders and were considered excellent by the multitude, such as 1. Purāṇa Kassapa, 2. Makkhali Gośāla, 3. Ajita Keśakambalī, 4. Pakuddha Kāccāyana, 5. Sañjaya Belaṭṭhiputta, and 6. Nigaṇṭha Nātaputta, (*i.e.* Mahāvīra). Those who want to and after going to them, asked these questions. They, being asked the questions by Sabhiya, the Pribbajaka, did not succeed (in answering them), and not succeeding they showed wrath and hatred and discontent, and they also in return put questions to Sabhiya the Paribbajaka.

"Then this came to the mind of Sabhiya, the Paribbajaka, 'Whatever *Śramaṇas* and *Brāhmaṇas* there are, that have an assembly (of *Bhikkhus)* and a crowd of followers), and are well-known teachers, famous leaders, considered excellent by the multitude, as Purāṇa Kassapa, Makkhali Gośāla, Ajita-Keśa Kambalī, Pakuddha Kāccāyana, Sañjaya-Ballaṭṭhiputta, and Nigaṇṭha-, Nātaputta they being asked questions by me, did not succeed in answering them, and not succeeding they showed wrath and hatred and discontent, and they also in return put questions to me in this matter, surely I think I shall go back to what I have left, and enjoy sensual pleasures.''

"Then this came to the mind of Sabhiya, the Paribbajaka : 'This *Śramaṇa* Gautama, *i.e.* Buddha, too has an assembly (of *Bhikkhus)* and a crowd (of followers), and is a well-known teacher, a famous leader, and is considered excellent by the multitude; surely I think I shall go to him and ask him these questions'. Then this came to the mind of Sabhiya, the Paribbajaka. Whatever *Śramaṇas* and *Brāhmaṇas* there are, decayed, old aged, advanced in years having reached old age, experienced elders, long ordained having assemblies (of *Bhikkhus)* crowds (of followers), being teachers well-known, famous leaders, considered excellent by the multitude, such as 1. Purāṇa Kessapa, 2. Makkhali Gośāla, 3. Ajita Keśakambalī, 4. Pakuddha Kāccāyana, 5. Sañjaya Belaṭṭhiputta and 6. Nigaṇṭha Nātaputta, (*i.e.* Mahāvīra) and they, being asked questions by me, did not succeed (in answering them) and not succeeding they showed wrath and hatred and discontent and they also in return put questions to me in this matter. (I should like to know) whether *Śramaṇa* Gautama (*i.e.* Buddha), will be able to explain them to me, for *Śramaṇa* Gautama is both young by birth and new in ascetic life'. Then this came to the mind of Sabhiya the Paribbajaka : '*Śramaṇa* Gautama is not to be slighted because he is young; even if the *Śramaṇa* Gautama is young, yet is mighty and powerful : surely I think I shall go to *Śramaṇa* Gautama and ask these questions."[145]

3. [146] Thus have I heard :

"Once the Exalted One was staying at Rājagṛha in the Mango Grove of Jīvaka Komarbhacca, together with the large order of monks, numbering one thousand two hundred and fifty.

Now at that time, when it was the night of the full-moon day of the observance-day, the full-moon day being the Kaumudī of rainy-season (*i.e.* the full-moon day in the month of *Aśvina* or *Kārtika*,[147] Ajātaśatru, the king of Magadha, the son of Vaidehi, surrounded by the ministers of the kingdom, was sitting on the terrace of the best palace. Then King Ajātaśatru expressing praise of the observance day (*i.e.* the full-moon day), said 'Ah'!

> How charming is the night illuminated by the light of the full-moon!
> How beautiful is the night illuminated by the light of the full-moon!!
> How handsome is the night illuminated by the light of the full-moon!!!
> How pleasant is the night illuminated by the light of the full-moon!!!
> How exquisite is the night illuminated by the light of the full-moon!!!

Buddha, we do not have a chronological account in the main (at such a pleasant time) to which *Śramaṇa* (recluse) or *Brahmin* should we go to pass our time in the company of the good (man), so that his company may please our minds?

"On his saying so one of the ministers of his kingdom said to Ajātaśatru, the king of Magadha the son of Vaidehi : 'Sire! there is one Purāṇa Kassapa, who has his order of disciples and his crowd of followers who is the teacher of disciples, well-known and reputed founder of a school of doctrine, esteemed as good man by the multitude, experienced, long-ordained, advanced in years and having reached old age. The king, sire, should have a religious discussion with Purāṇa Kassapa. The religious discussion with Purāṇa Kassapa even for a little time will delight your heart'. On his saying so, Ajātaśatru, the king of Magadha the son of Vaidehi, kept silence".

"Another minister said this to Ajātaśatru the ...... Vaidehi : 'Sire, there is one Makkhali Gośāla (*i.e.* of the cattle pen) who has his order of disciples, ... reached old age. The king, sire, should have religious discussion with this Makkhali Gośāla. The religious discussion with Makkhali Gośāla even for.......... kept silence.

"Another minister said this....... there is one Ajita Keśa Kambalī who has.......... old age. The king with this Ajita Keśakambalī........ The religious discussion with Ajita Keśakambalī even for...... kept silence."

"Another minister said this........ there is one Pakuddha Kāccāyana who has........ old age. The king......with this Pakuddha Kāccāyana. The religious discussion with Pakuddha Kāccāyana even for .... kept silence."

"Another minister said this....... there is one Saññajaya Belaṭṭhiputta who has .... old age. The king .... with this Saññajaya Belaṭṭhiputta. The religious discussion with Saññajaya Belaṭṭhiputta even for .... kept silence.

"Another minister said this .... there is one Nigaṇṭha Nātaputta (*i.e.* Mahāvīra) who has .... old age. The king .... with this Nigaṇṭha Nātaputta. The religious discussion with Nigaṇṭha Nātaputta even for...... kept silence.

"At that time Jīvaka Komārabhacca was sitting silently near Ajātaśatru, the king of Magadha, the son of Vaidehi. Then Ajātaśatru, the king......... Vaidehi, said to Jīvaka Komārabhacca. 'Why, good Jīvaka you are keeping complete silence?

"Sire, this Lord the Perfected One and the wholly Awakened. One (*i.e.* Buddha is staying in my Mango Grove together with a large order of monks numbering one thousand two hundred and fifty."

The auspicious fame of such Lord Gautama has spread thus—he is the Lord the Perfected One, the wholly Awakened One, having knowledge and conduct, having reached the best life (*Sugata)*, knower of the world, an unparalleled whip for restraining people (*i.e.* for bringing people on the virtuous path) the instructor (*i.e.* preacher) of the Gods and men, and the Enlighted One Sire; Your Majesty should go to him and have religious discussion with him. By having a religious discussion with him, perhaps your Majesty's heart will be delighted.

A Critical Examination

These three allusions are so explicit in themselves to prove the seniority of Mahāvīra to Buddha that it would be entirely needless to reconcile or explain them.

In this way the three allusions (quoted before) prove that Mahāvīra a predeceased Buddha and the other three allusions (quoted now) prove that Mahāvīra was senior to Buddha, and that too not only from the point of view age but also from the point of view of knowledge, influence and period of Monkhood.

These allusions themselves speak eloquently that when Buddha had just started his preaching work, Mahāvīra by that time, had already done a good deal in that direction.

The veracity of the above allusions is also proved by the fact that the Buddhist *Tripiṭakas* themselves accept the juniority of Buddha. If Buddha had been regarded senior from the point of view of age, period of Monkhood and influence by Buddhist *Tripiṭakas,* we would have questioned their credibility. On the ground that the compilers of the Buddhist scriptures might have done so in order to enhance the glory and fame of their religious preceptor, but acknowledging the juniority of one's religious preceptor cannot be regarded as a means of fostering the sentiment of sectarian egoism.

The already stated fact, *viz*. Mahāvīra was a senior, contemporary of Buddha, is also substantiated by the fact that the Jain canons are as reticent about Buddha as the Buddhist canons are eloquent about Mahāvīra. The possible reasons thereof are as follows :

A budding religious leader generally speaks much about his senior rivals. He has psychologically a feeling of equating himself with his senior rivals, and hence, he endeavours to show himself superior and his rivals inferior. Consequently, refers every now and then to the weak points of his rivals. This very process is reflected in the Buddhist canons which are replete with the allusions about Nigaṇṭha Natāputta (and also other five religious teachers) and the doctrines of the Nigaṇṭhas (*i.e.* the Jains).[148] On the contrary the Jain canons do not mention even the name of Buddha as the sponsor of Buddhism. This also signifies the same fact that those who have already earned the name and fame and become dignifying and dominating figures, shrink from giving an importance to the rival budding power all of a sudden.

Another possible reasons is that the teaching of Mahāvīra had already been compiled in the form of 12 *Aṅgas,* comprising the most original portion of the Jain canonical literature, by the eleven *Gaṇadharas* soon after Mahāvīra's attainment of omniscence. Now because Buddha's advent was not even 'in the air' at that time, How could we expect to find allusions in those canons about the life of Buddha? Also, on the other hand, if Buddha were really a senior contemporary of Mahāvīra, how the Jain canons could have refrained from referring to the events of Buddha's life.[149]

Again because Buddha was a junior contemporary of Mahāvīra and the Buddhist canons were compiled after the *Nirvāṇa* of Buddha by his perfected disciples, it is quite natural that the *Tripiṭakas* afford us with a lot of allusions about Mahāvīra's life.

Contemporaneity and Chronology

On the basis of the facts discussed in the preceding sections, we indubitably reach the conclusion that Mahāvīra predeceased Buddha and that Mahāvīra was a senior contemporary of Buddha. Now, it remains to decide the period of other contemporaneity, *i.e.* how long they lived in the presence of each other. But we can know this completely only after chronologizing the chief events of their life. Though the *Āgamas* and the *Tripiṭakas* afford us the account of the days and the months of their birth and death, they do not mention the years of these events in terms of any prevalent era. This might have happened on account of the fact that no such systematized era, was in vogue at that time. Thus the only means at our hand to determine their correct dates is the use of other chronicles after having attested their veracity on the touchstone of history.

First we shall consider the chronology of Mahāvīra, for it is rather more unequivocal and less controversial than that of Buddha.

Chronology of Mahāvīra

In the foregoing chapter it has already been elucidated that the most unequivocal date of Mahāvīra's *Nirvāṇa* is 527 B.C.[150] This date is substantiated by an extraordinary evidence : History accepts 322 B.C. as the date of the accession of Candragupta Maurya to the sovereignty of Magadha.[151] The historians call this date a 'light house' in the dark period of Indian history.[152] They decide the chronology of hundred of years, posterior and prior to this period, on the basis of this unanimously accepted and definitely verified date. According to the chronology adpoted by some ancient Jain traditional works, such as *Titthogali Paiññaya, Titthodhara Prakraṇa.* Merutuṅga's *Vicāraśreṇi,* etc., the event of Mahāvīra's death had taken place 215 years before Candragupta's accession. It should also be remarked here that the above work speak of Candragupta's accession to the throne of Avanti, and not that of Magadha. It is also a historical fact that in 312 B.C. (*i.e.* 10 years after Candragupta's accession to the throne of Magadha) Candragupta acquired the kingdom of Avanti.[153] Thus, the Jain chronology and the historical chronology endorse each other and the date of Mahāvīra's *Nirvāṇa* is confirmed in 312 + 215 = 527 B.C.

The Vikrama Era

The above date of Mahāvīra's *Nirvāṇa* is also supported by the historical dates of Vikrama, Śaka and Gupta eras. The ancient chronicles and works of Jain tradition state that Mahāvīra's *Nirvāṇa* took place 470 years before the commencement of the Vikrama era.[154] According to the unanimous opinion of historians, the Vikrama era started in 57 B.C.[155] This clearly implies that Mahāvīra died in 57+470 = 527 B.C.

The Śaka Era

According to both the traditions of Jains—Śvetāmbara and Digambara, the Śaka era commenced 605 years and 5 months after Mahāvīra's *Nirvāṇa.*[156] According to history, the Śaka era started in 78 A.C.[157] Hence, the date of Mahāvīra's *Nirvāṇa* comes out to be 605-78 = 527.

The Gupta Era

Dr. Vasudeva Upadhyaya, M.A., Ph.D. discussing about the Gupta era, writes in his famous historical work on Gupta period.[158] "On the basis of the account given by some Jain writers of centuries prior to Alberuni, it is found that there is an interval of 241 years between the Śaka and Gupta eras. One of these writers, Jinasena, who flourished in the 8th century A.D., states[159] that 605 years and 5 months after Mahāvīra's *Nirvāṇa*, the Śaka king flourished and 231 years after the Śaka, Gupta's reign began, during which was born the Kalakirāja. Another Jain auther Guṇabhadra writes in his work *Uttara purāṇa*[160] (889 A.D.), that 1000 years after Mahāvīra's *Nirvāṇa*, the Kalakirāja was born. The statements of Jinasena and Guṇabhadra are seconded by a third writer, Nemicandra.

"Nemicandra writes in his work *Trilokasāra.*[161] 'Śakarāja was born 605 years and five months after Mahāvīra's *Nirvāṇa* and Kalakirāja was born, 394 years 7 months, after the Śaka era.' Thus, 605 years 5 months + 394 years 7 months, = 1000 years. In this way on the basis of these three Jain writers, the time of Śakarāja as well as that of Kalakirāja are ascertained." In this way, after ascertaining the times of Śaka and Kalaki on the basis of some Jain works, Dr. Vasudeva Upadhyaya has proceeded further to find out the interval between the Śaka era, and the Gupta era on the basis of Khoha inscription of king Hastina. In conclusion of the whole discussion, he writes[162] : "On the basis of the above discussion, it can be said that adding the number 241 to a date in Śaka era, we get the corresponding date in Gupta era. Also, the statement of Alberuni is substantiated by this extensive discussion. It can be definitely concluded that the Gupta era began 241 years after Śaka era (*i.e.* in 319 A.D.)."

The above quotation shows how the date of Mahāvīra's *Nirvāṇa* has become the base of the chronology upto the beginning of Gupta era. Dr. Upadhyaya, as shown above, has reached at the date of the Gupta era by starting from the date of Mahāvīra's *Nirvāṇa* Now, if we employ just the reverse process we reach back to the date of Mahāvīra's *Nirvāṇa* as 527 B.C. For, the beginning of Gupta era—319 A.D. Interval between Mahāvīra's *Nirvāṇa* and the beginning of era—846 years..... Date of Mahāvīra's *Nirvāṇa*—527 B.C.

Astrological Calculations

The learned *Ācāryas* of *Terāpantha* have also accepted 527 B.C. as the date of Mahāvīra's *Nirvāṇa*. They have supported their belief by the astrological calculations. According to the Jain scriptures, at the time of Mahāvīra's death, an asterism of ashes (*Bhasma-graha)* entered into the sign of Zodiac under which Mahāvīra was born (the birth-rāśi) and it continued to stay for 200 years.[163] According to fourth *Ācārya of Terāpantha,* Śrīmad Jayācārya, that asterism left the sign of Zodiac of Mahāvīra's birth in the year 1531 of Vikrama era.[164] Again, the scriptures have predicted that a comet *(Dhūmaketu)* of duration of 333 years, will set in, 1990 years after Mahāvīra's death.[165] According to Śrīmad Jayācārya,[166] the comet left the sign of Zodiac of Mahāvīra's birth in the year 1853 of Vikrama era. On the basis of the above two astrological evidences, we reach 527 B.C. as the date of Mahāvīra's *Nirvāṇa* as follows :

Total duration of asterism of ash—200 years.
Date of its leaving the birth-rāśi—1473 A.D.
Date of Mahāvīra's Nirvāṇa—527 B.C.

Similarly, 1990 + 333 years after Mahāvīra's death, the comet left the birth-rāśi, so that—

Total duration of comet—2323 years.
Date of its leaving the birth-rāśi—1796 A.D.
Date of Mahāvīra's *Nirvāṇa*—527 B.C.

Traditional Era of Vīra—*Nirvāṇa*

The era of Mahāvīra's *Nirvāṇa*, which is in vogue at present in the Jain traditions, is also based on the date 527 B.C. It is remarkable that this era is unanimously and uncontrovertibly accepted by all the sects of Jains. At present, in the year 1963 A.D., the era of Mahāvīra's *Nirvāṇa* is 2490, which is 527 years ahead of Christian era, as it should be.

Chronology of Mahāvīra's Life

After having decided the date of Mahāvīra's *Nirvāṇa*, now we can easily chronologize the important events of Mahāvīra's life as follows :

B.C.	*Event*
599	Birth
569	Initiation into ascetic life
557	Attainment of omniscence
527	Final emanicipation

Traditional Dates of *Nirvāṇa*

It is not so easy to discover a unique date for Buddha's *Nirvāṇa* as in the case of

Mahāvīra. More than a millenium ago, there existed ambiguity about it and even today it persists to a great extent. Famous Chinese traveller Fa Hien, who visited India in 400 A.D., remarks.[167] "Up to now, 1497 years have passed since the *Nirvāṇa* of the Blessed One (Buddha)". Another well-known Chinese traveller Hiuen-Tsang who toured in India in 630 A.D., wrote.[168] "Lord Buddha lived for 80 years, There is a great controversy over the date of his *Nirvāṇa*. Some believe that Buddha attained the *Nirvāṇa* on the full-moon day of *Vaiśākha,* while the Sarvastīvādins take the full-moon day of the month *Kārtika* as the day of *Nirvāṇa*. Some people say that 1200 years have passed since the *Nirvāṇa*, while others contend that 1500 years have passed, and some other believe that 900 and a few more years have passed since the *Nirvāṇa*". On the basis of these beliefs, the dates of Buddha's *Nirvāṇa* come out to be 570 B.C. 870 B.C. and a few years earlier than 270 B.C. respectively. But all these dates have no more value than the legends.

At present, these are several dates prevalent on the basis of different Buddhist traditions. One of these is based on the Ceylonese chronicle, *Mahāvaṁsa.*[169] According to this, the *Nirvāṇa* of Buddha took place in 544 B.C. (This is popularly known as 'Ceylonese date'). Another date is based on the "dotted record of canton".[170] Saṅghabhadra brought this news to China. The people of Canton established a "Dotted record", the starting dot of which synchoronised with the year of Buddha's *Nirvāṇa*. Then, every year a dot was added to it. This tradition continued up to 489 A.D. When all the dots were counted, they were found to be 975, on this basis, the date of Buddha's *Nirvāṇa* was calculated to be 486 B.C.

There is a third date, prevailing in Chinese Turkestan. This is also known as 'Khotan tradition'.[171] "It place, *Dharma*—Asoka 250 years after the *Nirvāṇa* of Buddha, and makes him contemporary with Chinese emperor Shih Huang-Ti (Chin), the builder of the great wall, who came to throne in 246 B.C., became, universal emperor in 221 B.C. and reigned up to 210 B.C." On the basis of this tradition, some scholars affirm that Buddha died in 246+250 = 496 B.C.[172]

Historian's Date of Buddha's *Nirvāṇa*

It is really surprising that in spite of the extensive research work, that has been carried into the problem of Buddha's date, the historians failed to reach an unanimous decision regarding it. Most of the scholars have put forth new opinion, and thus, they have elongated the list of these dates. The dates, suggested by the prominent scholars are enlisted here :

Name of the Scholars	*(Date of Buddha's) Nirvāṇa in B.C.*
E.J. Thomas and a	
Japanese Scholar[173]	386
Rhys Davids[174]	412
Max Müller[175] and Jarl Charpentier[176]	477
Gen.... Cunnigham[177] and	
Diwan Bahadur	478
Svāmī Kanna Pilley[178]	480
Oldenberg[179]	481
Ferguson[180]	
Dr. Buhler[181]	In between 483 & 471
Dr. Wheeler, Gelger,[182]	
Dr. Fleet[183]	483
Tukārāma Kṛṣna Laddu,[184]	
Pt. Rahul Sankrityayana,[185]	
Dr. Jacobi[186]	
Dr. H.C. Ray Chaudhri,[187]	
Dr. Smith's later view,[188]	487
Prof. Kern[189]	488
Dr. Smith's Earlier Views,[190]	
Dharmānanda Kauśāmbī[191]	543
Pt. Bhagavān Lal Inderji[192]	638

It can easily be inferred, from the above list that out of the twenty two opinions quoted, nineteen hold that Buddha's *Nirvāṇa* took place later than 527 B.C. If 527 B.C. is accepted to be the correct date of Mahāvīra's *Nirvāṇa* Buddha can be considered as a Junior contemporary of Mahāvīra in opinion of the above 19 scholars.

Though in course of time, new changes have entered in the opinion regarding the date of Buddha's *Nirvāṇa*, not a single view has been propounded so as to reconcile the events of Buddha's life connected with Mahāvīra, Gośālaka, Bimbisāra (Śreṇika), Ajātaśatru (Konika), etc. This suggests that there has remained some fundamental mistake in our way of approach to the problem. It is nothing but the adoption of the chronology of Ceylonese chronicles as the basis.

Problem of Chronology

There are mainly three sources, which throw light on the ancient chronology of India :

1. Purāṇic,
2. Jain,

3. Buddhist.

The first of these, viz., the *Purāṇic* chronology is based on the Purāṇa such as *Viṣṇu Purāṇa, Matsya Purāṇa, Vāyu Purāṇa, Bhagvat-Purāṇa,* etc. The second one, *i.e.* the Jain chronology is found in the ancient works of Jain tradition such as, *Titthogali Paiññaya,* Merutuṅga's *Vicāra Śreṇi,* etc. The Buddhist chronology is based on the Ceylonese chronicles *Dīpavaṁsa* and *Mahāvaṁsa.*

The first of the above source is the earliest of all. The *Purāṇas* cited above according to the historians, were compiled in the fourth century B.C.[193]

Titthogali Paiññaya, the work of the Jain tradition describing the chronology of ancient India, is believed to be composed in the 3rd or the 4th century A.D.[194]

The Ceylonese chronicles, date back, according to the scholars[195] to the 4th or 5th century of our era.

The *Purāṇic* and the Jain chronologies are wholly Indian, and endorse each other.[196] It is worth noting that the authority of the Purāṇic chronology has been accepted by the historians.[197] The Buddhist chronology is non-Indian, in as much as the Ceylonese chronicles were composed in Ceylon. Dr. Rhys Davids writes[198] : "In the fourth century of our era, some one collected such of these Pāli verses, as referred to the history of Ceylon, piecing them together by other verses to make a consecutive. He called his poem, thus constructed, the *Dīpavaṁsa,* the Island Chronicle...."

"As generation afterwards Mahānama wrote his great work, the *Mahāvaṁsa.* He was no historian, and has, besides the material used by his two predecessors, only popular legends to work on. "This quotation of the renowned scholar clearly indicates of the unauthenticity of the Ceylonese chronicles. The greatest weakness of the Ceylonese chronology is that it shows a great discrepancy with the *Purāṇic* and the Jain chronologies.[199]

Reconstruction of Chronology

We have already reached a definite conclusion about the following dates :

Birth of Mahāvīra	599 B.C.
Accession of Ajātaśatru	544 B.C.
Death of Gośālaka	543 B.C.
Nirvāṇa of Mahāvīra	527 B.C.
Accession of Candragupta (at Magadha)	322 B.C.
Accession of Candragupta (at Avanti)	313 B.C.

Now, we should try to reconstruct the whole chronology from the king Śiśunāga, the founder of the Śrī Śuṅga dynasty to the end of Nandas rule.[200] As we have seen, the Jain sources assign 60 years to the rule of Palaka dynasty and 155 years to that of Nanda dynasty over the kingdom of Avanti, after the death of Mahāvīra in 527 B.C. Thus in Avanti, the Palaka dynasty rule from 527 B.C. to 467 B.C., and the Nanda dynasty ruled from 467 B.C. to 312 B.C.

Now regarding the chronology of Magadha, we find that after the *Nirvāṇa* of Mahāvīra, the Śiśunāga dynasty continued to rule of 54 or 53 years,[201] after which the Nanda's rule began in Magadha.

In terms of chronology, rule of the Śiśunāga-dynasty ended and that of Nanda-dynasty began in Magadha in 474-3 B.C.[202] Again, according to the *Purāṇas,* the ten kings of Śiśunāga-dynasty reigned Magadha for 333 years.[203] Hence, the beginning of Śiśunāga dynasty[204] dates back to 807 B.C.

Thus, the rule of the ten kings of Śiśunāga dynasty in Magadha lasted from 807 B.C. to 474 B.C. by accepting the regnal period given in the previous footnote, the accession of Bimbisāra falls in 582 B.C.[205] As we have already seen Ajātaśatru's reign began 17 years before the death of Mahāvīra (527 B.C.) and ended 30 years after it. Thus, Ajātaśatru reigned from 544 B.C. to 497 B.C. Then, Udayi[206] reigned for 16 years *i.e.* from 497 B.C. to 481 B.C. As stated before the Śiśunāga dynasty was succeeded by the Nanda dynasty. The first Nanda, probably called as Nandīvardhana,[207] acceeded to the throne of Magadha in 473 B.C.

This Nandīvardhana, conquered the kingdom of Avanti and established the Nanda's rule there in 467 B.C., thus ending the rule of the Palaka dynasty or "Pradyotas".[208] After conquering Avanti, it seems that Nandīvardhana attacked Kaliṅga and brought a Jain-statue to Magadha. On the basis of the Hāthīgumphā inscription of Khāravela, this event should have been taken place in 466 B.C.[209] Thus, after having established the rule of the Nanda-dynasty within 16 or 18 years, Nandīvardhana, the first Nanda king died in 456 B.C.[210]

It may be remarked here that this date (474-456 B.C.) of Nandīvardhana, the first Nanda king, is also corroborated by the date of famous grammarian Pāṇini, who is proved to be his contemporary and to have lived in 480-410 B.C.[211]

Nandīvardhana was succeeded by his son Mahānadina, whose regnal period according to the *Purāṇas* in 83 years.[212]

Thus, in 413 B.C., Mahāpadma Nanda acceeded to the throne of Magadha. He is said to have established "*Ek rat*" Kingdom in India.[213] He is assigned a regnal period of 88 years by the *Purāṇas,*[214] and hence, his rule must have ended in 326 B.C.[215] The remaining Nandas are assigned totally 12 years as their regnal period, and hence, the Nanda dynasty should have ended in 313 B.C.[216]

Thus, we have reconstructed a complete chronology of the kings from the foundation of Śiśunāga-dynasty to that of Maurya-dynasty. We give it here in a tabular form :

Event		*Date (B.C.)*
Foundation of Śiśunāga-dynasty		807
Accession of	Śiśunāga	747
" "	Kṣemavardhana	711
" "	Kṣemajita	661
" "	Prasenjita	625
" "	Bimbisāra	582
" "	Ajātaśatru	544
" "	Udayi (in Paṭaliputra)	497
" "	Darṣka or Nāgadaśaka in Rājagṛha	497
" "	Aniruddha-Muṇḍa	
Foundation of Nanda-dynasty		
Accession of Nandīvardhana (in Paṭaliputra)		
" " "	(in Avanti)	467
" "	Mahānandi	456
" "	Mahāpadama Nanda	413
" "	eight son of Mahāpadma	325
Foundation of Maurya-dynasty (in Magadha)		322
Accession of Candragupta Maurya (in Magadha)		
" "	Chandragupta, Maurya (in Avanti)	313

Inconsistencies in Ceylonese Chronology

Some inconsistencies in the chronology described by the Ceylonese chronicles are so obvious that it surprises us how they were accepted as the authoritative sources by the historians. For instance, the *Purāṇic* and the Jain chronologies assign 100 and 150 years respectively to the Nanda dynasty, whereas the *Mahāvaṁsa* ascribes only 22 years to the whole dynasty, and more surprisingly, we find that no place is given to this important dynasty of India in the chronological list supplied by the *Dīpavaṁsa*.[217] Another inconsistency of the Ceylonese chronology is that whereas in the *Purāṇas* the king Śiśunāga Kākavarṇa, etc., are enumerated as the predecessors of Ajātaśatru, the Ceylonese works enlist them as the successors of Ajātaśatru.[218] This can be said to be an untolerable blunder from the historical point of view. Besides such inconsistencies, the chronological beliefs of the *Mahāvaṁsa* such as "Buddha's death in the 8th years of Ajātaśatru's reign,[219] "Asoka's coronation (anointment) 218 years after Buddha's *Nirvāṇa* contradict not only *Tripiṭakas* and more genuine literary works, but also run counter to the fundamental historical facts.

Dr. Vinsent Smith had long ago warned the historians against the over-estimation of the value of the Ceylonese chronicles.[220] Dr. H.C. Raychaudhuri has also maintained that these Ceylonese legends cannot be made basis of the historical conceptions.[221] Dr. Shanti Lal Shah has already found out the reason of the discrepancy which is found in the Ceylonese chronicles, and which he terms as a deliberated perversion.[222] He writes[223] : "The peculiarity of the Buddhist tradition (The Ceylonese tradition) is that it confines itself firstly to the history of the Hīnayāna Buddhism and secondly to the history of its development in Ceylon, since Buddhism although originating in India, had found its development in Ceylong. Because of this territorial limitation, which has been a great factor for the preservation of the history of Ceylon, the account of this tradition about Ceylon is much more perfect than that about India. One who is acquainted with the scheme and content of the *Dīpavaṁsa* and *Mahāvaṁsa* will hardly fail to notice that the account of the North Indian kings in these two books is only occasional and of minor importance. This conclusion is absolutely borne out by the typical construction of the *Dīpavaṁsa* and *Mahāvaṁsa*".[224]

In spite of all these inconsistencies, in the most of the approaches made up to now to fix the date of Buddha's *Nirvāṇa*, the Ceylonese chronology has been accepted as the main basis. This seems to be the main reason responsible for the discrepancy created between the chronology of Buddha and the genuine life-events of Buddha.

The Chronology of Buddha

In such a condition, when the chronoloy of Buddha itself is dubious and uncertain, in order to compute the period of contemporaneity of Mahāvīra and Buddha, the life-events depicted in the *Āgamas* and the *Tripiṭakas*, serve as the most authentic means. Out of the six contemporary rivals of Buddha. Mahāvīra was the most prominent one. The *Tripiṭakas* bear testimony to their intimate relations, either bad or good. Hence, complete consistency in their life-events will reveal their period of contemporaneity, and consequently, the chronology of Buddha.

According to the Jain canon *Bhagvatī Sūtra,* Makkhali Gośālaka, the leader of the Ājīvakas, died 16 years before the *Nirvāṇa* of Mahāvīra. Also, as we have already proved,[225] Bimbisāra's (Śreṇika's) death and Ajātaśatru's accession took place 17 years before the *Nirvāṇa* of Mahāvīra. On the basis of the foregoing discussion, it has also become clear that Ajātaśatru fought the *Mahā-Śīlakaṇṭaka* war and the *Ratha mūsala* war with the Vajjis of Vaiśālī, in the first year of his regin.

The following four facts are quite obvious in the light of the foregoing discussion of the life-events of Mahāvīra and Buddha, as dipicted in *Āgamas* and the *Tripiṭakas :*

1. Mahāvīra was elder than Buddha, the former having lived for 72 years, while the latter for 80.

2. Mahāvīra's omniscience is antecedent to Buddha's enlightenment, Mahāvīra attained omniscience at the age of 42, while Buddha attained enlightenment at the age of 35.
3. When Gośālaka died, Mahāvīra was 56 year old.
4. Buddha's enlightenment had taken place before the death of Gośālaka,[226] *i.e.* Mahāvīra. Buddha as well as Gośālaka were alive at the time of *Mahā-Śīla-Kaṇṭaka* war.

On the basis of the above facts, the following conclusion can easily be deduced—When Mahāvīra was 56 years old, Buddha must be at least 35. So, the maximum possible seniority of Mahāvīra could be 21 years, and because Mahāvīra died at 72 and Buddha at 80, the maximum possible interval between their *Nirvāṇa* could be 29 years.

Again, as stated above, Mahāvīra attained omniscience 14 years before Gośālaka's death. Consequently, on the basis of fact No. 2, Buddha could not have attained the enlightenment prior to this. At the most, he could have attained it in the same year. If we suppose so, Buddha would be 35 and Mahāvīra 42 at that time. Therefore, the minimum possible seniority of Mahāvīra could be 7 years and the minimum possible interval between their *Nirvāṇa* could be 15 years.

Thus, Mahāvīra's seniority to Buddha lies between 21 and 7 years, and the interval between their *Nirvāṇas* lies between 29 and 15 years.

We get another way to reach a more definite period within the possible range stated above. The *Aṭṭhakathā* of *Aṅguttara Nikāya* supplies us a complete chronological list of the places where Buddha passed his rainy seasons after his enlightenment.[227] According to the above work, in Rājagṛha, Buddha spent his 2nd, 3rd, 4th, 17th and 20th rainy seasons after the enlightenment.[228] Now, according to the *Sāmmānnyaphala Sutta* of *Dīgha Nikāya,* the event of Ajātaśatru's only call upon Buddha, during which the king Ajātaśatru asked Buddha a question about the fruitfulness of monkhood and repented for murdering his father, took place during one of the rainy seasons passed by Buddha at Rājagṛha.[229] Again, this event should have happened in the first year of Ajātaśatru's reign, in as much as soon after his accession, he had transferred his capital to Campā, on account of the great sorrow he felt over his father's death. Now, if we supposed that the above event recorded by the *Sāmmānnyaphala Sutta* had taked place in the 17th or 20th rainy-season after Buddha's enlightenment, the fact No. 2 (stated above) is violated. For, as shown before,[230] Ajātaśatru's accession took place in the 13th years after Mahāvīra's attainment of omniscience. So, the possibility of the above event taking place in 17th or 20th rainy-season is ruled out. Consequently the event should have taken place either in the 2nd or 3rd or the 4th rainy season after Buddha's enlightenemnt.

Thus, it was the 13th year after Mahāvīra's omniscience and the 2nd, the 3rd, or the 4th years after Buddha's enlightenment. This means that Mahāvīra was, at that time 55 years old, and Buddha either 36, 37 or 38. In other words Mahāvīra was 19, 18 or 17 years older than Buddha, and attained the *Nirvāṇa* 27, 26, 25 years earlier than Buddha.

Further to reach to a definite conclusion out of these three alternatives, we fortunately get a small way out—If we suppose that the event of *Sāmmānnya-phala Sūtra,* had taken place in the 2nd or 3rd rainy season after Buddha's enlightenment, it would mean that Ajātaśatru's accession and Bimbisāra's death took place only one or two years after Buddha's enlightenment, that is to say, the contemporaneity of Bimbisāra with enlightened Buddha was of one or two years. But a closer study of the Buddhist *Tripiṭakas* reveal that it should be slightly wider than this. Therefore, it will be consistent to take the 4th rainy-season after enlightenment to be the year of Ajātaśatru's accession. This will allow a period of three years which is fairly long, for the contemporaneity of Bimbisāra with enlightened Buddha. Thus, by taking the last alternative, we reach the final conclusion that :

1. Mahāvīra was 17 years older than Buddha.
2. Mahāvīra attained the *Nirvāṇa* 25 years earlier than Buddha.
3. The total contemporaneity of their life was 55 years, the contemporaneity of their life as religious leaders was 20 years.

It should be borne in mind that the above conclusion is based only upon the life-events of Mahāvīra and Buddha. Even if we suppose them to have lived in any period of history, this conclusion will hold good. In order to accomplish our discussion, it is essential to think over it from the chronological point of view.[231]

It has already been made clear that the chronology of Buddha is in itself quite uncertain. Also, it has been shown that the chronology of Mahāvīra in itself is almost unanimous and certain. Hence, on the basis of the unequivocal date of Mahāvīra, the above conclusion can be put in chronological terms. The date of Mahāvīra's *Nirvāṇa* is 527 B.C. Therefore, that of Buddha's *Nirvāṇa* should be 502 B.C. Now as we have found out the date of *Nirvāṇa*, we can easily compute the dates of the important events of his life as follows :

Date	*Event of Buddha's Life*
582 B.C.	Birth
554 B.C.	Renunciation
547 B.C.	Enlightenment
502 B.C.	*Nirvāṇa*

The comparative chronological table of the important events of their life is as follows :

	Mahāvīra	*Buddha*
Birth	599 B.C.	582 B.C.
Renunciation	569 B.C.	554 B.C.
Enlightenment (Omniscence)	557 B.C.	547 B.C.
Nirvāṇa	527 B.C.	502 B.C.

Thus Mahāvīra and Buddha lived contemporarily from 582 B.C. to 527 B.C., *i.e.* for 55 years. As religious leaders, their contemporaniety lasted from 547 B.C. to 527 B.C. for 20 years.

It should also be noted here that Buddha had attained *Nirvāṇa* in 42nd year of Ajātaśatru's reign; and that Candragupta Maurya and Asoka acceded to the throne of Magadha 180 and 229 years after Buddha's *Nirvāṇa* respectively.

CORROBORATION OF THE CONCLUSION

We have reached the above conclusion regarding the date of Buddha's *Nirvāṇa* solely on the basis of historical and mathematical methods. Hence, it can be regarded as a 'self evident' fact. But, because it is being disclosed to the field of history of the first time, it will not be unnecessary to corroborate it by some other evidences which directly corroborate the above conclusion. They are as follows :

1. Tibetan Tradition

According to the Buddhist tradition of Tibet, the day on which Buddha was born, was also the birthday of the king Canda Pradyota (also known as Mahāsena) of Avanti.[232] The same tradition also records that Buddha's enlightenment and Pradyota's accession took place on the same day.[233]

The king Pradyota is mentioned in all the three traditions—Buddhist, Jain and Purānic. According to the *Purāṇas* such as *Vāyu Purāṇa,*[234] *Matsya Purāṇa,*[235] *Bhagvat Purāṇa,*[236] etc. and the famous literary works like *Kathāsaritsāgara,*[237] *Svapanavāsvadattā,*[238] *Mṛcchakaṭika*[239] etc., and the Jain works like *Āvaśyaka-Niryukti-Dīpikā,*[240] Pradyota was succeeded by his son Palaka. Now, as we have already seen the king Palaka acceded to the throne of Avanti in the same night on which Mahāvīra passed away.[241] Thus, it becomes clear that the king Pradyota was born on the day of Buddha's birth, he acceded to throne on the day of Budha's enlightenment, and lastely, his reign ended on the day of Mahāvīra's *Nirvāṇa*. The Purāṇic chronology unequivocally ascribe 23 years to Pradyota's rule.

"*Trayovimśat samarāja bhāvita sa narottamaḥ*"[242] that is "Best among men (Pradyota) will rule for 23 times (years)".

Thus, when Buddha attained the enlightenment at the age of 35, Pradyota became the king, and when Mahāvīra attained the *Nirvāṇa* at the age of 72, Pradyota's rule ended.[243] Therefore, at the time of Pradyota's accession, Mahāvīra must be 72–23 = 49 years old, and Buddha was 35 years old. Hence, we conclude that Mahāvīra was 14 years older than Buddha. This conclusion nearly endorses our conclusion that Mahāvīra was 17 years older than Buddha.

2. The Traditional Date of Chinese Turkestan

Our conclusion is also quite consistent with the traditional date of Buddha's *Nirvāṇa*, prevalent in Chinese Turkestan,[244] and also known as "Khotan Tradition".

This tradition places the King Asoka 250 years after the *Nirvāṇa* of Buddha by taking him as a contemporary of the Chinese emperor Shih-Huang-Ti. Some scholars, on the basis of the fact that Shih-Huang-Ti's accession took place in 246 B.C., have accepted (246+250 = 496 B.C.) as the date of Buddha's *Nirvāṇa*.[245] It may be noted that there is only a nominal difference of 6 years between this date and our conclusion. But, it seems that the interval of 250 years between Buddha's *Nirvāṇa* and Asoka should, in reality, be the one between Buddha's *Nirvāṇa* and the famous third Buddhist council, that had taken place in the 18th year after Asoka's consecration, and according to historians, in 252 B.C.[246] Hence, the date of Buddha's *Nirvāṇa*, on the basis of the above tradition should be 252 + 250 = 502 B.C. which exactly coincides with our conclusion.

3. Asoka's Edicts

The stone (rocks) and pillars inscribed by Asoka the great Mauryan emperor, are, in fact the foundation-stones and foundation pillars of Indian history. Many a doubtful facts regarding history were made undoubtful on the basis of the above inscriptions. The present conclusion regarding the date of Buddha's *Nirvāṇa* is too corroborated by these edicts. The edicts are mainly divided in the following types :

5	Minor Rock Edicts
14	Rock Edicts
4	Minor Pillar Edicts
7	Pillar Edicts

3 Cave Edicts
6 Miscellaneous Edicts

The following is the text of the Minor Rock Edicts No. 1, which is found at Rūpanātha, Sahasarāma and Vairāṭa.[247]

"Devanaṁ piye evaṁ aha (:-) Satilekani adhatiyani vayo sumipaka savake no cu vadhi pakate; satilake cu chavachare ya sumi hakaṁ saṁghe upete.

"Badhi cu pakate. Yi! imaya kalaya jambudipaṁsi amisa deva husu te dani misa Kata. Pakamayi hi eṣa phale. Noca eṣa mahātata pāpotave. Khudakena hi ka!

"Pi parumaminena sakiye pipule pi svage aroghave! Etiya athaya ca savane kate Khudaka cha udhala ca pakamantu ti ata pi ca janamtu iyaṁ pakakha.

"Kiti(?) cirathati ke siya. Iya hi athe vadhi vadhisiti vipula ca vadhisiti. Apalaghiyena diyadhiya vadhisata (.) iya ca athe pavatisu lekhapeta valatahadha ca (.) athi.

"Silathame silathambhasi lakhapatavayata Etina ca vayajanena yavataka tupaka ahale savara vivasetavayuti. Vyuthena savane kate 256 Satavivasata!"

The following is the translation :

Thus saith His sacred Majesty : For more than two and a half years I became a disciple, without, however exerting myself strenously. But it is more than a year since I joined the Order, and have exerted myself strenously.

In the mean time the Gods that were regarded as true have been proved false.

"For this is the fruit of exertion. Nor is this to be attained by a great man only, because even by the small man who chooses to exert himself immense heavenly bliss may be won."

"For this purpose has the precept been composed : 'Let small and great exert themsleves."

"My neighbours too should learn this lesson : and may such exertion long endure."

"And this purpose will grow, yea it will grow immensely at least one-and-a-half-fold will it increase in-growth."

"And this purpose must be written on the rocks, both and here afar of; and wherever there is a stone-pillar, it must be written on stone-pillar". And according to this text, so far as your jurisdiction extends, you must send it out everywhere".

"By (me) was the precept composed, when 256 years had passed since the *Nirvāṇa* of Buddha."

In the Minor Rock Edict No. 2, which is found at Brahmagiri Sidhapur, and Jatiṅga-Rāmeśvara, we find the same thing repeated with a slight difference. Emperor Asoka writes there[248]:

"Suvannagiri te aya Aputasa mahāmatanaṁ ca vacanena isilasi Mahāmata arogiyaṁ vātavīya. Hevaṁ ca vātavīya". Devānāṁ piye anapayati!

"Adhikanai adhati yāni vaya sumi....diyadhiya vadhisiti! Iyaṁ ca savane savapate vyudhena 256."

The translation is "By command of the Prince and high officials at Suvaraṇagiri, the high official at Isila are to be addressed with greetings, and further addressed as follows :

His sacred majesty gives commands : 'For more than two and half....grow one had a half fold. And this discipline was preached by? (me) in 256th (year) after Buddha's *Nirvāṇa*'.

There are mainly two things in the above edicts to be noted : The first in concerning Asoka's joining order, which is experessed by the words "*Saṁghe upete";* the second one—the date inscribed in the end of the edicts *viz.* 256 years after Buddha's *Nirvāṇa*, expressed by the words "*Vyuthena savane kate 256 Satavivasata.*"

The words "*Saṅghe upete"* used in the above Edicts have become a matter of controversy amongst the scholars and different scholars have tried to interpret them in different ways. Dr. Radha Kumud Mukherjee, discussing about this controversy, writes[249] : "It is difficult to understand what Asoka exactly intends by the expression on *Saṅghe upete*, which has been translated above to mean that he lived with, entered or visited the *saṅgha,* and the opinion of the scholars is sharply divided on this point. Some scholars hold that Asoka actually became a Buddhist monk *(Bhikkhu).* Others, however, take the expression simply to mean that Asoka made a state-visit to the Saṅgha and publicly proclaimed his faith as the Siṁhalese chronicle informs us. The former view is, however, supported by the statement of I-tsing that he actually saw a statue of Asoka dressed as a monk. A third possibility is that Asoka lived with the *saṅgha* for more than a year, without taking orders.

"Among those who assume that Asoka became a monk, there is again difference of opinion. Some hold that during the period Asoka was a monk, he must have ceased to be a monarch, for monastic life is hardly compatible with royal duties. Others, however, point out actual examples of kings who were monks at the same time and find no reason for the assumption that Asoka, even temporarily abdicated the throne.

"Whatever may be the right interpretation of this association with the *Saṅgha,* there is no doubt that since this event, Asoka exerted himself with unflagging zeal for the propagation of Buddhism, or at least that part of it which he accepted as his *Dharma*. He not only set up a net-wrok of missions to preach the doctrine both in and outside India, but himself undertook tours for this purpose and took various other steps to the same end."

Dr. Mukherjee has not emphasised a particular view regarding the interpretation of the expression, *Saṅghe upete*. Nevertheless, it is easily understood even by, glancing at the different interpretations, that the event of Asoka's *"Saṅghe Upete"* is related with his historical religious tour or pilgrimage, which is explicitly mentioned even in Asoka's own edicts. In the Rummindei Pillar Edict, Asoka writes[250] : *"Devan piyena piyadasin lajina visati-vasabhisitena atana agaca mahiyite! Hiya buddhe jate śākya muniti silavigada bhica kalapita silathama ca upa papi te hida bhagavaṁ jate ti luminigame uvalike kate athabhagiye ca*[251]."

In means, "His Sacred and Gracious Majesty the King, when he had been consecrated twenty years, having come in person, did reverence; and because "Here Buddha was born, the Śākya sage", a great(?) railing of stone was prepared and a stone pillar erected.

Because "Here the Venerable one was born" the village of Lumbinī was made free of religious cesses and decalred entitled to the eighth share (of the produce claimed by the crown).

In addition to this, the way in which the famous Buddhist work *Asokavādāna* describes the pilgrimage of Asoka, suggests that the expression *"Saṅghe-Upete"* is a quite competent with the pilgrimage of Asoka. 'The pilgrimage of Asoka' is described thus[252] :

"The King said 'I desire to visit all the places where the venerable Buddha stayed, to do honour unto them, and to mark each with an enduring memorial for the instruction of the most remote posterity'. The Saint (Upagupta) approved of the project, and undertook to act as a guide. Escorted by a mighty army, the monarch visited the holy places in Order.

"The first place visited was the Lumbinī garden. Here Upagupta said : 'In this spot, great king, the Venerable one was born; and added : 'Here is the first monument consecrated in honour of the Buddha, the sight of whom is excellent. Here, the moment after his birth, the reculse took seven steps upon the ground'.

"The king bestowed hundred thousand gold pieces on the people of the place, and built a *Stūpa*. He, then passed on to Kapilavastu.

"The royal pilgrim next visited the Bodhi-tree at Bodhi Gaya, and there also gave a largesse of hundred thousand gold-pieces, and built a Caitya. *Ṛṣipatana* (Sāranātha) near Banaras, where Gautama had turned 'the wheel of law' and Kuśīnagara where the teacher had passed away, were also visited with similar observances. At Saravastī the pilgrims did reverence to the Jetavana monastery, where Gautama had so long dwelt and taught, and to the *Stūpas* of his disciples, Sāriputra, Maudgalāyana, and Mahākassapa. But when the king visited the *Stūpa* of Vakkula, he gave only one copper coin, in as much as Vakkula had met with few obstacles in the path of holiness and had done little good to his fellow creatures. At the *Stūpa of* Ānanda, the faithful attendant of Gautama, the royal gift amounted to six million gold pieces."

Many a scholars are of the view that Asoka had also become a Buddhist monk in his life-time may it be only for a short time. It seems most probable that the pilgrimage was undertaken by Asoka in the form of a Buddhist monk. But it does not mean that he ceased to be the king at that time.

Thus, the purport of the expression "*Saṅghe-Upete*" also become meaningful. Asoka has stated in the above edicts that he became a lay-disciple two are half years before his stage of "Joining the Order" (*Saṅghe-Upete).* Now, if Asoka "Joined the Order" 20 years after his consecration, as stated by him in the Rummindei Pillar Edict, he must have become a lay disciple seventeen and half years after his consecration. This is exactly the time of the 'Third Buddhist Council.[253] Though generally, it is helt that Asoka became a follower of Buddhism 9 years after his consecration, it seems that he considered himself initiated into "formal *Upāsaka-dharma* (rules of the lay-disciple)" from the time of the Third Buddhist Council. Thus, we can say that Asoka became a lay disciple seventeenth and half years after his consecration; he "joined the order" 20 years after his consecration; and he wrote the above inscriptions (Minor Rock Edict Nos. I and II), slightly more than 21 years after his consecration.

"This second thing, to be paid attention to, in the aforequoted edicts, is the last time of the inscription *viz.* "*Vyuthena savane kate 256 satavivasata.*" This line has also been interpreted differently by different scholars.

Etymologically, *vyuthena* is the Apabhraṁśa of the Sanskrit word *vyustena* and *vivasa* that of *vivasat. Vyusta* is formed by adding the termination *kta* to the root *vi + vas* (forming the part participle), and *Vivasa* is formed by adding the termination *ghan* tothe root *vi+vas*. According to the distinguished scholars like Dr. Bühler, Dr. Fleet etc. *Vyuthena* means 'one who has passed away' *i.e.* Buddha, and *vivasat* means 'the *Nirvāṇa* (of Buddha)'.[254] Dr. Fleet also observes[255] : "It is quite probable that king Asoka would have become a monk by abdicating the throne 255 years and 7 or 8 months after the *Nirvāṇa* of Buddha and since then he would have "joined the Order". When 8 months and 16 days were thus completed, on the 256th night, Asoka would have written these inscriptions (Minor Rock Edict Nos. I and II). But a question arises that why Asoka specially mentioned 256th night in these inscriptions. The answer is 256th year from Buddha's *Nirvāṇa* had just completed on the 256th day or night of Asoka's tour, and to mark the 256th anniversary of Buddha's *Nirvāṇa,* Asoka wrote these inscriptions. Thus, it is proved that the number 256 mentioned in these inscriptions is indicative of the fact that Buddha's *Nirvāṇa* took place 256 years before Asoka."

The above view of Dr. Fleet and Dr. Bühler is based on a critical study of the inscriptions of Asoka. But the modern historians, however, accept it only partly. According to them,[256] it can only be said that the distinguished was written on the 256th departure from staging-place or on the '256th day of the tour', but to say that it was written to observe 256th anniversary of Buddha's *Nirvāṇa*, does not seem to be correct.

The only reason behind this view of the modern historians seems to be that the period which is 256 years precedent to Buddha's *Nirvāṇa*, does not synchronize with the whole period of Asoka (273-236 B.C.) on the basis of any prevalent date of Buddha's *Nirvāṇa*.[257]

Hence, they say,[258] "The number 256 in the earliest edict has no bearing upon chronology". But their argument is neither justifiable nor correct. Dr. Max Müllar, the profound Oriental Scholar, has criticized this trend of the historians, and supported the view of Dr. Bühler. He writes,[259] "I fully admit the difficulties in the phraseology of these inscription but I ask, "Who could have written these inscriptions, if not Asoka? and, how if written by Asoka, can the date which they contain mean anything but 256 years after Buddha's *Nirvāṇa*? These points, however, have been argued in so masterly a manner by Dr. Bühler in his 'Second Notice' that I should be afraid of weakening his case by adding anything of my own, and must refer my readers to his 'Second Notice'.

Now, the remarkable and important thing regarding this matter is that the "number 256 years" of the above inscriptions becomes quite consistence, with the date 502 B.C., which we have proved in this book to be the date of Buddha's *Nirvāṇa*. It has already been made clear that the above inscriptions were written by Asoka a little more than a year since he "joined the Order", and he "joined the Order" 20 years after his consecration. Here, we reach a definite point regarding the chronology which is unanimous and certain. It is the date of Asoka's consecration 269 B.C. Thus,

Asoka's consecration	269 B.C.
Asoka "Joined the Order "in	248 B.C.[260]
The date of the minor Rock Edicts I & II	247 B.C.

Hence, by going 255 years back from
247 B.C. we, reach the date of Buddha's *Nirvāṇa*.
247+255 = 502 B.C.

4. Burmese Tradition

The most sound evidence among the traditional evidences is that of Burmese tradition. There prevails an era called "Eetzana era" in Burma.[261] Eetzana is the Burmese term for Anjana, who was the Śākya king of Devadaha which is the Burmese for Devadaha Country and who was also the maternal grandfather of Buddha.[262] The chief events of Buddha's life have been chronicled in the Eetzana era and the tithis, (the lunar days), the week-days as well as the constellations with which the moon was in combination on these days, have also been recorded with reference to the different years of that era, which would seem to have been current at that ancient time :

1. Birth of Buddha[263] on Friday the full-moon day of the month Katson which is Burmese for the Indian lunar month *Viśākhā,* combined with the constellation *Viśākhā*, which is Burmese for the 16th lunar mansion *Viśākhā* in the 68th year of the Eetzana era.
2. Renunciation[264] (Departure from the household life and initiation into ascetic life); On monday full-moon day in the month of July, *i.e. Āṣāḍha* (the Indian lunar month), combined with the constellation Ootharāthana, which is Burmese for the 21st lunar mansion *Uttarāṣāḍhā* in the 96th year of the Eetzana era.
3. Enlightenment of Buddha.[265] On Wednesday the full-moon day of Katson = *Vaiśākha,* combined with the constellation Withaka = *Viśākhā* in the 103rd year of the Eetzana era.
4. *Parinirvāṇa* of Buddha[266] : On Tuesday the full-moon day of Katson = *Vaiśākha* combined with the constellation Withaka = *Viśākhā,* in the 148th years of Eetzana era.

According to the Burmese tradition, the Eetzana era began on Sunday which was the 1st lunar day of the waxing moon of the month Tagoo, *i.e.* Burmese for the Indian month *Caitra.*[267]

A research scholar Mr. M. Govind Pai has found out the corresponding English dates of the above Burmese dates. According to his conversations the chronology date is as follows :

1. Birth of Buddha 30th March, 581 B.C.
2. Renunciation of Buddha; 18th June, 553 B.C.
3. Enlightenment of Buddha; 3rd April, 546 B.C.
4. *Parinirvāṇa* of Buddha; 15th April, 501 B.C.
5. Beginning of Eetzana era; 17th February, 648 B.C.

Thus, it can be seen that the Burmese tradition is in perfect congruence with the chronological date of Buddha's life-events, which we have deduced in the last chapter.

It is really a surprising coincidence that the Burmese tradition and our approach arrive exactly at the same fact, for the author of this book was not at all aware of the Burmese tradition till he reached the conclusion.

The author came to know about the Burmese tradition only after the whole book had already been published in the form of articles in the journals like *Jaina Bhārati*, *Anekānta,* etc.

Well, the four evidences cited above have corroborated our conclusion in the same way as the fourway farers from different directions would confirm the reality of the pole by arriving at the same polar point.

REFERENCES

1. Scholars like Prof. Lassen regarded Buddha and Mahāvīra as identical, because the Jaina and Buddhist traditions are almost on some points (*cf.* the Jaina Sūtras, *Sacred Books of the East*, Vol. XXII, introduction, p. XIX).
2. According to the Jains, the chief disciple of their *Tīrthaṅkara* Mahāvīra was called Gautama Svāmī (*Ward's Hindus* II, p. 247, and *Colebrooke's Essays,* Vol. II, p. 279) or Gautama Indrabhūti, whose identity with Gautama Buddha was suggested both by Dr. Hamilton and Major Delamaine and was accepted by Colebrooke.

   "This is what Colebrooke says in his *Essays*, Vol. II, p. 276. In the *Kalpa Sūtra* and in other books of the Jains, the first of Mahāvīra's disciples is mentioned under the name of Indrabhūti, but in the inscriptions under that of Gautama Svāmī. The names of the other ten precisely agree, whence it is to be concluded that Gautama, the first one of the first list, is the same with Indrabhūti, the first of the second list. It is certainly probable, as remarked by Dr. Hamilton and Major Delamaine, that the Gautama of the Jains and the Gautama of the Buddhists is the same personage. Two out of eleven disciples of Mahāvīra survived him, *viz.* Sudharma and Gautama Svāmī. Sudharma's spiritual successors are the Jain priests, whereas the Gautama's followers are the Buddhists".

   —Manmath Nath Shastri, M.A.M.R.A.S., *Buddha : His life, His Teachings, His Order*, 1940 (Second Edition), pp. 21-22.
3. *Dīgha Nikāya, Mahāparinivāṇa Sutta*, 2-3-16.
4. *Kalpa Sūtra*, 147.
5. Although Dr. Jarl Charpentier first dealt with the subject specially with a view to decide the chronology of Buddha and Mahāvīra, but Dr. Jacobi is responsible for the primary research in this field.
6. There are 50 volumes in his series, out of these the Vol. XXII contains the translations of the *Ācārаṅga Sūtra* and the *Kalpa Sūtra*, and the Vol. XLV contains the translations of the *Sūtrakṛtāṅga Sūtra* and the *Utarādhyayana Sūtra*.
7. *Sacred Books of the East*, Vol. XLV. Introduction to the *Jain Sūtras*, Part II, p. XXI, 1894.
8. *Sacred Books of the East,* Vol. XXII, Introduction to the *Jain Sūtra*, Part I, pp. IX to XIX, 1884.
9. During his second visit to India (March 1914) he met Ācārya Śrī Kālugaṇi, the 8th Ācārya of Terāpantha Sect and held important discussions with him for three days.
10. *S.B.E.* Vol. XXII, Introduction, pp. XVII, XVIII.
11. *S.B.E.* Vol. XXII, Introduction, p. XXXVII.
12. *A.V.* means "after the death of Vīra" (*i.e.* Mahāvīra).
13. *S.B.E.* Vol. XIV, Introduction, p. XI.
14. *S.B.E.* Vol. XLV. Introduction, p. XXXVII, quoted from *S.B.E.* Vol. X, p. XXXII; *S.B.E.* Vol. XXII, p. XLII.

15. See *Cullvagga* II, 12-1-1; Buddha Carya by Rahul Sankrityayana, p. 556; *Political History of Ancient India*, by H.C. Raychoudhuri (Sixth Edition) 1953, p. 228.
16. *Bhāritiya Vidyā*, Vol. III, No. I, July, 1944.
17. *Śramaṇa* Vol. XIII, No. VI-VII, 1962.
18. *Ibid.*, Vol. XIII, No. VII, p. 10.
19. *Ibid.*, Vol. XIII, No. VII, preface to the essay of Dr. Jacobi, p. 9.
20. Op. cit., pp. 9-10.
21. *Śramaṇa*, Vol. XIII, No. VII, p. 35.
22. *Dīgha Nikāya Sāmānnya-phala Sutta*, 1-2.
23. *Buddhist India*, pp. 15-16.
24. *Hindu Sabhyatā*, p. 191.
25. Tassanam Koniyassa ekke purise viulakae vihie bhagvau pavittivaue, bhagvau taddevasiyaṁ pavitti nivei! Tassanaṁ purisassa behave anegapurisa dinabhatti bhattaveyana bhagvato pavittivauya bhagvato taddevasiyaṁ pavittiṁ nivedamti!
Aupapatika Sūtra, *Samavasraṇa Adhikāra*, 10.
26. Tenaṁ kalenaṁ tenaṁ samaenam konie raya bhambhasaraputte bahariya uvatthanasalae anega gaṇanāyaka damdanayaga....... Saddhiṁ samparivude viharai! Tenaṁ kalenaṁ tenaṁ samayenaṁ Samane bhayavaṁ Mahāvire....... Suhamsuhe Viharamane campaenayarie bāhiya uvanagaragamaṁ uvagae! Campanagari punnabhadda ceiyaṁ samosariokame! Tattenaṁ se pavittivaue imlse kahae laddhatthe samane......campanayarie majjhamm-ajjhenaṁ.......jeneva koniyassarannegihe....... jeneva koniyaraya bhambhasaraputte teneva uvagcchai, uvagacchitta....... evaṁ vayasi....... jassanaṁ devanuppiya damsanaṁ kamkhanti, jassanaṁ devanuppiya damsanaṁ patthanti jassanaṁ deva damsanaṁ abhilāśanti jassanaṁ deva nabhagottassavi savanattae hatthatuttha java hiyaya bhavanti senaṁ samāne bhagavaṁ Mahāvīre....... campaenayarie uvanagaramgamaṁ uvagae, campanagari punnabhaddaceie samasariakame! Taenaṁ devanu ppipyanāṁ piyatathayae piyani vedemi piyambhe bhavao! Tattenaṁ se Konie raya bhambhasaraputte tassa pavitti vauyassa antie eyayatthaṁ soccani-sammahatthatutthe java hiyaye....... simhasanao abbutthei....... egasadiya uttarasaṅgaṁ karei....... añjali maulīya hatthe titthayarabhimuhe sattattha payai anugacitti...... tikattu evaṁ vayasi .... namotthunaṁ arihamtanaṁ....... sampattanaṁ....... *Ibid.*, 11-18.
27. The uttarasaṅga position is the one, in which a Jain layman bows down; he has to mask his mouth with a scarf, which should be a single piece of cloth without any joints, in order not to kill the lives of air.
28. Namotthunaṁ, which is also known as Sakkathui, (Śakrastuti), is a hymn to pay homage to the *Tīrthaṅkaras*. This also indicates that Konika was a Jain 'Śrāvaka'.
29. Namotthunaṁ samanassa bhagavao Mahāvīrassa adikārassa, tithakarassa Java sampaviokamassa mamadhimmaigarassa dhammovadesagassa vamdaminaṁ bhagavaṁ tatthagayaṁ ihagate pasaume bhagvaṁ tathāgae ihagayaṁ tikattu, vamdamti namaṁ samti'.
—*Aupapatika Sūtra*, *Sāmavasaraṇa Adhikāra*, 18.
30. *Ibid.*, 102-37.
31. *Pariśiṣṭa Parva* of Hemacandrācārya, cantons IV v.v. 15-54.
32. *Buddhist India*, p. 88.
33. *Ibid.*, pp. 15-16.
34. *Saṁyukta Nikāya*, 1-81 (*The Book of Kindred Sayings*, Tr. by Mrs. Rhys Davids, Vol. I, p.109.
35. *Ibid.*, Vol. I, p. 109.
36. *Vinaya Piṭaka*, *Culla Vagga*, VII 3-6 (*The Book of Discipline*, Tr. by I.B. Horner, Vol. V, p. 268).
Cf. also "Śrīchand Rāmpuriā" in Chapter V of this book.
37. *Āvaśyaka Cūrṇī*, Part I, leaf 245.
38. *Ibid.*, uttarārdha, leaf 164; Triśaṣṭiśalākāpuruṣa Caritra of Hemacandrācārya, parva, X, cantos VI, v. 188; Upadeśamālā, (with commentary) leaf 238; *Uttarapurāṇa*, p. 483.
39. *Dīgha Nikāya*, *Mahā-Parinivvāna Sutta*.

40. *S.B.E.*, (Vol. XXII, Introduction, p. XIII.)
41. See, for these allusions, *'The Event of Mahāvīra's Nirvāṇa in Buddhist Tripiṭakas'* in chapter VII of this Book.
42. *Śramaṇa*, Vol. XIII, No. VI, pp. 14-15.
43. *Ibid.*, p. 15.
44. *Ibid.*, p. 16.
45. *Kalpa Sūtra*, 128; *cf. S.B.E.* Vol. XIII.
46. *Darśana Digdarśana*, p. 444n.
47. Bhagvāna Mahāvīra ki Nirvāṇa Bhūmi Pāvā ki Sthiti, an aritical in *Mahāvīra Commemoration Volume*, Vol. I 1948-48, pp. 45-9, and *Bhārīiya Itihāsa ki Bhūmikā* (Prācīna Bhārata), Part I, p. 83.
48. *Jain Sāhitya Aura Itihāsa*, p. 189.
49. *Uttara Pradeśa Meṁ Buddha Dharma kā Vikāsa*, p. 10.
50. *Śramaṇa*, Vol. XIII, No. VI, p. 26.
51. *Jaina Bhāratī*, Vol. Jan, 1951, p. 17.
52. *Vaiśālī*, pp. 85-87.
53. Pt. Rahul Sankrityayana identifies it with the present Papahura, a village near Ramkold Rly. Station in Gorakhpur Distt. (Loc. City); Cunningham identifies it with Paḍarauna in Devaria Distt. while Dr. Rajbali Pandey (*cf. op. cit.*, pp. 47-8) and Ācārya Vijayendra Suri (*cf., op. cit.*, pp. 85-7) refute both these views on the basis of the geographical reasons and identify Pāvā, the place of *Nirvāṇa* with the ruins of Sathiyamva Fazilanagara, 9 miles south-east of Kuśīnagara in Meveria District. They have corroborated their views by quoting an archaeologist named Karlayle, who, on the basis of his archaeological survey, had identified Pāvā with the above place.
54. *Mahāvaṁsa,* Pariccheda, IV-V.
55. *Op. cit.* p. 10.
56. See, "*Date of Mahāvīra's Nirvāṇa*" in Chapter VII of this book.
57. Evaṁ ca śrī Mahāvīramuktervarsasate gate!
    Pañc pañcasadadhike Candragupto bhavennṛpaḥ!!
    –*Pariśiṣṭa Parva*, VIII, V. 339.
58. *Titthogali Paiññaya*, 620-21.
59. *Epitome of Jainism*, Appendix A, IV.
60. Published by Asiatic Society, Calcutta.
61. Asmin nirvanato varasasatya(ta) nyamayasodasa!
    Navaśaṣṭiśca yasyanti yadā tatra pure tadā!!
    Kumārapalabhūpālo, caulukyakula—candramāḥ!
    Bhaviṣyati mahābāhuḥ pracaṇḍakhaṇḍasasanaḥ!!
    –*Triśaṣṭiśalākāpuruṣacaritra*, parva X, cantos XII, vv. 45-46.
62. *An Advanced History of India* by R.C. Majumdar, H.C. Raychaudhuri, and K.K. Datta, p. 202.
63. *Śramaṇa,* vol. XIII, No. VI., p. 10.
64. Ajātasattuputto taṁ, ghātetvadayabhaddako!
    Rajjaṁ solasavassani, karesi mittādubbhiko!! 1!!
    Udayabhaddaputto taṁ, ghātetva anuruddako!
    Anuruddhassa putto taṁ ghāteva muṇḍanamako!! 2!!
    Mittadduno dummatino, te pi rājjaṁ akarayuṁ!
    Teśāṁ ubhinnaṁ rājjeṣu aṭṭhavassanatikkamuṁ!! 3!!
    Muṇḍassa putto pitaraṁ ghātetava nagadasako!
    Catuviśati vassani rājjaṁ karesi papakko!! 4!!
    Pitughaṭakavamsoyaṁ iti Kuddhatha nagara!
    Nagadasakarajanaṁ apnetva samāgata!! 5!!
    Susunagoti pannataṁ amaccaṁ sādhu sammataṁ!
    Rājje sambahisiphicisuṁ savvesiṁ hitamanasa!! 6!!
    So aṭṭharasa vassani rājā rājjaṁ akāryi!
    Kalasoko tassa putto aṭṭhavissati kāryi!! 7!!

Atite dasame vasse, kalasokassa rājino!
Sambuddha parinivvāna, evem vassasatam āhu!! 8!!

–*Mahāvamsa*, Pariccheda, IV, 1-8.

Kalasokass putta tu, ahesum dasa bhatuka!
Dvāviśati te vassani, rājjam samanusasisum!! 14!!
Nava namdatatoasum kameneva narādhipa!
Tepi dvāviśa vassani, rājjam samanusasisum!! 15!!
Moriyanam khatiyanam vanase jatam siridharam!
Candaguṭṭoti panatam, caṇakko brahmaṇe tatto!! 16!!
Navamam dhananamdam tam, ghatetva caṇḍakodhava!
Śakale jambudāpamsmim, rājje samabhi sisciso!! 17!!

–*Mahāvamsa*, Pariccheda, V, vv. 14-17.

65. *Cf. Political History of Ancient India*, by Dr. H.C. Raychaudhuri, p. 225; *Bhārata Kā Itihāsa*, by Prof. Śrīnetra Pandey, Part I, (4th edition), p. 243.
66. *Op. cit.*, p. 10.
67. It may be noted that the chronology discribed in *Mahāvamsa* the Ceylonese chronicle has been found, in general, to be erroneous on historical tests; see, for the detailed discussion of this, '*Inconsistencies in Ceylonese Chronology*' in Chapter I of this book.
68. Tassavina vajjassa pacchanattha aimaim aṭṭha carmaim pannavei, tamjaha-carime pane, charime geye, carime natte, carime añjalikamme, carime pokkhalassa sam-vattage mahamehe, carime seyanae gandhahaṭṭhi, carime Mahāśīla Kamtae Saṅgame.

–*Bhagavati Sūtra*, Śataka, XV.

69. For, taking 484 B.C., as the date of Buddha's *Nirvāṇa*, Konika's accession, which according to Dr. Jacobi took place 7 or 8 years before the *Nirvāṇa* of Buddha, falls in 491-92 B.C., and the date of Mahāvīra's *Nirvāṇa* is 477 B.C. Hence, the maximum possible interval is 15 years.
70. Punarvijñpayamasa Ninendram magdhadhīpaḥ!
Bhagavān kevalajñānam kasmin uvycchedameśyati!!
Nathapyākarhayat pāsya vidyunmāli surohyasau!
Samaniko brahmendrasya caturdevī Samavṛtaḥ!!
Ahnomuṣmat saptamehni cyutva bhavi pure tava!
Śresthī-ṛsabhadattasya Jambu hutrontyakevali!!

–*Pariśiṣṭa Parva*, cantos I, vv. 262-64.

71. Sudharama Svāmīnaḥ paddanapadambhodhitarakan!
Pañcangasprṣta-bhūpithaḥ sa prāṇyjyam parmeśvara!!
Samsārasāgaratarim pravajyam parmeśvara!
Mama sasvajansyapi dehi dhehi kṛpam mayi!!
Pañcamaḥ śrīgaṇadhara pyevamabhyarthitastada!!
Tasknai saparivardya dadau dīkṣam yathāvidhi!!

—*Ibid.*, cantos III, vv. 287-89.

72. The total age of Jambu Svāmī was 80 years, out of which 16 years were spent in the household life, the next 20 years as a monk in non-omniscent stage, and the last 44 years in the omniscent stage. Also, he attained the *Nirvāṇa* 64 years after Mahāvīra's *Nirvāṇa*. It means that he was initiated into monkhood in the same year in which Mahāvīra attained the *Nirvāṇa*.
73. See, *Traditional Dates of Buddha's Nirvāṇa*, in Chapter VII of this book.
74. The essay of Dr. Jacobi was published originally in 1940.
75. *Darśana Aura Cintana*, Part II, pp. 47, 48.
76. The following is the translation of that Chapter of the *Mahāparinivvāna Sutta* :
"Now, when the Blessed one had stayed as long as was convenient at Ambalaṭṭhika, the addressed the venerable Ānanda, and said : Come Ānanda, let us go on to Nālandā".
"So be it Lord!" said Ānanda, in assent, to the Blessed one.
Then the Blessed one proceeded, with a great company of the brethren of Nālandā, and there at Nālandā, the Blessed one stayed in the Pavarika mango grove.

Now the venerable Sāriputta came to the place where the Blessed one was, and having saluted him, took his seat respectfully at his side and said : "Lord! Such faith have I in the Blessed one, that me thinks there never has been, nor will there be, nor is there now any other, whether *Śāmaṇa* or *Brāhmaṇa*, who is greater and wiser than the Blessed one, that is to say, as regards the higher wisdom".

"Grand and bold are the words of the mouth, Sāriputta! Veṛily, thou hast burst forth in a song of ecstasy! Of course then thou hast known all the Blessed ones who in the long ages of the past have been Arahat Buddhas, comprehending their minds with yours, and aware what their mode of life, and what salvation they attained to?"

'Not so, O Lord!'

'But at last then, O Sāriputta! Thou knowest me as the Arhat-Budda now alive, and hast penetrated my mind (in the manner I have mentioned)'.

'Not even that, O Lord!'

'You see then, Sāriputta! that you know the hearts of the Arhat Buddhas of the past and of the future. Why, therefore, are your words so grand and bold? Why do you burst forth into such a song of ecstasy?'

'O Lord! I have not the Knowledge of the heart of the Arhat Buddhas that have been, and are to come, and now are. I only know the lineage of the faith just, Lord! as a king might have a border city, strong in its foundations, strong in its ramparts and *toraṇas*, and with one gate alone; and the king might have a watchman there, clever, expert, and wise, to stop all strangers and admit only friends. And he, on going over the approaches all round the city, might not so observe all the joints and crevices in the ramparts of that city as to know where even a cat could get out. That might well be. Yet all living things of larger size that entered or left the city, would have to do so by that gate. Thus only is it, Lord, that I know the lineage of the faith. I know that the Arahat Buddhas of the past putting away all lust, ill will, sloth, pride, and doubt; knowing all those mental faults which make men weak; training their minds in the four kind of mental activity, throughly exercising themselves in the sevenfold higher wisdom, received the full fruition of Enlightenment. And I know that the Arhat Buddhas of the times to come will (do the same). And I know that the Blessed one the Arhat Buddha of today, has (done so) now".

Tr. by T.W. Rhy Davids, *Buddhist Sutta the Sacred Books of the East Series*, Vol. X, pp. 12-14.

The renowned Buddhist Scholar Rahul Sankrityayana commenting on this Chapter of *Mahā-Parinivvāna-Sutta* writes that the name of Sāriputta has been referred to here on account of the error committed by the Bhāṇakas the persons who used to learn the Scriptures by heart (*Buddhācārya*, p. 525). If we suppose so, can it not be probable that the whole event of Vassakara is also compiled in the *Mahā-Parinivvāna-Sutta* only erroneously?

77. *Āvaśyaka Kathānka*.
78. *Mahā Parinivvāna Sutta*, Tr. By T.W. Rhys Davids; *S.B.E.* Vol. XI, p. 3.
79. *Indian Antiquary*, *'The date of Mahāvīra'* Vol. XLIII, 1914, pp. 118 ff. 125 ff. 167 ff.
80. See, *'Mahāvīra's Nirvāṇa in which Pāvā'*, in the Chapter III of this book.
81. *Journal of Bihar and Orissa Society*, XIII, pp. 240-246.
82. See, *'The Chronology of Mahāvīra'* in Chapter VII of this book.
83. *Journal of Bihar and Orissa Research Society*, XIII, p. 246.
84. Dr. R.C. Majumdar, Dr. H.C. Raychaudhari and Dr. K.K. Datta, *An Advanced History of India*, p. 85.
85. 1. Dr. R.C. Majumdar, Dr. H.C. Raychaudhari and Dr. K.K. Datta, *An Advanced History of India*, p. 85.
    2. Vikramarājjarambha parao siri vīra nivvui maniya!
    Sunna muni veya jutto vikkama-kalau Jina-kala!!
    —*Vicura Śreṇi*, pp. 3, 4.
86. *Hindi Sabhyatā* (Tr. by Dr. V.S. Aggrawal), pp. 210-224.
87. *Ibid.*, pp. 216, 223, 224.

88. *Bhagavāna Mahāvīra Aura Mahātmā Buddha*, pp. 110-115.
89. *Ibid*, pp. 114, 115.
90. See, '*The Seniority of Mahāvīra*' in Chapter VII of this book.
91. *Bhagavāna Buddha*, pp. 33, 115.
92. *Ibid.*, preface, p. XII.
93. Hesting's *Encyclopaedia of Religion and Ethics*, p. 261.
94. *Vīra Nirvāṇa Saṁvat Aura Jaina Kālagaṇanā*, preface, p. 1.
95. The date of Mahāvīra's *Nirvāṇa*, though precisely is November, 528 B.C., is usually written as 527 B.C., the reason being that there is only an interval of two months between January, 528 B.C. and November 528 B.C. Muni Kalyāṇa Vijayajī has also used the date (527 B.C.) frequently in his book.
96. See, *Bhagvatī Sūtra, Śataka*, p. 15.
97. *Vīra-Nirvāṇa Saṁvat Aura Jaina Kālagaṇanā*, p. 15.
98. *Śataka*, p. 15.
99. *Op. cit.*, p. 160.
100. See, *The date of Buddha's Nirvāṇa*, in Chapter VII of this book.
101. *Op. cit.*, p. 160.
102. *Ibid.*, p. 3
103. For example, in the *Saṁyukta Nikāya, Dahar Sutta*, 3-1-1, the name of Nigaṇṭha Nātaputta appears in the third place; in the *Dīgha Nikāya Sāmānyaphala Sutta*, 1-2, it occurs in the fifth place (See the Hindi translation by Rahul Sankrityayana, p. 21).
104. *Op. cit.*, p. 4.
105. Avyaṁ deva nigaṇṭho nātaputto saṅghi ceva gani ca gaṇacariyo ca nato yasassi titthakaro sādhusmmato bahujanassa rattassu cirapavvajito addhagatavayo anupattati.
–*Dīgha Nikāya*, Vol. I, pp. 48, 49 (Quoted from *ibid*, p. 4).
106. In the original Pāli text, here, two words—'*addhagato*' and '*Vayoanupatta*' are used. We find a frequent use of these words in the Pāli texts. See, for example, Culla-vagga, Saṅgha Bhedaka Khaṇḍaka, Sutta Nipāta, Sabhiya Sutta; Rhys Davids has translated these words as 'he' has accomplished a long journey; and this term of life is nearly run'. (*S.B.E.* Vol. XVII); V. Fousboll has translated them as 'advanceed in years' and 'having reached old age' (*S.B.E.* Vol. X. p. 86) Rahul Sankrityayana translates them '*adhvagata*, and *vayaḥ anuprāpta*' (See, his Hindi Translation).
107. *Op. cit.*, p. 2.
108. *Op. cit.*, p. 2.
109. See for detailed discussion of all these references, '*Seniority of Mahāvīra*' in Chapter VII of this book.
110. *Op. cit.*, p. 7.
111. See also Editor's Notes for the contradiction between the belief and the *Buddhist Scriptures*.
112. See, for the establishment of this fact,—'*Contradictions*' in Chapter III of this book.
113. *Tīrthaṅkara Mahāvīra* (in two Volumes) published by Kāśinātha Saraka Yaśodharma Mandira, Bombay, 1963.
114. *Tīrthaṅkara Mahāvīra*, Vol. II, pp. 319-324.
115. *Ājīvakas*, p. 75.
116. *Tīrthaṅkara Mahāvīra*, Vol. II, p. 32.
117. *Ibid.*, p. 326.
118. *Ibid.*, p. 326.
119. *Ibid.*, p. 326.
120. Publisher's name is not printed on the book.
121. *Chronological Problems*, Preface, p. 1.
122. *Op. cit.*, p. 23.
123. *Op. cit.*, p. 68.
124. See, '*Date of Buddha's Nirvāṇa in Traditions*' in Chapter VII of this Book.
125. *Jain Bhāratī* (Weekly), Year 12, No. 1, Jan. 1951; pp. 5-21.

126. *Ibid.*, p. 15.
127. *Majjhima Nikāya*, Abhaya Kumāra Suttanta.
128. *Vinaya Piṭaka*, Cullavagga, VII, 3-41. Translated by Oldenberg, *S.B.E.*, XVIII.
129. *The Life of Buddha*, by Edward J. Thomas, pp. 140-141.
130. For the detailed discussion of this, see, *The Chronology* in Chapter VII of this Book.
131. Ajātaśatru Mathame Yasse Buddhe Parinivvaute, *Mahāvaṁsa*.
132. *Op. cit.*, p. 17.
133. *Mahā-Parinivvāṇa Sutta, Digha Nikāya* Tr. by T.W. Rhys Davids *S.B.E.* Vol. XI, pp. 103-106.
134. Maṅkhali Gośālaka died 16 years before Mahāvīra's *Nirvāṇa* (see, *Bhagavati Sūtra*, Śataka 15). In the chronology adopted by Dr. Jacobi, Dr. K.P. Jayaswal, Muni Kalyāṇa Vijayjī, Dr. A.L. Basham, Gośālaka's death occurs before the *Nirvāṇa* of Buddha as well as that of Mahāvīra. Purāṇa Kassapa had also died during the life-time of Buddha; see, *Dhammapada Aṭṭhakathā*, 4-2. (Also, *Buddhācārya*, by Pt. Rahul Sankrityayana, p. 86).
135. Here, instead of 'forty-five years' it should be 'forty-two years'. It seems that it is printed through a mistake (for 528–486 = 42; by taking 45, Buddha could not achieve enlightenment at that time.
136. *Ibid.*, p. 84.
137. *Majjhima Nikāya, Samāgama Sutta*, 3/1/4.
138. *Dīgha Nikāya*, Pasadika Sutta 3/6.
139. *Dīgha Nikāya*, Saṅgiti Priyāya Sutta 3/10.
140. The plusibility suggested is only conjectural. Yet it is possible on the basis of the hints given in the above allusions that the origin of the schism of the Jain order into Śvetāmbara and Digambara Sects, may lie somewhere here. The researchers should pay attention to this.
141. See, *Pārśvanātha kā Cāturyāma Dharma*.
142. *Op. cit.*, p. 11.
143. *Ibid.*, pp. 12-13.
144. *Bhagavatī Sūtra*, Śataka XV.
145. *Ibid.*, Śataka IX, uddeśaka VI, Sūtra 386-87.
146. *Saṁyutta Nikāya, Dahara Sutta* 3/1/10 (*Cf. The Book of the Kindred Sayings*, Tr. by Mrs. Rhys Davids, Vol. 1, pp. 93-96).
147. *Sutta Nipāta Sabhiya Sutta*, III-6 (*Cf.* Tr. by V. Fausboll *S.B.E.*, Vol. X, Part II, pp. 85-86). It may be remarked here that in the canonical literature of the Buddhist, the Mahāva of the Sutta Nipāta is considered to be very old. V. Fausboll has observed : "The collection on discourses of (*Sutta Nipāta*) which I have here translated is very remarkable, as there can be no doubt that it contains some remains of primitive Buddhism, consider the greater part of Mahāvagga Sutta Nipāta and nearly the whole of, Aṭṭhaka vagga as very old, (*Cf. op. cit.*, Introduction, p. I).
148. *Dīgha Nikāya, Samañjhaphala Sutta*, 1/2. (*Cf. Dialogues of the Buddha*, Tr. by T.W. Rhys Davids, Vol. 1, p. 51).
149. Kaumudi is full-moon day in *Aśvina* or *Kārtika Cf. Sanskrit-English Dictionary* of Vaman Shivaram Apte, Ed. by P.K. Gode and C.G. Karve, Part I, p. 611.
150. See, for the detailed discussion of these allusions the author's article titled '*Pāli Vāṅmaya Meṁ Bhagavāna Mahāvīra* in *Bhikṣusmṛti Grantha*, Part II, pp. 6-10.
151. Though in the Jain canons such as the *Sūtrakṛtāṅga Sūtra*, etc., we find a mention of some beliefs of the Buddhists, it is quite negligible. Also, because the later patriarchs of Jainism possessing the knowledge of the *Pūrvas* (the most important portion of the Jain canons, but not available now) had made additions and alterations in the original *Aṅgas*, the above stated fact is not violated.
152. Many an authoritative historians and scholars have approved this date; see for example,
    (a) Mahamahopadhyaya Raya Bahadur Gourī Saṅkara Ojhā, *Śrī Jain-Satya Prakāśa*, Vol. II, Nos. IV-V, pp. 217-81.
    (b) Dr. Baladeva Upadhyaya, *Dharma Aura Darśana*, p. 89.

(c) Dr. Vasudeva Saran Agravala, *Tīrthaṅkara Mahāvīra*, Vol. II, preface, p. XIX.
(d) Dr. Hira Lal Jain, *Tattva Samuccaya*, p. 6.
(e) Mahamahopadhyaya Pt. Vishveshar nath Rey, *Bhārata ke Prācīna Rājavaṁśa*, part II, p. 436.

153. *Candragupta Maurya and His Times*, by Dr. Radha Kumud Mukherjee, pp. 44-46; *Bhārata kā Bṛhat Itihāsa*, part I, (*Prācīna Bhārata*), by Śrīnetra Pāṇḍeya, 4th Edition, p. 242.

154. To these sources, Indian history is also indebted for what has been called 'the Sheet-anchor' of its chronology, for the starting-point of Indian chronology is the date of Candragupta's accession to sovereignity.
–*Candragupta Maurya and His Times*, by Dr. Radha Kumud Mukherjee, p. 3. Also, see, *Ancient India*, by Rapson, pp. 20-21.

155. The date 313 B.C. for Candragupta's accession, if it is based on correct tradition, may refer to his acquisition of Avanti in Malva, as the chronological datum found in a verse, where the Maurya king finds mention in the list of successors of Palaka, the king of Avanti.
–*Political History of Ancient India*, by Dr. H.C. Raychaudhuri, p. 295.
The Jain date 313 B.C., if based on correct tradition, may refer to his acquisition of Avanti (Malva).
–*An Advanced History of India*, by Dr. R.C. Majumdar, Dr. H.C. Raychaudhuri, K.K. Datta, p. 99.
Although the date 313 B.C. for Candragupta's accession is based on correct tradition it refers to his victory over Malva or Avanti, because the verse, in which this chronology is adopted, mentions Candragupta in the list of the successors of king Palaka of Avanti.
–*Śrīnetra Pāṇḍeya, op. cit.*, pp. 245-246.

156. Jaṁ rayanim Kalagao, ariha titthyamkaro mahāvīro.
Taṁ rayaniṁ avanivai, ahisitto palao raya!! 1!!
Saṭṭhi Palayaranno (60), Panavannasayam tu hoi nandanam (155)!
Aṭṭhasayaṁ muriyanaṁ (108), tisa ciyaya pusamittassa (30)!! 2!!
Balamitta-bhānumitta saṭṭhi (60), vari-sani caṭṭa nahavane!
Taha gaddabhilla-rājjaṁ tessa (13), varisa sagassa cau (varisa) (4)!! 3!!
Śrī Vikramādityaśca pratibodhitastadrajyaṁ tu Śrī virasaptati catustaye (470) samjātaṁ!
–*Tapagaccha Paṭṭāvali* by Dharmasāgara Upadhyaya (Ed. and Tr. by Panya Kalyāṇa Vijayajī), pp. 50-52.

157. Vikramarajjarambha parao siri vira nivvu bhaniyal
Sunnamuniveya jutto vikkama kalau jinakalo!!
Vikramakalajjinasya virasya kalo jinakalaḥ śūnyaḥ (0) muni (7), veda (4) yuktaḥ! Catvāriṁśatāni saptatyadhikavarśani śrīmahāvīranikra-madityayorantaramityarthaḥ! Nanvayaṁ kālaḥ viravikramayoḥ kathaṁ ganyate, ityaha vikramarājyarambhāt parataḥ paścāt śrīvīranirvṛtiratra bhānita! Ko bhavaḥ śrīviranirvanadinadanu, 470 varse vikramādityāya rājyarambhadinamiti!
—*Vicāra-śreṇī by Merutuṅga*, pp. 3-4.

158. Punarmannirvanāt Saptyadhikachath śatavarṣe (470) Ujjayinyaṁ śrīvikramādityo rājā bhaviṣyati ...... svanamna ca saṁvatsarapravṛtiṁ kariṣyati!
—*Śrī Saubhāgyapañcamyadīparvakathāsaṅgraha, Dipamālikā Vyākhyāna*, pp. 56-57.

159. Mahāmukkha gamanao palaya-nanda-candaguttairaiṣu bolineṣu causaya satterehiṁ vikkamaicco raya hohi! Tatthā saṭṭhi varisanaṁ palagassa rājjaṁ, panapannamsayaṁ nandanaṁ, atthottara sayaṁ moriyam vaṁśanaṁ, tisaṁ pusamittassa, saṭṭhi, balamitta-bhānumittanaṁ, calisaṁ naravahanassa, terasa gaddabhillassa, cattari sagassa! Tao vikkamdi cco!
—*Vividha tīrthakalpa* (*Apapabṛhat-kalpa*), pp. 38-39. Causaya sattari varise (470) viraro vikkamo jao—Pañcaka vāstu.

160. *An Advanced History of India*, p. 118, *Gupta Sāmrājya kā Itihāsa*, Vol. I, by Dr. Vasudeva Upadhyaya, pp. 182-183.

161. Jaṁ rayniṁ siddhigao, araha titthaṅkaro Mahāvīro.

Tam raynimavantie, abhisitto palao raya.. 620 ..
Palaya ranno satthi, puna pannasayaṁ viyaninadanaṁ
Muriyanaṁ satthisayaṁ, panatisa pusamittanaṁ (ttassa) 621 ...
Balamitta-bhānumitta, sattha cattaya honti nahasepe.
Gaddabhasayamegam puna, padivanno to sagoraya ... 622 ..
Pañca ya massa pañca ya, vasa chachceva honti vassaya.
Parinivvuassarihato, toauppan (Padivanno) sago raya raya... 623 ..
—*Titthogali Paiññaya*, Vss. 520-623.

162. Śrī viranirvṛtervarsaiḥ ṣadbhiḥ pañcottaraiḥ sataiḥ! Śaka saṁvatsarasyaisa pravṛttirbharate (a) bhavāt!!
—Merutuṅaga's *Vicāra-Śreṇi* (*Jaina Sāhitya-Saṁśodhaka*, Vol. II, Nos. III-IV, p. 4).

163. Chahini vasana saehiṁ pañcahiṁ vasehiṁ pañcamasehiṁ!
Mama nivvana gayassa upajjissai sago raya!!
—Nemi Candra's *Mahāvīra Cariyaṁ*, leaf, 94-01. Vs. 2169.

164. Panachassayavassaṁ panamasajudaṁ gamiya-vira-nivvuīdo!
Sagarājo to kakki Cadunāvatiyamahiya sagamasaṁ!! 850!!
—*Nemicandra Siddhānta-cakravartī's Trilokasāra* Vs. 65.

165. Varsanaṁ satsatiṁ tyaktvā pañcagrām māsapañcakaṁ!
Muktiṁ gate Mahāvīre śakarājastato (a) bhavat!!
—*Jinasenācārya's Harivaṁsa Purāṇa*, Adhyāya IX, Vs. 549.

166. "Nicvane virajine chacvasa sadeṣu pañcvariseṣu!
Panamāseṣu gadeṣu sañjado saganio ahava!!
—*Tiloyapannatti*, Part 1; 341.

167. "Pañca ya māsa pañca yā vāsa chacceva honti vasassasaya!
Sayakālena ya sahiya thaveyavvo tado rāśi!!
—*Dhavala*, (Jain Siddhānta Bhavana, Ara), leaf 537.

168. *An Advanced History of India*, p. 120; *Gupta Sāmrājya kā Itihāsa*, Part I, pp. 182-83.
169. *Ibid.*, Part 1, p. 382.
170. Guptanaṁ ca Satadvayaṁ.........!
Ektrimśacca varśāni kalavidbhirudahṛtaṁ.....!!
Dvicatvāriṁśadevataḥ Kalkirājasya rajata.......!
Tato (a) jitañjayo rājā syādindrapura-saṁsthitaḥ.....!!
Varṣāni śatsatia tyaktvā pañcagrāṁ māsapañcakaṁ.....!
Muktiṁ gate Mahāvīre śakarāja tato (a) bhavan......!!
—*Jinasena Harivaṁsa Purāṇa*, Adhyāya LX, VSS. 547-49.
171. *Indian Antiquary*, Vol. XV, 143.
172. Paṇa chasayṁ assaṁ panamasa judam gamīya virāni vuido Sagarāja to Kalkicadukakatiya mahiya Sasamasa, *Trilokasāra*, p. 32.
173. *Op. cit.*, 181.
174. *Kalpa Sūtra*, vs. 129 (*S.B.E.* Vol. XXII).
175. *Bhrama Vidhavaṁsanam*, Preface.
176. *Baṅkaculiā*.
177. *Op. cit.*
178. *Bhāratīya Prācīna Lipimata*, by Rayabahadur Mahamahopadhyaya Gourishankar Hirachand Ojha.
179. *Ibid.*
180. *Early History of India*, by Vincent A. Smith, p. 49.
181. *Journal of Royal Asiatic Society*, Great Britain, 1905, 51.
182. Sarat Chandra Das, *Journal of Asiatic Society*, Bengal, Part I, 1886, pp. 193-203, Tchang, Synchroismes Chinois; *Early History of India* by V.A. Smith, pp. 49-50.
183. *Buddhakālīna Bhārata*, by Janardana Bhatt, p. 371.
184. *B.C. Law Commemoration Volume*, II, pp. 180-22.
185. *Buddhism*, pp. 212-13.

186. *Introduction to Dhammapadda, S.B.E.* Vol. pp. X, XII.
187. *Indian Antiquary*, Vol. XLIII, 1914, pp. 126-133.
188. *Corpus Inscriptionum.* Indicarum, Vol. I, Introduction, p. II.
189. *An Indian Ephamenish*, Part I, 1922, pp. 471 ff.
190. *Introduction to Vinaya Piṭaka, S.B.E.* Vol. XIII, p. 22 and *The Religions of India* by E.W. Hopkins, p. 310.
191. *Journal of Royal Asiatic Society*, IV, p. 81.
192. *Indian Antiquary*, VI, p. 149, ff. (Also, see, *Buddhism in Translation*, p. 2).
193. *Mahāvaṁsa*, Geigar's Translation, XXVIII and *Journal of Royal Asiatic Society*, 1909, pp. 1-134
194. *Journal of Royal Asiatic Society*, 1908, pp. 471 ff.
195. Quoted from *Vīra Nirvāṇa Saṁvat Aura Jaina Kālagaṇanā*, p. 155.
196. *Buddhācārya*, preface, p. 1.
197. *Op. cit.*, p. 11.
198. *Political History of Ancient India*, p. 227.
199. *Early History of India*, p. 46.
200. *Der Buddhisumus*, Jar-Telling, II, p. 63.
201. *Early History of India*, 1924, pp. 49-50.
202. *Bhagavāna Buddha*, p. 89.
203. *Indian Antiquary*, XIII, 1884, pp. 411 ff.
204. The Purāṇa certainly existed in any form in the fourth century B.C., for we find in Kauṭilaya's *Arthaśāstra,* a reference to the Purāṇa.—Janardana Bhatta, *Bhaudha Kālīna Bhārata*, p. 3. In the opinion of scholars, the administrative system, described in Kauṭilya's *Arthaśāstra* is, in reality, an elaborated discussion of Candragupta Maurya's administration. So, the date of *Arthaśāstra* is, in no case, later than 3rd century B.C. Hence, it can be said that the Purāṇas were composed much earlier than 3rd century B.C. Hence, it can be said that the Purāṇas were composed earlier than the 3rd century B.C.
Shri Baladeva Upadhayaya, *Ārya Saṁskṛti Ke Mūlādhāra*, p. 164.
205. Muni Kalyāṇa Vijayajī, *op. cit.*, p. 30n.
206. Dr. Vincent A. Smith, *Early History of India*, p. 11.
207. Muni Kalyāṇa Vijayajī has discussed this point at length in his *Vīra Nirvāṇa Saṁvat Aura Jaina Kālagaṇanā*, pp. 15-29.
208. Modern European writers have inclined to disparage unduly the authority of the Purāṇic lists, but closer study finds in them, much genuine and valuable historical tradition.
—Dr. V.A. Smith, *op. cit.*, p. 12.
The Modern scholars have now accepted the view that the *Purāṇas* give authentic account of ancient chronology. The facts described in them have been corporated by the edicts, the coins and the reminicences of the foreign travellers. The learned historians, therefore, state that these materials should be regarded as genuine and acceptable.
—Shri Baladeva Upadhyaya, *op. cit.*, p. 167.
209. *Buddhist India*, pp. 277-78.
210. It is to be noted that the Buddhist tradition runs counter to the Brāhmanical and Jain traditions. *Chandragupta Maurya and His Time* by Dr. Radha Kumud Mukherjee, p. 20.
211. Muni Kalyāṇa Vijayajī (*op. cit.*, pp. 25-29) and Dr. Tribuvandas Laherchand Shah (*Prācīna Bhārata Varṣa)* have on the basis of a comparative study of the Jain, Purāṇic and Buddhist traditions, computed the regnal period of the kings of Śiśunāga and Nanda dynasties. We refer our readers to these sources for the detailed discussion of the topic.
212. According to Dr. T.L. Shah (*op. cit.*), after the death of Mahāvīra, Ajātaśatru reigned for 30 years, Udayi for 16 years and Aniruddha-Muṇḍa for 8 years, thus, assigning Mahāvīra's death in 527 B.C., the rule of Śiśunāga dynasty of Mahāvīra's death in 437 B.C.
According to Muni Kalyāṇa Vijayajī (*op. cit.*, p. 28), Ajātaśatru and Udayi reigned for 37 and 33 years respectively. But Mahāvīra's death took place 17 years after the accession of Ajātaśatru. Thus, 53 years after the death of Mahāvīra, ended the rule of Śiśunāga dynasty, so that 474 B.C. is the starting point of Nanda's rule at Magadha.

213. Nanda's rule at Magadha started in 474-3 B.C. and at Avanti, It started in 467 B.C. It is a well-known historical fact that at that time, there was a keen struggle between the kingdoms of Magadha and Avanti. It is quite probable that 6 or 7 years after having established his reign at Magadha, the first Nanda king would have conquered the kingdom of Avanti. It is unanimously accepted by the historians that the Nandas had established *'Ek rāt', i.e.* One umbrella kingdom in India (See, *Political History of Ancient India* by Dr. H.C. Raychaudhuri, p. 234, *Age of Nandas and Mauryas* by Nilkantha Shastri, pp. 11-20).

214. According to T.L. Shah (*op. cit.*) 'Śiśunāga was the founder of the Śiśunāga dynasty (*cf. Vāyu Purāṇa*, ad II c, vs 314). After the death of Aśāvasena, the king of Kāśī and the father of 23rd *Tīrthaṅkara* of Jain Lord Pārśvanātha, Śiśunāga established his kingdom in Kāśī. Then Śiśunāga himself went to Magadha and enthroned his son Kākavarṇa in Kāśī (*cf. Matsya Purāṇa*, ad CCLXXI, V-5). 'Śiśunāga was followed by Kākavarṇa Kṣema-Vardhana and Kṣemajita. The fifth king of the Śiśunāga dynasty was Prasenjita (The name of Prasenjita is omitted in the Purāṇas, but according to the Jain tradition the famous king Bimbisāra was the son of Prasenjita. Also the Buddhist work Divyavadāna (p. 369) enlist Prasenjita in the successors of Śiśunāga and Kākavarṇa, *cf.* Raychaudhuri, *op. cit.*, p. 222). 'It was Prasenjita, who transferred his capital from Kuthalnagar to Girivrija, Prasenjita was succeeded by Bimbisāra, Ajātaśatru, Uday Anuruddha and Muṇḍa'. (The Purāṇas enumerate Nandivarādhana and Mahānanda as the successors of Udayi, while the Buddhist chronology enlist Anuruddha-Muṇḍa. It will be shown below, Nandīvardhana and Mahānandi were Nanda kings, and not Śiśunāgas).' The regnal period of each of these ten kings is as follows :

1. Śiśunāga	60	years
2. Kākavaraṇa	36	"
3. Kṣemavaradhana	50	"
4. Kṣemajita	36	"
5. Prasenajita	43	"
6. to 10. Bimbisāra to Muṇḍa	108	"

Though the *Purāṇas* ascribe slightly different regnal-periods to these kings the above regnal-period assigned by T.L. Shah seems to be more correct.

215. It may be remarked here that though the Pūrāṇas state that the 10 kings of the Śiśunāga-dynasty reigned for 362 years, the total of the regnal period was assigned by them to these kings come out to be 333 years, (*Cf. Vāyu Purāṇa*, a ic, vss. 315-321, *Prācīna* by Mahamahopadyaya Vishaveshar Nath Reu, Vol. II, p. 54).

216.		
Śiśunāga	807 B.C.	747 B.C.
Kākavarṇa	747 B.C.	711 B.C.
Kṣemavardhana	711 B.C.	661 B.C.
Kṣemajita	661 B.C.	625 B.C.
Prasenjita	625 B.C.	582 B.C.

217. The *Purāṇas* insert Darśaka in between Ajātaśatru and Udayi. Also the famous Sanskrit play *Svapanavāsavadattā* speaks of Darśaka as the King of Rājagṛha. But it seems that Darśaka was really a king of viceregal throne at Rājagṛha and not that of the regnal throne of Magadha at Campā or Pāṭaliputra. (*cf.* Muni Kalyāṇa Vijayajī) (*op. cit.*, pp. 22-23) some scholars have considered it probable that Darśaka might be one of the many sons or grand sons of the King Bimbisāra (cf. Dr. Sita Nath Pradhan, *Chronology of Ancient India*, p. 217. "The order of succession in the *Viṣṇu Purāṇa*, which inserts Darśaka between Ajātaśatru and Udayaśva must be rejected. Also *cf. ibid.*, p. 212—Darśaka may be one of Bimbisāra's many sons who managed the state affairs during the life time of his father. Also, of Raychaudhuri, *op. cit.*, p. 130; Geiger, *Mahāvaṁsa*, Parichhedo IV, VV 1-2). Hence, in the chronological list of the main Śiśunāga dynasty, we need not count Darśaka.

218. According to the Buddhist Chronology Aniruddha-Muṇḍa were succeeded by Magadasaka (*Mahāvaṁsa* parichhedo IV, vs. 4) and Śiśunāga (Ibid., parichhedo IV, vs). Nāgadaśaka

and Śuśunāga are ascribed 24 and 18 years respectively as their regnal periods. (Ibid., l. c. cit). On the other hand, the *Purāṇas* assign Darśaka and Nandīvardhana a period, of 24 and 42 or 40 years respectively. *Vāyu Purāṇa*, II c. vs. 320 *Matsya Purāṇa*, ad. CCLXXI, vs. 10). Now, it seems that Darśaka of the Purāṇa and Nāgadaśaka of the Ceylonese chronicles are one and the same person. (cf. E.J. Rapson, *Cambridge History of India*, p. 279; Dr. Radha Kumud Mukherjee, *Hindu Sabhyatā*, p. 265). This Darśaka or Nāga-daśaka, after having ruled for 24 years at Rājagṛha (Viceregal throne), acceeded to the regal throne of Magadha at Pāṭaliputra. Because he belonged to the Śiśunāga dynasty, he can be called as "Śiśunāga". He it seems then assigned a new name "Nandi Vardhana" and found as a new dynasty—the Nanda-dynasty after his new name. He must have reigned for 16 or 18 years, for the Buddhist-chronology assign this period to Śuśunāga. Also, the Purāṇas have ascribed 40 or 42 years out of which 24 were spent at Rājagṛha as "darśaka" and the remaining 16 or 18 years must have spent as "Nandīvardhana." It should also be remarked here, that Udayi and Aniruddha Muṇḍa reigned for 24 years at regal-throne of Magadha and at the same time. Darśaka reigned at Rājagṛha for the same period. Thus the Purāṇas count 24 years of Darśaka twice which is an error, while the Buddhist chronology counts it only once which is correct.

219. According to the *Purāṇas* (*Vāyu Purāṇas*, a Ic, vs. 309-314, *Matsya Purāṇa*, ad CCLXXI, vvs, 1-4), Pulaka (or Śunaka) killed his master Ripuñjaga, the last king of the Bṛhadratha-dynasty, and enthroned his son Pradyota. Thus, when the rule of Vitihotras and Bṛhadrathas ended in Avanti, the rule of the kings called Pradyotas commenced. The following five kings are called Pradyotas :

1. Pravdyota (Mahāsena or Candpradyota)
2. Palaka (Son of Pradyota)
3. Viṣakhyupa
4. Ajaka or Gopālaka
5. Avantivardhana (Or Vartivardhana)

As we have already seen, according to the *Jain Tradition*, Palaka acceeded to the throne of Avanti on the very day on which Mahāvīra died, and his dynasty reigned for 60 years. Now, the Purāṇas assign 20 years to Palaka's reign (*cf.* Pargiter, *Dynasties of the Kali Age*, p. 19, note 26. In some Purāṇas, 24 years are assigned; but the scholars have relied on the above version. cf. Dr. Shanti Lal Shah, *Chronological Problems*, p. 26). The third Pradya king Viṣakyūpa is assigned a period of 53 (or 85) years. But the scholars, on the basis of other literary works like Mṛcchakaṭika, have proved that Ajaka or Gopālaka succeeded Palaka and therefore Viṣakyūpa should be omitted form the Palaka dynasty, (*Cf.* Dr. Shanti Lal Shah *Chronological Problems*, p. 27, "What about Viṣakyūpa who occurs in the *Purāṇas* in between Palaka and Āryaka? According to the family history of Pradyota which we have seen just now, there is no place for Viṣakyūpa in between Palaka and Ājaka as reported; "also cf. Majumdar Shastri *Journal of Bihar and Orissa Research Society*; vol. VII., p. 116. "Viṣakyūpa has been introduced between Palaka and Ājaka, but as that name does not occur, in all Mss, we thought to take no notice of him", also, *cf.* Dr. Ramashanker Tripathi, *Prācīn Bhārata kā Itihāsa*, p. 72. "The *Purāṇas* insert a third name—Viṣakyūpa in between Palaka and Ājaka, is probably a mistake." Ājaka is assinged a regnal period of 21 years, after which his son Avantivardhana reigned for 20 yeras. Thus the three kings Palaka, Ājaka and Avantivardhana ruled for 61 years. Then, the rule of Pradyotas ended. Thus both the Jain and *Purāṇic* Chronology agree that the Palaka-dynasty reigned for 60 or 61 years. (*cf.* Dr. Shanti Lal Shah, *Chronological Problems*, pp. 25-27).

220. A Nanda king is twice mentioned in the Hāthīgumphā inscription of king Khāravela of Kaliṅga (Orissa) (cf. E.J. Rapson, Cambridge, *History of India*, Vol. I, p. 280). The sixth line of the inscription is : "Pañcame cedanti vase nandarāja- ti-vasa-sata ogahitaṁ tamsuliya-vatabandi (m) nagaraṁ (paveśayati).......", (which means, "And now in the fifth year (of

his reign), he (Khāravela) brings into capital Tosāla or Taṁsuliya (or entered a particular town through or executed some public work associated with) the canal excavated by the king Nanda 300 years before". The word "tivasa-sata" has been translated as in 103rd years (of Nanda king) by some scholars, the conscientious scholars like Dr. K.P. Jayaswal, Dr. R.D. Banerjee, etc. have translated it as "300 years" (*cf. Journal of Bihar and Orissa Research Society*, Dec. 1917, pp. 425 ff) Dr. Shanti Lal Shah has made the following remark : "That ti-vasa-sata means" 300 years and not 103, is certain. See Dr. Banerjee's artical in *J.B.O. R.S.* Vol. III, p. 496 ff. 9 May add here that because the years are expressed in compound the word 'Śata' is used in the singular instead of the plural". (*Op. cit.* p. 41n).

Thus, the above Nanda king flourished 300 years before the fifth year of Khāravela's reign Dr. Jayaswal has also shown that this Nanda king was no other than Nandīvardhana *cf. op. cit.*, Vol. XIII p. 240).

Again, the sixteenth line of the inscription shows that the thirteenth year of Khāravela's reign synchronized with 165th year of Maurya Era. The inscription reads : "Panamtariya sathivasasata Rāja Muriyākāla, vocainam ca coyatiaga śataka turiyam Upadayati", which means, "He (Khāravela) caused to be made (the things described in the foregoing lines) in the 165th years of the Rāja Muriyā Era (of which) 164th year has just terminated (Vocinam). Here, also, though some scholars translate the above line in a different way and deny the existence of any date in the above inscription, others have critically refuted their view (*cf.* Dr. Shanti Lal Shah, *op. cit.*, pp. 47, 48). The famous historian E.J. Rapson has made the following remark : "Even the fundamental question whether the inscription is dated or not is still in dispute. Some scholars contend that a passage in the sixteenth line can only be interpreted to mean that the inscription was engraved in the 165th year of the Maurya kings, or of the Maurya king), while others deny the existence of any such date. The discussion of problems of this kind does not fall within the scope of present work; but may be pointed out here that the acceptance of the supposed date would seem to involve no chronological impossibilities, and that, in any case, the inscription probably belongs to about the middle of the second century B.C. We know from analogous instances that the origin of imperial eras is usually to be traced to the regnal years of the founder of the empire. A Maurya era, therefore, would naturally date from the accession of Candragupta C. 321 B.C.; and, if such an era is actually used in the present instance, the inscription must be dated c. 156 B.C. and the beginning of Khāravela's reign c. 169 B.C. With this hypothetical chronology other indications of date seem to agree.

Epigraphical consideration shows that the Hāthīgumphā inscription of Khāravela and the Nānāghāṭa inscription of Naganika, the queen of Śātakarṇi, belong to same period as the Nasika inscription of Kṛṣṇa. (Bühler, *Archaeological Survey of Western India*, V, p. 71; Indishe Palaeographie, p. 39). Even, therefore, if it must be admitted that the Hāthīgumphā inscription is undated, there is still reason to believe that Khāravela may have been contemporary with Śātakarṇi in the first half of the second century B.C. Moreover, a Śātakarṇi is actually mentioned in the Hāthīgumphā inscription is Khāravela's rival; and it appears most probable that he is to be identified with the Śātakarṇi of the Nānāghāṭa inscription. (*Op. cit.*, pp. 481, 482).

Thus, by taking 322 B.C., the date of Candragupta's accession, as the year of beginning of Maurya Era, Khāravela's accession should fall in 170 B.C., and the fifth year of his reign in 166 B.C. Consequently, Nandarāja's (*i.e.* Nandīvardhana's) attack on Kaliṅga must have taken place in 466 B.C. This Nanda-king is again mentioned in the 12th line of the inscription, which means, "In the twelfth year of his reign, Khāravela produced consternation among the king of Uttarapatha, created fear in the people of Magadha, made his elephants to enter into "Suganageya", humbled Bṛhaspatimitra, the king of Magdha and brought back to Kaliṅga the Jain statue which had been carried away by the Nanda-king, and also gained some Jewels from Aṅga and Magadha as an evidence of victory" (*Cf. Journal of Bihar and Orissa Research Society*, Vol. IV, p. 401, Vol. XII, p. 732). This line also confirms the date of Khāravela, decided above. For, 'Bṛhaspatimitra' mentioned in the inscription is identified with Puṣyamitra, the Suṅaga-king, who flourished in 185-150 B.C. according to the Purāṇic chronology, and the 12th year of Khāravela's reign falls in 159 B.C. which synchronises with the reign Puṣyamitra. (*Cf.* Chiman Lal Jee Chand Shah, M.A., *Jainism in North India*, (Gujarati Translation), pp. 159-162; Dr. V.A. Smith, *Journal of Royal Asiatic Society*, 1918, p. 554; Dr. K.P. Jayaswal, *op. cit.*, Vol. III, p. 447, Dr. Shanti Lal Shah, *op. cit.*, pp. 53-55).

Our view that this Nanda-rāja was no other than Nandīvardhana, is supported by some famous historians, Dr. V.A. Smith observes, "The Nanda-rāja referred to appears to be Nandīvardhana, the ninth Śiśunāga king of the Purāṇas. It seems to be necessary to treat him and his successor Mahānandin, No. 10 as Nandas distinct from the nine Nandas who come between No. 10 and Candragupta. In the third edition of Early History of India (1914) I placed the accession of Nandīvardhana about 418 B.C. He must now go back to c. 470 B.C. or possibly to an earlier date". (*Journal of Royal Asiatic Society*, 1918, p. 547). E.J. Rapson, the editor of *Cambridge History of India* (Vol. 1), concludes : "If tivasa-sata in line 6 of the inscription can mean 'three centuries before (the fifth year of Khāravela's reign), we must suppose that in the middle of the fifth century B.C., Kaliṅga was under the rule of a Nanda king, and it is natural to associated him with the well-known predecessors of the Mauryas". (*op. cit.* p. 484).

This date is also approved by the fact that according to Alberuni, the Nanda era commenced 400 years before the Vikrama-era (56 B.C.) (*Cf.* Dr. K.P. Jayaswal, *op. cit.*, vol. XIII, p. 240, also, *cf.* Ganga Prasad Maheta, *Prācīna Bhārata*, p. 103). It is quite probable that to mark the death of the founder of Nanda-dynasty, the Nanda-era was started in 456 B.C.

The ancient Brāhmanical as well as Buddhist traditions show Pāṇini to be contemporary with a Nanda king. It is mentioned by Taranath, the famous Tibetan writer, that Pāṇini was a friend of the Nanda-king, Mahānandin, the father of Mahāpadma Nanda. (History of *Buddhism*, p. 1608). The Buddhist work Mañjuśrī-Mūlakalpa records.

> Tasyapantro rāja Nandanama bhaviṣyati!
> Puṣpakhye nagre Śrīman Mahāsainyo mahābalākā.
> Bhaviṣyati tadā kāle brāhmaṇastarkika bhuvil!
> Tebhi parivarito rājā vai!
> Asyapyanatamaḥ sakhyaḥ Pāṇinirnama mānavaḥ!!

Patal III, pp. 611-12; *Studies on Mañjuśrī-Mūlakāla* by Jayaswal p. 14.

This means—"There will be a Nanda-rāja in Puṣpapura (Pātaliputra) and a *Brāhmaṇa* called Pāṇini will be his intimate friend. In the court of the king, there will be many Brāhmaṇas who will be logicians and the king will honour them by gifts".

Besides these evidences, Somdeva's Kathāsaritsāgara and Kṣemendra's Bṛhatkathāmañjarī bear testimony to the contemporaneity of Pāṇini with the Nanda-rāja the records of the Chinese traveller Hieun-Tsang also support this view. (*Cf.* Dr. Vasudeva Saran Aggrawal, *Pāṇinikālīna Bhāratavarṣa*, pp. 467-480), Dr. Vasudeva Saran Aggrawal has shown on the basis of literary, historical and traditional evidences that the correct date of Pāṇini is about 480-410 B.C. Dr. Aggrawal has also endorsed the view of Jain chronology that the Nanda-dynasty ruled in C. 473-323 B.C. (*op. cit.*, p. 473). Dr. Aggrawal has also accepted that in 465 B.C. Nandīvardhana, the first Nanda king was reigning at Pāṭaliputra (*op. cit.*, p. 474). Dr. Aggrawal has also cited an allusion from the grammar of Pāṇini, which records that Nandīvardhana was the first Nanda king and that Mahānandin his son was the second Nanda-king (*Loc. cit.*).

221. *Vāyu Purāṇa*, adh, ICV 320; *Matsya Purāṇa* adh CCLXXI, vs. II.
222. *Vāyu Purāṇa*, adh, Ic, V. 327.
223. *Ibid.*, *loc. cit.*
224. It is remarkable that Dr. Smith, who has established his chronology on different basis, has also ascribed the period of 88 years from 413 B.C. to 325 B.C. to Mahāpadma Nanda.

225. Candragupta Maurya acceeded to the throne of Magadha in 322 B.C., but the Nandas continued to reign at Avanti, upto 313 B.C. As already discussed before, Candragupta Maurya acquired the kingdom of Avanti in 313 B.C., and this ended the rule of the Nanda-dynasty.
Some historians have called the first two Nanda-Nandīvardhana and Mahānandi as old Nandas and Mahāpadma Nanda and his dynasty as Neo-Nanda (Nanira-Nanda) or new Nandas. (*Cf.* Dr. Shanti Lal Shah, *Chronological Problems*, pp. 34-37; also *Cf.* E.J. Rapson *Cambridge History of India*, pp. 279-280; Dr. K.P. Jayaswal, *Journal of Bihar and Orissa Research Society*, Sept., 1915, p. 21).

226. *Cf.* The following chronologies supplied by the Mahāvaṁsa, Dr. Smith and Dr. Shanti Lal Shah respectively :
(i) *Mahāvaṁsa*, Pariccheda V, V.
(Taking Buddha's *Nirvāṇa* in 544 B.C., the eighth year of Ajātaśatru's reign; the dates refer to the accession of the kings mentioned).

	Regal Period	*B.C.*
Ajātaśatru	32	551
Udayibhadda	16	519
Aniruddha-Muṇḍa	8	503
Nāgadaśaka	24	495
Śiśunāga	18	471
Kālaśoka	28	453
Kālaśoka's sons	22	425
Nava Nandas	22	403
Candragupta	24	381
Dr. Smith : (*Early History of India*)		
Bimbisara	31	582
Ajātaśatru	24	551
Darśaka	24	527
Udayi	23	503
Nandīvardhana	24	480
Mahānandina	43	456
Mahāpadma Nanda	88	413
Sons of Mahāpadma Nanda	12	325
Candragupta		313
Ajātaśatru	32	551
Darśaka	18	519
Udayina	33	501
The Old Nandas		
Nandīvardhana	20	467
Kākavarṇa and Mahānandina	43	447
The New Nandas		
Nanda (Barber)	22	404
Nanda II (Mahāpadma)	66	382
Candragupta	24	316

227. Refer to Muni Kalyāṇa Vijayajī, *op. cit.*, p. 24, for a detailed discussion of the topic Prof. Lassen had observed long ago. "In den Berichten die Nandas herrschtin den Singhalesischen Schriften offenbareine Verwirrung". (*Indian Antiquary*, Vol. II, p. 64). "The account about the Nandas recorded by the Singhalese chronicles reveal a confusion". Dr. Smith (*op. cit.*) and Dr. Radha Kumud Mukherjee (*Hindi Sabhyatā*, p. 267) have explicitly refuted this belief of Ceylonese chronicles.

228. The greatest blunder committed by the historians in believing the Ceylonese chronology which states Śiśunāga as the successor of Ajātaśatru, is probably due to the misinterpretation of the following verse of the Pūrāṇa.
Astatrimsacchataṁ bhāvya pradyotahpancate sutaḥ!
Hatvā teṣāṁ yaśaḥ risanaṁśiśunako bhaviṣyati!!
The meaning of this verse becomes clear in the light of the foregoing discussion. To make it more clear, we should know that in *Purāṇas*, the name of the king of the dynasties of Kāli age are mentioned in the following order :

(i) The king of Pāṇḍava-dynasty from Abhimanyu, who fought in the Mahābhārata war, to Kṣemaka, the fourth king to reign after Udayan, the contemporary of Buddha. this dynasty first reigned at Hastināpura and later on removed the seat of its rule to Kauśāmbī, during the reign of Nicakṣus, the successor of Adhisimakriṣṇa.
(ii) The king of Ikṣavāku-dynasty from Bṛhadvalo, who fought in the Mahābhārata war, to Sumitra, the fourth king to reign after Prasenjita, the contemporary of Buddha. This dynasty reigned at Srivasti in Kosala.
(iii) The king of Lunar dynasty of Pāṇḍava and successors of Bṛhadratha from Sahadeva, who fought in the Mahābhārata war to Ripuñjya, the predecessor of Caṇḍa Pradyota (Mahāsenā), the contemporary of Buddha. The successors of Baṛhadratha (*i.e.* Barhadrathas) are also called Magadhas probably because they belonged to the dynasty of Bṛhadratha, Jarāsandha, etc., who were the rulers of Magadha, and also Somadhi, the son of Sahadeva established his reign of Girivraja in Magadha after the Mahābhārata war. But, after giving the chronology of the twenty-two kings, the *Purāṇas* say :

Pūrṇa varṣasahasraṁ vai teṣāṁ rājyaṁ bhaviṣyati!!
Bṛhadratheśvatiteṣu vitihotreśvavantiṣu!
Pulakas svāmināṁ hatvā svaputṛmabhiṣekṣyati!!
(*Vāyu Purāṇa*, adh. Ic, VV. 309-310; *Matsya Purāṇa* adh. CCLXX V. 30; ad. CCLXXI, V.1).

These verses explicitly indicate that when the rule of the kings Vitihotras and Bṛhadrathas was over in Avanti, Ripuñjaya the last king was killed by his minister Pulaka (or Punika or Sunaka) and his son Pradyota was enthroned. (We have already discussed Pradyota's rule in Avanti). Thus, though the rule of the Barhadrathas was established in Magadha in the time of Somādhi, later on it must have been transferred to Avanti.
(iv) The king of Pradyota dynasty from Pradyota to Avantivardhana. This dynasty reigned in Avanti.
(v) The king of Śiśunāga-dynasty from Śiśunāga to Mahānandi. This dynasty reigned in Magadha.

These dynastic lists clearly show that the dynasities mentioned are not in succeeding order but are more or less contemporary. Udayana of the first dynasty, Presenjita of the second dynasty, Pradyota of the fourth dynasty and Ajātaśatru (and Bimbisāra) of the fifth dynasty are undoubtedly contemporary kings of Vatsa, Kosala, Avanti and Magadha respectively. (cf, Rapson, C.H. 1. p. 277). Thus, it would be mistake if we take the fifth as the successor of the fourth dynasty, although the fourth dynasty is explicitly mentioned to have succeeded the thrid dynasty. Also, because the Barhadrathas transferred their seat from Magadha to Avanti, the Śiśunāgas are justified as the rulers of Magadha and the contemporaries of the later Barhadrathas of Avanti. The only question which remains still to be answered is that during whose reign the Barhadrathas changed their seat from Magadha to Avanti. It is possible that when Śiśunāga became powerful in northern India and when he established his kingdom in Magadha (in c. 807 B.C) the Barhabrathas king ruling at that time of Magadha, would have escaped to Avanti and established his kingdom there. Then onwards, the Śiśunāgas ruled in Magadha and the Barhadrathas in Avanti contemporarily. The Barhadrathas were succeeded by the Pradyotas, who, as already shown, were succeeded by Śiśunāga Nandīvardhana, the first Nanda king.

The above interpretation of the Purāṇic verses is also compatible with the chronology described therein. According to the Purāṇas, the twenty two kings of the Barhadratha-dynasty ruled for 100 years as follows :

	Name of the King	*Regnal period*	
1.	Somadhi	58	years
2.	Śrutaśrva	60	"
3.	Ayutayusa	36	"
4.	Niramitra	40	"
5.	Sukṣketra	56	"
6.	Bṛhatkarmā	23	"
7.	Senajita	50	"
8.	Śrutañjaya	40	"
9.	Mahābāhu	28	"
10.	Suci	64	"
11.	Kṣema	28	"
12.	Bhuvrata	64	"
13.	Dharmanetra	35	"
14.	Vivṛti	58	"
15.	Suvrata	38	"
16.	Dṛḍhasena	48	"
17.	Mahīnetra	33	"
18.	Sucala	32	"
19.	Sunetra	40	"
20.	Satyajita	83	"
21.	Viśvajit	35	"
22.	Ripuñjaya	50	"
		999	years

Thus, 1000 years for 22 kings are exactly computed. Also by taking arithmetical average of these regnal periods, we find that each king is alloted 45.45 years. This means "that the six kings ruled for 45.45 x 6 = 273 years, which is also the exact total of the last six rulers, Now, we know from other sources that Pradyota acceeded to the throne of Avanti (by ending the rule of Ripuñjaya) in 549 B.C. (see '*Tibetan Tradition*' in Chapter VIII of this book). This means that Ripuñjaya's rule ended in 549 B.C. By calculating the dates of the last six kings and by comparing them with those of the first six kings of the Śiśunāga dynasty, we find that their contemporaneity is surprisingly proved :

	Barhadratha king	*Date (B.C.)*	*Śaiśunāga king*	*Date (B.C.)*
1.	Ripuñjaya	599-549	Bimbisāra	582-544
2.	Viśvajita	634-599	Prasenjita	625-582
3.	Satyajita	717-634	Kṣemajita	661-625
4.	Sunetra	757-717	Kṣemavardhana	711-661
5.	Sucala	789-757	Kākavarṇa	747-711
6.	Mahīnetra	823-789	Śiśunāga	807-747

Ajātaśatru the 7th king of the Śiśunāga dynasty and Prodyota, the 7th king in the line of Avanti-rulers also become contemporary as followers :

Ajātaśatru : 544-497; Pradyota 549-527.

Thus, the whole chronology becomes complete.

It may be indicated here, that the date of *Mahābhārata* is also fixed to a great certainty in c. 1559 B.C. This is also confirmed by another chronological fact of the *Purāṇas* and the *Mahābhārata* that the Nanda's rule commenced 1050 years after the *Mahābhārata* war, which is thus, dated in 474 + 1050 = 1524 B.C. (*Cf. Vāyu Purāṇa* adh. to v.v, 217-329; *Matsya Purāṇa*, adh. CCLXX v.v. 30 adh. CCLXXI, v.v. 1-20 adh. CCLXXII. v. 35 *Mahābhārata* XIV = 66-70, also *cf. Buddha Parva kā Bhāratīya Itihāsa*, by Missra & Missra, pp. 30-171; Pargiter, *The Dynasties of Kali age*, pp. 20 ff. 65 ff.; Dr. Sita Nath Pradhana, *Chronology of Ancient India*, pp. 100-230.

229. *Cf.* Editior's Note, p. XII.

(4) *Cf.* T.W. Rhys Davids, *Introduction to the Mahāparinirvāṇa Sutta S.B.E.* vol. XI, p. XLV; "According to the *Rāja-paramparā* or line of kings, in the Ceylon chronicles, the date of great decease would be 543 B.C., which is arrived at by adding to the date 161 B.C. (from which the reliable portion of the history begins), two periods of 146 and 236 years. The first purports to give the time which elapsed between 161 B.C. and the great Buddhist church council held under Asoka, and in the eighteenth year of his reign at Patna; and the second to give the interval between that council and the Buddha's death.

"It would result from the first calculation that the date of Asoka's coronation would be 325 B.C. (146 + 161 + 18). But we know that this must contain a blunder or blunders, as the date of Asoka's coronation can be fixed, as above stated with absolute certainty within a year or two either way of 267 B.C.

Would it then be sound criticism to accept the other, earlier period of 236 years found in those chronicles a period which we cannot test by Greek chronology—and by simply adding the Ceylon calculation of 236 years to the European date for the 18th years of Asoka (*i.e.* circa 249 B.C.) to conclude that the Buddha died in or about 485 B.C.?

"I cannot think so. The further we go back, the greater does the probability of error become, not less, The most superficial examination of this earlier period shows that they are unreliable and what reliance would it be wise to place upon the total, apart from the details, when we find it mentioned for the first time in a work Dīpavaṁsa, written eight centuries after the date it proposed to fix?

If further proof were needed, we have it in the fact that the Dīpavaṁsa actually contains the details of another calcuation-based on the lists of king (*Rājaparamparā*), but on a list of There as (*Theraparamparā)* stretching back from Asoka's time to the time of the great Teacher which contradicts this calculation of 236 years".

230. *Early History of India*, p. 11.

231. *Political History of Ancient India*, p. 6.

232. *Chronological Problems*, p. 41.

233. *Op. cit.*, p. 19.

234. The content of *Mahāvaṁsa* are as follows :

1. The visit of the Tathāgata.
2. The race of Mahāsammata.
3. The first council.
4. The second council.
5. The third council.
6. The coming of Vijaya.
7. The consecration of Vijaya.
8. The consecration of Pāṇḍu Vasudeva.
9. The consecration of Abhaya.

— See Giger Tr. of Dr. *Mahāvaṁsasa*, p. VIII.

235. See, '*Inconsistencies*' in Chapter III of this book.

236. The *Tripiṭakas* tell us the six religious teachers Purāṇa Kassapa, Makkhali Gośālaka, Nigaṇṭha Nātaputta, Ajita Keśakambalī, Sañjya Vellaṭthiputta and Pakuddha Kāccāyana had already announced themselves as '*Tīrthaṅkaras*' and had started preaching their religions before the enlightenment of Buddha. Also, when Buddha attained the enlightenment, all of them were alive. Makkhali Gośālaka was the founder of the Ājīvaka sect. When, just after having attained the enlightenment, Buddha was travelling from Gayā to Sāranātha in the way he met an Ājīvaka monk called Upaka. Buddha said to him, "I have attained enlightenment". But Upaka, being not convinced of this, paid no heed to him, Having said, "May be, perhaps, Upaka went away by another road. *Vinaya Piṭaka, Mahāvagga*, I, also see Buddhācārya by Rahul Sankrityayana, p. 21 and Bhagvāna Buddha by Dharmānanda Kauśāmbī, p. 137. This incident makes it clear that at the time of Buddha's enlightenment, Makkhali Gośālaka had already become an eminent religious leader.
237. *Aṅguttara Nikāya, Aṭṭhakathā*, 2-4-5.
238. According to Rhys Davids, Buddha passed his 4th rainy-season in Mahāvana (Vaiśālī) : (Buddhism by Rhys Davids quoted by M.N. Shastri in *Buddha : His Life, His Teaching, His Order*, p. 120). But the *Aṭṭhakathā* states that the 5th rainy-season was spent at Vaiśālī in the same way *Aṭṭhakathā* states that Buddha passed his 6th rainy-season at Maṅkula Parvata". While Rhys Davids has stated that he passed the 5th rainy-season, at Maṅkula Pravata. It seems, that in the calculation of Rhys Davids, there is an error of 1 year.
239. This Sutta has been quoted in Seniority of Mahāvīra, in this Chapter.
240. See, '*Inconsistencies*' in Chapter III of this book.
241. Dr. Radha Kumud Mukherjee has rightly remarked, "Chronology is essential to biography. An individual cannot rank as a historical person, unless his life and work are placed in time".

—*Candragupta Maurya and His Times*, p. 2.

242. *Life of Buddha* by Rockhill, p. 17.
243. *Ibid.*, p. 32.
244. *Vāyu Purāṇa*, Adhyāya IC V. 312.
245. *Matsya Purāṇa*, Adhyaya CCLXXI V. 3.
246. *Bhāgawata Purāṇa*, Skandha, XII, Adhyāya V. 3.
247. *Kathāsaritsāgara* 3/5/58.
248. *Svapnavāsavadattā* of Bhāsa.
249. *Mṛcchakaṭika* of Śūdraka.
250. *Ayasyuka-Nirukti*, Dīpikā, part II, pp. 110-11, V. 1282.
251. *Tithogalipaiññya*—quoted in "*The Date of Mahāvīra's Nirvāṇa* in Chapter VII of this book.
252. *Vāyu Purāṇa* Adhyāya IC V. 311.
253. Pradyota's ended in 527 B.C. Hence, his accession should have taken place in 527 + 23 = 550 B.C. *Cf.* foot note.
254. See, *Traditional Dates of Buddha's Nivāṇa* in Chapter VII of this book.
255. See, for example Janardan Bhatt, *Buddha Kālīna Bhārata*, p. 213.
256. Dr. Ramashankar Tripathi, *Prācīna Bhārata kā Itihāsa*, p. 129.
257. *Asoka ke Dharma Lekha*, by Janardan Bhatt.
258. The edicts of Sahasārāma and Vairāṭa read "Upāsake".
259. *Asoka ke Dharmalekha*, by Janardan Bhatt.
260. The Age of Imperial Unity. (*The History and Culture of Indian People*, Vol. II), pp. 75-76.
261. *Asoka ke Dharama-lekha*, by Janaradan Bhatt.
262. *Asoka*, by Vincent A. Smith, p. 199.
263. Translated from *Asokāvadāna* by Dr. Vincent A. Smith, in *Asoka* (The Rulers of India), pp. 227-228.
264. *Cf. Asoka*, by V.A. Smith, p. 211.
265. *Journal of Royal Asiatic Society*, 1904, pp. 1-26, Dr. Bühler, '*Second notice, Indian Antiquary*, 1893'.

266. *Journal of Royal Asiatic Society*, 1910, pp. 1301-8, 1911, pp. 1091-1112 (quoted from Janardan Bhatta, *Asoka ke Dharmalekha*).
267. For the view of the modern history, see Vincent A. Smith *Asoka*, p. 150; Dr. F.W. Thomas, *Indian Antiquary*, 1908, pp. 19-23, Dr. H.C. Raychaudhuri, *op. cit.*, p. 341 n; Yadhunadana Kapur, *Aśoka*, p. 128, etc.

5

PREVIOUS BIRTHS

We are provided with a similiar discussion about the previous births of Bhagavān Mahāvīra and Gautama Buddha in the Jaina and Buddhist traditions respectively, and there is a very extraordinary similarity between the two accounts. We have it in the Jaina tradition that many many lives before the birth of Mahāvīra, the first *Tīrthaṅkara* Ṛṣabhadeva had revealed about Tāpasa Marīci. This monk would be the last *Tīrthaṅkara* Mahāvīra. In the same way, we have it in the Buddhist tradition that many many *kalpas* before the birth of the Buddha, Dīpaṅkara Buddha had revealed about Tāpasa Sumedhā, 'One day, he will be the Buddha'. The forecast about Mahāvīra was made 25 lives before his birth as Mahāvīra, while that about the Buddha was made 551 lives prior to his birth as the Buddha.

TĀPASA MARĪCI

Marīci's vacillation

Marīci was the son of Bharata. He was greatly impressed by the festivities organised by the gods and the demons on the occasion of the attainment of omniscience by Bhagavān Ṛṣabhadeva, and he became a monk along with his 500 brothers. Marīci was the master of 11 *Aṅgas,* and day after day, he followed Bhagavān Ṛṣabhadeva as his shadow. It so happened once that he was exceedingly tired because of terrific heat. His whole body was soiled by sweat, and his body and clothes emitted a foul smell. Besides, he was very much thirsty. Because of heat and hardships, he lost his patience, and he slipped out from the *śramaṇa* order and fell a prey to inferior thoughts. Thought he in his mind,

> 'I am the grandson of the first *Tīrthaṅkara* Bhagavān Ṛṣabhadeva. I am the son of the first World-monarch Bharata who had conquered all the six regions (or Bhāratavarṣa). In the presence of the four orders, I courted monkhood out of indifference to wordly life. It will be shameful for me to give up discipline and return home. But at the same time, the fact remains that I cannot bear the heavy responsibility of monkhood on my weak shoulders. It is impossible for me to practise the great vows, and

> yet in giving them up and returning home, I shall be staining the family line. Thus, I have a tiger on one side, and a river on the other. But just as in climbing a mountain, there is always a narrow foot-path, so by the side of this most difficult road (*i.e.*, religion, there should be an easy way).

Marīci as a tridaṇḍī monk

Lost in the tangle of his own thoughts, Marīci further pursued his contemplation :

> 'The monks in the order of Bhagavān Ṛṣabhadeva conquer mind, speech and body, and I have conquered all the three. So I shall be a *tri-daṇḍī* (triple-wanded). The *śramaṇas* with their senses subdued tonsure their hairs and become bald. I shall also tonsure my hairs except a few at the crest. The Nirgranthas desist from killing all forms of live, minute as well as big, but I shall desist from killing big lives. (But) I shall not give up possession (property), and I shall use foot-wear. I shall apply sandal paste and others to perfume my body. I shall spread umbrella over my head. Being wholly free from passions, these monks put on white robes, but since I am not wholly free from passions (called/*kasaya),* I shall put on *kasaya* (saffron-coloured) garments. These monks do not drink fresh (unboiled) water, but I shall take bath with a limited quantity of fresh water and drink the same.'

He gave effect to his thought and changed his dress and way of life, but he did not give up the company of Bhagavān Ṛṣabha. He always moved in the group of his monks. When perople saw a peculiarly-dressed monk in the group of *nirgrantha* monks, they felt a curiosity about him and asked him about his religion. But to everyone he spoke about his original religion (*i.e.*, *śramaṇa* religion, and nothing about his new religion). When people asked him why he did not follow it in his own life, he frankly confessed his own inability. If anyone got inspiration from his words and desired to be initiated into the holy order, he always referred him to Bhagavān Ṛṣabhadeva and advised him to join his order.

Kapila

Marīci spent many years with Bhagavān Ṛṣabhadeva. Once he fell seriously ill and there was none to take care of him. For the first time, he experienced the misery ofa solitary life, and he thought that he should take some direct disciples of his own. One day, as Bhagavān Ṛṣabhadeva was delivering a sermon, a prince Kapila was present in the assembly. Somehow, he did not like sermon and he felt a disgust for it. So he looked around, and his eyes fell on Tridaṇḍī Marīci who conspicuous for his dress. So he got up from his seat, came to Marīci and asked him about his religion. Said Marīci,

"I have no religion to offer to you. If you care for it at all, then I would advise you to seek the protection of the Bhagavān."

So, the prince came back to his own seat and tried to concentrate again on the sermon. But despite his best effort, he found no interest in it. So, he came back to Marīci and said,

"Don't you have some inferior staff with you on which you may advise and direct me. If you have none, then why have you taken a friar's robe?"

When Marīci heard these words, thought he,

"It seems that this fellow bears similarity with me. They say–birds of the feather flock together. Very well. He will be a good companion to me."

Then he said aloud,

"You have religion with the Bhagavān as you have it with me".

This is a false statement that Marīci made, and because of this falsehood, he enlongened his span of worldly existences. However, he initiated Kapila as his own disciple, taught him his 25 'fundamentals', and started a new school. According to the Jaina *Purāṇas,* Kapila took a disciple in Āsurī, and the latter in his turn took a disciple in Sāṅkhya. Kapila and Sāṅkhya together elaborated the 25 fundamentals of their preceptor Marīci, and thus became the first philosophers of the new school. Their philosophy which has come down to us is known as the philosophy of Kapila or of Sāṅkya, though, it must be borne in mind, that the real founder of the school was Marīci.[1]

As Future Tīrthaṅkara

Once Bharata submitted to Bhagavān Ṛṣabhadeva,

"Bhante! Is there any soul present in this assembly who, like your worthy self, will establish the order and consecrate the land of Bharata?"

Ordained the Lord,

"Your son Marīci is the first Tridaṇḍī Parivrājaka, His soul is still impure because of the dirt of *karma.* But gradually it will be purified with the help of white (pure) meditation (*śukla-dhyāna).* (Thereupon, after having passed through several lives), he will be the first Vasudeva named Triprṣṭha at Poṭṭanapur in Bhāratavarṣa in the down phase of the time-

> cycle. Then passing through several more lives, he will be born in western Videha as a son unto King Dhanañjaya and his queen Dhāriṇī when he will be named Priyamitra, and he will be a world-monarch. Thereafter, to close his chapter of worldy glidings, he will become the 24th *Tīrthaṅkara* in this group of 24 (headed by me), and at that time, he will bear the name Mahāvīra. He will (re-)establish the order, on this earth, and will be perfected, enlightened and liberated."

Marīci felt elated—Bharata became exceedingly happy to hear these words of the Lord. He was proud that his son would be the first Vasudeva, a world-monarch and the last *Tīrthaṅkara*. In order to communicate this great news to his son Parivrājaka Marīci, he hurried to him from the proximity of Bhagavān Ṛsabhadeva, and narrated all that he had heard about his future greatness. Marīci's joy too knew no bound. He clapped his hands thrice in joy, sprang up in the sky and praised again and again his own good luck. Shouted he,

> "How great is my line! How noble is my line! My grand-father is the first *Tīrthaṅkara*, my father is the first World-monarch, and I shall be the first Vāsudeva, a world-monarch and the final *Tīrthaṅkara*. All my great ambitions will thus be fulfilled. My line is the best of all."

Because of this ego, Marīci acquired great *karma* that gave him a lowly birth. This is the reason why, though he was marked to be the last *Tīrthaṅkara* Bhagavān Mahāvīra, and he should have been placed in a *Kṣatriya* womb, to start with, he had to spend some time in the (lowly) womb of the *Brāhmaṇa* lady Devānandā.[2]

We get an account of total 27 (past) lives of Mahāvīra of which he hived two before he was born as Marīci, and the rest afterwards. Of the 27, he lived the first life as Nayasāra Karmakāra. In this life, he had offered food to a meritorious monk because of which he acquired right faith. But later, when he lived as a World-monarch as also as a Vasudeva, he had acquired great sins because of which he had been assigned to the hells, as low as the seventh one. In his 25th birth, he propitiated the 20 *nimittas* (list given at the end of this Chapter) which are basic to the attainment of Tīrthaṅkarahood, and the acquired thereby auspicious *karma* to give him the name and line *(nāma-gotra)* of a *Tīrthaṅkara*. He spent his 26th life in the 10th heaven named Pranata, and in his 27th life, he was born to be Śramaṇa Bhagavān Mahāvīra.

TĀPASA SUMEDHĀ

Sumedhā was born in Brāhmin family in the city of Amarāvatī. He lost both his parents in his infancy. Thereupon, be became indifferent to the world, and was initiated as *tāpasa* monk.

Immersed in deep thinking, he had a realisation as follows :

> 'There is suffering in the next life. I must find out the way what would liberate me from rebirth. There must be some such way. As happiness and misery are two counterparts, so there must be a counterpart to this life to end further life. Heat goes with the emergence of cold; so does the fire of attachment, etc., with liberation.'

This thinking gave a further stimulus to his indifference. He built a cottage on the Himālayas and settled there. He spent his time mostly intrance and meditation.

At that time, Dīpāṅkara Buddha, the Leader of mankind, was preaching in the world and served as a becon-light. While on his tours, once he arrived at the great *vihāra* (Buddhist resting place) named Sudarśana in the city of Rammaka. The people of the city welcomed the great teacher with the offerings of incences and wreaths, and paid their homage and obeiscance to him. They attended his sermons, invited him to take food from them on the following day and returned home. On the next day, the Buddha would enter the town to beg. So, the town was being decorated to recieve him. The ditches on the streets, through which water flowed, were filled up with dust. Thereon they spread white sand as bright as silver, and scattered on it fried rice and flowers. Flags of various hues were unfurled, and all important places were decorated with rows of banana trees and filled-up jars. Groups of happy people were strolling all over the city. All that time, Tāpasa Sumedha who had come out of his cottage (on the Himālayas) was flying through the sky on some business. When he saw the decoration of the city, and groups of merry people moving about, he had a desire in his mind to know the reason for all this. So he descended from the sky to the ground and made enquiries when was told by the people, in part, as follows :

> "*Bhante!* Revered Dīpāṅkara who has become a Buddha and is currently preaching the best religion to mankind is at this moment stationed at the great *vihāra* named Sudarśana outside our city. We have invited him to our city, and he is scheduled to visit us to-day. So, we are decorating the route through which the Buddha will pass."

On hearing these words, Sumedhā thought,

> 'What to speak of being born as a Buddha in this world, it is a rare luck even to hear the word (Buddha). I should also join with these people to decorate the path of the Buddha.'

At once, he applied himself to the work. Within a short time Dīpāṅkara Buddha arrived. The bugles were sounded heralding his entry into the city. Men as well as gods shouted joy at his sight, and *mandāra* flowers were showered on him from the sky. Sumedhā untied his matted hairs, spread his bark, saffron robes and (deer) skin on the ground, lay on it and thought.

> 'It will do me the greatest good if Dīpāṅkara Buddha touches my body with his feet.'

From his bed, be beheld the great leader and witnessed in him the lustre of Buddhahood. Thought he,

> 'I can attain liberation by ending all misery, but that is not my objective. Like Dīpāṅkara Buddha, I must attain the Great Enlightenment, and help the people to cross through the worldly ocean by boarding on the ship of religion. Thereafter, I should attain liberation.'

He felt an intense desire within himself to attain Buddhahood. For this, he was even prepared, to sacrifice his life.

The Buddha came to Sumedhā and said,

> "Behold this matted monk. One day, he will become the Buddha. This is the explicit meaning of Buddhahood".

'One day, he will become the Buddha'—when men and gods heard these words, they became immensely happy and said,

> "Monk Sumedhā is the seed of future Buddha, he is the sprout of the future Buddha. The 'progeny of the Jina' (*jina-putra,* which should mean in this context the progeny of the Buddha) moved round Sumedhā (thrice). People said,
> "Holy sir! You will surely become a Buddha. Exert yourself with all your might, move on forward, retrace no backward."

When Sumedhā heard these words, thought he,

> 'The Buddha's words cannot be wrong.'

Now, he concentrated all his efforts for the attainment of Buddhahood. He looked for the path that would entitle him to this great status, and he exhibited great enthusiasm in his search for this. He practised 10 *pāramitās* (list given at the end of the Chapter) which had formerly been practised by the Bodhi-sattvas.

Sumedhā received the Buddhist disciplines from the living Buddha and bowed before him. From now on, Sumedhā started his penances and passed through 550 lives. Thereafter, he was born in what is called Tuṣit-loka (which is stated to be the abode of the Bodhi-sattvas). In this world (of the would-be Buddhas), a thousand years prior to the Great Enlightenment, there arose a din that Sumedhā's success was now a certainty. Having descended from the Tuṣit-loka, he entered as an embryo into the womb of Queen Māyādevī, and on the arrival of the right moment, he was born as the next Buddha.[3]

There are many items of researchers' interest in the two accounts given above, such as the glidings of the two, their life-span, etc., Twenty *nimittas* have been considered a must for the attainment of Tīrthaṅkarahood, as 10 *pāramitās* are a must for the attainment of Buddhahood. It is interesting that both the lists have many similar items. The lists are as follows :

***20 Nimittas*[4]**

1. Devotedness to the *Arihantas* (Worthy Onces).
2. Devotedness to the *Siddhas* (Perfected Souls).
3. Devotedness to the Teachings (*pravacana*).
4. Obedience to the Preceptor.
5. Obedience to Senior Monks (*sthaviras*).
6. Obedience to Canonists (scholars).
7. Obedience to the Austere Monks.
8. Perpetual Activity of Knowledge.
9. Pure Right Vision (*samyak darśana*).
10. Humility/Discipline (*vinaya*).
11. Practise of six essentials as per prescription (*e.g.*, practice of equanimity, eulogy of 24 *Tīrthaṅkaras*, obeisance, confession, suspension of bodily acticivity, and renunciation).
12. Unfailing pursuit of celibacy (*brahmacarya*).
13. Meditation (*dhyāna*).
14. Penances (*tapaḥ*).
15. Offerings to the Apt Ones (*pātra-dāna*).
16. Service to the distressed or ill monks (*vaiyavṛtya*).
17. Tranquilizing the Perturbed Monks.
18. Unprecedented Practice of Knowledge.
19. Devotion to Canons.
20. Propagation of Spiritual Discipline (*pravacana-pravavana*).

***10 Pāramitās*[5]**

1. Offerings (*dāna*)
2. Discipline (*śīla*)
3. Detachment (*naiṣkramya*)
4. Wisdom (*prajñā*)
5. Exertion (*vīrya*)
6. Forgiveness (*kṣānti*)
7. Truth (*satya*)
8. Firmness (*adhiṣṭhāna*)
9. Compassion (*maitrī*)
10. Equanimity (*upekṣā*)

While there is much similarity between the 20 *nimittas* (of the Jainas) and the 10 *pāramitās* (of the Buddhists), there is, however, a basic difference between the two traditions. The (would-be) Buddha is determined for the attainment of Buddhahood, and all the practices are directed to the same end. In contrast, in the Jaina tradition, all efforts (even by an would-be *Tīrthaṅkara*) are to be concentrated on attaining supreme indifference (*vītarāga*) (what the Buddhists have called the Arhathood). Tīrthaṅkarahood is indeed a glorious state, but it cannot be coveted; it comes of itself on the accumulation of merit. To direct prescribed penances to the attainment of a transcient goal is, in Jaina terminology, a *nidāna*,[6] the very reverse of true devotion. To practise penances with a material end is a sacrilege.[7] In the Buddhist tradition, Buddhahood had been considered to be a coveted thing, because herein personal liberation is secondary, the primary mission of the Buddha being the liberation of the world. The implication is that the Jainas have viewed Tīrthaṅkarahood as a state, but the Buddhists have viewed Buddhahood as a mission for doing good to others. This relative difference has been the fundamental cause of difference between the two traditions. (For the rest), doing good to others is not wholly undesired in Jainism, nor is the desire for status glorified in Buddhism. The difference thus turns out to be one of presentation.

REFERENCES

1. Based on *Triṣaṣṭi-śalākā-puruṣa-caritraṃ*, Parva 1, Sarga 6, Ślokas 1′-52; *Ādi-purāṇa*, Parva 18; and *Āvaśyaka Sūtra Niryukti, Malayagiri Vṛtti*, pp. 232.2 to 234.1.
2. *Triṣaṣṭi-śalākā-puruṣa-caritraṃ*, Parva. 1, Sarga 6, Ślokas 370-90. Also *Āvaśyaka Sūtra* as above, 244 to 245.1.
3. *Jātaka-aṭṭhakathā*, Dūre Nidāna, pp. 2 to 36.
4. *Cf. Nāyādhammakahāo*, Adhyayana 8, Sūtra 70, imehi ya ṇaṁ vīsāehi ya kāraṇehimāseviyabahulī kaehiṁ titthayara-nāma-goyaṁ kammaṁ nivattiṁsu taṁ jahā :

arahanta siddha pavayaṇa guru thera, bahussue tabassīsuṁ vacchallayā ya tesiṁ abhīkṣṇ-ṇāṇovayoge ya 1
daṁsana viṇaya ābassae ya sīlabbae ṇiraiyāraṁ
khanalava tava cciyāe veyavacce samāhī ya 2
apubba-ṇāṇa-gahaṇe suyabhattī pavayaṇe pabhāvaṇayā
e-e-hiṁ kāraṇehiṁ titthayarattaṁ lahai jīyo 3

5. *Bauddha Dharma Darśana*, pp. 181-182; Also *Jātak*, Vol. I, pp. 110-113.
6. *Dassasūyakkhandha*, Nidāna Prakaraṇa.
7. *Cf. Dasāveāliyaṁ*, Adhyayana 9, Uddeśaka 4 :
caubbihā khalu tavasamāhi bhavai taṁ jahā : no ihalogaṭṭhayāe tavamihiṭṭhejjā no paralogaṭṭhayāe tavamihiṭṭhejjā no kitti-vaṇṇa-saddasilogaṭṭhayāe tavamahiṭṭhejjā nannattha nijjaraṭṭhāe tavamahiṭṭhejjā.

6

BIRTH AND INITIATION

The original version of the life-story of Bhagavān Mahāvīra is contained in the two Jaina *Āgamas*, the *Āyāraṅga* and the *Kappa.* This version has been further elaborated in the commentaries, *cūrṇies, niryukties* and poetical works. The earlier lives of Bhagavān Buddha are mainly contained in the *Jātakas.* Of course, in their entirety, the *Āgamas* and the *Tripiṭakas* are virtually the life-stories of these two great men, but in the aforesaid texts, (*i.e.*, the *Āyaraṅga* and the *Kappa,* and the *Jātaka*) the two life-stories have been given in biographical forms. There are indeed similarities as well as differences between the two descriptions regarding the birth and initiation of these two great men, and these similarities and differences are especially important for understanding the difference between the two cults, viz., Jainism and Buddhism. These apart, the two accounts throw ample light on popular usages, social customs and religious traditions of that age.

Both Mahāvīra and Buddha think towards the end of their previous birth about their next live; but there is difference in the thinking of the two. For, whereas Mahāvīra thinks where he is going to be born, the Buddha thinks where he should be born.

About the time of his birth, the Buddha thought,

> 'I should be born at the time when the span of human life is more than a hundred years but less than 1,00,000 years. That time is good for *nirvāṇa.*'

In the Jaina tradition too, that period has been considered most propitious for the birth of a *Tīrthaṅkara* when the span of human life is of medium size.

The Jambūdvīpa of Mahāvīra is stated to be 1,00,000 *yojanas,* but that of the Buddha (only) 10,000 *yojanas.* Mahāvīra was born at Uttara-kṣatriya-Kundapura in South India in Jambūdvīpa, and the Buddha was born at Kapilavastu in the central part of Jambūdvīpa. The two places were in closest proximity; only their names were different.

When Mahāvīra came in the *Brāhmaṇa* line in the womb of Devānandā, Indra thought as follows :

> 'The Arahantas have never been born outside the *Kṣatriya* line, among the *Brāhmaṇas, Vaiśyas* or *Śūdras*, nor will they be so born. So, I should remove him from the womb of Devānandā and place him in the womb of the *Kṣatriya* woman Triśalā.[1]

At the command of the Indra, the god named Harinaigameśī performed the job. (In the Buddhist tradition), the Buddha thought himself,

> 'A Buddha is born as a *Brāhmaṇa* or *Kṣatriya*, but never as a *Vaiśya* or a *Śūdra*. At this moment, the *Kṣatriyas* are the superior of the two; so I should be born as a *Kṣatriya*.'

Thus according to the Indra, a *Tīrthaṅkara* could be born only in the *Kṣatriya* line, but according to the Buddha, a Buddha could be born either in the *Kṣatriya* line or in the *Brāhmaṇa* line.

At the time of her conception, Mahāvīra's mother dreamt 14 dreams, such as, a lion, an elephant, an ox, and so on; but the Buddha's mother dreamt only a single dream. In both the cases, the next morning, the dream-interpreters were called in. For Mahāvīra, they predicted that he would either be a *Cakravartī* or a *Tīrthaṅkara;* in the case of the Buddha, they predicted that he would either be a *Cakravartī* or a Buddha.

The occasion of the birth in both the cases in commemorated by the association of gods. The descriptions in both the traditions are hyperbolic; (but compared to the Jaina tradition), the description in the *Jātaka* in more elaborated and exaggerated. Both Mahāvīra[2] and the Buddha were free from dirt as they emerged from the wombs of their respective mothers.

Suddhodana (Gautama Buddha's father) desired to place the child at the feet of a holy man named Kāladevala; but before he could do so, the Buddha's feet touched the matted hairs of the monk. For, the Buddha is supposed not to bow before anyone. We read of no comparable incident in the life of Mahāvīra; but the *Tīrthaṅkaras* too are governed by a similar rule, *viz.*, that they bow before none.[3]

Mahāvīra as a child was taken care of by five trained nurses. They had different assignments like cleaning the boy, dressing him, feeding him, carrying him on the lap, etc. The Buddha as a child was taken care of by dirt-free nurses.

Neither Mahāvīra nor the Buddha had formal schooling in crafts, grammar, etc. Mahāvīra came to the school for a day when he displayed his profound enlightenment by solving the most difficult questions on grammar put to him by no less a person than the Indra. In the case of the Buddha, we have it that one day, he demonstrated his craftmanship in an assembly of technicians.

Mahāvīra started his married life on maturity (this is not accepted by the

Digambaras, as already stated); whereas the Buddha did the same when he was sixteen. The *Jātaka* narrates his affluence by stating of his three Palaces, one being his winter resort, another his summer resort , and the third one his resort during the rainy season. In the Jaina tradition, Mahāvīra's palaces have been described as 'wide and vast' (*vistīrṇa* and *vipula).*[4] We have it from other sources that in those days, the affluent people had several mansions which they used during different seasons, and as the seasons changed, they moved from one mansion to the other.[5]

For the Buddha's enjoyment, there is mention of 44,000 dancing girls.

When the time for his initiation and come, the *Lokāntika* gods came to Mahāvīra and reminded him of his great mission; in the case of the Buddha, this purpose is served by the sight of a old man, an ailing man, a corpse and a monk. On the attainment of Enlightenment (*Bodhi*) by the Buddha, Sahampati Brahmā arrived and requested him to introduce the wheel of Religion (*dharma-cakra*) for the good of the world.[6] Before his initiation, Mahāvīra gave in alms enormous treasures for a full year; but in the life of the Buddha, we do not have any mention of an analogous event.

As the Buddha moved out of the city precincts (on his way to courting monkhood), Māra came to him and said,

> "On the seventh day from to-day, a Wheel of Paramontcy (*cakra-ratna*) will be born; so renounce not your home."

In the Jaina tradition, too, the birth of a Wheel of Paramontcy is conceived in the case of a would be world-monarch.[7]

The occasion of Mahāvīra's initiation was celebrated by the gods headed by the Indra and by men headed by Nandīvardhana. They decorated him with ornaments and placed him on palanquin, took out a procession, till they saw through the whole process of initiation. In the case of the Buddha during the night when the Buddha left his home, at the command of the Indra, gods came after the Buddha had finished his bath, and remaining invisible from the rest of the people who had assembled, they dressed and decorated him.

Placed side by side, it should appear that the process of initiation as described in the *Āgamas* has been followed in (describing the initiation of the Buddha in) the *Jātaka.* In the Buddha's eventful march for initiation, the association of the gods is not difficult to add. As the Buddha rode on his horse-back, it is stated, 60,000 gods moved with him from all directions with torches in their hands, without disturbing the silent environment of the night.

In the Jaina tradition, the throne of the Indra is shaken on the occasion of the birth, initiation and other special events in the life of a *Tīrthaṅkara;* but in the Buddhist tradition, it becomes hot on such occasions.

At the time of his initiation, Mahāvīra uprooted five handfuls of hairs from his head; the Buddha cut his long hairs with a sword. Mahāvīra's hairs were received by the Indra on a saucer made from *vajra-ratna* and were immersed in the Ocean of Milk. The Buddha, in contrast, hurled his hairs in the sky where, at a height of a *yojana,* they became fixed. Indra collected them from the sky in a pot made from gems and gave them the shape of a *caitya* named Cūḍāmaṇi in the Trayas-triṁśaloka.

It has been stated about Mahāvīra that his hairs, beard, pore-hairs and nails were fixed and did not grow *(avaṭṭhie keśmaṁṣu romaṇahe).*[8] From the time of his initiation, the Buddha is also stated to have his hairs fixed. This has been considered to be a miracle in both the traditions.[9] Both are stated to have curly hairs.[10]

The name of the horse on which the Buddha rode (while renouncing his home) was Kanthaka. From his neck upto the tall, the horse was =18 cubits in length.

The Buddha is said to have the physical strength equal to that of 1000,00,00,000 elephants. In the Jaina tradition, a *Cakravartī* has the strength of 40,00,000 *aṣṭapadas* (an animal, believed to be extinct now, which was stronger than the lion), and a *Tīrthaṅkara* has infinite strength. Mahāvīra rid the Indra and other gods of doubt about himself by shaking Mount Meru by the touch of the first finger of his leg just at his birth. Though no such miracle is recorded about the Buddha, still, by dint of his great yogic powers, he is stated to have performed many a miracle.

BHAGAVĀN MAHĀVĪRA

Of the current down-phase of the time-cycle, the double-bracing period (*suṣama-suṣama*) had gone out (long ago); even the bracing phase (*suṣama)* had ended; and so did the bracing-non-bracing phase (*suṣama-duṣama*); and a good part of the non-bracing-bracing phase *(duṣama-suṣama)* was also out. Of the last mentioned phase, only 75 years and 8 months still remained. At this time, in the fourth month of the summer season, during the eighth fort-night, on the sixth day of the bright half of the month of *Āṣāḍha,* when the star Hastottara was in conjunction with the moon, Bhagavān Mahāvīra descended from the great *vimāna* named Puṇḍarīka in the tenth heaven named Prāṇata on completion of his celestial life-span of 20 *sāgaropamās.*

In the southern part of Jambūdvīpa, in Bhāratavarṣa, at a village named Dakṣiṇa-Brāhmaṇa-Kuṇḍapura, Mahāvīra descended to enter into the womb of the *Brāhmaṇa* women Devānandā of the Jālandhara line, the wife of one Ṛṣabhadatta of the Koḍāla line. For a moment, all the living beings were liberated from their painful experiences. The three worlds witnessed joy and light.

At that time, Bhagavān Mahāvīra was the master of three types of knowledge, *mati, śruta* and *avadhi.* He realised that it was time for him to descend from celestial life. Having descended, the realised that he was safely lodged in the womb of the *Brāhmaṇa* woman Devānandā. But what he did not know was his descent because it was completed within a very short time.[11]

When a god has only six months of his life left in heaven, his wreath dries up, the *kalpa* tree shakes. His grace becomes dim, his beauty fades away, his clothes lose their brightness, he looks pale, his sleep is gone, his desires end, his body loses its vigour, his eyes lose their vision, he shivers and his entire time is spent in distressing thoughts. But Mahāvīra was an exception. He did not undergo these 12 experience.

At the time of Mahāvīra's entry into the womb, Devānandā, half asleep and half awake, dreamt 14 dreams. At once, she got up in a happy mood and narrated her dreams to Ṛsabhadatta. Ṛsabhadatta was also very happy to hear about them. Said he.

> "Lucky woman! These dreams are very important; they are good, blissful and worthy; they give health and well-being. As a result of these dreams, you will get wealth, affluence, son and happiness. You will give birth to an extraordinary boy on the expiry of 9 months and 7 days. The hands and feet of that boy will be very tender, his organs of senses pleasant and duly developed, and his body beautiful and well-proportioned in every limb. He will be rich in signs, marks and merits. He will be placid like the moon, beloved of all, beautiful and pleasant."

(Continued the *Brāhamaṇa:)*

On completion of his childhood, when he will step into his youth, his knowledge will be widely extended. He will be the master of the *Ṛkveda*, the *Sāmaveda,* the *Yajurveda* and the *Atharvaveda,* History and Lexography, with all their complementary texts. He will expound their deepest mysteries. He will revive the lost meanings of the Vedas. He will be thorough in the six *Āṅgas* and in *Ṣaṣṭī-tantra* (of Kapila).. He will be an expert in Mathematics, Astronomy, Grammar, Brahmanical lores, the holy books of the Parivrājaka order, etc., etc.

Transfer of the embryo—When, by dint of his clairvoyant knowledge, Indra came to know that Mahāvīra had descended on the earth to be born, and had entered the womb of lowly (*Brāhmaṇa*) woman, he had a sudden thought in his mind,

'The (would-be) *Tīrthaṅkaras, Cakravartīs, Baladevas, Vāsudevas* to not descend in a caste which is *Śūdra,* lowly, insignificant, having few kinsmen, poor, miserly, begging, or Brāhmanical. They descend in such royal families as the Jñātṛ, the Ikṣvāku, the Hari or some other *Kṣatriya* line.[12]

At once, he looked for the god Harinaigameṣī and commissioned him to transfer the embryo. It was the midnight of the 13th day in the dark half of *Āśvina*. The star *Uttarā-phālguṇī* was in conjunction with moon. Mahāvīra had already spent 82 day-nights in the womb of Devānandā. On the 83rd day, at mid-night, Harinaigameṣī transferred the embryo from the womb of Devānandā and placed it in the womb the *Kṣatriya* woman Triśalā. Mahāvīra was already equipped with three types of knowledge, and so he knew of it before the transfer and also after the transfer, and he did know when he was being transferred.[13]

In the latter half on the night, Triśalā dreamt the following objects in fourteen dreams : a lion, an elephant, an ox, Goddess Lakṣmī, a pair of wreaths, the moon, the sun, a pitcher, a lotus tank, ocean of milk, a celestial *vimāna,* a heap of jewels and smokeless fire. She woke up, and in a happy frame of mind, she came to King Siddhārtha and narrated her dreams. On hearing all about them, the king was also very much delighted. The kind addressed the following words of Queen Triśalā :

> "You have dreamt very worthy dreams, as a result of these, we will have wealth, affluence, son and happiness; and the kingdom also will prosper. Some great soul is coming to us."

The queen was delighted to hear this precise explanation in the outcome of her great dreams from King Siddhārtha. From the king's bed-room, whe came back to her own. In order to retain in tact the good effects of the dreams, she spent the rest of the night in practising spiritual vigil.

In the morning, King Siddhārtha got up. He was in very high spirit. Having finished his morning duties, he repaired to the gymnasium. There he practised the use of arms, jumping, wrestling, etc., various sitting and respiratory postures (*āsanas*). To get his fatigue removed, he had his body massaged with *śatapāka* and *sahasrapāka* oils. Then he entered into his bath room and finished his bath. After bath, he had sandal paste besmeared on his body, put on clothes and ornaments, and with the decorations of the highest office, he came to the assembly hall. Beside the king's throne, behind a tapestry, was placed an excellent chair for Queen Triśalā which was bedecked with jewels. Orders were issued to invite to the assembly all the leading dream-interpreters of the city.

Dreams interpreted—On receiving the invitation, the dream-interpretors took their bath, worshipped gods, wore *tilaka* mark on the forehead, and performed the propitiatory rights with curd, *dūrvā* grass and rice to drive away evils. Then passing through the heart of the city of *Kṣatriya*-Kuṇḍapura, they arrived at the palace entrance. There they discussed among themselves and chose a leader. Then they entered into the assembly and bowed before the king.

The king received them with due honour, explained to them the purpose for which they had been brought in and asked them about the outcome of the dreams.

After a threadbare consideration and scrutiny of the dreams, the interpreters submitted :

> "Oh King! In the text-books on Dreams, there are on record 42 types of dreams which yield ordinary results, and 30 types of dreams which yield good results. In all there are 72 types of dreams. Of the latter 30 the mothers of the would-be *Tīrthaṅkaras* and *Cakravartīs* dream 14, those of the *Vāsudevas* 7 those of the *Baladevas* 4 and those of the *Māṇḍalikas* only one."
>
> The experts continued :
>
> "Queen Triśalā has dreamt 14 good dreams and so it is a certainity that you will have wealth, affluence, son and happiness. On the expiry of 9 months and 7 day-nights, the queen will give birth to a son who will be (like) the ensign of the family the light of the family, the crown of the family, the *tilaka*-mark of the family. He will ennoble your family line, and widen its achievements, prosperity and fame. He will have his organs of senses in right proportion, with his limbs tender and graceful. He will have good marks and signs on his body, and will be pleasant-looking and gentle.
>
> "Even at the expiry of his childhood the boy will be mature in knowledge. On stepping into his youth, he will be a great philanthrophist and a great hero and thereafter he will either be a *cakravartī* commanding all the four directions, or he will be a *Tīrthaṅkara* who would help living beings in the four existences to terminate their rebirth."

Then the dream-experts analysed each one of the 14 dreams separately and in complete details. The delight of King Siddhārtha and Queen Triśalā increased a hundred-fold. The king offered them ample wealth and gifts, honoured them and bade them good-bye.

Affection for the Mother

While stationed in the womb, once Mahāvīra thought as follows :

> 'If I move, it cause pain to my mother. So, I should not move and cause her trouble.'

> So, he fixed his limbs and not stir. When the embryo in the womb did not stir, this became a source of great anxiety to the mother : 'Has the child been stolen from my womb by some god? Is it dead? Is it dilapidated?'

These and similar other mental worries made Queen Triśalā extremely restless. She felt very much depressed and began to weep. Here distress was so heavy that she fell down in a swoon. Her maids rushed forth to help her and restore her to her senses. They made enquiries about the safety of the embryo. The elderly ladies performed various expitiatory and propitiatory rites, and the astrologers were called in to throw light on various queries. When King Siddhārtha heard the news, he also felt a great anxiety. The ministers did not know what to do in the situation. There was a shadow of unknown apprehension all over the palace.

By dint of his *avadhi* knowledge, Mahāvīra came to know all this. Thought he,

> 'It withheld the movement of my limbs to save pain to my mother, but the outcome has been far from good.'

So, to relieve his mother of unnecessary anxiety, he began to move. This was an indication to the queen that the child was in good health, and this gave her a great delight. She regretted for her earlier apprehensions. She was now fully convinced that neither the child had been stolen, nor was it lost or dilapidated. So, she thought that henceforth, she should entertain no such evil ideas in her mind. The queen's happiness restored the palace to its own cheerfulness.

The above event took place about the time when Mahāvīra had already lived in the womb for six months and a half. This cast a profound impact on his mind. Thought he :

> 'How very deep will be the sorrow of my living parents, if I renounce the world during their life-time!'

In consideration of this distress to his parents, he made the following decision while he was still in the womb :

> 'I shall not renouce the world so long as my parents, live.'

On the realisation that the child in the womb was in perfect order, Queen Triśalā took her bath, said prayers and performed her propitiatory rites. Then she put on her dress and ornaments. For the good of her child, she gave up food which was too hot (to touch) or too cold, too sour, too pungent, too hot (to taste), too oiled or too rough. She took care to protect herself from too much anxiety, too much grief, too much meanness, too much joy, too much fear and too much terror.

Keeping in view the suggestion of the elderly and experienced ladies in the household, she walked slowly and infrequently, indulged not in anger or loud laughter, ate only wholesome food, avoided garments that were tight at the waist, kept aside from uneven and rough grounds, and was especially careful, and never sat under the bare sky.

Ever since Mahāvīra came into the household of King Siddhārtha, his wealth and grains increased. At the order of Śakra, the *Indra* of the gods, the valet-gods (Jrmbhakas) of *Vaiśravaṇa,* the keeper of the celestial treasures, transferred to King Siddhārtha's household all sorts of treasures that were buried under ground, treasures of which there was no owner or no protector, even treasures whose existence was not known to anyone, and treasures from villages, towns, forests, highways, tanks, holy places parks, vacant chambers, caves and many other resorts. Wealth, grains and vehicles of diverse sorts increased manifold in the kingdom.

Desire of a Pregnent Women

According to the *Kalpalatā* commentary of the *Kalpa Sūtra,* during his pregnancy, Queen Triśalā felt a yearning to put on the ear-rings of the consort of Indra, though (she knew well that) it was an impossible desire. So, she became depressed. Suddenly, the throne of Indra shook, and by dint of his *avadhi* knowledge, he saw the cause of it. To safeguard against this position, he took his principal consort and other nymphs with him, and in a very dangerous valley on an inaccessible mountain, he built a celestial city and took shelter there. When King Siddhārtha came to know this, he came to that valley with his army, and demanded the surrender of the ear-rings. But Indra was not prepared to oblige him. So, there started a war between the two. Although Indra was quite capable to fight, somehow in the present case, he failed to do so for long, and after some time, he took to his heels. King Siddhārtha plundered the nymphs. Thereafter, he snatched the ear-rings from Indra's queen and gave them to Triśalā. The queen wore them, and thus her desires were fulfilled.

At the mid-night of the 13th day of the bright half of *Caitra,* the embryo had completed the stay of 9 months and 7½ day-nights in the womb and was now mature for birth. Mahāvīra was born in good health. At the time of his birth (as it happens in the case of the gods), he was perfectly clean, and had no coat of blood and other dirts. During that night, all the seven stars were high up in the sky and the stars *Uttarā-phālguṇī* was in conjunction with the moon. The Universe was lit with a wonderful light. Heavenly drums sounded in the sky.

For a while, even the infernal beings enjoyed a bracing respiration. All the directions were placid pure. All omens forecast victory and success. Wind was blowing gently and favourably. The clouds sent a delightful shower. The landscape was green with corn. The whole country was full of joy.

Celebrations at Birth

At the time of Mahāvīra's birth, 56 divine damseld (*dik-kumāris*) came and served as midwives. At the *Saudharma-kalpa,* the throne of Indra was shaken. By dint of his *avadhi* knowledge, he realised that the final *Tīrthaṅkara* Mahāvīra had been born. Being highly delighted at this realisation, he set out for *Kṣatriya*-Kuṇḍapura in the company of all members of his family. He had with him four species of gods *viz.,* the *Bhavanapatis,* the *Vāṇavyantaras,* the *Jyotiṣkas* and the *Vaimanikas* and many other Indras. All the gods were anxious to be the first to reach King Siddhārtha's palace. Indra moved round Mahāvīra and Triśalā thrice and bowed before them. Thereafter, Indra made a dummy of Mahāvīra and placed it beside the mother. The mother was then hypnotised to sleep and real Mahāvīra was carried to the summit of Mount Meru There all the gods stood in readiness to pour water on him brought from eight sources 8064 pitcher Indra, the Lord of Saudharma-kalpa became alarmed at the thought of the heavy shower of water that the just-born baby would be required to undergo.[14]

By dint of his *avadhi* knowledge. Mahāvira came to know of Indra's apprehension. To remove this, he gave a little pressure on Mount Meru with his left leg and the mountain began to shake. To ascertain the cause of this sudden quake, Indra applied his own knowledge, and he was convinced of the infinite power of Mahāvīra. At once, he begged to be forgiven (for his unnecessary apprehension). Then Indra and other gods bathed him with water, chanted prayers before him, and placed him again by the side of his mother, Queen Triśalā.

At day-break the good news (about the birth of a son to him) was conveyed by the slave-girl Priyamvadā to King Siddhārtha. The king became very much delighted, and rewarded her by giving to her all the ornaments that he had on his body, except the crown. Besides he restored her freedom for the rest of her life. He sent for the jailors, and to mark the special occasion, he ordered them to set free the convicts The debtors were relieved of their debts. In the markets people who had no purchasing power, were given leave to purchase whatever they needed against payment assured from the Treasury. Weights and measures for all things were increased. The city was cleaned everywhere. Scented water was sprinkled at all places. Temples and highways were decorated. At the market place and elsewhere, temporary seats were erected for the members of the public to sit comfortably and watch the celebrations. The walls were white-washed and decorated with paintings in traditional style. Invitations were sent to actors, dancers, rope-players, wrestlers, boxers, jesters, jumpers, swimmers, readers, acrobats, musicians and instrument players of all sorts, and they were required to display their skill in squares, at places where three roads meet, where four roads meet, and at all other public places. Accordingly, all the aforesaid artists turned up and displayed their skill.

King Siddhārtha came to his gymnasium and took exercise as usual. Then he took his bath, put on his royal robes and ornaments and came to the assembly hall. He ordered the celebration of *sthiti-patita* (a celebration at child birth) for 10 days with pomp and grandeur. On the third day, Mahāvīra was exposed to the moon and the sun. On the sixth day, there was a complete vigil at night and people of the royal household did not sleep during that night. The naming ceremony took place on the twelfth day. On that day, King Siddhārtha invited all his friends, relatives, kinsmen, officers and slaves and entertained them at a great banquet, and give them clothes and ornaments. Addressing his guests, the royal host said :

> "Ever since the boy has come into the family, we are passing through a period of unusual growth of wealth, grains, treasures, granaries, man-power, kinsmen and territory. So, I suggest that he may be named Vardhamāna (ever-growing)."

The proposal was unanimously approved. Thus, Mahāvīra was named Vardhamāna (by his parents). Later, after he had entered into a hard life of penances, and remained unshaken in the midst of unbearable, terrific and dreadful hardships, the gods named him Mahāvīra (the great hero) by which name he bacame famous.

Childhood

Mahāvīra's childhood was spent like that of any other prince in the midst on plenty and pleasures. He had five trained maidst to look after him. They had their duties carefully assigned, and they performed them carefully at proper hour. The duties included feeding, washing, dressing, playing and carrying on the lap, Mahāvīra was not fond of games and plays. But still he played sometimes in the palace garden in the company of his peers. Once when he was less than 8 years of age, he was playing a game called saṁkuli. In this game, the target was a tree at which all the boys ran. On reaching the tree, they were required to climb up and get down. One who completed the process in the minimum time was declared to be the most successful. Other participants would then carry him on their shoulders to the place wherefrom the race had started.

Once pointing to Mahāvīra who was at play, Śakra, the Indra of the gods, said in the assembly of gods,

> "Though a child, Mahāvīra is very powerful and brave. None, not even an Indra, a god a demon, can defeat him."

One of the gods, who did not believe in these words of the Indra thought at once of holding a test of the child and arrived at the place where Mahāvīra was at play with his friends. The god turned himself into a dreadful snake, coiled round the trunk of a banyan tree and began to hiss. Mahāvīra was at that time climbed on the same tree. When the boys saw the snake, they were terrified and ran away, but Mahāvīra sat perfectly unconcerned. With is right hand, he caught the snake and placed it aside.

The boys met again started a fresh game called *tiṇḍusaka.* In this game also, a tree was chosen as target, but the boys were paired, and both were required to run at the same target. Of the two, he who touched the target first was declared successful, and then he would enjoy a ride on the defeated partner to the place wherefrom the race had started. The aforesaid god changed himself into a boy and got mixed into the group. He managed to pair himself with Mahāvīra, but was defeated by the latter. As per the rule of the game, Mahāvīra rode on the boy's back and was on his way to the place wherefrom he had started. May be to terrorise him or hide him from others, the god enlongened his body to the length of seven palms and looked severely dreadful. All the boys became alarmed. Some began to shout and others began to cry bitterly; but Mahāvīra remained free from fear. He measured the extent of his wickedness and gave him a severe blow on the head and another on the back. The blows were too powerful for the god to bear, and be began to sink into the ground. Quickly he changed his form and fell at Mahāvīra's feet. Said he,

> "Indra spoke highly about your courage and bravery, but, I think, you surpass all description."

The god went back to his heavenly abode. After the god had departed, Indra came himself and congratulated Mahāvīra for his masterly demonstration of courage.

Physical strength

About Mahāvīra's physical strength; the widely held belief is as follows :

In strength,
12 soliders are equal to 1 ox;
10 oxen are equal to 1 horse;
12 horses are equal to 1 buffalo;
15 buffaloes are equal to 1 elephant;
500 elephants are equal to a lion with mane;
2000 maned lions are equal to 1 *aṣṭapada;*

1,00,000 *aṣṭapadas* are equal to 1 *Baladeva;*
2 *Baladevas* are equal to 1 *Vāsudeva;*
2 *Vāsudevas* are equal to 1 *Cakravartī;*
1,00,000 *Cakravartīs* are equal to 1 Indra of the Nāgakumāra gods;
An infinite number of Indras is equal to the smallest finger of the *Tīrthaṅkara.*

Education

When Mahāvīra had crossed his eighth year, his parents sent him to school. The teacher was given a cocoanut as his fee and costly gifts of cloths and ornaments. Sweets were distributed among the students, and they were given things necessary for scholars. The teacher arranged a separate seat for the prince.

Indra was surprised at his arrangement made by King Siddhārtha and Queen Triśalā for the education of their boy. For, it was very much unbecoming to send one endowed with three types of knowledge to a school to be taught by an ordinary mortal. So, Indra came there at once in the guise of a *Brāhmaṇa.* He put some typical questions on grammar to Mahāvīra in the presence of the teacher and senior students; but to the surprise of everybody, Mahāvīra took no time to provide the correct answers. The teacher and the students became very much surprised. Some of the answers even the teacher himself did not know and they got enlightenment from the answers given by Mahāvīra. After this demonstration, Indra said to the teacher.

"Sir! This is an exceptionally gifted boy. He is the Master of all arts."

On the basis of Mahāvīra's answers to his queries, Indra produced a new grammar to be called *Indra's Grammar.*

Marriage

When Mahāvīra stepped into his youth, his parents desired that he should marry and take a wife. Mahāvīra had no desire to lead a married life, but at the same time, he did not wish to disappoint his dear parents. So he married Yaśodā, the daughter of a *Mahāsāmanta*[15] from Vasantpura by his wife Padmāvatī.[16]

In the various *Āgamas,* we have an elaborate record about the members of his family. Supārśva was the name of his uncle, and Nandīvardhana that of his elder brother. His elder sister was Sudarśanā, and his daughter was Priyadarśanā who was married with Jamālī. The name of his grand-daughter (his daughter's daughter) was Śeṣavatī or Yaśasvatī.

From his very birth, Mahāvīra was indifferent to worldly life. His body was strong and highly graceful. All objects of pleasure were readily available to him, but he had no fascination for them. Both his parents were the followers of Pārśva, and were very pious souls. They lived a long life as devoted followers, and before their final exit, they devoted themselves to the practise of the vows like *ahiṁsā,* etc., discussed, decried and denounced their sins, performed *pratikramaṇa,* etc., and at last courted fast unto death. Thus closing their earthly chapter, they were born in *Acyutakalpa.*

By the time Mahāvīra was 28, he had lost both his parents, and so he desired to fulfill the resolve he had made earlier. He placed before his elder brother a proposal about his own renunciation and initiation. Nandīvardhana was deep-hurt to hear such untimely request. The parents had just died, and Nandīvardhana was not mentally prepared to let his brother go at this time. So, at the pressing request of his elder brother, he agreed to defer his exit by two years. Meanwhile, rumour had spread far and wide that as Mahāvīra's mother had dreamt 14 dreams, he was now sure to become a world-monarch. So, the leading kings of that period sent their sons, Śreṇika, Caṇḍa Pradyotana and many others to serve under him.[17] But Mahāvīra was not in the least interested to be a world-monarch. For one who was ear-marked to be a *Tīrthaṅkara,* the position of a world-monarch was too insignificant. Although Mahāvīra was still living at the palace, he was virtually living like a monk, almost renounced in everything. He did not drink raw water, did not take food at night and remained strictly celibate. He slept on the ground, and to quench the fire of passions, he was always immersed in deep concentration on Self. He spent a year like this. After this, he commenced his final year in the household and during the whole of this year, he gave alms (*varṣī-dāna).* He gave out 1,08,00,000 gold coins per day, so that during the year, he gave 3,88,80,00,000 gold coins in all.

Great Renunciation

At the age of 30, Mahāvīra completed his resolve. As per their convention, they came to Mahāvīra and submitted as follows :

Jai jai khattiya vara vasabha
bujjhahi bhayavaṁ
savva jagajjīva hiyaṁ arahaṁ
titthaṁ pavvattehi.

(Oh Bull among the noblest *Kṣatriyas!* Victory be to thee. Now, it is for thee to get initiated and organise the holy order for the good of all living beings on earth).

Mahāvīra now placed his firm resolve regarding his own initiation before his elder brother Nandīvardhana, his uncle Supārśva and his other kinsmen. All the kinsmen approved of his resolve.

Nandīvardhana started the celebrations to mark the occasion of the great renunciation. He ordered his men to procure jars made from eight substances (*viz.,* gold, silver, jewels, gold-silver, gold-jewels, silver-jewels, gold-silver-jewels, and simply clay), 1008 of each variety. The order was immediately put into effect. To participate in the celebrations, Śakrendra arrived with his entire family. Then, Nandīvardhana, Śakra and other gods placed Mahāvīra on a golden throne facing the east and poured water on him from the eight varieties of jars (as aforesaid). His body was then dried with a scented saffron cloth, and divine sandal paste was applied to it. Then he was made to wear light but costly robes and ornaments. Having gone through these initial rites, Mahāvīra sat on a spacious and decorated palanquin named Candraprabhā. Śakra himself, men and gods together shouldered the palanquin. Followed by a vast crowd, the procession passed through the heart of Kṣatriya-Kuṇḍapura and stopped beneath an excellent *aśoka* tree in a park named *jñātṛ-khaṇḍa*. There Mahāvīra took off all his clothes and ornaments with his own hands. Then he plucked out five handfuls of hair from his head. Śakra received the hairs on a saucer made from *vajra-ratna* in a kneel-down posture, and immersed them in the ocean of milk. Henceforth, Mahāvīra had only a single divine cloth to cover his body.

On that day (of his initiation), he was on a two-day fast missing six meals in all. His tinge was pure. It was the season of winter. It was the 10th day of the month of *Mārgaśīrṣa.* The day was named as *Suvrata,* the moment as *Vijaya,* and it was the fourth quarter of the night when the star *Uttarā-phālguṇī* was in conjunction with the moon. While bowing to the liberated souls, asceticism in the great assembly of gods and men, he accepted based on equanimity (*sāmayika)* and uttered the following words :

> *Savvaṁ me akaraṇijjaṁ pāvakammaṃ*
> (From this day, I desist from all sinful acts).

There was silence everywhere. That day, the winkless eyes of thousands of gods and men witnessed the superb scene. Just then, the *manaḥ-paryayā* knowledge (knowledge of the fourth type) was attained by him.

Resolve—Immediately after his initiation, Mahāvīra took leave of his friends, relations and kinsmen, and dismissed them. Thereon he resolved as follows :

> 'Henceforth for 12 years, I shall remain indifferent to my body and take no care of it. If during this period any disturbance is created by gods, men, animals or birds, I shall bear it with perfect equanimity.'

Thereafter, he moved out from the *Jñātṛ-khaṇḍa* park. On the same day, just a *muhurta* (48 minutes) before sun-set, he reached a village named Kumāra and stood in meditation.

BHAGAVĀN BUDDHA

When the *Bodhi-sattva* was in the *Tuṣit-loka* there arose a din about (the imminent birth of) the Buddha. Having learnt that on the expiry of a thousand years, the omniscient Buddha would be born in the world, the *Lokapāla* gods stirred all over, addressing their friends, and announcing.,

> 'On the expiry of a thousand years from now, the Buddha will be born in the world.'

Being inspired by the announcement, all the gods residing in the 10,000 *cakravālas* (each *cakravāla* is a world by itself, with a diameter of 12,03450 *yojanas* and circumference of 36,10,350 *yojanas)* assembled. They enquired who the next Buddha was, and having observed his prior marks they came to him and prayed. When the marks had become explicit, all the gods from the *cakravālas,* such as Caturmahārājika, Śakra, Suyāma, Santuṣit, Paranirmita-vaśavartī, and others, met in the same *cakravāla* with the *Mahābrahmas*, and held consultation among themselves. Thereafter they came to the *Bodhi-sattva* in the *Tuṣitloka* and prayed unto him :

> 'Friend! You have acquired the 10 *pāramitas* not to win the seat of Indra, nor to usurp the position of *Māra*, *Brahma* or a *cakravartī*, but you have done so in order to save the world and attain enlightenment for yourself. Friend! We have come to tell thee that it is time for thee to become the Buddha.'

Five great selections

Without committing anything to the gods, the *Bodhi-sattva* analysed threadbare five items, the time (period) of his birth, the isle (continent), the country (region), the parental line and the span of his life. The first item up in his thought was whether the time was propitius or not. When people had a life-span of more than one lakh years, that period was not propitious for the birth of a Buddha; for, with such a long life, people did not have the experience of birth, old age or death, nor are the preaching by the Buddhas (during this period) free from transcience, misery and emphasis on non-self. During this period, people did not pay heed to these preachings, and had no respect for these. Rather, they made adverse comments. (During this phase), people were not conscious about the utility of religion, and unless they were so conscious, the preachings by the Buddha had no impact on them. So, such a period (when people lived more than one lakh years) was not suitable (for the birth of a Buddha).

Likewise, a life-span of less than a hundred years was equally unsuitable.

For, when life-span was very short, it had the dominance of malice and attachment, and in such a situation, all words of wisdom fell as if on deaf ears. Just as a line drawn in water with the help of a stalk dipped in it disappears in no time, so good counsel would get lost (with people who had a very short life). So, this period also was not suitable.

Most favourable was the period when life-span was less than one lakh years and more than a hundred. (He saw that) the current time was like that. So, (he was statisfied that) it was the proper time for the birth of a Buddha. Considering next the isles (continents), he gazed at the four isles with their peninsulas. Aparagoyana, Pūrvavideha and Uttara-kuru,—these three were not suitable for the birth of a Buddha; he could be born only in the Jambūdvīpa. So, he decided in favour of this isle.[18]

Now, (in the Buddhist tradition), the Jambūdvīpa is of the size of 10,000 *yojanas.* So, while thinking of the region (suitable for the Buddha's birth, he looked at the central part (of the Jambūdvīpa). In the eastern part of this region, there was a village named Kajaṅgalā; beyond that, there was a forest of grown-up *sāla* trees. Between the two (*i.e.*, the village and the forest) follwed the river Salalavatī. In the south, there was a village named Setakannika, and in the west, a *Brāhmaṇa* village named Thūṇa. In the north, there was the mountain Uṣīradhvaja which was 300 *yojanas* in length, 250 *yojanas* in breadth and 900 *yojanas* in circumference. It was this region that was most suitable for the birth of a Buddha, a *Pratyeka-Buddha, Agraśrāvaka* (leadingmost disciple), *Mahāśrāvaka,* 80-*Mahāśrāvaka, Cakravartī* rulers, and the most powerful and affluent among the *Kṣatriyas,* the *Brāhmaṇas* and the *Vaiśyas.* The city of Kapilavastu was located in this very region. So, he decided to be born in this city.

Considering next the parental line, he took the following decision about it :

> 'A Buddha is never born among the *Vaiśyas* or the *Śūdras.* He may be born either in the *Brāhmaṇa* or in the *Kṣatriya* caste which are revered by the people. These days, the *Kṣatriya* caste is more respected; so I shall be born in this caste. King Suddhodana would be my father.'

Analysing the nature and behaviour of his (would be) mother, he thought as follows :

> 'The mother of the Buddha is free from restlessness and addictions to drinking, etc. She needs to be one who has been fulfilling the *pāramitās* for a lakh innumerable) *kalpas,* and who, since her birth, practises the *pañcaśilas* without a break. Queen Mahāmāyā fulfils these conditions very admirably. So, let her be my mother.'

But when he considered the remaining part of her life-span, he found that she had only 10 months and 7 days more at her disposal on this earth.

Having considered the five items and made his selections, he made the following announcement :

"This is time for me to be the Buddha."

The gods were delighted to hear this, and then they departed. Then in the company of the other gods of the *Tuṣit-loka*, he entered into the park named Nandana. There (in the park) they enjoyed a promenade in the course of which the gods reminded the *Bodhi-sattva* of the coveted existence that he would attain after he would move out from there (*Tuṣit-loka*), and of the states he would experience because of his pious *karma* in the past.

Thereafter he descended from there to enter into the womb of Queen Mahāmāyā.

Dreams of the Queen

At that time, all the residents of Kapilavastu were celebrating the *Āṣādha* festival. (It started a week before the full moon night). At the commencement of the week, she decorated herself with wreaths and perfumes, and participated in the celebrations. On the seventh (last) day, she got up in the morning and took her bath with scented water. She offered alms amounting to a total of 4 lakhs. Then she took very delicious food. After this she took a vow called *uposatha* and lay on a beautiful couch in a well-decorated room. While asleep, she dreamt four dreams which were as follows :

> 'Four great kings, Lords of the four directions, lifted me with my couch and took me to some part of the Himālayas. They placed me on a slab of stone named *Manaḥśilā* which had a dimension of 60 *yojanas* under an excellent *sāla* tree whose shadow covered an area of 7 *yojanas* and stood aside. Then the consorts of these Lords of the directions took me to a lake named *Anotapta.* They bathed me in order to remove the human dirt from my body, dressed me in divine clothes, sprayed perfumes on me and decorated me with divine flowers. There is a mountain nearby named *Rajat,* where there is a golden palace (*vimāna).* There they lay me on a divine couch with my head towards the east. The *Bodhi-sattva* who had become a beautiful white elephant came to a mountain named *Suvarṇa* which was very adjacent, and from there, he climbed the northern part of *Rajat* mountain. He came there from the north. There was a white lotus in his trunk which looked like a silvery garland. Trumpeting sweetly, he entered into the golden palace. Thrice he moved round the couch, and then he entered into my womb by piercing through the right.'

That day, the star *Uttarāṣāḍhā* was in conjunction with the moon.

Next day, Queen Mahāmāyā narrated her dreams to King Suddhodana. The king sent for 64 leading *Brāhmaṇas.* In order to accord them a befitting reception, the ground was purified with a coast of cowdung, propitiation was done with paddy sheaves and costly cushions were spread. They *Brāhmins* came and sat on those excellent seats. They were served with *khīra* (rice boiled in milk) dressed and sweetened with ghee, honey and sugar which was served on silver saucers, each such saucer being covered with another. Then they were honoured with the gift of clothes and *kapilā* cows. Having thus fulfilled all the wishes of the invited *Brāhmaṇas,* the king drew their attention to the dreams which they were to interpret. Said the *Brāhmaṇas* in reply,

> "Great King! Have no anxiety. The child in the womb of the great queen is a boy, not a girl. You will have a son. If he remains in worldly life, he will be a world-monarch, but if he renounces the world, he will be mightily enlightened to be the Buddha."

When the *Bodhi-sattva* entered into the womb, the 10,000 *cakravālas* were, in a sense, shaken. Thirty-two auspicious prior omens appeared. In the 10,000 *cakravālas*, there was a non-ending lustre, and, as if to witness this lusture, the blind people regained their vision, the deaf their capacity to listen, the dumb to speak, the hunchback to stand erect, and the lame men to walk properly. Living beings who were chained and handcuffed, or who were tied with fetters became free. Fire in the hells was extinguished. The evil spirits had their hunger and thirst quenched. The beasts became free from fear. All the living beings were cured of diseases. All the living beings became sweet-tongued. The horses neighed sweetly, and sweetly did the elephants trumpet. All musical instruments gave out music themselves. The bangles on human hands jingled even without a clash. All the directions became quiet. Pleasant, gentle and cool air began to blow. There were untimely showers of rain. Water rushed out from the earth and flowed. The birds stopped flying in the sky. The rivers stopped flowing. The water of the great oceans became sweet. The entire landscape became covered with lotuses (flowers) of five colours. All the flowers of land and water became blossomed. Flowers on the trunks of the trees, on the branches of the trees and on the creepers became blossomed. Even stone-slabs pierced to emit forth bunches of seven flower each. Hanging flowers blossomed in the sky. There were showers of flowers everywhere. Divine instruments played in the sky. In all the directions, all the 10,000 worlds looked like a bunch of garlands, or like garlands pressed and tied together, or like a decorated garland-seat, or like columns of garlands, or like a full-blown *camara* scented with flowers, incences and perfumes.

From the time the *Bodhi-sattva* entered into the womb, four gods stood ready closeby with swords in hand to keep out any disturbance to the child or the mother. Henceforth, the mother of the *Bodhi-sattva* lost all hankering for the male (husband). She attained great benefit and fame, and she lived in a happy frame free from fatigue. She could see the *Bodhi-sattva* in her womb as one can see a yellow thread passing through an exquisite gem. Now, the rule is that like a diety's abode in a temple, the womb occupied by the *Bodhi-sattva* cannot afterwards be occupied or enjoyed by another being. This is why the mother dies a week after the birth of the child and she is then born in the *Tuṣit-loka*. Unlike other women who give birth to a child in sitting or lying posture after having carried the child in the womb for 10 months more or less, the mother of the *Bodhi-sattva* carries the child in the womb exactly for ten months and then she gives birth to the child in a standing posture. That is typical of the *Bodhi-sattva's* mother.

Birth

When the time of delivering the child came, Queen Mahāmāyā expressed a desire to go to her parental home. The king got the road connecting Kapilavastu with Devadaha repaired, and then had it decorated with banana trees, filled-up jars, ensigns, flags, etc. Then the queen started on a golden palanquin being accompanied by a thousand officers and many valets and maids. Half-way between the two cities, and used by the citizens of the two cities, there was a park named Lumbinī which was full of excellent *sāla* trees. At this season, the trees in the park were in full bloom from top to bottom. Between the twigs and between the blossoms, bees hummed sweetly and birds chirped gently. The entire park of Lumbinī was in full decoration. Queen Mahāmāyā expressed a desire to take a stroll in the park. The attending officers at once carried out her wishes. The entire party moved into the park. When the queen came under an excellent *sāla* tree, she desired to capture a branch. At once the branch bent itself and came within her reach. The queen stretched her hand and caught it. Just then, she had her labour pain. At once an enclosure was put up and all people stood apart. As the queen stood holding the branch in her hand, the child was born. The child was received on a golden net by the four *mahābrahmas* of pure heart who had arrived there in time for this purpose. They placed the child in the presence of the mother and said,

> 'Queen! Be pleased to learn that you have given birth to a very powerful son.'

Like other beings, the *Bodhi-sattva* is not besmeared with dirt and blood at the time of his birth. He comes out from the mother's womb, wholly clean, like a spiritual teacher coming down from a holy seat, or like a man descending from a staircase, with both his hands and feet stretched, like one in a standing posture, glittering like a jewel placed on a clean and pure silk from Kāśī. For the use of the *Bodhi-sattva* and his mother, two flows of water rushed forth from the sky, and they cooled the body of the two.

From the hands of the (four) *mahābrahmas,* the child was received by the four Lords of the directions on soft deer skin which was considered auspicious. From them (the Lords of the directions), men received them on a piece of folded silk. But the child slipped from the hands of men and stood on the earth. He cast his glance towards the east. In that direction, several thousand *cakravālas* had been mixed up as if into a single surface. From there, gods and men worshipped him with incences and flowers, and submitted :

> "Noble sire! In this direction, what to speak of one excelling thee, there is not even one to be equal with thee."

In the same manner, the *Bodhi-sattva* looked in all the directions and sub-directions very thoroughly, and when he found that there was no one to equal him, he walked seven steps towards the north. At this time, the *Mahābrahma* held a white umbrella on his head, the Suyamas fanned him with palm leaf, and other gods held other royal objects *(kakudhabhaṇḍas,* such as sword, umbrella, crown, sandals and fan) in their hands and followed him. At the seventh step, the *Bodhi-sattva* stopped and spoke the following fearless words of the best among men :

> "I am the best in the Universe."

Then he gave a tremendous yell.

Thus immediately on coming out from the mother's womb, the *Bodhi-sattva* spoke in the same manner as he had done (in two of his previous births) when he was born as Mahāuṣadha and Vessantara.[19] As at the time of his entering into the womb, so at the time of his birth, 32 auspicious omens appeared. When the *Bodhi-sattva* was born in the Lumbinī park, Queen Rāhul-mātā, minister Channg (Chandaka), minister Kāla-Udāi, *Hastirāja* (elephant) Ājānīya, *aśvarāja* (horse), Kanthaka, *mahābodhi* tree and four pitchers full of treasure were also born. The pitchers were placed respectively at a distance of one *gavyūti* (*i.e.*, at a distance of 1/4 *yojana), (1/2 yojana),* 3 *gavyūtis* (3/4th of a *yojana)* and one *yojana.* The residents of the two cities together came to Kapilavastu with the *Bodhi-sattva.*

Tāpasa Kāladevala

Hermit Kāla-devala who was the master of eight *samādhis* was held in the highest esteem in the family of Suddhodana. One day, having finished his dinner, the *Tāpasa* went to the *Trayastriṁśa-loka* for the purpose of a change and recreation. To the gods who were having a nice time, he said,

> "Will you kindly tell me what it is that makes you so very gay and playful?"

The gods said,

> "Dear me! Don't you know that? A son has been born unto king Suddhodana. He will sit beneath the Bodhi tree, be enlightened himself and then he will introduce the Wheel of Religion (*dharma-cakra).* We will have unlimited opportunity to see his great activities and hear *dharma* from his lips. This explains why we are so happy and gay."

Without losing any further time, the monk hurriedly descended from heaven and came to Suddhodana's palace. (He was duly received). Having taken his seat, he said to the king,

> "King! A son is born to thee. I want to see him."

The king sent for the boy, and (after he was brought in,) he advanced to place him at the monk's feet, But (before he could do so), the *Bodhi-sattva's* feet touched the matted hair of the monk. In his life as a *Bodhi-sattva,* he bows before none. If, through ignorance, the *Bodhi-sattva's* head were placed at the feet of the monk, then, the latter's head would have broken into seven pieces. But no monk would desire his own annihilation. So, no sooner was the child was ushered in than the monk stood up from his seat and bowed before him. The king witnessed this unusual event and himself bowed before the boy. The monk was in possession of the superhuman power of seeing through a time-sapn of 40 *kalpas* on both sides. he observed very carefully the physical marks of the boy to make sure if he would be a Buddha, and he had now no doubt about it. He saw that this was a wonderful personality. So, he smiled within himself. Next moment, he thought if he would live enough to see him become a Buddha; but after thinking for some time, he saw (to his greatest disappointment) that he would not live to see him (become a Buddha). (He saw that) before the boy would attain Buddha-hood, he would pass away to be born in the *Arūpa-loka* where he would not be enlightened even till the descent of a hundred, nay, a thousand, Buddhas. He began to cry on his own ill-luck. The people present were surprised and asked,

"Holy sire! Just a moment ago, we saw you gay, but so soon you weep. Did you notice any difficulty for prince?"

The monk became serious and firmly asserted,

"He will have no difficulty. He will undoubtedly be a Buddha."
"Then what's it that makes you so restless and unhappy?"

The monk's voice was faltering. He said :

"I myself won't live to see him be a Buddha."

The monk extended his thought to see if any one from his own family line would witness this great event, and he saw that his own nephew (sister's son) Nālaka would do so. At once, he reached the house of his sister and enquired,

"Where's Nālaka?"

The sister said,

"He is at home."
"Call him hither at once,"
said the monk.

When Nālaka came to him, the monk said,

"My dear child.' A son has been born to King Suddhodana. He is the Buddha in the making. Thirty-five years from now, he will become the Buddha, and you are lucky enough to be able to witness it. So, I wish, renounce this very day."

Thought the boy,

"Though I am born in a household which possesses a huge treasure worth 87 crores, my maternal uncle does not desire me to be entangled this source of evil."

So, he ordered to be brought from the market a saffron robe and a clay bowl. He tonsured his hairs and shaved his beard, and put on the monastic robe. Then he said,

"I get initiated in the name of one who is the best among men in the world."

Uttering these words, he paid his obeisances to the *Bodhi-sattva* by folding hands and bowing five limbs. Then he put the earthen bowl in a bag, hung it from his shoulder and became settled in the Himālayas observing the conduct and practices of a *śramaṇa.* To anticipate the story of the later part of his life, after Tathāgata had become a Buddha, he came to him, received instructions from him, and went back to his seat in the Himālayas. There he became an *arhat* and attained the most exquisite state. (After this event), he lived for seven months, and then, he entered into an exclusive *nirvāṇa* in a standing posture.

Question on the Future

On the fifth day, the *Bodhi-sattva* was given a bath from his head down. The naming ceremony was performed. The palace was besmeared with four perfumes. Four types of flowers with stalks were scattered. *Khīra* was boiled in milk without water. The king invited (to dinner) 108 *Brāhmaṇas* who were versed in the three Vedas. The *Brāhmaṇas* included eight scholars, named Rāma, Dvaja, Lakṣmaṇa, Mantrī, Kauṇḍinya, Bhoja, Suyama and Sudatta, who were masters of the six *Aṅgas*. It was these (eight) who chanted the *mantras*. It were these again who had earlier interpreted the dreams. They (eight) were given seats inside the palace, served excellent food and duly honoured and then they were requested to give their considered views about *Bodhi-sattva* :

> "What about the future of this boy, learned *Brāhmaṇas!"*

Of the eight *Brāhmaṇas*, seven raised two fingers each and predicted either of the two futures for the boy :

> "With marks like these, if the boy sticks to the household, he will be a *Cakravartī*; but if he renounces, he will be a Buddha."

Then they tendered a complete accounts of the grandeurs of a *Cakravartī.* But the youngest *Brāhmin*, who belonged to the *Kauṇḍinya* line, raised only one finger to give a definite reading of the boy's future and firmly asserted :

> "I do not see any chance of his remaining in the household. He will acquire profound knowledge and become a Buddha. Most deserving, and holding the final body, he excels any other person. Such a man cannot, by any chance, remain in the household. He will surely become a Buddha."

The King interrupted,

> "Sir! What will be my son's immediate inducement(s) to renunciation?"
> —"Four prior scenes."
> —"What four scenes, pray?"
> —"An old man, a sick man, a corpse and a monk."

The king at once issued a strict order as follows :

> 'None of these four should, by any chance, be allowed to come near the prince. I am not interested in his becoming a Buddha. I wish to see him as overlord of four great isles surrounded by 2000 smaller islands, seated at the head of a vast assembly hall as much as 36 *yojanas* in circumference, and freely flying through the unobstructed firmament.'

At the order of the king, check-posts were set up all around the city at a gap of three *korśas* from one another. The guards were asked, on pain of severe punishment, not to allow anyone of these four inside the city.

On that day, at the place where ceremonies were performed, 80,000 kinsmen and relatives declared.

> 'No matter whether the prince becomes a Buddha or a *Cakravartī,* we shall offer him one son each. If he becomes a Buddha, he will be surrounded by 80,000 *Kṣatriya* monks; and if he becomes a *Cakravartī,* he will be surrounded by 80,000 *Kṣatriya* warriors.'

A Miracle

To take care of the *Bodhi-sattva,* the king empolyed five very exquisitely beautiful and blemish-free maids. In a vast family, the *Bodhi-sattva* was growing in grace and majesty. It was the occasion of the farm festival in the city. On this occasion, people decorated the city very beautifully so that it acquired the look of a heavenly *vimāma*. All the king's valets, slaves, etc., put on new clothes, scented themselves, wore wreaths and assembled at the palace. The king himself possessed a vast farm which needed a thousand ploughs to cultivate. He had eight hundred less one (799) silver ploughs bedecked with gold and jewels. The horns of the bulls as also their whips and bridles were similarly decked with gold. The king came to the farm in the company of the prince and the entire retinue. In the farm, there was a berry tree which was vast and shady. A bed was spread for the prince beneath the tree. A canopy was hung above it with the help of golden threads. Then it was enclosed on all sides and guards were placed outside the enclosure.

Thereafter, the king, in the company of his ministers, went out to plough.

The king held a golden plough, the ministers held 800 less 1 silver ploughs and other men held other ploughs. They started ploughing the land from one end to the other.

There assembled a vast crowd of men to witness the occasion. Even the maids who held charge of the prince inside the enclosure could not check the temptation of coming out and be eye-witness of the occasion. When the *Bodhi-sattva* saw that there was no one near him, he got up quickly, controlled his respirations and sat down in meditation for the first time. At that time, the shadow of all the trees had changed their direction (*i.e.*, became enlongened), but the shadow of the tree beneath which the *Bodhi-sattva* sat remained round, without a change. This attracted the attention of the maids who hurried inside the enclosure to find the *Bodhi-sattva* on his bed sitting in meditation. They were taken by surprise and rushed to the king to report about this miracle. The king too rushed to the spot, witnessed the miracle. The king too rushed to the spot, witnessed the miracle and became surprised. At once, he bowed before his son, saying,

> "My son! This is the second occasion when I bow before thee."

The *Bodhi-sattva* grew to become 16. The king erected three palaces to be used by his son during three seasons. One of these was nine-storeyed, another seven and the third one five. He employed 40,000 dancing girls to amuse the prince all the time. Like gods surrounded by nymphs, he was surrounded by these finely dressed girls who, in their turn, were attended by trained female instrument players. Thus, the prince lived amidst grandeur, and moved from one palace to another with the change of season. (The prince was, however, already married, and) Rāhul-mātā was his principal consort.

Displaying technical skill

One day, there was a discussion among the relatives and kinsmen as follows :

> 'The prince is planted amidst, pleasure all the time. He takes no interest in learning crafts. How will he fare in case there is a war?'

The king who had heard this discussion sent for the *Bodhi-sattva* and said unto him,

> "My son! You have not learnt any craft. Is it good? Does it help?"

The *Bodhi-sattva,* however, replied with confidence :

> "There is no craft which I do not know. You issue forth a proclamation that on the seventh, I shall display my skill in public."

The king did accordingly. On the appointed day and at the appointed place, there assembled a vast crowd of thousands of people. Sixty thousand expert archers having diverse proficiency were special invites for the occasion. The *Bodhi-sattva* put on a suit of armour. He wore a turban on his head. He tied a thread of light yellow colour on a bow made from a ram's horn, and tied a bucket full of arrows at his back. He hung a sword at the waist on the left. Then dangling an arrow with a *vajra* tip on his finger, he came forward. The people welcomed him with a great applause. Addressing the king, the *Bodhi-sattva* said,

> "Sire! From among the archers who are assembled here, the leading-most four who can hit the target in no time, hit a fixed target, follow with an arrow the course of sound, and hit an arrow in motion, maybe sent forth to me."

The king did accordingly. The *Bodhi-sattva* erected a square platform and placed the four archers at the four corners. Each archer was given 30,000 arrows and an expert to assist each. The *Bodhi-sattva* took his position at the centre of the platform. He was still dangling the same arrow with a vajra tip on his finger. Addressing the king, he said,

> "Sire! These worthy archers may be asked to discharge volleys of their arrows at me. I assure you, their arrows will not touch me."

> "Great king! We are trained in archery. We are respectively a quick shot, a fixed shot, expert in following the course of sound with an arrow and expert in hitting at an arrow in motion. The prince may be induced to disist from this daring feat. He is still a notice, and we do not desire to discharge our arrows at him."

The *Bodhi-sattva* protested,

> "Hit me if you can. This is my challenge to you."

The archers accepted the challenge and discharged their arrows at a time. The *Bodhi-sattva* cut their arrows before they could touch him. With his own arrows, the *Bodhi-sattva* created an enclosure round himself so that the arrows discharged by the adversaries could not even come near him, whereas the arrows discharged by him puzzled his adversaries very severely. When the archers had exhausted all their arrows, the *Bodhi-sattva*, without dismantling his own enclosure of arrows, gave a jump and stood before the king. The people shouted a deafening applause, and offered him gifts of costly ribes and ornaments which made a huge pile. The value of the treasure was 18 crores.

The king was the proud father of such a meritorious son. He received the *Bodhi-sattva* very cordially, and asked the name of this particular skill and that of the master-archer who had devised it. Said the *Bodhi-sattva*,

> "Sire! This skill is called arrow-resisting (*bāṇa-varodhini*), and in the whole of the Jambūdvīpa, there is none who excels me in this."

The king—"My dear son! Display another skill."

The *Bodhi-sattva* started,

> "Sire! These four skilled archers could not hit me though they enjoyed vantage over me in their corner positions. Now, from my position at the centre, I shall pierce all the four with a single arrow."

But the archers had no more courage to face his arrow and they withdrew, whereon four banana trees were placed at the four corners. A red thread was put through the eye at the far end of the arrow and it was then discharged by the prince at one of the banana trees. The arrow passed through a tree, took a turn, passed through the second tree, took a turn again, passed through the third, and likewise it passed through the fourth tree, and returned into the prince's hand. Thus, the four trees were placed on a single thread. The people were delighted to witness this wonderful feat and hailed the prince with a tremendous applause.

The *Bodhi-sattva* displayed a few more skills named *śara-yaṣṭi* (stick), *śara-rajju* (rope), *śara-veṇī* (braid), *śara-prāsāda* (palace), *śara-maṇḍapa* (platform), *śara-sopāna* (staircase), *śara-puṣkariṇi* (pond), *śara-padma* (lotus) and *śara-varṣā* (shower of water). In all, he displayed 12 superhuman skills. After this, he pierced through seven very thick objects with his arrow. Among other things, these included wooden planks from *fig* tree of the thickness of eight fingers each (4 inches), copper sheets of the thickness of two fingers (1 inch) and iron sheets of the thickness of one finger (1/2 inch). Then he pierced 100 planks tied together. After these superhuman demonstrations, no one had even an iota of doubt about the skill and craftsmanship of the prince.

Four scenes

One day, the *Bodhi-sattva* expressed a desire to go to the garden. He asked his charioteer to make his chariot ready which he did. The chariot was decorated, and four excellent horses from the Sindhudeśa were yoked to it. When the chariot was ready, it was announced to the prince. The *Bodhi-sattva* sat on the chariot, which looked like a divine thing, and started his journey. Meanwhile the gods thought that the time when the prince would become a Buddha was fast drawing near so that it was time for them to prepare and present before him the four scenes. So they deputed a young god in the guise of an old man who had lost his teeth, whose hairs had turned grey, whose body was bent under the weight of age, whose feet had become unsteady and who could move with great difficulty with the support of a stick. The old man appeared Siddhārtha and his charioteer who alone could see him (and none else). Said the *Bodhi-sattva* to the charioteer,

> "*Saumya!* What sort of man is this? Why are his body and hairs different from those of others?"

Charioteer—"Deva! This man has grown old due to age."

Bodhi-sattva—"What do you mean by grown old due to age?"

Charioteer—"*Deva!* The body of this man is worn. So he is called old. He will not live long on this earth."

"Then, does it mean that I shall also grow old some day? Is it an unavoidable law?"

"*Deva!* Such is the law. For you, me and everyone else, old age is unavoidable."

"*Bhadra!* I have no more desire to go to the garden. Turn the chariot and get me back to the palace."

The charioteer did as he was asked to do. The *Bodhi-sattva* came back to his apartment. His mind had moved away from everything and wholly concentrated on what the charioteer had said, 'Old age is unavoidable.' These words raised a tremendous storm in his mind.

The king noticed that the prince had come back so soon. He had no doubt that the prince did not go to the garden. So, he made an enquiry, and he was told that he had seen an old man on the street. At once, the king's mind went back to the day when a young *Brāhmaṇa* had predicted that the sight of an old man would be one of the inducements for the prince to renounce the world. So, he ordered that dances and merry-making should commence at once to divert the mind of the prince. For, he was still sure that the prince could be held back through such means. Besides, all around the city, upto a distance of half a *yojana,* check-posts were extended, and watchmen were ordered to be especially vigilant.

One day, the *Bodhi-sattva* was on his way to the garden. The gods placed a sick man on the road, and the *Bodhi-sattva's* eyes fell on him. The man was besmeared with his own excreta, and could not even move or turn his body without help. The *Bodhi-sattva* saw the man from a distance, and said to his charioteer :

> "Who is this fellow? His eyes are so different. Even his voice is different."

Charioteer— *"Deva!* He is a sick man. His body has become weak due to disease. Perhaps he cannot rise now."

Bodhi-sattva—"Does it mean that I too am under the same inexorable law about disease? Is sickness unavoidable?"

Charioteer—*"Deva!* It is so. It cannot be avoided."

This came as a shock to the *Bodhi-sattva.* At his order, the chariot was at once turned back towards the palace.

The prince's indifference did not escape the attention of the king, and as a further precaution, he extended the check-posts upto a distance of three quarters of a *yojana*.

One day, the *Bodhi-sattva* was out in his chariot. On the way, he saw a scene again placed by the gods. He saw that at a distance, some men were busy making something. The *Bodhi-sattva* asked his charioteer what these men were busy at. Said the charioteer,

> *"Deva!* It seems that somebody is dead. The members of his family, friends and kinsmen are preparing for his creamation."

The *Bodhi-sattva* directed the charioteer to proceed thither. When the *Bodhi-sattva* had reached the spot, he saw the dead body and said,

> "What do you mean by 'dead'?"

Charioteer—*"Deva!* Now, this fellow has no more relation with his parent, friends or kinsmen. Neither will he see them any more, nor will they. His relation with them is now cut off for ever."

Bodhi-sattva—"Am I too subject to the same inexorable law about death? Is death unavoidable?"

Charioteer—*"Deva!* It is so. It cannot be avoided." With an air of indifference, the *Bodhi-sattva* said, "I have no more intention to proceed. Turn the chariot and take me back to the palace."

The king learnt all this. He was struck with deep anxiety. Check-posts were extended upto one *yojana* beyond city precincts, and strict orders were issued to the guards to be particularly vigilant. Meanwhile, all sorts of pleasures were provided for the diversion of the prince.

One day, the *Bodhi-sattva* was again on his way to the garden. The gods placed a monk on the road. The *Bodhi-sattva* saw the strange man who had a tonsured head and who had saffron clothes on. On seeing him, the *Bodhi-sattva* said,

> "*Saumya!* Who is this fellow? He has no cover of hair on his head and he puts on a different cloth."

Charioteer—"*Deva!* He is renounced."

Bodhi-sattva—"*Saumya!* Why does a man get renounced."

Elaborating the objectives of a renounced person, the charioteer said,

> "*Deva!* This he does to practise virtue, to attain bliss, to perform good deeds, to acquire merit, to observe non-injury, and to have compassion for all. For these, he has renounced."

The *Bodhi-sattva* directed the charioteer to go near the monk. He observed him most closely, and asked him many questions. He enquired about the merits of monkhood. He felt an attraction for the life of a monk. This time, he did not return to the palace at once, but proceeded to the garden.

(Elderly Buddhist monks who can freely recite *Dīgha Nikāya*, called *Dīgha-bhāṇaka*, are of the view that the *Bodhi-sattva* witnessed the four scenes in course of a single day).

A Son is Born

He spent the whole day in the garden enjoying diverse pleasures. He took bath in a beautiful tank. Then in the evening, he sat on a stone slab in order to be decorated. His attendants stood around him with wrappers of various colours, ornaments, garlands, perfumes, etc. in their hands. Just then, the throne of Indra became hot. He became angry and thought,

> "Who is this that desires to remove me from my throne?"

But at once he realised that it was time for the *Bodhi-sattva* to decorate. He became pacified and sent for Viśvakarmā at once. When Viśvakarmā arrived, Indra said to him,

> "*Saumya!* At midnight to-day, there will be the great renunciation by Prince Siddhārtha. His decoration to-day will be his last. You go yourself to the garden and adorn him with divine ornaments."

By dint of his divine power, Viśvakarmā came to the garden at once. He changed himself into one of the valets attending the prince and got mixed up with them. He took a wrapper from the hands of another attendant, and began to wrap it round the *Bodhi-sattva's* head. From the touch of his hand, the *Bodhi-sattva* realised that this was no ordinary human being but some divine personality. No sooner was the wrapper given a single turn round the head than, like jewels in the crown at the head, it produced forth a thousand wrappers, and like this, ten such turns produced 10,000 wrappers. The biggest of these wrappers had the weight of a flower of *śyāmā* creeper, while others had no more than that of a *kuṭumvaka* flower for each. The head of the *Bodhi-sattva* looked like a *kuyyaka* flower. After he had been decorated in all respects, the *Brāhmaṇas* who were experts in musical rhythms displayed their skill. Then, after being honoured by the eulogies and propitiatory words of the bards, and beings adorned in all respect, he sat on the chariot.

Just then, a son was born to Rāhula-mātā. When this report reached King Suddhodana, he sent forth messengers at once to convey this good news to the prince at the garden. These men came running to the garden and communicated the good news to the prince. When the *Bodhi-sattva* heard the news, the following words suddenly dropped from his lips :

> 'A Rāhu-fetter is born.'
> (In India, Rāhu is considered to be an inauspicious planet that swallows the moon and the sun during an eclipse).

When the men came back to the palace, the king enquired about the reaction of the prince. On being asked like that, the men tendered a *verbatim* account, where on the new-born babe was named Rāhula.

The *Bodhi-sattva* returned to the city. At that time, a *Kṣatriya* girl, Kṛśā-Gautamī by name, was observing the beauty of the city from the top of her mansion. Her eyes fell on the *Bodhi-sattva,* and on seeing his grace and adornment, she expressed a great joy and uttered a happy couplet (*udāna*) which as follows :

> "Perfect calm have the parents
> who have a son like this,
> Perfect calm has the woman
> who has a husband like this."

This joyous couplet reached the ears of the *Bodhi-sattva*, and his thought became concentrated on this. Thought he,

What's that whose calmness imparts calm to the heart?

As he became indifferent to attachment and other causes of misery, his thoughts reached a depth :

> 'Perfect calm is attained only when the fire of attachment, aversion and delusion is put out. Perfect calm is attained only when the dirt of ego and wrong out-look is washed away. This girl has uttered words that are good for me. I am in search of *nirvāṇa.* I must give up my home this very day move out in search of *nirvāṇa.*'

At once, he took out a pearl necklace from his neck and gave it to Kṛśā-Gautamī who had shown him the way. The girl was very much delighted to receive such a costly gift from the prince. She thought that the prince had been exceedingly good to her and loved her.

Departure from home

The *Bodhi-sattva* returned to the palace. He stretched himself on the couch. At once, he was encircled by nymph-like beautiful girls who were nicely dressed and adorned, and who were proficient in music and dancing. They were playing on instruments. They tried their best to relieve the prince of his fatigue and make him happy and gay. But to-day, the *Bodhi-sattva* was somewhat indifferent and taking no interest in them. So, all the efforts by the girls failed. The *Bodhi-sattva* retired, they stopped their music and dances, and lay on the floor. Lamps filled with perfumed oils were still burning. At the dead of night, the *Bodhi-sattva* woke up. He sat on his couch. His eyes fell on the girls lying on the floor. What he saw there created a great reaction in him. Some of these girls had their dresses soiled by saliva which came out from their mouth; some were rattling their teeth; and some were coughing or murmuring. Some had their mouths agape and some were undressed in a shameless manner. These very ugly scenes that he witnessed within his own chamber made him all the more detached to worldly life. At that moment, that grand palace appeared to him to be no better than a crematorium filled up with dilapidated corpses. It appeared to him that all his three palaces were ablaze. In such a situation, the following words dropped from his lips,

> "What a sorrow! What a grief!"

His mind was now fully turned towards renunciation. He resolved,

> "I must move out from my home this very night."

He came out from his bed, reached the door and called out,

"Is there anyone?"

Chandaka who sat reclined against the wall responded,

"Āryaputra! I am Chandaka here, ever at your service."
"I want to go out. Prepare a horse for me."

Chandaka took the necessary outfit and proceeded to the stable. In the light of the lamp, he saw an excellent horse named Kanthaka standing on a beautiful ground beneath a well-decorated canopy. Chandaka considered him to be the best for the purpose in his view. He prepared and disciplined it in the best possible manner. Kanthaka had a very natural thought at this moment that the night's preparation was somewhat unusual. He had a feeling that his master was not going out to the garden to come back after some time; it was his final exit from home on a noble mission. So, in a delightful mood, he gave out a loud neigh. This neigh would have been audible all over the city, but the gods prevented it in time from spreading.

When Chandaka went out to prepare the horse, the *Bodhi-sattva* turned his steps towards the apartment of his wife to have a look at the son. He opened the door a jar. An oil lamp was burning inside the chamber. Rāhula-mātā lay fast asleep on her bed which was covered with sweet flowers as much as one *ammana* (*i.e.*, 11 *droṇa*), with one of her hands placed on the head of the new-born babe. Standing at the door, the *Bodhi-sattva* saw the mother and the child. He desired to hold his son on his own lap, but soon he desisted thinking,

'If I do this, this may disturb the mother and wake her up. If that happens, that may foil my own plan. So it is better that when I am enlightened, I shall come back and see my son.'

According to the *Jātaka Kathā* written in old Ceylonese language, when the prince left his home, Rāhula was seven days old.

The *Bodhi-sattva* came down from his palace. He came near Kanthaka and said,

"Kanthaka! My child! You help me to cross through during this one night. With this co-operation from your side, when I shall be enlightened, I shall help the entire universe, including the gods, to cross through."

So saying, he gave a jump, and was straight on the horse's back. Kanthaka was a colossal steed who was 18 cubits in length from his neck till the tail; he had a great speed, and he had the hue of a cleaned conch. (He had the speciality that) if he neighed or struck with his hoofs, the sound went far throughout the city. (At the *Bodhi-sattva's* words, the horse neighed again, and again the gods prevented the sound from going far. All along the route, the gods made the horse trot on their own palms so that the horse's movement was silent and free from any sound. Chandaka held the horse's tail in his hand. At mid-night, all the three arrived at the city-gate.

The king always held the apprehension that the prince might escape during some night. So, to render that impossible, he made the doors so very heavy that they could not be moved by less than a thousand people. But (the king knew not that) the *Bodhi-sattva* was even more powerful. He commanded a strength which was as much as that of 10 crores elephants or a hundred crore men. Arriving at the gate, the *Bodhi-sattva* thought,

> 'If the door does not open, then, seated on the horse, with Chandaka at the horse's tail, I shall press the horse with my legs and make it jump across the 18 feet rampart.'

Chandaka had his own thinking,

> 'If the door fails to open, then, I shall place the prince on my shoulder, hold the horse in my arms, and jump across the rampart.'

And the horse thought,

> 'If the door fails to open, then, having the prince on my back, and the horseman at my tail, I shall jump across the rampart.'

Had not the door been open, each would perhaps have acted as per his thinking; but this was rendered unnecessary. The gods opened the gate at once.

At this moment, to induce the *Bodhi-sattva* to retrace, *Māra* stood ready in the sky. Said he,

> "Good friend! Do not renounce the kingdom. On the seventh day, a Wheel of Paramountcy (*cakra-ratna*) will arise to help thee. You will have a vast empire extended over four great isles and 2000 islets. So, come back. Do not go further."

Bodhi-sattva—"Who are you?"
Māra—"I am a god belonging to the Heaven of Vasavarti."

Bodhi-sattva—"I know it perfectly well that a wheel of Paramountcy will arise before me; but I am not keen to have an empire. I shall be a Buddha inspiring and resounding through thousands of human material."

But *Māra* issued forth his warning,

> "Let me see how you do not fall a prey to the thoughts regarding lust, malice and causing injury even once."

Thereafter, he followed him like a shadow.

In this manner, the *Bodhi-sattva* abandoned the empire of a *Cakravartī* like a spittle and moved out from his own city in the full-moon night of *Āsādha* when the star *Uttarāṣāḍhā* was up. No sooner had he moved out of the city than he felt a desire to have a look at the city. At once, the Earth began to shake like the potter's wheel as if communicating her disapproval in the following words :

> 'Great man! In the course of your life, you have never turned to look at the rear.'

At the place where the *Bodhi-sattva* felt the desire to look at the city, a *caitya* came up named Kanthakanivartaka-caitya. He resumed his journey again attended with respect and fortune. At the time, 60,000 gods were moving with him, on his left and right and on his rear, with burning torches in their hands. At the doors of the *cakravālas*, innumerable torches were lit. Many gods, *nāgas, suparṇas,* and others appeared at the sky and worshipped the *Bodhi-sattva* with divine incences, wreaths, powders and perfumes, and scattered various flowers like *pārijāta, mandāra,* etc. Divine melodies were sung. In all the four directions, eight types of instruments totalling 68,00,000 in all were playing. Moving with exceptional good look, in course of a single night, the *Bodhi-sattva* passed through three kingdoms, Śākya, Koliya and Rāmagrāma, leaving them behind. He covered a distance of 30 *yojanas* and reached the bank of a river named Anomā.

Kanthaka was a very powerful horse. Setting out in the morning, he could trample under his hoof the central circle of *cakravāla,* like a circle trampled on the ground, trot at all the points on it and come back to his original position in time for his mid-day meal. But during this night, he could cover only 30 *yojanas* and there was sufficient reason for that. For, the gods had showered so many flowers and so much of other stuff that he was buried upto his hips. It was for this reason that his speed had been very much slowed down, and every time he took a step, he had to make a tremendous effort.

Initiation into Monkhood

Standing on the bank of the river, the *Bodhi-sattva* enquired what the name of the river was.

"Anomā," said Chandaka.

Thought the *Bodhi-sattva* at once,

> "*Anomā-na avam.* Then my initiation too cannot be in vain."

At once, he directed the horse with his heel, and at on jump, the horse reached the other bank of the river which was as much as 8 *rṣabhas* (1 *rṣabha* = 140 cubits) in width. The *Bodhi-sattva* alighted from the horse and stood on the sandy bank which was silvery (in hue) and soft like silk. Adressing Chandaka, he said,

> "*Saumya!* Chandaka! You take my ornaments and Kanthaka back home. I am going to be initiated."

Chandaka—"*Deva!* I shall follow thee. I intend to be initiated."

Very distinctly did the *Bodhi-sattva* say,

> "You cannot be initiated. Get back, as I say."

Chandaka had no other alternative but to obey. He handed over his ornaments and the horse to Chandaka. The *Bodhi-sattva* thought.

> 'The (long) hairs of mine do not make me appear like a *śramaṇa.* For cutting the hairs of the *Bodhi-sattva,* no instrument is good enough except a sword. So, I should apply the sword.'

He held the sword in his right hand and the bunch of hairs with the peacock plume in his left hand and cut them. Only very short hairs as big as two fingers (1 inch) remained, which, turning from the right, stuck to his head. Till the last day of his life, this remained the size of his hairs. And the same was the size of his moustache and beard. Henceforth, he needed no more hair cut.

He hurled the bunch of hairs in the sky thinking that if he was destined to be a Buddha, they should remain in the sky; otherwise, they should come down. That bunch attained a height of a *yojana* in the sky and remained there. Śakra, the Indra of the gods, saw them with his divine vision. He held them in a pot made of gems, and erected with them the Cūḍāmaṇi-caitya in the Trayastriṁśa heaven.

The *Bodhi-sattva* thought again,

'These clothes made at Kāśī are of no good for a monk.'

Just then, Mahābrahma, a contemporary of Kāśyapa-Buddha, thought,

'My friend has renounced his home to-day. I must provide him with all the things he would need as a monk.'

At once, he took three robes, a pot, a razor, a needle, a belt and a piece of cloth to filter water—in all eight things, and gave them to the *Bodhi-sattva.* The *Bodhi-sattva* put on the excellent dress and accepted the other objects used by an *Arhat,* and dismissed Chandaka saying,

"Chandaka! Console my parents on my behalf."

Chandaka moved round him thrice, bowed before him and departed. Kanthaka heard the conversation between the *Bodhi-sattva* and Chandaka. When he understood that he would never again see his master, he could not bear the separation. He died on the spot and was born as a god named Kanthaka in the Traystriṁśa heaven. Chandaka who was already deeply wounded at the renunciation by his master was now doubly grieved by the death of his dear horse. Weeping bitterly, he turned his steps towards the city.

REFERENCES

1. The Digambaras do not accept the event of the transfer of the embryo.
2. *Tri-ṣaṣṭi-śalākāpuruṣa-caritraṃ* (Hindi ed.) Parva I, p. 139.
3. *Kalpasūtrārtha Prabodhinī*, p. 127.
4. *Cf. Uvavāī, Sūtra* 6 : vicchiñña-viula-bhavana.
5. *Cf. Vijāha-Paññatti* (Bhagavatī), S. 9, U. 33.
6. *Jātaka-aṭṭha-kathā,* p. 154.
7. *Cf. Tri-ṣaṣṭi-śalākāpuruṣa-caritraṃ*, Parva I, Sarga 3, Śloka 513.
8. *Cf. Samavāyāṅga*, Sama, 34.
9. *Cf. Samavāyāṅga,* Sama, 34, and *Uvavāī Sūtra* 10 which contain reference to 34 miracles of a Jina. Worthy of note is that the words Jina and Buddha are used as synonyms.
10. About Mahāvīra, we have it in the *Uvavāī, Sūtra* 10, nikuraṁba-niciya-kuñciya-payāhiṇāvattamuddhasiraye.
11. *Āyāraṅga*, 2/15, pp. 388/1.
12. *Kappasutta*, 17-18.
13. According to the Kappasutta, the act of transfer was unknown to Mahāvīra. This may need explanation. As Mahāvīra was endowed with a *avadhi* knowledge, there is no reason that he did not know the act of transfer.
14. *Kappasutta, Kalpalatā commentary*, pp. 108/2, 109/1.
15. According to *Vaijayantī Koṣa*, 'sāmanta' meant a neighbouring king. This is supported from Kauṭilya's *Arthaśāstra*. The leadingmost among the neighbouring kings was called mahā-sāmanta.
16. We have it in the *Harivaṁśa Purāṇa* of the Digambaras that Mahāvīra's parents desired their son to marry and take a wife, and that many kings wanted to bestow their daughters on him. Particularly deserving of mention is King Jitaśatru who wanted to marry his daughter

Yaśodā with him; but Mahāvīra declined to marry.

17. *Kappasutta, Kalpalatā commentary*, p. 123/1.
18. According to the Jainas, too, Pūrva-videha, Paścimavideha, Uttara-kuru, etc., were portions of Jambūdvīpa.
19. For what did the Buddha speak in these two births, see *Jātaka*, No. 546, 547.

7

SPIRITUAL EXERTIONS

The period of penances of Mahāvīra lasted for 12 years and 13 fortnights and that of the Buddha for six years. In the life of both these great man who marked their epoch with great achievements, we find hard penances, harder perseverance and still harder concentration. In the early part of his career as a monk, the Buddha like Mahāvīra, lived like an ordinary monk, and became lean and pale, and one day he fell down on an alter named Caṅkarmaṇa. Then he realised that this sort of hard penance did not lead to enlightenment. So, he again started taking food, and before he attained *bodhi,* he had taken *khīra* served by Sujātā. He accepted that it was meditation that led to enlightenment. In reviewing through the stages of his penance, it should appear that he considered them as unpalable as a farmer wrongly attributes germination to a shower that comes after germination. The farmer fails to realise that not this shower alone, but the entire process like digging the earth, sowing seed, rainfall, all these taken together help in the germination.

Mahāvīra used cloth for slightly more than a year (after initiation), and thereafter he moved about without any cloth.[1] The Buddha put on saffron robe at the time of his initiation.[2]

There is much similarity between the two in their spiritual exertions. Mahāvīra lived on dried rice, *manthu* and *uḍad* and the Buddha lived on sesamum, rice, etc. When for the first time, the Buddha took these coarse things, he felt a severe reaction in within his body, but he checked himself and ate. In both the traditions, we get a very exhaust account of the coarse food-stuff obtained from begging.

Regarding Mahāvīra, we have the following from a discourse between Monk Ārdraka and Gośālaka :

> "Mahāvīra wandered alone in the beginning," said Gośālaka, "but now he wanders with a vast group. This is his method of earning a living."

Likewise, after the Buddha had attained his enlightenment, monks from the rival (five) orders said as follows about him,

> "Gautama Buddha is now serious about building up accumulations, and he has deviated from his spiritual exertions... In the beginning of his life as a monk, he was thin and ematiated, but now he is nourished with rich food."

To prepare *khīra* for the Buddha, Sujātā fed 500 cows with the milk of 1000 cows, and in this descending order, she gave at last the milk from 16 cows to 8. In the Jaina traditions, too, we have similar account for making milk more palatable, delicious and nourishing. Take for instance *khīra* prepared for a *Cakravartī,* we read that the milk from 1,00,000 cows who had grazed in a sugar-cane farm was given to 500 vows, and that, in this descending order, the milk obtained from the last cow was used to prepare *khīra.* This was considered to be (very tasteful, and also) a very wholesome food. Only Goddess Śrī and a *Cakravartī* was capable to eat this, and they alone could digest this.[3]

Mahāvīra's Exertions for Attaining Kaivalya

We have a detailed account of the spiritual exertions of Mahāvīra in the *Ācārāṅga Sūtra.* In the *Sūtra,* these exertions have been described as follows :

At the time of his initiation, Mahāvīra had only one cloth on his body. For about 13 months, he kept that cloth on his shoulder. In the second year, when half of winter had passed, he gave up that cloth, and became a monk without cloth. He never folded his arms as a protection against cold, but wandered with his arms stretched. In winter, when there was chilly wind, and it was terribly cold, other monks ran about in search of some warm shelter, wrapped themselves with cloth, or, as did he *tāpasa* monks did, burnt wood in order to warm themselves up; but Mahāvīra remained in an exposed place without any cloth, and he never desired to protect himself. In such a place, he would sit to mediate. Being unclad, he was not only exposed to heat and cold, but he also suffered innumerable hardships due to bite from insects and mosquitoes, and due to touches hard as well as soft.

For his halting, Mahāvīra sometimes used lonely cottages, sometimes he chose inns, alms-houses, shades put up for weekly (bi-weekly), market (*hāṭa),* black-smith's workshops, and even gardeners' homes, and sometimes he lived in towns, cremation grounds, discarded homes, even under the shed of the trees or mere thatched roofs. Sometimes he was bitten by snakes and other poisonous creatures, and sometimes he was pecked by hawks and similar giant birds. He was often put into trouble by wicked people. (Taking him to be a thief), many village watchmen caned him with their sticks or hurt him with their javelines. Many lusty women who were attracted by his grace tried to cast their snares round him. He had to bear many hardships inflicted by men and beasts, and many harsh and terrific yells which were intended to frighten him. Security men were very much annoyed to see him alone in lonely places; they beat him, chastised him with rebukes and asked him to quit. But inspite of all these tortures and hardships, he remained unmoved in his meditation, and when he was asked to quit, silently he moved elsewhere.

Mahāvīra was very much restricted in his diet. Though enjoying a good health, he took a measured quantity of food. He begged from door to door without caring for warm or cold reception; but he never humbled himself before the donor. He felt no greed for dainties and delicacies, and he did not at any time look for them. Whatever he got from begging, no matter whether it was coarse food, cold food, food cooked on a previous day, *uḍad,* dry rice, *manthu*, barley, or any other, he ate with peace and contentment. Once, for a stretch of eight months, he lived on such coarse things. If on any day he was offered nothing, he did not feel miserable. Sometimes, he did not drink water for a fortnight, for a month or even for six months. He moved out (from his halting place) even during a fast. He was never a daily eater, and he took his meal, irrespective of its quality, at a gap of three, four or five days. Thus the conquest of appetite (taste) was an important item in his programme. If in the course of his begging mission he came across a pigeon or only other bird picking grains, he would not scare them in any way but retraced his steps and went back. If at the house of a donor he came across a *brāhmaṇa,* a *śramaṇa,* a beggar, a guest, an untouchable, a cat or a dog standing in expectation of food, he did not disturb them but silently left the place. In this manner, he carefully avoided all occasions that would rouse anger or jealousy in others.

Exceptionally thrilling is the account of his indifference to his own person. He never used medicine even when he was unwell. He never used purgatives, massage, etc., nor did he take bath or clean his teeth. He never desired his feet to be pressed for the sake of comfort. If any particle of dust fell into his eye, he did not care to remove it, nor did he rub his eye in order to be relieved of it. He did not itch his skin at any time.

Mahāvīra did not enjoy a sleep. (It is believed that in the long period of his career as a monk, only once did he sleep for a *muhūrta* which is equal to 48 minutes). He kept awake all the time, immersed in meditation or *kāyotsarga* practice.

While living in homes, he was never attracted by music, dancing or drama. He was neither interested to witness duels nor to watch wrestling. He was never attracted by the lusty words of women, or love-making by a young married couple. Unholding his supreme detachment, he remained indifferent to objects of senses.

While in meditation, he sat in various postures, such as *utkaṭuka, godohikā, vīrāsana* and others. In winter, he practised meditation in some cool place, but in summer, he sat in *utkaṭuka* or some other posture wholly exposed to the scorching sun. On many occasions, when he halted in some home, many beautiful women felt attracted by his graceful personality, but he did not care to look at them. He was wholly turned inward (and did not care for external things). He did not establish any (friendly) relation with the householders. While in meditation, he did not give reply to any query. He spoke little, and was very much measured in his speech. He did not lose his patience, and rigorously held his tongue against all ridicules and provocations. Some praised him, but others poke ill of him, lashed a cane at him, pulled his hairs or gave scratches on his skin; but he remained perfectly unconcerned to all these praises and blames. In this manner, Mahāvīra spent his time, with perfect peace and forbearance, wholly liberated from passions, immersed in pious thoughts and concentrated on self.

While walking, he fixed his eyes in his front over the ground as long as a man, but never looked in the rear or on the sides. (In other words), he walked with proper precaution fixing his gaze on the way in front of him. He did not talk while walking.

At the time of his initiation, many perfumed objects were pasted on his body. Because of these, for more than four months, bees and other flying insects were attracted to his body eating at his flesh or sucking his blood; but Mahāvīra never lost patience with them. What to speak of killing them, he never desired even to remove them.

Mahāvīra wandered through the most inaccessible regions named *Vajra-bhūmi* and *Śubhra-bhūmi* in the country named *Lāḍha.* In this country, he had to face most severe difficulties. The people were very much after him, and he had the greatest difficulty in getting even very coarse and commonplace food. Shelter was equally difficult to get, and even when he got one, it was unfit for habitation. On many occasions, people set dogs on him, and there was none to help him, still less to protect him. Even in such difficult situations, he never wished ill to his adversaries, nor did he ever think of taking revenge on them or inflicting any punishment on them. With perfect patience, he bore all the harsh words of the wicked people.

Sometimes it so happened that even after wandering for a long time, (*i.e.*, despite persistent effort), he was prevented from coming near a village. As he approached a village, the barbarians chased him out, abused him and shouted, 'Go away from here.' On many occasions, they bit him with sticks, fists, spears, stones and bones and created deep wounds on his body. When he was in meditation, they scratched his flesh, showered dust on him, raised him up and dropped him, or pushed him down from his seat.[4]

In many ancient texts of the Jainas, we have authentic accounts of Mahāvīra's fasts when he took no food or water. Once he was on a fast without food and water for 6 months, once for 5 months and 25 days, nine-times for 4 months, twice for 3 months, for two and half months, six times for two months, twice for one and half months, 12 times for 3 days, 229 times for 2 days, and he practised the following *pratimās* at least once, viz., *bhadra, mahābhadra* and *sarvatobhadra*.[5] Of the 4515 days of his life as a monk, he spent 4165 days fasting, and he took food and drink only for 350 days. Thus compared to the penances of the other *Tīrthaṅkaras*, his penances were doubtless more severe.[6]

Buddha's Exertion for attaining Sambodhi

Immediately after his initiation, the Buddha spent a week comfortably in a mango grove named *Anūpiyā*. Starting from there, he covered a distance of 30 *yojanas* in a day, and reached Rājagṛha. He went into the city to beg his food. Like a palace at the entry of Dhanapāla, the god of Wealth, or a heaven at the entry of Camarendra, the Indra of the Asuras, the city of Rājagṛha became delighted at the sight of such a charming monk. The king's officers at once reported about him to the king.

> "Your Majesty! A wonderful man is begging in the street of our city. We cannot say if he is a human being, a *deva* a *nāga* or a *garuḍa*."

The king came at the roof of his palace and looked at the man. He was himself amazed. His men had not exagerated. He said to his men,

> "You follow this wonderful man. If he be a spirit, he will disappear as soon as he goes out of the city; if a *deva*, he will fly away through the sky; if a *nāga*, he will craw into the earth; but if he be a human being, he will sit somewhere in order to eat whatever he has got."

When the Buddha had collected enough food for himself, he moved out by the same gate through which he had entered into the city, sat down in the shadow of a mountain named *Pāṇḍava* and began to eat. When he saw the coarse and tasteless food before him, he had from within himself a severe reaction as if his entire digestive system revolted. He had never seen such a bad food in his life. To get over this feeling of misery, he argued with his own self in part as follows :

> 'Harken thou myself! You were born in an affluent home where there was plenty of food. You were served with most delicious dishes prepared from three-years old fragrant rice. But you came across poor monk, in rags and you thought, if there would ever be an occasion in your life when you will beg your food like that. It is this though which induced

you to renounce your home. Oh my Mind! Why then do you feel miserable now?'

Having argued like that with himself, he ate that abominable food without any reaction.

The king's men who watched him from a distance reported it to the king. Thereon, the king came personally to the Buddha. Being impressed by his simplicity, the king offered him riches; but the Buddha declined the offer saying,

"Oh King! I care neither for 'pleasures nor for riches. I have renounced my home in order to attain the great *sambodhi."*

The Buddha agreed and departed from the place. In the course of his wanderings, he came to *Ālār-kālām* and the king tried his utmost to induce the Buddha to accept his offer, but he failed. At last, the king made a humble request :

"Sir! May I beseech you that as soon as you attain the great *sambodhi,* you will first lay your feet on my kingdom."

Uddāk-Rāmputra from whom he learnt the art of total absorption *(samādhi).* But after some time, he realised that this was not the path to *sambodhi, Samādhi* appeared to him to be a very inadequate tool for *sambodhi.* So, in order to display his energy and powers to all men and gods, and to acquire the highest truth, he came to *Uruvelā.* The place was delightful and he liked it. He stayed on at this place and started his exertions.

Five *Parivrājaka* monks, including Kauṇḍinya, who walked through villages and towns and capital-cities begging their food, came where the Buddha was to felt that this new monk was soon going to be enlightened. So, they had come. For ful six years, they lived with him, served him in all manners and waited eagerly for the day when he would become the Buddha. During these years, the Buddha practised severest penances living only on sesamum and rice. On many occasions, he observed a complete fast when he did not even touch these. On these occasions, to save his life, the gods poured energy into his body through his poreholes, but as he did not take food, he became very weak. He lost his golden complexion and became blackish. The 32 marks of greatness on his body became invisible. (He had become so weak that) one day, when he had controlled his respirations and was in meditation, he fell senseless on an altar named Caṅkramaṇa. Some of the *devas* said,

'*Śramaṇa* Gautama is dead.'

The Buddha realised that even severe penances were not the way to attaining *Sambodhi.* So, once again, he started begging food from villages and market-places and ate freely. The golden hue of his body was restored. The aforesaid *Parivrājaka* monks thought,

> 'Despite very hard penances for six years, this fellow could not become a Buddha. Now that he accepts food from villages and other places, how does he aspire to attain his goal? He has become greedy, and has slipped from the hard path of penance. What purpose will be served if we still continue to follow him? (The sooner we give up, the better for us).'

So, they gave up his company, picked up their belongings and started in the direction of *Ṛṣipaṭṭana* which was at a distance of 18 *yojanas.*

In a religion named *Uruvelā,* in a village named *Sanānī,* Sujātā was born as a daughter upto one Senānī Kuṭumbī. At her youth, she prayed to *Baragada* (Banyan tree) :

> 'If I am married in a family which has an equal status with my parental family, *i.e.*, if I have an endoganous marriage, and if my first child is a boy, then, every year, I shall spend a lakh to worship you.'

Her wishes were fulfilled. This happened about the time when the Buddha was about to close his six-year long chapter of hard penances. It was the full-moon day of *Baiśākha.* With a view of offer the promised workshop. Sujātā gave the milk of 1000 cows who had grazed on a sugarcane farm to 500 cows, the milk of these 500 cows she gave to 250 cows, and so on, till at last, she gave the milk of 16 to 8 cows. The idea in doing so was to increase the density, sweetness and strength of the milk. Having done so, she milked these eight in the very early hours of the morning, and with this milk, she prepared *khīra* in a brand new pot.

Sujātā asked her maid Pūrṇā to clean the god's alter outside beneath the tree. The maid went out. She came beneath the tree. During the same night (when Sujātā was preparing the milk for her worship), the Buddha dreamt five great dreams on the basis of which he felt sure that the time of his attaining *sambodhi* was imminent. When the night was over he performed his morning duties, and sat beneath the (same) tree waiting till the arrival of the time for begging. As he sat beneath it, the whole tree looked radiant by his brilliance. When Pūrṇā came there, he was sitted with his face turned towards the east. When Pūrṇā saw this brilliant man, she thought as follows :

> 'Meseems that the god has come down in person to receive the offer with his own hands.'

At once, she turned her steps and went back to her mistress to report about the arrival of the god in person. When Sujātā heard the tale narrated by the maid, she too became very much delighted and said,

> "Pūrṇā, my dear child! What lovely tidings you have broken before me! From this day, I shall look on you as my own eldest daughter. You dwell with me like my own child."

So saying, she gave her many gifts of clothes and ornaments. Then she poured *khīra* on a golden saucer, covered it carefully with another similar saucer, and securely tied the whole thing in a piece of cloth. Then she herself wore dress and ornaments suitable for the occasion of worshipping god. After he had been ready, she placed the golden saucers on her head and came beneath the tree. When she saw the Buddha there, she became immensely happy. She thought that this was the deity of the tree.

Sujātā stood at the place wherefrom she had first seen the Buddha. Then she plucked down the saucers from her head, took the one containing *khīra* in one hand, took a jar of scented water in the other, and stood before the Buddha. The earthen bowl which was provided to the Buddha by Ghaṭikār Brahma, and which was with him upto this time disappeared at this moment. When the Buddha did not find the bowl near him, he extended his right hand and accepted the jar of water. Sujātā then placed the saucer containing *khīra* in his other hand. The Buddha looked at Sujātā. Sujātā understood his mind. She said,

> "Ārya! I offer this to you. Be pleased to accept it and thereafter repair wherever thy convenience suit thee."

Then Sujātā bowed before him and said,

> "As my heart's desire has been fulfilled, so, may your desire be fulfilled as well."

As one discards a used leaf-plate, so Sujātā did not care for her golden saucer worth a lakh. She left it there and departed from that place.

The Buddha stood up from that place. He moved round the tree and came to the bank of the Nirañjanā. He placed the saucer containing *khīra* on the river bank, went inside the water, took his bath and came out, and he sat facing towards the east. It was this food that sustained him for 49 days when, after attaining the Buddhahood, spent seven weeks in the Bodhi bower *bodhi-manda*). During these 49 days, he did neither take food, nor bath, nor did he clean his mouth. He spent these seven weeks in the joy of meditation, in the joy of the path and in the joy of the result. Having taken the *khīra,* the Buddha threw the golden saucer into the river.[7]

DREAMS

On the last night of his life as a monk, Mahāvīra dreamt 10 dreams which were the precursors of his future life. The Buddha also dreamt five dreams at the end of his careers of spiritual exertions, and these were intimately related with the future course of his life. The details of the dreams dreamt by the two are very much different, but they have some similarity as well in their content.

Dreams of Mahāvīra

During the period of his penances, Mahāvīra slept only once, and that for a *muhūrta* when he dreamt dreams as follows :

1. He saw that he was killing a dreadful *piśāca* as big as palm tree.
   Implication—annihilation of attachment.
2. He saw that a white male cuckoo had come into his presence.
   Implication—white (pure) meditation.
3. He saw that a multi-coloured male cuckoo had come into his presence.
   Implication—gave the contents of 12 *Aṅgas* full of deep thoughts of various sorts.
4. He saw before him two garlands of gems.
   Implication—enunciation of Law (*dharma)* for the monks *(anāgāra)* and for the householders *(āgāra).*
5. He saw before him a herd of white cattle.
   Implication—he would be served by a four-fold order.
6. He saw before him a lake with blossomed lotuses.
   Implication—he would preach before four species of gods.
7. He saw that he had crossed a vast ocean full of mighty waves only with the help of his own hands.
   Implication—he would put a stop to his own glidings into life, (*i.e.*, he would stop his rebirth).
8. He saw that a blazing sun was giving light to the whole universe.
   Implication—attainment of supreme and unobstructed vision—knowledge *(kevala-darśana-jñāna).*

9. He saw that he had encircled the Mānuṣottara mountain with his own sinews which were of the colour of cat's-eyes.
   Implication—his fame would spread in the world of men as well as in heavens occupied by gods.
10. He saw that he sat on the crest of Mount Meru.
   Implication—he would give discourses on *dharma* in the assembly of gods and of men.[8]

Dreams of the Buddha

1. The Buddha saw that he lay on a vast couch. The Himālayas served him as his pillow. His left hand touched the Eastern Ocean and his right hand touched the Western Ocean.
   Implication—attainment of complete *bodhi* by Tathāgata.
2. The Buddha saw that a tree named *titiyā* grew on his palm, and soon it touched the sky.
   Implication—propagation of the eight-fold path.
3. The Buddha saw that white insects with black tips were coming upto his knees.
   Implication—white-robed householders would take shelter with him.
4. The Buddha saw the four multi-coloured birds came from four directions. They fell at his feet, and at once they became white.
   Implication—men belonging to four castes *(varṇa)* would be sheltered with him and would be liberated.
5. The Buddha saw that he was walking on a hill of cow-dung, but he did neither slip nor fall.
   Implication—indifference to the easily available wordly objects.[10]

REFERENCES

1. *Āyārāṅga*, Śrutaskandha One, Chapter 9.
2. *Lalit Vistara*, Also, Mookerjee, *Hindu Civilisation* (Hindi), p. 238.
3. *Cf. Jambūdvīpa-paññatti Vṛtti*, Vakṣa, 2 :
   Cakravartī-sambandhinīnāṁ puṇḍrekṣu-cāriṇināmānataṅkānāṁ gavāṁ lākṣāsyardhārdha-krameṇa pītagokṣīrasya paryante yāvadekṣyāḥ goḥ sambandhi yat kṣīramtat-prāptakalamaśāli-paramānnarūpam-anekasaṁskāraka-dravyasammiśraṁ kalyāṇa-bhojanaṁ iti prasiddhaṁ cakrīṇāṁ strīratnāṁ ca vinā anyasya bhoktur-durjaraṁ mahat unmādakaṁ ceti.
4. Based on *Āyārāṅga*, 9/1-4.
5. *Triṣaṣṭiśalākā-puruṣa-caritraṃ*, Parva 10, Sarga 4, Śloka 652-57; *Āvaśyaka Niryukti, Haribhadrīya Vṛtti*, 227-2 to 229-1 : *Malayagiri Vṛtti* pp. 298-2 to 300-2; *Āvaśyaka Niryukti Dīpikā*, Part I, pp. 107-1 to 108.
6. *Cf. Āvaśyaka Niryukti*, Gāthā 262 :
   uggam ca tavokammaṁ viśeṣato Vaddhamāṇassa.

7. *Jātakaṭṭhakathā*, Nidāna.
8. *Viaha Paññatti* (*Bhagavatī*) Ś. 16, U. 6, Sū. 579. Also Ṭhāṇāṅga, Ṭhā, 10, U. 3; *Āvaśyaka Niryukti, Malayagiri Vṛtti*, p. 270.
9. In the Jaina view, the outcome of this dream is the attainment of complete liberation (*mokṣa*) from that very birth. Compare, *Bhagavatī*, S. 16, U. 6, Sūtra 580.
10. *Aṅguttara Nikāya* 3-240; also *Mahāvastu* 2-136; E.J. Thomas, *Life of Buddha*, p. 70, fn. 4.

8

HARDSHIP AND FORBEARANCE

Unlike Buddha, there are many thrilling accounts of a number of difficult events experienced by Mahāvīra in the course of his penances. There are, however, a few such events which happen more or less identically in the lives of these two great men. To cite an instance, the story of the snake *Caṇḍa-kauśika (Caṇḍa-Kauśika-udbodhana)* in the life of Mahāvīra and that of *Caṇḍa-nāga* (*Caṇḍa-nāga-vijaya)* in the life of the Buddha come very near to each other.

Mahāvīra fixing Caṇḍa-kauśika on Spiritual Path

While wandering from village to village, Mahāvīra was once on his way to the city Śvetāmbika. As the way was blocked by a dangerous snake named *Caṇḍa-Kauśika*, some people requested him not to go by that way. They said,

> "Oh monk! A glance of the snake is enough to kill a man. Thousands of men have lost their lives in this manner. This fact is well-known to the travellers and they discard this path as a prohibited one. So, in the interest of your own safety, please do not take this path."

From the day Mahāvīra was initiated as a monk, he had given up all attachment to the body, and lived on with exclusive reliance on penances. So, he never cared to change his course or retrace his step simply because there was some danger or hardship on the way. So, although he gave a patient hearing to all that these men said, he was neither influenced by them, nor did he like to change his course. He walked on at his usual pace. When he had reached near the snake's hole, the snake lay in a coil on the surface outside. When Mahāvīra stepped into that way, the snake had observed it. He was very much surprised. For, it was after a very long time that a human being had stepped into that way. The snake glanced at the sun and blew out a terrific fire in his hiss at Mahāvīra. Mahāvīra stood firm in meditation. The hiss failed to have any effect on him. He stood motionless with his eyes shut. When the snake saw that his venom, which he had known to be non-failing, had failed in this case, he became all the more infuriated, and his rage knew no bound. So, he crawled towards Mahāvīra and gave him a severe bite at the finger on the leg. Even then the poison had no effect. So, he crawled on the body and gave a severe bite at the shoulder; but still the poison failed to overpower him. Mahāvīra stood firm and motionless as before, completely immersed in meditation *(dhyāna-mudrā)*. The snake found that the man's blood was very tasteful and sweet. So, he started sucking more and more of it. But soon he felt a curiosity at this wonderful event. His poison had never failed to act on a human body. But this was the first occasion when it had failed. He wondered as to how this happened. As he concentrated on his own thinking, at once he revived his memory of his previous birth, and he realised that the man who stood in his front was no less a person than the 24th *Tīrthaṅkara,* Mahāvīra, At once, he became very much alarmed. Thought he,

'In biting him, I have committed the greatest sin.'

He crawled down from his body and rolled in remorse at his feet. At this moment, he remembered not only his present crime, but all the crimes committed by him throughout his life, and even those committed by him in his previous life on account of his outrageous nature, discussed them, described them, returned to his hole, gave up his attachment to his own body and started living without taking anything. He gave up his natural instinct of giving a bite to human beings and other animals, big as well as small. Totally unmindful of the body, he concentrated wholly on his own self.

When people saw that inspite of their repeated warnings, the monk did not pay any heed to them but proceeded on the same route, they were taken by surprise. Some people followed him at a safe distance. When they witnessed the whole episode, their surprise knew no bound. The complete pacification of such a dreaded reptile could not but be viewed as a very unusual event. After having witnessed the episode, the people came back, and discussed it with others in the same village, and with people in the neighbouring villages. It became widely known that the snake Caṇḍakauśika had become perfectly peaceful and had given up the administration of his venom to others. People became immensely happy. The snake had changed into a god in their eyes. So, they came to worship him everyday with milk and sugar. They placed these before him and went away. The smell of these things attracted many pests and ants round the snake at all hours, and these made his life extremely miserable; but the snake had been inspired to the great ideal of Mahāvīra, and so he did not display anger or restlessness in any way. He held fast to the great ideal of forbearance. What to speak of hurting or disturbing any insect in any way, he did not change his place (to save his own life). Bearing pain with calm and equanimity, he died and was born in heaven as a god.[1]

The Buddha's Victory over Caṇḍa-nāga

The Buddha reached the cottage of Uruvela Kāśyapa Jaṭila and said to him,

> "If it causes you no inconvenience, then, I desire to take shelter in your sacrifical cottage (*agni-śālā).*"

On hearing these words of the stranger, Uruvela Kāśyapa said,

> "Great *Śramaṇa*! You are perfectly welcome to stay at my cottage. It will be a pleasure for me, except for the fact that here lives a king-cobra who is extremely severe and who possesses great divine power too. I am afraid, he may cause you great harm."

The Buddha repeated the request for the second time, and then for the third time, and said,

> "Kāśyapa! That snake will do me no harm. You give me shelter in your cottage."

Uruvela permitted him to stay. The Buddha spread some hay in a corner, prepared his seat on it, sraightened his body, fixed his mind and sat on it. King-cobra saw him on his seat. He became angry and started emitting fire. The Buddha had a thought in his mind,

> 'Without causing any harm to his skin, flesh, sinews, bones and marrows, I shall suck out his power.'

He did as he had thought by dint of his spiritual power. He himself started emitting fire. The cobra found this fire more powerful than his own and was soon ablaze. Even the Buddha became ablaze like fire. The brilliance coming out of the two brightened the whole cottage as if it was on fire. Uruvela Kāśyapa moved round the cottage and lamented,

> "Alas! The *Mahāśramaṇa* has been killed by the snake."

The night ended. In the morning, without causing the snake any physical pain, he sucked its venom making him wholly harmless, placed him in a basket, held him before Uruvela Kāśyapa and said,

> "I have sucked the cobra's prowess. He is now powerless. He can do no harm to anyone."[2]

Hardships caused by the Gods

In Mahāvīra's life, the hardships caused by a god named Saṅgama are very famous; and likewise in the life of the Buddha the hardships caused to him by Māra. The similarity between the two accounts is astonishing.

The Story of the God Saṅgama

Starting from Sānulaṭṭhiya, Mahāvīra directed his steps in the direction of Dṛḍhabhūmi. He arrived at a *caitya* named Polāśa in a park named Peḍhāla in the vicinity of a village bearing the same name Peḍhāla, and went on a fast for three days missing eight meals. He reclined slightly against a rock and spread his hands. He fixed his vision on a rough object, exercised full control on his mind and did not allow his eyes to wink. This sport of penance is called *mahāpratimā.* At this place, Mahāvīra remained in meditation of a whole night. Observing this excellent method of penance, Indra spoke the following words in his assembly of gods :

> "At this moment, in the entire land of Bhārata, there is no one more patient and firm in meditation than Mahāvīra. No power is capable to shake him from his standing posture of meditation."

All the gods were very much delighted to hear these observations of Indra. There was, however, one god named Saṅgama who did not like these words. He protested and said,

> "There can be no one holding a human body who will not yield before divine power."

To establish that the Indra had made a wrong observation, he declared,

> "I can shake him; he will have to yield before my power."

Adding strength to what he had observed earlier, Indra re-affirmed,

> "Neither has this happened, nor will this ever happen that a *Tīrthaṅkara* in meditation is shaken by any wound or by sharp words."

But Saṅgama protested again with equal vehemence,

> "I must hold a test of his firmness."

To give effect to his ignoble design, he came down at once and arrived at the polāśa *caitya*. To shake him during the same night, he caused him 20 very severe pains one after another. They were in the following order :

1. He produced a terrific dust storm as if the deluge was imminent. Mahāvīra's eyes, ears and nose were all choked with dust.
2. He produced poisonous ants who gave severe bites all over Mahāvīra's body.
3. He produced swarms of mosquitoes and released them on Mahāvīra. They sucked his blood to their heart's content.
4. He produced sharp-mouthed white ants. They stuck to Mahāvīra's body and gave him severe bites which swelled his pore-holes.
5. He produced a vast army of scorpions who launched a simultaneous attack on Mahāvīra, and pinned his whole body with their stings.
6. He released many mongeese who cracked down on Mahāvīra with a terrific noise and tore off his flesh.
7. He released on him snakes with sharp teeth and a lot of venom. They gave bites to him again and again till they were exhausted when they fell aside.
8. He produced a horde of rats who gave sharp bites to his body and passed urine on it.
9. He produced an elephant with a very long trunk. The elephant coiled Mahāvīra with his trunk and hurled him in the sky again and again. As he was dropped to the ground, he was trampled by the elephant under his feet and struck with his sharp tusk.
10. He produced a she-elephant with a long trunk. She too coiled Mahāvīra in her trunk and hurled him in the sky again and again. As he was dropped to the ground, she trampled over him and wounded him severely with her tusk.
11. He appeared in the guise of a fierce-looking *piśāca* (spirit), and while giggling bitterly, he leapt on Mahāvīra with a dagger in his hand. He sank the dagger into his body with all the strength he could command.
12. Guised as a terrific tiger, he pierced Mahāvīra's body with his thunder-like sharp teeth and trident-like claws.
13. Guised as Siddhārtha and Triśalā (Mahāvīra's parents), he uttered a heart-rending lament and said, "Where have you fled leaving us without support our old age?"
14. Between Mahāvīra's two legs, he lit a fire and set a pot on it to cook food. But Mahāvīra stood firm, and the red flame added to his own brilliance.
15. He hanged birds' cages on Mahāvīra's body. The birds gave him bites with their beaks and claws.

16. He raised a severe cyclone which uprooted many trees and swept away innumerable thatches. The terrific roar of the wind created a severe panic everywhere. In that terrific cyclone, Mahāvīra himself was raised up several times and dropped down.
17. He created a whirlwind in which Mahāvīra was entangled several times.
18. He hurled a death-trap in consequence of which Mahāvīra sank into the ground upto his knees.

    When he saw that Mahāvīra was not perturbed by all these hardships, the god felt somewhat ashamed. But he did not stop. Now he tried several favourable means to break his meditation.
19. Flying in an air-chariot, he came to Mahāvīra and said, "Speak out what you want, heaven or liberation *(mokṣa)*. I shall fulfil your wishes."
20. At last, he brought a nymph and placed her before Mahāvīra. By her lusty overtures, she sought to disturb his meditation, but she could do nothing.[3]

By this time, the night was over. In the morning, Mahāvīra's meditation was over. So, he departed on the way to *Vālukā.*

An unsuccessful person does not give up his wicked thoughts so soon. He is bent on achieving success by hook or by crook. Although the god was completely perplexed to find Mahāvīra unshaken like Mount Meru, still he did not give up his evil designs. On the way to *Vālukā,* he created a habitation of 500 thieves. But Mahāvīra remained undaunted. He neither changed his route nor slowed down his pace of movement. He passed by the abodes of the thieves and crossed through a number of villages such as Suyoga, Succhetā, Malaya and Hastiśīrṣa. At each one of these places, the wicked god Saṅgama was after him and he continued to create diverse troubles for him.

Mahāvīra reached a village named Tośali and went into meditation in the park. Guised as a monk, Saṅgama went into the village and broke into a house through the wall. People took him to be a thief, caught him and beat him very severely. While howling, Saṅgama said,

> "Why do you beat me? I am innocent. I am only carrying in out my *guru's* order."

The people shouted,

> "Who is your *guru?* Where is he?"

Saṅgama led the people into the park and pointed to Mahāvīra who was still in meditation. Now the people launched an attack on him. They tied him and started preparations to take him to the village. Just then, a magician named Mahābhūtila came there. He revealed the identity of Mahāvīra to the villagers and got his release. The people were now looking for the so-called monk who has posed as a disciple, but he was nowhere to be found. The villagers were now convinced that there was some conspiracy behind the whole thing.[4]

From Tośāli, Mahāvīra reached Mośāli. He was in meditation in the park when Saṅgama again charged him of being a thief. The policemen came and arrested him. He was brought before the king. King Siddhārtha's friend, one Sumāgadha who was present at the court at this time recognised him at once. He stood up and saluted him. He introduced Mahāvīra to the king and got him released. Mahāvīra came back to the park and started his meditation again.[5]

Once, Mahāvīra was in meditation in a *kāyotsarga* posture. Saṅgama placed some booty beside him. People took him to be a thief, caught him and brought him before the *Kṣatriya* Chief of Tośāli. The chief asked him many questions and wanted to know who he was, but Mahāvīra spoke nothing. His silence evoked greater suspicion. The chief consulted his council of advisers, and they came to the decision that this was not a real monk. So they ordered that he should be hanged. The executioners at once became active to give effect to the order. They brought him to the scaffold and placed the nook round his neck. But the nook dissipated and dropped to the ground. They tried this seven times, and every time, they had the same experience. This was a great surprise for the *Kṣatriya* Chief and his counsellors. They had now no doubt that this must be a very exceptional man. At once, the king expressed regret and released him.[6]

Mahāvīra now reached Siddhārthapura. Because of the trap already laid by Saṅgama, even here, he was caught as a thief, but was released when his identity was revealed by a hourse-dealer named Kauśika. Starting from there, he reached Vajragrāma. On that day, people were celebrating some festival. So, *khīra* had been cooked in every home. Mahāvīra got up to beg his food. Saṅgama did not lag behind. Before Mahāvīra reached a home, Saṅgama was already there, and the prior presence of a monk at the donor's home made the food unacceptable for him. Mahāvīra realised at once that this was the trick by the same god. So, he left the village and went elsewhere.[7]

For full six months, Saṅgama continued to pursue Mahāvīra harming and harrassing him in every manner. In this, he had degraded himself to the nadir of indecency and meanness. But still Mahāvīra did not budge from his way. Saṅgama was now ashamed in his mind (for his misbehaviour towards a great monk). He realised beyond all doubts that despite his vilest efforts, Mahāvīra had continued to add to his mental stature and attained a colossal spiritual height. He had never allowed himself to be overpowered by his meanness. Being thus defeated, he appeared before Mahāvīra, and revealing the identity, he submitted,

"The praise given by the Indra about you is true to the last word. You are a man very firm in your resolve. I have fallen from my promise. No power, howsoever great, can force you off your path. In future, I promise, I shall never be mean like this with any one."

Mahāvīra was balanced in his mind. He was neither bothered about his past meanness, nor did he rejoice at his promise to improve in future. Saṅgama returned to his abode in heaven. The Indra became much displeased with him, rebuked him severely and turned him out from heaven. After being exiled, Saṅgama came to the Summit of Mount Meru with his wife and settled there.

The Story of the God Māra

When the Buddha made a firm determination for the attainment of *Bodhi*, and sat down for the purpose, Māra thought as follows :

"The prince wants to get out from my authority; but I won't let this happen."

So Māra repaired to his army camp, equipped all his soldiers for an onslaught and set forth to launch an attack on the Buddha. It was a vast army which covered a very wide expanse and altitude of many *yojanas*. Māra himself took weapons in his one thousand hands and started on the back of an elephant called Girimekhalā. His soldiers were not only equipped with arms, they were also diversely painted so that they looked very dreadful as they marched. As Māra and his entire entourage came near the *bodhi*-altar, one by one, all his soldiers dropped out. They could not stare at the unusual brilliance of the Buddha. Māra became conscious of his own limitation, and while looking for an alternative route to divert his army, he decided as follows :

"There is no one equal to the Buddha in power, I can never win a victory over him by launching an attack from the front; so I must launch my attack from the rear."

So, he directed his army to the Buddha's rear. The Buddha saw that the army of Marā was advancing on him from the north only; all other directions were perfectly free. Thought he,

'Such a vast number of gods have been mobilised against me. On my side, there is no one-neither my parents, brothers or kinsmen. So, the ten *pāramitās* are like my own relations. So, I must make a shield of them for my own protection and throw the same as my weapon, and in this manner, I must finish my adversaries.'

The Buddha invoked the ten *pāramitās* to come to his aid and sat tight on his seat. Māra started his onslaught to disolodge him from this place. He caused him troubles which were as follows :

1. He started a severe dust storm. The summits of mountains were separated and these began to fly, trees were uprooted; towns and villages lost their trace. But the Buddha sat unperturbed. As the moving storm reached the proximity of the Buddha, it had already lost its rigour, and not even a corner of his garment was disturbed.
2. Having failed to harm him with the dust storm, Māra attempted to drown him in heavy downpour. The streaks of water were so very sharp that they bored the earth with holes at many places. The flood-water reached the top of the trees in the forest; but the Buddha's garment did not recieve even as much exposure as in a mist.
3. He started a shower of pebbles. Even big rocks emitting smoke, even whole summits blazing with fire came floating through the sky, but no sooner did they reach the vicinity of the Buddha than they changed into boquets of flowers.
4. This was followed by a shower of arms—one-edged weapons, two-edged weapons, swords, spears, arrows and many others incessantly disgorging fire, but no sooner did they reach the vicinity of the Buddha than they changed into heavenly flowers.
5. Then he started the shower of burning charcoal. Hot and red charcoal incessantly dropped from the sky, but on the Buddha's feet, they scattered like flowers.
6. Then he created a shower of ashes. Burning ashes dropped from the sky, but as they reached the Buddha's feet, they changed into powder of sandalwood.
7. Then he started a shower of dust. Dark, blazing and very fine particles of dust started pouring from the sky, but it turned into heavenly flowers on the Buddha's feet.
8. There was a shower of mud. Grey and boiling mud trickled from the sky, but it fell as a divine paste at the Buddha's feet.
9. There emerged a pitchy darkness from all around, but before it could engulf the Buddha, it cleared away as does the night at sunshine.
10. When Māra failed to make the Buddha flee by his storm, rain, pebbles, weapons, charcoal, ashes, dust, mud and darkness, he thundered at his stalwarts,

"Why stand ye cowards inactive? Take this young fellow, beat him and put him to his heels."

He himself did not remain idle. Seated on his elephant Girimekhalā, with a wheel in his hand, he rushed at the Buddha and shouted,

"Ye Siddhārtha! You get out from this seat. It has not been meant for thee; it is mine."

The Buddha reacted,

"Māra! You have neither fulfilled the ten *pāramitās,* nor sub-*pāramitās,* nor the supreme *pāramitās.* You have not even made the five great renunciations, nor done anything either for the good of the clan nor for that of humanity. You have not even acquired knowledge. So, how can this seat be for thee; it is mine."

Māra could no longer restrain his fury. He hurled his wheel at the Buddha. The Buddha at once remembered his ten *pāramitās.* The wheel become a canopy of flowers over his head. Be it mentioned that the wheel was so very powerful that it could smash even a solid pillar made from a rock as if it were a blade of grass. The stalwarts of Māra showered many rocks and stones at the Buddha to make him flee, but because of the protection given to the Buddha by the *pāramitās,* all these turned into garlands of flowers and fell on the ground within a short range of the Buddha.

Standing at the brink of the *cakravālas,* the gods witnessed the scene with the greatest suspense. From time to time, all of them had the same apprehension in their mind,

'Siddhārtha has lost all his grace. What will he do now?'

"The seat which is allotted to the *Bodhi-sattvas* fulfilling the *pāramitās* on the day they attain Buddhahood is mine; you are a pretender."

When Māra uttered this, the Buddha asked him,

"Māra! Who bears witness of your donations?"

Māra stretched his hands to his stalwarts and said,

"Why? All these you see are my witnesses."

At this hint from Māra, his soldiers shouted in one voice,

> "We are his witnesses. We shall testify."

The noise was so very tremendous as if the earth had fallen into pieces.
Māra—"But, pray, who bear witness to your own donations?"
The Buddha firmly declared,

> "These bear witness to your donations; but I have no witness of mine who is alive. So, let alone the donations made by me in other births. But the donations I made for seven weeks when I was born as Vessantara, even this solid and unconscious earth will testify."

The Buddha took out his right hand from under his cloth. Addressing the Great Earth, he said,

> "Do you bear witnesses to the donations made by me for seven weeks during my birth as Vessantara?"

The Great Earth—"Yes, I do."

So saying, she gave out tremendous roars, hundreds, thousands, millions, so that the army of Māra disappeared in utter confusion.
Māra's defeat was complete. Agreeing wholly with the Buddha, he said,

> "Siddhārtha! I admit, you made great donations. You made excellent donations."

The moment Māra concentrated on the Buddha's donations in his life as Vessantara, his elephant Girimekhalā stooped low on his knees. Just then, the army of Māra fled in confusion in whatever direction they could without caring for their dress and ornaments. In the great confusion that prevailed, not two could go by the same route.
The gods witnessed the victory of the Buddha and the defeat of Māra. They were very happy. They came to the Buddha and worshipped him.[8]

Conclusion

There are important similarities between the hardships inflicted by Saṅgama and those inflicted by Māra; but there are significant differences too. The hardships inflicted by Saṅgama acted straight on the person of Mahāvīra, but he was so firm in his physique that he did not care. But the phenomena created by Māra did not operate on the Buddha's body. When they came into his proximity, the Buddha invoked the *pāramitās,* these helped him to change them into flowers or some other excellent objects, and did not allow them either to touch the person of the Buddha or cause him any pain. At no time did Mahāvīra enter into any dialogue with his foe, but in the case of the Buddha, there were challenges and counter-challenges, and even sharp exchanges of words. In the end, however, both the adversaries were defeated,—Saṅgama in the hands of Mahāvīra and Māra in the hands of the Buddha. The event took place in the eleventh year of Mahāvīra's life as a monk.[9] (This was one year before he attained omniscience). The praise by the Indra of Mahāvīra's firmness in meditation was the immediate provocation for the episode that unfolded intself. Saṅgama has been considered to be a god with a false belief. In the case of the Buddha the Māra episode took place in the last year before his Enlightenment. Having taken the *khīra* served by Sujātā, the Buddha took the vow that he would not leave his seat till he was enlightened. Then he successfully passed through the ordeal and attained the Buddhahood. Thereafter, he changed his seat and spent under *Ajapala* banyan, and during the third week, he was in *samādhi* under the shade of the *mucalinda* tree, spent under *ajapala vargada,* and during the third week, he was in *Samādhi* under the shade of the *mucalinda* tree. During that week, trouble was caused to him by the appearance of unexpected clouds. There were chilly winds giving severe bites on the flesh. At that time, there arrived a cobra named *Mucalinda* who made seven coils round the Buddha's body and spread its hood over the Buddha's head. In this manner, the snake protected the Buddha from heat and cold, mosquitoes, wind, sun, insects and reptiles, etc.[10]

These (last-mentioned) hardships of the Buddha are comparable to those undergone by Arhat Pārśva in the hands of Kamaṭha. In his career as a monk, Pārśva stood in meditation near a well under the shade of a banyan tree. His enemy from his previous birth, a god of the name Meghamālī, started a terrific shower with thunder and hail. The rivers and canals became overflooded, and it seemed that the deluge is not far. Pārśva was drowned upto his neck. It was at this time that god Dharaṇedra and his consort Padmāvatī saved his life by making him stand on a lotus shooting out from their novels, and a cobra which they created provided him with an umbrella with its hood. In this manner, he was protected by the divine couple for three days.[11]

REFERENCES

1. *Triṣaṣṭi-śalākā-puruṣa-caritraṃ*, Parva 10, Sarga 3. Also, *Āvaśyaka Niryukti, Malayagiri Vṛtti*, Gāthā 466-67, pp. 273-74.
2. *Vinaya Piṭaka*, Mahāvagga Mahākhandhaka,
3. Based on *Āvaśyaka Cūrṇī*, Part I, p. 311, The order and nature of hardships delineated in the Kappa Sutta are somewhat different.
4. *Āvaśyaka Niryukti*, Gāthā 508.
5. *Ibid.*, Gāthā 509.
6. *Ibid.*, Gāthā 509.
7. *Ibid.*, Gāthā 510.
8. *Jātaka-aṭṭha-kathā*, Nidāna.
9. *Āvaśyaka Niryukti, Malayagiri Vṛtti*, Gāthās 498-517.
10. *Vinaya Piṭaka*, Mahāvagga, Mahākhandhaka.
11. For details, see *Triṣaṣṭi-śalākā-puruṣa-caritraṃ*.

9

OMNISCIENCE AND ENLIGHTENMENT

On Mahāvīra's attainment of Omniscience

"Mahāvīra spent a long term of 12 years in enriching his soul by excellent knowledge, vision and conduct, by simplicity, study, energy, lightness, forgiveness, detachment (greedlessness), controls, contentment, truth, restraint, penance and excellent practice, and by the purusuit of the surest way to the ripe fruit of liberation. In the thirteenth year of his career, one day, he was in meditation in a milking posture (*go-dohikāsana)* exposing himself to the blast of the blazing sun under a *sāla* tree, in the north-eastern direction, neither near nor far from the *Vyāvṛta caitya,* in a farm belonging to a *gāthāpati* named Śyāmaka, on the bank of the *Ṛjubālikā* outside the village named Jambhiya. On that day, he was on fast without water missing altogether six meals. It was the tenth day of the bright half of *Vaiśākha.* The shadow had fallen towards the east. It was the final quarter of the day. The name of the hour (*muhūrta)* was *Vijaya,* and the name of the star was *Uttarā-phālguṇī,* Mahāvīra was immersed in pure (white) meditation with a fine concentration in the midst of an environment which was perfectly serence and silent. At this time, Mahāvīra, the great master of exertions, reached the acme of spiritual practices. He exhausted his four terminable *karmas,* and attained supreme (*kevala)* knowledge and vision, which were final, excellent, unsurpassed, unlimited, expansive, all-round, unshrouded and unobstructed. On the attainment of these, the became capable to know and see the diverse mental states and categories of all living beings in the worlds of men, gods and demons".[1]

No sooner did he attain omniscience that there was light in heaven. The seats of the gods moved. The *Indra* of the gods, the *Sāmānika gods,* the *Trayas-triṁśaka* gods, the *Lokapālas,* their principal consorts, gods who were members of their families, commander gods, body-guard gods, valent gods,—all descended in a hurry to be the first to reach the world of men. At a several places *en route*, the gods met in meetings. The goddesses smiled and chanted sweet hymns. All the directions were becoming placid and pure. The whole earth became bright with an exceptionally strange light. Heavenly drums sounded in the sky. Infernal beings enjoyed a pleasant respiration. Gentle and comfortable breeze started blowing. Many unusual events took place.[2]

On the Buddha's attainment of Enlightenment

During the day, the Buddha was wandering in the well-blossomed *sāla* forest on the bank of the river. In the evening, he started from there and came near the *bodhi* tree. On the way, he met a grass-cutter named Śrotriya who was carrying grass. He gave eight handfuls of hay to the Buddha. With these, the Buddha ascended the *bodhi* altar and reached the southern corner where he stood turning his face towards the north. At this, the southern horizon became depressed to reach the hell named *Abīci,* and the northern horizon soared high as if it touched the crest of the world. The Buddha realised that he would not attain enlightenment at this place. So he moved from there, and, giving a round, he reached the western corner, and stood with his face turned eastward. At this, the western horizon sank to the hell *Abīci,* while the eastern horizon rose at if it touched the crest of the world. Wherever he stepped, the great earth became curved like a wheel spread on the support of its spokes. Even this place he did not find suitable for the attainment of his enlightenment. So the moved out from there, went to the north, and stood with his face turned southwards. At this, the northern horizon sank to the hell *Abīci* and the southern horizon kissed the crest of the world. Even this place he rejected as being unsuitable for the attainment of enlightenment. He moved round, went to the east, and stood with his face turned westward. At once, a thought came to his mind :

> 'This is the place unrejected by the Buddhas. This is the most suitable place for ending all misery.'

Then he caught the tips of the grass and gave a jerk. At once, the grass spread to make a cushion which was 14 cubits in length. The form in which the grass spread was very beautiful. Not even an artist or a skilled craftsman could have produced such a superb thing. The Buddha turned his back towards the *bodhi* tree, and with a complete concentration of mind, he resolved.

> 'Even if I am reduced to mere skin, sinews or bones, even if my body, flesh and blood dry up, I shall not move out from this seat till I attain enlightenment.'

Having made a resolve like this, he sat in an appropriate posture on his cushion which was proof even against the stroke of lightening.

To remove him from that seat, *Māra* created storm, rain, shower of stones, of weapons, of burning charcoal, of hot ashes, of dust and of mud; he created dark shadows; but he could not be effective. Before the sun was down, he admitted his own defeat and departed. At that time, the sprouts of the *bodhi* tree were dropping on the Buddha's garment, and it looked as if he was being worshipped by the shower of red *mūṅga.* During the first one-third of the night (*yāma),* he received Enlightenment about his previous birth; during the second one-third, his divine sight became purified; and in the final one-third, he witnessed Dependent Origination (*paṭicca-samuppāda).* The 8000 space-gaps (*lokāntara)* between the *cakravālas,* which were never sufficiently lighted even by the rays of the seven suns, became lighted at this time in all the directions. The waters of the great oceans, 84000 *yojanas* deep, became sweet. The flow of the rivers came to a standstill. The born-blind got vision, the deaf had their faculty of hearing resotred, the lame walked. The hand-cuffs and chains of the convicts broke and dropped down; they were thus liberated. Many surprising events took place at this time.[3]

The description of *bodhi* is much more hyperbolic than that of the *kaivalya.* In Mahāvīra's attainment of the *kaivalya,* we have description of the arrival of gods; in the Buddha's attainment of the *bodhi,* we have description of the arrival of men. Both the accounts are, however, similar in their description of strange and supernatural events.

Conclusion

On the question of omniscience, the Buddhistic view is that whatever the Buddha desired to know, he could know, while the Jaina view is that whatever was worth-knowing, Mahāvīra knew in the first moments of his attainment of the *kaivalya.* On the attainment of the *bodhi* but before he started preaching, Buddha thought,

> 'To whom do I preach this religion? Who is capable to accept this religion at once?'

At once, he remembered,

> '*Ālāra-kālāma* is intelligent, brilliant and for ever with little dirt of mind. Why do I not make a beginning with him'? He will accept it immediately.'

Remaining in hiding, the gods reported,

> '*Bhante! Ālāra-kālām* died a week ago.'

Just then, knowledge and vision came to the Buddha with which too he knew of it. He thought,

> '*Ālāra-kālāma* was highly receptive. If he had heard of this religion, he would surely have accepted it.'

Then he looked for the next suitable man, and his choice fell on Uddakrām-putra. Thought he,

> 'Uddakrām-putra is intelligent, bright and for ever with little dirt of mind. Why don't I first preach to him? He will soon accept this religion.'

But again from hiding, the gods informed him,

> '*Bhante!* He has died last night.'

The Buddha also learnt this by his own knowledge and vision.
Starting his search again, the Buddha thought,

> 'The *pañca-varga* monks were of great help to me. During my penances, they rendered me a lot of service. Why don't I first start with them?'

Thinking further ahead, he tried to locate them :

> 'Where are they at this moment?'

With his superhuman, pure and divine vision, he saw,

> 'At this moment, they are wandering in the deer-park at Rsipattan in Vārāṇasī.'[4]

Thus on the attainment of the Buddhahood, the Buddha's choice of his first disciple fell on such persons as were already dead. On each occasion, this was pointed out to him by gods, and then he saw it with his own knowledge and vision. It is worth noting that in both the Jaina and Buddhist traditions, the two words, knowledge and vision *(jñāna-darśana)* have been used together. Thus, we have that Mahāvīra acquired *kevala-jñāna-kevala-darśana,* and the Buddha learnt about the death of Ālāra-kālāma and Uddakrām-putra with the help of his *jñāna-darśana.* In the Jaina view, there are five types of knowledge (*mati, śruta, avadhi, manaḥ-paryāya* and *kevala)* and four types of vision *(cakṣu, a-cakṣu, avadhi, kevala).* The third type of knowledge (and a vision) is *avadhi* (or *Vibhaṅga)* in which one with this knowledge perceives the knowledgeable object only by concentrating on it. The Buddha's knowledge appears to be of the same order as the Jainas have termed *avadhi* knowledge (or *Vibhaṅga,* depending on the person concerned). A further reason may be adduced in support of this view, which is that the Buddhist canons have, while conceiving *kevala-jñāna* as unreliable and impossible for all times and in all countries, never hesitated to hurl a ridicule on it. For instance, we have the following in the *Sandaka Sutta* :

> "Here is a spiritual leader who claims to be all-knowing, all-seeing, a master of unlimited knowledge-and-vision. As he walks, stands, lies or sleeps, these are stated to be ever present with him. And yet he goes to an empty home for begging where he gets no food; furthermore, he is bitten by a dog or is confronted with an uncontrollable elephant, a powerful horse or a violent bull. Though claiming to be all-knowing, he asks men and women their name and the line to which they belong. He also enquires about the name of the village and the road leading to that village. When people say, 'Sir, you are all-knowing and yet you ask such simple questions', he replies, 'I went to an empty house because this was so pre-determined'. He says, 'Not getting food was pre-determined, and I did not get food. Being bitten by a dog was pre-determined, and so I was bitten by a dog. Being confronted by an elephant, a horse and a bull was pre-determined, and so I was confronted by these.'[5]

It is not intended to go into the merit or otherwise of observations like these. What, however, is intended is that the *kaivalya* and the *bodhi* are not synonymous. The omniscience of the Jainas have always remained like a query-mark with the Buddhists. In the present age, omniscience is indeed a disputed field. In the new ideas (of contemporary life), Mahāvīra's omniscience enters into the realisation of,

> *Uppannei vā vigamei vā dhuvei vā*
> (reality persists through creation and cessation)[6]

and the Buddha's *bodhi* merges with

> *Yat sat tat Kṣaṇikam*
> (Whatever exists is momentary).

REFERENCES

1. *Āyārāṅga, Śru.* 2 Adhyayana 15;
   Kappa Sutta, Kalpa-druma Kalikā Vṛtti.
2. *Triṣaṣṭi-śalākā-puruṣa-caritram*, Parva 10, Sarga 5.

3. *Jātaka-aṭṭha-kathā*, Nidāna.
4. Based on *Vinaya Piṭaka*, Mahāvagga, Mahākhandhaka.
5. Also *Majjhima Nikāya*, Majjhima Paññāsaka, Parivvājaka Vagga.
6. *Bhagavatī, Śataka* 5, Uddeśaka 9, Sūtra 225.

10

THE MONASTIC ORDER AND ITS EXPANSION

The Monastic order of Mahāvīra contained, according to the scared texts, 14,000 monks and 36,000 nuns.[1] But it is difficult to get a definite and undisputed statement about the number of monks and nuns in the monastic order of the Buddha. We find a mention that when sometime after the attainment of the Buddhahood, the Buddha came to Rājagṛha, he had 1093 *bhikṣus* with him. At Rājagṛha, Sāriputta Moggallāna joined the order of the Buddha with their 250 *parivrājaka* monks. Thus at Rājagṛha, the number of his disciples swelled to 1345. When he first came to Kapilavastu, he had with him 20,000 *bhikṣus.* According to *Lalita Vistara*, at the time of his arrival at Śrāvastī, he had 12,000 *bhikṣus* and 32,000 *bodhi-sattvas* with him.[2]

The organisation of the respective orders started with the attainment of omniscience by Mahāvīra and of enlightenment by the Buddha. Groups of thousands of people were initiated into monkhood at special occasions. Among those so initiated, the largest number came from the Vedic scholars, *parivrājaka* monks and the *Kṣatriya* princes. The accounts of initiations in both the traditions are highly inspiring and entertaining.

At several places, there is a striking similarity between the two accounts. Thus, we have (in the Jaina account that Mahāvīra accepted within his order 11 *Vedic* scholars headed by Indrabhūti along with their 4400 *Brāhmaṇa* disciples; and likewise, (in the Buddhist account), we have that the Buddha accepted into his order three *Jaṭila* leaders headed by Uruvelā along with their 1000 disciplines. Further we have it that Indrabhūti initiated three *tāpasa* leader named Koḍinna, Dinna and Sevāla slong with their 1500 *tāpasa* disciples.

On coming back to his own birth-place, Mahāvīra initiated into monkhood his own son-in-law Jamāli with a family of 500 and his own daughter Priyadarśanā with a family of 1500 people. Likewise, on coming back to Kapilavastu, the Buddha initiated into monkhood, 10,000 citizens, his own son Rāhula, and also Nanda who was the son of *Mahāprajāpati* Gautamī.

Are the Buddhist Accounts Exaggerated

Dharmānanda Kośāmbī, a Buddhist scholar, is of the view that the number of the Buddhist *bhikṣus* is exaggerated to the point of rousing doubt their correctness. To quote him,

> "At Vārāṇasī, the Buddha got 60 *bhikṣus*......Did the number of *bhikṣus* whom the Buddha could claim in his order till he reached Rājagṛha exceed these 15 (*i.e.*, five *pañcavarga* monks, Yaśa and his four friends, three Kāśyapa brothers, and the two disciples of Sañjaya named Sāriputta and Moggallāna)? He added 60 at Vārāṇasī (as aforesaid), 30 on the way to Uruvelā, and 1000 (1003 according to some) at Uruvelā, so that with a group of 1093 *bhikṣus,* the Buddha might have come to Rājagṛha. At Rājagṛha, 250 disciples of Sañjaya came with Sāriputta and Mogallāna and joined the Buddha's order, raising the total to 1345."
>
> But there is no mention in the *Sutta-piṭaka* of there being such a big group with the Buddha. It is stated in the *Sāmanaphala Sutta* that one or two years before he passed away, when the Buddha came to Rājagṛha, he had 1250 *bhikṣus* in his company; but we have a figure of 500 in eight *suttas* in *Dīgha-nikāya,* from which it appears that there were only 500 *bhikṣus* who followed the Buddha's body after he had passed away. The first Buddhist Council meeting at Rājagṛha after the death of the Buddha was attened by 500 *bhikṣus* only, from which also it would be a safe surmise that till his death, the total number of monk in the Buddha's order did not exceed 500.
>
> "It was perhaps after the death of the Buddha that exaggerated figures were produced about the number of the *bhikṣus.* At the opening chapter in *Lalita Vistara*, it has been stated that at Śrāvastī, the Buddha had 12,000 *bhikṣus* and 32,000 *bodhi-sattvas.* About this time, the practice of giving exaggerated figures of monks in previous times started in order to give prestige to their own order, and later, the canonists of *Mahāyāna* sect observed no restraint in giving such figures. This was a main cuase of the decline of Buddhism. To create glamour for their own order and religion, the Buddhist *bhikṣus* started fabricating many cock-and-bull stories, but the *Brāhmaṇas* went further ahead than the Buddhists in this enterprise and ultimately inflicted a complete defeat on the Buddhist *bhikṣus."*[3]

In this manner, Kośāmbī has put up the thesis that the accounts about the numerical strength of the Buddhist *bhikṣus,* are completely exaggerated. In his zeal, however, Kośāmbī may have somewhat overstated his position. It is quite plausible that the non-canonical literature of both the Jainas and the Buddhist have many exaggerated accounts; but it may not be fair to reject the figures about initiates as wholly imaginary. Man always lives in the midst of his environment and moves with the current. The age of Mahāvīra and the Buddha was one when religious consciousness must have been at its height. In this age, renunciation was considered to be the pinacle of spiritual behaviour. It was also an age of devotion. Lofty examples were set by the kings, princes and rich merchants who took to the spiritual path. In an atmoshpere like this, it should not be particularly surprising that a large number of people renounced their homes at a time and became initiated as monks. Whatever that may be, we should strive to understand the accounts of the two traditions with due respect and sympathy, and with an open mind.

The accounts of initiations in the two tradition that have been restated below have neither been in chronic order nor have they been drafted in toto. Some of the more important accounts are presented at random.

Initiations in the Nirgranṭha Order

1. *Eleven Gaṇadharas*—A *Brāhmaṇa* named Somila had started a grand sacrifice at Madhyama Pāvā. There was a great enthsiasm all over the city. Many renowned scholars near and far came with their disciples to participate in the celebrations. The better known among them were Indrabhūti, Agnibhūti, Vāyubhūti, Vyakta, Sudharmā, Maṇḍita (Maṇḍika), Mauryaputra, Akampita, Acalabhrātā, Metārya and Prabhāsa. Indrabhūti, Agnibhūti and Vāyubhūti belonged to the Gautama line and were the residents of a village named Gobara in Magadha. All the three were masters of the 14 branches of learning, and each had a band of 500 disciples. Vyakta and Sudharmā were from a village named Kollāga, the former being in the Bhāradvāja line and the latter in the Agni-vaiśyāyana line. Both had 500 disciples each. Maṇḍita and Mauryaputra came from a village named Maurya, the former being in the Vāsiṣṭha line and the latter in the line of Kāśyapa. They had 350 disciples each. Akampita came from Mithilā and belonged to the Gautama line. Acalabhrātā came from Kośala and he belonged to the line of Hārita. Metārya was a resident of Tuṅgika, a place near Kauśāmbī, and Prabhāsa came from Rājagṛha, and both belonged to the Kauṇḍinya line. All the four had 300 disciples each. The presence of these eleven renowned scholars in the elaborated arrangement of the sacrifice added to the elegance of the grand celebration.

All these eleven scholars were the accepted commentators of their respective schools of philosophy, besides being great researchers in deepest mysteries. They were also acquainted with the philosophy of the other schools. But despite so profound a scholarship, not one of them was wholly free from doubt, though they never allowed these to be known to their disciples. Their doubts concerned the following :

1. Indrabhūti—whether the soul exists.
2. Agnibhūti—whether *karma* exists.
3. Vāyubhūti—whether the conscious principle and the body are the same.
4. Vyakta—whether there are five elements.
5. Sudharmā—whether in the next birth, one is the same as he is now.
6. Maṇḍita—how are fetters of, and liberation from *karma.*
7. Mauryaputra—whether heavens exist.
8. Akampita—whether hells exist.
9. Acalabhrātā—whether there are virtue and vice.
10. Metārya—whether there is life hereafter.
11. Prabhāsa—whether there is liberation.

On the second day after the attainment of omniscience, Bhagavān Mahāvīra arrived at the same place (Madhyama Pāvā) and halted in the Mahāsena park. A congregation was organised. The people of the township hurried at a rapid pace to be the first to reach the park. Even the gods were not lagging behind. When the *vedic* scholars saw air-chariots of the gods coming through the sky, they felt elated at the successful performance of the sacrifice. But within a short time, their happiness turned into dejection. For, the air-chariots of the gods did not halt over the sacrificial ground, but proceeded towards the park. With a feeling of depression, the scholars felt curious as to the destination of the gods. Who was this great soul in the neighbourhood that had attracted the gods from heaven? Men were sent in all directions to procure the information. Soon it became known to them that this exceptional man was none other than the all-knowing Mahāvīra. They learnt further that the gods had come to pay their homage and obeisance to him. At this, Indrabhūti thought in his mind,

> 'In the presence of such an ominiscient person like me, who is this other omniscient person that has come? Common folks may be deceived by anyone, but, it seems, this fellow has deceived even the gods. This is the reason why instead of coming to me, they are going to him.'

Immersed in his own thought, Indrabhūti felt a doubt about the gods. Thought he again,

> 'Maybe, they are as much gods as this fellow is omniscient. Whatever that may, but two swords cannot be placed in the same sheath. When I am present here, I cannot tolerate the presence of another all-knowing person.'

Indrabhūti saw people returning after having paid their homage and obeisance to Mahāvīra. He asked them many questions about him :

"Did you see this omniscient person? What sort of omniscient person is he? How does he look like?"

Being asked like this by Indrabhūti, people spoke at great length about the superhuman qualities of Mahāvīra. Indrabhūti felt in his mind,

'This must be a hypocrite, a dissembler, who has hypnotised the entire populace. He has entrapped them all in his snares. For, otherwise, so many could not have been deceived at a time. I cannot allow this sort of deceiptfulness being practised here. I have silenced so many great scholars. What is he in comparison to them? My scholarship is so far-reaching that being afraid of me, many have fled from their motherland. It is silly that a pretender should dominate like this in my presence.'

He gave a severe kick at the ground and stood up in anger. He printed a dozen *tilakas* on his forehead, hang a golden thread from his neck, wore yellow robes and took *darva*-cushion and water-pot. Then surrounded by 500 disciples, Indrabhūti set out and came straight to Mahāvīra.

No sooner did Mahāvīra saw Indrabhūti then he said,

"Hallow Indrabhūti of the Gautama line! You have doubt about the existence of the soul. It does not come to visual perception in the same sense as a jar does. You believe that anything which cannot be perceived by the sense organ is very much unreal as a flower blossoming in the sky."

Indrabhūti was surprised at the way in which Mahāvīra deciphered his inner thought. This was followed by a long discussion on the Soul in which his doubt was completely resovled. Inrabhūti accepted Mahāvīra as his spiritual master, and with all his disciples, he took shelter in Mahāvīra's spiritual order.

In the same manner, the remaining ten *Brāhmaṇas* came one after the other, and in the same manner, they too had their doubts resolved, and along with their followers, they joined the *nirgrantha* order. These 11 became famous as the *Gaṇadharas* (segment-leaders) in the spiritual order of Mahāvīra. Thus, the spiritual order of Mahāvīra started with a total strength of 4411 disciples all of whom were *Brāhmaṇas* converted to Jainism.

Indrabhūti became well-known as Gautama (which the name of his line).

At the liberation of Mahāvīra from this worldly life, Sudharmā succeeded him as *Ācārya* to the spiritual seat.

According to the Digambaras, it was Gautama who was the first successor of Mahāvīra to the spiritual seat.[4]

2. *Candanavālā*—In the Buddhist order, for some time, women were not initiated as nuns; but in the *nirgrantha* order, even at the first congregation of *Bhagavān* Mahāvīra, women were initiated as nuns. Candanavālā was the first to join the order as a nun, and even when the strength of the nuns reached 36,000 she remained foremost among them. Once, Mahāvīra went on a fast for six months, whose termination depended on the fulfilment of certain conditions set by himself (*i.e.*, these were not known to others). These conditions were as follows :

As to object—this must be dried *uḍada*, and it must exist at the corner of winnowing fan.
As to place —the donor must have one leg inside the threshold and another outside it.
As to time — at the fag end of the usual begging time.
As to state — a princess, enslaved, chained, with head tonsured, crying and one fast for three days.

He would accept food if these conditions were fulfilled; otherwise, the fast would be extended for another six months.[5]

When there were five days to complete six months, all the conditions were fulfilled in the hands of Candanavālā. The life-story of this pious woman was full of events from the start through its middle till its end. She was the only daughter of Dadhivāhana of Campā from his queen Dhāriṇī. She had two names, Candanavālā and Vasumatī, and she was reared up with the greatest care and in the midst of all joys. Once, King Śatānīka of Kauśāmbī came with a vast army by the water route, and without giving any time, laid seize of Campā. Dadhivāhana was unprepared for this. So, he was completely defeated. For two hours, Śatānīka's men looted the city of Campā like free booters. One of the charioteers got into the *harem* and carried away Queen Dhāriṇī and princess Candanavālā.

After his success, Śatānīka returned to Kauśāmbī; but the charioteer carried the queen and the princess to a lonely forest. He wanted to enjoy a sexual intercourse with them. The queen tried to dissuade him from this mean design, but the rogue was not prepared to listen to entreaties or good counsel. As the fellow was about to transgress the bounds of decency, and rushed towards the queen, she committed suicide by pulling out her tongue. This came as a great shock to that man and he did not dare to repeat a similar behaviour towards the princess.

The charioteer came back to Kauśāmbī and sold out the princess as a maid-servant in the market. At first, she was bought by a prostitute, and she passed her on to a merchant with whom she lived like a maid-servant. In her behaviour, she never made a display that she was a princess. Rather, she was always as soft and agreeable as *Candana* (sandal), from which she took her name which later became famous.

Candanavālā had the knack to make each one of her acts especially attractive. She was laborious too. So, she was liked by everybody. Other servants and maids were happy at her popularity. Whatever the assignments, the pressure of work could not hide her personality. Candanavālā reached her youth, all her limbs had their full development. The merchant's wife Mūlā became jealous of her lest she should be replaced by this servant girl in the eyes of the merchant. So, she kept Candanavālā constantly under observation. As Candanavālā worked, the mistress would supervise her. Candanavālā, however, did not bother. She always looked on her benefactor and benefactress as her own parents, and she never let them know that she was a princess of the royal blood.

One day, the merchant returned home from another village. It was already past midday. He walked on foot, and was very hungry and thirsty by the time he reached home. So, on reaching home, he sat down to clean his feet. Candanavālā fetched water for him. As the merchant rubbed his feet, she poured water on it. Suddenly, her hairs became loose and scattered on the ground. To save them from being soiled in unclean water, the merchant gently picked up the bunch of her hairs and placed them on her back. Seated at the window, Mūlā observed all this. She was alarmed to discover that her apprehension was not unfounded. Her whole body was ablaze as if with fire, and from that very moment, she started her conspiracy against her.

The merchant regularly visited other villages on business. One day, when the merchant was absent from home, Mūlā caught hold of Candanavālā, cut her hairs, tied her legs with a chain and pushed her into a vault. Then she locked her home from outside and went to her parental home. The merchant was absent from home for three days. When he came back, the home locked. He had surprise as well as irritation.

He took another door to go inside the house. One by one, he checked all the rooms, and they were looked. Then he came near the vault at the basement, and heard somebody groaning inside. He shouted,

"Is it Candanā?"

"Yes, dad, I am here."

These words came in a very low voice. The merchant's sorrow knew no bound. With a great difficulty, the merchant rescued her from the vault. He asked,

"My daughter! Who did this to you?"

But Canadanavālā was calm. She did no lose her patience. She said,

"Dad! Could you help me with some food?"

The merchant came up at once. The kitchen was locked. While looking around, he found some dried *uḍada* lying an a winnowing fan. He came to her with the fan, placed it in her hand and said,

"My daughter! You help yourself with these. Mean-while, let me arrange for the removal of your irons."

The merchant went out. With great difficulty, Candanavālā reached the door. With her legs chained, her head tonsured, and without food for three days, Candanavālā while holding the winnowing fan with the dried *uḍada* at a corner in her hands, thought,

'If at this moment a *nirgrantha* monk comes, I shall deem it a great good-luck of mine to offer him a portion of my dry and rough food.'

Her luck favoured her. By chance, *Bhagavān* Mahāvīra who was on a conditional fast came there. He had already completed five months and 25 days of his condition. Candanavālā became thrilled to see the future *Tīrthaṅkara* at her door. All her pain turned into joy. Overflowing with joy, she prayed,

"Supreme Master! Be gracious enough to accept this pure food and fulfil my wishes."

Mahāvīra possessed *avadhi* knowledge. He checked if his conditions were fulfilled. He found that they were all fulfilled save one. Candanavālā had no tears in her eyes. Mahāvīra turned to go back. Candanavālā cried. Mahāvīra turned and looked at her. All his conditions were now fulfilled. He retraced his steps and proceeded towards her. With her eyes shedding tears and with her heart overflowing with joy, she offered the dry *uḍada* skin to Mahāvīra. Mahāvīra broke his fast at that place. There arose a din in the sky,

'A Great offer! A laudable offer!'

Five divine things made there appearance. There was a shower of 12,50,00,000 gold pieces. Candanavālā's beauty was at its best and her iron chains turned into gold ornaments. She was now hailed all over the city as a great lady.

The report reached the king's palace where the king and the queen heard about Candanavālā. It came to light that Mṛgāvatī was her own maternal aunt. She was at once taken to the palace. The king started looking for a suitable groom to settle her; but she made it clear that she was not keen to settle in domestic life.

After the attainment of omniscience, when Mahāvīra came to Madhyama Pāvā and held his first congregation, Candanavālā was initiated into his order as a nun. It was the occasion when Mahāvīra accepted many lay followers and administered them necessary vows. These became *śrāvakas* and *śrāvikās.* The fourfold order emerged in this manner, consisting of the monks, the nuns, male followers and female followers, and collectively, it was given the name *'tīrtha!'*, and as the organiser of the *tīrtha,* Mahāvīra became the celebrated *Tīrthaṅkara,* the Organiser of the Fourfold Order.[6]

3. *Meghakumāra*—Meghakumāra was the son of King Śreṇika. He was married to eight princesses. Once, *Tīrthaṅkara* Mahāvīra came to Rājagṛha. King Śreṇikas and the entire royal household came to pay their homage and tribute. After the sermon was over, people returned home. Even the king went back to his palace. Mahāvīra's words had, however, created a great inspiration in the mind of Prince Meghakumāra, and he saw a new way opened before him. He became keen to give up his life at the palace and take the life of a wandering monk. He came to his parents, and with folded hands, he submitted to them as follows :

> "You are my parents, and it is under your care and affection that I have grown. During the years of my life, you have taken great pains for me. But now I pray for one thing from you. I have seen through life and it holds no more attraction for me. At this moment, *Bhagavān* Mahāvīra is present in the city, and if you be so good as to permit me. I would like to utilise this chance and follow him like a monk in his order."

The king and the queen explained to him the difficulties and hardships of a monk's life, but the prince was firm in his resolve. He convinced his parents that his choice was not the result of emotion, nor was it based on ignorance.

When King Śreṇika found that the prince was decided, he made a last request to him :

"My dear son! You say that you have seen through life and that you are tired of the world. Very good. Neither kingdom, nor wealth or family attracts you to the rear. But I have a final request to you, and I hope, you will fulfil it. It is that at least for one day, you hold the reign of power and seat on the throne as king. I shall be happy if you agree."

Meghakumāra agreed to his parent's request. With complete celebrations and rituals, he was placed on the throne. There was rejoicing all over the city. The king was fully happy. With a filian affection, he looked at his son. The he said,

"My dear son! What can I do for you?"

With due humility, Meghakumāra said,

"Father! If you are pleased with me, then, get me from the market the duster, the wooden pot etc. Now, I want to go out as a monk."

King Śreṇika fulfilled all his requests. The duster cost a lakh of gold coins and the pot cost another lakh. Like his coronation, his initiation was also marked by great festivities. On beging initiated by *Bhagavān* Mahāvīra, Meghakumāra dedicated his life to spiritual pursuits.[7]

4. *Nandīsena*—Nandīsena was also a son of King Śreṇika. Once, Mahāvīra came to Rājagṛha when, in the company of the king and other members of the royal household, Nandīsena attended his congregation. Thousands came to pay their homage and obeisance and to listen, and there were questions and answers, whereupon, out of inspiration, thousands courted equanimity and became partially renounced; but Nandīsena was in favour of a total renunciation in order to be a monk.

People all over the city talked of his great resolve to give up non-ending pleasures at the palace and to go out like a begging mendicant. Suddenly, a voice was heard from the sky :

"Prince! Reconsider your decision. Your *karma* giving you a worldly life is yet to be exhausted. It exists and it must be gone through. Your resolve is indeed noble, but *karma* is more powerful and inexorable."

The prince smiled within himself. He was so full of the idea of renunciation that he said with courage :

"Does darkness withstand light? How long do the patches of clouds

> struggle against gusts of wind? On initiation, I shall submerge myself deep under hard penances, so that it would be impossible for *karma* to be effective. What can be the base of the future except the present? I shall spend every moment of my life carefully to the performance of penances, combined with studies, meditation and *kāyotsarga*. I will not let any evil force to strike any root there."

Thus completely unmindful of the favourable as well as unfavourable factors, a determined Nandīsena came to attend the congregation of *Bhagavān* Mahāvīra, and displaying supreme indifference to the mundane life, he joined the order of monks. But the possibility of harm makes a man vigilant every moment. To render the divine voice in efficacious, Nandīsena immersed himself into deep penances. In this manner, he turned his plump and powerful body into a skeleton devoid of all lusture. Only his bones were visible. He led a solitary life, and concentrated on the nature of the self. Fortnight after fortnight, and month after month, he lived on fast, and visited human habitation only on the fast-breaking day to beg food, but soon he came back to his own seclusion and concentrated on slef. In consequence, he acquired good many powers that come from penance.

While discharging pious duties, sometimes a man slips from his path, and gets entangled in an unexpected trap. One day, Nadīsena came to the village to beg food. It was a sheer accident that he found himself into a harlot's home. He met a lady inside. In his usual manner, he aksed,

> "May I get some right food here?"

The women observed the begger-like appearance and mean status of the man, and spoke out instantaneously,

> "One who is rich is welcome at my door, but a poor man, a beggar, has no place here."

These words of the fallen woman roused a strong ego in him. He thought that the woman had not yet recognised him, that she had no idea of the powers of his penances. He should display some. It was time for that. He picked up a stick from the floor and broke into two, and at once, there was a shower of gold coins from the stick. The woman looked at Nandīsena, as Nandīsena looked at her. She did not realise for once if this was a dream or a reality; but soon she recollected herself with great skill. She came forward and welcomed Nandīsena with all sorts of lusty overtures. This became an occasion for a straight clash between Attachment and Detachment. On one side, there were penances practised over years, and, on the other there was the sweet welcome that he had just received a couple of minutes ago. Nandīsena forgot all about his penances and responded to her overtures. He agreed to enjoy life in her charming company.

Knocked out from the spiritual path, Nandīsena dangled for some time between two extremes. The only bright spot was the vow he took even in this lowly position. The vow was as follows :

> 'Everyday, I shall send 10 persons to join as monks the holy order of Mahāvīra. Till this vow is fulfilled, I shall not touch any food.'

Nandīsena remained true to his vow. Everyday, he induced 10 persons to join the *nirgrantha* order and sent them to *Bhagavān* Mahāvīra. He took food only on fulfilment of his vow.

One day, he had nine persons on hand, and the tenth one was a goldsmith who proved to be a very hard nut to crack. He was not responding to his arguments and pursuasions. It was already very late, and the harlot was restless. She came to Nandīsena and asked him to take his food. But Nandīsena said,

> "How do I accept food till I have a tenth convert?"

The harlot had lost her patience. She retored,

> "In that case, why don't you offer yourself as the tenth convert?"

The words went deep to shake his heart. And as the harlot looked on, he came to *Bhagavān* Mahāvīra and became re-initiated into his order.[8]

5. *Ṛsabhadatta and Devānandā*—Having spent his thirteenth year at Rājagṛha, *Bhagavān* Mahāvīra turned his steps in the direction of Videha. On the way, he paid a visit to *Brāhmaṇa* Kuṇḍagrāma. In this village lived *Brāhmaṇa* Ṛsabhadatta and his wife Devānandā. The news of the arrival of Mahāvīra spread through the village with the speed of lightning. Ṛsabhadatta and his wife came to pay their homage to him. As they came near Mahāvīra, they took the five precautions. They gave up live objects, arranged their clothes in proper order, place a cloth on the shoulder, folded their hands and concentrated their mind. They then moved round Mahāvīra and sat down to listen his inspiring words. Now, the more the pious lady Devānandā looked at Mahāvīra, the more she became thrilled. Her breasts were swollen with motherly affection, and the eyes were wet with joy. But she did not realise why she was experiencing this change within herself. All of a sudden, her brassier lossened and milk flowed out from her breasts.

Gaṇadhara Gautama observed this unusual scence, and he had a curiousity about the implication of all this. He came forward, paid his homage and obeisance to Mahāvīra and submitted.

"*Bhante!* Why is Devānandā so much thrilled today? What is the special occassion for which milk has flown out from her breast?"

Bhagavān Mahāvīra explained,

"Gautama! Devānandā is my mother. I am her son. She has been so much thrilled because of her motherly affection towards me."

People were surprised at this unusual revealation. They had never heard of it before. But Gaṇadhara Gautama came out with a fresh interpellation :

"But, *Bhante*, we know that you are born of Queen Triśalā."

At this *Bhagavān* Mahāvīra revealed the whole story of the transfer of his own embryo. Till then the account was unknown to everybody. The joy of Ṛṣabhadatta and Devānandā knew no bound.

Bhagavān Mahāvīra delivered his sermon to Ṛṣabhadatta, Devānandā and all other people that had assembled there. The people became very much inspired. At this moment, Ṛṣabhadatta stood up and made the following submission :

"*Bhante!* I have faith in your religion. I have devotion for it. This religion helps one to terminate rebirth. I want to accept it and be sheltered in it, desire to be initiated as a monk and terminate my *karma* in its entirety."

So saying, he went to the north-eastern direction, gave up his ornaments, etc., uprooted five handfuls of hairs and stood before Mahāvīra. Then he moved round him thrice and paid him his homage and obeisance. Thereafter, he was initiated as a monk in the order.[9] Devānandā too did as her husband had done, and became a nun under the most illustrious Canadanvālā.[10]

6. *Jamāli and Priyadarśanā*—Jamāli who was a *Kṣatriya* prince was a resident of *Kṣatriya* Kuṇḍagrāma, he was a very rich man. He was the son of Sudarśanā, Mahāvīra's own sister. Jamāli was married with Mahāvīra's own daughter Priyadarśanā. So, on one side, he was Mahāvīra's nephew from his sister, and on the other, he was his own son-in-law.[11]

While wandering from village to village, Mahāvīra came to *Kṣatriya* Kuṇḍagrāma. People assembled round him and a congregation was held. After the meeting had been addressed by *Bhagavān* Mahāvīra, people returned home.

Now, Jamāli who had come to attend the sermon felt especially inspired. He stood before Mahāvīra and said,

> "*Bhante!* The words of the *nirgranthas* appeal to me. They appeared to be truths. I desire to give up my life as a householder and be initiated as monk."

Said *Bhagavān* Mahāvīra,

> "Do as it may suit your convenience, but delay not."

Jamāli returned to his own palace and discussed his intention with his parents. This came as a great shock to them. They argued with him in all manners, but all their efforts were in vain. At last, they had to give him permission. The initiation ceremony was organised with the greatest pomp. Thousands of citizens came to witness the occasion. They showered their blessings and good wishes on the new initiate.

Then, at a humble request from Jamāli and his parents, Mahāvīra took him in his holy order. On the occasion of Jamāli's initiation, 500 *Kṣatriyas* courted monkhood with him. Jamāli's wife, Priyadarśanā, who was Mahāvīra's own daughter, joined the holy order as a nun in the company of 1000 *Kṣatriya* women.[12]

7. *Jayantī*—From Vaiśālī, *Bhagavān* Mahāvīra proceeded towards Vatsa. Kauśāmbī was the capital of Vatsa. There, he took shelter in a *caitya* named Candrāvataraṇa. The ruling monarch was King Udayana, who was the son of Mṛgāvatī, the daughter of King Ceṭaka of Vaiśālī. Udayana's father was Śatānīka and his grand-father was Sahasrānīka. Jayantī happened to be Udayana's paternal aunt. She was a follower of the *śramaṇa* path and was well-known for her devotion and service to the monks. Any monk visiting the city came first Jayantī's abode and lodged there for some time.

When Jayantī came to know that *Bhagavān* Mahāvīra had arrived, she came to him in the company of her son to pay her homage and obeisance. She attended the sermon and asked questions on which she desired to be enlightened. The discussion was as under :

Jayantī—"*Bhante!* How does a living being quickly acquire heaviness?"

Mahāvīra—'Jayantī'. There are 18 lapses or sins, and by practising these, a living being quickly acquires heaviness. These 18 are : slaughter, falsehood, usurpation, sexual relation, possession anger, pride, deceit, greed, liking, disliking, quarrel, non-acqusitiveness, malice, back-bitting, attachment-detachment, falsehood to deceive and wrong outlook."

Jayantī—"*Bhante!* How does a living being become light?"

Mahāvīra—"He becomes light by desisting from these (eighteen) starting with slaughter. Just as slaughter, etc., increase wordly life, give it a longer span and make one to be born again and again, so abstension from them reduces wordly life, shortens its span and cuts out rebirth."

Jayantī—"*Bhante!* Does one become entitled to liberation through his own exertion or by some inexorable law?"

Mahāvīra—"One acquires title to liberation through his own exertion, and not by some in exorable law."

Jayantī—"*Bhante*! Do all the souls who are to be perfected in this life attain liberation?"

Mahāvīra—"That's right. Whoever be perfected in this life must attain liberation."

Jayantī—"*Bhante!* If all the would-be perfected souls are liberated, then there will be no more of them in the world."

Mahāvīra—"Jayantī! It doesn't happen like that. If from different categories of *pudgala* which are with a beginning, which are limited, and bounded (by nonsphere) on both ends, one atom is taken out during each (smallest) unit of time, and if the process is repeated over an infinite number of clock-wise and anti-clockwise phases of the time-cycle, still the different categories of atoms will not be exhausted; in the same manner, even though the would-be liberated souls who are to be liberated in this life are liberated, the world will not be empty of them."

Jayantī—"Is it good that a living being sleeps or wakes?"

Mahāvīra—"For some, it is good that they sleep; but for others, it is good that they wake."

Jayantī—"*Bhante!* Why is it so?"

Mahāvīra—Jayantī! Those who are habitually sinful, who follow sin, to whom sin is very dear, who explore sin, who inspire sin, who are addicted to sin, who take delight in sin, and who live on sin, for them it is good that they sleep. When they sleep, they do not be instruments of sorrow and pain to one-organ beings, to two-to-four-organ beings, to flora bodies and to the immobile beings. When they sleep, they save themselves as well as others from sinful acts. So, it is good that they sleep."

Bhagavān Mahāvīra went on :

> "Jayantī! Those who are pious, who follow *dharma,* to whom *dharma* is dear, who explore *dharma,* who uphold *dharma,* who are inclined to *dharma,* who derive delight in *dharma,* who live on *dharma,*—it is good that such be awake. When they wake, they do things which relieve

many of their sorrow and pain. When they wake, they become instrumental for pious deeds for themselves as well as for others. So, it is good that they wake. It was with this in view that I said that it was good for some to sleep, and for others to wake."

Jayantī—"*Bhante!* Is weakness or strength good for the living being?"

Mahāvīra—"Strength is good for some, and weakness is good for others."

Jayantī—"*Bhante!* How is to so?"

Mahāvīra—"Those who are sinful, and those who live on sin, it is good that they are weak. Their weakness makes them incapable to cause pain to others. But those who are pious,—for them it is good that they are strong. It is for this that I say that strength is good for some and weakness is good for others."

Jayantī—"Oh great monk, the very embodiment of piety! Is it good for the living beings to be exertive or to be lethargic?"

Mahāvīra—"For some, it is good to be exertive, while for others, it is good to be lethargic."

Jayantī—"Of thou the very embodiment of forgiveness! how it so?"

Mahāvīra—"Those who are impious, and those who move about performing sinful deeds, it is good that they are lethargic. But those who are pious, they should be energetic. For, in being energetic, a pious being is ever vigilant, and he is respectful of and serviceable to his preceptor, teacher, senior monks, other monks, segment (*guṇa),* order (*Saṅgha)* and breathren-in-faith."

Jayantī—"*Bhante!* By being a slave unto his organ of audition, what does a living being bind?"

Mahāvīra—"Not a slave unto his organ of audition alone, but being a slave unto all his five organs of senses, he glides back and forth in the world."

The devoted woman Jayantī was delighted to obtain solutions of all her difficulties from Mahāvīra. Having acquired the knowledge of Soul and Matter, she joined the order of Mahāvīra as a nun.[13]

8. *Kāśyapa*[14]—Kāśyapa Gṛhapati lived at Rājagṛha. He became a monk in the order of Mahāvīra. He mastered the 11 *Aṅgas* and practised servere penances. He continued to enrich his soul in the holy order for 16 years. Then he gave up his mortal frame on Mount Vipula by courting a fast unto death.[15]

9. *Parivrājaka monk Skandaka*—Mahāvīra moved out from *Guṇaśīla caitya*, and after passing through many villages, he came to Kayaṅgala. There he halted at a *caitya* named Chatrapalāśaka which was on the north-eastern side. The congregation of *Bhagavān* Mahāvīra met at this place.

Not far from Kayaṅgala was the city of Śrāvastī. There lived a *Parivrājaka* monk named Skandaka who belonged to the Kātyāyana line and who was the disciple of *Parivrājaka* Gardabhāla. He was versed in the *Vedas,* Itihāsa and *Nighaṇṭu.* He was a specialist in the *Ṣaṣṭitantra* of Kapila. He had mastered mathematics, phonetics, conventions, grammar, prosody, etymology, astronomy and many other profound texts produced by the Brāhmanical scholarship. In the same city, there lived a Vaiśālikaśrāvaka named Piṅgala who was a follower of Mahāvīra. One day, we came to the cottage of Skandaka and said to him,

> "Māgadha (*i.e.,* one born in Magadha)! Are the spheres with limit or without limit? Are the souls with limit or without limit? Is the above of the perfected beings with limit or without limit? Are the perfected beings with limit or without limit? By what death does a being enlongen his stay in various existences, and by what death does he cut short that stay?"

On hearing these questions, Skandaka was in confusion. He did not know the correct answer. Whenever he wanted to open his lips, the answer would not come. "Besides, he was not sure if his question would satisfy Piṅgala. Confused by his own thought, he could give no reply. He remained silent. Piṅgala repeated his questions with eagerness twice or thrice. But a hesitant and apprehensive Skandaka could give no reply. He lost confidence in himself. His intellect did not work.

One day, Skandaka heard people discussing about the arrival of Mahāvīra at the Chatrapalāśaka caitya outside the city. Thought he,

> "How very nice it would be, if I go to him and obtain solutions of these questions from him." He made his decision firm and returned to his cottage. Having returned, he picked up the triple stick, small cup, garland made from *rudrākṣa* beads, earthen pot, cushion, cloth for drying vessels, channalaya, hook, ring, wrist-band, umbrella, vanana, sandals and saffron robes, held them in proper manner and set out for reaching the city of Kayaṅgalā.

Just then, *Śramaṇa Bhagavān* Mahāvīra said to Gautama.

> "Gautama! Today will meet with your former companion."

Gautama—"*Bhante!* Who do you mean?"

Mahāvīra—"Skandaka *Parivrājaka* of the Kātyāyana line."

Gautama—"*Bhante!* When and how will the same *Parivrājaka* meet me?"

Mahāvīra—"At Śrāvastī, Piṅgala, who is a follower of the *nirgrantha* order, asked him some questions : but he could not give any reply. So, equipped with all the external marks and objects of his order, he is coming here. He has covered a good part of the way. He is on the road. Soon he would arrive here. You will meet him today."

Gautama—"*Bhante!* Is he fit to be your disciple?"

Mahāvīra—"Yes, he has it, and surely he will be my disciple."

As Mahāvīra and Gautama were conversing, Skandaka became visible. Gautama got up and advanced to welcome him. Said he,

> "Skandaka! Welcome to thee! A very hearty welcome to thee! The coming is good. But, Māgadha, tell me if it is true that Pingala, a follower of the *nirgrantha* order, asked you some questions, and that you could give no reply to them, and that this is the purpose of the coming here."

Hearing his own secret thoughts being uttered by Gautama so openly, Skandaka was taken by a great surprise. He said,

> "Gautama! Who is that wise man, or savant, who has known beforehand the inner thoughts of mine so soon?"

Gautama had a feeling of wholesome pride. Said he,

> "Skandaka! My spiritual master, my spiritual preceptor, *Śramaṇa Bhagavān* Mahāvīra is the holder of supreme knowledge (*kevala darśana).* He is an Arhat, a *Jina* a *Kevalin,* a knower of the past, present and future, all-knowing and all-seeing, None of your thoughts could remain unknown to him."

Skandaka expressed his desire to pay homage and obeisance to Mahāvīra. Gautama conducted him before his Master, and Skandaka felt very happy to see him. With due regard, he moved round him thrice and bowed before him. Then addressing Skandaka, Mahāvīra said,

> "Indeed, Skandaka, in the city of Śrāvastī, the Vaiśālika-śrāvaka Piṅgala had said unto thee as follows : 'Oh Māgadha! Are the spheres with limit or without limit? Are the souls with limit or without limit? Is the abode of the perfected beings with limit or without limit? Are the perfected beings with limit or without limit? By what death does a being enlonged his stay in (various) existences, and by what death does he cut that stay short?'"

Skandaka—"*Bhante!* You are correct, He asked me these questions."

The *Bhagavān* Mahāvīra started his answers which were as follows :

"The spheres have to be viewed from four angles, *viz.*, as substance, as place, as time and as phenomena."

As to substance, the spheres are one and with limit.

"As to place, the spheres are said to be extended over innumerable crores of *yojanas* in length and breadth, and over innumerable crores of *yojanas* in circumference, but sitll with limit."

"As to time, the spheres existed in the past, they exist in the present and they will exist in the future. There was, there is and there will be no time when there were no spheres. The spheres did exist, and will continue to exist. The spheres are fixed, eternal permanent, non-depreciating, non-wearing-out, ever-existent, and without limit."

"As to phenomena, the spheres are with limitless colours, smells, substances and touches, with limitless physical structures, with limitless heaviness and lightness, with limitless non-heaviness, non-lightness, and without limit."

"So, you see, Skandaka, as to substance, the spheres are with limit, and so they are with limit as to place; but as to time, the spheres are without limit and so also without limit they are as to phenomena."

"As to souls, think in terms of the same four items. As to substance, the souls are one and with limit. As to place, souls are with innumerable space-units, holding innumerable space-units, but still with limit. As to time, there was no time, nor there will be any, when souls did not, do not any will not exist, till ever-existent and without limit. As to phenomena, souls are in possession of limitless knowledge, of limitless vision, of limitless conduct, of limitless non-heaviness non-lightness, and again without limit. So, you see, as to substance, souls are'with limit, and so also as to place, they are with limit; but as to time, without limit, and so as to phenomena, *i.e.*, without limit."

"And so you had in your mind whether the abode of the perfected souls is with limit or without limit. On this too, I ordain that the abode of the perfected souls is to be viewed from four angles, *viz.*, substance, place, time and phenomena. As to substance, the abode of the perfected souls is one and with limit. As to place, this abode of the perfected souls extends over an area of 45,00,000 *yojanas* in length, and so also in breadth, and with a circumference which is 142,30,249 hundred-thousand *yojanas* more or less, but still with limit. As to time, there was no time, nor there will be any, when the abode of the perfected souls did not, does not and will not exist. As to phenomena, the same as with the spheres. So, you see, the abode of the perfected souls is, as to substance, with limit, and so also as to place; but without limit as to time, and so also without limit as to phenomena."

"And Skandaka, you had in mind whether the perfected souls are with limit or without limit. Here, too, you have to consider them in terms of the same four, *viz.*, as to substance, as to place, as to time as as to phenomena. As to substance, the perfected souls are one and with limit; as to place, the perfected souls are in possession of innumerable space-units and hold innumerable space-units, but still with limit; as to time, the perfected souls are with a genesis but without limit; as to phenomena, the perfected souls are in possession of limitless knowledge, limitless vision, till in possession of limitless non-heaviness, limitless, non-lightness, still without limit. So, you see, the perfected souls are, as to substance, with limit : as to place, with limit : but as to time, without limit, and so without limit as to phenomena."

"And then, Skandaka, you had in mind, by what death does a being enlongen his stay and by what death does he shorten it. On this, I say that death is of two types, *viz.*, death of the fool (*bāla-maraṇa)* and death of the prudent (*paṇḍita-maraṇa).*

"And what about the death of the fool?"

"Wells, it may occur by 12 causes which are,

1. due to starvation and thirst,
2. due to too much submission to the organs of senses,
3. due to inner thorn,
4. death called tadbhāva condemning one to rebirth in the same existence again and again,
5. death due to a fall from a mountain,
6. due to a fall from a tree,
7. due to drowning in water,
8. due to entering into fire,
9. due to taking poison,
10. due to wound from some deadly weapon,
11. due to hanging, and
12. due to piercing by some wild animal."

Death due to any one of these causes enlongen stay in the infernal existence, or in animal, human and celestial existences. One dying due to any one of these causes continues to glide back and forth in the wilderness, without a beginning and without an end, in the infernal, subhuman, human or even celestial existences. Hence, he enlongens his stay by dying the death of a fool."

—"And pray what about dying the death of the prudent?"

—"Death of the prudent may take in either of the two ways, which are, by lying steadfast (till death) like a tree (*padapopagamana)*, and lying without intake (*bhattapacca).* Lying steadfast till death may be of two types, which are, lying in the midst of a human surrounding, and lying far away from human habitation. Even death by renouncing intake of food may be of two types, which are, lying in the midst of a human surrounding, and lying far away from human habitation. A monk, who dies in an *upāśraya* (monks' abode), either by lying steadfast or by renouncing intake, has to be cremated outside the monks' abode or outside the city because of which such death is called *nirhārima*. A monk who dies in a forest in either of the two ways need not be taken out of the forest for cremation because of which such death is called a *nirhārima*. *Pādapopagamano* death, no matter where *nirhārima* or *anirhārima*, restricts all physical activities (*apratikarma)*, for which such death prescribes no duty to preceptor, teacher, and others on the part of the dying monk. Dying by giving up all intakes, no matter whether *nirhārima* or *anirhārima*, does not restrict physical activities. (In other words, it is *sapratikarma)*. Hence, in this, duty to preceptor, teachers and others (till death) is not forbidden. Skandaka! People who die in either of these ways do neither go to hell, nor do they pass through an infinite number of briths. They shorten their long stay."

On receiving the reply to all his question, Skandaka became very happy. He expressed full confidence in the words of *Bhagavān* Mahāvīra and expressed a desire to court monkhood. Mahāvīra initiated him and gave him complete instructions about the life of a monk.[16]

10. *Śramaṇa Keśīkumāra*—While wandering from village to village, once *Bhagavān* Mahāvīra turned his steps towards Hastināpur. The whole party of monks, including Gaṇadhara Gautama and others, headed by the Leader, arrived at Śrāvastī and camped at a caitya named Koṣṭhaka. Outside the same city, there was a part named Tiṇḍuka which was already occupied by *Śramaṇa* Keśīkumāra and his disciples who belonged to the order to Arhat *Pārśva*. Keśīkumāra was initiated into monkhood at a very early age. He was foremost in knowledge and conduct and possessed three types of knowledge, *viz.*, *mati, śruta* and *avadhi.*

(When the two groups were camped side by side), it was but natural that the monks of the two groups, compared their respective orders, tenets and practices. Arhat *Pārśva* had propagated religion based on 'four vows'; but *Bhagavān* Mahāvīra lay emphasis on 'five vows'. When the striving of both the groups was towards the same goal, the differences needed justification. One had suggested the use of cloth, and the other had preferred nudity for the monks. These differences highlighted the discussions between the monks of the two orders. The situation reached a stage when it became necessary for the top people of the two orders to meet and settle the points at issue. In the company of his own disciples, one day, Gaṇadhara Gautama came to the Tiṇḍuka park. *Śramaṇa* Keśīkumāra was there with his own monks. When Keśīkumāra saw that Gautama was coming to him, he came forward to receive him with due respect and honour. A cushion made from *palāla*, *kuśa* and other grass was spread for the honoured guest. The meeting of the two monks attracted many people at the park who were eager to know the outcome.

Being requested by Gautama, Keśīkumāra started the discussion.

Keśī—"Mahābhāga! I find that *Bhagavān Vardhamāna* lay emphasis on five vows, whereas *Arhat Pārśva* did on four. Oh learned monk! When our goals are the same, why should there be so much difference in our ways? When there is so much difference in our ways, why don't you feel inquisitive about it?"

Gautama—"In a religion which deals with such fundamentals as *jīva, ajīva* and so on, it is intellect alone that can probe into them. By virtue of the period to which they belonged, the monks of the first *Tīrthaṅkara* were simple and unwise (*ṛju-jaḍa)* and those of the last *Tīrthaṅkara* are crooked and unwise (*vakra-jaḍa);* in contrast, the monks of the remaining 22 *Tīrthaṅkaras* were simple and wise (*ṛju-prajñā).* This is why there are differences. The age of the monks of the first *Tīrthaṅkara* was difficult to purify and that of the last *Tīrthaṅkara* is difficult (for spiritual exertions), but the ages of the intervening *Tīrthaṅkaras* were easy to purify and easy for spiritual exertions."

Keśī—"Gautama! You have given a very satisfactory reply to my first question. Now, I have a second question which, I hope, you will answer. Now, *Bhagavān Vardhamāna* has prescribed nudity for the monks, but Arhat *Pārśva* suggested that they should use clothes. Why this difference between the two when the goal is the same? What is the special reason for this? Famous monk! When there is so much difference in the externals, does it not raise a querry in your mind?"

Gautama—"You will agree with me that an external mark is necessary to create a confidence in the people, to uphold restraint during the rainy season, to practise restraint in the course of one's wanderings, to recive knowledge, etc., (which are bestowed on those who possess such mark), or simply to be congnizable that 'this is a monk'. *Bhagavān!* Both the *Tīrthaṅkara* hold the undisputed view that the necessary equipments for a monk who is dedicated to the attainment of liberation are Knowledge Vision and Conduct."

Keśī—"Noble sire! You are standing surrounded by several thousand foes. They are advancing on you in order to conquer you. How do you win victory over them?"

Gautama—"When I overpower one, five have been overpowered; and when I have overpowered five, ten have been overpowered, and in this manner, I win victory over thousands of my foes."

Keśī—"Whom do you call your foes?"

Gautama—"Great monk! The foes consist of the wandering (*i.e.*, not concentrated) mind, four passion and five organs of senses."

Keśī—"Oh monk! In the world, we see many beings who are fettered; but how have you liberated yourself of fetters and move about by being light?"

Gautama—"Monk! I have cut the fetters in all ways; and so they don't claim me, I move about free and light."

Keśī—"*Bhante!* Whom do you call fetters?"

Gautama—"*Bhagavān!* Fetters consist of liking and disliking and deep affection which are very dangerous. I have uprooted them with endeavour, and live free and light."

Keśī—"Gautama! How did you uproot the creeper whose root goes to the depth of the heart, and whose fruits are highly poisonous?"

Gautama—"I have wholly uprooted that creeper, cut it into pieces and thrown out. Now I am wholly liberated from the intake of the poisonous fruits."

Keśī—"Great soul! Whom do you call the creeper?"

Gautama—"Great monk! In this world, desire is the most dangerous creeper, and it gives very dangerous fruits. Having duly uprooted it, live on."

Keśī—"Wise monk! There is a severe, a tremendous fire raising in the body. It will reduce the body to ashes. How did you cool it? How did you put it out?"

Gautama—"Great sage! I keep this fire under check by pouring water which is born in a great cloud, which is excellent and pure. Thus watered, the said fire causes me no trouble."

Keśī—"Great soul! What is this fire and what is this water?"

Gautama—"Wise monk! The passions are the fire. Scriptures, discipline and penance are the great clouds. Controlled by the pour of *śruta,* water this fire causes me no trouble."

Keśī—"Oh monk! A brave, dreadful and wicked horse is running about in all the directions. Though you are riding on this horse, how is it that it does not take you in the wrong direction?"

Gautama—"Great sage! I keep the running horse tied with the bridle of *śruta* so that it cannot run in the wrong direction; it proceeds in the right direction."

Keśī—"Famous man! What is this horse?"

Gautama—"Oh monk! Mind is the most tremendous and dreadful horse. It runs about in all the directions. Like Kanthaka-horse, it is kept under control by me by spiritual instructions."

Keśī—"Great monk! In the world, there are many bad ways which degrade a man from the honest track. But how is it that you, while moving on the honest track, are never taken off it?"

Gautama—"Oh leading-most among the monks! I know well those who move on the right track and also I know those who follow the wrong track. So, I do not deviate from the right track."

Keśī—"Oh wise man! What is the right track and what is the wrong track?"

Gautama—"Oh sage! The heretics who believe in wrong prescriptions are on the wrong track. The right track has been described by the *Jinas.* And decidedly this track is the best one."

Keśī—"Great monk! What is the island which provides succor and stability to living beings who are flowing in the current of a vast water?"

Gautama—"Great monk! There is a vast island. It is widely extended. But the flow of the water is completely helpless here."

Keśī—"Wise monk! What is that great island?"

Gautama—"Great monk! For living beings drowning in the flow of old age and death, the isle of religion provides the shelter, and to take shelter on it is good."

Keśī—"In a sea of mighty waves, you are on board a ship which is haphazardly moving across the current. I beg to ask how do you reach the other shore?"

Gautama—A boat with leaks does not reach the other shore, but a boat without leak reaches the other shore."

Keśī—"What is that boat?"

Gautama—"The body is the boat; the soul is the sailor; the world is the ocean which great sages easily cross through."

Keśī—"Many living beings live in the midst of a great darkness. For these living beings, what serves as the beacon light?"

Gautama—"The sun which has risen is the beacon light for all the living beings."

Keśī—"Pray, whom do you call the sun?"

Gautama—"One whose attachments are exhausted such a Sun, Victor, an Omniscient has already risen. He is the beacon light in the whole world."

Keśī—"For living beings, tortured by physical and mental pain, which place do you consider wholesome, full of bliss and free from obstruction?"

Gautama—"There is a permanent place at the crest of the sphere where there is no old age, death, disease or pain. But to reach there is extremely difficult."

Keśī—"What palce is that?"

Gautama—"That place attained by the great sages has been variously called *nirvāṇa, avyābādha, siddhi, lokāgra, kṣema, śiva* and *anābādha.* Oh monk! This is a place where one may eternally live, which is at the crest of the sphere, but which is most difficult to attain. Great souls who attain this position terminate the long course of wordly life and be free anxiety."

Concluding the discussion, Keśīkumāra said,

"Great monk Gautama! Your wisdom is profound. You have uprooted my doubts. So, oh one who is free from all doubts, oh one who has mastered all the *Sūtras,* I bow to thee."

Having bowed to *Gaṇadhara* Gautama, *Śramaṇa* Keśīkumāra, with his vast body of monks accepted the religion of 'five vows' with deep devotion and joined the holy order of *Bhagavān* Mahāvīra.[17]

Like *Śramaṇa* Keśīkumāra, many others, notably monk Kālāsaveśīyaputta,[18] monk Gaṅgeya,[19] Peḍhālaputta Udaka,[20] and others, held discussions on the fundamentals and changed over from the religion of 'four vows' to one of 'five vows.'

The above account brings to our knowledge the history of the absorption of the Order of *Arhat Pārśva* by the emerging Order of *Bhagavān* Mahāvīra, as also the points of difference or divergence between the two which kept them separate till this absorption.

11. *Śālibhadra and Dhanya*—The Jaina tradition has been enriched by the exceedingly charming and widely known life-story of Śālibhadra and Dhanya. The two were closely related as brothers-in-law, one having married, another's sister, and both were the followers of Mahāvīra.

Śālibhadra was the son of *Gṛhapati* Gobhadra, an affluent resident of Rājagṛha. His mother's name was Bhadrā and that of his sister was Subhadrā. When Śālibhadra was still a child, his father died. So, his mother had an extra affection for him and he was brought up in the midst of all comforts. It is stated that after his death, Śālibhadra's father was born in heaven, and he supplied everyday 33 boxes full of clothes and ornaments (33 boxes of clothes, 33 boxes of ornaments and 33 boxes of sweeets, according to another reading) for his son and his daughters-in-law. Bharda managed the affairs of the entire household. Śālibhadra spent his days at the seventh floor of his mansion enjoying the finest pleasures of life.

One day, some dealers in *ratna-kambala* (blankets made of fine gems) came to the city. They carried a stock of 16 pieces each valued at 1,25,000 gold pieces. But they could not find a single buyer in the entire market of Rājagṛha. At last, they came to King Śreṇika. The blankets were liked by the queens, but they were too costly even for the king's treasury. The king did not buy a single piece.

Seated outside their hotel in the shade of a tree, the dealers discussed among themselves that if in a place like Rājagṛha, they could not get a buyer, how did they expect to sell the blankets elsewhere. At that time, Śālibhadra's maids were passing by them on their way to the water tank. On their way back, they stood for a while and started a conversation with the blanket dealers,

> "Hello gentlemen! It appears that you are in the midst of some great difficulty. Will you share it with us?"

The dealers—"Our difficulty could not be resolved even by King Śreṇika. Being mere drawers of water, what can you do to relieve us of the difficulty?"

The maids—"Gentlemen! Sometimes help comes even from unexpected quarters."

To get rid of the interrupting maids as early as possible, the dealers narrated their story rather coldly and in few words. Said the maids,

> "Oh! Your difficulty is a trifle. Come with us. It will be solved in no time. We shall help you to sell the entire lot in one deal."

The merchants became serious and asked who could that buyer be. The maids gave them an idea of the wealth of their master Śālibhadra. The merchants now followed the maids to Śālibhadra's house. Even from outside, the mansion was more magnificent and grand than the king's palace. They were now at the first floor and they were surprised at its furnishing. Said the maid,

> "Sir! This portion is meant for the servant's use."

They were now at the second floor and were struck at its lavishness. This floor was occupied by the writers and then they were at the third floor which was occupied by Bhadrā herself. The dealers were introduced to her. Said the dealers.

> "Madam! We have come to meet Śālibhadra. We intend to show our blankets to him for sale."

Bhadrā—"But, sir, you cannot see him. You may display them before me, if you please."

Partly with hesitation and partly with surprise, the blanket-merchants sat before Bhadrā. The took out a piece and placed it in Bhadrā's hand. Without bothering to ask its value, Bhadrā enquired how many pieces they had with them. Said the merchants,

> "Madam! We have sixteen."

Bhadrā—"But, you see, I need 32. I have 32 daughters-in-law. If the number is less than that, then, the distribution becomes difficult."

The dealers—"But, Madam, you should know the price per piece."

Bhadrā—"Don't you worry, sir. Whatever the price, it will be paid."

The dealers were surprised. They were not sure if they were moving in dreamland. Said Bhadrā,

"All right. You leave all your blankets here."

The dealers did accordingly. Bhadrā sent for the chief manager and asked him to make payment. The manager took them to the cash section and asked,

"Gentlemen! How much is the price of each piece?"
—"1,25,000 gold coins."

The manager asked the cashier to make payment for 16 blankets at this rate. This was done. The dealers were happy as well as surprised. While coming out of the mansion, they remembered the maids with gratitude. But for their assistance, it would have been impossible for them to sell their wares. In fact, they had given up the hope of being able to sell a single piece.

On the next day, Queen Cellanā, the principal consort of King Śreṇika, became insistent that the must at least have a piece of blanket for herself. Śreṇika was helpless. He sent out his men to look for the dealers. The dealers were at once brought before the king. They said,

> "Your Majesty! After we left from here, we have been able to seel all the sixteen pieces at a single deal."

King Śreṇika was surprised to hear this. He sent his Chief Minister Abhayakumāra to Bhadrā to enquire if she could spare one for the queen. Abhayakumāra came to Bhadrā and said,

> "Madam! I understand you have bought sixteen blankets. Could you spare at least one piece for the king? He is prepared to pay for it."

Bhadrā—"Sir! I am very sorry, I have already cut each into two pieces and distributed them to my 32 daughter-in-law.

Abhayakumāra—"Then get me two such pieces. They will serve my purpose of pacifying the queen."

Bhadrā sent a maid to her daughter-in-law. They said that they had put their pieces as towels to clean their feet. This information was given to the Chief Minister.

Having collected the information, the Chief Minister, came back to the palace. Bhadrā, too, followed him with suitable gifts for the monarch. She said to the king,

In presenting her gifts to the king, she said,

> "Sir! Please take no offence, but Śālibhadra and his wives put on divine robes. You know, after his death, my husband has been born in heaven.

Everyday, he supplies clothes, ornaments and sweets for the use of his son and daughters. The blankets were somewhat coarse. So, my daughters have used them as towels to clean their feet."

When the king and people at his court heard this account, they were all taken by a great surprise.

As a matter of courtsey, Bhadrā invited the king to see her at her own residence. The king was already very curious about Śālibhadra and his fabulous wealth and he wanted to see this exceptional man. So, at once he welcomed the invitation. Bhadrā returned home and started preparations to receive the king at her house. The king came in a magnificent royal style. He was duly received. The king was surprised to see the divine furnishing of the house. He was seated at the fourth storey. The sole thought in his mind was the owner of so much grandeur. Śālibhadra was still in his own apartment. After the king had been received, Bhadrā came to her son and said,

"My son! King Śreṇika has come to see you. Come, meet the king and salute him."

Śālibhadra—"Mummy! Why do you trouble me? You are the mistress of the house. You pay the price and buy Śreṇika."

Bhadrā—"My son! You have not understood me. Śreṇika is not a vendible commodity. He is our monarch, our master. He has been king enough to respond to my invitation. So, you come down and salute the king."

These words from his mother came as a shock to Śālibhadra. Then he was not his own master! thought he. There was someone above him who was the master! He felt that he should look for the way where he could be his own master.

At the bidding of his mother, Śālibhadra came to Śreṇika and saluted him. The complexion, colour and youthfulness of Śālibhadra was a fresh surprise for the king. When Śālibhadra came near the king, he received him by the hand and made him sit on this lap. But so very tender was Śālibhadra that the temperature of the king's body was too hot for him and he began to perspire all over his person. He felt extremely uneasy. The king understood this. Śālibhadra was given a separate seat wherefrom he talked with the king.

Thrilled and surprised, Śreṇika returned to his palace. Śālibhadra went back to his apartment at the seventh floor. His mind had been severely shaken by the words of his mother, '...... the king...... he is our master'. Then, was he not the master of his own self?

One day, there came a monk named Dharmaghoṣa to the city. He halted at a park to the north-east of the city. Thousands of people moved out to pay their homage and obeisance to the celebrated monk. From his apartment at the seventh floor, Śālibhadra witnessed vast waves of crowd moving towards the park. He enquired where for the people were bound, and having obtained the information, he thought of meeting the monk about the solution of his own personal problem. With this end in view, he got ready and slipped out of the house. From the inspiring sermon of the monk, he realised the transitoriness of wordly pleasures. He found that a monk alone was his own master. So, he decided to be a monk.

Śālibhadra returned home and shared his own thoughts with his mother. This came as a great shock to her. She tried her best to change the son's mind, but her efforts were in vain. At last, it was settled as a compromise that instead of being initiated on that very day, he should renounce at the rate of one wife per day, and should be initiated at the expiry of 32 days. When his wives learnt this, they felt very much disturbed, and they tried their best to keep him back. But Śālibhadra had his mind made up. He gave up one wife per day.

Śālibhadra's own sister Subhadrā was married to Dhannā, who was the son of another very rich man in the same city of Rājagṛha. Dhannā had in all eight wives. One day, all the wives were helping Dhannā to bath at the Asoka garden. Just then, Subhadrā had a thought in her mind that her dear brother was soon going to renounce the world and be initiated as a monk, and she had her eyes filled with tears. A drop of hot tear fell on Dhannā's back. When Dhannā turned to look at her, he found that her eyes were wet. Said Dhannā,

> "Why this? My dear! What makes you grieved at this joyful moment?"

Subhadrā—"Sir! My brother is going to be initiated very soon. Each day, he is giving up one wife."

With indignation, Dhannā looked at Subhadrā's face and said,

> "Your brother is very weak and cowardly. If he is decided to be a monk, why should he renounced his wives at this rate? It is just ludicrous."

These words were too hard for Subhadrā's self-respect. She retored,

> "My dear Sir! It is easy to say like that; but difficult to do so. Can you do this?"

Dhannā felt as if he had been lashed. His mind revolted. Addressing all his wives, he said,

> "Keep apart. I have already renounced you all."

The wives were struck dumb at this unexpected turn of events. Other members of the family tried their best to change his mind. A right man takes decision but once. Dhannā at once came to Śālibhadra's house. He was Śālibhadra and said,

> "Why are you wasting your time. Come with me. This very day, we go to *Bhagavān* Mahāvīra and be initiated."

Śālibhadra had his mind already made up; if still he had deferred his action, he did so at the pressing request of the mother. (Now that the final call had come), he renounced the remaining wives at once. Both came to the congregation of Mahāvīra and joined his holy order as monks.[21]

12. *Rājarṣi Udayana*[22]—In ancient times, Sindhu Sauvīra was considered to be one of the biggest states of *Bhāratavarṣa.* It consisted of 16 big provinces and 363 cities and towns. The name of the king was Udayana. Ten crowned kings headed by Caṇḍa-Pradyotana were always at his service. The name of his queen was Prabhāvatī who was the daughter of King Ceṭaka of Vaiśālī. The name of the crown-prince was Abhīcakumāra, and that of the king's nephew (son of his sister) was Keśī. Queen Prabhāvatī was the follower of the *nirgrantha* path, but the king was the follower of the *Tāpasas.* After her death, Queen Prabhāvatī was born in heaven. From there she effectively induced the king to change over to the *nirgrantha* way. In this manner, the king became a staunch convert to the faith of his wife.

One day, the king was performing *pauṣadha* in his *pauṣadha* room. While he was undergoing a vigil at night, he had a thought in his mind,

> 'Fortunate are those villages, towns and cities which are sanctified by the dust from the feet of *Bhagavān* Mahāvīra. If some day, my city Vītabhaya has a similar good-luck (*i.e.*, if *Bhagavān* Mahāvīra is gracious enough to visit this city), I shall give up the life of a householder and follow him as a monk.'

Bhagavān Mahāvīra was an omniscient personality. He came to know at once the toughts of Udayana and turned his steps towards his country. It was a very long trek of 700 *kroṣas*. The way was uneven and exceedingly difficult. Some of the monks died on the way due to extreme hardship. (At last, the party of Mahāvīra reached Vītabhaya). The king was immensely delighted to receive *Bhagavān* Mahāvīra in his own city. He attended the congregation of Mahāvīra, and expressed his mental resovle of very long standing of joining the holy order as a monk. Said he,

> "*Bhante!* Till I come back after placing my son on the throne, please be not in a hurry to move out from here."

"But don't be careless and slow in this matter", advised the master in reply.

The king came back to his palace. On his way, he gave his mind to the arrangement he would make for the kingdom after he would be initiated into monkhood. He thought,

> "If I place my own son on the throne, he would grow attachement for it, and continue gliding back and forth in wordly existences. (In other words, he would be a perpetual victim of rebirths). And I shall be the cause of his fetters. I can save him if, instead of placing him on the throne I place my nephew on it. This will save the prince."

The king took a final decision on it and made it effective. Having completed the necessary rituals he moved out, and followed the footsteps of Mahāvīra as a monk.[23]

13. *Tāpasa monks*—A group of 1503 *tāpasa* monks were going up on the Aṣṭapada mountain. Koḍinna, Dinna and Sevāla were the leaders. In other words, each headed a family of 500 monks. All of them were thin and emanciated because of hard penances. Koḍinna and his group reached upto the first stage on the Aṣṭapada mountain, Dinna and his party upto the second stage and Sevāla and his monk upto the third satge of the mountain. The Aṣṭapada mountain had in all eight stages, each being at the distance of a *yojana* from the other. The monks found themselves incapable to go any further up.

(As the *tāpasa* monks watched), *Gaṇadhara* Gautama reached the top of the mountain by dint of his spiritual powers. When the *tāpasas* saw this unusual feat, they were very much impressed. The monks decided that when the monk would come down from the Aṣṭapada mountain, they would all become his disciple.

When Indrabhūti Gautama descended from the Aṣṭapada mountain, all the *tāpasa* monks prayed,

> "Sire! You are our *guru* and we are your disciples."

Thereon, Indrabhūti reinitiated the 1503 monks, and by dint of his spiritual power called *akṣīṇa-mahānasalabdhi,* he produced a pot of *khīra* with which all the monks were fed. The newly reinitiated monks became obliged to him at this second display of spiritual power by their *guru.*[24]

(The authenticity of this account has not been accepted by some sects of the Jainas).

14. *King Daśārṇabhadra*—Daśārṇabhadra was the king of Daśārṇapura. He maintained a harem of 500 queens, and had a very large army. Having finished his lunch, the king was comfortably seated enjoying various pleasures. Suddenly, the keeper of the royal garden rushed in and announced,

"Deva! Today, the last *Tīrthaṅkara, Bhagavān* Mahāvīra, has arrived at the garden."

The king became very happy to get this good news. He came down from his throne at once, and bowed with his head bent low in the appropriate direction where Mahāvīra was. Then he dismissed the gardener with suitable gifts for conveying such a hearty news. The king then had a thought in his mind,

"Tomorrow in the morning, I shall call on *Bhagavān* Mahāvira with unprecedented grandeur and pay homage and obeisance in a manner never witnessed before."

At once, he sent for his army chief and asked him to keep his soldiers ready on the following day in the morning. He asked another officer to make the city thoroughly clean, to sprinkle perfumed water everywhere, to shower flowers, to decorate the streets with jars and suitable hangings of leaves and flowers, and decorate the whole city with flags and ensigns. To still another officer he assigned the task of mobilising all the feudal chiefs, ministers and leading citizens on the following day in the morning with a directive that they should all be properly dressed for the occasion.

"We are to go together to pay homage and obeisance to the *Śramaṇa Bhagavān* Mahāvīra", added he.

King Daśārṇabhadra himself got up early in the morning, took his bath, rubbed sandal paste on his body, put on the finest fabrics and adorned his person with gold and costly jewellery. The he sat on the principal elephant.

An umbrella was held over his head. The camara-bearers fanned the king with camara. After the king thousands of feudal lords and citizens riding on elephants, horses and chariots. The entire army followed. Five hundred queens started in their own chariots. Thousands of flags touching the sky were unfurled. The sound of music became a sort of link joining the earth with the sky. Thousands of chanters repeated auspicious hymns. Thousands of singers sang to the great delight of the listners.

Attended by the display of an unusual pomp and followed by his entire family, the king came to attend Mahāvīra's congregation. On reaching the garden, the king alighted from his elephant and discarded the royal umbrella, camara and other external marks of kingship. Then he moved round Mahāvīra, paid his homage and obeisance, sang in praise of him and took his seat in the assembly.

Meanwhile, Śakra, the Indra of the gods, came to know about the arrogant intentions of the king. Thought he,

"Daśārṇabhadra has a profound respect for Mahāvīra, but he should not be too proud."

He became ready to caution the king. He asked a god named Airāvaṇa to create a vast herd of 64,000 brilliant and lofty elephants. Each elephant had 512 faces, each face had eight tusks, each tusk had eight holders, each holder had eight lotuses and each lotus had one lakh petals. On each petal were being performed 32 dramas. At the centre of each lotus, there stood a palace with openings on four sides. From all the palaces, the Indra witnessed the dramas in the company of his eight consorts. Thus attended by a great pomp, the Indra covered the entire firmament and arrived to pay his homage and obeisance to Mahāvīra. King Daśārṇabhadra saw all this, At once, the king turned his gaze inward and thought,

"In vain did I boast of my riches. In comparison with this vast wealth of the Indra, my own pales into insignificance. Only a fool boasts of his riches. The only atonement for what I have done is to court monkhood and attain liberation which is free from old age, death and diminution."

The king rose from his seat, came near Mahāvīra and submitted,

"*Bhante!* I am tired of mundane life. Please oblige me by giving me a place in your order."

Śakra, the Indra of the gods, witnessed the king being initiated. He felt that he had been paid back in his own coins. He came to monk Daśārnabhadra and praised his act with an open heart. Thereafter, the Indra returned to heaven and monk Daśārṇabhadra became immersed in spiritual exertions in the holy order of *Bhagavān* Mahāvīra.[25]

In this manner, many people became initiated as monks in Mahāvīra's order. They have been introduced as follows :

"They were from the *Ugras,* the *Bhogas,* the *Rājanyas,* the *Jñātas* or the *Nāgas,* the *Kurus* and the *Kṣatriyas.* There were many chroniclers, warriors, army-commanders, spiritual teachers, merchants and commoners. Many came from noble families from the sides of both their parents. Many of them were foremost in beauty, humility, knowledge, appearance, grace and power. They were second to none in wealth and excellence. They were rich in wealth, grains and families. They had ample supply of objects bestowed by their respective kings to give happiness to their five organs of senses, and they could have enjoyed a comfortable life if they had so wished. But they considered these to be of no more worth than *kimpāka* fruits. They took life to be transcient like a dew drop at the tip of a *Kuśa* grass. They were ever prepared to thrown out riches and ephemeral objects in the same manner as one throws out dust deposited on cloth. They joined the order of monks by giving up vast stores of silver, gold, wealth, grains, army, vehicles, treasures, granneries, kingdoms, states, cities, seraglios, riches, bullion, gems, jewels, pearls conches, corals, *padma-rāga* (a precious stone with lotus tinge) and many other valuable things."[26]

The Upasampadās of the Buddha[27]

1. *The Pañcavarga Bhikṣus*[28]—These *bhikṣus* lived at Ṛsipattan (present Sāranātha) in Vārāṇasī. The Buddha who was seriously considering after his Enlightenment whom he should first give the knowledge of the four 'noble truths' *(ārya-satya)* arrived at the same place. The *bhikṣus* saw him from a distance and thought.

"Here comes Gautama Buddha who has fallen from the spiritual path and is now after wealth. So, let us not receive him, let us not saltue him, let us not stand in honour of him, nor assist him by holding his begging bowl, garments, etc. We should only keep a seat for him. If he desires, he may take it."

But as the Buddha approached near, they could not remain firm in their decision. Some went forward to receive his begging bowl, garment, etc.; some spread cushion for him; and some came with water, wooded seat and towel and held these before him for his use. Gautama Buddha sat and washed his feet. When the *bhikṣus* addressed him as '*ābus*', he protested,

"*Bhikṣus!* The *Tathāgata* should not be addressed as '*ābus*' or by some lowly expression. The *nathāgata* is an *Arhat* who is duly enlightened. Pay attention to him, and then he will share with thee the immortality of which he is the possessor. If thou follow his advice, then, in this very life, and that too very soon, thou will be in possession of great merits."

But the *bhikṣus* retored,

"*Ābus!* Gautama! When you practised servere penances and underwent great exertions and seriously cultivated knowledge-and-vision, you could neither attain speciality, nor divine power. How do you claim to be duly enlightened when you have slipped from austerities, eat as you please and accumulate riches?"

The *Tathāgata* protested and repeated what he had said before; but the monks persisted. They did this for a second time and for a third time. In the end, the *Tathāgata* said,

"*Bhikṣus!* Did I ever speak like this in the past?"

The *bhikṣus* were silenced to think, and after a while they said,

"No, never in the past, did you speak like this."

"Then why don't you pay heed to my words. I have found the way to immortality. If you accept this, you too will soon be liberated."

The *Tathāgata* became successful with the *bhikṣus.* With rapt attention, they listened to his words. For the first time, the Buddha gave them the *Dharma-cakra-pravartana Sūtra.* Said he,

"*Bhikṣus!* A monk should neither be a slave unto his senses, nor should he inflict too heavy a torture on his body. He should avoid extremes. This is the Middle Path (*madhyama pratipadā*)."

Being thus equipped with seen-religion (*dṛṣṭa-dharma),* known-religion (*vidita-dharma)* and the middle path, Kauṇḍinya submitted to *Bhagavān* Buddha,

"*Bhante!* May thou initiate me! May thou confer on me the *upasampadā!*"

Said the *Bhagavān,*

"*Bhikṣu!* I welcome thee. This religion is duly propounded. To terminate all misery, practise carefully the ways of a *śramaṇa.*"

Kauṇḍinya was thus initiated. Later, other four followed him. Thereon, the Buddha imparted to them the necessary training by dint of which the *bhikṣus* were cleaned of their mental dirt (*āśrava)* and became liberated.[29] At that time, there were six *Arhats* in the world.

2. *Yaśa and others*—Yaśa was a darling son of a *śreṣṭhis* (honorary magistrate or notary) at Vārāṇasī. He had three palaces which he used at different seasons. He never came down from his apartment. Living at a top floor, he spent his life happily enjoying sweet music flowing from exquisitely beautiful maidens. One day, Yaśa Kula-putra (which was his full name) was sleeping in

his chamber. Suddenly, he awoke and opened his eyes. In the light of the dim lamp, he looked at the girls all asleep, some with *vīṇā* in their arms, some with *mṛdaṅga* hanging from their neck, some with their hairs dishevelled, some pouring out saliva from their mouth and some snoring aloud. It was for him a ghastly sight, and he felt a disdain for the whole lot. His heart revolted. Suddenly, the following words dropped from his mouth,

"Oh ye miserable! Oh ye wretched!"

Putting on his golden slippers, Yaśa Kulaputra came down and moved out of the house. Passing thrugh the city-gate, he came to the deer-park at Ṛṣipattana where the Buddha was gently pacing on the open ground. When he saw that Yaśa was coming to him, he sat down on his seat. Yaśa came to him and repeated what had earlier dropped out from his lips :

"Oh ye miserable ! Oh ye wretched!"

Said the Buddha,

"Here there is neither misery nor wretchedness. Come, take a seat. I shall show you the way."

Yaśa enjoyed a real peace of mind. He removed his golden slippers, came near the Buddha, saluted him and took his seat. The Buddha spoke to him about the bad outcome of the desire for objects, and about the great utility of keeping away from mundane activities. When the Buddha saw that he had been fixed in his mind, light in his mind, receptive in his mind and delighted in his mind, he spoke at length on misery, on the cause of misery, on the annihilation of misery and on the way of becoming free from misery. Just as a clean and stain-free cloth nicely takes any hue, in the same manner, seated on his cushion, Yaśa Kulaputra had his pure, spiritual eye opened.

Meanwhile, Yaśa's mother came to his place apartment. When she did not find her son there, she rushed to her husband reported the matter to him. The *Gṛhapati* sent men in all directions to look for him. Even he himself went out. As luck would have it, he proceeded towards the deer-park at Ṛṣipattana. On the way, he detected the mark of his son's golden slippers on the ground. He pursued them. When the Buddha saw the merchant at a distance coming towards him, he thought that he should better make Yaśa invisible to his father by dint of his own spiritual powers, and he did accordingly. The Śreṣṭhī came to the Buddha and said,

"Bhante! Did you by any chance see anywhere my son Yaśa Kulaputra?"

The Buddha—"*Gṛhapati!* Take your seat. You will be able to see your son here."

The *Gṛhapati* became happy. He saluted the Buddha and sat down. The Buddha gave a sermon for him. On hearing this, the *Gṛhapati* had his pure, spiritual eye opened on his seat. Being thus inspired into religion, he uttered,

> "*Bhante!* It's wonderful. *Bhante!* It's simply wonderful. Just as something turned upside down in put again in its right posture, just as something covered is uncovered, just as one who has lost his way is put back to his track, just as an oil-lamp removed darkness so that one may see as with his own eyes, so thou hath revealed religion from diverse facets. So, I seek refuge unto the Buddha, unto the *Dharma,* unto the *Saṅgha.* From this day, therefore, be gracious to accept me as a follower *(upāsaka)* who has sought refuge with thee with folded hands."

Thus in the world, the *Gṛhapati* became the first lay follower by taking refulge with the Buddha, the *Dharma* and the *Saṅgha.*

The son heard the sermon given for the benefit of the father, and having pondered over it deeply, his mind became detached and free from sin (*āśrava).* The Buddha realised the situation. He had a firm belief that inspite or all efforts, Yaśa was henceforth no more capable to enjoy pleasures of life in the manner he did before. So, he removed the veil he had created by dint of his spiritual power. From his own seat, Yaśa became visible to his father. Said the *Gṛhapati* to him.

> "My son! Since your disappearance, your mother is completely upset. She is weeping bitterly out of grief. You should save her life."

Yaśa looked at the Buddha. The Buddha said at once,

> "*Gṛhapati!* Just as you have received a glimpse of *Dharma* by your imperfect knowledge-and-vision, has not Yaśa done the same? On seeing, knowing and realising, his mind is now detached from everything and free from sin. In his present position, can he enjoy the pleasures of life in the same manner as he did before?"

Out of devotion, the *Gṛhapati's* head bent low, and the following words spontaneously slipped from his mouth,

> "*Bhante!* He cannot."

The Buddha spoke again,

> "Yaśa Kulaputra's mind has moved away from mundane life. He is no loger fit for it."

The *Gṛhapati*—"*Bhante!* It has thus happened for the good, for the real good of Yaśa Kulaputra. You take him as a monk who will be following you, and be pleased to accept food from my household today."

Having received a silent assent, the *Gṛhapati* rose from his seat, moved round him and saluted him, and departed. Thereafter, Yaśa Kulaputra begged for his own initiation as a monk and for being awarded the *upasampadā*. Said the Buddha,

> "*Bhikṣu!* I welcome thee. *Dharma* has been well-enunciated. To end misery in the best possible manner, you practise celebacy."

In the manner, he was the first to be given the *Upasampadā.* At that time, there were seven *Arhats* in the world.

Four young men from the families of *śreṣthis* and other merchants at Vārāṇasī who were named Vimala, Subāhu, Pūrṇajit and Gavāṁpati were Yaśa's peers. When they heard that Yaśa had been initiated as a monk, they thought,

> "Surely the order in which Yaśa is a monk cannot be an ordinary one. It must be an important one."

So, they started from their respective homes and came to *Bhikṣu* Yaśa. They saluted him and stood on one side. *Bhikṣu* Yaśa introduced them to the Buddha and requested him to give sermon for them. The Buddha gave a lofty sermon for them. All the four were attracted to *Dharma.* They sought their own initiation as monks in the order and to be admitted in the *upasampadā*. The Buddha at once favourably responded to their request. As they heard his words, they became free from sin. At that time, there were 11 *Arhats* in the world.

Fifty friends from the households who lived in the villages heard the story of Yaśa's initiation as a monk, and they felt an attraction for the Buddha's order. On hearing the sermon, they became monks, and their minds became free from sin. At that time, there were 61 *Arhats* in the world.[30]

While staying at Vārāṇasī, the Buddha gave the *upasampadās* to the aforesaid 60. To these sixty, he gave his well-known message, *Carata bhikkhava cārikāṁ, Carata bhikkhava cārikāṁ* at Vārāṇasi, and at this very place, he empowered his monks to give *upsampadā* themselves. It appears that for the future growth of the Buddhistic order, the message of *cārikā* and the power conferred on the monks to give *upasampadā* acted like a boon.

3. *The Bhādravargīyas*—For the propagation of the message of *cārikā,* the Buddha sent his 60 disciples in different directions. Starting from Vārāṇasī, he himself came to Uruvelā. He took rest under a tree in a park which was somewhat a far from the road. At that time, thirty friends from *Bhādravarga* were having a nice time with their wives in the same park. One of them had no wife; so he hired a woman to give him company. They indulged in revelry and merry-making to the extent that they lost all senses. The hired woman made full use of the situation. She removed their ornaments and disappeared with them. When the young people had recovered their senses, they realised what had happened to them. They searched every part of the garden. While looking for the woman, they came to the same tree under which the Buddha sat. They narrated the incident, and enquired if he had seen the woman coming thither.

The Buddha asked them back,

> "Young folks! You consider a search for the woman more important, or a search for your own self?"
>
> —"For us, a search for the self (soul) is the most important."

The Buddha gave sermons for them. All the *Bhadravarga* friends became fixed in religion. They were admitted in to the *upasampadā* by the Buddha.[31]

4. *The Parivrājakas—Bhagavān* Buddha reached Uruvelā. At this place, three friends (brothers) named Uruvelā Kāśyapa, Nandī Kāśyapa and Gayā Kāśyapa, all nick-named *Jaṭila* because of their matted hairs, were practising penance by offering oblation to the fire. The Buddha reached the cottage of Uruvelā Kāśyapa *Jaṭila* and took shelter in his sacrifice room (where burnt the fire). During the first night, he deprived the cobra of his venom and finished his virility.

This strange event made a deep impression on Uruvelā Kāśyapa. He was convinced that his guest was a man with a great divine power and experience. He requested him to stay in his cottage and accept food from him.

The Buddha conceded to his request. Once a proposal has come to Uruvelā Kāśyapa to be the chief priest at a great sacrifice. A large number of men from Aṅga and Magadha were expected to participate in it with vast supplies of food with them. Uruvelā thought :

> "On the occasion of this sacrifice, many people will come to attend. If, on this occasion, the great *śramaṇa* displays his occult powers before the crowd, then, in their estimation, he will go up, and I shall go down. So, it will be better if he goes out from here before this occasion."

The Buddha came to know the wishes of Uruvelā Kāśyapa. He left his cottage and arrived at Uttarakuru. Having begged food from that city, he sat on the bank of a tank named Anavatapta and ate. He spent the day there. Next day, Uruvelā Kāśyapa came to the Buddha and said,

> *Mahāśramaṇa!* It is time to dine. Cooked rice is ready. But why didn't you turn up yesterday?

The Buddha had no intention to hide the reasons for which he did not return on the pervious day. He stated it in clear terms and added,

> "It is for this that I did not stay there yesterday."

Uruvelā Kāśyapa realised that the great monk was no ordinary person; he was in possession of great powers. He knew easily in his own mind what was there in the mind of others; but still, thought he,

> "He is not as great an *Arhat* as I am."

The Buddha accepted the food provided by Uruvelā Kāśyapa and continued to stay on in that forest-strip. Once he got some old clothes and he thought where he should clean them. Śakra, the Indra of the gods, came to know his wishes and dug a tank with his own hands for the Buddha's use. Then he said to him,

> "*Bhante!* You may wash your clothes here."

Immediately thereafter, the Buddha had another thought, 'Where should I strike them to make the clean'?
At once, Śakra placed a big slab of stone for his use.
The Buddha then had a third thought in his mind :

> "With what support shall I get down into the tank?"

At once Śakra provided a branch of a *kakudha* tree.
And the Buddha thought again,

> "Where shall I spread them to dry?"

Having known his mind, Śakra, the Indra of the gods, placed another big slab of stone for his use. The night was over. Uruvelā Kāśyapa came to invite the Buddha to receive food from him. On seeing the unusual tank, the stone slabs and the branch of the *kakudha* tree, he asked the Buddha about them whereon the Buddha narrated the whole story. On hearing this, Uruvelā Kāśyapa thought that the great monk was no ordinary person, but that he was still not as great an *Arhat* as he himself was. The Buddha accepted the food but continued to stay on in the same place.

Once there was an untimely shower. There was almost a flood. The region where the Buddha lived was submerged. Thought the Buddha,

> "Why don't I remove water from all around myself and live on a dry ground?"

He did accordingly. Elsewhere, Uruvelā Kāśyapa had a sudden thought in his mind that the great monk must have been drowned in the flood-water. With other people of his clan, he rushed forth with a boat to rescue him. He found to his surprise that the Buddha was on a dry plot. With a great surprise, he said,

> "*Mahāśramaṇa!* Are you the same person?"

Said the Buddha,

> "Yes, I am."

The Buddha flew in the sky and stood on board the vessel. Uruvelā Kāśyapa thought again that the great monk was no ordinary person, but that he was still not as great an *Arhat* as he himself was.

In this manner, the Buddha displayed before him 15 surprises, but Uruvelā continued to have similar thinking in his mind about the Buddha being a lesser *Arhat* than himself. In the end, in order to remove this thought from his mind, the Buddha said,

> "Kāśyapa! You are neither an *Arhat* nor on the road to be one. You have not even the idea as to what it is that makes an *Arhat,* or how to be an *Arhat.*"

At these words of the Buddha, Uruvelā's head bent low out of respect. He placed his head at his feet and said,

> "*Bhante!* I beseech to be initiated by thee, to be given *upasampadā* by thy hand."

The Buddha said in a very soft voice,

"Kāśyapa! You are the leader of 500 *Jaṭilas*. You think of them."

Uruvelā Kāśyapa understood the hint dropped by the Buddha. He came to his men and apprised them of his intention of being initiated by the great monk. He advised his men to feel free and act according to their discretion.

They thought for a while and then said in one voice,

> "We too have respect for the great monk. If you intend to be initiated by him, we shall follows you."

All the *Jaṭilas* rose in a body. They immersed their hairs, mats, begging cloth, ghee pot, fire oven, etc., in the water and came to the Buddha. With their heads bent low, they prayed to be initiated and to be given his *upasampadā*. The Buddha accepted their prayer and gave them the *upasampadā*.

Nandī Kāśyapa observed the various objects (of the *Parivrājaka* monks) being carried away in the flow of the river. He was surprised. He apprehended that some disaster must have befallen his brother. So, in the company of his own followers he rushed to look up his brother. But when he saw him as a monk, his surprise-knew no bound. Suddenly, the following words dropped from his mouth.

"Kāśyapa! Have you done a good thing?"

Uruvelā Kāśyapa said in reply,

"Yes, *abus,* I have done a good thing."

Nandī Kāśyapa and all his 300 men immersed their belongings in the river and accepted *upasampadā* from the Buddha.

Gayā Kāśyapa also saw the objects being carried by the river. He came to his brothers and enquired all about them. He was pleased to hear their account, and in the company of his 200 *Jaṭilas,* he too accepted *Upasampadā* from the Buddha.

Starting from Uruvelā, the Buddha came to Gayā with his great *Saṅgha* only recently expanded by the inclusion of 1000 *Jaṭila* initiates.[32]

5. Sāriputta and Moggalāna—At Rājagṛha, there lived *Parivrājaka* Sañjaya with his 250 followers. Sāriputta and Moggallāna were the leadingmost among them. They were undergoing a training in the practice of *brahmacarya* under the direction of Sañjaya. One day they decided that whoever obtained Truth *(amṛta)* first would communicate it at once to the other.

One day, in the forenoon, *Bhikṣu* Aśvajit, equipped with his begging bowl and cloth, entered into Rājagṛha, with a noble demeanour, excellent movement, with his eyes bent low and walking at a measured pace, in order to beg. Sāriputta saw him. He was much impressed by his calm and thoughtful appearance. Thought he,

> "Among the *Arhats* or would-be *Arhats* in the world, this monk may be one. Why do I not ask him by whom has he been initiated, who is his preceptor, and what spiritual line he belongs to?"

But at the very next moment he thought,

> "The monk is on a begging mission. This is not an appropriate time to ask a question. Why do I not follow him and obtain my answers in his cottage?"

Having begged his food, *Bhikṣu* Aśvajit came back to his shelter. Sāriputta entered just after him. He enquired about his welfare and stood on one side. While speaking highly of Aśvajit, he said,

> *"Abus!* Delightful are your organs of senses. Noble and bright is your stature. Who is you initiator? Who is your preceptor? What is your line?"

Aśvajit—"There's a great monk named Śākyaputra who is born in the Śākya line. I have accepted him as my preceptor and I have been initiated by him. He is my guide and I follows him."

Sāriputta—"What are the principal teachings he follows?"

Aśvajit—"I am only a recent entrant. So, I cannot give you the details of his teachings. But I can surely give you a concise idea of them."

Sāriputta—"Concise or detailed, abus, I don't mind. Tell me what you know about it. Even a brief account will serve my purpose. I am not interested in details.

Aśvajit stated in brief the four fundamentals of his religion, (viz., misery, cause of misery, annihilation of misery and the way to liberation. In concluding his statement he said,

> "Such are the teachings of the *Mahāśramaṇa."*

Immediately on hearing this, Sāriputta acquired the pure, spiritual eye. As per his prior agreed, he rushed to Moggallāna to convey to him the Truth he had obtained. Moggallāna saw him from a distance. He was impressed by his calm demeanour, his restrained and slow pace. Suddently, he said,

> "Have you attained the Truth?"

Sāriputta expressed himself in the affirmative. Moggallāna enquired where he got it. Sāriputta gave a complete account. Moggallāna was especially delighted to hear it. He too had his pure spiritual eye opened. Both of them at once took a decision that they should go to the Buddha and accept him as their guide. They brought their decision to the notice of other 250 *parivrājaka* monks so that they would be able to take a decision about themselves.

All the *parivrājaka* monks hailed their decision and expressed their intention to follow them and take shelter with the great guide.

Sāriputta and Moggallāna brought this collective decision to the notice of *Parivrājaka* Sañjaya. He did not like it. To induce them not to give effect to it, he said,

> "*Ābusas!* You do not go there. I am prepared to share my leadership position with you."

But Sāriputta and Moggallāna did not agree. They reaffirmed their decision for a second time, and then for a third time. From his own side, Sañjaya repeated his disapproval. Hot blood flowed out from his mouth. Sāriputta and Moggallāna gave up the company of Sañjaya and arrived at Veṇuvana in the company of other fellow *parivrājakas*. The Buddhas saw them coming from a distance and said as follows to his own monks :

> "Kolita (Moggallāna) and Upatiṣya (Sāriputta), the two friends will be my principal disciples, a couple of noble souls."

The two *parivrājaka* leaders and their families saluted the Buddha. They received *upasampadā* at the hands of the Great Monk, and lived on true to their new faith.[33]

6. *Mahākātyāyana*—Mahākātyāyana was born in the family of a priest at Ujjaini. He belonged to the Kātyāyana line. When he grew up, he mastered the three *Vedas,* and after the death of his father, he was installed as a priest. Once King Caṇḍapradyota said to his ministers,

> "The Buddha has been born in the world. Someone should go and bring him here."

At this, the ministers made the following suggestions,

> "Sir! We think that *Ācārya* Kātyāyana is the most suitable person for this commission. So, you may be pleased to give this to him."

The king sent for Kātyāyana and repeated his wishes to him, but Kātyāyana set condition :

> "Sir! I am prepared to take up the commission provided I am given leave to be initiated into monkhood."

In accepting his condition, the king said,

> "I don't mind what condition you set, but I insist that the *Tathāgata* must be brought to our city."

Ācārya Kātyāyana agreed to undertake the commission. While making preparations to depart, he thought that in carrying this invitation, he should not be accompanied by a crowd. He took only seven persons with him and came to the Buddha. The Buddha gave sermons for them. All of them were enlightened and attained *arthat*-hood. The Buddha extended his hand to them and said,

> "*Bhikṣus!* You are welcome."

At once, all of them became tonsured, were equipped with begging bowls and clothes and looked like a-hundred-year old monks (*sthaviras*). After his initiation, *Sthavira* Kātyāyana did not sit idle. He extended invitation to the Buddha to come to Ujjaini. The Buddha gave him a patient hearing and said,

> "The Buddha does not go to a place rendered unworthy even by a single cause. So, *Bhikṣu,* you go yourself. The king will be happy to see you."

Kātyāyana reviewed the situation within himself : 'The Buddha never reconsiders.'

So, he saluted the *Tathāgata* and started back for Ujjaini with his seven companions. In the way, they came to a village named Telappanālī in order to beg food. In that village, there lived two girls. One of them was born in a very poor family. She lost her parents in her infancy, and was brought up by a maid servant. She was extremely charming and possessed long hairs. The other girl was born in the family of a rich merchant, but she was without hair. She sent a proposal to the poor girl :

"If you give me your hairs, I shall pay you a thousand coins."

But the poor girl refused to part with her hairs.

The poor girl saw *Sthavira* Kātyāyana moving in the village for the purpose of begging. The monk had received nothing in his bowl so far. Thought the girl,

"If I had the necessary wherewithal, I would not let this happen."

Just then she remembered the proposal sent by the merchant's daughter about the sale of her hair. She decided at once that with the money she would get by selling her hair, she would buy food and offer it to the monk. No sooner had she taken the decision than she gave effect to it. She sent her foster-mother to invite the monks to her house. Meanwhile, she cut her hairs and said to her,

> "Mummy dear! Please send my hairs to the merchant's daughter. The money these would fetch, I shall use to help the monks."

Her foster-mother felt very sorry at the poor girl cutting her hairs. But what could she do now? She wiped her tears and tried to be patient. Then she received the hairs and proceeded to the merchant's home to sell them. Even the finest things on earth receive no appreciation when they come unwanted. This happened to the hairs. When the merchant's daughter saw the hairs, she thought,

> "I offered a fabulous price for these hairs, but then she did not sell. But now they are cut. So I shall pay what I consider just."

Turning to the maid, she said,

> "The price of the hairs of a living person is no more than 8 *kārṣāpaṇas*. She took the hairs and thrust the coins into the maid's hand. The maid gave the coins to the poor girl. She used these eight coins to procure eight varieties of food and offered them to the monks. *Sthavira* Kātyāyana realised the noble intentions of the donor and said to the maid,
> "Where is the girl, our benefactress?"

The maid—"*Ārya!* She is in."

The monk—"Call her hither."

When the girl came to know that the monks have known her noble intentions, she was very much impressed. She felt a great respect for them in her mind.

She came and bowed before the monks. As offer made to a worthy person always yields a great result. As the girl bowed before the monks, she had her hairs restored. The monks ate the food. As the girl looked on, they flew through the sky and reached Kāñcana-vana, the park in their own city Ujjainī. The report of their arrival was conveyed to King Caṇḍapradyota by the gardener :

> "Your Majesty! The noble priest Kātyāyana has become a monk along with his companions. He is in the park waiting for Your Majesty's orders."

The king was delighted to hear the news. He himself came to the park. After the monks had taken their food, the king saw them. He bowed before them with his five limbs and said,

> "*Bhante!* Where is *Bhagavān* Buddha?"

Kātyāyana—"Mahārāja! The Great Teacher has not himself come. He has sent me instead."

The king—"Where did you get your food today?"

The monk narrated the most difficult feat performed by the poor girl. The king was very much impressed by this. He arranged for the monks' lodging, invited them to receive food at the palace and came back. He sent his men to bring the poor girl. When she came, the king married her and made her the first queen. She became the most beloved of the king. The king paid full attention to the monks.

The new queen gave birth to a son who was named Gopālakumāra, after his maternal grand-father and the mother was nicknamed *Gopāla-mātā.* At her request, the king erected a *vihāra* in the Kāñcana-vana for the use of the monks. The monks provided inspiration to the entire populace of Ujjainī and converted them to the new faith and returned to the Buddha.[34]

7. *Nanda, Rāhula and others*—King Śuddhodana learnt that having gone through severe penances, his son had attained the status of the Buddha and had rolled the Wheel of Religion *(dharma-cakra).* He learnt further that at that time, he was staying at Veṇu-vana (in the outskirts of Rājagṛha). He said to his minister,

> "You go to Rājagṛha with a thousand men with you and tell the Buddha, 'Your father King Śuddhodana desires to meet you'. You bring him here with you."

The minister obeyed the king's order. With one thousand men in his company, he covered a distance of 60 *yojanas* and arrived at Veṇu-vana in Rājagṛha. At that time, the Buddha was delivering a sermon in a four-fold assembly comprising of the monks, nuns and male and female followers. The minister and his 1000 men entered into the *vihāra.* Without communicating the message they stood in one corner and became engrossed in listening. Standing there, the minister and his 1000 attained *arhat*-hood. They prayed to the Buddha for their own initiation into his order. The Buddha extended his hand and said,

"Oh *bhikṣus!* You are welcome."

In a moment, as if by magic, all of them became equipped with the begging bowl and cloth and looked like a-hundred-year-old *sthaviras*. In becoming an *arhat*, one attains the middle state. This happened to the minister and his 1000, and they forgot to deliver the invitation sent by the king to the Buddha.

The minister did neither deliver the king's message to the Buddha, nor did he go back to his city. After waiting for some time, the king sent another minister with a thousand men with him as before. They too became *arhats* and did not come back to report. Thereafter, in succession, the king sent out more ministers, in all nine, with a thousand men with each; but all of them became involved in their own spiritual growth, and no one came back to report to the king. The king became very anxious, Thought he,

'All these men had so much affection for me, but none returned to give me any tiding. In this situation, who will obey my orders'? In deep anxiety, he looked at his council. His eyes fell on Kālaudāī. Kālaudāī was very dear to the king, very faithful, on whom the king depended in all matters. He was born on the same day with the *Bodhisattva.* Both were great friends in thier childhood. Addresing Kālaudāī, the king said,

> "My child! I am keen to see my son. I sent nine thousand men, but not a single person came back to report. I do not know how long I shall live. I want to see him once during my life. Can you show me my son?"

Kālaudāī—"*Deva!* I hope to be able to fulfil your wishes, but please permit me to be initiated."

The king—"My dear child! Whether you be initiated or not, you bring my son to me once."

With the assignment from the king, Kālaudāī set out. He arrived at Rājagṛha. Standing at one end of the assembly, he heard the sermon given by the Buddha. In the company of his men, he attained *arhat*-hood.

On the attainment of Enlightenment, the Buddha spent his first rainy season at Ṛsipattana (Sāranātha). Then he came to Uruvelā and stayed there for three months. There he acquired the three *Jaṭila* brothers with their fellow *parivrājakas* into his own order. Then with a family of 1000 monks, he arrived at Rājagṛha on the full-moon day of the month of *Pauṣa*. He lived there for two months. Since he departed from Vārāṇasī, five months were over. It was seven or eight days since *Sthavira* Udāī had arrived there.

On the full-moon day of the month of *Phālguna,* he thought,

> "The winter is over. It is spring. The farmers have harvested the crop and so the way is free. The earth is covered with green grass, and the forest-strip is fully blossomed. The way is comfortable for movement. This is the most appropriate time for the Buddha to acquire converts from his own clan."

So he came to the Buddha and submitted,

> "*Bhante!* At this time, it is neither very hot nor very cold. Food is not difficult to get : The earth is green with grass. It is a nice time for you to pay a visit to your own city."

The Buddha—Udāī! Do you really think so?"

Udāī—"*Bhante!* Your father King Śuddhodana is keen to see you. You should also have recruits from your own people."

The Buddha—"Very good. I shall receive converts from my own people. Meanwhile, tell the monks to get ready to depart."

When the Buddha started, he had a following of 10,000 from Aṅga and Magadha, and another 10,000 from Kapilavastu. These 20,000 were *arhats* with little (no) sin. Travelling at a speed of a *yojana* per day, they reached Kapilavastu in sixty days. On hearing that the Buddha had arrived to their city, all the Śākyas held a meeting and chose the Nyagrodha garden for his stay. They cleaned it and decorated it in a beautiful manner. To receive him, they sent young boys and girls, nicely dressed and wearing ornaments, with flowers, incences, etc., in their hands. They were followed by princes and princesses. In this manner, offering him ovation and worship, they brought him to the Nyagrodha halt. The Buddha resumed an appropriate seat (*buddhāsana)* established by his 20,000 *arhats.*

On the following day, followed by his monks, the Buddha entered into Kapilavastu to beg. In the city, no one invited them to dinner, and none held their begging bowls. The Buddha stood on the Indra-kīla and thought,

> "How did the Buddhas in the past beg in their own cities? Did they beg

from the selected affluent homes, or, did they beg from one end without discrimination?"

He learnt that they discarded no home but begged all from end to end. He thought again,

"As a Buddha, I belong to the same line. Then I must adhere to the practice of my line. In future, my followers will follow the practice I uphold before them and fulfil the rule of begging."

So, he started begging from one end.[35]

It became widely known throughout the city that Prince Siddhārtha, the noble soul, was begging in the city out of curiosity, the citizens stood at their respective windows to witness the unusual scence.

Rāhula's mother, Princess Yaśodharā also beheld him from her own window. It occurred to her,

"At one time, *Āryaputra* (husband) used to drive through the city in a golden chariot with full pomp and dignity; but now with his hairs and bear cut, with saffron robes on, with his forehead held in his hand, he is out to beg. Does it look nice?"

She drew the attention of the king. Shaken with nervousness, the king hurried to the Buddha and said,

"*Bhante!* Why do you put me to an awkward situation? Why do you beg? Do you want to prove that I do not have enough food to feed you monks?"

The Buddha—"*Mahārāja*! This is the practice of my line."

The king—"*Bhante!* Ours is a great *Kṣatriya* line started by *Mahāsammata*. None from this line has ever begged."

The Buddha—"*Mahārāja!* You belong to that royal line. But I belong to the line of the Buddhas laid by Dīpaṅkara and others. Thousands of Buddhas in the past had been begging mendicants. They had laid down this way to livelihood."

The king received the Buddha's bowl in his own hand and with the entire body of monks, he returned to the palace. They were served with excellent food. After the dinner, all the inmates of the harem, except Rāhula's mother, came and bowed before him. Rāhula's mother had only one explanation,

"If I have merit, then the *Āryaputra* will come to see me, and then I shall bow before him."

The Buddha gave his begging bowl to the king, and then with his two leading disiples (Sāriputta and Moggallāna), he came to the bed-chamber of the Princess (Yaśodharā). To both his leading disciples, he gave the following instruction,

"Let the Princess bow as she pleases. Do not obstruct her in any way."

Then he sat down on a cushion that was already spread. The Princes came at a hurried pace. She held the Buddha's feet, placed her head thereon and bowed as she pleased. As to Yaśodharā, the king said to the Buddha,

> "*Bhante!* From the day you took the saffron robes, she too has done the same. When she came to know that you take food only one time per day, she started the same. She has given up sleeping on a couch, but spends her nights on a wooden plank. Since you do not use garlands, perfumes, etc., she too has given them up. Several invitations came from her parental home, and her own people desired to help her; but she did not even care to read them."[36]

Approving the words of the king, the Buddha said,

> "*Mahārāja!* There is nothing to be surprised in this. Besides being in your protection, she herself is very mature in her senses. She is capable of providing her own protection. Even in the past, under very adverse circumstances, and without sufficient maturity, she protected herself at the foot of a mountain."

The Buddha rose from his seat and departed. On the third day, Prince Nanda was to be the crown-prince; he was to enter into a new palace and he was to be married. So on that day, three auspicious ceremonies were to be celebrated for him. The Buddha arrived on the spot on the same day to induct him into his own order as a monk, he placed a begging bowl in Nanda's hand, uttered some auspicious words and departed from there. While returning, he did not take the bowl back. The prince too was very much overwhelmed at the greatness of the Buddha (and at the great favour he did to him by giving him the begging bowl), that he could not ask the Buddha to take the bowl back. He thought that the Buddha would take the bowl at the staircase, but he did not do that, nor did he take it at the bottom of the staircase, nor in the courtyard. He went on. When the people saw this, they said to Janapada Kalyāṇī Nandā,

> "Behold! The *Bhagavān* is taking away Prince Nandā. He will separate you from him."

With water dropping from her uncombed hairs which she carelessly held, she went up and shouted from her window,

> "*Āryaputra!* Come back soon."

But the words rebounded and pricked her heart like a javeline. But still the Buddha did not take back the begging bowl from his hand. Out of bashfulness, Nanda too could not utter a word. They come to the lodge. To Nanda he asked,

> "Do you like to be a monk?"

Out of hesitation he said,

> "Yes, I like to be a monk."

The Leader at once ordered,

> "Initiate Nanda into monkhood."

In this manner, on the third day of his arrival at Kapilavastu, Nanda was taken as a monk.[37]

On the seventh day, Rāhula's mother dressed and decorated her son and sent him to his father saying,

> "My dear son! In the centre of 20,000 monks, the man with a golden, excellent complexion is your fater. He possessed enormous wealth, but ever since his initiation, this is nowhere to be found. You pray to be given this wealth. Tell him also that you are a prince, and that you would like to be a world-monarch after you are coronated as a king. For this purpose, wealth is needed. So, please give me wealth. The son inherits the wealth of the father."

In the early part of the day, the Buddha, equipped with his begging bowl and cloth, came to Śuddhodana's house to beg.

After lunck, being sent by his mother, Prince Rāhula came to the Buddha said,

> "*Śramaṇa!* Pleasant is thy shadow."

The Buddha left the place. But Rāhula followed him shouting,

> "*Śramaṇa!* Give me my paternal property. Give me my paternal property."

The Buddha did not ask the prince to go back, nor did the kinsmen prevent him from going with the Buddha. He came upto the Buddha's camp. The Buddha thought,

> "The treasure he is asking for is wordly treasure. It is liable to destruction. Why don't bestow on him seven noble treasures (viz., devotion, conduct, humility, fear of public censure, knowledge of scriptures, renunciation and wisdom)[38] by inducting him into the order. I shall make him the master of this unusual realm."

At once, he called Sāriputta and said,

> "Initiate Prince Rāhula as a monk."

Sāriputta—"Bhante! By what mode should I initiate Prince Rāhula?"

On this issue, the Buddha delivered a sermon, and then addressing the monks, he said,

> "*Bhikṣus!* I order an initiation called *Srāmaṇera* for him. This prescribes the seeking of shelter with three. It involves the following practices : the hairs on the head and the beard need be cut; saffron clothes need be put on; a piece of cloth needs be placed on the shoulder; then he should be made to bow at the feet of the monks; then he should be made to sit in the *utkaṭuka* posture, and with folded hands, he should say,
>
> I take shelter with the Buddha
> I take shelter with the *Dharma*
> I take shelter with the *Saṅgha.*"

Sāriputta initiated Prince Rāhula in the manner prescribed by the Buddha. When Śuddhodana came to know of this, he rushed to the Buddha submitted,

> "*Bhante!* I seek a boon."

Being permitted by the Buddha, Śuddhodana said,

> "I became immensely unhappy when you were initiated. I became

unhappy again when Nanda was initiated. Now, I am most unhappy when Rāhula has been initiated. *Bhante*! Affection for my progeny is piercing through my skin; it is piercing through my flesh; and then penetrating through my flesh, it is piercing through my veins; then penetrating through my veins, it is piercing through my bones; and then penetrating through my bones, it has shattered me. *Bhante*! The monks should not initiate anyone without the prior permission of the parents."

Thereafter, on the point made by Śuddhodana, the Buddha gave a sermon. Śuddhodana stood up from his seat, bowed, moved round the Buddha thrice and departed. After he had gone, the Buddha said to the monks,

"Let not the monks initiate anyone without the prior permission of the parents. Anyone violating this commits the sin of having performed a prohibited act."[39]

8. *Śākya Princes and Upāli*—Having initiated Prince Rāhula, the Buddha departed from Kapilavastu, and while performing the *cārikā,* he arrived at the mango park outside city of Anūpiyā in Malladeśa. At that time, many Śākya youths from noble families were being initiated into the Buddha's order on their own initiative. There were two Śākya brothers, Mahānāma and Anuruddha by name. Anuruddha was the younger of the two, and he had three mansions for his use during fall, summer and rains respectively. He was at that time residing in his monsoon mansion. He never came down. When Mahānāma heard that many Śākya youths were joining the monastic order of the Buddha, he came to his younger brother Anuruddha, narrated the recent initiations and said,

"From our family, no one has yet joined the Buddha's monastic order. So, between us two, at least one must be initiated."

Anuruddha said at once.

"I am yet too young. I cannot give up my home and join the monastic order. So, you consider the matter for yourself."

With profound affection for his brother, Mahānāma said,

"My dear brother Anuruddha! I agree. Let me explain to you the affairs of our household."

Anuruddha became all attention, and Mahānāma started,

> "First, plough the farm; then sow the seed and water the farm. Thereafter, drain out the excess water and dry the farm. When the crops are ready, harvest them, bring them up, make them straight, spread them, have them molested, take out the straw, dehusk them, winnow them and then place them in the granneries. Do in this order every year. The work will never suffer nor come to a stand still."

Anuruddha—"But tell me when the work ends so that I may return to my carefree life and enjoy five types of pleasure."

Mahānāma—"Brother Anuruddha! The work never ends, nor is it possible to know its finale. Our own parents and grand-parents died even before they could finish the work."

Suddenly, the seed of renunciation sprouted in Anuruddha. He said,

> "You better look after the household and let me go."

Anuruddha came to his mother. He explained his inclination to her and sought her permission. The mother, however tried her best to dissuade him.

> "Anuruddha, my child, both you and your brother are my darling sons. I shall not turn away from you even after my death. So, how I permit you to go when I am still alive? I cannot give you permission."

Anuruddha did not give up his hope. He repeated his intention for a second time, and then for a third time. But the mother remained firm about her disapproval. At last, she devised a strategy to prevent him, which was as follows. At this time, Bhaddīya was the king of the Śākyas. He happened to be a great friend of Anuruddha. The mother knew for certain the Bhaddīya would never be ready to join the monastic order. So she said,

> "If Bhaddīya joins the monastic order, then, I may permit you to do the same."

On getting such a straight reply to his difficult question, Anuruddha came to Bhaddīya and said,

> "Friend! My own initiation depends on you."

Bhaddīya—"If that be so, I permit you very gladly to be initiated and be in the monastic order."

Anuruddha—"But, friend, let us go together."

Bhaddīya—"I am not interested. But I shall gladly do anything for you. Go ahead, my dear fellow."

Anuruddha explained to him the condition laid down by his mother for his own initiation and emphatically affirmed.

> "You must come wih me. You are bound by your own words. You cannot go back on your words. We must tread on the same path."

People in that age used to be truthful. Bhaddīya said to Anuruddha,

> "I am not going back on my words. But I must be spared for seven years to get ready, and after that, I may go with you."

Anuruddha—"But seven years is too long a time. I cannot wait for such a long period."

Bhaddīya reduced it to six years. But, for Anuruddha, who was keen for initiation, even a six-year period was too long. So, he protested. Bhaddīya cut it down, by stages, to five years, then to four, three, two, one, to six months, five, four, three, two, one, and at last to a fortnight. But even a fortnight was too long for Anuruddha. So, he rejected this too, and insisted on him to get ready at once. Bhaddīya said at last,

> "Give me at least a week's time so that I may properly give charge of my kingdom to my sons and brothers."

Anuruddha agreed. As the week went out, the Śākya king Bhaddīya, Anuruddha, Ānanda, Bhṛgu, Kimbila, Devadatta, and a Barber named Upāli, these seven were taken to the park accompanied by the four-fold army. After the procession had covered a great distance, the army was ordered to return. Thereafter, the seven moved on. Having crossed into another kingdom, they took out their ornaments and valuables and tied them in a piece of cloth. Then they entrusted the bundle to Barber Upāli and said,

> "You go back from this place. These will be enough to support you through life."

Upāli returned with the bundle. While still on the road, he thought,

> "The Śākyas are by nature haughty. When they will know that I have returned with ornaments and valuables, they will at once suspect that I

> have murdered the princes and robbed them of their valuables and jewels. They will at once kill me. If Bhaddīya, Anuruddha and others, who are princes, are going to be initiated, then, why should I not follow them?"

Having thus taken a firm decision, he hanged the ornaments from a tree and shouted,

> "Whosoever sets his eyes on these may take these."

Upāli started back and soon overtook his companions. On seeding the barber return so soon, the princes asked,

> "Upāli! Why have you come back"?

Upāli apprised them with his own thinking and narrated to them how he had disposed off the ornaments.

The Śākya princes approved his action and added,

> "You are very correct. The Śākyas are, by nature, very haughty. Your apprehension is not baseless."

With Upāli in their company, the Śākyas came to the Buddha. They saluted him and sat in one corner. They submitted,

> "*Bhante*! We, the Śākyas, are a proud people. This fellow, Barber Upāli, has for ever been our servant. Please initiate him first so that (being senior in initiation), we shall be liable to salute him, revere him and tender him our services. If this is done, then alone our pride in being Śākyas will be duly tempered."

The Buddha accepted the request of the Śākya princes. Upāli was the first to be initiated as a monk, and then the other six princes followed.[40]

REFERENCES

1. *Aupapātik-sūtra*, 10; *Kappa Sūtta* Su. 134-135.
2. Dharmānanda Kośāmbī, *Bhagvān Buddha*, p. 154.
3. *Ibid.*, pp. 153-54.
4. Based on *Gaṇadhara-vāda*; *Avaśyaka Niryukti*, Gāthā 17-65.
5. *Cf.* sāmī ya imaṁ etārūvaṁ abhiggahaṁ abhigeṇhati cauvvihaṁ dabbato 4; davvato kumāse suppa-koṇeṇaṁ khittao eluyam vikkhamvaitta kalao niyatteṣu bhikkhayareṣu bhavato yadi rayadhuya dasattanaṁ pattanīya labaddha muṇḍiyaśira royamani aṭṭhaṁ-vattiya abaṁ

kappati śeṣaṁ na kappati kalo ya poṣa-bahula padibao, ebaṁ abhiggahaṁ ghettunaṁ kosāmbīya acchati.

—*Ābaśyaka Cūrṇi*, Part I pp. 316-317.

Also *Āvaśyaka Niryukti, Malayagiri-vṛtti*, pp. 294-295; *Śrī Kalpasūtrārtha Prabodhini*, p. 154.

We have a mention of the duration of the fast for six months in.

6. *Āvaśyaka Cūrṇi*, Part 1.
7. Based on *Naya-dharmma-kahao*, Adhyayana 1.
   On the attainment of Enlightenment, the Buddha spent.
8. Based on *Triṣaṣṭi-śalākā-puruṣa-caritraṃ*, Parva 10, Sarga 6.
9. After his initiation into monkhood, Ṛṣabhadatta duly studies the 11 *Aṅgas*. He practised many fasts missing six, eight, ten or more meals at a time and lived for many years attaining higher spiritual levels. In the end, he courted fast till death, observing it for 30 days when he passed away, and became liberated.
10. After her initiation in the order of nuns, she studied the 11 *Aṅgas*. She practised various penances enriching her soul. In the end, she was liberated.
11. *Viśeṣāvaśyaka-bhāṣya, Saṭīka* (with commentary), p. 935.
12. For Jamāli's initiation, *Bhagavatī*, Śataka 9, U. 33. For the initiation of Priyadarśanā, *Triṣaṣṭi-śalākā-puruṣa-caritram*, Parva 10, Sarga 8.
13. Based on *Bhagavtī*, Śataka 12, Uddeśaka 2.
14. He is not the same person as Kāśyapa of the Buddhist tradition.
15. *Antagadādasao*, Varga 6.
16. *Bhagavatī*, Śataka 2, Uddeśaka 1.
17. Based on *Uttarājjhayānani*, Adhyayana 23.
18. *Bhagavatī*, Śataka 1, Uddeśaka 9.
19. *Ibid.*, Śātaka 9, Uddeśaka 32.
20. Suyagadang, *Śruta* 2, Adhyayana 7.
21. Based on *Triṣaṣṭi-śalākā-puruṣa-caritram*, Parva 10, Sarga 10. In the Jaina tradition, there are many legends and poems on Dhanyā and Śālibhadra.
22. In *Tīrthaṅkara Mahāvīra*, Part, II p. 509, Vijayendra Sūrī has called him as Udrāyaṇa. This is not correct. Compare, for instance, senam udayaneraya. Also vide *Bhagavatī*, Sa. 13, U. 6.
23. After his initiation, we have the following account of his life :

   The royal-monk practised severe penances. He underwent many fasts from one-day to 30 days durations. He enriched his soul by studies and meditations. Because of too many fasts and intake of coarse and dry food, his body became very thin and he lost his physical strength. He was frequently ill and his condition worsened. He could no longer study or mediate with the same ardentness as he previously did. The doctors suggested that he should take curd. As it would be easy for him to obtain curd from a cow-herds' village (*gokula*), the royal-monk begged from that village.

   Once in the course of his wanderings, he visited his own city Vītabhaya. A wicked minister told King Keśī that the royal-monk had returned to recover his kingdom and he warned him to be very watchful. King Keśi took the counsel in all seriousness and issued strict orders that the former king should not be given shelter by anyone in the city. The royal-monk moved from one end of the city to the other calling at every door, but no one was prepared to receive him. At last, he was received by a potter in his workshop. King Keśī tried to poison the former ruler on several occasions, but his life was saved by the grace of a goddess. But one day, when the goddess was away, the royal monk was given some food which contained poison. As the royal monk ate, the poison ran through his whole body. Since then the royal monk went on fast and remained like that for a whole month. In this state, on the expiry of a month, he obtained omniscience and passed away while he was in meditation.

   When on her return the goddess came to know that the royal-monk had been killed by the evil design of King Keśī, she became furious in rage and started incessant showers of dust on the city. The whole city of Vītabhaya was buried. The solitary exception in this total carnage was the potter's cottage.

24. Based on *Śrīkalpasūtrārtha Prabodhinī*, pp. 169-171; also, *Kalpasūtra Balavabodha*, p. 260.
25. *Uttarājjhyānāni, Vṛtti* by Bhāvavijaya Gaṇi, Chapter 18, pp. 375-379.
26. *Uvavai*, Su. 14.
27. In the Buddhist tradition, the order of the *Śramaṇas* is called *pravrajyā* and that of the *bhikṣus* is called *Upasampadā*.
28. Rāma, Dhvaja, Lakṣmaṇa, Mantrī, Kauṇḍinya, Bhoja, Suyāma and Sudatta—these *Brāhmaṇas* had mastered the Vedas with their six *Aṅgas*. Seven from among these had predicted at the birth of the Buddha that if he would remain in the household order, he would be a world monarch and if he would renounce, he would be a Buddha. Kauṇḍinya who was the youngest of them predicted only one future for the child, *viz.*, that he would be a Buddha. The former seven advised their sons to join the holy order of Prince Siddhārtha when he would be a Buddha. By the time the prince renounced his home, all these *Brāhmaṇas* were dead except Kauṇḍinya. He brought it to the notice of the sons of his former colleagues that the prince had left his home and that he would definitely be a Buddha. Added he in the end, "So let us also be wandering mendicants." Only four young men responded to his call. They were Vāṣpa (vappa), Bhadrīka, Mahānāma and Aśvajit. Later, these were called *Pañcavarga bhikṣus*.
29. Based on *Vinaya Piṭaka*, Mahāvagga, Mahākhandhaka, 1-1-6 & 7.
30. *Ibid.*, 1-1-8 to 10.
31. *Ibid.*, 1-1-13.
32. *Ibid.*, 1-1-14 & 15.
33. *Ibid.*, 1-1-18.
34. *Aṅguttara Nikāya Aṭṭhakathā*, 1-1-10.
35. *Cf. Daśaveyalīyam, Agastyasinha Cūrṇi*, Adhyayana 5, Uddeśaka 2, Gāthā 25.
36. *Jātaka Nidāna 4, Mahāvagga Aṭṭhakathā*, Mahākhandhaka, Rāhulvastu.
37. *Udāna Aṭṭhakathā*, 3-2; *Aṅguttara Nikāya Aṭṭhakathā*, 1-4-8; *Vinaya Piṭaka, Mahāvagga Aṭṭhakathā*.
38. *Jātak* (Hindi) Part 1, p. 118.
39. *Jātaka Aṭṭhakathā, Nidāna* 4; *Vinaya Piṭaka*, Mahāvagga, Mahākhāndhaka, 1-3-11.
40. Based on *Vinaya Piṭaka*, Cullavagga, Saṅghabhedakaskandhaka, 7-1-1 & 2.

11

MONKS AND NUNS

It is an inevitable fact of history that certain persons acquire immortality because of their association with the great men of their age. We have many such personalities associated with the lives of both Mahāvīra and the Buddha.

Eleven *Gaṇadharas* of Mahāvīra have become immortal with him. They were the leaders of their respective teams called *gaṇa*. It is they who preserved the great treasure of 12 *Aṅgas*.

1. *Indrabhūti Gautama*—He was the foremost among Mahāvīra's disciples, and is inseparable from him. He used to ask from the most commonplace to the most difficult questions to the Master, and based on these questions and answers, there has been the compilation of the biggest of the Jaina *Āgamas, Vihāya* Paññatti, popularly called *Bhagavatī*. He was also famous for his great spiritual powers.

Gautama had the deepest affection for the Master. On the occassion of Mahāvīra's death, this affection overpowered him completely like a river flooding both the banks, and Gautama was deeply aggrieved at the apparent lack of reciprocation from the other side. But soon he controlled himself. He recognised the supreme detachment of the Master and his own attachment. From the outward, he turned to the inward. The veil of ignorance was torn. He attained the supreme and limitless knowledge and himself became *Arhat*.

Once, Gautama felt a great mortification for his own self for not attaining the supreme knowledge. To rid him of this, Mahāvīra said,

> "Gautama! For a very long time, You are tied with me by affection. You have been all praise about me for a very long time. We have been acquaintances for ever, and for ever you have served me, for ever you have followed me, and for ever you have carried out my orders. In your previous lives, whether as a god or as a human being, you were always linked with me, and what more, after we die, and when this body is destroyed, we shall be together again, in the same state, as liberated souls."[1]

The above should indicate how very intimate was Gautama's relation with Mahāvīra.

2. *Candanabālā*—She was the foremost in Mahāvīra's order nuns. Her position in the order was called *pravartinī*. She was a princess, but her life was full of many vicissitudes. She spent a part of her life as a maid-servent. She underwent the experience of being in chains. But in the closing chapter of her life, we see her holding the most illustrious position of being the head of Mahāvīra's order of nuns.

According to the Thānāṅga and the *Samavāyāṅga*,[2] 700 in Mahāvīra's order attained Omniscience,[3] 1300 attained *avadhi* knowledge, 500 atained *manaḥ-paryava* knowledge, 300 were the masters of the 14 Pūrvas, and there were many other monks and nuns who held great powers, who had practised hard penances, who were great debators, and so on.

At times, Mahāvīra even mentioned about the specialities of his monks and nuns.

In the *Tripiṭakas,* too, we have accounts of monks who lived around the Buddha, foremost among them being Sāriputta, Moggallāna, Ānanda, Upāli, Mahākāssapa, Ājñākoḍinna, and so on. In the Jaina order, the *Gaṇadharas* enjoyed a dignified position and were entrusted with a well-defined responsibility. In the Buddhist order, there is no counterpart of Jaina *Gaṇadhara;* but Sāriputta and others held quite high positions of honour and responsibility in that order.

3. *Sāriputta*—As was *Gaṇadhara* Gautama go Mahāvīra, so was Sāriputta an inseparable companion of the Buddha. He was highly intelligent and learned and was a great commentator. The Buddha depended on him in various matters. On one occassion, the Buddha had observed, "Sāriputta! In whichever direction you go, you emit the same sort of light as the Buddha does."[4]

The *Tripiṭakas* give an illustration of Sāriputta's intellect. When the Buddha's recalcitrant disciple *Devadatta* broke away from the order with 500 Vajjī monks, it was mainly the wit of Sāriputta that could reclaim these 500 from the clutches of the rebel.[5]

Once the Buddha said to Ānanda,

> "How do you like Sāriputta?"

Ānanda said in reply,

> *"Bhante!* Who will not like the long-lived Sāriputta unless he is a fool, a wicked person, or one with an unbalanced mind? The long-lived Sāriputta has a great knowledge and a great wisdom. His wisdom is as delightful as it is sharp."[6]

At Sāriputta's death, the Buddha observed,

> "A vast branch of *Kalpa*-tree of Religion is gone."

The Buddha nick-named him as the spiritual commander.

4. *Moggallāna*—Moggallāna, like Sāriputta, was among the foremost disciples of the Buddha. He was a great monk and was considered to be endowed with the greatest power.[7] As in the Jaina tradition we have many examples of the occult powers *(labdhi)* of Gautama, so in the Buddhist tradition, we have many stories about the occult powers *(ṛddhi)* of Moggallāna.

With Sāriputta, Moggallāna too had a hand in the reclamation of the 500 Vajjī monks for the Buddha's order from the clutches of rebel Devadatta.[8]

Viśākhā, a female devotee of the Buddha had decided to erect an abode (*vihāra*) for the Buddha and his monks on an outlay of 27,00,00,000 gold coins. She prayed to the Buddha to give her a monk who could help her in supervising this work. Said the Buddha,

> "You pick up the begging bowl and the rag of the monk whom you intend to have for this purpose."

Viśākhā thought the Moggallāṇa commanded great powers by dint of which he could help her in the quick construction of the shelter. So, she named him and the Buddha agreed. It is stated that because of the occult powers of the great Moggallāna that Viśākhā's masons were able to mobilise big trees and stone-slabs from a distance of even 60 *yojanas* in course on a single night.[9]

The Jaina tradition, however, does not permit a monk to assist in this sort of enterprise, nor does it consider worthwhile to permit a monk to display his occult powers. But even in this tradition, (in somewhat different contexts) we have on record many strange accounts of *labdhi*-power and its application. We have noted elsewhere how Nandīsena, a son of Śreṇika, who had joined the monastic order of Mahāvīra, displayed his power to stupefy a prostitute.

We have in the Jaina tradition the story of Mahāvīra shaking the whole of Mount Meru by the touch of his thumb in order to alert the Indra. Likewise, we have in the Buddhist tradition the story of Moggallāna shaking a palace named Jayanta by the touch of his thumb for a similar purpose.[10] It is stated that once the Buddha, Moggallāna and others were at the topmost floor of a shelter (*pūrvārāma*). At the ground floor of the same building, some misguided monks were making a noise and indulging in indecent talks. To warn them, Moggallāna shook the whole palace by dint of his occult power. When these misguided monks became thrilled and alarmed, the Buddha spoke to them words of enlightenment.[11]

About the monks of Mahāvīra, we have the following in the *Uvavai*[12] :

> There were many who could mentally curse or favour anyone.

There were many who could do the same by their speech.

There were many who could do the same by physical activity.

There were many who commanded *śleṣmauṣadha labdhi;* with their pheegm could be cured even most difficult diseases like leprosy.

There were many who commanded *jallauṣadha labdhi;* their body-dirt could cure any disease.

There were many who commanded *amarṣauṣadha labdhi;* a drop of their urine could cure any disease.

There were many who commanded *amarṣauṣadha labdhi;* a touch of their hand could cure any disease.

There were many who commanded *sarvauṣadha labdhi;* their hairs, nails, porehairs, in brief, everything, served as medicine.

There were many monks who commanded *padanusarī labdhi;* on hearing a couplet, they could hear many such couplets.

There were many monks who command *saṁbhinnaśrotṛ labdhi;* with any one sense organ, they could take the objects of all the sense organs. (For instance with their eyes, they could not only see, but also hear, smell, taste and touch).

There were many monks who commanded *akṣiṇamahānasa labdhi;* they could feed hundreds, even thousands, with food they had begged before they themselves ate.

There were many monks who commanded *vikurvaṇa labdhi* by dint of which they could assume any form.

There were many monks who commanded *jaṅghācāraṇa labdhi* by placing their hand on the upper part of the leg, they could, in a single flight, reach the 13th Rucakavara Isle or the summit of Mount Meru.

There were many who commanded *vidyācārana labdi;* by a slight *upaṣaṭambha,* in two stages, they could reach the eighth Isle named Nandīśvara or the summit of Mount Meru.

There were many who commanded *ākāśātipāti labdhi;* they could fly into the sky and shower from there silver and many other wholesome and unwholesome objects.

It is, however, stated that Moggallāna had a very tragic end. People of other faiths became so very jealous of him that they beat him to death like a beast. His bones were smashed to small particles so that no single particle was bigger than a grain of rice. It is further stated that he could have saved himself by dint of his spiritual powers, but he did not do that. He submitted to the torture silently taking it to be the outcome of his past karma.[13]

5. *Ānanda*—In several respects, Ānanda was more intimate with the Buddha than either Sāriputta or Moggallāna. His relation with the Master makes an interesting and inspiring account. He was associated with many historic events which have become immortal in the Buddhist tradition. The inclusion of nuns in the Buddhist order was the outcome of his zeal. The Buddha was never in favour of it. He saw many faults in it. It was at the suggestion from Ānanda that he initiated *Mahāprajāpati* Gautamī as a nun. But at the same time, the Buddha said,

> "If, without nuns, this order would have lasted for a thousand years, now, it will remain for not more than 500. The initiation of a woman in my order has knocked out half its life-span."

The *Tripiṭakas* were compiled at the first Buddhist Council. Among the 500 *arhat-bhikṣus* who attended, Ānanda was the only one who had an authoritative knowledge of the *Sūtras*. It was on his exclusive authority that the *Suttapiṭaka* was compiled. It is, however, interesting that for not obtaining the necessary clarifications about the texts from the Buddha during his life-time, Ānanda had to make atonements before the whole *Saṅgha*. But by far the most surprising thing is that the *Saṅgha* penalised him on account of his proposal to the Buddha for the inclusion of women in the monastic order.[14]

Ānanda was the Buddha's personal attendant (*upasthaka*). The story of his attaining this position is very interesting. At his 56th year, the Buddha called all his monks and said,

> "*Bhikṣus!* Engage an attendant for me. In the absence of one, I am not getting proper attention. I say, go by this route, and the *bhikṣus* go by another route. Carelessly they place my bowl and cloth on the ground. Overriding the claim of Sāriputta, Moggallāna and others, the Buddha took Ānanda as his personal attendant."[15]

From that time, Ānanda became the Buddha's inseparable companion. Sometimes he put questions to the Buddha as *Gaṇadhara* Gautama did to Mahāvīra, and sometimes he gave his suggestions. Just as it stated that Gautama was linked to Mahāvīra in his previous births, so we have many accounts in the *Jātaka* about Ānanda's link with the Buddha in his previous births. When strangers came to see the Buddha, they had invariably to apply through him. Just as after the passing away of Mahāvīra, Gautama became very much overwhelmed with grief, so was Ānanda after the passing away of the Buddha. As Ānanda had come to know before hand that the Buddha would pass away on that day, he went aside, took the support of a pole and wept bitterly. In the case of Gautama, he became omniscient during the same night when Mahāvīra passed away. Ānanda attained *arhat*-hood after a considerable gap but before he went to attend the first Buddhist Council. Like Gautama who felt a remorse till he became omniscient, Ānanda too passed through a similar state till be became an *arhat*. Thus, there is much similarity between the two events.

Mahāvīra too had a devoted follower bearing the same name (Ānanda),[16] but he was a householder. Beyond a similarity of the two names, there is nothing to cause confusion between the two. There was still another Ānanda who was a monk in Mahāvīra's order. It was to this (third) Ānanda that Gośālaka had said,

> "By the stroke of my fiery powers, Mahāvīra will soon meet with his end."

6. *Upāli*—At the first Buddhist Council, it was Upāli who reproduced the *Vinaya-sutta.* He had memorised this during his intimate association with the Buddha. (A barber by birth), he was initiated as a monk in the company of five Śākya princes named Bhaddīya, Ānanda and others.

7. *Mahākāśyapa*—He was one of the very hard-working disciples of the Buddha. His early life was also very illustrious and inspring. The legend of Pippalīkumāra and Bhadrākumārī,[17] is based on his life. In the Buddha's monastic order, the same Pippalīkumāra became the long-lived Mahākāśyapa. Touching his delicate and costly garment, once the Buddha spoke highly of it. He offered his garment to the Buddha, when the Buddha said,

> "Supposing I accept your garment, can you use my old, coarse and dirty rags?"

Mahākāśyapa was ready whereon there was an exchange of robes between the two. This has been considered to be a historic event in the life of the Buddha, as also in the Buddhist tradition.

Mahākāśyapa was a learned man. He became famous as the commentators of the Buddhist suttas. At the Buddha's funeral, again, it was he who directed the funeral rites. On the day and at the time when the Buddha was to be cremated, he came in the company of 500 monks to the cremation ground.[18]

It was at his suggestion that King Ajātaśatru preserved the bones of the Buddha in a metal casket which, at a later period, was opened by Emperor Aśoka, and portions of the same sent to far-off lands.[19] He was one of the leading organisers of the first Buddhist Council.[20]

There were many other monks such as Ajña-koḍinna, Anuruddha and many others who were intimately associated with the Buddha.

8. *Gautamī*—In the Buddhist tradition, the name of *Mahāprajāpati* Gautamī is a much famous as that of the great nun Candanavālā in the Jain tradition. There is, however, no common ground between the early lives of the two, thought both were the first women disciples of their respective masters, and both headed the orders of nuns in the two orders.

Two things in the life of Gautamī are deserving of special attention. She not only induced the Buddha to accept women in his monastic order, but also suggested that the nuns should be given equal status with the monks. But in accepting Gautamī in his monastic order, the Buddha imposed a number of conditions. One such condition was that even a fresh monk would be entitled to homage and obeisance from a veteran nun. Gautamī agreed, but very soon after her initiation, she took the matter up with the Master. She submitted,

> "*Bhante!* Why do you insist that a veteran nun must pay homage and obeisance even to a newly initiated monk? Why should it not be to the contrary that a newly initiated monk should pay his homage and obeisance to a veteran nun?"

On this, the Buddha said,

> "Gautamī! Such is not the practice even in religious orders which are lesser than mine; and, you know, mine is a very superior religious order."[21]

The question raised by Gautamī about the status of women in the Indian society at a distance of about 2500 years has not lost its significance even now. In contrast with the importance of the issue, the reply given by the Buddha would appear to be very evasive. The reply would give the impression that even among the great men, there are few who are prepared to give recognition to fresh values; most of them prefer to adhere to established practices and conventions. It is true that even now women are fighting to improve their status in a society which is dominated over by men; but the fact remains that even 2500 earlier, there was a woman in this country who had made it an important issue no less a man than the Buddha himself.

Gautamī apart, a number of other nuns, notably Khema, Utpalavarṇa, Paṭacara, Bhadra, Kuṇḍala keśa, Bhadra Kapilayanī and many others, became famous in the Buddhist order. In naming the etadagga vagga (foremost among the foremost),[22] the Buddha himself has honoured the names of 41 monks and

12 nuns, giving specifically the best quality in each. The list would run as follows :

1. Ajña-kauṇḍinya—for his devotion to the Buddha; a *Brāhmaṇa* from Droṇa vastu near Kapilavastu in the Sākya country.
2. Sāriputta—for his wisdom; a *Brāhmaṇa* from Upatiṣya (Nalaka) which was not far from Rājagṛha in Magadha.
3. Mahāmoggallāna—for his spiritual powers; a *Brāhmaṇa* from Kolita near Rājagṛha in Magadha.
4. Mahākāśyapa—for his renunciation; a *Brāhamṇa* from Mahātīrtha Brāhmaṇagrāma in Magadha.
5. Anuruddha—for his divine vision; a *Kṣatriya* from Kapilavastu in Śākya country. He was the cousin of the Buddha, being the son of his uncle Amṛtaudana.
6. Bhaddīya Kaligodhā-putra—for his noble parentage; a *Kṣatriya* from Kapilavastu in Śākya country.
7. Lakuṇṭaka Bhaddīya—for his mild voice; a Dhanī (*Mahābhoga)* from Śrāvastī in Kośala.
8. Piṇḍola Bhāradvāja—for his roaring voice; a *Brāhmaṇa* from Rājagṛha in Magadha.
9. Pūrṇa Maitrāyaṇi-putra—for being the best speaker of spiritual lores; a *Bhāhmaṇa* from Droṇavastu near Kapilavastu in Śākya country.
10. Mahākātyāyana—foremost among commentators; a *Brāhmaṇa* from Ujjainī in Avanti.
11. Cullapanthaka—for his mastery in giving shape to imagination and for his expertise in psychiatry; a son of a Śreṣṭhi's daughter from Rājagṛha in Magadha.
12. Mahāpanthaka—for his mastery of definitions (concepts); son of a Śreṣṭhi's daughter from Rājagṛha in Magadha.
13. Subhūti—foremost among those who were liberated from pains; a *Vaiśya* from Śrāvastī in Kośala.
14. Revata-khadira-vaniya—foremost among the forest-dwellers; a *Brāhmaṇa,* Sāriputta's younger brother, from Nālaka Brāhmaṇagrāma (near Rājagṛha) in Magadha.
15. Kaṅkha Revata—foremost among mediators; a *Mahābhoga* from Śrāvasti in Kośala.
16. Soṇa Koḍivīsa—most enterprising; a Śreṣṭhī from Campā in Aṅga.
17. Soṇa Kuṭikaṇṇa—foremost among speakers; a *Vaiśya* from Kuraravara in Avantī.
18. Sīvalī—foremost among the covetous of spiritual gains; son of

Supravāsā, daughter of Kolīya; a *Kṣatriya* from Kuṇḍiya in Śākya country.

19. Vakkali—foremost among the most devoted; a *Brāhmaṇa* from Śrāvastī in Kośala.
20. Rāhula—foremost among those who observed the discipline of the *Saṅgha*; son of Siddhārtha, a *Kṣatriya* from Kapilavastu in Śākya country.
21. Rāṣṭrapāla—foremost among those who were initiated for their devotion; a *Vaiśya* from Thullakoṇṇita in Kuru.
22. Kuṇḍadhāna—first to pick up the stick (*Śalākā*); a *Brāhmaṇa* from Śrāvasti in Kośala.
23. Vaṅgīśa—foremost among the writers of verses; a *Brāhmaṇa* from Śrāvastī in Kośala.
24. Vaṅganta-putra—foremost among the most graceful; Sāriputta's younger borther; a *Brāhmaṇa* from Nālaka Brāhmaṇa-grāma in Magadha.
25. Malla-putra Dravya—foremost among those who were in charge of beds and cushions; a *Kṣatriya* from Anūpiyā in Malla.
26. Pilindivātsya—foremost among the beloved of the gods; a *Brāhmaṇa* from Śrāvastī in Kośala.
27. Vāhiya-dāru-cīriya—for his sharp intellect; a Kullaputra from Vāhiya-rāṣṭra.
28. Kumāra Kāśyapa—among extempore speakers; from Rājagṛha in Magadha.
29. Mahākosṭhita—foremost among the most consoled souls; a *Brāhmaṇa* from Śrāvastī in Kośala.
30. Ānanda—foremost among the most well-versed, with keenest memory, most progressive outlook, with greatest perseverance and among the most intimate companions of the Buddha; son of Amṛtadoṇa; a *Kṣatriya* from Kapilavastu in Śākya country.
31. Uruvelā Kāśyapa—foremost among the councellors; a *Brāhmaṇa* from Vārāṇasī in Kāśī.
32. Kāla-udāyī—foremost among those who had brightened their lines; born in the family of a minister from Kapilavastu in Śākya country.
33. Bakkula—foremost among those enjoying a most perfect health; a *Vaiśya* from Kauśāmbī in Vatsa.
34. Śobhita—foremost among those who had a memory of their previous birth(s); a *Brāhmaṇa* from Śrāvastī in Kośala.
35. Upāli—foremost among the most courteous; a Barber from Kapilavastu in Śākya country.
36. Nandaka—chief adviser in the affairs of the order of nuns; from a noble family at Śrāvastī in Kośala.

37. Nanda—foremost among those who had subdued their senses; son of Mahāprajāpatī; a *Kṣatriya* from Kapilavastu in Śākya country.
38. Mahākappina—chief adviser in the affairs of the monks; born in a royal household from Kukkuṭavatī on the frontier.
39. Svāgata—foremost among experts in *teja-dhātu*; a *Brāhmaṇa* from Śrāvastī in Kośala.
40. Rādha—for his great brilliance; a *Brāhmaṇa* from Rājagṛha in Magadha.
41. Mogharāja—foremost among those who put on coarse rags; a disciple of Bāvarī; *Brāhmaṇa* from Śrāvastī in Kośala.

The following is the list of the foremost among the nuns :

1. Mahāprajāpati Gautamī—for her great devotion for the Buddha; wife of Śuddhodana; a *Kṣatriyāṇī* from Kapilavastu in Śākya country.
2. Khemā—for her geat wisdom; wife of Bimbisāra, king of Magadha; a princess from Sāgala in Madras.
3. Utpala-varṇā—for her great spiritual powers; born in a *Śreṣṭhī* family of Śrāvastī in Kośala.
4. Paṭācārā—foremost for her courtsey; born in a *Śreṣṭhī* family of Śrāvastī in Kośala.
5. Dhammadinnā—foremost among discourse-givers; wife of Viśākha *Śreṣṭhī* of Rājagṛha in Magadha.
6. Nandā—foremost in meditation; daughter of Mahāprajāpati Gautamī; from Kapilavastu in Śākya country.
7. Soṇā—most enterprising from a noble household at Śrāvastī in Kośala.
8. Sakulā—foremost among those endowed with a divine vision; from a noble household at Śrāvastī in Kośala.
9. Bhadrā-kuṇḍalakeśā—the most brilliant; born in a *Śreṣṭhī* family Rājagṛha in Magadha.
10. Bhadrā Kapilāyanī—for her memory of previous birth(s); wife of Mahākāśyapa; a *Brāhmaṇī* from Sāgala in Madras.
11. Bhadrā-kātyāyanī—for her divine powers (*abhijñā*); daughter of Rāhulamātā who, in turn, was the daughter of Suprabuddha, a resident of Devadāhā; a *Kṣatriyaṇī* from Kapilavastu in Śākya country.
12. Kṛśā Gautamī—for her use of coarse rags; a *Vaiśya* from Śrāvastī in Kośala.
13. Śṛgāla-mātā—the most respectful; born in a *Śreṣṭhī* family at Rājagṛha in Magadha.

In the Jaina Āgamas, we do not come across any list of the foremost among the foremost as we have in the Buddhist texts cited above; but the figures in the Kappa Sutta of the omniscients and others and the account in the Uvavai give an idea about the length of penances of the *nirgrantha* monks and their other multifarious qualities. As to penances, it is stated, in part, as follows :

> "Many monks practised a penance called *kanakāvalī*, many practised *ekāvalī, laghusiṁha-niṣkrīḍita, mahāsiṁha-niṣkrīḍita, bhadra-pratimā, mahābhadra-pratimā, sarvatobhadra-pratimā, ayaṁvila-vardhamāna, tapaḥ pratimā* for one month, for two months, and so on, till seven months, *pratimā* for one, two or three weeks for whole day and night, *pratimā* for one day-night, *pratimā* for one night, seven *saptamikā pratimā, yava-madhya-candra-pratimā*, and many practised *vajra-madhya-candra-pratimā*."

As to qualities of the monks, it is stated in the same Sūtra :

> "The monks were endowed with knowledge, with vision, with conduct, with humility and with simplicity. They were endowed with oration, brilliance, speech and fame. They had conquered senses, slumber and hardships. They had no expectation from life and no fear from death. They were experts in arts like *prajñapti*, etc., and in the use of *mantras*. They were excellent, wise, restrained from sex, truthful and clean. They wore a beautiful complexion. They had overcome all the wordly desires. They were above all curiousities, careful about the observance of rules prescribed for a monk and experts in breaking both the external and internal ties. They were well-acquainted with their own philosophies as well as those of others. They were foremost in defeating their rivals who held different views. They new well the 12 *Aṅgas* and were the masters of all the *gaṇipiṭakas*. They knew all word-formations and all languages. Although they were not yet complete *jinas*, they were very much near them."[27]

The life-story of many monks and nuns remains scattered here and there in the entire Āgamic literature from which it is possible to gather their individual traits.

9. *Dhanya of Kākandī*—Dhanya of Kākandī became a monk by giving up 32 young maidens and 32 seraglios. Under the guidance of Mahāvīra, he practised very severe penances so that his body was reduced to a mere skeleton. On a point of enquiry about him by King Bimbisāra, Mahāvīra said, in part, as follows :

> "In a group of 14,000 monks, this monk Dhanya is about to perform something most difficult by dint of his penances, his spiritual exertions."[24]

10. *Meghakumāra*—During the first night after his initiation, Meghakumāra, the son of King Bimbisāra, deviated from his path. Thought he,

> "Till yesterday, when I was a prince, all the monks took care of me and expressed their affection and respect for me. Today, I have become a monk, but where are their affection and respect for me gone? Without caring for me, they run about their own affairs. They do not assemble round me as they did in the past. The place allotted to me for taking rest (sleeping) is the last one near the door so that while going out or coming in they disturb me all the time. What sort of behaviour is this towards me? At dawn, I shall return my monk's garment to *Bhagavān* Mahāvīra."

In the morning, as he stood before *Bhagavān* Mahāvīra, the latter know his mind by dint of his omniscience and said,

> "Meghakumāra! Last night, you had such and such thoughts in your mind, and you have made up your mind to go back to your palace-home by handing over the monk's pot, duster, etc. Is it correct?"

> "*Bhante*! Every word of what you have stated is correct."

In order to refix him in necessary restraint, Mahāvīra gave him necessary advice and spoke to him revealing life in the previous birth whereon Meghakumāra was refixed in restraint.

Meghakumāra acquired the knowledge of his previous birth. He studied and mastered 11 *Aṅgas*. He practised the most difficut of penances named *guṇa-ratna-saṁvatsara* and also 12 *pratimās*. In the end, with the permission of Mahāvīra, he courted death by a long fast unto death, and was born as a god in an excellent existence.

11. *Nanda*—In the Buddhist tradition, a new initiate named Nanda (the Buddha's Cousin) underwent a similar predicament as did Meghakumāra in the Jaina tradition. Remembering the final entreaties of his newly-wed bride Janapada-Kalyāṇī Nandā, he was shaken immediately after his initiation. The Buddha came to know this and went to reclaim him. The Buddha pointed to a she-monkey on the street whose ears, nose and tail were cut, whose hairs were burnt, whose skin was wrecked and blood dropped therefrom, and said,

> "Is your wife more beautiful than this?"

> —"Sure, of course"!

Thereafter, the Buddha took him to the Trāyastriṁśa heaven. The Indra along with him nymphs bowed before him. Pointing to the nymphs, the Buddha said,

> "If your Janapada-Kalyāṇī Nandā more beautiful than these?"
>
> —"No, sir, to these, Janapada-Kalyāṇī stands in the same position as the lame monkey does to her."

The Buddha said,

> "Then why are you so much excited for her? Observe the rules of monkhood, and you will acquire nymphs like these."[25]

Nanda was refixed in the monastic order. His motive for a material gain was, however, completely erased only after he was ridiculed by 80 monks including Sāriputta who said that Nanda had become a monk in order to win the nymphs. In this manner, Nanda was freed from desires and he became an *arhat.*[26]

The facts over which Meghakumāra and Nanda became perturbed were somewhat different, but the course of events for both bears a lot of resemblance. Mahāvīra refixed Meghakumāra by showing him the scene of tenacity and perseverance which he possessed in his previous life, whereas the Buddha reclaimed Nanda by pointing to the joy he will be entitled to by leading the life of a monk. Deserving of special note is that like Meghakumāra who was an elephant in his previous birth, we have it on the authority of the *Jātakas* that Nanda was also an elephant in his previous birth.[27]

12. *Śālibhadra*—Śālibhadra of Rājagṛha, whose treasures had been a cause of wonder of King Bimbisāra, became an excellent monk in his life. He regularly practised fasts for one, two or even three months at a time. Once Mahāvīra came to Rājagṛha in the company of a large number of monks. Śālibhadra was in the group. On the day they arrived, Śālibhadra was to break his fast for a month. So, with his head bent low, he sought permission from *Bhagavān* Mahāvīra to move into the city to beg. Said *Bhagavān* Mahāvīra.

> "You go and receive food from your mother's hand."

Śālibhadra came to his mother Bhadrā. Bhadrā was busy in her own business and did not pay attention to the monk. Other members of the household did not recognise him. Śālibhadra returned empty-handed. On the way, he met a milk-maid who carried a pot of curds on her head. When she saw the monk, she felt a sponteneous affection for him. A spark of thrill ran through her body, and milk flowed out from her breasts. She requested the monk to accept some curd from her. The monk accepted it and returned to the shelter. After he had broken his fast, he made the following submission to *Bhagavān* Mahāvīra.

> "*Bhante!* You asked me to receive food from my mother's hand in order to break my fast. How is it that it did not materialise?"

Said *Bhagavān* Mahāvīra.

> "Śālibhadra! You have broken your fast with food received from your mother's hand. The milk-maid was your mother in the previous birth."

On the same day, with the permission of *Bhagavān* Mahāvīra, Śālibhadra went up the Baibhāra hill and courted fast unto death. Meanwhile, Bhadrā came to Mahāvīra's congregation. From *Bhagavān* Mahāvīra, she got a complete account about her son from the time he visited his former home in order to beg food to break his fast till now when he was on a fast unto death. The mother's feelings for her darling child are easier to imagine than state. At once, she rushed to the hill and went up. She was completely overwhelmed and shaken to see the ematiated frame of her son, now dedicated to death by a fast. She began to cry aloud. King Bimbisāra spoke words to console the mother's grief and took her back home.

Having discarded his mortal frame, Śālibhadra became a god in heaven. He had started the life on the pinacle of wealth and affluence; but when it closed, he was on the pinacle of restraint and renunciation.

13. *Skandaka*—He had been inducted from the order of *parivrājaka* monks into the monastic order of Mahāvīra. It is extremely noteworthy that, a highly accomplished man as he was, he not only changed over to another order, but soon gained for himself a noteworthy position in the new order of his adaptation. We have it in the *Āgamas* that monk Skandaka walked carefully, stopped carefully, sat carefully, slept carefully, ate carefully and spoke carefully. He practised restraint towards one-organ beings, two-to-five-organ beings, flora-bodies and static beings. Skandaka had courted the five precautions, was restrained in mind, in words and in body, was devoid of desires and of restlessness and was rooted in restraint. Skandaka mastered the 11 *Aṅgas* under the guidance of the senior monks, and with the permission of *Bhagavān* Mahāvīra, performed a prolonged penance named *guṇa-ratna-saṁvatsara.* As a result of this severe penance, his body which was beautiful, well-proportioned and pleasant became rough, dry and emaciated. All his flesh was gone, and he was reduced to a mere skeleton with a cover of skin on it. When he moved, his bones rattled like a moving cart loaded with dry leaves or with charcoal. But he shone all the time due to brilliances acquired through severest penances.[28]

What to speak of talking, Skandaka felt weak even when he desired to talk. Considering the state of his body, one day, he came to *Bhagavān* Mahāvīra and sought his permission for a fast unto death. Having obtained the necessary permission, and duly attended by fellow monks, he proceeded to Mount Vipula where he courted the fast as per rules. After fulfilling the fast for a month, he passed away to be born as a god in a heaven named *Acyuta-kalpa*. Among the monks around *Bhagavān* Mahāvīra, he held a very important position.

Among the nuns in Mahāvīra's order, Candanavālā was indeed the leadingmost; but others deserving mention were Mrgāvatī, Devānandā, Jayantī, Sudarśanā and others.

Such is the briefs account of the monks and nuns who lived with and around the respective leaders of the two order, Mahāvīra and Buddha.

REFERENCES

1. *Bhagavatī,* Śataka 14 Uddeśaka 7.
2. *Thānanga,* Sutta 230; *Samavayanga*, Sāma, 110.
3. According to the *Kappa Sutta* (Sutta 144), 700 monks and 1400 nuns were perfected.
4. *Anguttara Nikāya,* Aṭṭhakathā, 1-4-1.
5. *Vinaya Piṭaka,* Cullavagga, Saṅgha-vedaka-khandhaka.
6. *Saṁyutta Nikāya,* Anāthapiṇḍikavagga, Susima Sutta.
7. *Anguttara Nikāya*, 1-14.
8. *Vinaya Piṭaka*, Ibid.
9. *Dhammapada Aṭṭhakathā*, 4-44.
10. *Majjhima Nikāya,* Cūla-taṇhā-sāṅkhaya Sutta.
11. *Saṁyutta Nikāya*, Mahāvagga, Ṛdhipāda, Saṁyutta Prāsāda-kampana-vagga, Mauggallāna Sutta.
12. *Uvavaiya*, Sutta 15.
13. *Dhammapada Aṭṭhakathā,* 10-7; *Milinda-pañña*, Pari. 4, Varga 4, p. 229.
14. For detail, Chapter 18 at the end.
15. *Anguttara Nikāya* Aṭṭhakathā, 1-4-1.
16. *Uvasaga-dasao*, Adhyayana 1.
17. *Āgama and Tripiṭaka* Vol. 2.
18. *Dīgha Nikāya*, Mahāparinivvāṇa Sutta.
19. *Dīgha Nikāya,* Aṭṭhakathā, Mahāparinivvāna Sutta.
20. *Vinaya Piṭaka*, Cūllavagga, Pañcaśatikā Khandhaka.
21. *Vinaya Piṭaka*, Cūllavagga, Bhikkhunī-Khandhaka.
22. *Anguttara Nīkaya*, Ekeka-nipāta 14.
23. *Uvavaiya*, Sutta 15-16.
24. *Aṇuttarovavai-dasao*, Varga 3, Adhyayana 1.
25. The story of Sundarī Nanda in the Jaina tradition bears resemblance with this Buddhist story. The only difference between the two stories is that in the Jaina story, the brother-monks of Sundarī Nanda showed him, by dint of their spiritual powers, a she-monkey, vidyādharī and a nymph in order to refix him in restraint, whereas in the Buddhist story, this is being done by the Buddha himself to reclaim his own cousin. Vide *Āvaśyaka Sutta*, Malayagiri Commentaries.
26. *Sutta-nipāta Aṭṭhakathā*, p. 272; *Dhammapada Aṭṭhakathā,* Part 1, pp. 96-105, *Jātaka* 182; *Theragāthā* 157; *Dictionary of Pāli Proper Names*, Vol. 1, pp. 10-11.
27. *Sangamāvacara Jātaka* 182, (Hindi ed.) Vol. 2, pp. 248-254.

12

LEADING FOLLOWERS (UPĀSAKAS)

Wending through the *Āgamas* and the *Tripiṭakas,* one comes across ample material about the followers and disciples of both Mahāvīra and Gautama Buddha. To signify these, both the orders have used a common term, *śramaṇopāsaka.* Both Jainism and Buddhism were parts of a common cult called *śramaṇa,* and the term *śramaṇopāsaka* reveals the common source of the two. Even the word *śrāvaka* has been used in both the traditions; but whereas in the Jaina tradition, a *Śrāvaka* is a lay-follower, in the Buddhist tradition, it may be monk as well as a follower, *e.g., bhikṣu-śrāvaka upāsaka-śrāvaka.*[1]

Leading Jaina Upāsakas

The accounts about the leading followers are more organised and detailed in the *Āgamas* than in the *Tripiṭakas*. Among the 11 *Āgamas* in the Jaina tradition, the seventh one is devoted to the life-story of 10 leading *Śrāvaka.* This apart, the *Bhagavatī* and many other canonical texts have noticed innumerable followers, both male and female. The account of 10 *śrāvakas* in the Uvāsagadasao gives details of their conversion to the *nirgrantha* faith, their families, their business, their riches and their cowherds. Each one of these 10 *śrāvakas,* it possessed 24,00,00,000 gold coins and 80,000 cow-heads. The Buddhist follower Viśākhā is stated to have even a much greater amount of wealth with her and she to have spent 27,00,00,000 gold coins in the construction of *pūrvarām*, a shelter for the use of the Buddhist monks. We further learn from the *Tripiṭakas* that the Buddhists followers, too, maintained large herds of cattle. The main traits of the Buddhist followers have been stated to be lavish outlay on the construction of shelters for the monks and on making offers of food, clothing, etc., to the monks. In contrast, the principal traits of the Jaina followers have been the fulfilment of 12 vows, practice of equanimity, penances, etc. We have thrilling accounts of the disturbances created by gods (with wrong outlook) in the performance of spiritual practices by the followers. In consequence, some slipped from their path, while others held firm. The ten leading followers of whom account is given in the Uvāsagadasao are as follows :

1. Ānanda from Vāṇijyagrāma possessed 40,000 cows and 12 crores of gold coins.
2. Kāmadeva from Campā possessed 60,000 cows and 18 crores of gold coins.
3. Culiṇīppiyā from Vārāṇasī possessed 80,000 cows and 24 crores of gold coins.
4. Surādeva from Vārāṇasī possessed 60,000 cows and 18 crores of gold coins.
5. Cullaśataka from Ālambhikā possessed 60,000 cows and 18 crores of gold coins.
6. Kuṇḍa-kolika from Kāmpilyapura possessed 60,000 cows and 18 crores of gold coins.
7. Śakaḍāla-putra from Polāśapura possessed 10,000 cows and 3 crores of gold coins.
8. Mahāśataka from Rājagṛha possessed 80,000 cows and 24 crores of gold coins.
9. Nandinī-pitā from Śrāvastī possessed 40,000 cows and 12 crores of gold coins.
10. Sālihī-pitā from Śrāvastī possessed 40,000 cows and 12 crores of gold coins.

Apart from these 10 leading followers, *Bhagavān* Mahāvīra had many others of whom the following are deserving of mention :

> Śaṅkha [2], Pokhalī [3], Sudarśanā [4], Sulasā [5], and Revatī [6]. It has been stated that Mahāvīra had a total of 1,59,000 male followers and 3,18,000 female followers[7]. But it is not indicated what type of followers they were, *i.e.*, whether they were ordinary followers of Mahāvīra or they practised the 12 vows prescribed by him.

Leading Buddhist Upāsakas

The foremost-among-the-foremost *(etadagga-vagga)* list of the Buddha accords place to the following leading followers[8] :

1. Foremost among those who first sought refuge with the Buddha were Tapassu and Bhalluka, both Kuṭumbika-geha from the city of Asitañjana.
2. Foremost among the donors was *Gṛhapati* Sudatta Anāthapiṇḍika, son of *Śreṣṭhī* Sumana from Śrāvastī in Kośala.
3. Foremost among the deliverers of spiritual discourses was *Gṛhapati* Citra who was born in a *Śreṣṭhī* family at Macchikāṣaṇḍa in Magadha.

4. Foremost among those who supplied for essential objects to the people at the congregation was Hastaka Ālavaka, a prince from Ālavī in Pañcāla.
5. Foremost among the donors of excellent objects was Mahānāma Śākya, *a Kṣatriya* (elder brother of Anuruddha) from Kapilavastu in Śākya country.
6. Foremost among the donors of dear (pleasing to the mind) objects was *Gṛhapati* Ugra who was born in a *Śreṣṭhī* family at Vaiśālī in Vajji.
7. Foremost among the servants of the order was *Gṛhapati* Udgata who was born in a *Śreṣṭhī* family at Hastigrāma in Vajjī.
8. Foremost among those with the most cheerful disposition was Śūra Ambaṣṭa who was born in a *Śreṣṭhī* family at Śrāvastī in Kośala.
9. Foremost among the self-delighted (*i.e.*, one how was made of pleasant matter) was Jīvaka Kumāra Bhṛtya, born of Sātavalikā who was Abhayakumāra's concubine. He belonged to Rājagṛha in Magadha.
10. Foremost among the most faithful was *Gṛhapati* Nakulapitā (father of Nakula) who was born in a *Śreṣṭhī* family at Samsumāra Giri in Vagga.

The following is the list of *upāsaka-śrāvikās* (female followers) as given by the Buddha :

1. Foremost among those who first took refuge with the Buddha was Sujātā, daughter of Senānī Kuṭumbika from Uruvelā Senānī *grāma* in Magadha.
2. Foremost among the donors was Viśākhā, mother of Mṛgāra, a *Vaiśya* from Śrāvastī in Kośala.
3. Foremost among the well-versed was Khujjauttarā, daughter of the nurse of a *Śreṣṭhī* named Ghoṣaka from Kauśāmbī in Vatsa.
4. Foremost among those who were most friendly to the monastic order (*maitrī-vihāra)* was Śāmāvatī, queen of King Udayana of Vatsa. She was the daughter of a *Śreṣthi* named Bhadravāṭikā. Later, she became a foster-daughter of *Śreṣṭhī* Goṣita from Kauśāmbī in Vatsa. She belonged to the city of Bhadrikā in Bhadravatī.
5. Foremost among the experts in meditation was Uttarā, mother of Nanda, who was the daughter of one Pūrṇasiṁha, who worked under a *Śreṣṭhī* named Sumana. She belonged to Rājagṛha in Magadha.
6. Foremost among the donors of the *praṇita* objects was Supravāsā, daughter Kolīya. She was the mother of Śivalī, and she belonged to Kuṇḍiyā in Śākya country.
7. Foremost among those who nursed the sick monks was Ṣuprīya who was a *Vaiśya* from Vārāṇasī in Kāśī.
8. Foremost among those who had a pleasant disposition was Kātyāyanī, mother of Soṇakuṭikaṇṇa. She was a *Vaiśya* from Kuraraghara in Avantī.

9. Foremost among the faithful was the mother of Nakula, a housewife who belonged to Samsumaragiri in Vagga.
10. Foremost among the self-delighted was Kālī who was born in a noble family at Rājagṛha in Magadha and who was married at Kuraraghara in Avantī.

Some of the above followers, male as well as female have just been mentioned, while others have received a more detailed attention. Of these, Tapassuka and Bhalluka made the offer of *modaka* and *dodhi* to the Buddha after his Enlightenment and were the first to take refuge with him. Both of them were travelling merchants, and both met the Buddha by sheer accident.

Householder Citra was an ideal follower of the Buddha and he was a discussing follower. He held discussions even with *Nigaṇṭha* Nātaputta (Mahāvīra). Once he differed from a monk named Sudhamma. When Suddhamma appealed to the Buddha for arbitration, the latter said,

"Sudhamma! You are at fault. You seek forgiveness from Citra."

This account bears resemblance with the one in which Mahāvīra said something very similar to Indrabhūti Gautama about Ānanda (a lay follower).

When the final moments for householder Citra on this earth were drawing near, gods approached him with a request to be their Indra. They said,

"Sir, please decide to be our Indra."

Citra said in reply,

"I do not entertain a desire for the ephemerals."[9]

The Jaina *Āgama Bhagavatī*[10] contains a similar account about a *tāpasa* monk Tāmalī who had courted a fast unto death and who was approached by the gods with a request to be their Indra; but Tāmalī thought that it was unwholesome and unprofitable to bargain with his penances and made no reply to the request made by the gods.

Jīvaka Kumāra Bhṛtya was the place physician to King Bimbisāra. He was well-known to royal families and *śreṣṭhī* families even in far-off lands. He had exceptional skill in many surgical cases. in appointing him as his palace physician, King Bimbisāra also assigned to him the duty of attending the Buddha and the monks of his order. Jīvaka was the son of a well-known public woman of Rājagṛha named Sālavatī.[11] As he was abandoned at his birth on a heap of rubbish, he was brought up later in the palace of (minister) Abhayakumāra. He had his education at Taxila. *Aṅguttara Nikāya Aṭṭhakathā, Vinaya Piṭaka* and many other Buddhist texts contain interesting accounts of the remarkable skill of this surgeon which he applied even on the person of the Buddha and many other distinguished people of that age.

In the Buddhist tradition, Jīvaka Kumāra Bhṛtya was a very distinguished person of his time. It was he who had introduced Ajātaśatru to the Buddha. The Jaina *Āgamas* or *Purāṇas* take no note of him.

Ānanda and Sulasā have, however, been taken to be the representative-most lay followers of the Jaina tradition, as Anāthapiṇḍika and Viśākhā (mother of Mṛgāra) have been taken to be the representative-most lay followers of the Buddhist tradition. A brief account of each follows :

Ānanda

Jitaśatru was the ruling monarch at Vāṇijyagrāma. To the north-eastern direction of the city, there was a garden named Dyutipalāśa. In the same garden, there was a *caitya* which was dedicated to a spirit of the same name (*i.e.*, Dyutipalāśa). In fact, the garden took its name from him. Householder Ānanda lived in the same city. The name of his wife was Śivānandā. She was a very beautiful, a devoted wife and highly skilled in arts. So, the conjugal life of Ānanda was one of great happiness. Besides, he had a vast property. He had four crores of gold pieces in reserve, four crores lent out as loans, and four crores invested in business. To add to these, he possessed four herds of cattle each having 10,000 cows. He was therefore called an affluent person (*mahārdhika)* because of his vast wealth and cattle herds.

Ānanda was highly trusted and respected person of his city. Kings, princes, chief of the town police, frontier kings, village administrators, merchants, exporters, importers and many others consulted him and took advice from him on many matters, including confidential correspondences and deals.

In the north-eastern direction of Vāṇijyagrāma, there was a prosperous satellite town named Kollāga. A large number of friends and relatives of Ānanda live there. Once, wandering from village to village, *Bhagavān* Mahāvīra came to Vāṇijyagrāma. People assembled round him in a holy congregation. King Jitaśatru himself and thousands of people of his kingdom came to pay their homage and obeisance to *Bhagavān* Mahāvīra and derive inspiration from his words. There was an unusual enthusiasm in the city at his coming. Ānanda also heard the happy news of the arrival of *Bhagavān* Mahāvīra and became delighted and pleased. He thought that it was profitable to see the Lord. So, he decided to come and see *Bhagavān* Mahāvīra and worship him. He took his bath, put on clean clothes and ornaments, and then being surrounded by his men, he walked on foot through the heart of the city. The canopy held over his head was decorated with a garland of *koraṇṭa* flowers. Thus Ānanda arrived at the Dyutipalāśa caitya where Mahāvīra had camped. He moved round him thrice, paid his homage and obeisance and took his seat in the assembly. When the sermon was over, the people went away. Householder Ānanda became exceedingly delighted and happy to hear the sermon. He submitted,

> "*Bhante!* I have devotion for the prescription of the *nirgranthas.* I have faith in them, I have taste for them. These prescriptions are the same as they have been stated by you. You are very correct. I hold this religion in the highest esteem, in the greatest esteem. *Bhante!* Many kings, princes, commanders, city guards, *maṇḍala* chiefs, respectable persons, merchants exporters and importers and many others have tonsured their heads and joined your order as monks by throwing out their wordly responsibilities. I am, however, incapable to bear the hardships of a monk's life. So, I intend to court the 12 vows of the lay followers."

In giving his approval to this submission by Ānada, *Bhagavān* Mahāvīra spoke the following words :

> "Ānanda! Do as it may suit your convenience, but delay not."

In courting the 12 vows of a lay follower, Ānanda said,

> "*Bhante!* With two instruments and three modes, I give up injury to life, falsehood and acquisition of anything not duly bestowed on me. Except for the company of my own wife Śivānandā, I shall look on every other woman as my mother. I restrict my possession to 4 crores in hard cash, 4 crores in loans and 4 crores invested in business, and beyond this, I renounce all other possessions. I shall keep no more than four herds of cattle. On my farm, I shall have no more than 500 ploughs. I shall have 500 carts to go abroad and another 500 for local use, but not more than that. I shall have four vessels for overseas trade and four boats for inland trade, but no more than that. I discard the use of all clothes after bath except the use of a perfumed towel. I shall use nothing except *madhu-yaṣṭi* as my tooth-stick. I give up all fruits except *kṣīrāmalaka.* I renounce the use of all clothes except a pair of silk and of all ornaments except a ring with my name printed on it, and a pair of ear rings."

Whereon said *Bhagavān* Mahāvīra as follows :

"Ānanda! A follower of the *śramaṇa* path who has knowledge of fundamentals, like soul, non-soul, etc., and who strictly lives within his bounds, should also have knowledge about slips or transgressions, and in fulfilling his spiritual routine, he should carefully avoid them."

On a request from Ānanda, *Bhagavān* Mahāvīra elaborated at length the various slips of transgressions. Thereon Ānanda courted five *aṇuvratas* and seven *śikṣāvratas*. In reciting one of these vows, he said,

"*Bhante!* From this day onward, I affirm that I shall not pay homage and obeisance to a heretic, to the gods of the heretics or to the *arihantas* (great souls) of the heretics. Unless addressed by them, I shall not talk to them, nor enter into discussion with them, nor consider them worthy of my offer of food, drink, dainties and delicacies. From the purview of this vow, however, the following will be excluded : the king, the sect, the strong, the pressure from the gods, the advice of the preceptor, an inclement situation as in a forest only when I may make an offer of food, etc."

Expressing his firm devotion to religion, house holder Ānanda said,

"*Bhante!* I affirm that I shall offer pure and prescribed food, drink, dainties and delicacies, cloth, blanket, bowl, duster, back-plank, bed-plank, bed-wrapper, medicine and herbs to the *nirgrantha* monks."

Having courted the 12 vows of a lay follower, householder Ānanda asked many questions and tried his best to get into the fundamentals of religion. Then he thrice moved round *Bhagavān* Mahāvīra, bowed before him and returned home. Being delighted beyond limit, he said as follows to his wife Śivānandā :

"Today, I have heard about religion straight from the mouth of *Bhagavān* Mahāvīra. This is very good for me. This is very helpful to me. My deer! It is my sincere wish that you too go to him, pay him homage and obeisance, worship him and court from him five *aṇuvratas* and seven *śikṣāvratas* which are meant to be practised by the householders."

Being thus directed by her husband, Śivānandā became very happy. She took her bath, put on clean clothes, decorated herself with light but costly ornaments, and then being surrounded by her maids, she sat on an excellent chariot and arrived at the *caitya* named Dyutipalāśa in order to attend the congregation of *Bhagavān* Mahāvīra. She took her seat in the vast assembly and attentively listened the Lord's soul-stirring words and became thrilled at her heart. She accepted the 12 vows of the householder from *Bhagavān* Mahāvīra nad returned home.

Gaṇdhara Gautama put the following question to *Bhagavān* Mahāvīra,

> "*Bhante!* Is your disciple and follower (*śramaṇopāsaka*) Ānanda fit to be initiated as a monk in the order?"

To this enquiry, *Bhagavān* Mahāvīra gave reply as follows :

> "Gautama! He is not. For may years to come, he will continue practising the vows of a householder, and then he will discard his mortal frame by a fast unto death and will be born in a *vimāna* named *Aruṇābha* in *Saudharma-kalpa* with a life-span of four *palyopamas.*"

Concentrating on the categories of soul and non-soul, Ānanda and Śivānandā lived happily on. They spent 14 years of their life in fulfilling *Śīlavratas, guṇavratas,* and practising formal renunciations, *pauṣadha* and fasts. The fifteenth year was now running. One night, during the second half, while Ānanda was awake on a spiritual vigil, he took a decision as follows :

> "I am a tower of strength to the king, the crown prince, the city guard, the city administrator and many others. About many of their affairs, they discuss with me. Being too busy and too much involved in their affairs, I have not been able to do full justice to the vows I accepted from *Bhagavān* Mahāvīra. How fine it will be if at the dawn of the day, tomorrow, I invite my friends, relations and kinsmen, entertain them with food, drink, dainties and delicacies, hand over the charge of the household to my eldest son and settle myself in the *pauṣadha* room of the Jñātrs at Kollāga to fulfil the spiritual assignments I have taken from *Bhagavān* Mahāvīra."

At the next morning, he gave effect to his thought of the previous night. He invited his friends and relations at his house, and in the presence of these, he entrusted the responsibility of his household to his eldest son. Thereafter, he said,

> "Henceforth I have decided to spend my life in total seclusion."

With the permission of his kinsmen, householder Ānanda came to the *pauṣadha* room at Kollāga. He cleaned the room and he selected a place for passing urine and depositing his excreta. Then he spread *darbha* grass, sat on it and devoted himself to fulfilling the assignment for which he was committed to Mahāvīra.

Householder Ānanda practised the 11 *pratimās* of a lay follower. He did so with his body, as per the sacred texts (*sūtra),* as per *kalpa,* as per the path (*mārga)* and as per the fundamentals (*tattva)* and duly fulfilled them. By avoiding carefully the slips and transgressions, he became pure. Even after time allotted to *pauṣadha* was over, he overstayed in his spiritual practices.

It was on account of performing the *pratimās* and the austerities involved in them that Ānanda became very lean and emaciated. His veins became prominent over the skin. One night, while he was practising a spiritual vigil, he had a thought in his mind which was as follows :

> "Because of these spiritual practices, I have been reduced to mere skeleton. But still sheltered within me are endeavour, *karma,* strength, energy, exertion, power, devotion, patience and earnestness. So, (when there's time), why don't I renounce food and drink for ever and court fast unto death. I think, that is good for me."

He gave effect to his thought.

As he was on fast unto death, one day, because of his pious effort, pious outcome and gradually purifying tinges, *karma* which enshrouded Ānanda's knowledge and exhausted, and he came to acquire a very extensive *avadhi* knowledge because of which he could know and see in the north as far as the Himālayas, in the south, the east and the west over an expanse of 500 *yojanas* till the salt ocean, till the *Saudharmakalpa*, and underneath, till the dreary cells in the first hell.

In those days, *Bhagavān* Mahāvīra arrived at Vāṇijyagrāma. On that day, Indrabhūti Gautama had completed a tow-day fast, and, with the permission of *Bhagavān* Mahāvīra, he moved into the town to beg. There when he heard people talk about Ānanda's fast unto death, he felt a keen desire to call on him. So, he turned his steps in the direction of the *pauṣadha* room where Ānanda was and arrived there. Ānanda had become too weak to get up from his bed to receive such a distinguished caller. So, from his bed, he expressed his homage and obeisance and touched Gautama's feet. Said Ānanda to *Bhagavān* Gautama,

> "*Bhante!* Is it possible for *avadhi* knowledge to be generated in a householder who is committed to fast unto death?"

Gautama—"Yes, it is quite possible."

Ānanda—"Sir, I am glad to tell you that I have generated within me such knowledge which is widely extensive in all directions."

Gautama—"Ānanda! A householder, to my mind, cannot acquire so extensive an *avadhi* knowledge. While you are on a fast unto death, I am afraid, false words have been uttered by you. So, you should discuss and make atonement for them."

Ānanda—"Respected sir! Under the spiritual governance of Mahāvīra, is atonement to be practised for falsehood or for truth?"

Gautama—"Why, for falsehood, I am sure!"

Ānanda—"Then, sir, I think, it is you who have to make atonement yourself, as you have indulged in a falsehood."

These firm words of Ānanda gave a servere jerk to Gautama. Starting from there, he came straight to *Bhagavān* Mahāvīra and narrated the whole conversation to him, whereon *Bhagavān* Mahāvīra said,

> "Gautama! You have been wrong. You go to Ānanda at once, and beg to be forgiven by him."

So, Gautama came back to Ānanda and said,

> "Ānanda! I have it from *Bhagavān* Mahāvīra that what you have said is correct. Please forgive me for starting a futile controversy."

Householder Ānanda lived the life of a devoted follower for full 20 years. After his death, he was born in a *vimāna* named Aruṇābha in *Saudharma kalpa.*[12]

Sulasā

At Rājagṛha, there lived a charioteer named Nāga. Sulasā was the name of his wife. Both Nāga and Sulasā were the followers of the *nirgrantha* path. Being very devoted followers, they were known as *dṛḍha-dharmī* (firm-in-faith) or *priya-dharmī* (in-love-with-faith). Their equanimity was pure and firm, and they sincerely fulfilled the vows of a lay follower. Sulasā was, however, more devoted of the two. They happily lived on performing spiritual exercises.

One day, Nāga saw some boys who were at play in the courtyard of a merchant. These boys were tender, playful and lovely. The courtyard looked gay as they played. The scene created a delightful impression on the mind of Nāga. Since that day, Nāga often felt in his mind that a home without playful children in it was absolutely useless. But this was something beyond human control, and man was no free agent to fill his home with children. Nāga was now keen to have at least a son, and all the time he was thinking how to fulfil this desire. For the fulfilment of this desire, he was henceforth very much after popular gods, astrologers, priests and *brāhmaṇas*. When Sulasā came to know this, she said to her husband in very clear terms :

> "Sir! One gets a son, fame, wealth, etc., as per his past *karma*. In these matters, human effort and the grace of gods are no more than secondary aids. If one does not get a coveted object, it must surely be attributed to the obstructing *karma*. I do not understand how this can be done away with by the advice of the astrologers, by the grace of gods or by any other means. I thinks it is better for us that we devote a greater part of our time in making offers (of food, etc., to worthy monks), in improving conduct, in practising penances and other spiritual exercises. These may help us to loosen the fetters of the obstructing *karma,* and as a conquence, we may attain the coveted objects. But I am afraid, you cannot get a son from me. So, I suggest that you take another wife."

Nāga—"But, my dear, if I am to have a son, it must be from you, and none else. I am not going to marry again."

Sulasā—"But that is just a matter of chance or, if I may say so, a piece of good luck. We should not be overjoyous when we have, as we should not feel morose when we have not. If we rise above such petty desires, we may surely attain our goal."

Nāga was somewhat reconciled at these wise words of his wife. Their life flowed on like this.

One day, a monk came to Sulasā's home. He begged to be given *lakṣapāka* oil which he needed for the use of an ailing monk. Sulasā became delighted to see a monk at her house to beg. At a hurried pace, she came to her room to get the oil. As she picked up the jar, it slipped accidentally from her hand. It fell on the ground and broke into pieces so that oil flowed on the floor. This happened for the second time and again for the third time, so that the whole supply of the medicated oil flowed on the ground. On an occasion like this, it is but very usual for the person concerned to be filled with rage and disgust; but Sulasā did not lose control by herself. With perfect peace in her mind, she came out and narrated the incident to the monk. The monk observed her very carefully and founder to be perfectly at ease. He found that inspite of her loss, which was in a sense due to the monk, she was as respectful to him as ever before. The monk now changed his guise and appeared before Sulasā in his original form as a god from heaven. Sulasā felt completely lost and did not know what to say or do. The very next moment, the god started.

"Worthy lady! In the assembly of gods, Śakra, our Indra, our king, spoke very highly of your great forbearance. Śakra intended to convey that you are so very firm in your equanimity and so very sincere in the practice of the vows of a devoted follower that neither a god nor a demon, still less a human being, was capable to throw you out from your coveted path. These words of Śakra induced me to come down in order to see you. I appeared before you as a monk and it was by dint of my power that all the three jars slipped from your hand and broke into pieces. But I saw that despite so much loss, you did not lose control on self, nor be disrespectful of me in any way. I am very much impressed by your self control. I am more than convinced that Śakra, our India, did not exaggerate. I am very happy and I request you to ask for anything."

Sulasā smiled and said,

"Divine sir, I am in no dearth of money, property or respect from fellow men. But you know very well that I have a hankering for something which is a normal hankering of any woman, and the absence of which hurts her in life. But I am pretty certain that even this hankering of mine will be fulfilled at appropriate time."

The god felt a profound respect for the lady. In order to share in her joy and grief, he said,

"My dear sister. You take these 32 pills. Take one at a time whenever you please, and these 32 pills will give you 32 sons. Thus, your desire will be fulfilled. This apart, if you ever stand in need of any assistance from me, please do not forget to remember me."

Sulasā accepted the pills and the god disappeared.

Sulasā thought that 32 sons would be too many for her. To brighten a childless home, one meritorious son was enough. She felt that perhaps this purpose would be served if, instead of taking the pills one by one, she took all the 32 at a time, so that she would give birth to a son possessing all the (32) qualities. So, she took all the pills at a time. After some time, (when the 32 pills turned into 32 embryos), she felt a severe pain in her abdomen. She became extremely restless and found no means of getting any relief. So, at last, she remembered the god who appeared before her at once. When Sulasā had narrated all that she had done with the pills, the god said to her.

"Worthy lady! You have committed the greatest mistake. Since you have taken 32 pills at a time, you have acquired 32 embryos. Now, the position is that at appropriate time, 32 sons will be born to you; but if perchance anyone of them dies, then, all the other 31 will follow him. This is inevitable."

Sulasā—"Divine sir! Ultimately it is Destiny that is the final arbiter of a man's life. But I was wondering if you could do something with your divine power to relieve me of my present suffering."

The god took pity on her, and by the application of his divine power, he alleviated a good part of her suffering at that very instant. At suitable time, Sulasā gave birth to 32 sons. All the 32 were identical in features and similar in behaviour. Their loveliness, brilliance and grace attracted everybody. Henceforth, the home of charioteer Nāga wore a cheerful look. When he looked at his sons, his heart leapt with joy. All the 32 sons grew up to their youth when they were married with 32 beautiful girls from respective families. The brothers and their wives lived together and worked together.

All of them got employed as the aide-de-camp to King Śreṇika. They were experts in the art of welfare. Once when King Bimbisāra eloped with Celaṇā, daughter of Ceṭaka, through an underground tunnel and was pursued by Ceṭaka, these 32 brothers prevented the latter to proceed any further. This enabled Śreṇika to return to his palace safely. After Śreṇika had escaped, there started a fierce battle between the two camps in which one of the aides of Śreṇika lost his life, and at once the other 31 fell dead on the ground. In this manner, the 32 sons of Sulasā met with their end.

The simulataneous death of all her sons was the severest blow that Sulasā received in her life. Although she was a pious woman, she was overwhelmed with grief. No less a person than chief minister Abhayakumāra came to console her. Sulasā recollected herself and devoted herself to pious meditation.

While wandering from village to village, *Bhagavān* Mahāvīra once came to the city of Campā. A congregation was organised outside the city. People assembled to pay their homage and obeisance and listen the inspiring words of the Lord. A follower *(śrāvaka)* named Ambaḍa from Rājagṛha had also come for the same purpose. Ambaḍa was in command of magical power *(vidyās)* by dint of which he could change his form. When the sermon was over, he submitted to *Bhagavān* Mahāvīra.

"*Bhante!* My life has been worth living to attend thy sermons. My plans are to depart for Rājagṛha today. May I do anything for you!"

Bhagavān Mahāvīra—"At Rājagṛha, I have a very devoted follower named Sulasā. She is very firm in her devotion to religion. So, much devotion in a lay follower is very rare. Look her up if you can."

These words of praise about Sulasā uttered by no less a person than *Bhagavān* Mahāvīra made people think that she must be a highly meritorious and fortunate lady about whom the Lord spoke so eloquently. But Ambaḍa had a different thought in his mind. He became inquisitive about the special qualities of Sulasā and he decided that he must hold a test. So guised as a *parivrājaka* monk, he came to Sulasā's house and said to her,

> "Pious lady! Give me some food. In doing so, you will acquire great merit."

Sulasā—"Sir! I know well what offer earns merit and what offer is just a matter of course."

The monk went away. He started wonderful penances and in *padmāsana* postue, he remained pending in the sky. It was a wonderful feat. Thousands of people were attracted to see it. Thousands came from far-off districts and they spoke eloquently about the great powers of the monk. Sulasā heard all about him, but she felt no curiosity to see, nor did she make any inquisitive enquiry about him. People invited the monk to receive food at their homes, but the monk declined to everyone. This surprised the people all the more. They asked him wherefrom would he receive his food. The monk's instant reply was,

> "From Sulasā."

People at once turned their steps towards Sulasā's home. Within a short time, a vast crowd had assembled there. The people brought her the good news that the exceptional monk had chosen her for receiving his food. They said,

> "This great monk has expressed a desire to receive food from your hands even though you have not extended any invitation to him. Now, we think, you should come forward and make a formal request to him to receive food. You are such a lucky woman."

But a curt reply from Sulasā disheartened them all. She said,

> "Well, you may call him great, but I attach no value to his feats. They are all a sham."

People were surprised to hear these words from the mouth of so pious a lady as Sulasā. They came back to the monk and reported him. Ambaḍa had now no doubt that Sulasā possessed excellent right outlook and she did not revere anyone who was not an *arihanta* or a *nirgrantha.* He was convinced that no power on earth was capable to disturb her in her faith. Ambaḍa now changed his guise and came to Sulasā's home as a *nirgrantha* monk. He had not merely copied the external form of such a monk, but also evinced his sensibility. When Sulasā saw the monk, she bowed before him and expressed her profound regard for him. Now, Ambaḍa stood before her in his real form and conveyed to Sulasā verbatim what *Bhagavān* Mahāvīra had said about her. On his own behalf, too, he expressed a deep admiraion for her and praised her steadfastness in religious matter.[13]

Because of her great qualities, Sulasā acquired *karma* that imparts to one the name and lineage of a *Tīrthaṅkara.* Among the forthcoming group of 24 *Tīrthaṅkara* (in the following up-phase of the time-cycle), she would be born as the fifteenth *Tīrthaṅkara* named Nirmana.[14]

Anāthapiṇḍika—Anāthapiṇḍika Sudatta was householder who lived in the city of Śrāvastī. He was the son of a *Śreṣṭhī* name Sumana and brother-in-law (sister's husband) of another *Śreṣṭhī* named Rājagṛhaka. Once he came to Rājagṛha on business. At that time, *Bhagavān* Buddha was staying at Sīta-vana outside the city. Anāthapiṇḍika had heard that the Buddha had already been born in the world, and he had an ardent desire to meet him if he could. It was such a happy co-incidence that brother Rājagṛhaka (with whom Anāthapiṇḍka was staying as a guest), had invited the Buddha with all his monks to receive food from his house on the following day. So, he directed all his men and slaves to cook some gruel, rice and soup in time. (As all these preparations were going on), Anāthapiṇḍika thought in his mind,

'Usually when I come here, my brother-in-law is all attention to me; but to-day, he appears to be somewhat disturbed in his mind, and busy giving orders to his men and slaves to prepare food. I wonder if there is some wedding at the house, or some great sacrifice, or if Śreṇika, the King of Magadha, is coming to his house with all his men to dine.'

When at last *Śreṣṭhī* Rājagṛhaka found time to come to him and welcome him to his house, Anāthapiṇḍika enquired about the special occasion for which all his men were so very busy. Said the *Śreṣṭhī,*

> "There is no wedding in the house, nor any sacrifice. I have not even invited Śreṇika, the King of Magadha, to dinner, But I have invited *Bhagavān* Buddha with all his monks to come and receive food at my house."

Anāthapiṇḍika felt a pleasant surprise when he heard these words. Said he,

"What did you say, the Buddha!"

And as if mechanically, he repeated this thrice. The *Śreṣṭhī* said,

"You are right. The Buddha is coming to my house."

Anāthapiṇḍika

"It's a rare chance even to hear the word 'Buddha' being mentioned. (I am so fortunate that I shall have a chance to meet him). May I go at once to see the duly Enlightened, the *Bhagavān,* the *Arhat!"*

Śreṣṭhi—"No, this is no appropriate time to see him."

Anāthapiṇḍika somehow passed the night. During the night, he got up thrice and intended to go, but in the prevailing stillness, he could not gather necessary courage to step out. But he could neither remain in bed, (so great was his uneasiness), and got up pretty early. He started to see the Buddha. But when he arrived at the city gate, it was not yet open. But the gods came to his aid and the gate was opened. Anāthapiṇḍika came out of the city. After he had gone some distance, the city lights came to an end and it was all pitchy dark. Anāthapiṇḍika was simultaneously shocked, alarmed and thilled. His legs refused to carry him further. A spirit (*yakṣa)* named Śivaka gave him inspiration from the sky :

"Go on, *Gṛhapati,* move fast. It is good for you to step forward, not backward."

Suddenly, the veil of darkness was lifted up and the way became visible. His fear, shock and thrill were gone. Anāthapindika moved forward with confidence. But he was swallowed by darkness again, and the felt alarmed. He lost courage to move up. He had this experience thrice, but on each occasion, and invisible voice from above continued to inspire and direct him. Anāthapiṇḍika gathered courage on each occasion and moved further on. At last, he was within sight of Sīta-vana. At that early hour of the morning, the Buddha was having his usual constitutional in the fresh air of the morning. When he saw Anāthapiṇḍika at a distance coming towards him, he went back from the place where he was pacing and took his seat to receive the guest. Addressing Anāthapiṇḍika, the Buddha said,

"Sudatta! I welcome thee."

Being thus welcomes by the mention of this name, Anāthapiṇḍika became immensely overwhelmed. He reached near the Budha and fell at his feet. He enquired about his welfare and said,

> "*Bhante!* May I hope that you had a nice sleep at night."
>
> —"Thank you for the expression of a fine sentiment. But you know that one who has attained *nirvāṇa* always enjoys a nice sleep at night."

And at once the Buddha started his inspiring sermon for Anāthapindika. Just as a clean and dirt-free cloth takes any hue, so, while seated on the cushion, Anāthapiṇḍika became free from sin, and his pure spiritual eye opened as he listened the sermon from the Buddha. When in this manner Anāthapiṇḍika acquired the fundamentals of religion and became free from all doubts, he prayed for his own admission into the Buddha's order. Submitted he,

> "*Bhante!* It's wonderful. As a thing turned upside down is put back in its right posture, as a covered think is uncovered, as one who has missed his path is restored to the right track, as an oil-lamp shows the way in the midst of darkness so that one may see with his own eyes, so, *Bhante*, you have given the Law *(dharma)* in diverse ways. I take shelter unto the Buddha. I take shelter unto the *Dharma.* I take shelter into the *Saṅgha.* From this day, please count me as one come to thy succour with folded hands, and for tomorrow, please accept invitation to receive food with thy monks from me."

The Buddha conveyed his assent through silence. Anāthapiṇḍika bowed and returned home.

When *Śreṣṭhī* Rājagṛhaka heard that the Buddha had been invited by Anāthapiṇḍika on his own behalf, he hurried to Anāthapiṇḍika and said to him.

> "*Gṛhapati!* You are my guest. So please let me bear the cost of serving food to the Buddha and his monks, and you supervise over the management."

Anāthapiṇḍika—"Please allow me to avail this chance of serving food to the Buddha and his monks. I hope, you agree."

When the *Naigama* (which is a higher position than that of a *Śreṣṭhī*) of Rājagṛha heard this, he offered to bear the cost himself; but Anāthapiṇḍika declined the offer again.

Thus, *Gṛhapati* Anāthapiṇḍika arranged to receive the Buddha and his monks at the residence of *Śreṣṭhī* Rājagṛhaka. A party was sent to bring the

Buddha to the *Gṛhapati's* house. In the forenoon, the Buddha came duly covered, with the begging bowl and cloth in his hand, to the residence of *Gṛhapati* Rājagṛhaka. He sat on the cushion already spread for him. Anāthapiṇḍika served him food with his own hands. After the Buddha had dined, *Gṛhapati* Anāthapiṇḍika sat near him and submitted,

> "*Bhante!* I inivite you with your monks to spend the next monsoon at Śrāvastī."

The Buddha—"Gṛhapati! The *Tathāgata* stays only in vacant homes."

The Gṛhapati—"Bhante! I understand what you mean. *Sugata!* I understand what you mean."

Gṛhapati Anāthapiṇḍika had many friends at Rājagṛha. After he had finished his business in the city, he started for Śrāvastī. In all the way-side villages he stopped and said as follows to the villagers.

> "*Aryas!* Build up shelters at every *yojana*. Erect *vihāras*. The Buddha has been born in the world. I have invited him to come to Śrāvastī. He will come by this route."

Those people, who could so afford, built up shelters and *vihāras* at their own cost. For those who did not have the necessary wherewithal, the finance was provided by Anāthapindika.[15] At the inspiration and leadership provided by him, all the villages between Rājagṛha and Śrāvastī was duly provided with shelters and *vihāras*.

Having reached Śrāvastī, Anāthapiṇḍika looked for a place all over which would be suitable for the construction of a shelter for the monks. The place must be neither too near nor too far from the city. It should be easily accessible to the people who would come to see the Buddha. It should not be too much crowded during the day, nor too much noisy at night, fairly secluded, so that it might be a good place for purposes of meditation. For this purpose, he selected a garden belonging to Prince Jeta; for, this appeared to him most suitable in all respects. So, he came to the prince and said,

> "Noble sir! Please give me your garden wherein I intend to construct a shelter for the monks."

Prince Jeta—"*Gṛhapati!* I can't sell it even for a crore."

Anāthapiṇḍika—"Noble sir! I have already bought it."

Prince Jeta—"No, *Gṛhapati,* you have not."

They referred, the matter to the Justice who ruled,

"Since a price has been quoted, it has been acquired."

Anāthapiṇḍika ordered to be brought cart-loads of gold coins which were to be used to cover the entire garden (in fact, this was the price he had agreed to give for Jetavana). In this manner, one vault containing 18 cores was exhausted.[16] There was only a small place near the entrance which remained uncovered. Anāthapiṇḍika ordered more coins to be brought to cover this vacant spot. All of a sudden, the Prince thought,

> "This fellow appears to be lavish in spending so much gold on this project. Surely there must be something especially important in this. Why do I not join with him?"

So, he said to Anāthapiṇḍika,

> "*Gṛhapati!* Leave this portion uncovered. You needn't pay for this. Let this be my contribution to your project."

Anāthapiṇḍika had a different thought in his mind : Prince Jeta is a respectful person. It's good that he feels attracted to my project.

So, he left the portion uncovered, and the prince constructed a big hall on it. Anāthapiṇḍika constructed a *vihāra* at Jetavana which had a reading room for the monks, residential rooms, assembly halls, rooms for boiling water, stores, latrines, urinals, *caṅkramaṇa* altar, *caṅkramaṇa* rooms, *propā, prapā* rooms, bathrooms, tanks, *maṇḍapas*, etc.[17] Thus, he spent 8 crores in building a *vihāra* which stood on a plot 8 *kroṣas* in area.[18]

Wandering through Vaiśālī and many other places in his *cārikā* mission, *Bhagavān* Buddha came to Śrāvastī. He stayed at the newly constructed *vihāra* at Jetavana. Anāthapiṇḍika felt immensely obliged. He bowed before the Buddha and sat on one side. He invited the entire group of monks to dinner on the following day. The Buddha communicated his assent through silence. From early in the morning, Anāthapiṇḍika made elaborate preparations for the cooking of food. At the appropriate hour, the Buddha arrived with his monks. Anāthapiṇḍika served food with his own hands. When, after dinner, the Buddha sat, Anāthapiṇḍika made a humble submission :

> "*Bhante!* What should I do about Jetavana?"

The Buddha said,

> "You dedicate it for the use of the monks, present as well as future, coming from anyone of the four directions."

Anāthapiṇḍika accepted the Buddha's suggestion and dedicated it at once for the use of the monks, present as well as future, coming from anyone of the four directions. The Buddha gave his approval to the gift made by Anāthapiṇḍika and departed.[19]

After this, the Buddha paid frequent visits to Śrāvastī and he mostly stayed at the *vihāra* in Jetavana. It was from this place that he propounded many rules for his *Saṅgha.*

When his life on this earth was about to come to a close, Anāthapiṇḍika became ill. He sent the following message to the Buddha :

> 'I am ill. I send my homage and obeisance from here. Please accept them.'

To Sāriputta he sent the following message :

> "Be good enough to come so that I may bow before thee."

Sāriputta came to his house with Ānanda. Anāthapiṇḍika was completely bed-ridden with several complications. Sāriputta spoke to him of the utility of restraining one's organs of senses and also on the utility of detachment. With an exuberance of emotion, Anāthapiṇḍika began to cry. He said,

> "*Bhante!* All through my life, I have heard many things from the Great Leader; but the words you spoke today stand unique and without parallel."

Sāriputta went away.

Anāthapiṇḍika died and was born in a heaven named Tuṣitakāya. From his abode in heaven, he came down to Jetavana to pay his homage and obeisance to his spiritual guide.[20]

The coming of Sāriputta at the house of Anāthapiṇḍika before his death has a close resemblance with the coming of Indrabhūti Gautama to see *śrāvaka* Ānanda before he passed away.

Viśākhā, Mother of Mṛgāra

Viśākhā was born at the city of Bhaddīyā in Aṅgadeśa. *Gṛhapati* Meṇḍaka was her grand-father, Dhanañjaya was her father and Sumanā was her mother. With Jotiya, Jaṭila, Puṇṇaka and Kākabaliya, Meṇḍaka ranked among the 'big five' most affluent and most fortunate people of the time. All the five lived in the empire of Śreṇika Bimbisāra, the ruler of Magadha. Each one of these, again, had a family of five, and all of them were endowed with divine powers. In the family of *Gṛhapati* Meṇḍaka, these five were Meṇḍaka himself, his wife Candrapadmā, his eldest son Dhanañjaya, Dhanañjaya's wife whose name was Sumanā and their attendant named Pūraṇa. All these five had very pious souls.[21]

(The divine powers enjoyed by them were as follows). When, after taking his bath, *Gṛhapati* Meṇḍaka had his granneries cleaned and he sat at their doors, grains were showered from the sky, and his granneries were filled up with these grains. His wife Candrapadmā was capable to feed up any number of her servants, slaves and workers out of a bowl of rice and soup, and till she got up from her seat, these would not be exhausted. The special capacity enjoyed by Dhanañjaya was that he placed a thousand coins in his purse, and with these he could settle the pay of all his servants, slaves and workers for six months. Daughter-in-law Sumanā enjoyed the special capacity to offer grains sufficient for six months to any number of servants, slaves and workers out of a jar where initially she had placed only four *droṇas* of grains, and till she got up from her seat, the jar was never empty. The special capacity of Pūraṇa, the attending slave, was that he could furrow seven lines with a single plough.

When Śreṇika Bimbisāra, the ruler of Magadha, heard about the special capacities of *Gṛhapati* Meṇḍaka and of other members of his family, he sent one of his most efficient ministers to gather complete information about them. The minister came to Meṇḍaka's house, saw with his own eyes these exceptional gifts of all the five persons and submitted his report to the king.[22]

Once the Buddha came to Bhaddīyā. When *Gṛhapati* Meṇḍaka heard the news, he asked Viśākhā to arrange a suitable reception for him and his monks. Viśākhā started with 500 girls from her family and 500 maids on 500 chariots. As far as the chariots could go, they rode on them, and thereafter they covered the remaining distance on foot and at last they came to the Great Leader. They saluted the Buddha and stood on one side. The Buddha gave a sermon for them and they had their pure, spiritual eye opened. Even *Śreṣṭhī* Meṇḍaka came to the Buddha, heard his sermon and acquired a similar state. For the following day, Meṇḍaka invited the Buddha and his monks to receive food at his house. He entertained the Buddha and his monks with excellent dishes. This he continued to practise for full eight months because of which he acquired the merit of a 'great offer' (*mahādāna).* Having spent his time happily at Bhaddīyā, the Buddha departed.

King Bimbisāra and King Prasenajit of Kośala were brothers-in-law. Once King Prasenajit of Kośala thought,

> "King Bimbisāra is very lucky to have the 'big five' within his realm, but I do not have a single person equal to them in my kingdom. I think, I should request King Bimbisāra to send one of them to me."

With this end in mind, King Prasenajit arrived at Rājagṛha. Bimbisāra received him very cordially, and asked him about the purpose which had brought him to his city. After Prasenajit had explained his purpose, Bimbisāra said,

"How can I ask anyone of them to go and settle in your kingdom? They are after all free agents."

Prasenajit—"But I am not moving out from here till my purpose is fulfilled." Bimbisāra held consultaion with his minister who gave advice as follows :

"To ask any one of the big five to go is as difficult as to shake the earth. So, it is not worth trying. A comparatively easier job may be to induce Dhanañjaya, son of Meṇḍaka, to migrate, and if he agrees, that will be equally good."

Bimbisāra sent for Dhanañjaya. When Dhanañjaya came, he said to him,

"The King of Kośala has come to invite you to the position of a *Śreṣṭhī* in his kingdom. The offer is open. Are you agreeable to it?"

Very humbly did Dhanañjaya submit,

"Your Majesty! If that be your pleasure, I must abide by it."

The king became very happy to hear this reply. He said,

"Very nice. Then you get ready to go."

Dhanañjaya made necessary preparations, and came back ready to depart. Bimbisāra welcomed him and handed him over to Prasenajit as a gift unto him. The King of Kośala was very much delighted and obliged to receive him, and taking Dhanañjaya with him, he started for his own capital Śrāvastī. Having spent a night on the way, they were now in the vicinity of the capital which was no more than seven *yojanas* from that place. Dhanañjaya said to the king,

"Sir! Whose kingdom is this?"

Prasenajit—"This is mine."
Dhanañjaya—"How far is Śrāvastī from here?"
Prasenajit—"Only seven *yojanas*."
Dhanañjaya—"Sir! If you kindly permit me to submit, the big cities are usually very congested places. I maintain a fairly large household. So, if you kindly permit, I would like to settle at this place."

The king agreed. A township came up there within a short time. The king bestowed that town and 14 other villages on Dhanañjaya. As Danañjaya had spent a night (*sāyaṁ*) there in the company of the king, his town came to be called Sāketa.[23]

At Śrāvastī, there lived a *Śreṣṭhī* named Mṛgāra. He had a son named Pūrṇavardhana. When he grew up to his youth, preparations were made for setting him in marriage. *Śreṣṭhī* Mṛgāra sent out matchmakers in all directions in the capital to look for a suitable bride for his son, but they did not find a suitable girl in the whole of Śrāvastī whom Mrgāra could accept as his daughter-in-law. So, the matchmakers came to Sāketa. Viśākhā was at that time celebrating a festival in the company of 500 girls on the bank of a big tank. These matchmakers who had passed through the lanes and bylanes of Sāketa but did not find a suitable girl came out of the city and held consultations about their next plan. Suddenly, there started a heavy shower. Five hundred girls who accompanied Viśākhā were in a great confusion. They ran towards a shed at the speed they could command and took shelter therein. Standing at a short distance, the matchmakers observed all these girls, but none was suitable for their purpose. Viśākhā was the last to reach the shed and she came at a gentle pace. When the matchmakers saw her, they were at once impressed by her gaiety and grace. But they thought that in the selection of a bride, physical grace should not be the only consideration, and that a still more important thing was to make sure that the girl was sweet tongued. So, with a view to open conversation with her, they said,

> "Mother! Are you sufficiently old?"
>
> *Viśākhā*—"Sir! Why do you ask such a question?"

The men—"We observed that your companions hurriedly took shelter under the shed in order to save themselves from the shower, but you came walking very slowly, like an aged woman, without caring so much for your *sārī* which has been spoiled. Will you move in the same manner if you are chased by a horse or an elephant?"

There was softness in Viśākhā's voice. She said,

> "Sir! Sārī is not very important for me. A young girl is, so to say, a vendible ware. If she fractures a limb, she is useless. People start hating her, and nobody wants to marry her. This is why I walk carefully and at a gentle pace."

The people were deeply impressed at these words. They saw that the girl was not only beautiful, but also very considerate and sweet-tongued. Whatever words she spoke, she did so after great consideration. They rolled a garland and threw it over her head. Instantaneouly, Viśākhā felt that while a moment ago, she belonged to no one, now she had been taken over. Out of bashfulness, she sat down on the ground. Later, surrounded by her companions, she returned to her home.

The matchmakers came to Dhanañjaya's house and introduced themselves. When Dhanañjaya asked about the cause of their coming, they said,

> "Sir! Our master *Śresthī* Mrgāra has a son whose name is Pūrṇavardhana. He is an excellent young man, with fine health, physical grace and merits. If your daughter is united with him in marriage, then, we think, that will be ideal for both."

To this, Dhanañjaya made the following reply,

> "Your master is somewhat inferior to me in wealth, but in lineage, we are about equals. It is difficult to find one who is equal in all respects. So, I think, your proposal is good, and I welcome it. You convey my consent to your master."

Śreṣṭhī Mrgāra's men hurried back and gave the good new to him, adding in the end,

> "Viśākhā, daughter of *Śreṣṭhī* Dhanañjaya, who lives at Sāketa, will make a good bride for our boy."

Śreṣṭhī Mrgāra became highly pleased to hear this. He felt honoured to think that he would be able to establish a connection with such a noble family. At once, he scribbled a letter addressed to Dhanañjaya which was as follows :

> "I am starting to receive your daughter as bride for my son. Please make necessary preparations."

Dhanañjaya sent the following reply,

> "There will be no difficult at this end. You go ahead with your own preparations."

Śreṣṭhī Mrgāra came to the King of Kośala and submitted,

> "Your Majesty! I have a wedding at my house. *Śreṣṭhī* Dhanañjaya will

settle his daughter Viśākhā in marriage with my son Pūrṇavardhana. So, please permit me to go to Sāketa."

In giving his permission, the king said,

"Do you invite me also to go with the party?"

Mṛgāra—"Your Majesty! I would deem it to be a great good-luck for me."
The King—"I shall also go. Dhanañjaya of very noble descent will be happy to receive me."

King Prasenajit came to Sāketa in the big marriage party of *Śreṣṭhī* Mṛgāra. Dhanañjaya welcomed the two great guests, the king and the *Śreṣṭhī,* with great warmth, Suitable arrangements were made for their stay and enormous supplies of garlands, perfumes, robes, etc., were arranged. Everyone had a feeling as if he was receiving personal attention from Dhanañjaya himself. The party had already been there for a number of days, and there was yet no preparation in sight to see the party off. So, one day, the king sent the following note Dhanañjayas :

"We do not want to stay permanently as your guests. So, fix a suitable date when you may let us depart and bid farewell to your daughter."

Dhanañjaya's reply followed immediately :

"The rainy season had already started. So, you cannot go for four months. Whatever you may need, please send me your orders. You can depart only after I send you my consent."

At Sāketa, there was festivity everyday. Three months passed in this manner. A costly ornament named *mahālatā* for the use of Viśākhā was not yet ready.

One day, the cooks came to *Śreṣṭhī* Dhanañjaya and said, "Sir! We have everything else in plenty, but we are running short of fuel for cooking."

The *Śreṣṭhī* ordered at once,

"Take out the big poles from the elephant-stables, horse-stables, cow-sheds, and use them all as fuel."

This was done; but they were used up in a fortnight's time, and again there was the same difficulty. When the matter was brought to the notice of the *Śreṣṭhī,* he said,

"At this time, it is difficult to get fuel in the market. So, open the godowns where cloths is in stock. Roll cloth into thich wicks, moist them in oil, burn them and use them as fuel."

At last, the four months of the rainy season were over. The *mahālatā* for the use of Viśākhā was also ready by that time. Now, Dhanañjaya decided to let his daughter go to her new home. He invited her near him and imparted to her ten instructions which, he said, she whould be well-advised to follow in her new career. These were :

1. Do not take fire out from inside the home.
2. Do not take fire into the home from outside.
3. Give to those who are worthy.
4. Do not give to those who are not worthy.
5. Give to both who can or cannot return.
6. Sit comfortably.
7. Eat comfortably.
8. Lie (sleep) comfortably.
9. Behave as you would towards fire.
10. Bow before family deities.

When Dhanañjaya was imparting the above advice to his daughter, *Śreṣṭhī* Mṛgāra overheard it from outside.

At the time of departure of the marriage party, Dhanañjaya invited all the people to come and assemble. Then in the presence of all, he handed over the charge of his daughter to eight elders saying.

"If in her new home my daughter errs in any way, please correct her."

Dhanañjaya decoreated his daughter with he most precious *mahālatā* which had cost him nine crores. Besides, he bestowed on her a profuse dowry. They took in all 5500 trucks to carry. Treasures, ornaments, gold, silver, copper and utensils were each loaded on 500 trucks. Similarly, ghee, rice and paddy were each loaded on 500 trucks. Fifteen hundred trucks were loaded with farm products. There were 500 excellent chariots with three maids in each. There were as many milch cows as could stand on a plot 3/4 *gābuta* by 8 *yaṣṭi*. When these started moving towards Śrāvastī, other cattle-heads belong to Dhanañjaya numbering 60,000 oxen and 60,000 cows left their sheds and followed them.

Dhanañjaya had 14 villages under him. When Viśākhā was to depart, people from all the villages became very sorry. Dhanañjaya gave the following orders.

"If anyone wanted to go with Viśākhā and settle in her city he is given leave to do so."

Viśākhā was popular with all her people. As soon as the people heard this announcement, all of them moved out and the villages were virtually depopulated. This became a source of great anxiety for *Śresṭhī* Mṛgāra who was worried about the cost of maintenance of such a large population. He requested them all to return to their homes.

Starting from her parental home, Viśākhā and her party arrived at the city gate of Śrāvastī. Suddenly, she thought whether she should enter into the city in a covered vehicle or whether she should stand in an open chariot. For, if she entered into the city in a covered vehicle, the people would not get a change of seeing her precious *mahālatā* ornament. So, she entered into the city in an open chariot. The people of Śrāvastī witnessed with their own eyes the grace and affluence on Viśākhā's person and lauded her and welcomed her with their finest expressions. People who had gone out with the marriage party had reason to be particularly happy at the grand reception and hospitality they received from *Śresṭhī* Dhanañjaya, and they bestowed many gifts on Viśākhā. She distributed them to people in all walks of life.

During Viśākhā's first night at her new home, a mare in the stable had a severe labour pain. When Viśākhā heard this, she went out from her chamber. She was attended by her maids who carried torches in their hands. The mare was given a hot bath and oil was rubbed on her body. After she was safely delivered, Viśākhā returned to her chamber.

The marriage festivity lasted for a whole week. *Śresṭhī* Mṛgāra was a follower of the *nirgranthas.* To mark the last day of the festivity, the *Śresṭhī* invited many *nirgrantha* monks to his house to the utter exclusion of the Buddhist Monks. The *Śresṭhī* sent a message for Viśākhā.

"The *Arhats* have come to our house. So, come and bow before them."

Viśākhā was an inspired *Ārya śrāvikā*. When she heard that the *arhats* had come, she became very happy. She took no time to get ready and appear before the monks to pay her obeisance. But when she saw so many nude monks at a tine, she felt a severe reaction from within her, and the following words spontaneously dropped from her lips,

"Do *arhats* look like these? Why did my father-in-law ask me to come in the presence of these shameless *śramaṇas?* What a shame!"

Viśākhā's behaviour gave affront to the nude monks. They lodged a strong protest against her with *Śreṣṭhī* Mṛgāra. Said they,

> "Couldn't you get a better bride for your son? Why did you bring to your home a worthless follower of *Śramaṇa* Gautama? Get rid of her as early as you can."

Śreṣṭhī Mṛgāra was between the horns of a dilemma. Thought he,

> 'Viśākhā comes of a good family. She cannot be driven out like this at the bidding of the monks. But if I do not do something in the matter, the rage of the monks will not be pacified.'

He begged the monks to forgive him and saw them off. After the monks were gone, he sat down to eat. He started eating sweet *khīra* with a golden spoon from a golden saucer. The *khīra* was boiled in milk to which no water was added. Just then an elderly monk who was out on a begging mission arrived at the *Śreṣṭhī's* door. Viśākhā saw him but did not consider it fit to announce him to her father-in-law. So she moved a little aside so that it would be possible for the *Śreṣṭhī* to see the monk himself. But the foolish *Śreṣṭhī* did not care to respond. With his face bent low, he remained deeply absorbed in eating. When Viśākhā saw that her father-in-law was perfectly unmindful to the monk's presence at the door, she could no longer check herself. She shouted to the monk,

> "*Bhante!* Better try your luck elsewhere. My father-in-law is subsisting on a cold stuff saved from the previous day."

The *Śreṣṭhī's* temper was already ruffled by Viśākhā's behaviour towards nude monks. But when he heard her say that her father-in-law was subsisting on a cold stuff saved from the previous day, he lost all control on himself. He withdrew his hand from the food and said to an attendant boy,

> "Take away this saucer and ask Viśākhā to leave my home at once. In such a pious home, she calls me to be an eater of impure food."

The servants of the Śreṣṭhī's house were very much obliged to Viśākhā. They held her in the greatest esteem. So, what to speak of turning out from the house, none dared to utter an undignified word in her presence. To her father-in-law, Viśākhā said,

"Sir! I am not to be turned out like this. I did not join this house as a water-maid. When my parents are alive, you cannot behave towards a daughter-in-law in this manner. The day I was seen off by my father, he handed over my charge to eight elders. They must be called in to rectify my mistake, if any."

Śreṣṭhī Mṛgāra assembled the elders, and in great excitement, he narrated the account. The elders wanted Viśākhā to defend herself. Viśākhā said,

"May be my father-in-law intends to be an eater of impure food, but I made no such attribution to him. A elderly monk who was out on a begging mission stood at our door. The *Śreṣṭhī* did not care to observe him, still less to receive him, but remained busy with his food. When I saw this, I said to the monk, '*Bhante!* My father-in-law is not keen to earn fresh merit in this body; he wants to live on his past acquisitions'. Please tell me, considering the situation, if I committed a crime in saying like this."

The elders found Viśākhā innocent on this count. They said, "This is no crime. Our daughter has pointed at a right thing."

Changing the topic, the *Śreṣṭhī* came out,

"During her first night at my house, this girl, without caring for my son, went out, I know not where. Was it worthy of a freshly wed bride?"

The elders turned to Viśākhā to receive her explanation about the charge. Viśākhā said,

"I did not go to any undesirable place. In this very house, a mare was suffering acutely from labour pain which I could not just overlook. So, with torches and with attendant maids, I went to the stable to help the mare to deliver safely."

On hearing this, the elders gave the following verdict,

"*Ārya!* Our daughter served as a midwife to your mare which, we suppose, not even the maid-servants in your household would attend. We see nothing wrong in this."

But *Śreṣṭhī* Mṛgāra was blind with rage. He said,

"In your view, gentlemen, this has been an act of merit. But let me cite another instance. When she was to depart from her father's home, her father said to her, 'Do not take fire out from inside the home'. When there are good neighbours on both the flanks of our home, is it honestly possible to practise this precept?"

The elders now turned to Viśākhā who explained,

"My father-in-law has misunderstood the whole meaning. What my father intended to convey is that one should not discuss the affairs of the family with servants and maids. For, that may start a quarrel in her family. This is what he intended to convey through this aphorism."

As *Śreṣṭhī* Mṛgāra was fast losing his ground, he repeated one after another all the words that *Śreṣṭhī* Dhanañjaya had given to his daughter at the time of her departure, He said,

"She may be innocent about the first aphorism; but what about the second? Her father had said to her, 'Do not take fire from outside into the home'. Please tell me if such a maxim is practicable in life. When the fire in the home is extinguished, can you stick to this advice?"

Viśākhā explained,

"My father did not mean that. He intended to convey that the lapses, shortcomings and errors of servants, and maids, as they come to one's notice, should not be discussed with other members of the family. For, in that case, they would lose faith in the servants."

Śreṣṭhī Mṛgāra shouted,

"But her father said so many other things. What did he mean? I want a complete explanation."

Viśākhā started explaining,

"My father said, 'Give to those who are worthy; do not give to those who are not worthy'. These words were directed to beggars. Next he said, 'Give to both who are capable and incapable to make a return'. You see, even among our own people, all are not equally affluent. Some are rich and some are poor. So, you understand the implication of his words. Next, he said, 'Sit comfortably', by which he meant that a daughter-in-law should not sit at a place frequented by the elders. (In sitting in such a place, she has to stand up everytime an elderly person comes, making herself uncomfortable). Then he said, eat comfortably, by which he meant that a daughter-in-law should never dine before her parents-in-law and her husband had taken food. She should take her meal only after making enquiry that everyone in the house has been duly fed. And then he said, 'Lie comfortably', by which he mean that a daughter-in-law should retire only after the elders had retired. And then he said, 'Behave as you do towards fire', by which he meant that a daughter-in-law should view her parents-in-law, even her own husband, as she would view a heap of fire, or even king cobra. And my father's final words were, 'Bow before family deities', by which he meant that the guests arrived at the house should be duly taken care of."

Even before Viśākhā had stopped, the elders said to *Śreṣṭhī* Mṛgāra,

"Sir! Does your ethics debar you from giving food to the mendicants?"

The *Śreṣṭhī* could give no reply. He bent his head low.
Being now confident about heir own strong position, the elders said,

"*Śreṣṭhī!* Is there any other thing on which you intend to charge our daughter?"

Finding that the *Śreṣṭhī* had nothing more in his stock, they said,

"Then why do you intend to turn her out from your home?"

Viśākhā's self-respect flared up. Addressing the elders, she said in an angry voice,

"It was not proper for me to get out at the bidding of my father-in-law. My father had placed my charge in your worthy hands and requested you to rectify me in case I committed any error. You have now exonerated me from the charges levelled against me by father-in-law. So, now I feel free to depart of my own."

Then turning to her maids, she said,

"Get my chariot ready at once."

Śreṣṭhī Mṛgāra looked blank. He knew not what to say or do. In deep penetence, he pathetically appealed to Viśākhā's good sense :

"My daughter! All I said and did was the outcome of my own studpidity and ignorance. Please forgive me."

Viśākhā said,

"Sir! I am born in a family which is devoted to the Buddha. I am used to serving the Buddhist order of monks. If I am permitted freedom of faith and conscience, then only I may live in your house."

Śreṣṭhī Mṛgāra agreed to everything. He gave her leave to invite the Buddha with all his monks. As for himself, he said that he would keep himself wholly out of her way.

Viśākhā invited the Buddha and his monks on the following day. When the Buddha arrived, the whole house was filled up with his monks. Viśākhā welcomed the party. When the nude *śramaṇas* heard that the Buddha had been received at the house of *Śreṣṭhī* Mṛgāra, they came running and besieged the house. Meanwhile, Viśākhā gave water to the Buddha and the monks to wash and sent words to her father-in-law to come and serve food to the Buddha. But Mṛgāra was afraid of the nude monks and so he did not shows his face. After the Buddha and his monks had dined, Viśākhā again sent words to her father-in-law to come and listen the sermon from the Buddha. The *Śreṣṭhī* thought that it would not be decent on his part to decline. So he came out of his room. The nude monks tried their best to prevent him, but at last they yielded to some extent,

"If you must attend, do so from outside."

Addressing *Śreṣṭhī* Mṛgāra, the Buddha said,

"You may choose to sit behind the tent, a wall, a mountain or at the far-end of the Cakravala; I am Buddha and hence can make you listen to the *sermons.*"

The Buddha started his sermon. Like a branch of a mango tree, laden with ripe golden mangoes with drop when the branch is shaken, so, as the Buddha progressed in his sermon, the sins of the *Śreṣṭhī* started dropping out, and by the time the Buddha ended, the *Śreṣṭhī* had his pure spiritual eye opened. The curtain was removed. The *Śreṣṭhī* moved forward, lowered his five limbs till the ground and bowed at the feet of the Great Leader. In the august presence of the Buddha, he said to Viśākhā,

"From this day, you are no longer my daughter, but my mother, and as 'mother', I shall address you."

He bowed before her as one does before his mother and sucked her breast. From that day, Viśākhā became known as Mṛgāra-mātā or mother of Mṛgāra. One of Viśākhā's own sons was also named Mṛgāra.[24]

The *Śreṣṭhī* organised a grand celebration to mark the occasion of his accepting Viśākhā as his mother, and the Buddha and his monks were invited to attend. She was bathed with 15 jars full of flower essence and was given an ornament named *ghana-matthaka-prasādhana* by the *Śreṣṭhī.* It was worth a lakh.[25]

Mṛgāra-mātā Viśākhā invited 500 monks everyday to dine at her house.[26] She was very regular at the Buddha's sermon, she personally looked after and took care of guests, patients, outgoing monks, incoming monks, junior monks, and others sheltered at the *vihāra*.[27]

It was a festive day. Dressed in their finest clothes, people on the road to the *vihāra* where they were to attend a lecture on *dharma*. Viśākhā took her food at the festival canteen and proceeded straight to the *vihāra.* She had her *mahālatā* ornament on that day. So, on reaching the *vihāra,* she took out her *mahālatā* and other lesser ornaments, and entrusted them to a maid saying to her,

"I shall take them on my way back from the Leader."

Viśākhā attended the sermon and returned to receive her jewellery. Meanwhile, the maid had forgotten all about the ornaments so that they were lying uncared for. Now, it was a self-allottd duty of Ānanda that after the people dispersed, he checked carefully if anyone had left any personal belonging in the assembly hall, and if he found any, he carried it and placed before the Leader. While on this usual round, Ānanda came across the discarded ornaments. At once he placed them before the Buddha who asked him to keep them aside in safe custody. Ānanda deposited them near the staircase. When after fulfilling her work at the *vihāra* she asked the maid to give her ornaments back, the maid suddenly woke up to her absent-mindedness and looked alarmed. Viśākhā read into the situation and said,

"Go and get them back if they are there where I gave them to you. But remember that if perchance they have been taken care of by *Sthavira* Ānanda, then do not ask for them. I shall prefer to leave them with the great monk."

The maid went to the spot inside the *vihāra* where she was entrusted with the ornaments. Ānanda at once observed her and asked her the cause of her coming back. When maid Supriyā explained the position, Ānanda said to her,

"I have kept them near the staircase. Pick them up from there."

But Supriyā made no secret to tell Ānanda that since the ornaments had been touched by him, they were no longer fit to be used by her mistress. When Viśākhā heard all about them, she gave them to the monks. But then she had a thought in her mind that in leaving such valuable ornaments with the monks, she would be putting them into difficulty about their safe keeping. So, she decided to take them back and put them to some worthy use for the monks. So, she asked the maid to get them back.

Viśākhā did not use the ornaments. She decided to sell them. The jewellers who were called into make the valuation stated at fabulous price of nine crores, with an extra one lakh for their making. She asked the jewellers to sell them for her, but they expressed difficulty about finding a suitable customer for such costly things. So, she bought them herself. She loaded nine crores and one lakh coins on heavy trunks, arrived at the *vihāra,* saw the Buddha, bowed before him and said,

> "*Bhante!* My ornaments had been touched by the hands of *Sthavira* Ānanda. So, I could not use them any more. I decided to make a gift of them to the monks. But monks have no use with ornaments. So, I decided to sell them so that the money could be used for the benefit of the monks. But the next problem was to find a buyer of such costly things. So, I decided to repurchase them myself which I have done, and I have brought the wherewithal to pay for them. Please direct me on which one of the four objects used by the monks I may spend this money."

The *Tathāgata* directed her to erect a shelter at the eastern gate of the city. Viśākhā at once started preparations to give effect to the suggestion. She purchased a plot of land for nine crores and the construction work was taken on land.

The Buddha's routine was to beg at Viśākhā's house and to return to his camp at Jatavana by the southern gate. The day he received food at the house of Anāthapiṇḍika, he went out of the city by the eastern gate and lived in the shelter in the east. But when he turned his steps to the northern gate, that was an indication to the people that the Buddha was moving out from the city on his *cārikā* mission. One day, Viśākhā observed that the Buddha had turned his steps in the direction of the northern gate. At once, she hurried after him, bowed before him and asked him with deep anxiety,

> "*Bhante!* Do you intend to move out on your *cārikā* mission?"
>
> —"Yes, Viśākhā, I do."

Viśākhā was full of emotion, as if her heart had reached the throat. In a choked voice, she said,

> "*Bhante!* I am erecting this shelter for your use, and you are going away. No, I will not allow this. Please come back."

The Buddha—"But, Viśākhā, I have already started on my mission. I cannot get back."

Viśākhā—"Then, *Bhante,* at least leave a veteran monk here who may continue to enlighten us."

The Buddha—"Viśākhā, you pick up the begging bowl of anyone whomsoever you intend to retain."

Viśākhā thought at once of picking up the begging bowl of *Sthavira* Ānanda. But the next moment she changed her mind.

> 'The long-lived Moggalāna is in command of great spiritual powers. He will be useful for my construction work now in progress. He will help me to complete the construction soon.'

So she picked up the begging bowl of Moggallāna. Moggallāna looked at the Buddha. The Buddha said,

> "Moggalāna! Stay back with your entire family of 500 monks."

So, Moggalāna stayed. The work of construction became pretty easy under his supervision. With the support of his occult powers, Viśākhā's masons could carry heavy trees and rocks from as far as 50 or 60 *yojanas* in course of a day. They found no difficulty in loading heavy trucks with trees and rocks, and the axles of the wheels never gave way under such heavy weight. The two-storeyed shelter was ready for use. It had 500 rooms, big and small at each floor. The whole cost of construction was nine crores.

On the completion of his *cārikā* mission for nine months, the Buddha came back to Śrāvastī. By that time, the shelter was ready for the use of the Buddha and his monks. But the Buddha was proceeding towards Jetavana. When Viśākhā heard this, she came to him and requested him to stay at the new shelter four months of the rainy season. The Buddha agreed.

One day, a friend of Viśākhā came to her. She brought with her a carpet which was worth a lakh. She said to Viśākhā,

> "I want to spread my carpet somewhere in your new guesthouse. Where shall I do so?"

Viśākhā—"If I say that no portion of the floor is uncovered, you will not believe me. You will feel that I do not intend to take your carpet. So, it is better that you look up yourself. See if you can spread it somewhere."

The lady moved all over the building but in vain. She did not find any portion of the floor which was uncovered. Wherever she set her foot, she came across a costlier stuff than her own already spread. She became depressed and began to weep. *Sthavira* Ānanda observed this and enquired the cause of her grief. When she explained, Ānanda tried to console her. He said,

> "You may spread your carpet between the staircase and the bathroom. It will be useful for us to wipe our legs. The monks would wash their legs and dry them with your carpet."

(It is necessary to add that) this portion of the floor escaped the attention of Viśākhā and remained uncovered.

Viśākhā served the Buddha and his monks for four months with food and shelter. On the last day of their stay, she distributed clothes among them. The cheapest cloth given to a new initiate cost a thousand. Besides, she filled their begging bowl with ghee, jaggery, etc. The entire cost of enertaining the monks before their departure was nine crores. In this manner, Viśākhā spent a total amount of Rs. 27 crores—nine crores on land, nine crores on building and nine crores on gifts. For Viśākhā who was married in a home which was not a Buddhist, the total amount spent by her for the order of the Buddha has no parallel.[28]

Starting from Vārāṇasī, the Buddha came to Śrāvastī. He stayed at Jetavana. Viśākhā came to pay her homage and obeisance. The Buddha delighted her and inspired her with his profound sermon. For the following day, Viśākhā invited the Buddha and his monks to receive food from her. With his silence, the Buddha signified assent.

As the day dawned, there was a heavy downpour as if the clouds from the four isles (continents) had come together to crack down. The Buddha said to his monks,

"Like the heavy shower at this Jetavana, there is a severe downpour all over the four isles. These are the last great clouds of the season over the four isles. So you take your bath in the rain water."

The monks obeyed. They removed their clothes and started taking bath. Meanwhile, Viśākhā sent a maid to the *vihāra* with the word that the food was ready. When the maid came, she saw the naked monks taking their bath in the rainwater. At once, she felt embarassed and turned her steps back. She reported to Viśākhā,

"Madam! They do not look like the Buddhist monks. They are all *Ājīvakas.* They are taking their bath naked in the rain water."

Viśākhā was very intelligent. She read through the whole situation at once. She asked the maid to go again. The maid came back to the monks' abode. By that time, the monks had finished their bath, dried their bodies, put on their clothes and gone back to their respective rooms. So, she did not see any monk. She came back again and reported to her mistress that the monks were not there. Viśākhā understood the position again and asked her to go back and try again in their rooms.

At the appropriate time for dinner, the Buddha asked the monks to get ready to go, which they did. Like a man who can spread his arm and withdraw it at ease without any special effort, so the Buddha disapppeared from Jetavana without any effort and appeared at the house of Viśākhā and took his seat with his monks. Said Viśākhā with a great surprise,

"Truly praiseworthy is the great power of the *Tathāgata.* The whole township is flooded upto the knee, or even upto the waist, but not a single monk of the order has his legs or cloth drenched in rain water."

With great joy in her mind, Viśākhā served food to the Buddha and his monks and fed them. When the Buddha had finished his meal, she sat in one corder and made following submission :

"Bhante! Please permit me to seek some boons from thee."

—"But you know, Viśākhā, the *Tathāgata* is far away from boon."

—*"Bhante!* What I ask for are permitted and free from fault of any kind."

Being permitted by the Buddha she made the following submission,

1. For the rest of my life, please permit me to offer bathing suits to the monks for their use during the rainy season.
2. For the rest of my life, please permit me to feed the newly arrived monks.
3. For the rest of my life, please permit me to feed the outgoing monks.
4. For the rest of my life, please permit me to feed the ailing monks.
5. For the rest of my life, please permit me to feed the people who would take care of the ailing monk (*i. e.,* nurses).
6. For the rest of my life, please permit me to supply medicine in the ailing monks.
7. For the rest of my life, please permit me to supply breakfast *(yavāgū)* to the monks.
8. For the rest of my life, please permit me to supply *(udaka-sāṭikā)* to the nuns.

When the *Tathāgata* asked about the cause the induced her to ask for these boons, she explained each one of them as follows :

"*Bhante*! Nudity is hateful, base and low. So, I wish to supply bathing suits to the monks which they may use during the rainy season. This I propose to do till I die.

"Bhante! Incoming monks are not acquainted with the roads at Śrāvastī. Besides, they are tired. If they are permitted to take food at my house, then, they will at leisure pick up acquaintance with all the roads, lanes and bylanes in the city, and being relieved of their exhaustion, they will be able to beg their food later.

"Bhante! When the monks are to move out from Śrāvastī, a good part of their useful time is wasted in begging food. Due to this, at times, they are separated from the party, or each their destination at a very odd hour. If they are permitted to receive food at my house, then, I am sure, both these risks may be easily eliminated. They will not run the risk of being separated from their fellow monks, nor reach their destination at odd hours. Besides, they will not be exhausted on account of their trek. It is due to consideration like this that I beg leave to supply food to the outgoing monks.

"Bhante! If the ailing monks do not get right food, their suffering augments, and they may even die before their time. If they are permitted to receive food from me, they will be safeguarded against both the possiblities.

"Bhante! If the people who are to attend the ailing monks are busy procuring their own food, they will be delayed in coming to the patients, and if they are punctual, they may miss their food. If they received food at my house and if they carry food for the patients from my house, such a situation will not arise.

"*Bhante!* If the ailing monks do not receive suitable medicine, their suffering will increase. If they accept good medicine from me, their suffering will not increase, (rather it will diminish), and the chance of dying before time (on account of taking improper medicine) will be very much reduced.

"*Bhante!* Keeping in view the ten merits, you have permitted the distribution of morning food to the blind. On a similar consideration, I want to supply morning food to the members of the holy order.

"*Bhante!* Once it so happened that the nuns were obliged to take bath in the river Aciravatī at the same bathing spot where harlots were taking bath. These fallen women said curtly to the nuns, 'You are so young. Why do you keep away from men? At this age, you should enjoy life, and you will have enough time to practise celibacy in your old age. If you do this, you will do full justice to both parts of your life.' The nuns could give no suitable reply. Nudity among women is particularly hateful and mean. So, I intend to supply *udaka-sāṭikā* to the nuns."

The Buddha—"Viśākhā! What special merit have you detected in these which you intend to acquire?"

Viśākhā—"Having completed their withdrawal during the monsoon months at various places in all directions, monks will flock to Śrāvastī to pay their homage and obeisance to thee when they will ask, '*Bhante*! Monk so and so is dead. What will happen to him? Is there a next life?' And at that time, in reply, those will explain at length the outcome of *srotāpatti* (*i.e.,* to be firm on the roral to liberation), of *sakṛdagāmī* (*i.e.,* one on the road to liberation who is busy exhausting fetters of sin), of *arhat*-hood, and so on. I shall enquire from the monk if ever the dead monk had come to Śrāvastī or not. If I learn that the dead monk had visited this city during his life-time, I shall be able to check at once if he received a bathing suit from me, or incoming monk's diet or outgoing monk's diet, if he received a patient's food, 'or a nurse's food, or medicine or daily *yavāgū.* A remembrance like this will give joy to my mind, joy will give happiness and happiness will generate peace in the body. Physical peace will enable me to enjoy bliss, and bliss will help my mind in attaining concentration. These chain reactions will give me thought of my senses, thought of my power and thought of the *bodhi-aṅga* (which are seven, *viz., smṛti, dharama-vicaya, vīrya, prīti, prakṣabdhi, samādhi* and *upekṣā).* I think, I shall benefit in this manner from these boons."

The *Tathāgata* approved of her thoughts, praised her and granted her all the eight boons. Thereafter, the Buddha stood up from his seat and departed. Having reached the *vihāra,* he called the monks in his presence and gave them permission about the eight items.[29]

One day, Viśākhā came to the Buddha with a towel in her hand. She bowed before him and sat on one side. In offering the towel to the Buddha, she said,

"*Bhante!* Please accept this. This will give me perpetual peace and happiness."

The Buddha accepted the towel and delighted and inspired her by his sermons. After Viśākhā had gone, he called the monks in his presence and permitted them to accept a towel, it offered to clean dry their face.[30]

REFERENCES

1. *Aṅguttara Nikāya*, Ekakanipāta, 14.
2. *Bhagavatī*, S. 12, U.I.
3. *Ibid.*
4. *Ibid.*
5. *Āvaśyaka cūrṇī.*
6. *Bhagavatī*, S. 15.
7. *Samavayāṅga*, Sū. 114-115.
8. *Aṅguttara Nikāya*, Ekakanipāta, 14.
9. *Samytta Nikāya*, 39.1.11. Also *Dictionary of Pāli Proper Names*, Vol. 1, p. 866.
10. *Bhagavatī*, S.3, U.1.
11. According to *Aṅguttara Nikāya* (II. p. 399), he was the son of *Abhayakumāra.*
12. *Uvasagdāsao*, Ad. 1.
13. *Avaśyaka Cūrṇī*, Second half, p. 164: *Bhārateśvara Bāhubalī Vṛtti*, pp. 248/2, 255/1. *Upadeśa Prasāda*, Stambha 3, Vyākhyāna 36.
14. *Ṭhāṇāga Sūtra* Ṭhā. 9, U. 3, Sūtra 691.
15. *Vinaya Piṭaka*, Aṭṭakathā.
16. *Ibid.*
17. *Vinaya Piṭaka*, Cullavagga, 6.3.1.
18. *Vinaya Piṭaka*, Atthakathā.
19. *Vinaya Piṭaka*, Cullavagga, 6.3.6.
20. *Majjhima-nikāya*, Anāthapiṇḍikovāda Sutta, 3.5.1.
21. *Dhamapada*, Aṭṭhakathā, 4-8.
22. *Vinaya Piṭaka*, Mahāvagga, 6. 6. 1. and 2.
23. *Dhammapada*, Aṭṭhakathā, 4-8.
24. *Ibid.*
25. *Dictionary of Pāli Proper Names*, Vol. II, p. 902.
26. *Jātaka* (Hindi), part IV, p. 144.
27. *Dhammpada*, Aṭṭhakathā, I-128.
28. *Ibid.*, 4-4.
29. *Vinaya Piṭaka*, Mahāvagga, 8-4-5 & 6
30. *Ibid.*, 8-3-5.

13

DEFIANT DISCIPLES

Both Mahāvīra and Buddha collected many worthy men around them who, by dint of their dedication, service, submission and brilliant exertions, created history; but at the same time, they had same bad disciples who built a parallel history of defiance and opposition. Two such leading disciples who became foremost rebels were Gośālaka and Devadatta, the former rebelling against Mahāvīra and the latter against the Buddha. Both had received their initation at the hands of their respective masters and both were advanced enough to acquire occult powers through their penances, but in the end, both turned agains their masters. Gośālaka called Mahāvīra *Ajina-Jina* and himself a *Jina.* Likewise, in a great assembly, Devadatta said to the Buddha,

> "Sir! You are now aging and are worn out. So, you hand over the charge of the *Saṅgha* to me. I shall be its leader."

Both Gośālaka and Devadatta conspired to kill their respective masters and this became a cause of concern in both the camps. When, on hearing about this, Ānanda was completely upset, Mahāvīra said to him and to other disciples,

> "A Jina cannot be killed before he reaches the time of his exit. He does not die premature."

In the same manner, the Buddha told his disciples,

> *"Bhikṣus!* The Buddha cannot be killed before his time. He dies only at the appropriate time. Not can kill him."

A striking resemblance between the two events is thaṭ while Gośālaka used Ānanda to carry his message to Mahāvīra, Devadatta used (another) Ānanda for a similar errand to the Buddha. The reactions of Mahāvīra and the Buddha, too, have striking similarity.

Both the rebel disciples became very influential for some time. Gośālaka had a large following. Devadatta could mobilise the partonage of King Ajātaśatru. The king was under his personal influence.

But it is worth while to note that at the closing time of their life, both regained reverence for their respective masters. Both died of similar diseases.

After his death, Devadatta was born in a hell named Avīci. He will be there for 1,00,000 *kalpas*, after which he will get his release from the hell and be born as Buddha, and will then enter into liberation. But it was the reverse with Gośālaka. After his death, he was born in a heaven called *Acyutakalpa.* When he will descend from there, he will have to spend many lives in infernal and sub-human existences. In the end, he will be perfected, enlightened and liberated.

The Gośālaka episode is recorded in the *Bhāgavatī* and has been incorporated earlier in this volume. The Devadatta episode is contained in the *Saṅgha Bhedaka Khandhaka Prakaraṇa* in the *Vinayapiṭaka Cullavagga.* A summary from the same source is given below. Both stories are important in so far as they throw ample light on contemporary religious movements, social and political conditions and communal mentalities of the people. Both the narratives appear to be very much distorted and full of rancour and bitterness. But a researcher's eye may still discern some useful material from them.

Devadatta

Starting from Anupiya, *Bhagavān* Buddha arrived at Kauśāmbī. He encamped at a shelter named Ghoṣita. Monk Devadatta was seated in a secluded corner thinking, "Whom should I cultivate in order to earn a great merit"?

Suddenly he thought of King Ajātaśatru and he thought, 'King Ajātaśatru is young and promising. He had a bright future before him. I should please him. This will give me much gain and prominence!

Devadatta picked up his cushion and begging bowl and took the road to Rājagṛha. Having arrived there, he changed himself into a boy, wore an ornamental chain (as was used by young childern) round his waist and appeared straight on the laps of Ajātaśatru. At this unusual appearance, Ajātaśatru became somewhat afraid, alarmed and terrified. Said the body to the king,

"Prince! are you afraid of me?"

Ajātaśatru—"Yes, I am. Who are you"?

Devadatta—"I am Devadatta."

Ajātasatru—"*Bhante!* If you are Devadatta, as you say, please appear in your proper from."

At this, Devadatta gave up his disguise and appeared before Ajātaśatru in his proper from with his begging bowl and cloth in his hand. Ajātaśatru was very much impressed by this wonderful feat of the monk. Since this event, Ajātaśatru became a rugular visitor to Devadatta every morning and evening. He was followed by 500 chariots and he supplied 500 dishes of food everyday for the use of Devadatta and his monks.

Having thus gained royal favour, prestige and prominence, Devadatta thought,

'Now, I should be the leader of the *bhikṣus*.'

No sooner did he think like that than his spiritual power was gone.

Starting from Kauśāmbī, *Bhagavān* Buddha came to Rājagṛha. He halted at Veṇu-vana which belonged to Kalandaka Nīvāpa. Many monks came to the Buddha. They paid him their homage and obeisance and sat on one side. They narrated the account of the honour conferred on Devadatta by Prince Ajātaśatru. When the Buddha heard this, he observed,

> "Don't ye be covetous of royal patronage, prestige and prominence that have been acquired by Devadatta. So, long as prince Ajātaśatru continues his patronage, Devadatta will be a loser rather than a gainer. He will wane in spirit. He will not enrich his own self. This royal favour is a prelude to his defeat and annihilation, just as it happens to a banana tree, a bamboo tree and a *narakaṭa* tree which die after their first fruit, or even to an *aśvatarī* who becomes pregnant in order to die at the birth of its offspring. The same will be the case with Devadatta. You should not attach too much importance to it."

On Kakudha Koliyaputra who was a devoted follower of long-lived Mahāmoggalāna had died about that time and was born in a heaven named *Manomaya.* His body was as large as two or three farms at Magadha. But such a large body caused inconvenience neither to him nor to others. This Kokudha Devaputra came to the long-lived Moggalāna, saluted him, stood on one side and submitted,

> "*Bhante!* Aspirant Devadatta has a thought like this : 'I must assume the leadership of the monastic order'. No sooner did he entertain such a thought in his mind than he lost all his spiritual powers."

Having communicated this, Kakudha Devaputra disappeared at once.

Moggalāna came to the Buddha and narrated the account tendered to him by Kakudha Devaputra. Said the Buddha to Moggalāna,

"Did you yourself verify the same by dint of your spiritual power"?

To this Moggalāna humbly submitted,

> "*Bhante!* I feel that whatever Kakudha Devaputra has tendered is correct. There is no distortion in it."

The Buddha was speaking before a vast assembly. Prince Ajātaśatru was also present. In this assembly, Devadatta stood up, paid his obeisance and with folded hands said,

> "*Bhante!* You have become old, aged and worn. Now, you should retire from all responsibilities and lead a carefree life. You should hand over the responsibility for the monastic order to him. I am prepared to take it over."

The Buddha retorted at once,

> "Stop, Devadatta! You are not fit to be the leader to the monastic order."

Devadatta repeated the same words thrice. But the Buddha protested emphatically everytime :

> "Devadatta! You should know for certain that I am not going to pass on the leadership of the monastic order even to such worthy disciples as Sāriputta and Moggalāna. I do not understand how do you cherish the idea of becoming the leader of the monastic order though you are no better than an worthless fellow."

But all the time Devadatta was boiling within himself. He shouted,

> "In this grand assembly, where even the Crown-prince, the future monarch, is present, you have insulted me by calling me an worthless fellow. In contrast, you have extolled Sāriputta and Moggalāna as being every worthy disciples."

He was very angry and unhappy. He saluted the Buddha, moved round him and quitted the place at once. This was the first revolt by Devadatta.

The Buddha called the monks around him and said,

> "*Bhikṣus!* At Rājagṛha, the monastic order should expose Devadatta in the following manner : Devadatta was a different person in the past, but

he has totally changed now; and whatever Devadatta does now in body and speech, neither the Buddha, nor *Dharma* nor *Saṅgha* is in any way responsible for that. Devadatta alone is responsible for all he does."

The Buddha continued,

"I suggest that this should be brought to the notice of the entire monastic order, this should be made known to them, and the following should be repeated again and again : 'The *Saṅgha* agree with this and accepts this tacitly.' I accept this."

Addressing "Sāriputta! You take the responsibility of exposing Devadatta at Rājagrha."

Sāriputta—"Bhante! In the past, at Rājagṛha, I have spoken words of praise about Devadatta. I have said, "Godhiputra (Devadatta) commands great powers. '*Bhante*! Should I now speak just the reverse in order to expose him"?

The Buddha—"Sāriputta! In the past, you showered praise on him which he rightly deserved. Is that right?"

Sāriputta—"Bhante! It is so."

The Buddha resumed,

"In the same manner, Sāriputta, you expose him as he is now."

Sāriputta accepted the order of the Buddha. To the monastic order, the Buddha said,

"May the monastic order nominate Sāriputta to the task of exposing Devadatta at Rājagṛha."

Then he himself explained how Sāriputta should be given the necessary nomination :

"The monastic order should first interview Sāriputta; then it should bring this to the notice of the wise and able people in the order; and thereafter, it should be made known, announced and upheld."

Having been given the nomination by the monastic order, Sāriputta entered into Rājagṛha with a large body of monks. There they exposed Devadatta. The kind-hearted, wise and intelligent people thought that this exposure of Devadatta in the city at the instance of the Buddha was too important an event to be lightly overlooked.

Devadatta rushed to Prince Ajātaśatru and said to him,

> "Prince! In the past, people enjoyed a long life, but now life has become very short. Who knows you may die as a prince (and never get a chance of sitting on the throne). So, Prince, I suggest that you assassinate your father and ascend on the throne, and I do the same to the Buddha and occupy his position in the monastic order."

Ajātaśatru hid a dagger beneath his trousers and suddenly burst into the seraglio at noon hour. He was afraid, alarmed, anxious and shaken. In that state, he was caught by the palace guards who said to the prince,

> "Speak the truth why you entered into the seraglio at this very odd hour. What is in your mind?"

Ajātaśatru—"I came to kill my father."
The guards—"But who inspired you to do such a mean thing?"
Ajātaśatru—"*Ārya* Devadatta."

Some guards said that the prince, his instigator and all the Buddhist monks should be beaten up; but others did not agree. They were of opinion that this should be brought to the notice of the king and then they should leave the whole matter to His Majesty's discretion.

The guards conducted the prince to the presence of King Bimbisāra and tendered a complete account of all that had happened. The king asked the guards what they thought about it, and these men submitted as they deemed appropriate in a situation like this, whereon the king gave the following order :

> "Guards! I do not think that in this matter, the Buddha, his *Dharma* or his *Saṅgha* is responsible in any way. The expulsion of Devadatta from the order has already been announced by the Buddha at Rājagṛha. So, those men from the palace guards who had suggested that the prince, Devadatta and all the Buddhist monks should be beaten up should be dismissed forthwith; and those who had suggested that the matter should be brought to my notice and that the action should be left to my discretion should be promoted at once to higher positions."

Having given these, orders about the palace guards, the king turned to Ajātaśatru and said,

> "Prince! Why did you intend to kill me?"

Ajātaśatru—*"Deva!* I wanted to be the king myself."

At once, Śreṇika Bimbisāra handed over the kingdom to his son.

Now that Ajātaśatru had become the king, Devadatta came to him and exposed before him his own desings about himself. In the end, he added,

> "Oh King! Send your men with necessary orders to kill the Buddha."

Ajātaśatru who was already very much impressed by the great ability of Devadatta readily agreed. He ordered his faithful men to act accordingly. Devadatta elaborated on that. Addressing the first man, Devadatta said,

> *"Ābusa! Śramaṇa* Gautama is encamped at such and such place at that time. Kill him and come back by this very road."

After he had gone, he placed on the same road two guards and said to them,

> "If you see a single man coming by this road, you kill him at once and come back by this very road."

In the same manner, (at a certain distance from the previous party of guards, he placed four guards, and likewise eight and sixteen guards, with a similar instruction. All the guards took positions as directed, ready to execute the order. Equipped with a sword and a shield, the first man came to the Buddha's camp. He was afraid, anxious and alarmed, looking completely blank. As he was of a very mild tone, he said to him,

> "Come, *ābusa* I welcome thee. Have no fear."

The man threw aside his sword and shield, fell down at the Buddha's feet and said,

> *"Bhante!* Like a child, a fool, an ignoramous, I have committed the meanest crime against thee. With a wicked design in my mind, I came to kill thee. Please forgive me my sin."
> *"Bhante!* Please forgive me for what is past now; and for the future, please fix me in *Saṁvara* (restraint)."

In consoling him, the Buddha said,

> "Although you have committed a great sin, still, penitent as you are,

> and you are keen to recitfy for the future according to the Law *(dharma),* I accept your words and grant you reprive."

Then the Buddha spoke to him words of enlightenment and the man had his pure, spiritual eye opened at once. Said he to the Great Leader.

> "*Bhante!* From this day, please accept me who is come to this succour with folded hands as a devoted follower of thee."

By dint of his divine powers, the Buddha saw the whole trap laid by Devadatta and so he changed the route of the man's going back. In consequence, he did not go by the route assigned to him by Devadatta, but he went by a different route. The two guards were anxiously waiting for this man to return, but after waiting for a long time when they found that nobody did come back, they themselves proceeded in the same direction to check. They came across the Buddha seated beneath a tree. They saluted him and stood on one side. The Buddha spoke to them words of enlightenment, and both the guards had their pure, spiritual eyes opened at once. With folded palms, they took shelter with him. In the same manner, the four, eight and sixteen guards came to him, heard his inspiring words and with their folded palms, all of them took refuge with him. For each party, the Buddha changed the route of their return (in the same manner as he had done to the first man). Meanwhile, the first man returned to Devadatta and narrated his experience adding in the end,

> "*Bhante!* I could not kill the Buddha. He is a great soul with great powers."

In a fit of absent-mindedness, Devadatta said,

> "All right. If you have failed to kill *Śramaṇa* Gautama, I must do it with my-own hands."

The Buddha was now pacing on the shady side of the Gṛdhrakūṭa mountain. Devadatta reached the peak of the mountain and rolled a rock down to crush the Buddha. But the rock was held between two (minor) peaks. But a small portion of the rock fragmented out and hit the Buddha's leg which started bleeding at once. The Buddha turned his gaze upward and said to Devadatta.

> "Notorious man! You have acquired a great sin by making the Buddha bleed."[1]

Then addressing the monks he said,

"Devadatta has erected the first rock to his own liberation."

When the monks came to know about the mean conspiracy by Devadatta, they started a strict vigil of the place (where the Buddha was lodged) and read aloud their sacred texts. The Buddha asked Ānanda to send the monks to him. To the monks he said,

> "*Bhikṣus!* It is not possible that the *Tathāgata* can be killed by the conspiracies of any one. The *Tathāgata* never courts death from another's hand; he passes away only when it is time for him to enter into liberation. So, you relax in your own rooms. The *Tathāgata* needs no protection."

At Rājagṛha, there lived an elephant named Nālāgiri who was extremely turbulent and played havoc with human life. One day, Devadatta came to the keeper of the said elephant and said,

"When *Śramaṇa* Gautama comes by this route, you place your elephant before him. (You will be rewarded for this)." The keeper agreed to oblige him. Next morning, the Buddha followed by the monks entered into Rājagṛha to beg food. The elephant-keeper released the elephant towards the Buddha. The monks became very much confused and alarmed and requested the Buddha to move aside from the road for his own safety. Many people went atop their own houses or stood at the windows witnessing with concern the scene of the turbulent elephant chasing the Buddha. There were also many among them who had no respect for the Buddha, or were really wicked people who said,

> "The so-called *Mahāśramaṇa* is going to be trampled and crushed to death under the feet of the elephant."
>
> Those who were wise and had respect for him said,
>
> "One *nāga* (elephant) will fight with another *nāga* (meaning the Buddha)".

When the Buddha saw the elephant at a distance, he tamed him through his own affectionate feelings for him. The elephant came near the Buddha and stood motionless with his trunk hanging down. The Buddha touched the elephant with his own hands. The elephant touched the Buddha's feet with his trunk, licked some dust from them and placed it at his crest. Then he moved to go in backward steps, without turning his rear portion towards the Buddha. This form he did not change till the Buddha was visible to him, and then he returned to his own shade' and stood at his own place. This roused a wide gossip all over the city. People openly said,

> "How vile and mean Devadatta must be to hatch an ignoble plot to kill such a worthy man with great divine power and influence!"

Devadatta moved down in their estimation, while the Buddha moved up.

Unsuccessful Devadatta was, however, not to sit quiet. He set his mind to devising more effective plans for the Buddha's annihilation. He came to Kokālika Kaṭamoratissaka and *Khaṇḍa Devīputra* Samudradatta. In order to inspire them to effect the split of the *Saṅgha,* he placed before them a proposal for their consideration which was as follows :

> "I intend to request *Śramaṇa* Gautama to prescribe five new rules for the monks of his order. These rules are as follows :
>
> 1. The monks should remain throughout life in the forests, and never in the villages (or towns).
> 2. The monks should subsist on begging, and should never expect to be invited.
> 3. The monks should put on rags; they should not use cloth supplied by the householders.
> 4. The monks shoud live at the foot of the trees.
> 5. The monks should not touch fish or meat throughout their life.
>
> I am sure *Śramaṇa* Gautama will never accept these rules for his monks, in which case it will be easy for me to turn the people against him and for myself."

With his followers, Devadatta came to the Buddha. He saluted him and placed before him his well-conceived plan for his consideration. The Buddha said in reply :

> "Devadatta! These are all right. I have already asked the monks to live in the forest as well as in the villages; to live on begging as well as to accept invitation to receive food; to put on rags as well as clothes provided by the householders; to sit and lie under the shade of the trees; and I have asked the monks to subsist on meat. They have three conditions to fulfil *viz.,* not seen the slaughter, they have not heard that the slaughter has taken place for their sake, and they have no hunch that the slaughter has been effected for them. I see no sin in these."

When the Buddha rejected the proposals made by Devadatta in this manner, the latter became very happy and returned to Rājagṛha. In his effort to expose the Buddha to the people, he said,

> "The lord supports and prescribes little desire, contentment, penance, simple living, *prasādika,* renunciation and endeavour for the monks. So, I placed before him for his consideration for making five rules for the members of the monastic order, but be did not approve of them. I approved these five rules."

When the disrespectful and foolish people heard these words, they said,

> "Born in the Śākya line, the Buddha is a false and property-earning monk. He builds up property and inspires people to do the same."

The devoted and wise people, on the contrary, became sorry at this mean attiude of Devadatta. All of them denounced him in the same manner saying,

> "Devadatta is trying for a cleavage in the Buddhist order."

The monks heard the people discussing these. They came to the Buddha and reported. The Buddha's reactions were as follows :

> "We should be very careful so that Devadatta may not create a cleavage in the order. This is a hineous crime. He who strives to divide a monastic order which is united acquires a life in hell as long as one *kalpa.* He rots in hell for one *kalpa.* He who unites a divided order acquires great merit. He enjoys life in heaven for one *kalpa.* So tell Devadatta that it is not good on his part to try to create a split in the monastic order."

In the morning, the long-lived Ānanda entered into Rājagṛha to beg food. When Devadatta saw him, he called him. He said to Ānanda,

> *"Ābusa* Ānanda! From this day, I shall perform *upasatha* outside the Buddha's monastic order and fulfil rituals outside the order."

Having finished his begging, Ānanda returned and reported to the Buddha,

> *"Bhante!* From this day, Devadatta is separated from our order. He will create a charge in the order today carry on his spiritual practices outside the order. When I went to the city to beg, he himself told me like that."

At this, the Buddha utered a maxim as follows :

> "It is easy to be honest with honest people but honesty is difficult to practise with the sinful. Sin is easy with the sinful, but difficult with the *Āryans* (honest people)."

It was about this time that 500 Vajjīputtakas had been initiated into monkhood at Vaiśālī. But they were not familiar with the code to be followed by the monks. One day, when they were practsing *upasatha*, Devadatta said to them,

> "*Ābusa!* I placed five rules before *Śramaṇa* Gautama for his acceptance, but he declined. But I shall put them into currency. He who is ready to follow them may pick up a stick."

So, saying, he extended the sticks towards the initiates. The initiates thought,

> "This is *dharma.* This is *Vinaya.* This is the direction given by the Leader!"

All of them picked up the sticks.

Thus, Devadatta created a split in the monastic order and won over 500 monks on his side. In the company of his monks, he started for Gayāśīsa on a *Cārikā* mission.

Sāriputta and Moggalāna brought this event to the notice of the Buddha. The Buddha said,

> "Sāriputta, Do you not feel any compassion for these new initiates? You should try to save them before they are in deeper water."

Sāriputta and Moggalāna started at once and came to Gayāśīsa. Devadatta was then delivering a sermon before a vast assembly of men. He saw the two at a distance coming towards him. He became very happy and said to his monks,

> "You see how very well prescribed is my religion. Being attracted by this, Sāriputta and Moggalāna, the two stalwarts of the Buddha have broken away fròm the order and are coming to me. They have high regard for my way."

Kokālika lodged a mild protest against what Devadatta had said :

"Sir! Do't be so very cockish about Sāriputta and Moggalāna. They are sinfully inclined."

But Devadatta repeated what he had said earlier,

"No, we must welcome them. They have faith in my way."

By this time, Sāriputta and Moggalāna had come nearer. Devadatta invited Sāriputta to share his seat, but Sāriputta and Moggalāna sat on separate cushions on one side. Meanwhile, Devadatta started his sermon for the monks. The sermon continued till very late hours in the night, but the monks were deeply absorbed in the flow of the discourse. On seeing this, Devadatta said to Sāriputta,

"*Ābusa!* At this time, the monks are free from fatigue and deceit and deeply concentrated in the holy discourse. I do not want to disturb their concentration. But I am already red and must retire now. You take my place and carry on."

Sāriputta started his discourse to the monks. Meanwhile, Devadatta spread his bed on one side and stretched on it turning to the right. Being lightened from the burden of memory and *samprajanya,* Devadatta was soon fast asleep. Sāriputta and Moggalāna took advantage of the situation. Sāriputta addressed the monks on the wonders of *ādesanā* and *anuśāśānīya* and Moggalāna did the same on *ṛddhi.* On hearing these discourses, all the initiates had their pure spiritual eyes opened.

With 500 monks with them, Sāriputta and Moggalāna took the road to Veṇuvana at once. When Kokālika saw this, he gave a sharp pull to Devadatta and said,

"I had already warned you not to rely on these two. They are going away with our 500 monks."

On hearing this sad news, Devadatta vomitted hot (fresh) blood.

With 500 monks, Sāriputta and Moggalāna now stood before the Buddha and prayed as follows :

"*Bhante!* We submit and pray that these 500 monks who broke away from the order may be readmitted into the order."

Ordained the Buddha,

"Sāriputta! It should not be done like this. First make them at one for the great sin they committed, and till they do so, they cannot be admitted into the order."

Changing the topic, the Buddha said,

"Sāriputta! How did Devadatta behave towards you?"

Sāriputta narrated his experience as follows :

"*Bhante!* Till very late hours in the night, Devadatta continued to stimulate and humour the monks with his speech. Then he was fully exhausted and retired asking me to carry on the sermon in his place for the benefit of the monks who were neither fatigued in their body nor exhausted in their mind. Then I took over from him. This is how he behaved towards me."

Addressing the monks, the Buddha said,

"In ancient times, there was a great pool. There lived many elephants in its neighbourhood. Everyday, they came to the pool, pulled out the lotus stalks, washed them clean and ate them. This (diet) contributed to their beauty and physical strength and relieved them of all sufferings. Now, some young jackals started imitating the elephants. They also started eating the lotus stalks, but they did not care to clean them. So, they were steadily losing their physical stamina and grace. They felt very unhappy and miserable. So you see, oh monks, in trying to imitate me blindly, Devadatta will die as a bankrupt. He is ominous, hellish, destined to a long span of a *kalpa* and beyond any remedy."[2]

For vomitting hot (fresh) blood, Devadatta fell seriously ill. For full nine months, he continued to suffer great pain. In his last days, he woke to his follies. With deep regret, to enquired where the Buddha was at that time. He was told that he was in Jetavana. He requested his followers to carry him thither so that he could at least see his former preceptor before he left this earth. His followers placed him on a cot and started. (But he could never reach his destination). In the vicinity of a tank near Jetavana, he fell into a crater and lost his life. He took birth in a hell named *Avīci* where he will spent his life for 1,00,000 *kalpas,* and thereafter he will be born as a Pratyeka-Buddha named Aṭṭhissāra, and in that birth, he will attain his liberation.[3]

According to another source, (after his sojourn in hell), he will be born as a Buddha named Davarāja .[4]

Jamāli

Gośālaka apart, another illustrious name among the rebel disciples of Mahāvīra is that of Jamāli who happened to be his nephew as well as his son-in-law. The account of his early life and initiation have been narrated earlier in this volume. He was initiated in the company of 500 *Kṣatriya* youths. We have a complete account in the *Āgama*[5] why Jamāli rebelled against Mahāvīra. It is given below : One day Jamāli came to *Bhagavān* Mahāvīra and said,

> *"Bhante!* If you kindly permit me, I intend to move in some other area in the company of 500 monks".

Mahāvīra heard Jamāli's prayer but gave no reply to him. He remained silent. Jamāli repeated his prayer thrice, but when there was still no reply from Mahāvīra, he did not care any more for his permission, but moved out for another region in the company of his 500 monks.

Once monk Jamāli was stationed in a *caitya* named Koṣṭhaka at Śrāvastī. As he was living on poor, dry, cold and inadequate food, he had an attack of yellow fever. He had a severe pain and burning sensation all over his body. He asked his monks to spread the bed for him. The monks were busy with other duties. But Jamāli could sit no longer. Even a moment's delay was oppressive for him. He shouted,

> "Is my bed ready?"

The monks said,

> "No, sir, it is not yet ready. It will be ready soon".

On hearing these words, Jamāli hit on an important point. Thought he,

> 'According to *Bhagavāna* Mahāvīra, what is being done has already been done, what is moving is already moved, and so on. But I find that this is totally wrong. Till the bed has been spread, and not still in the process of being spread, how do I correctly say that the bed has been spread?'

He called the monks round him and shared his thought with them. Some monks agreed with his logic, but some others did not. The former remained with him, and the latter went back to Mahāvīra.

Monk Jamāli recovered after some time. Starting from Śrāvastī, he came to Campā. At that time, *Bhagavān* Mahāvīra was also encamped at the same city. Jamāli came to Mahāvīra and said,

> "Many of your monks are ordinary persons, not *kevalins.* But I am fully equipped with *kevala* knowledge and *kevala* vision. I am an *arhat, Jina,* and I am moving about as an omniscient person."

Gaṇadhara Gautama protested. He said,

> "The knowledge of an ominiscient person is never obstructed by a mountain or any other thing. If you are a *kevalin,* please give reply to my question: Is the sphere eternal for transcient? Is *Jīva* eternal or transcient?"

Jamāli could give no reply. He held his tongue. Addressing him, *Bhagavān* Mahāvīra said,

> "Jamāli! You should know that many of my disciples can give reply to these question. Still they do not declare themselves to be *Jinas* or *Kevalins."*

Jamāli did not relish these words of Mahāvīra. He stood up and left the place. He lived separately, and in this manner, he spent many years of his life implanted in falsehood built up by an erroneous logic. In the end, he died of starvation without discussing his sins and without performing *pratikramaṇa,* and he was born in a heaven named Lāntaka as a junior god *(kilviṣika).*

When Jamāli was still alive, Priyadarśanā (she was Mahāvīra's daughter Jamāli's wife) arrived at Śrāvastī with her nuns. There she took shelter in the workshop of a potter named Ḍhaṅka. Ḍhaṅka was a devoted follower of Mahāvīra. In order to reawaken her and reclaim her to the right path, (for, like her husband, she, too, was misguided and rebelled against the monastic order and broke away from it), the potter set fire to her *saṅghātī.* As it was burning, Priyadarśanā shouted,

> "The *saṅghātī* is burnt."

Said Ḍhaṅka,

"The *saṅghāṭī* is still burning and is not yet been burnt. Why do you utter false words?"

At this, Priyadarśanā realised her mistake and understood the implication. She went back to reenter Mahāvīra's order.[6]

REFERENCES

1. For a similar story of one Kūlabālaka who made a plot of kill his preceptor, vide *Uttarājjyayanani*, Lakṣmīballabha Gaṇi's Commentary, pp. 8-9.
2. *Vinaya Piṭaka*, Cullavagga, Khandha-bhedaka Khandhaka.
3. *Dhammapada Aṭṭhakathā*, Part I, p. 125.
4. *Saddharma Puṇḍarīka*, Chapter 11.
5. *Bhagavatī*, S. 9, U. 33.
6. *Viśeṣāvaśyaka Bhāṣya*, Gāthā 2324-2332.

14

FOLLOWER KINGS

ŚREṆIKA BIMBISĀRA

Among the lay followers of Mahāvīra and the Buddha, there were many kings. It is somewhat surprising that some of these kings and princes have been claimed as 'followers' by both the Jainas and the Buddhists. Among the most important names that fall in this group are Śreṇika-Bimbisāra, Koṇika (Ajātaśatru) and Abhayakumāra. Both the religious are vociferous in claiming them as very staunch suporters. The *Āgamas,* the *Tripiṭakas* and the *Purāṇa* literature of both the religious are full of accounts about them. These accounts have attracted the attention of researchers, and they hae arrived at diverse conclusions. Some of these hold that all the three aforesaid persons were the followers of Mahāvīra, while others are of opinion that they were the followers of the Buddha. A third line of thinking is that Śreṇika was at first a Buddhist and then he became a Jaina, and a fourth line would reverse the order, making him a Jaina first and then a Buddhist. Effort is being made in the following pages to collect and analyse the available material about him and to try to arrive at a conclusion.

First Acquaintance

The first acquaintance of Bimbisāra with the Buddha appears to have teken place long before the latter's enlightement, and shortly after his initiation into monkhood. The young monk, the Buddha, entered into the city of Rājagṛha in order to beg. His charming personality attracted the attention of thousands of men and women. In the words of the great poet Aśvaghoṣa,

> "People had their eyes arrested on eye-brows, forehead, face, eyes, body, hands, feet or the movement of the Buddha wherever they set first."[1]

While begging in Rājagṛha, the Buddha's eyes were firm. He walked keeping his vision restricted within a very short distance no longer than a *Jua.* He was mute. His pace was slow and restricted. His mind was under full control .[2]

Even. Bimbisāra saw this extraordinary monk from his palace and was deeply impressed. He wanted to talk with him. He met the monk on the Pāṇḍu (Ratnāgiri) hill in Rājagṛha.

Bimbisāra made a request to the Buddha to accept and enjoy his kingdom and other objects of pleasure. In declining the request, the Buddha explained to the king the evil effects of wordly pleasures and said,

> "I have courted monkhood not to win a kingdom but to attain the state of Buddhahood."

Said Bimbisāra,

> "Sir! May your wishes be fulfilled! When you become a Buddha, please pay a visit to this city."[3]

According to the Jaina sources, it appears that King Bimbisāra had his first acquaintance with Monk Anāthī. This meeting too bears a close resemblance with the other one just noted. Near the city of Rājagṛha, there was a garden named Maṇḍī-kukṣī which was full of many flowers and was exceedingly charming. One day, King Śreṇika came to that garden for holiday-making. He saw a great *nirgrantha* monk in that garden. He was seated under the shade of a luxuriant tree. His look was tender and impressive. He was young in age. He had endless peace stamped on his face. No sooner did the King of Magadha see him than the following words came out from his mouth,

> "What a fine complexion! How very beautiful! What an embodiment of serenity is that noble soul! How very lofty is his forgiveness, his renunciation, his detachment!"[4]

King Śreṇika came to the monk and said,

> "Monk! You look very young. How did you court monkhood in such a tender age when one is supposed to be enjoying the pleasures of life?"

"Oh King"! replied the monk, "I was anātha (helpless)."

The King—"Oh Monk! A man of such unusual fortune calling himself *anātha!* I shall be a parent unto thee. I request you to come back to wordly life and enjoy pleasures of life."

The Monk—"But, Oh King of Magadha, you are yourself *anātha* (helpless). How can you be a succour unto me?"

The King—"You say I myself am helpless? What do you mean?"

The monk started the account.

> "There was a city named Kauśāmbī. There lived my father Prabhūta-dhana-sañcaya who justified his name by the accumulation of a vast fortune. Beside, I was fortunate to have the pleasant company of my mother, wife and friends. Once I was severely affected by eye sore, and I ran high temperature with burning all over the body. It was terrific and unbearable. Top physicians and reputed charmers were called in, but they failed to give me any relief. Oh King! believe me, my father was prepared to give away his all for my sake, but still he could not relieve me of my pain. Such was the state of my helplessness. My mother looked at me with tearful eyes, but could not free me from the clutches of pain. Such was the state of my helplessness. No more effective were my own brothers and sisters to relieve me from pain. Such was the state of my helplessness. My wife stood by me all the while shedding tears on my chest, but even this was of no use. Such was the state of my helplessness."

Continuing, the great monk said to the King of Magadha,

> "Oh King! Finding myself helpless in all aspects, I placed myself under the protection of relatives, I made a resolve, 'If I am relieved of pain, I shall be a monk!' Next day, the pain subsided, and I became a monk."

A complete account of the conversation between Monk Anāthī and King Śreṇika is the subject-matter of Chapter 20 entitled *'Mahānirgranthīya'* in the *Uttarādhyayana Sūtra.* In this context, the illustrious monk narrated another type of helplessness which overtakes when a monk, duly initiated, does not abide by the code of conduct prescribed for a monk. Denouncing laxity in the strongest possible terms, the great monk said,

> "Oh King! Hear from me with full attention another type of helplessness in man. There are such weak souls who become lax in discipline even when they are the recipients of the benefit of the *nirgrantha* religion."[5]
>
> "Just as alkaline soil is unfertile, just as a debased coin has no currency, in the same manner, monks who use only the external marks of monkhood are worthless. Even a jewel made for glass may shine bright like a saphire, but to an expert it has no value. In the same manner, from one's external marks, one may look like a monk; but when the

monk uses only the external marks he does not carry any value in the eyes of wise people."[6]

"A dishonest person (monk) who makes use of omens, dreams, etc., and who had addiction for ceremonials, wastes his life on false and wonder-generating arts. When his sins fructify, he has no escape."[7]

"A dishonest person (monk) who does not discard anything including food brought for him, food bought for him, regular food and food to be searched, who is all-eating like fire, acquires life in hell."[8]

Having described the conduct of monks who did not observe restraint, Monk Anāthī said to King Śreṇika the following very outspoken words :

soccāṇa mehāvi subhāsīyaṁ imaṁ anuśāsanaṁ nānaguṇovaveyaṁ
maggaṁ kuśīlāna jahāya savvaṁ mahānīyanthānavae pahenaṁ

(Oh intelligent man ! Having heard this discourse full of merit and knowledge, and having discarded the path of bad men, follow the path chalked out by the *Tīrthaṅkaras).*

On hearing all this, King Śreṇika became immensely happy. Out of gratitude for the monk, he submitted with folded hands,

"Great Monk! You have given me a real insight into the state of helplessness. Fruitful is thy life. You are well-protected and with good friends; for, you are firmly fixed on the best of ways, the *Jina* way. I invited you to enjoy pleasures, I disturbed you in your meditation, for which I beg to be forgiven. I accept the direction given to me by you."[9]

Concluding this chapter, a couplet in the *Uttarādhyayana Sūtra* runs as follows :

"In this manner, the lion among kings bowed before the lion among monks, and with his family and kingsmen, he befriended the *nirgrantha* religion."[10]

Surprisingly enough, there is much common ground between the two accounts. In both the accounts, the King of Magadha is attracted by the grace and serenity of a young monk; in both the cases, he induces the monk to come back to wordly life, and in both the cases, the invitation evokes a similar reply. All this makes one inclined to think if it were not copied by one from the other. The garden named Mandikucchi has been rendered Maddakucchi in the Buddhist account.[11] Excepting for this chapter, monk Anāthī has not received attention anywhere else. It is not known for certain if he belonged to the order of Mahāvīra or to that *Pārśva.* It is not mentioned if he ever met Mahāvīra. It is probably on account of these reasons, Radhakumud Mookerjee has linked up the whole account of Mahāvīra on the basis of such expressions as 'Lion among monks' which could not apparently be an epithet of Monk Anāthī. He suggests that this was really a meeting between Mahāvīra and King Śreṇika.[12] Although the acceptance of such an interpretation would impart a great historical value to the meeting between the two, on a deeper consideration, there does not appear much basis for it. 'City of Kauśāmbī, 'Sresṭhī Prabūta-dhana-sañcaya,' 'eye-sore,' etc., are some important items in the account which would support that the monk referred to was some other than Mahāvīra.

Coming to differences in the two accounts, as per the Buddhist account, King Śreṇika merely requests the Buddha to look him up in his own city Rājagṛha after he became a Buddha; in the Jaina account, in contrast, the meeting with Monk Anāthī induced King Śreṇika to accept *nirgrantha* religion with the members of his family.

In his description of the second type of helplesseness, monk Anāthī administered severe lashes at the monks who relished in wordly pleasures. One explanation of this may be that thereby he tried to remove the king's patronage to these monks with lax habits. But the account is insufficient to indicate to which sect his reference was made, or to which sect Śreṇika himself belonged. As per the account, the exposure related to the lax *nirgrantha* monks, but the account does not indicate which particular sect of the *nirgranthas* had become so very lax at that time. If these were some monks of the order of *Pārśva,* then the event must be placed somewhere before Mahāvīra attained omniscience and came to Rājagṛha when the lax monks of the order of *Pārśva* dominated over the society.

IN THE TRIPIṬAKAS

In the *Tripiṭakas,* we have a few clear records of King Bimbisāra having embraced Buddhism. The early mention is in the *Vinaya Piṭaka* which states, in part, as follows :

> "Having initiated into monkhood a thousand *Jaṭilas* headed by Uruvelā Kāśyapa, the Buddha came to Rājagṛha. King Bimbisāra heard this news. He waited on him in the company of 12 lakh *Brāhmins* and householders, all residents of Magadha. At that time, the Buddha was at the Laṭṭhivana. He delivered a sermon for the benefit of King Bimbisāra and his party of 12 lakhs. On hearing the pious words of the Buddha, 11 lakh residents of Magadha had their pious spiritual eye opened on the same seat and

they realised that 'whatever is born is transcient.' The remaining one lakh people become lay followers."[13]

Being thus converted to the religion of the Buddha, Bimbisāra submitted,

> "*Bhante!* In my youth, when I was a prince, I cherished five desires which were : (a) may I be coronated as a king, (b) may the Buddha come to my kingdom, (c) may I have a chance to serve him, (d) may he deliver a sermon for my benefit and (e) may I know him. They have been fulfilled in due order, one after the other, till this day. May I now request you to accept food for tomorrow in the company of all the monks of your order."

So, on the following day, Bimbisāra, the King of Magadha, served food to the Buddha and his monks with his own hands, and dedicated a royal garden named Veṇuvana for the use of the monks of the order.[14]

The *Kūṭadanta Sutta* of the *Dīgha Nikāya* contains something which would give support to the above account. Said Kūṭadanta to other monks who were his companions and counsellors,

> "Why should not go to see *Śramaṇa* Gautama? Śreṇika, the King of Magadha, with his sons, wives and ministers, has taken shelter with the Buddha, and dedicated his life for him."[15]

A similar assertion is made by *Brāhmaṇa* Sonadaṇḍa in the *Sonadaṇḍa Sutta.*[16]

Beginning of Uposatha

There are many accounts indicating the relation between Bimbisāra on the one hand, and the Buddha and his monks on the other. The *Vinaya Piṭaka, Mahāvagga* has several accounts of the meeting between the Buddha and Bimbisāra. In the course of one of these meetings, Bimbisāra made a request as follows:

> "On the 8th, 14th and full-moon days of the fortnight, people of other faiths meet together and hold discourses. *Bhante!* I wonder why this cannot be introduced for our own order of monks."

The Buddha at once gave his approval to this request.

Prohibiting the Initiation of Soldiers

In another meeting with the Buddha, Bimbisāra requested the Buddha not to initiate into monkhood men of the armed personnel. At that time, a war was going on at the frontier of the kingdom for which men were sent to the frontier in order to fight. In order to escape from this to save their life, many got initiated into the order as monks. The request was granted by the Buddha.

Once King Bimbisāra assembled round him the representatives of 80,000 villages which were under his administration. He gave them necessary direction about social, political and economic matters. In the end, he added,

> "All that I have said so far pertain to this world. For a knowledge of things beyond this world, you should take shelter with the Buddha."

Thereafter, all of them came to the Gṛddhrakūṭa mountain and placed themselves under the protection of Buddha.[17]

It has been noticed elsewhere in this volume that King Bimbisāra engaged the famous royal physician Jīvaka Kaumārabhṛtya for the treatment of the Buddha and his monks. There are also records of King Bimbisāra having erected shelters for the residence of the monks and the nuns of the order.[18]

According to the *Peṭāvatthu Aṭṭhakathā* King Śreṇika practised *uposatha* on the 8th and the 14th days of the fortnight and also on the new moon and full-moon days.[19]

The Buddha's Appearance in Prison

According to the *Amitāyurdhyāna Sutta* of the Mahāyāna Buddhism, when in the last part of his life, Śreṇika Bimbisāra was lodged in prison. Monk Moggalāna appeared in his cell by dint of his supernatural powers and gave out a discourse for him. While in prison, Bimbisāra had desired this, and this desire was fulfilled. Vaidehī, who was Bimbisāra's queen, was imprisoned in another cell. It is on record that at her prayer, the Buddha visited her in the cell.[20]

According to the *Dhamamapda Aṭṭhakathā,* on accepting on invitation from Mahālī, who was an emissary of the Licchavīs, the Buddha turned in the direction of Vaiśālī, King Bimbisāra came to see him off till the bank of the Gaṅgā. On this occasion, he constructed a road from Rājagṛha upto the bank of the Gaṅgā decorated it with flowers, and had guest houses erected all along the road. The Buddha took his seat on the boat and the boat sailed. Bimbisāra held the boat and followed it inside water till he was deep into water upto his chin. Then he turned his back. Till the Buddha came back from Vaiśālī, he remained camped on the bank of the Gaṅgā. After the Buddha's return, he came back to Rājagṛha with him.[21]

Lalitavistara records that for the Buddha and his monks, travelling by boat was made free of charge for all times.

Awakening of Pakkusati

The *Aṭṭhakathā* of the *Dhātuvibhaṅga Sutta* of the *Majjhima Nikāya* as follows :

Once some traders from Texila came to the court of King Bimbisāra. In the course of converastion, they spoke highly of the qualities of their king, Pakkusāti. In age as well as in qualities, they said, he was similar to King Bimbisāra himself. Soon a friendship was established between the two kings. Traders from Taxila were exempted from the customs at Rājagṛha, as traders from Rājagṛha were accorded a similar privilege at Taxila. Pakkusati sent five colourful, printed shawls as gifts for King Bimbisāra. In return, King Bimbisāra had scribed on a golden plate a hymn to the Buddha and sent it to Pakkusati. Pakkusati came to Rājagṛha all along on foot in order to see the Buddha and entered into his order as a monk.

After his Death

The *Janavasabha Sutta* of the *Dīgha Nikāya* gives a description of Bimbisāra's life after death. Said Ānanda,

> "*Bhante!* You have narrated the life after death of many a follower from many lands. Śreṇika Bimbisāra was a pious man, who was under the protection of the Buddha, the spiritual king. Will you kindly state which life did he attain after death, in which world was he reborn?"

On hearing this request from Ānanda, the Buddha went into a trance. He concentrated his soul power and strove to decipher the joys and sorrows Bimbisāra was then passing through. Thereon a *Yakṣa* appeared and said,

> "I am Janavasabha, I am Janavasabha. I am Janavasabha. I am Bimbisāra."

Then the Buddha came to know all about him and said to Ānanda,

> "Bimbisāra has become a *Yakṣa* named Janavasabha."

According to the *Ṭherī Gāthā,* Queen Khemā, .wife of Bimbisāra, joined the Buddha's order as a nun, and she was named by the Buddha as the wisest among the wise.

IN THE ĀGAMAS

All the above accounts are clear in themselves. If we have to arrive at a conclusion exclusively on their basis, we have to accept that Śreṇika Bimbisāra was a follower of the Buddha. But when we penetrate into the world of the *Āgamas,* we have a much more vigorous and forceful evidence on hand to suggest that King Bimbisāra was a Jaina.

In Touch with Mahāvīra

It has been stated above that King Śreṇika got a direction from the *nirgrantha* monk Anāthī about religion. The *Daśāśruatkṣandha* contains a brilliant account of his direct relation with Mahāvīra and the great esteem in which he held him. The account is as follows :

> In that period, at that time, there was a city named Rājagṛha. There was a garden named Guṇaśila outside the city. Śreṇika was the ruling monarch. One day, seated on his cushion in his spiritual chamber, he sent for his officers, and after they had come, he said to them,
>
> "Of beloved of the gods! You go outside the city of Rājagṛha to all rest houses, gardens, workshops, hill temples, public halls, hill water stores, shops, restaurants, quarries, wood shops, coir shops, etc., and tell their owners, 'Oh beloved of the gods! King Śreṇika Bimbisāra so orders, when *Śramaṇa Bhagavān* Mahāvīra comes to this city, you give him shelter, cushion, bed, etc., and convey the news of his arrival to the king.'"

The officers carried out the orders of the king.

In that period, at that time, *Śramaṇa Bhagavān* Mahāvīra came to Rājagṛha. People met in a congregation. The above-mentioned owners of rest houses, etc., met together to hold discussion, and then they came to Śreṇika in a group and said, "Your Majesty! *Bhagavān* Mahāvīra, the founder of religion, *Tīrthaṅkara,* all-knowing and all-seeing, whom you were keen to see, the mention of whose name and face pleases you, is at the Guṇaśīla caitya."

On hearing this news, King Śreṇika was delighted and happy. Coming down from his throne, he moved seven or eight steps forward, and from there, he paid his homage and obeisance for *Bhagavān* Mahāvīra. Then he profusely rewarded those people who had brought the good news, sent for his army commanders and keepers of royal vehicles and ordered them to make ready the fourfold army and to decorate all the chariots for the spiritual mission to pay a visit to *Bhagavān* Mahāvīra.

Having done all this, he came to Queen Celanā and said, "Oh beloved of the gods! Highly fruitful is the visit to the *Bhagavān* Arihanta. So, let us go, pay homage and obeisance to *Śramaṇa Bhagavān* Mahāvīra, welcome him in our midst and adore him. He is the giver of the greatest goods, the greatest bliss. He is even superior to Gods and immensely wise. Let us go to him and worship him. This will be good for us in this life, and also in the next life, for our happiness, for our welfare, for our liberation, till for terminating the bondage of rebirth."

On hearing all this, Queen Celanā became immensely delighted and happy. She took her bath and put on costly garments and jewellery. With King Śreṇika, she sat on the special chariot that was to carry them to *Bhagavān* Mahāvīra. They arrived at Guṇaśīla caitya. Taking precedence, she stood in front of *Bhagavān* Mahāvīra, moved round him thrice and bowed before him. Enquiries were made about health and well-being, and then the king taking precedence over her, the royal couple resumed their seats to attend the sermon.

Bhagavān Mahāvīra delivered his sermon. After the sermon was over, people went away. Some of the monks of the order who were immensely impressed by the display of the wealth of King Śreṇika, had a thought as follows in their mind,

> "How very fortunate must be King Bhambhasāra who has a queen like Celanā and a kingdom like Magadha. If our austere penances have any effect, we would like to have fine wordly pleasures like this."

Seeing the great fortune of Queen Celanā, some of the nuns thought in their mind,

> "How very fortunate must be Queen Celanā! If our austere penances have any effect, we would like to have a fine wordly life like this."

By dint of his supreme knowledge, *Bhagavān* Mahāvīra came to know about the thinking of these monks and nuns. He collected them round him and apprised them of the evil consequences of this kind of thinking. Thereon the monks and nuns confessed their guilt.

The above account indicated not only the great esteem in which Śreṇika Bhambhasāra held Mahāvīra, but it also indicates in all probability that this was their first meeting. It is explicit in the account that the queen took precedence, apparently to introduce the king to *Bhagavān* Mahāvīra, and thereafter, while taking their seats, she yielded the precedence to the king. According to the Jaina tradition, in his early life, Śreṇika was the follower of some heretical creed, but Celanā imbibed Mahāvīra's religion in her parental home. It was, therefore, in the fitness of things that she introduced the king, as in a first meeting. The sort of thinking that the monks and nuns had about the great wealth and fortune of King Śreṇika and Queen Celanā was also a natural thing for a first meeting.

It has been recorded in the *Anuttarovavai-dasao* that King Śreṇika called on *Bhagavān* Mahāvīra, and, having attended his sermon, he made the following submission,

> "*Bhante!* Among your 14,000 monks, Indrabhūti and others, who, in your considered opinion, performs maximum penances and exhausts *karma* fetters to the highest extent?"

Said *Bhagavān* Mahāvīra,

> "Śreṇika! Monk Dhanya has maximum penances and maximum *karma* exhaustion to his credit."

The king was delighted to hear this. He came to Monk Dhanya and said,

> "Oh beloved of the gods! You are fortunate. You have the highest merit to your credit."

From there, he came back to Mahāvīra, paid his homage and obeisance, and went back to his palace.[22]

Chapter 13 of the *Nayadhammakahao* has an account of Śreṇika's visit to Mahāvīra with his household and retinue.

Initiation of the Princes

On the solemn occasion of the initiation of Meghakumāra into monkhood, King Śreṇika showered praise on the religion of the *nirgranthas* in the following words :

> "*Nirgrantha* religion is based on truth, is foremost and complete; it is a way to liberation; it transcends all logic and is unprecedented. Its fulfilment is as difficult as the chewing of iron chocolates."[23]

Nandīsena, another son of Śreṇika, was initiated into monkhood in one of Mahāvīra's congregations.[24]

There is on record that once King Śreṇika declared in the presence of the members of the royal household, feudatory kings and ministers that he would not prevent any one who desired to be initiated into monkhood by *Bhagavān*

Mahāvīra from doing so.[25] It is further stated that being inspired by this proclamation, 23 sons of Śreṇika, Jāli, Mayāli and others,[26] and 13 queens, Nandā, Nandamatī, and others,[27] were initiated at the hands of Mahāvīra.

Going to Hell and Subsequent Tīrthaṅkarahood

Once Śreṇika was present at the congregation of *Bhagavān* Mahāvīra. Just then a leper came and sat beside him. Meanwhile, Mahāvīra sneezed, when the leper remarked,

> "You die."

He was followed by Śreṇika who sneezed when the leper commented,

> "You live."

The third to sneeze was Abhayakumāra when the leper commented,

> "Live or die."

And then sneezed the great butcher, Kālaśaurika, when the leper's curt comment was,

> "Neither live nor die."

On hearing these irrelevant and uncalled for comments of the leper, Śreṇika's soldiers wanted to put the man under arrest; but they failed to do so because the fellow had already disappeared. When Śreṇika requested Mahāvīra to explain the singnificance of this mysterious episode, the latter observed,

> "This leper was a god, and whatever he has observed is perfectly correct. He asked me to die because liberation lies ahead of me. He asked you to live because you are marked for hell hereafter. As for Abhayakumāra, he is in human existence in this life (the most coveted even of the gods), and, besides, he is a pious man. When he goes out from here, he goes to heaven. So, it is immaterial whether he lives or dies. This explains his comment about him, 'Live or die!' The great butcher, Kālaśaurika, has a miserable life on this earth, and hereafter he goes to hell, which is equally bad. So, he said to him, 'Neither live nor die'."
>
> "*Bhante!* Does every person who worships thee get this sort of result?"

Said Mahāvīra,

> "Oh king! It's not like that. But because of your excessive love for hunting, you have already tied a life in hell. But the outcome of worshipping me will be that, just as you see, I am the last of a group of 24 *Tīrthaṅkaras,* so, immediately on coming out of your infernal life, you will be the first of the next group of 24 *Tīrthaṅkaras* named Padmanābha in the new era."[28]

On hearing this great news, Śreṇika was immensely delighted and happy. Śreṇika enquired if there was a way whereby he could escape life in hell. Said Mahāvīra,

> "If you can make the *Brāhmaṇa* lady Kapilā to give alms and the great butcher Kālaśaurika to give up animal slaughter, then you may escape hell."

Śreṇika sent his request to both Kapilā and Kālaśaurika, but it was entertained by none. When Kapilā was forced to give alms, she said,

> "It's not I but the king who is making the offer."

When Kālaśaurika refused the request, he was thrown into the well where he produced 500 buffaloes out of clay and slaughtered them.[29] The implication was that these two were as impossible as Śreṇika's averting life in hell.

The Jaina literature has on record many occasions to remind one of the meeting beween *Bhagavān* Mahāvīra and King Śreṇika. In this connection, there is an interesting episode which also involves the royal-monk Prasannacandra. Prasannacandra was the King of Potanapura. He was initiated into monkhood by Mahāvīra himself. One day, at Rājagṛha, as the congregation met, Prasannacandra stood in meditation outside the paṇḍāl. When Śreṇika's party arrived there, his army commander Durmukha pointed to the royal monk and remarked.

> "This man is a hypocrite and unenlightened too. He has entrusted his kingdom to a young prince who is in the prime of life, and has himself escaped to be a monk. His ministers are conspiring against him in collusion with the enemy kings and have already started usurping his kingdom."

These words reached the ears of the royal monk as he stood in meditation.

He felt a confusion within himself. He had within him a feeling of anger against his enemies and ministers.

Śreṇika made a formal bow to the royal monk and hastened to the presence of Mahāvīra. Coming there, he put the follow-question,

> "*Bhante*! If Prasannacandra, who is standing here outside in meditation, dies just now, what state does he attain?"

—"Nineth hell."

Śreṇika was taken competely aback.

After a short gap of time, he asked again,

"*Bhante*! If he dies now, then?"

—"He goes to *Sarvārtha Siddha;* the above of the Liberated Souls at the crest of the sphere, which is the highest form of divine existence. But, King, there is nothing to be surprised at this. The main determinants of his future state are the states of his mind from time to time. At the moment when you put your first question to me, he was in the midst of a profound mental conflict. By the time you put your last question, he had regained full self-control and was busy with the purification of self."

As Śreṇika was having the conversation with Mahāvīra, the royal monk standing outside in meditation attained omniscience. Heavenly drums were beaten in the sky. Seeing this glory of the spiritual governance of the *Arhats,* Śrenika felt a delightful surprise.[30]

According to the *Caupanna Mahāpurisa Cariyam,* one day Indra praised Śreṇika in the following manner,

> "At this moment, there is no one on the earth as pious and devoted as King Śreṇika."

Having heard these words of Indra, one god came down to this earth in order to hold the test, but when he found that Śreṇika was very firm in his devotion to the *nirgrantha* religion, he was very happy. While taking leave, this god bestowed on Śreṇika a very precious eighteen-fold necklace which later became the cause of the *Rathamūsala* and the *Mahāśilā-Kaṇṭaka* wars.

According to the Digambara belief, the first serman of Mahāvīra was delivered on the Vipulācala mountain at Rājagṛha on the first day of the dark half of *Śrāvaṇa.* Śreṇika, the king of Magadha, and his family attended that historic sermon. King Śreṇika and Queen Celanā were the foremost among the lay followers of Mahāvīra.[31]

A JAINA OR A BUDDHIST

If one depends wholly on the Jaina sources, one will hardly have occasion for doubt that Śreṇika was not a staunch follower of the *nirgranthas.* But when the Buddhist and the Jaina sources are placed side by side, the attention tends to be bifurcated. One finds it difficult to be dogmatic if he was one or the other. But in looking at the historical value of the above accounts, one is bound to find that many of these were later interpolations. Thus, for instance, Rhys Davids has written, "The *Kūṭadanta Sutta* appears to be fictitious. There is no proof anywhere to support that there was a man named Kūtadanta" (translated from Hindi).[32]

Edward Thomas has expressed the following opinion :

> "The importance of the first meeting between the Buddha and Śreṇika is no more than a fiction. This account has taken diverse forms in diverse texts. There is nothing of this sort in the older Pāli texts." (translated form Hindi)."[33]

A review of the Jaina sources too would place some of them in the category of fiction. But then sometimes it is very difficult to draw a straight line between fiction and reality. When we think that a particular account is fictitious, that thinking may itself be rooted in fiction. Under the circumstances, a consideration of fiction or reality does not take us to a sure enough ground.

In this respect, the only dependable clue may be a consideration about the time when Mahāvīra, Gautama Buddha and Śreṇika lived. This point has been already discussed in and earlier chapter wherein it has been shown that the contemporaneity of Mahāvīra after his attainment of omniscience and Śreṇika lasted for 13 years, but the same in the case of the Buddha after his attainment of the Buddhahood lasted for only 3 years. And during these 3 years too, Mahāvīra was still alive. Mahāvīra's first monsoon retreat after the attainment of omniscience was spent at Rājagṛha. At the commencement of this period, Śreṇika courted the view of equanimity[34] and Abhayakumāra and many others courted the vows of the householders.[35] It has already been stated in the account of Monk Anāthī that Śreṇika courted the *nirgrantha* religion. Maybe, this account came to assume a proper form here. There is no occasion for doubt that a close link came to be established between Mahāvīra and Śreṇika in the very first year of the attainment of omniscience by the former. As an outcome of this very intimate relation, Śreṇika gave leave to his queens and princes to join Mahāvīra's order as monks and nuns, and the king himself organised necessary celebrations for each. Both Meghakumāra and Nandīsena were initiated into monkhood during this very first year.[36] It is quite likely that because of this extraordinary devotion of Śreṇika, Mahāvīra very often spent his monsoons there.

By his very nature, Śreṇika was a man of religious disposition. Before the Buddha had come into prominence, Mahāvīra had been a frequent visitor to Rājagṛha. It cannot be conceived that in a situation like this, Śreṇika would not become a follower of Mahāvīra. And it is equally difficult to conceive that in the last four years of his life, Śreṇika would give up the *nirgrantha* religion, particularly when Mahāvīra was still alive, and court the religion of the Buddha, the more so when many of his queens and princes were in the order of Mahāvīra as monks and nuns. Dalsukh Malvanīya's suggestion that Śreṇika courted Buddhism because of Mahāvīra's prediction about him that he would go to hell after death is not at all convincing.[37] Had it been so, then, why should Mahāvīra reveal at the same time that on completion of his life in hell, Śreṇika would be a *Tīrthaṅkara* like himself and be named Padmanābha?

The *Mahāvaṁsa* which is a Buddhist text states, in part, as follows :

> The Buddha was senior to Bimbisāra by five years. The Buddha attained Buddhahood at the 35th year of his life and came to Rājagṛha. Bimbisāra ascended the throne at the age of 15. In the 16th year of his reign, *i.e.*, when he was 31, he placed himself under the protection of the Buddha. Then during the next 37 years of the Buddha's life, Bimbisāra was still alive. The Buddha passed away in the 8th year of the reign of Ajātaśatru.[38]

The record of *Mahāvaṁsa* is not correct. This has been discussed threadbare in an earlier chapter on the determination of time.

There is a further proof of Śreṇika's intimate link with the *nirgrantha* religion which is that the number of queens and princes who were converted by the Buddha was insignificant compared with those converted by Mahāvīra.

Evidence is also available to suggest that Śreṇika was a Jaina by birth. It has been said about his father that he belonged to the order of *Pārśva* and had courted the vow of equanimity and also the the 'lesser vows.'[39] According to Dr. Kāśī Prasāda Jaiswal, Śreṇika's ancestors came from Kāśi to Magadha.[40] He has further suggested that his was the same family in which once *Tīrthaṅkara Pārśva* had been born. On the basis of this source, it is plausible to think that Jainism was his family religion. According to some Jaina view, though Śreṇika was a Jaina by birth, he became hostile to it during his banishment. It is quite likely that during this period of his banishment, he became the admirer of *Śramaṇas* with lax morals, of which there is hint in a the account of monk Anāthī. All things considered, it was natural for Śreṇika to be a Jaina when his ancestors were Jainas and his father was a Jaina.

During the last four years of his life, Śreṇika had a link with the Buddha and his order of monks; but this does not appear to be anything more than a relationship of friendliness and mutual appreciation.

There is a strong proof in support of this view which is that Rājagṛha happened to be the main centre of activity of Mahāvīra and his order of monks. Mahāvīra spent 14 monsoons in this city. On many occasions, he spent time immediately preceding the commencement of monsoons in that city. Even from an earlier period, people of that city belonged to the sect of *Pārśva*. Under the circumstances, there should be no doubt that Rājagṛha became the principal centre of activity of Mahāvīra and his order of monks mainly because they could count on the ruling monarch among their principal followers.

The main centre for the Buddha and his monks was not Rājagṛha but Śrāvastī. Jetavana of Anāthapiṇḍika and Pūrvarāma of Viśākhā Mṛgāramātā where the Buddha and his monks often lived were both located at Śrāvastī. Prasenajit who happened to be a great follower of the Buddha reigned in that city. The Buddha spent 26 monsoons there as against only 5 at Rājagṛha. Mahāvīra spent only one monsoon at Śrāvastī. It is worth while to note that just as Mahāvīra predicted a future *Tīrthaṅkarahood* for Śreṇika, so did the Buddha predict a future Buddhahood for Prasenajit.[41]

On the whole, therefore, it appears certain that Śreṇika was a follower of Mahāvīra and Prasenajit was a follower of the Buddha.

Regarding Śreṇika, Vincent A. Smith has expressed the following opinion :

> "He appears to have been a Jaina in religion, and sometimes is coupled by Jaina tradition with Aśoka's grandson Bamprati, as a notable patron of the creed of Mahāvīra."[42]

Further, he writes,

> "Being related through his mother to the reigning King of Videha, Magadha and Aṅga, he was in a position to gain official patronage for his teaching and is recorded to have been in personal touch with both Bimbisāra and Ajātaśatru who seem to have followed his doctrine."[43]

About the Name–Bhimbisāra

Bhimbisāra, etc.—Various words like Bhambhasāra, Bhimbhasāra, Bhimbhisāra, etc., have been used in the Jaina *Āgamas* as the names of Śreṇika.[44] In later *Saṁskṛta Prākṛta* texts the name more frequently used has been Bhambhasāra.[45] bhambha, Bhimbha and bhimbhi, these three words are accepted as synonyms for a musical instrument called *behrī* (cf. *Pāyiya-Sadda-mahāṇṇavo,* pp. 794, 807. In diverse texts, the interpretation that has been given to this name of Śreṇika is that during the outbreak of fire at the palace once, while other princes ran away with diverse objects, Śreṇika, to whom the bhambha alone stood important as the royal insignia ran away with it. Hence, he was given the name Bhambhasāra.[46] According to Vijayendra Sūri 'Bhambhasāra' was the only correct name, all others being incorrect.[47] This explanation is far from satisfactory. The *Āgamas* have used all the froms, and, therefore, even if the contention of Vijayendra Sūri be accepted, still it has to be said that all these words, the of bhambha, bhimbha, etc., are associated with Śreṇika. Being used as proper nouns, they refer to the same person. There can be no question of the proper nouns used by the monks to be incorrect. In support of his view Vijayendra Sūri has quoted the following line from the *Thānāṅga Vṛtti,*

bhambha tti dhakkā sā sāro yasya sā bhambhāsār

But it appears that he has quoted this evidence out of a faulty outlook in order to support his own viewpoint. For, the same text from which he has quoted his also the following line,

bhimbhi tti dhakkā sā sāro yasya sa tathā bhimbhisārh.[48]

The excerpt that is being discussed here is distinctly as follows :

seṇie rāyā bhimhisāre.

Commentator Abhayadeva Sūri has clarified the point as follows:

tena kumāratve pradīpanake jayadhakkā gehānniṣkāsitātatha pitrā bhimbhisāra ukt.[49]

Dr. Pichel too has accepted 'Bhimbhisāra' to be the correct word.[50]

Bimbisāra—In the Buddhist tradition, the name of Śreṇika that has gained acceptance is Bimbisāra. 'Bimbi' stands for gold. He was given the name Bimbisāra because of his golden complexion.[51] According to the Tibetan tradition, the name of Bimbisāra's mother was Bimbi from which the son took the name Bimbisāra.[51]

The words 'Bhimbhisāra' and 'Bimbisāra' come very near to each other. This may be a very important point for investigation. It may be that the two words are identical, but they are pronounced differently in different vocabulary.

About the Name-Śreṇika

The name 'Sreṇika' has been equally used in both the Jaina and the Buddhist traditions. In both the traditions, it has been mostly used as a compound, 'Śreṇika Bhimbhisāra' in the Jaina tradition, and 'Śreṇika Bimbisāra' in the Buddhist tradition. There is also much similarity in the etymological meaning of the word 'Śreṇika.' According to the Jaina interpretation, he was named Śreṇika because he established 'śreṇi' or 'clans.'[53]

According to the Buddhist interpretation, he was named Śreṇika becuase he was made the overlord of sixteen clansby his father.[54] Both the traditions have recounted 18 clans.[55] Even the names of the clans bear a striking similarity between the two in many respects. The *Jambūdīpa-paññatti* which is a Jaina *Āgama,* gives details about 9 clans named Nārus[56] and another 9 named Kārus.[57] In the Buddhist tradition, in contrast, we do not get these names in a consistent form. The names given in the Mahāvastu[58] bear much resemblance with those given in the *Jambudīpa-paññatti,* but they have been 30 in number. Basing on diverse texts, R.C. Majumdar has compiled a list of 27 clans, but in doing so, he has totally overlooked the Jaina source book *Jambūdīpa-paññatti.* Otherwise, he would not have written that it was difficult to say that what these 18 clans were.[59] Some scholars are of opinion that he was called Śreṇika because of his vast army *(Senā),* or because the name of his family line was Seṇiya.[60]

Father's Name

According to the Śvetāmbara tradition of the Jainas, Prasenajit was the name of Śreṇika's father.[61] In the *Uttarapurāṇa* of the Digambaras, his father's names has been stated to be Kuṇika,[62] which apparently is not correct. According to the *Bṛhad-kathā-koṣa* by a Digambara *Ācārya,* Hariṣeṇa, (story 55), the name of Śreṇika's father has been stated to be Upaśreṇika.[63] *Śrīmad Bhāgavat Purāṇa* has called Śreṇika as Vidhisāra, and his father as Kṣetrajña.[64] Elsewhere we find his name as Bhaṭṭiya, Mahāpadam, Hemajit, Kṣetrojā, Kṣetprojā, etc.[65]

Queens of Śreṇika

In the Jaina texts we find the names of 25 queens of Śreṇika. Of these, 13 names, Nandā and others, and another 10 names, Kālī, Sukālī and others, are contained in the Jaina text *Antagada-dasao.* All of them joined Mahāvīra's order of nuns after the death of Śreṇika. The *Daśasūyakhandha* has described Celaṇā as the Empress. The *Niśītha Cūrṇī* has the name of Apatagandhā as the queen of Śreṇika, but this name is not very well-known.[66] The *Nayadhamma-kahao* gives a detailed description of Dhāriṇī another queen of Śreṇika.[67]

According to the *Vinaya Piṭaka,* King Bimbisāra had 500 wives.[68] Once Jīvaka Kaumāra Bhṛtya, the royal physician, cured the king of fistula by a single application of ointment because of which the king rewarded him with as many ornaments as his 500 women could use at a time. From this, however, it is difficult to state that these 500 women were the queens of Śreṇika.

According to the Buddhist view, Kośalā Devī, the sister of King Prasenajit was Śreṇika's principal consort. As a dowry from this marriage, Bimbisāra got a village which yielded him a revenue of one lakh *karṣapaṇas.*[69]

Queen Kṣemā was a princess from Madra. She was proud of her beauty. She received spiritual inspiration under proper guidance, and was initiated at the hands of the Buddha.[70]

A prositute named Padmāvatī who hailed from Ujjain has also been called to be a wife (concubine?) of Śreṇika.[71]

There is a reference in the *Amitāyurdhyāna Sūtra,* the Vaidehī Vāsavī was a queen of Bimbisāra.

About the queens of Bimbisāra, the Jaina and the Buddhist sources are widely apart from each other. It appears that Bimbisāra had many queens. Different traditions have given different importance to different queens depending on their relations. It is quite likely that some queens have figured in the two traditions under different names.

Princess (Sons of Śreṇika)

Śreṇika's successor was Prince Kūṇika, also called Ajātaśatru. The Buddhist tradition names only some of these princes. Abhayakumāra has been called the son of a concubine named Padmāvatī.[72] Another prostitute Ambāpālī gave birth to a son for Bimbisāra who was named Vimala Kodamna. At a later period, he became a Buddhist monk.[73] Another son of Bimbisāra named Śīlavā (Śīlavat) also became a Buddhist monk, and later an *Arhat.*[74] Bimbisāra had another son named Jayasena.[75]

In the Jaina tradition, Kūṇika apart, there is a consistent account of many other princes. The *Aṇttarovavāyīya* gives the following ten names :

> 1. Jālī, 2. Mayālī, 3. Uvayālī, 4. Purimaṣeṇa, 5. Vāriṣeṇa, 6. Dihadanta, 7. Laṭṭhadanta, 8. Vehalla, 9. Vehāyasa and 10. Abhayakumāra. Of these, the first seven were by Queen Dhariṇī, Vehalla and Vehāyasa by Celanā and Abhyakumāra by Nandā.[76]

Elsewhere in the same *Āgama,* the following names are given of 13 princes :

> 1. Dīhaseṇa, 2. Mahāseṇa, 3. Laṭṭhadanta, 4. Gūḍhadanta, 5. Śuddhadanta, 6. Halla, 7. Duma, 8. Dumaseṇa, 9. Mahādumaseṇa, 10. Sīha, 11. Sīhaseṇa, 12. Mahāsīhaseṇa and 13. Puññaseṇa.

According to *Niriyāvalikā,* the following ten princes were born of Kālī, Sukālī and other queens of Śreṇika :

1. Kālakumāra, 2. Sukālakumāra, 3. Mahākālakumāra, 4. Kaṇhakumāra, 5. Sukaṇhakumāra, 6. Mahākaṇhakumāra, 7. Vīrakaṇhakumāra, 8. Rāmakaṇhakumāra, 9. Senakaṇhakumāra and 10. Mahāseṇa-kanhakumāra.

Two princes, *viz.,* Meghakumāra and Nadīsena have been very famous in the Jaina tradition.

The Jaina *āgamas* not only mention the names of the aforesaid princes, they give an appropriate places their biological sketches in very consistent forms. Of these, ten, Kālakumāra and others, died in the *Mahāśilākaṇṭaka* war and the remaining princes became monks.

Ajātaśatru Kūṇika

Like Śreṇika, even Kūṇika (Ajātaśatru) enjoys a respectable position in both the Jaina and the Buddhist traditions. Both claim him as a close follower, and both come forward with evidence in support of this claim. According to the Buddhist tradition, the *Sāmañjaphala Sutta* deals with the first meeting between the Buddha and Ajātaśatru. According to the same text, during this meeting, he took the protection of the Buddha, the *Dharma* and the *Saṅgha.* One important example of his great devotion to the Buddha that has been put forward is that he erected a vast *stūpa* on the bones of the Buddha. So, goes the account that when the last remains of the Buddha, bones and ashes after the funeral, were going to be distributed, at that time, Ajātaśatru, too, sent the following message to the Mallas at Kuśīnārā,

> "The Buddha was a *Kṣatriya.* I am also a *Kṣatriya.* Of his last remains, I must also have a share."

On the advice of the *vipra* Droṇa, he got a portion of the bones over which he erected the *stūpa.*[77]

According to the *Sāmañjaphala Sutta,* during a fullmoon night in the month of *Kārtika,* Ajātaśatru came to know of the Buddha from the royal physician Jīvaka Kumāra Bhṛtya, and during the same night, followed by his 500 queens seated on 500 elephants, he met the Buddha. It is difficult to say when he first met Mahāvīra; but all the accounts suggest an old acquaintance between the two in which Ajātaśatru held Mahāvīra in the highest esteem. The *Uvavai,* which is the first *Upāṅga* of the Jainas, throws light on the relation between Mahāvīra nd Kūṇika. The same text contains beautiful description about the city of Campā and also about Kūṇika's kingdom. Regarding the great esteem in which Kūṇika held Mahāvīra. It is stated therein, in part, as follows :

"He had an officer to report about the daily routine of Mahāvīra to him. He was very lavishly paid. His duty was to report to the king about the day-to-day affairs of Mahāvīra. The officer had a vast supporting field staff through whom he collected all the information about Mahāvīra and reported it to the king."[78]

The *Uvavai Sutta* has a detailed and illuminating discussion on Mahāvīra's arrival at Campā and the honour shown to him by Kūṇika. Had the researchers been attracted to this account, it would have been as useful a material as the account in the *Sāmañjaphala Sutta.* The researchers have, in general, neglected the *Āgamas* totally and have relied exclusively on the *Tripiṭakas*. The views expressed by the researchers could have been more balanced and useful if they had used both the sources of information for the purpose of their investigation. It is more particularly so about Ajātaśatru Kūṇika of whom the account in the *Tripiṭakas* is scrappy, and not as much detailed as the account in the *Āgamas.*

The meeting between Mahāvīra and Kūṇika took place at Campā. Wandering through village to village in the company of 14,000 monks and 36,000 nuns, Mahāvīra reached the suburb of that city. The officer on Mahavīra's daily routine was delighted and happy when he got the information about his coming. He took his bath, put on clean clothes, decorated himself in light-weight high-cost ornaments and moved out of his residence. Passing through the heart of the city of Campā, he came to the court of Kūṇika, son of Bhambhasāra, wished victory to the king and submitted, in part, as follows :

> "Wandering through village to village, *Śramaṇa Bhagavān* Mahāvīra, whom you wanted to meet, whose sight is so much coveted by you, and whose name and family line are a source of delight to your ears, has arrived in the subrub of this city, Campā, and the party is about to reach the Pūrṇabhadra caitya very soon. May this news be a source of delight for your majesty."

On hearing this news from the officer, Kūṇika, the son of Bhambhasāra, became very happy. His face and eyes beamed with joy. In a hurry, he got up from the throne and removed his slippers. He took out the five emblems of kingship, sword, umbrella, crown, foot wear and camara. He retained only a single piece of cloth on his person. Then with folded hands he moved seven or eight steps in the direction of Mahāvīra, contracted his left leg and placed the right one on the ground. Thrice he touched the ground with his forehead. Then rising slightly, he folded his hands, with which he touched his head, and bowed in the usual *'namotthuṇam'* posture, saying,

"May my homage and obeisance reach *Śramaṇa Bhagavān* Mahāvīra, who is an *Ādikara,* a *Tīrathaṅkara,* till entitled to the seat of the Liberated Souls, who is my spiritual guide and *ācārya.* From here I send my homage and obeisance to him to where he is at this moment. May the *Bhagavān* view me from there!"[79]

Having paid his homage and obeisance the king again sat on the throne. He rewarded the officer with 1,08,000 gold coins and said,

"Please send me information as soon as the *Bhagavān* reaches the Pūrṇabhadra caitya."

Decorated with a thousand rays, the sun rose in the sky. In that serene atmosphere of the dawn, *Bhagavān* Mahāvīra stepped into the Pūrṇabhadra caitya. He set up his camp there and lived in restraint and penance. All over the city of Campā, in the parks and squares, and at the confluence of roads, people said,

"*Bhagavān* Mahāvīra has come to our city. He is staying at the Pūrṇabhadra caitya. The mention of his name and that of his family line give a great merit, what to speak of the merit in seeing him with our own eyes. Oh beloved of the Gods ! Let us go and pay homage and obeisance to *Bhagavān* Mahāvīra. That will be for our good, and for our happiness in this life and in the next one."

Thereon the people took their bath, put on clean clothes and decorated themselves with garlands. Then, some on horse back, some on elephants, some on palanquins, but the largest majority on foot, started on their way to see *Bhagavān* Mahāvīra.

The officer in charge of Mahāvīra's routine communicated this happy news to the king. This time, the king gave him a reward of 12,50,000 gold coins.[80] Then Kūṇika, son of Bhambhasāra, sent for his army commanders and said,

"Decorate the best of elephants and make them ready for me. Mobilise the four-fold army for a full procession. Prepare the chariots for the queens, Subhadrā and others. Clean the city of Campā both from inside and outside. Erect platforms at various places for the use of the members of the public. I shall go to pay me homage and obeisance to *Bhagavān* Mahāvīra."

All preparations were ready as per the king's order. The king sat on the best of elephants. Subhadrā and other queens took their seats on the chariots. Followed by the magnificient fourfold army, the king set out to see *Bhagavān* Mahāvīra and pay his homage and obeisance.[81] Passing through the heart of Campā, the royal party reached the vicinity of the Pūrṇabhadra caitya. As the superhuman marks announcing the presence of a *Tīrthaṅkara* came with in his sight from a distance, he gave up the elephant, and discarded the five emblems of kingship. From there, walking, he came within the august presence of *Bhagavān* Mahāvīra, and bowed before him in due manner. Then he took his seat, worshipping the *Bhagavān* with his mind, words and body.[82]

Bhagavān Mahāvīra gave out his sermon to the assembly, and he spoke in *Ardha-Māgadhī* language. In the course of the sermon, he said,

> "There is the sphere, and there is the non-sphere. Likewise, there are soul and non-soul, bondage and liberation, virtue and vice, influx of *karma,* their check, their experience, their exhaustion, etc. There are slaughter, falsehood, usurpation, sex indulgence accumulation, anger, pride, attachment and greed. There are abstention from slaughter, from falsehood, from usurpation, from sex indulgence, from superfluous accumulation, till from the thorn of wrong faith. There is *astihood* in all the *astis* and *nāstihood* in all the *nāstis.* Good deeds yield good results as bad deeds yield bad results. All souls touch virture and vice, pass through life and death and allow virtue and vice to fructify. There are two types of religion, religion of the homeless *(anagāra)* monks, and religion of the householder. The former religion demands that a person gets tonsured, and goes out from the state of a householder to be a homeless monk, to desist from killing, etc., all forms of abstention. The latter religion prescribes 12 items, *viz*., 5 'lesser vows' *(aṇuvratas),* 3 vows prescribing controls *(guṇavratas)* and 4 educational vows *(sikṣāvratas)."*[83]

Having attended the sermon on religion, the assembly dispersed. Kūṇika, the son of Bhambhasāra, also got up. Having paid his homage and obeisance, he submitted,

> *"Bhante!* Your sermon on the *nirgrantha* religion has been well delivered, full of information, well said, well expressed, well conceived and insurpassed. While discussing religion *(dharma),* you passed on to tranquility *(upaśama),* thereform to conscience *(viveka),* thence to abstention *(viramaṇa),* to non-doing *(akāraṇa)* of sinful deeds. What

to speak of excelling thee, no other *Śramaṇa* or *Brāhmaṇa* could have given such a brilliant exposition of religion as thou hast done."[84]

So saying, the king went away in the direction from which he had come.[85]

A Jaina or a Buddhist

If the *Sāmañjaphala Sutta* and the *Uvavai* are placed side by side, then the *Uvavai* will appear more profound in depth and penetration. The only line in the *Sāmañjaphala* that would give support to Ajātaśatru's having become a Buddhist is :

"From this day, the *Bhagavān* may accept me as a follower who has come to his protection with folded hands."

In contrast, the *Uvavai* has a more detailed account of the information given by the officer in charge of Mahāvirā's routine, Ajātaśatru's coming down from the throne, expressing his homage and obeisance with the familiar utterance of *'ṇamotthuṇaṁ'* his meeting with Maḥāvīra, etc. His concluding words, "What to speak of excelling thee, on other *Śramaṇa* or *Brāhmaṇa* could have given such a brilliant exposition of religion as thou hast done," signify his full confidence in the religion of the *nirgranthas.* Therefore, Ajātaśatru's utterance to the Buddha were a mere formality befitting a meeting with a holy man, and does not prove that he had ever become a follower of the Buddha.

Whereas Ajātaśatru met the Buddha only once[86], he had several meetings with Mahāvīra.[87] Even after the death of Mahāvīra, he was present at the Council that met under the guidance of *Sudharmā,* the successor of *Bhagavān* Mahāvīra to the spiritual throne.[88]

Vincent Smith has written,

"Both Buddhists and Jainas have claimed him as one of themselves. The Jain claim appears to be well founded."[89]

According to Radha Kumud Mookerjee, "so long as both Mahāvīra and the Buddha were alive, Ajātaśatru was a follower of Mahāvīra."[90] He writes further,

"As it is often found in the Jaina tradition, both Ajātaśatru and Udāibhadda have been described as men of good character because both were the followers of the Jaina religion. And this is the reason why the Buddhist texts have given a black paint on their character." (translated from Hindi).[91]

There are other evidences too which would suggest that he could not have been a follower of the Buddha, *viz.*, his intimacy with Devadatta, who happened to be an enemy of the Buddha, his enmity with the Vajjīs who were the great favourites of the Buddha, and the last but not least, the war with Prasenajit who was a great devotee and follower of the Buddha.

The Buddhist tradition has described him to be a patricide.[92] But after he had confessed his guilt and expressed repentance, the Jainas have called him to be obedient to his father.[93] These events are sufficiently expressive of his nearness to one religion and distance from the other.

That the Buddha was unfavourably disposed towards Ajātaśatru should be clear from the fact that after Ajātaśatru had held a discussion with the Buddha on the outcome of monkhood and departed, the Buddha is said to have made the following observations about him to his monks,

> "The background of this king has not been very good. He is very unfortunate. If he had not killed his pious father, then, today, he would have his dirt-free, spiritual eye opened on his very seat.[94] In the context of Devadatta, he said, "Monks! Ajātaśatru, the King of Magadha, who is an embodiment of sin, is his friend, is very intimate with him, and maintains a close relation with him."[95]

Once the Buddha was tendering some spiritual advice to Bimbisāra at the latter's palace. But instead of concentrating on the Buddha's words, he was all the time busy with patting his dear son. The Buddha invited the king's attention towards himself and told him a story whose substance was that the boy for whom he had so much of affection would one day take his life.[96]

For the victory of the Vajjis, once Ajātaśatru sent his minister Vassakara to the Buddha. This was a conspiracy to ascertain beforehand as to who would win. Had Ajātaśatru been a follower of the Buddha, how would he have played such a mean trick with him?

It is said that 500 *nirgrantha* monks were butchered by the command of King Ajātaśatru after the murder of Moggallāna.[97] This would suggest that he was a staunch follower of Buddhism. But this record is only in the *Aṭṭhakathā,* and, therefore, it has no more value than a fiction.

The *Aṭṭhakathās* have other interesting records as well. For instance, it is said that after the death of the Buddha, the problem for his ministers was as to who would break this sad news to the king and how. They were particularly careful to make sure that the revelation of the said news of the demise of the Buddha did not overwhelm the king. So, the ministers organised a *'catu-madhura'* bath for the king as an antedote against evil dreams. In the pleasant surrounding created by the bath, they broke the news to Ajātaśatru. But no sooner did the king hear about the death of the Buddha than he fell down in a swoon. The administration of the same bath was repeated twice in consequence of which the king regained his consciousness and expressed a deep grief.[98] According to another account, minister Vassakara showed the king pictures on the life of the Buddha from birth till death, and in this manner, he broke the news to the king.[99] This has been cited as a mark of great esteem in which the Buddha was held by King Ajātaśatru. But since the accounts are of a much later period, they cannot be taken as authoritative and authentic.

Once Upaka, son of one Miṇḍikā, and a disciple of Devadatta, held a discussion with the Buddha. Then he came to Ajātaśatru and spoke ill about the Buddha. This irritated Ajātaśatru who asked him to get out.[100] The author of the *Aṭṭhakathā* has added that Ajātaśatru asked his men to turn him out by the neck.[101] But even this does not establish any more that he was a follower of the Buddha. For, any wise man will do the same to another who violates the code of decent behaviour or indulges in a mean denunciation. Besides, if Upaka knew for certain that Ajātaśatru was a follower of the Buddha, he would surely not have gone to him to discuss his own experiences with the Buddha. If still he went to him, he did so knowing fully well that the king was a friend of his own master, Devadatta.

In the later literature, there are on record certain episodes which would support Ajātaśatru's deep enmity towards Buddhism. According to the *Avadāna-śataka,* King Bimbisāra erected a *stūpa* on the nails and hairs of the Buddha even when the latter was alive. The women of the *harem* worshipped at this *stūpa* with incences, lamps and flowers. When Ajātaśatru ascended the throne, he ordered the worship to be stopped. Śrīmatī, a palace maid, disobeyed the order for which she had to pay dearly with her life.[102] According to the *Theragāthā Aṭṭhakathā,* Ajātaśatru even tried hard for the execution of his own brother, Śīlavat.[103] These illustrations do not support in any way that Ajātaśatru was a follower of Buddhism; rather, they point to the same conclusion that he was its inveterate enemy. But even these evidences may be rejected as not being very substantial.

Rhys Davids, who is an authority on Buddhism, has written,

> "At the end of the conversation, Ajātaśatru frankly accepted the Buddha to be his guide and expressed deep regret for murdering his father. But it has been stated without any doubt that his religion could not have been changed. There is not a single proof that even after this shocking event, he had become a follower of the Buddha's teachings. So far as I have been able to understand, after this meeting, he did not even meet

either the Buddha or any other monk of the Buddhist order, nor did he discuss about religion with any one of them; and it does not occur to my mind that he ever made any financial donation to the Buddhist order in the life-time of the Buddha."

"Of course, this much is known that he sent a request for a share of the bones of the Buddha; but his justification for this request was that "I am a *Kṣatriya,* and the Buddha was a *Kṣatriya."* And then he erected an altar on the bones. Second, in later texts, it is recorded that when, immediately after the death of the Buddha, the Buddhist Council met, Ajātaśatru had erected a conference hall at the entrance of the Saptaparṇī cave where the Buddhist *Piṭakas* were compiled. But the older Buddhist texts are silent on this. Therefore, it is very much likely that even without courting the religion of the Buddha, he had a great regard for this religion. In doing so, Ajātaśatru was only following the great tradition of kingship in India according to which it was the sacred duty of a ruler to extend protection to all religions" (translated from Hindi).[104]

Desire during Pregnancy and Birth of Kūṇika

The account of the birth of Kūṇika and of his revolt against his father is more or less similar in the two traditions. On this, the Jaina source book is *Nirayāvalikā,* and the Buddhist source book is the *Dīgha Nikāya* Aṭṭhakathā. According to both the sources, the name of his father was Śreṇika (Bimbisāra).

But his mother's name was Celanā according to the Jaina tradition, and Kośalā Devī according to the Buddhist tradition. The Jaina tradition believes that during her pregnancy the mother saw a lion in her dream, but the Buddhist tradition has nothing like this. During her pregnancy, the mother had a desire. According to the Jaina tradition, the desire was that he should eat the fried muscle of the heart of King Śreṇika and drink liquor; but according to the Buddhist tradition, it was to drink blood from the king's arm. According to both, the desire was fulfilled by the king. The Jaina source, however, holds that Abhayakumāra so contrived that the muscles of the king's heart had not really to be taken out, and yet the queen had the satisfaction that she had eaten the fried muscles of the king's heart. According to the Buddhist tradition, a surgeon took out the blood from the king's arm and the queen drank it. After the fulfilment of her desire, the queen was very much ashamed and sorry. She tried even to kill the child in her womb. This she tried because, as per the Buddhist tradition, the astrologers had forecast that the child would one day kill his father. As per the Jaina tradition, the queen could visualise herself what sort of child she was carrying in her womb who desire to taste the muscles of his father's heart.

Śreṇika's Love for his Son

According to the Jaina tradition, when the child was born, Celanā had it thrown out. From there, a cock took out his little finger. There started a profuse bleeding at the place wherefrom the finger had been pecked out. When King Śreṇika came to know of this incident, he became restless out of affection for the son. He picked up the boy, brought him back to the queen and repeatedly sucked at the wound to stop bleeding.

As per the Buddhist tradition, the officers of the king had the child removed at once out of fear lest the queen should kill it herself. After a gap of time, the child was restored to his mother. Then the queen felt an affection for him. Once boy Ajātaśatru had a boil on his finger. As the prince was bitterly crying, he was brought to the king at the court. The king held the finger in his mouth to warm the boil. After some time, the boil burst in the king's mouth. Out of affection for the son, the king did not spit the blood, but swallowed it in.

Imprisonment of the Father

Regarding his revolt against the father, we have it in the Jaina tradition that Kūṇika was a man with restless aspiration. So he won his brothers to his side, chained his father and imprisoned him, and himself ascended the throne.

According to the Buddhist tradition, the aspiration of Kūṇika was aflame at the povocation given by Devadatta. So he had his father locked up in a smoky cell.

Murder of the Father

According to the Jaina tradition, on a festive occasion, Kūṇika came to his mother to bow at her feet, but the mother did not respond. When she was asked about it, she narrated the old story of Śreṇika's affection for his son. She condemned Kūṇika for all he had done to such an affectionate father. At this touch on a delicate part, Kūṇika's affection for his father came up. At once, he picked upon axe in his hand and hurried to the prison cell to set his father free. But when Śreṇika saw him coming towards him with an axe in his hand, he thought,

> "So, he is now coming to kill me. It is better that I end my life with my own hands."

At once, he swallowed *tālapuṭa* poison and ended his life.

It has been said in the Buddhist tradition that no one was permitted to go to the former king inside the smoky cell except Kośalā Devī. Ajātaśatru wanted to starve him to death.

For, Devadatta had counselled him as follows :

> "The father cannot be killed by weapon. So, he has to be starved to death."

When Kośalā Devī went to see the king, she used to carry some food in a small wallet. When this was reported to the king, he ordered the guards not to allow the wallet to be taken in. So, next she used to carry some food hidden beneath her hairs. When this too was detected, she carried some food in her golden slippers. When even this was prohibited, the queen took bath in scented water and besmeared four coats of honey on her body with which she came to the king. The king licked this honey from her body and lived on. In the end, Ajātaśatru completely stopped her going to the king. Now, the king lived on the joy of *śrotāpatti.*

When Ajātaśatru saw that the king was not still dying, he sent for the barber and gave him the following order :

> "Pierce the legs of my father with a knife and pour salt and oil on the cut, and foment it hot with fire made from *khaira* wood."

When this was done by the barber, the king died.

Repentance

According to both the traditions, Ajātaśatru became repentant after the death of his father. As per the Jaina tradition, the repentance came much earlier when Ajātaśatru heard from the mother the great affection that his father always had for him. After the former king ended his life with his own hand, Ajātaśatru fell down in a swoon, like a *campaka* tree hewn by an axe. After a while, he regained consciousness and lamented grievously,

> "Alas ! How very unfortunate I am! How much devoid of virtue I am ! How devoid of meritorious deeds I am ! What a cruel act have I committed ! In chain did I tie my father who was god-like. It is because of me that King Śreṇika is dead."

Being overwhelmed with grief, he could no longer bear his residence at Rājagṛha and transferred the capital of Magadha to the city of Campā.

Coming to the Buddhist tradition, on the day Bimisāra died, Ajātaśatru had a son born to him. The king was beside himself with joy at the birth of the son. The affection for the son filled up his bones and marrows. He thought that his father too must have experienced a similar delight when he himself was born. At once he ordered his gaolers to set his father free. But just then he received a note conveying the death of the former king. As the king read it, he gave out a shriek of distress and rushed straight to his mother, He asked,

"Mother ! Did my father have affection for me?"

The mother narrated how the ex-king had sucked at his finger when he was afflicted by a severe boil on it. This redoubled his grief and he lamented for what he had done.

Biographical Sketch : A Review

Though the details of the mother's desire during her pregnancy, the finger boil, the imprisonment of King Bimbisāra, etc., are different, the two accounts run almost parallel. Keeping in view the fact that the two traditions are widely different, this much difference between the two need not be overemphasized. All great events gain currency in diverse forms even when they are a part of current history. The date of the writing of the Jaina *Āgama, Nirayālikā,* is accepted to be before the commencement of the *Vikrama* era,[105] whereas the Buddhist *Aṭṭhakathās* were written in the fifth century of the *Vikrama* era.[106] This is another reason for the difference between the two. Stories which were preserved in, and transmitted through, memory in different traditions were put to writing after a few centuries or at a gap of a few centuries.

The accounts of the murder of the former king make it clear that whereas the Buddhist tradition was bent on exposing the cruelty of Ajātaśatru, the Jaina tradition attempted a sort of compromise. The Buddhist account of the piercing of the legs, pouring salt and oil, etc., is extremely inhuman. In the Jaina account, Śreṇika was imprisoned, of course, but there is nothing to establish that he was starved to death. Whereas in the Jaina account, Śreṇika himself committed suicide, in the Buddhist account, he was actually killed. The softness of the Jaina account may be due to that fact the Kūṇika had an extraordinary devotion for Jainism.

About his Mother

The names of Kūṇika's mother have been differently given in the two traditions.

According to the *Jātakas,* Kośalā Devī was the daughter of Mahā-Kośala, the king of Kośala, and she was the sister of Prasenajit who succeeded on the throne.[107] On the occasion of this marriage, the village of Kāśī was given to Bimbisāra as a dowry. After the murder of Bimbisāra, so goes the Buddhist account, Prasenajit took that village back. There followed a war in which Prasenjait was defeated at first, but was successful later. As Ajātaśatru happened to be his own nephew (sister's son), he was spared his life, a peace treaty was entered into and Prasenjit's daughter, Vajirā, was married with him.[108] The same village, Kāśī, was given to him as dowry. The *Saṁyutta Nikāya* account has simultaneously called him as the 'nephew of Prasenajit' and as *'Vaidehī putta.'*[109] There is, however, no consistency between the two epithets. The meaning of the word *'Vaidehī'* is, as given by Buddhaghoṣa, not 'princess of Videha,' but *Paṇḍita.*'[110] The fact is that Queen Celanā was called "Vaidehi" in the Jaina tradition because she was the daughter of Ceṭaka, the head of the Vaiśālī confederacy. Kośalā Devī who has been described as a sister of Prasenajit might perhaps be one of the step-mothers of Ajātaśatru. According to the Tibetan tradition[111] and also the *Amitāyurdhyāna Sutta,*[112] the name of Ajātaśatru's mother was *"Vaidehī vāsavī,"* and the cause of her being called *"Vaidehī"* has been stated to be that she was a princess from Videha.[113] The word *"Videha"* has been used in a similar sense in many other places. Even *Bhagavān* Mahāvīra has been called *Videha Videhadinne Videhajacce.*[114] As he was born in Videha, he has been called *"Vaideha";* as his mother happened to be a princess from Videha he has been called "Videhadinne"; and as he was the best among all the *Videhans,* he has been called *"Videhajacce."*[115]

In his dramatic work, *Svapnavāsavadattam,* the great poet, Bhāsa has called Udayana as *Videhaputra,*[116] because his mother happened to be a princess from Videha. According to the Jaina tradition, Queen Celanā and Mṛgāvatī who was the mother of Udayana, were sisters. Both were the daughters of Ceṭaka, the chief of the Vaiśālī confederacy.[117] Triśalā who was Mahāvīra's mother was Ceṭaka's sister.[118] So, the adjectives like *Videhadinna. Videhaputta,* etc., become easily intelligible. In the Jaina *Āgamas,* even Kūṇika has been called *Videhaputtra.*[119] According to Rhys Davids, King Bimbisāra had two queens, one being Kośalā Devī, the sister of Prasenajit, and the other, a princess from Videha. Ajātaśatru was born of the latter.[120]

When King Bimbisāra was placed in the smoky cell, according to the *Aṭṭhakathā,* Queen Kośalā Devī was entrusted with the duty of taking care of him. According to the *Encyclopaedia of Buddhism,* the queen taking care of the ex-king in prison was Khemā, and she has been said to be a princess from Kośalā.[121] This is apparently a mistake. For, Khemā was from the country named Madra.[122] Maybe, Kośalā Devī has been confused with Khemā. According to the *Amitāyurdhyāna Sūtra,* as also the Tibetan tradition, the name of the queen looking after the ex-king was Vaidehī Vāsavī.[123] Radha Kumud Mookerjee has identified Vaidehī Vāsavī as Queen Celanā.[124] These conflicting views in the Buddhist tradition does not in any way disprove the fact that Ajātaśatru was born of a princess from Videha, and it was because of this that he was called *Vaidehīputra.* It is not known why Buddhaghoṣa made the confusion that *"Vaidehī"* stood for *"Paṇḍita,"* and that Ajātaśatru was the son of Kośala Devī, a princess from Kośala.

Difference in Name

Between the Jaina and the Buddhist traditions, there is a lot of difference about the names of Ajātaśatru. Whereas he has been called Kūṇika throughout the Jaina tradition, the Buddhist texts have consistently called him Ajātaśatru. The latter name, Ajātaśatru, has been used even in the *Upaniṣads,*[125] and the *Purāṇas.*[126] The fact appears to be that 'Kūṇika' was the original name and 'Ajātaśatru' was only an epithet added later. Sometimes, as it happens, the epithet acquires a wider currency than the name itself. For comparison, *'Vardhamāna'* is the original name and 'Mahāvīra' is only an epithet, but, for all practical purposes, the epithet 'Mahāvīra' has a wider currency. The writers of Indian history have used the name 'Ajātaśatru.' An inscription in the Mathurā museum has it as 'Ajātaśatru Kūṇika.' (*Vide* Journal of Bihar & Orissa Research Society, Vol. V, part IV, pp. 550-551). It is desirable that in future, this latter name is used in the history of India.

Two meanings are given to the word, 'Ajātaśatru' as follows :

(i) *nayātah śatrur yasya, i.e.,* one to whom on enemy has been born,[127] and

(ii) *ajātohapi śatruḥ, i.e.,* one who has been an enemy even from before his birth.[128]

The second meaning is due to Buddhaghoṣa, and is correct in a sense, and logical too, though the first meaning is more apparent, and comes at once. Kūṇika was a powerful and a brilliant monarch. He had overpowered many an invincible foes. So, the epithet Ajātaśatru, instead of standing as a condemnation (as in the interpretation of Buddhaghoṣa), should appropriately stand as an eulogy for his gallantry.

The word *'Kūṇika'* is derived from the word *"kūṇi"* which means sore of the finger.[129] hence, '*kūṇika*' should mean one who had suffered from soar finger. As Ācārya Hemacandra has written :

rūḍhavraṇāpi sā tasya kūṇitattavadaṅguliḥ,
tataḥ sapāṁśuramaṇaiḥ sohabhyaścīyata kūṇiha.

Kūṇika has been named 'Aśoka Candra' in the *Āvaśyak Cūrṇī*;[130] but this use is very rare.

MAHĀŚILĀKAṆṬAKA WAR AND THE CONQUEST OF THE VAJJĪS

One of the historical episodes in the life of Kūṇika was, to use a Jaina expression, the *Mahāśilākaṇṭaka* War, called the 'conquest of the Vajjīs' by the Buddhists. The causes of the war, the process of fighting and the termination of hostilities have been diversely described in the two traditions; but one truth that inevitably emerges is that Magadha achieved victory over the Vaiśālī confederacy. When this war broke out, both Mahāvīra and the Buddha were alive; both answered questions about the war. Most thrilling is the account of the war itself in the two sources, and sufficient light is thrown by them on the then political situation in the country. The main Jaina source books for this great event are the *Bhagavatī*, the *Nirayavaliya Sutta* and the *Āvaśyaka Cūrṇī*, their Buddhist counterparts being the *Mahāparinivvāna Sutta* of the *Dīgha Nikāya* and its *Aṭṭāhakathā*.

From the Jaina Sources

Having arrived at the city of Campā, Kūṇikā sent for his ten brothers, Kālakumāra and others. He divided the kingdom, army, wealth, etc., into eleven equal parts and lived on happily with his own share. Kūṇika had two brothers (from the same mother Celanā) named Halla and Vihalla.[131] During his lifetime, King Śreṇika had bestowed on them two gifts, *viz.*, one watering (secanaka) elephant, and another, an 18-fold divine necklace.[132]

Everyday, Vihallakumāra rode on this elephant with his harem to come to the river Gaṅgā and enjoyed water sports there. Seeding the happiness and joy of the prince, the people in the city said,

> "Vihallakumāra, and not Kūṇika, enjoys the real pleasures of the kingdom."

This gossip reached the ears of Queen Padmāvatī, wife of Kūṇika. She thought in her mind,

> "If I do not have this elephant and this divine necklace in my possession, then, what's the use of this kingdom?"

So, she shared her thinking with her husband Kūṇika at the first available opportunity and became excessively insistent in her demand. Kūṇika at last agreed to make a request to his two brothers to surrender these two precious objects. Accordingly, he sent for Halla and Vihalla and requested them to give the elephant and the necklace. But they were not ready to oblige him. They said,

> "These are gifts from our dear father to ourselves. Why should we part with them?"

The arrogant reply caused much annoyance in Kūṇika. Halla and Vihalla availed a chance and escaped to their maternal grandfather, Ceṭaka, along with their *harem* and valuable possessions. When Kūṇika came to know this, he despatched an envoy at hot haste to King Ceṭaka requesting him to send back Halla and Vihalla, the necklace and the elephant at once to Campā. In reply, the following message was received from Ceṭaka,

> "The elephant and the necklace rightfully belong to Halla and Vihalla. And they have taken shelter with me. They are my protege. I cannot surrender them. If Kūṇika, who is the son of Śreṇika and Celanā, and my own grandson, is prepared to surrender half his kingdom in favour of Halla and Vihalla, then I may arrange the return of the necklace and the elephant in exchange."

A second envoy came to Ceṭaka with a message as follows :

> "Halla and Vihalla have taken out the elephant and the necklace without my knowledge and permission. Both these things belong to the kingdom of Magadha."

Ceṭaka refused to abide by the request and dismissed the envoy. When the envoy came back and reported, Kūṇika became furious and lost control on himself. His lips were quivering; his eyes were bloodshot; he wore three distinct lines of from on his forehead. He bade the envoy,

> "Go for the third time. I am giving you my demand in writing. This note contains, 'Return the necklace and the elephant at once, or get ready for the war.' You go inside the court of Ceṭaka and kick at his throne. You deliver this latter to Ceṭaka from the tip of your sword."

The envoy started to fulfil his mission. He did all he was asked to do.

Ceṭaka became furious at the content of the letter and the behaviour of the envoy. Said he to the envoy,

> "I am ready for the war. May Kūṇika come. I am waiting here to receive him."

Ceṭaka's men turned out the envoy by the neck. Kūṇika got the full report from the envoy and at once sent for his ten brothers Kālakumāra and others. After they had come he said to them,

> "Hurry back to your respective kingdoms and return as early as possible with your full army. I am at war with Ceṭaka."

The brothers brought each 3000 elephants, 3000 horses, 3000 chariots and 3 crores of infantrymen. Kūṇika also made ready his own army of a similar size. With such a colossal preparation, he marched against Vaiśālī.

Ceṭaka, in his turn, invited his own allies, 9 Mallas and 9 Licchavīs, in all 18 kings of Kaśī-Kośala and conferred with them. He said to them,

> "Kūṇika, the son of Śreṇika and Celanā, my own grandson, has come to fight. Either we must fight, or we must surrender."

All the kings replied in one voice,

> "We shall fight; we shall not surrender."

Having arrived at this decision, the kings returned to their respective kingdoms. They came back each with 3000 elephants, 3000 chariots and 3 crores of infantrymen. Ceṭaka himself prepared a fourfold army of a similar size. Altogether, with 57,000 elephant, 57,000 horses, 57,000 chariots and 57 crores of infantrymen, Ceṭaka took the field.

King Ceṭaka was a devoted follower of *Bhagavān* Mahāvīra. He had courted the 12 vows of the lay followers. He was also bound by a promise not to shot an arrow more than once per day. He was the most proficient archer of his time and his shot never missed its target. On the first day of the war, Kālakumāra commanded the army of Ajātaśatru. He orgainsed the army in *'Garuḍa'* formation. Ceṭaka, in contrast, organised his army in 'chariot' formation. It was a terrific battle. King Ceṭaka shot his infallible arrow which killed Kālakumāra, the commander of Ajātaśatru's men on the first day.

On the nine following days, nine brothers of Ajātaśatru, who were named commanders one after the other fell in the same manner, *i.e.,* by the infallible arrow of King Ceṭaka. At that time, Mahāvīra was at the city of Campā. The mothers of the dead princes, queen Kālī and others, made enquiries about the war and their own sons, and Mahāvīra gave replies to their questions. These queens were then initiated in a body in the order of Mahāvīra.[133]

Help from Indra

Thereafter, Kūṇika practised penances for three days. He offered prayers to Śakrendra and Camarendra who appeared before hm. When the war started again, the battle on the first day was fought with Indras on the side of Kūṇika. Śakrendra provided Kūṇika with an impenetrable armour to protect him before he took the field. This was a sure protection against the arrow of Ceṭaka. There was a severe fighting. But, under divine influence, even pebbles, straw and leaves hurled by Kūṇika's men fell like rocks on the army of Ceṭaka. On that day, 84 lakh men lay dead on the battle field. On the second day, a divine chariot and mace were used. Kūṇika sat on the chariot driven by Camarendra himself. The chariot moved freely through the enemy columns throughout the day smashing innumerable men. Thus 96 lakhs lost their lives on the second day. Ceṭaka and his allies, the 18 kings of Kāsī-Kośala,—9 Mallas and 9 Licchavis—were completely defeated. Kūṇika won the laurels of victory.[134]

Storming of the Wall round Vaiśālī

Being defeated in the battle field, King Ceṭaka took shelter in his own city. The city gate was closed. Kūṇika was unable to break through the wall. Thus, Vaiśālī lay under a state of seize for many days. One day, an oracle was heard from the sky as follows :

> The day on which *Śramaṇa* Kūlavālaka[135] will be attracted by prostitute Māgadhikā will be the day on which Aśokacandra (Kūṇika) will occupy Vaiśāli.[136]

Kūṇika gathered information about *Śramaṇa* Kūlavālaka. Then he sent for the prostitute Māgadhikā. Disguised as a devoted follower, this fallen woman attracted the monk towards herself. Then disguised astrologer, Kūlavālaka intered into the city of Vaiśālī, of course with great difficulty. He learnt that the city was saved by an alter which was dedicated to *Muni* Suvrata. When people saw the astrologer, they enquired from him how their city would be saved from the enemy, when the astrologer said that the enemy columns would be broken only if the alter dedicated to *Muni* Suvrata was removed. The people now turned to the alter which they uprooted from the foundation and cleared. For once, the army of Kūṇika retreated. This it did by a prior arrangement. But as soon as the alter was removed, as per the signal given by Kūlavālaka, Kūṇika launched a sudden attack and pierced through the wall of the city.[136]

Halla and Vihalla tried to escape with the elephant and the necklace. They reached the city wall. Beneath the city wall, there burnt a secret fire. The elephant came to know of this by dint of his superior knowledge and stopped. When he was still forced to advance, he threw down both Halla and Vihalla and himself entered into the fire. The elephant died, but because of his pious endeavour, he was born in the first heaven. The divine necklace was picked up by the gods and taken away. Śāsana Devī, the administrative goddess of the Jaina order picked up Halla and Vihalla and carried them to Mahāvīra. There, they were given initiation into monkhood.[138]

King Ceṭaka courted a fast unto death. He attained an exalted state because of his pious endeavour.[139]

From the Buddhist Sources : Enmity with the Vajjīs

There was a diamond mine near a village on the Gaṅgā.[140] There was an agreement between Ajātaśatru and the Licchavis that they would have an equal share of diamonds. But on account of sheer lethargy, Ajātaśatru failed to collect his own share, and the whole lot of the diamonds was carried away by the Licchavīs. This happened many a time, and at last, Ajātaśatru became angry. He thought,

> "It is difficult to fight against a whole confederacy which is never unsuccessful infighting.[141] But whatever that may be, I must uproot these powerful Vajjīs, I must exterminate them."

He sent for his chief minister and said to him,

> "Go to *Bhagavān* Buddha. Apprise him with my thinking and get me his reply as early as possible."[142]

At that time, the Buddha was on the Gṛddhrakūṭa mountain at Rājagṛha. Vassakāra came to him. On behalf of the monarch, he enquired about his health and well-being, and then revealed the purpose of his mission, whereon the Buddha gave out to him the following seven fundamental rules which the Vajjīs observed with meticulous care and which made them so very powerful.

1. They have a cent per cent attendance in their meetings.

2. They sit in the assembly with a single mind and they rise with a single mind, they do the same deed, they assemble at the sound of the bugle, no matter whether they are dining, dressing or decorating at that time.
3. They do not honour the unwise, nor uproot the wise.
4. They honour the elderly people, respect them, have regard for them, and worship them.
5. They do not forcibly marry with their woman or maidens.
6. They adore the caityas inside as well as outside their cities; they do not at any time transgress their respectability.
7. They give a spiritual protection to the *Arhats* so that those *Arhats* who are with them live on happily, and those who are to arrive in future may easily come.

Till the Vajjīs continue to observe these fundamental rules, they will continue to attain greater and still greater heights, he said.[143]

Split among the Vajjīs

Vassakāra came back to Ajātaśatru and said,

> "Sir, as per what *Bhagavān* Buddha as revealed, the Vajjīs are in invincible people. They may be over powered only through corruption and split."
> — "But how do we expect to bring about a split among them?"
> —"Sir, I have a plan for this. Tomorrow, you speak someting against the Vajjīs at the court, and then I shall speak something in their favour. On account of that insubordination, you order the tonsure of my head and expulsion from the city. When I shall be taken out of the city, I shall shout, 'It is I who constructed the city wall and the ditch around it. I know all the weak spots. My name is not Vassakāra if soon I do not teach you a good lesson'."

All these things were enacted on the following day. When the news reached the Vajjīs, some of the said,

> "He must be a rogue. Don't let him come to his side of the Gaṅgā."

But many more said,

> "The whole incident goes in our favour. Upto this time, Ajātaśatru relied on Vassakāra's wisdom. The man is very intelligent. Why do we not

use him now? He happens to be the enemy of our enemy. So, we should welcome him."

Under this impression, the Vajjīs made him their minister.

Within a short time, he established his hold on the Vajjīs. Now it was time for him to create a split among them. Whenever many Vajjīs assembled at one place, he would take one aside and say,

"Have you started ploughing your farm?"

—"Yes, sir, I have."
—"You yoke two bulls, I suppose?"
—"Yes, sir, I do."

Then another Vajjīs would enquire.

"What confidential thing did the minister discuus with you?"

But even when he reproduced the conversation verbatim, the other fellow would not believe in him that the minister could talk of such flimsy things. He would then react.

"You are not speaking the truth. You are hiding. It seems that you have no faith in me."

Henceforth, they would be enemies for good.

Sometimes, Vassakāra would say to a Licchavi.

"What vegetables did you cook today in your house?"

And again the same thing would happen, a mutual disrust.

Someday, he would take a Vajjī aside and say,

"You are very poor."

To some he would say,

"You are very weak."

If the Vajjī enquired how he know about it, he would say,

"Such and such Vajjī told me."

Thus, within a short time, the split among the Vajjīs was complete, and no two of them would use the same road. To be further sure, one day Vassakāra had the bugle sounded, but not a single Vajjī turned up. Then he was convinced that it would be easy now to overthrow the Vajjīs. A secret message was sent at once to Ajātaśatru to launch an attack. Ajātaśatru did the same with his vast army. In the face of this imminent danger, the bugle was sounded asking the people not to allow the enemy to cross the Gaṅgā, but not a single Vajjī responded. The bugle was sounded again calling upon the people to shut the entrances to the city, but nobody turned up. Some of them said, "We are too poor to fight." Other said, "We are too weak to fight." Still other said, "Let those who are heroic fight." And so on. So, the city gates lay open. Ajātaśatru entered the city without resistance, ravaged it to a complete ruin and went back.[144]

According to the *Parinirvāṇa Sutta,* two great ministers of Ajātaśatru, Sunidha and Vassakāra, erected the city of Pāṭaliputra on the bank of the Gaṅgā in order to remain at a safe distance from the Vajjīs. When the city was being erected, by chance, the Buddha came there. On an invitation from Sunidha and Vassakāra he took his meal at their house. In the course of a conversation, the Buddha praised the city of Pāṭaliputra, and pointed to three difficulties of a city, viz., fire, water and mutual split among the people. According to the Buddha's advice, the two ministers consulted the *Trayaśtrimśa* gods about the construction of the city.

Review

Both the sources give, in their respective ways, the account of the victory of Magadha and the destruction of Vaiśālī, but the cause of the war and the description of battles are wholly different. In the Jaina tradition, Ceṭaka figures as the leader of the Vajjī (Licchavī) Confederacy; but in the Buddhist account, the Confederacy figures by itself. Some details of the Jaina account, 33 crores constituting the army of Kūṇika and 57 crores that of Ceṭaka, the collaboration of Śakrendra and Camarendra, death of one crore and 80 lakh people in course of two days, the oracle about Kūlavālaka, the forecast about the overthrow of the Vajjīs on the destruction of the sacred altar, etc., do not appear to be very convincing to a rational mind. The Buddhist account, in contrast, is easy and natural.

As a cause of the war, we have in one account a diamond mine, and in the other, a very costly divine necklace. This shows some similarity between the two. According to the Jaina account, the arrow of Ceṭaka never failed its target; in the Buddhist account, the description of the Vajjīs as the most invincible people makes almost a similar hint. In the Jaina account, an altar in the city protected the city of the Vajjīs; this may be compared with what the Buddha said, "So, long as the Vajjīs will honour the caityas both inside and outside their city, they will attain fresh heights and will never go down."

As to the main personalities of the war, the Jaina account is more detailed than the Buddhist. The latter does not even take note of Ceṭaka, who was the main adversary of Ajātaśatru, and his allies, 9 Mallas and 9 Licchavīs, the 18 kings of Kaśī-Kośala, who were the members of the Confederacy.

The use of a secret strategy has been admitted in both the accounts. The Jaina accounts gives two phases of war, viz., (i) straight fighting for a fornight, and (ii) storming of the wall round Vaiśālī. There is a time gap between the two phases. Radha Kumud Mookerjee is of the view that this gap could be as long as 16 years.[145] According to the Buddhist account, Vassakāra lived for three years in Vaiśālī and created a split among the Vajjīs. From this, the conclusion is unavoidable that the Buddhist account deals only with the second phase of the war.

Queens and Progeny of Kūṇika

In the Jaina account, we come across principally three names of Kūṇika's queens. They are Padmāvatī,[146] Dhāriṇī,[147] and Subhadrā.[148] According to the *Āvaśyaka Cūrṇī*. Kūṇika married eight princesses,[149] but we do not get any worthwhile detail about them for this source.

According to the Buddhist tradition, the name of Kūṇika's queen was Vajirā. She was the daughter of Prasenajit, King of Kośala. The name of Kūṇika's son, according to the Buddhist tradition, Udāyībhadra. He was born of Padmāvatī, according to the Jaina tradition, and of Vajirā, according to the Buddhist tradition. In being born of Vajirā, however, there arises one inconsistency, *viz.*, that whereas, as per the Buddhist tradition, Udāyībhadra was born on the dame day on which Bimbisāra died,[150] Vajirā was married after Bimbisāra's death.[151]

Death of Kūṇika

The account of the death of Ajātaśatru Kūṇika is widely different in the two accounts. According to the Jaina account, Kūṇika asked *Bhagavān* Mahāvīra,

> "*Bhante!* Where do the world-monarchs go after death?"
> —"A world monarch dying while in office goes to the seventh hell."
> —"Where shall I go after my death?"
> —"You will go to the sixth hell."
> —"Then am I not a world monarch?"
> —"No, you are not."

This made Kūṇika anxious to become a world monarch. He created 12 artificial jewels and set out for the conquest of the six regions of the world. When he reached the Timisra cave, however, he was stopped by a god who said,

> "Only a world monarch can pass through this cave, and already there have been 12 world monarchs."

On this, Kūṇika said,

> "Then count me as the thirteenth."

The god became enraged at this impossible request, and reduced him to ashes right on the spot.[152]

According to the Buddhist tradition, Ajātaśatru was murdered by his son, Udayabhadra, who was greedy of the kingdom.[153]

The only common element between the two traditions has been that after his death, Ajātaśatru Kūṇika went to hell, —*Tamaḥprabhāva* according to the Jaina, and *Lohakumbhīya* according to the Buddhist.[154] There are in all seven hells according to the Jainas,[155] and eight according to the Buddhists.[156] In the Buddhist version, after passing through many births, Ajātaśatru would be born as a Pratyeka Buddha, when he will will be liberated.[157]

Previous Births of Kūṇika

We have an account of Kūṇika's previous births in both the traditions.[158] Their factual details widely differ, but they have a similarity if fundamentals. the similarity is that in one of his previous lives, Śreṇika had murdered Kūṇika.

ABHAYAKUMĀRA

More mysterious than the life of either Śreṇika Bimbisāra or Ajātaśatru Kūṇika is the life of Prince Abhayakumāra. Not only the two traditions claim him to be their own follower, they go even so far as to claim him to have been initiated as a monk in their respective orders. According to the *Āgamas,* he was initiated by Mahāvīra himself, and according to the *Tripiṭakas,* by the Buddha himself.

Birth of Abhayakumāra

According to the Jaina account, he was born of Queen Nandā, wife of Śreṇika Bhambhasāra.[159] She was the daughter of a Śreṣṭhī named Dhanvāha who lived at Vennātaṭapura.[160] In his youth, when Śreṇika was exiled, he went to that city when he married her. Abhayakumāra spent first eight years of his life at the house of his maternal grand-father. After that, both mother and son were brought to Rājagṛha.[161]

Throughout the Buddhist accounts, Abhayakumāra has been consistently called 'Abhayarājakumāra.' According to this tradition, he was born as a son to Bimbisāra from his concubine Padmāvatī who hailed from Ujjain.[162] Bimbisāra heard stories about the beauty of this woman and was attracted towards her. He consulted his priest who propitiated *Yakṣa* named Kumbhira to help his king. The *Yakṣa* appeared and carried Bimbisāra to Ujjain. At Ujjain, Bimbisāra established contact with Padmāvatī. From the time of his birth, Prince Abhaya lived for seven years with his mother at Ujjain. After that, he came to Rājagṛha and was brought up with other princes.[163]

It is difficult to say anything about the mother of Abhayakumāra. On this, the two accounts widely differ. The Jaina sources on this are the *Āgamic* texts, while the Buddhist sources are the *Aṭṭhakathās*. The appearance of the *Yakṣa* and his carrying Bimbisāra to Ujjain are no more than fictions.

Habits and Personality

The Buddhist tradition does not depict Abhayakumāra as anything more than an ordinary prince. At the most, he has been presented as an expert charioteer.[164] In contrast, a Jaina text depicts him as follows :

> "Abhayakumāra, son of King Śreṇika and born of Queen Nandā was not a man of mean origin. He was handsome, expert in the four principles of state craft, *viz.*, *sāma, dāna, bheda* and *daṇḍa,* and he was expert in matters of commercial policy. He was versed in *ihā, apoha, mārganā, gaveṣaṇā* and *arthaśāstra,* He was endowed with four kinds of intellect, *viz., autpātikī, Vaināyikī, kārmikī* and *pāriṇāmikī.* In the discharge of many of his royal duties, in the matters concerning the *harem* affairs, in secret and confidential discussions, in diplomacy, he was worthy to be taken into confidence once, and again and again. For all people, he was like the *'medhī,'* the pole round which bullocks move in threshing grains. For them, he was the authority, the basis, the support, the very eye sight. He was a man who attained fame in everything he did, and he made a name everywhere. He was the administrator of justice, the man at the helm of the statecraft, and he personally looked after the kingdom, its administration, the treasury, grannery, army, vehicles, the city and the *harem.*[166]

According to the Jaina belief, Abhayakumāra was nominated by Śreṇika

Bhambhasāra as his minister.[167] As a minister, he was like a single (unfailing) solution in all the problems with which the king was faced. It was he who contrived to fulfil the desires of Queen Dhāriṇī, mother of Meghakumāra, during her pregnancy, and that of Queen Celanā, mother of Kūṇika, by dint of his sharp intellect. Even the marriage between his step-mother Celanā and King Śreṇika was wittily arranged by him.[168] For his fine intellect, Abhayakumāra became a famous man in the Jaina tradition. There are many episodes on record which are a proof of his great intellect.

On many occasions, Abhayakumāra averted political crises. Once Caṇḍapradyota, King of Ujjain, along with his 14 allies, launched an attack on Rājagṛha. Abhayakumāra had some gold pieces under the ground beforehand where the encounter between the two armies was about to take place. When Caṇḍapradyota besiezed the city, Abhayakumāra sent a note to him as follows :

> "I submit as your well-wisher that all your friends have now become the allies of King Śreṇika. They are about to tie you up very soon and hand you over to Śreṇika. They have already received huge quantity of gold from him. You will find a corroboration of this if you dig the ground on which stands your army."

When Caṇḍapradyota had the ground dug up, he found gold pieces buried everywhere. This made him nervous, and he fled back to Ujjain.[169]

There is no similarity in the two accounts about any episode in the life of Abhayakumāra, except a minor one. This is as follows. According to the Buddhist tradition, on the dexterous handling and settlement of a border dispute, Śreṇika rewarded Abhayakumāra with a fine dancing girl.[170] According to the Jaina account, however, King Śreṇika had a sister named Seṇā. She was married with a *Vidyādhara.* When Seṇā had been murdered by other *Vidyādharas,* her daughter was sent to Śreṇika. Śreṇika settled this girl as the wife of Abhayakumāra.[171]

Initiation into the Buddhist Order

It has been stated in the *Abhayarājakumāra Sutta* of the *Majjhima Nikāya,*[172] in part as follows :

Once *Bhagvān* Buddha was lodged at the Kalandaka Nivāpa in Veṇuvana at Rājagṛha. At that time, Abhayarājakumāra went to *Nigaṇṭha Nātaputta* who said to him,

> "Rājkumāra! Discuss the meaning of the *Sūtras* with *Śramaṇa* Gautama. This will help you to be famous. People will say, Abhayarājakumāra

discussed the meaning of the *Sūtras* with *Śramaṇa* Gautama who is such a powerful person."

"Bhante! How shall I open the discussion?"

In giving him the guidelines, Mahāvīra said,

> "You start like this : "Can *Tathāgata* speak such words as may sound harsh to others?" If *Śramaṇa* Gautama's reply be in the affirmative, then ask him about the distinction between the *Tathāgata* and an ordinary person. Even an ordinary person does the same. If the answer be in the negative, then ask him why he made a forecast about Devadatta that he was destines to go down, that he would go to hell and be lodged there for full one *kalpa* and that nothing would save him. Being querried thus from both the angles, *Śramaṇa* Gautama will be able neither to swallow nor to disgorge. His condition then will be like that of a man who has a hook stuck up in his throat which he can neither take in nor throw out."

Having saluted *Nigaṇṭha Nātaputta*, Abhayarājakumāra got up from there and came to the Buddha. He saluted him and took a seat. Finding the latter busy, Abhayarājakumāra thought in his mind,

> "Today, there will be no time to discuss the meaning of the *Sūtras* with *Bhgavān* Buddha. I shall do it tomorrow at my own residence where let me invite him."

So, he invited the Buddha with four monks to receive food at his house on the following day. The Buddha gave him his silent consent. Thereupon Abhayarājakumāra came back to his own palace. Next morning, the Buddha, dressed in his robe, and with the begging bowl and cloth in his hand, came to the house of Abhayarājakumāra. He sat on a cushion which was already spread for him. Abhayarājakumāra severed the Buddha with delicious food with his own hands. After the Buddha had dined and withdrew his hand, Abhayarājakumāra took a lower seat, and started his discussion on the meaning of the *Sūtras*.

> —*"Bhante!* Can the *Tathāgata* speak such words which may sound harsh to other?"
>
> "Rājakumāra ! No single answer is possible to this."

As the Buddha was speaking, Abhayarājakumāra spoke out,

"Bhante! The *Nirgranthas* are undone?"

"What did you say? The *Nirganthas* are undone? What do you mean by that?"

—*"Bhante!* I mean exactly what I have asserted. I have just been to *Nigaṇṭha Nātaputta.* It is he who has sent me hither to put this two-pronged question to you. He holds the view that being asked a question like this, you will be able neither to swallow nor to disgorge."

At that time, a very young but dull-looking child was seated on the lap of Abhayarājakumāra. Pointing to him, the Buddha said,

"Rājakumāra! Suppose due to your own carelessness, or to that of the attending nurse, this child places a piece of wood or pebble in his mouth. Then what will you do?"

—*"Bhante!* I shall take it out. If I cannot do so easily, then I shall hold his head with my left hand, and then with a finger on my right hand turned like it hook, I shall force it out, if necessary, with blood. I shall do so because I have great affection for the child."

Picking up the thread, the Buddha started,

"Rājakumāra ! The *Tathāgata* does not utter words which are meaningless, harmful and harsh. Though full of meaning, but harmful or harsh, the *Tathāgata* does not utter even such words. Though pleasant to others, but meaningless or worthless, even such words the *Tathāgata* does not utter. The *Tathāgata* who has full time sense speaks only what is meaningful and necessary, no matter whether words are palatable or harsh. This he does because he has compassion for all living beings."

—*"Bhante!* Scholars from among the *Kṣatriyas,* the *Brahmins,* the *Gṛhapatis* and the *Śramaṇas* prepare their questions, come to the *Tathāgata* and put their questions before him. Does the *Tathāgata* know beforehand that he will be asked such and such questions so that he will give such and such answers?"

—"Rajakumāra! put a question to you. You give whatever reply you like. I guess, you are an expert in the mechanism of a chariot."

—"Yes, I am. I know thoroughly the mechanism of a chariot."

—"Suppose, somebody points to a chariot and asks, what is this part of the chariot called. Do you think beforehand what reply you will give to such and such question? Or, you just give the reply as it may suit the occasion?"

—*"Bhante!* I am an experienced charioteer. I know all its parts. So, I can give the answer right then."

—"In the same manner, Rājakumāra, the *Tathāgatha* can give answer right then, because he is religion."

—*"Bhante!* How surprising ! How very wonderful ! You have expounded religion in diverse forms. I place myself under the protection of thy *Dhamma,* of thy *Saṅgha.* From this day, please accept me as a follower who has come to thee with folded hands."

In the *Abhaya Sutta* of the *Saṁyutta Nikāya.*[173] there is an account of a meeting between the Buddha and Abhayarājakumāra, in which the latter asks a question abut the position occupied by *Pūraṇa Kāśyapa* in the spiritual hierarchy.

Abhayarājakumāra had his pious, spiritual eye opened[174] when being overwhelmed with grief at the death of his dancing girl, he came to the Buddha, and the latter spoke words of inspiration for his benefit.[175]

According to the *Theragāthā.*[176] and its *Aṭṭhakathā*[177] being overwhelmed at the death of his father, Abhayarājakumāra was initiated into monkhood by the Buddha, and later he became an *Arhat.* The *Therīgāthā Aṭṭhakathā*[178] further states that during his monkhood, he inspired his mother, Padmāvatī, to take shelter in religion. She was also initiated into the order and attained the status of an *Arhat.*

Initiation in the Nirgrantha Religion

According to the Jaina belief, Abhayakumāra was a great devotee of Mahāvīra. Once a woodcutter (henceforth called Drumaka) was initiated into monkhood by Sudharmā Svāmī. When this monk entered into the city of Rājagṛha for begging, people laughed at him saying,

> "Here comes a great renouncer. He has given up his gold, wealth and everything."

The curt remarks hurt the new monk severely. He came back to the camp and narrated his experience to his spiritual master, Sudharmā. To help the monk out of this difficult situation, it was decided that the whole party of monks would depart immediately on following day. But the departure was cancelled at the pressing request of Abhayakumāra.

Coming back to the city of Rājagṛha, Abhayakumāra made three piles of gold coins, each having one crore pieces. Then the people of the city were invited to try their luck with these. All people were attracted at the prospect of a windfall gain. After the people had assembled, Abhayakumāra made the following announcement :

> "These three piles, each having one crore gold coins, will go to one who can give up for good his wife, water and fire."

This was too difficult a string and none dared to come forward. Thereon Abhayakumāra said,

> "You see how very noble is Monk Drumaka who has renounced for good woman, water and fire."

In this manner, Abhayakumāra put an end to the popular discussion about the monk.[179]

The Jaina tradition has many stories about the great devotion of Abhayakumāra towards religion. Speaking about him, Mahāvīra himself has called him intensely pious.[180] Sulasakumāra, son of the butcher Kālaśaurika, became a follower of the *nirgrantha* religion under his influence.[181] Ārdrakakumāra also became a monk under the inspiration given to him by Abhayakumāra.[182]

About the initiation of Abhayakumāra, it has been said that once when *Bhagavān* Mahāvīra came to Rājagṛha, Abhayakumāra called on him at the garden to pay him his homage and obeisance. When the sermon was over, Abhayakumāra made the following submission :

> "*Bhante!* Who will be the last king to attain liberation?"[183]

To this, Mahāvīra made the following reply :

> "King Udāyana of Vītabhayapura who has already recevied intiation from me will be the last king to attain liberation."

Abhayakumāra thought in his mind,

> "If I am initiated after I become a king, there will be no chance for me to attain liberation. So, why do I not be initiated in my youth?"

Abhayakumāra came to Śreṇika, and expressed to him his desire for instant initiation. After hearing him, Śreṇika made the following observation :

> "It is time for me to be initiated into monkhood. I am afraid, you are yet

too young for that. At this age, you should assume the responsibility of running the administration of the state."

But Abhayakumāra was adamant. So, Śreṇika said at last,

"Look here. On the day I am angry with you and ask you to get away, and not to show me your face, you will have your permission for initiation into monkhood."

After a gap of some time, Mahāvīra came again to Rājagṛha. It was a chilly winter. One evening, as King Śreṇika and Celanā were coming back after paying their homage to Mahāvīra, they saw a monk standing in meditation on the bank of the river. At night, a the queen lay in her bed, she woke up suddenly, and just then she remembered the said monk, when the following words slipped from her mouth,

"What he (the monk) may be doing at this moment?"

The king heard these words and had at once an apprehension about the chastity of his wife. Next morning, while going to pay his homage and obeisance to Mahāvīra, he gave the following order in Abhayakumāra :

"Reduce the *harem* into ashes. This has become the abode of impurity."

Abhayakumāra was in a dilemma; at the same time, he could not disobey the king. So, he took out the queens to a safe resort and set fire to the palace. On a point of enquiry by Śreṇika, *Bhagavān* Mahāvīra said,

"All your queens, Celanā and others, are spotlessly chaste."

On this, the king became penitent for the order he had given earlier. So, he rushed forth to save the situation. He saw Abhayakumāra on the way, and enquired,

"What have you done with the palace?"
—"Why? I have put it to flames."

The king became intensely sorry. He was also angry with Abhayakumāra for giving effect to such a silly order. And then suddenly the following words dropped from his mouth,

"Get away, Don't show me your face."

Abhayakumāra accepted the order of his father. He joined the order of monks of Mahāvīra wherein he was given initiation by the Master himself.

The king soon discovered that all the queens were safe. Then the only thought in this mind was that was that he should prevent Abhayakumāra from renouncing the world. As he rushed to Mahāvīra's camp, he found that Abhayakumāra had already been initiated.[184] The *Antagaḍadasao* mentions that Abhaya's mother, Nandā, too was initiated and liberated.[185]

After his initiation, Abhayakumāra studied all the 11 *Aṅgas,* performed the penance named *Guṇaratna* and became extremely lean and emaciated.[186] After his death, he was born in the celestial *vimāna* named Vijaya as a god, where he will live as long as 22 *sāgaropamas*, on completion of which he will be born in *Mahāvideha* and from there, he will attain the status of Liberated Souls.[187]

Gleaning carefully through the two accounts, one may be left free to wander why Abhayakumāra and Abhayarājakumāra should not be taken as two separate persons. Leaving aside the only fact that they had a common father, all other evidences would support the suggestion that they were two distinct persons. According to the Buddhist tradition, Abhayarājakumāra was the name of the father of the royal physician, Jīvaka Kaumārabhṛtya, but the Jaina tradition gives no hint to that effect. Coming to other differences, while the mother of one is the daughter of a merchant, that of the other is no more than a prostitute woman; while one is the chief minister of Magadha, the other is only an expert charioteer; while one is initiated by Mahāvīra, the other is initiated by the Buddha. Abhayarājakumāra is stated to have given up the *nirgrantha* religion and too shelter in the religion of the Buddha. Had Abhayarājakumāra been the same person as Abhayakumāra, how could there be an account of his initiation by Mahāvīra? Śreṇika Bimbisāra had many sons, and it should cause no surprise if two of them bore similar names.

Indeed, if all the discussion in the two traditions refer to a single person, then it is worthwhile to note that the Jaina account of his initiation in the *nirgrantha* religion is a part of the *Āgama* named *Aṅuttarovavayiyadasa,* which is one of the 11 fundamental texts. It must have been written prior to the second century of the pre-Vikrama era.[188]

The Buddhist account of his initiation is contained in the *Aṭṭhakathā* and *Thera Apadāna.*[189]

The *Aṭṭhakathā* is a posterior construction, and even Apadāna of the *Tripiṭaka* literature is considered to belong to a later period.[190]

'Udrāyaṇa' is one of the names of a king that figures in the list of those initiated in both the orders. According to the Buddhist work, *Avadānakalpalatā,*[191] the name is 'Udrāyaṇa,' and according to *Divyāvadāna,*[192] it is

'Rudrāyaṇa.' We get the name as 'Udrāyaṇa' in later-day Jaina literature.[193] Both the accounts are unanimous that he was the king of Sindhu Sauvīra. However, they differ as to how he came in contact with Mahāvīra and the Buddha. In the Jaina source, the name of his capital has been given as Vītabhaya and in the Buddhist source, as Rorūka. According to both the traditions, he received inspiration in religion from his deceased queen.

UDRAYĀNA

According to the Jaina account, Mahāvīra went to Sindhu Sauvīra in order to give him initiation in his own order, but according to the Buddhist account, the Buddha gave him initiation after the king came to him in Magadha. According to both the traditions, King Udrāyaṇa came back to his own capital after his initiation for a short visit, but he was murdered by the order of the king who was counselled to do so by his wicked ministers. We have it from the Jaina source that before he became a monk, Udrāyaṇa gave his kingdom to his nephew in order to save his son from the inevitable course of going to hell if he would administer a state. (In other words, he deprived his son of his rightful claim to the throne). According to the Buddhist source, however, he gave his kingdom to his own son, Śikhaṇḍī. Both the traditions agree that before he died, he became a *Kevalin Arhat,* after which his city was ravaged by the anguish of the gods.[194]

The account of *'Rudrāyaṇa'* is nowhere available in the Pāli literature, nor does it exist in the literature of the Hīnayāna sect. Both Divyāvadāna and *Avadāna-kalpalatā* are the texts of the Mahāyāna sect. The Mahāyāna *Tripiṭakas* are written in Sanskrit and belong to a much later period.[195] In itself, the *Divyāvadāna* is a mere compilation, and its date of compilation falls somewhere between 200-350 A.D.[196] Under this circumstance, it is very much likely that the Jaina account about Udrāyaṇa has been turned into *Rudrāyaṇāvadāna* by the Buddhist writers. Otherwise, how is it possible that the same king has been initiated both by Mahāvīra and the Buddha and he attained liberation? That the Buddhist work is a mere copy is further supported by the fact that in this work, Bimbisāra and Udrāyaṇa have been made to enter into friendship in same manner in which Abhayakumāra and Ārdrakakumāra did in the Jaina account,[197] or even as Bimbisāra and Pakkusāti did in the Buddhist tradition.[198] The Avadāna makes it perfectly clear that the account of his initiation by both Mahāvīra and the Buddha must in itself be an imitation of one account by the other. From very olden times, it has been a practice to enlist well-known names among the followers by each religion. This is the reason why Rāma figures as an ideal man in the Jaina, the Buddhist and the *Vedic* traditions alike. Each tradition has built up the Rāma story in its own way.

The Jaina account about Udayāna is contained in the *Bhagavatī Sūtra.*[199]

The *Uttarājjhayanānī* contains a concise account of the same.[200] The early texts apart, the story has figured in the later-day commentaries and Cūrṇī literature of the Jainas.

According to the Jaina *Āgamas,*[201] Abhīcakumāra who was the son of Udrāyaṇa, was also a follower of the *nirgranthas.* As he was deprived of the kingdom, he became angry with his father, and could never forget the injustice done to him, so that after his death, he was born as *asura.*

CAṆḌA-PRADYOTA

Like the names of Śreṇika Bimbisāra and Ajātaśatru Kūṇika, the name of Caṇḍa-pradyota also figures in both the traditions. Both the traditions agree that in his early life, Caṇḍa-pradyota was haughty, a lover of war, an addict who was fond of mischievous way. Both the traditions contain many accounts of his wars. Of these, a war between him and Udayana of Vatsa has been described with much similarity in both.[202] Even the *Paurāṇic* literature of the Hindus contain an account of this war.[203] On the basis of this very episode, the great poet, Bhāsa, produced his dramatic master-piece, *Svapanavāsavadattam.*

According to the Jaina account, Caṇḍa-pradyota fought with King Udayana of Sindhu Sauvīra,[204] Śatānīka of Vatsa,[205] Bimbisāra of Magadha,[206] and Dummaha of Pāñcāla.[207] He fought with Udayana for a servant maid named Svarṇa-gulikā, with Śatānīka for Queen Mṛgāvati, with Dummaha for a crown with two faces and with Bimbisāra for his growing power and influence which he could not tolerate. These accounts are thrilling as well as interesting.

According to the *Majjhima Nikāya,*[208] Ajātaśatru strengthened the fortification of Pāṭaliputra out of fear from Caṇḍa-pradyota. The Buddhist account has no record of other wars.

According to the Jaina belief, Caṇḍa-pradyota became a follower of the *nirgranthas* from the time he was released from his captivity of King Udayana who himself was a devoted follower of the *nirgranthas.*[209] Prior to this, he used to say, "My parents were Jaina *śrāvakas.*"[210] When at a congregation of Mahāvīra, Mṛgāvatī, queen of King Śatānīka, and Śiva and other consorts of Caṇḍa-pradyota himself were initiated, the latter king, witnessed the event by his personal presence.[211] That was his first meeting with Mahāvīra, and during that first meeting, he accepted the religion of the *nirgranthas* in proper manner.[212]

According to the Buddhist account, Caṇḍa-pradyota was induced to accept Buddhism by a monk named Mahākātyāyana. Before becoming a monk, Mahākātyāyana was the priest of Caṇḍa-pradyota. Caṇḍa-pradyota had sent him to invite the Buddha. The Buddha did not come, but he initiated

Mahākātyāyana into his own order and sent him back to Ujjain. It was he who converted Caṇḍa-pradyota to Buddhism.[213] The Buddhist literature contains no account of his meeting with the Buddha.

In the basic literature of both the traditions, there is no mention of Caṇḍa-pradyota having ever been a devoted follower of any religion, the account exists mainly in the story literature. The question is, therefore, still unresolved how he became a follower of either Mahāvīra or the Buddha. It is quite possible that he was the follower of one in early life, and then, later, he changed over to the other. It is also possible that he maintained a link with both the religions, and that this link was exploited by the story-writers who gave an exaggerated account of the connection in order to establish that he was a follower of their own religions, whatever that might have been.

UDAYANA

King Udayana of Kauśāmbī was also a historical person. The account of his life, with minor differences of details is available in the Jaina, Buddhist and *Vedic* traditions. This king had a vast collections of elephants who were caught by the music of the *Vīṇā* (a musical instrument) of strings popular in India).

According to the *Bhagavatī Sūtra* of the Jainas,[214]

> "At that time, there reigned a king named Udayana, who was the grandson of King Sahasrānīka, son of Śatānīka, born of his queen Mṛgāvatī, who was the daughter of King Ceṭaka, head of the Vaiśālī confederacy. He was a nephew of the celebrated Jayantī who was a pious follower of the Jaina path. At that time, *Bhagavān* Mahāvīra came to Kauśāmbī. When King Udayana got this news, he was happy and delighted. He called in his officers and gave them detailed instructions as Kūṇika had done in another account.[215]
>
> "The King came to attend the congregation of Mahāvīra with the display of same sort of pomp and grandeur as Kūṇika had done. He was accompanied by his mother Mṛgāvatī and aunt Jayantī.[216] All of them were present at the sermon."

The Jaina *Āgama Vipāka Sūtra*[217] has an account of the misconduct of Queen Padmāvatī, the consort of the king. On this, Gautama put many questions to Mahāvīra, and the latter gave his answers in details. The *Vipāka Sūtra* has described this king to be as great and noble as the Himālayas.

The Jaina story literature gives a detailed account of the war with Caṇḍa-pradyota and also about Vāsavadattā.

According to the Buddhist belief, in his early life, Udayana was hostile to the Buddha and his order. Once, three *Śreṣṭhīs* of Kauśāmbī named Ghoṣaka,

Kukkuṭa and Pāvārīya[218] invited the Buddha to their city. Now, Khujjuttarā, who happened to be the maid servant of Queen Śyāmāvatī, used to attend the Buddha's sermon every day. Then she started reproducing the words of the Buddha. Under her influence, even Queen Śyāmāvatī was attracted was attracted to the Buddha in her devotion. When the Buddha passed from beneath the palace, she used to pay him her homage and obeisance from her window. Her co-wife Māgandiyā reported all this to King Udayana. As Udayana happened to be hostile to the Buddha and his order, he became displeased with her. It was only through the divine grace that the queen could save her life. When at last the king's anger was pacified, at the request of Queen Śyāmāvatī, he gave permission for inviting the Buddhist monks to the palace for receiving food. After the monks had dined, the women of the palace desired to give them clothes, to which, again, the king raised objection. But after Ānanda had convinced him of its utility, he agreed.[219]

There is nothing on record to establish that Udayana ever met the Buddha. According to the *Saṁyutta Nikāya,*[220] the king saw Piṇdola Bhāradvāja at Ghoṣitārāma at Kauśāmbī. He discussed with him why young folks became monk and said in the end,

> " I take shelter with the Buddha, with the *Dhamma* and with the *Saṅgha*. May thou accept me as a follower who has come to seek protection with thee."

Review

All the Jaina records are unanimous in showering praise on him, while all the Buddhist records have nothing but indignation for him. There is a description even to the effect that once he had red ants sprayed on Piṇḍola Bhāradvāja. On hearing about this, the Buddha is reported to have said,

> "Not only in this life, but in his previous life, too, Udayana had been a source of pain to monk."[221]

From these, it may be definitely inferred that Udayana was at first a follower of Mahāvīra. The eulogistic records about him in the Jaina literature and contemptuous references in the Buddhist literature are not the only proofs in support of his being a *Jina.* A more convincing proof is that his father Śatānīka, his mother Mṛgāvatī, his aunt Jayantī, were all the followers of the Jaina path.

Once reason why he was not very respectful of the Buddha is the influence exerted by Queen Māgandikā on him. She was angry with the Buddha from a very young age. Her father was looking for a handsome groom for his daughter who was well-known for her beauty. He made a request to the Buddha to accept the hand of his daughter. The Buddha who was hurt by this request said,

"She whose body is full of urine and stool you call beautiful. I do not care even to touch her with my legs."[222]

Later, Māgandikā was settled in marriage with Udayana, but she remained ever hateful of the Buddha. Udayana was very much under her influence. Naturally, he could not be a follower of the Buddha.

The Buddhist account of his becoming a "follower who came under protection" would give the impression that in course of time his distance from the Buddhist order was obliterated and his hatred of it was wiped out.

The Buddha outlived Mahāvīra by 25 years. It is, therefore, just likely that Udayana was influenced by the growing strength of the Buddhist church and was converted to this religion by Piṇḍola Bhāradvāja. We have a description of his son, Bodhirājakumāra,[223] only in the *Piṭaka* literature, just as we have a description of his father only in the Jaina *Āgamas*. This will give a strong support to his being a Jaina in his early life, though at a later period, he might or might not have been converted to Buddhism.

PRASENAJIT

As a Follower of the Buddha

Prasenajit, who was the king of Kośala, was a contemporary of Mahāvīra and the Buddha, and was also a historical person. In the prime of his life, he a follower of the *Vedic* religion. He performed a number of sacrifices. According to the *Saṁyutta Nikāya,*[224] for one such sacrifice, he had collected as many as 500 oxen, 500 male calves, 500 she-calves, 500 goats, 500 rams, etc. But at the advice of the Buddha, he did not kill them, but released them.[225] In this manner, because of his frequent contact with the Buddha, he became his follower. It is well-known that the Buddha spent the last 25 monsoons of his life either at Jetavana or at Pūrvārāma Bihar at Śrāvastī. So, it was but natural that Prasenajit would have a constant and regular touch with him. On many occasions, on many matters, big and small, he put many questions to the Buddha. These questions and answers are contained in the Chapter on *Kośala Saṁyutta* in the *Saṁyutta Nikāya.*

The following is an interesting account worthy of quote :

"Seeing that King Prasenajit of Kośala was out of breath after he had taken food, the following couplet dropped from the mouth of the Buddha,

manujasa sadā satimato
mattaṁ jānato laddha-bhojane
tanu tassa bhavanti vedanā

> *saṇikaṁ jīrati āyu pālayaṁ"*
>
> (A man who is alert in his mind
> Who is measured in the intake of food,
> The Pain of such a man is less,
> His food is digested helping long life).

At that time, Sudarśana Māṇavaka was standing just behind the king. Addressing him, the king said, in part, as follows :

> 'Dear Sudarśana! Learn this couplet from the *Bhagavān.* You recite it everyday as I sit to dine. For this extra assignment, you will be paid 100 *karṣapaṇas* per day.'
>
> —'Your Majesty! I accept the assignment, and I shall do as you desire me to.'

So, saying, Māṇavaka learnt the couplet from the Buddha and recited it everyday as the king sat down to eat.

"Henceforth the kind ate just enough and no more."

Within a short time, he developed a fine and muscular body. Feeling his own cheeks with his hands, the king said to himself,

> *"Bhagavān* has been king to me in two respects, *viz.*, in matter pertaining to this life, and in matter pertaining in life hereafter."[226]

This apart, the *Tripiṭakas* have recorded at diverse places episodes on the life of King Prasenajit some of which have been noticed in this work.

Aṅgulimāla happened to be a famous robber of that period. He was the son of Gagga who was the preceptor of the royal household. One day, when Aṅgulimāla was seated near the Buddha after being initiated into his order as a monk, Prasenajit was out with 500 cavalrymen in search of him. The Buddha held the hand of the robber, and in presenting him to the king, he said,

> "Here's Aṅgulimāla you are looking for."

The king was terrified to hear these words, his pore-hairs stood erect on his body, and he was stunned. His whole frame was wet with warm sweat. The Buddha started again,

> "Have no alarm, oh king. You needn't be afraid of him any more."

By this time, Prasenajit was seized of the whole situation. He praised the Buddha for his wonderful feat in captivating such a notorious character.[227]

Cause of his Devotion for the Buddha

On being asked by the Buddha why the king was so much devoted to him, the king, in the main, assigned two causes which were as follows :

1. "I know many monks who have lived for 10 to 40 years and then come back to wordly life and plunged in worldly pleasures. But I have never seen a Buddhist monk indulging in such a behaviour. I have seen quarrelling parents and sons, kings and their vassals, but I have always found the Buddhist monks living in peace and amity. I have seen such monks who have become pale from disease, but I have never found a Buddhist monk like that. In the law courts, I have seen people indulging in incessant gossips, but in a gathering where the Buddha speaks, I have never seen anyone even coughing. Here nobody even asks a question as I have seen people doing in the congregations around other spiritual leaders.
2. "The *Bhagavān* is a *Kṣatriya* and so am I. The *Bhagavān* is a resident of Kośala and so am I. The *Bhagavān* is 80, and I am also 80. So, it is in the fitness of things that I show him respect and accord him diverse honours."[228]

Queen Mallikā was one of the principal consorts of Prasenajit. She was highly devoted to the Buddha. All the time she was exerting her influence on the king in favour of the Buddha. Vajirā who was married with Ajātaśatru was her daughter.

Vidūḍabha

In order to augment his proximity to the Buddha, Prasenajit wanted to marry a princess from the Śākya clan. But the Śākyas looked on him as being inferior to them in caste status and so they did not agree. But knowing him to be a powerful king, they dared not to disoblige him altogether. So, they married with him one Vāsava-khattiyā, daughter of Mahānāma Śākya by a servant maid. To keep it a close secret, from Prasenajit Mahānāma sat to dine with this servant girl. But as he lifted his first morsel of food, as per a previous arrangement, an errand-boy arrived with an urgent message, and, on the pretext of attending to it, he left the place in a hurry without touching any food. Prasenajit was under the impression all the time that he had married a *Kṣatriya* woman of a distinguished family, and he gave the lady the position of the first queen. From this marriage, a son was born who was named Vidūḍabha. He grew into an immensely powerful young man and he was given the command of the army at a pretty early age. At the age of 16, he came to the house of his maternal grandfather in the company of a large party of men. The Śākyas sent all the princes who were junior to him outside the city. Only the elders came forward to receive him and accord him a suitable welcome. Viduḍabha bowed before the elders one after another. But he was surprised to find that there was no one in the city, junior to him, who would bow before him. This created a suspicion in his mind. After he departed from the city, the wooden stool on which he sat was washed with milk and water. His valets gathered all this information, and as the prince was on his way back to Śrāvastī, they brought these to his notice. Soon he came to know that as he was the son of a maid, no one bowed before him, and the stool on which he sat was washed clean by milk and water, he became furious and resolved to uproot the Śākyas to their very root.

When King Prasenajit came to know that Vāsava-Khattiyā was the daughter of a maid servant, and was not a lady of high breed, he sent the mother and the son to live in the quarters assigned for the menials. The Buddha argued with him,

> "Oh King! Vāsava-Khattiyā is born of Mahānāma Śākya, and Vidūḍabha is born to you. Under the circumstances, the mother's line loses its importance."

On this, the king restored them to their original position.

Dīrghakārāyaṇa was an army commander of King Prasenajit. He was given the command after the murder of his maternal uncle. So in his heart, he was an enemy of the king. Once Prasenajit came to see the Buddha. Before coming to the Buddha's presence, he entrusted his sword and crown to Dīrghakārāyaṇa. With this important things in his possession, the general slipped out and joined with Vidūḍabha who he declared king. When the Buddha's sermon was over, the king came out but did not find his general there. Soon the whole conspiracy came before him. So he hurried to Rājagṛha with a view to get the necessary support from Ajātaśatru for his own restoration. When he came back, he found that the entrance to the city was closed. So he decided to spend the night in a charitable guest house outside the city. The king was very much tired by the scorching rays of the sun and by the blast of hot wind. At night, he died in the same guest house. In the morning, when the news reached Ajātaśatru about the sudden death of the deposed king, he arranged a suitable funeral to him.

Now, Vidūḍabha marched against the Śākyas. The Śākyas were very much afraid of his power. Those who submitted without resistance had their lives spared; the rest were butchered to death. This included breast-fed children even. The stool which he had once used was washed with the blood of the Śākyas. It is recorded that on this occasion, 77,000 Śākyas lost their lives.[229] The historians are of the view that after this carnage, the Śākya republic came to an end.[230]

But when Vidūḍabha was on his way back to Śrāvastī, he and his entire army were washed away by a bore in the river Acīravatī.[231]

While recounting to Sāriputta the future Buddhas, the Buddha announced that Prasenajit would become the fourth Buddha.[232]

In the Jaina Āgamas

The name of this Prasenajit is nowhere to be found in the Jaina *Āgamas* wherein the name of the king of Śrāvastī has been given to be Jitaśatru.[233] It is not even clear if he ever met Mahāvīra. Mahāvīra had two important followers from Śrāvastī. They were Nandinīpiā and Sahīlīpiā. About them, the record states, *Jahā ānanda tahā niggae* (the same in weal and woe). From the word *'tahā,'* it is inferred by some that it referred to Jitaśatru who came to pay his homage, but this sounds like a far-fetched meaning which is far from convincing. According to the writers of the *Āgamas*, the kings of Vāṇijyagrāma, Campā, Vārāṇasī, Ālambhiyā and many other places had the same name 'Jitaśatru."[234] It appears, therefore, that this name was very popular and widely used in those days. In the *Āgama* named *Rāyapaseṇīya*, there is some detail available about one Jitaśatru, but it is not mentioned anywhere that he had any contact whatsoever with Mahāvīra. According to the *Dīgha Nikāya,*[235] King Pradeśī was a vassal unto King Prasenajit. According to the *Rāyapaseṇīya,* Jitaśatru was a vassal unto King Pradeśī. Even if we do not enter into this disputed territory as to who was vassal unto whom, this much should be clear from what has been said that in the Jaina tradition at least, Prasenajit has been called Jitaśatru. It is also very likely that he was a great follower of the Buddha because of which the writers of the Jaina *Āgamas* have neither noticed his great achievements nor mentioned his name as Prasenajit. In the course of their discussion, wherever the mention of the king of Śrāvastī has been relevant, they have very coldly called him as Jitaśatru. From this, however, it does not follow that the same would apply to those kings who had been called Jitaśatru.

The king of Śrāvastī might not have been a follower of Mahāvīra, but there is no occasion for doubt that Śrāvastī was a principal centre of activity of the Jainas. The immortal discussion between Keśīkumāra and Gautama took place in this city. The sharp exchange between Gośālaka and Mahāvīra also took place in this city. There is also a record that the followers of Mahāvīra from Śrāvastī came to the city of Kayaṅgalā in order to pay their homage to their spiritual leader.[236]

CEṬAKA

Just as there is no mention about Prasenajit in the *Āgamas,* so there is no mention about Ceṭaka in the *Tripiṭakas.* Like Prasenajit, King Ceṭaka was also a historical personality. If still the *Tripiṭakas* did not notice him, it must be because he was a great follower of Mahāvīra. According to the Jaina tradition, he was not merely a follower, but a staunch follower too, of Mahāvīra. We have it in authoritative sources that he had a resolve not to settle his daughters with one who was a follower of some other religion. But, surprisingly enough, nowhere in the *Āgamas,* Ceṭaka has been called a follower of the *nirgranthas.* Only in the later Jaina texts like the *Āvaśyaka Cūrṇī* and others, there is nothing either in the Jaina or any other tradition to prove that he was anything other than a Jaina. Under the circumstances, it may be claimed that he was a Jaina.

His Family

Triśalā, Mahāvīra's mother was the sister of Ceṭaka. All the daughters of Ceṭaka were settled in marriage with the principal kings of the time, and were themselves well-known. They were : Prabhāvatī married to King Udayana of Vītabhaya, Padmāvatī married to Dadhivāhana of Aṅga, Mṛgāvatī married to King Śatānīka of Vatsa, Śivā married to King Caṇḍa-pradyota of Ujjain, Jyeṣṭhā married to Mahāvīra's elder brother, Nandīvardhana and Celanā married to King Bimbisāra of Magadha. One of his daughters, Sujyeṣṭhā, was initiated in the order of Mahāvīra.

Vaiśālī Republic

The kingdom of Ceṭaka was well-known as the Vaiśālī Republic, which consisted of many small and big kingdoms.[238] Together, these kingdoms constituted a 'federation' or 'confederacy.' According to the *Jātaka Aṭṭhakathā,*[239] the confederacy had 7707 members. All the members of the confederacy were called 'kings.' King Siddhārtha, Mahāvīra's father, has been stated to be a member of this Confederacy.[240] According to Pāṇinī,[241] these kings were coronated in the usual manner, and enjoyed full autonomy in their own territory. It was customary to call a coronated king as 'Rājanya.' We have it in the *Lalitavistara*[242] that the Licchavīs did not recognise any difference in status between one king and another, and each had a feeling, 'I am a king.' Each king had his own vassals, commanders, store-keepers, etc. Each member of the Confederacy maintained a palace, guest-house, etc., at the metropolis of the entire confederacy, Vaiśālī. The Assembly of the 7707 kings was called the confederate. Assembly and the entire Confederacy was called Vajjī or Licchavī Confederacy.

The Republic had two Committees consisting of nine members each. One looked after the administration of justice and the other took care of the external relations. It was this second Committee that was responsible for the building up of the Confederacy which claimed within its fold the Licchavīs, the Mallas and kingdom of Kāśī-Kośala, of which the head was King Ceṭaka.

Jitaśatru, Siṅgha and Ceṭaka

In his English translation of the *Uvāsagadasāo,* Dr. Hornell has confused King Jitaśatru of Vāṇijyagrāma with King Ceṭaka. This is not correct. When in the Vaiśālī confederacy, there were 7707 kings, there is no reason why the two should be confused as one and the same person. Dr. Otto Stein has, however, tried to throw light on this in diverse ways.[243]

Some people have stretched their imagination to suggest that Siṅgha Senāpati to the Buddhist tradition and King Ceṭaka were one and the same person.[244] The reason for his surmise may be that according to the Tibetan tradition,[245] Queen, Vāsavī, wife of Bimbisāra, was the daughter of Siṅgha Senāpati, and she was the mother of Ajātaśatru. But leaving aside the Tibetan tradition, this has not been corroborated by any other source. Had Siṅgha Senāpati been the father-in-law of Bimbisāra and maternal grand-father of Ajātaśatru, the *Tripiṭakas* would have taken pride to record this relation. Under the circumstances, this should not be given too much importance beyond what may be due to a popular gossip of the later period.

In the Buddhist literature, Siṅgha has been consistently called a *Senāpati'* or army commander, whereas Ceṭaka was the head of the most powerful confederacy of the time. This is not very likely that a king would be confused with an army commander by anyone. In the social hierarchy of the time, as also of later period, the position of the king and that ofa general were clearly distinct. Dr. Jyoti Prasad Jain is of opinion that King Ceṭaka had 10 sons of whom the eldest named Siṅgha or Siṅghabhadra was a famous general of the Vajjīs.[246]

The main Jaina sources on the life-story of King Ceṭaka are the *Nirayāvalikā* and the *Bhagavatī.* This story has been already recounted at length under the section on 'Ajātaśtru' above.

OTHER KINGS

Apart from the above-mentioned kings, many other names of kings exist in both the traditions. Many of them have been noticed in different contexts in this work. They were either the followers of Mahāvīra or of the Buddha and there is hardly any dispute about them. Their names have usually figured in the tradition to which they belonged, and they are by no means important for purposes of a comparative study. Therefore, they are not relevant for our present purpose.

REFERENCES

1. *Buddha Carita*, sarga 10, śloka 8.
2. *Ibid.*, sarga 10, śloka 13.
3. *Ibid.*, sarga 11, śloka 72.
4. *Uttarājjhayanāni*, adhyayana 20, gāthā 6.
5. *Ibid.*, adhyayana 20, gāthā 38.
6. *Ibid.*, adhyayana 20, gāthā 42, 43.
7. *Ibid.*, adhyayana 20, gāthā 45.
8. *Ibid.*, adhyayana 20, gāthā 47.
9. *Ibid.*, adhyayana 20, gāthā 54-57.
10. *Ibid.*, adhyayana 20, gāthā 58.
11. *Dīgha Nikāya*, Mahāvaggo, Mahāparinibbāna Sutta, p. 91.
12. *Hindū Sabhyatā* (Hindi), p. 185.
13. *Vinaya Piṭaka*, Mahāvaggo, Mahākhandhaka, p. 35-36.
14. *Ibid.*, pp. 37-38.
15. *Dīgha Nikāya* 1-5, pp. 111-112.
16. *Ibid.*, 1-4, p. 108.
17. *Vinaya Piṭaka*, Mahāvaggo, Cammakhandhaka, p. 199.
18. *Vinaya Piṭaka*, Cullavagga, Kṣudrakavastu-skandhaka, p. 458.
19. *Peṭavatthu Aṭṭhakathā*, gāthā 209.
20. *Sacred Books of the East*, Vol. XLIV, p. 166.
21. *Dhammapada Aṭṭhakathā*, Vol. 2, pp. 438 *et. seq.*; also *Dictionary of Pāli Proper Names*, Vol. 2, p. 288.
22. *Aṅuttarovavāi-dasāo*, varga 3, sutta 4.
23. *Nayadhammakahāo*, 1/1.
24. *Triṣaṣṭiśalākā-puruṣa-caritram*, parva 10, sarga 6.
25. Ācarya Guṇacandra, *Mahāvīra Cariyam*, p. 334-1.
26. *Aṇuttarovavāi-dasāo*, varga 1, adhayana 1-10, also 1-13.
27. *Antagaḍa-dasāo*, varga 7, adhyayana 1-13.
28. For details about *Tīrthaṅkara Padmanābha*, *vide Thāṇaṅga*, 9-3-693.
29. *Triśaṣṭiśalākā-puruṣa-caritram*, parva 10, sarga 9.
30. *Ibid.*
31. *Bhāratīya Itihāsa : eka Dṛṣṭi*, p. 65.
32. *Dialogues of Buddha*, Part 1, p. 163.
33. Edward Thomas, *Life of Buddha*, p. 68-80.
34. *Tīrthaṅkara Mahāvīra*, Part 2, p. 11.
35. *Triṣaṣṭi-śalākā-puruṣa-caritram*, parva 10, sarga 6, śloka 376. Also, Nemicandra, *Mahāvīra Cariyaṃ*, gāthā 1294.
36. *Tīrthaṅkara Mahāvīra*, Part 2, pp. 11-16.
37. *Sthānāṅga-Samavayāṅga* (Gujarātī), p. 741.
38. *Mahāvaṁsa*, Chap. 2, gāthā 26-32.
39. *Triṣaṣṭi-śalākā-puruṣa-caritram*, parva 10, sarga 6, śloka 8.
40. *Bhāratīya Itihāsa : Eka Dṛṣṭi*, p. 62.
41. *Anāgatavaṁsa*; also *Dictionary of Pāli Proper Names*, Vol. 2, p. 174.
42. V.A. Smith, *The Oxford History of India*, p. 45.

43. *Ibid.*, pp. 51-52.
44. *Naya-dhamma-Kahās*, śru 1, adhyayana 13 (pp. 189-92); *Dasāsuya-khandha* (10-1 *et seq*) have it, seṇie bhambhasāre; *Uvavai* (Sūrta 7, page 23; Sūtra 9, p. 25; Sūtra 29, p. 115); seṇie Bhambhasāre, seṇie bhimbhasāre; *Ṭhāṇāṅga* (Thā. 9, p. 458-2); seṇie bhimbhisāre.
45. *Abhidhāna Cintāmaṇi*, kāṇḍa 3, śloka 376; *Upadeśamālā Satika*, p. 334; *Ṛṣimaṇḍala Prakaraṇa*, p. 143; *Śrī Bharateśvara Bāhuvalī Vṛtti*, Part 1, p. 22; *Āvaśyaka Cūrṇī*, Second half, p. 158.
46. *Upadeśamālā Saṭīka*, p. 334-1.
47. *Tīrthaṅkara Mahāvīra*, Part 2, pp. 630-633.
48. *Āgamodaya Samiti* Prakāśana (1920).
49. P. 461-1.
50. *Gramatic der Prakrit Sprachen*, Para 201; Hemarandra Jośī, *Prākṛta Bhāṣāon kā Vyākaraṇa*, p. 313; Bihāra Rāṣṭra Bhāṣā Pariṣad, Patnā.
51. *Udāna Aṭṭhakathā*, 104.
52. W.W. Rockhill, *Life of Buddha*, p. 16.
53. *Abhidhāna Cintāmaṇi*, Svopajñavṛtti, Martya Kāṇḍa, śloka 376.
54. *Vinaya Piṭaka.*
55. *Jambuddīpa Paññatti*, vakṣa 3; Also, *Jātaka, Mūgapakkha Jātaka*, V. 6, 539.
56. They are
kumbhāra paṭṭaillā suvaṇṇakāra, sūvakāra ya
gandhavvā kāsavaggā mālākāra kacchakāra. //1//
tambolīyā ya e e navappayāra ya nārua bhaṇiyā
57. aha ṇam ṇavappayāre kāruovaṇṇe pavakkhāmi. //2//
cammayaru jatapīlaga gañchia chiṁpāya kaṁsāre ya
sīvaga guāra bhillaga dhīvara vaṇṇai aṭṭhadasa. //3//
58. Part 3, p. 113, also, pp. 442-443.
59. *Corporate Life in Ancient India*, Vol. 2, p. 18.
60. *Dictionary of Pāli Proper Names*, Vol. 2, pp. 289, 1284.
61. *Triṣaṣṭi-śalākā-puruṣa-caritraṁ*, parva 10, sarga 6, śloka 1.
62. *Uttarapurāṇa*, parva 74, śloka 418.
63. *Cf.* tathāsti magadhe deśe puraṁ rājagrahaṁ paraṁ
tatropaśreṇiko rājā tadbhāryā suprabhā prabhā. //1//
....
64. *Skandha* 12, adhyāya 1, p. 903.
65. *Political History of Ancient India*, p. 205.
66. *Sabhāṣya*, bha 1, p. 17.
67. *Nayadhamma-kahāo*, adhyayana 1, sūtra 8.
68. *Mahāvagga*, 8-1-15.
69. Jātaka, 2-403; *Dictionary of Pāli Proper Names*, Vol. 2, p. 286; *Saṁyutta Nikāya* Aṭṭhakathā.
70. *Therīgāthā Aṭṭhakāthā*, 139-143.
71. *Therī Gāthā*, 31-32.
72. *Ibid.*
73. *Theragāthā Aṭṭhakathā*, 64.
74. *Thera Gāthā*, 608-619.
75. *Majjhima Nikāya Aṭṭhakathā*, 2, 932.
76. *Anuttarovavāyīya*, varga 1.
77. *Buddhacaryā*, p. 509.
78. *Uvavai Sutta*, 8.
79. *Ibid.*, 12.
80. *Ibid.*, (Hindi), p. 133.
81. *Ibid.*, Sutta 28-31.
82. It appears that this description of paying a visit to the spiritual leader was later adopted by the Buddhists. In the *Mahāvastu* (translated by J.J. Jones Vol. 3, pp. 442-443) of the

Mahāyāna sect, there is an identical description when King Bimbisāra came to pay his homage and obeisance to Buddha.

83. For details, vide *Upāsaka-dasāṅga Sūtra*, Adhyayana 1.
84. *Uvavī Sutta*, 25.
85. *Ibid.*, 34-37.
86. *Buddhist India*, p. 88.
87. *Thānāṅga Vṛtti*, 4-3.
88. *Mayadhamma-kahāo*, 1 to 5; Pariśiṣṭa Parva, sarga 4, śloka 15-54.
89. V.A. Smith, *Oxford History of India*, Second Edition, 1923, p. 51.
90. *Hindū Sabhyatā*, pp. 190-91.
91. *Ibid.*, p. 264.
92. *Dīgha Nikāya*, Sāmaññjaphala Sutta, p. 32.
93. *Uvavaī* (Hindi), p. 26; also, *Senapraśena*, ullāsa 3, question 237.
94. *Dīgha Nikāya*, Sāmaññjaphala Sutta, p. 32.
95. *Vinaya Piṭaka*, Cullavagga, Saṅgha-bhedaka Khandhaka, 7.
96. *Jātaka Aṭṭhakathā*, Thusa Jātaka, sam. 338.
97. *Dhammapada Aṭṭhakathā*, 10-7.
98. *Ibid.*, Part 2-605-6.
99. *Encyclopaedia of Buddhism*, p. 320.
100. *Aṅguttara Nikāya*, 4-8-188.
101. *Encyclopaedia of Buddhism*, p. 319.
102. *Avadāna-śataka*, 54.
103. *Theragāthā Aṭṭhakathā*, 609-19.
104. *Buddhist India*, pp. 15-16.
105. Dalsukh Malvaniya, *Āgama yuga kā Jaina Darśana*, p. 29.
106. *Bhikṣudharma Rakṣita*, Ācārya Buddhaghoṣa, p. 7.
107. *Jātaka*, edited by Fausboll, Vol. 3, p. 121.
108. *Jātaka Aṭṭhakathā*, sam. 249, 283.
109. *Saṁyutta Nikāya*, 3-2-4.
110. *Cf.* vedehiputto ti vedehīti paṇḍitādhivacanaṁ etaṁ paṇḍititthīya putto ti attho. *Saṁyutta Nikāya*, Aṭṭhakatha, 1, 120.
111. Rockhill, *Life of Buddha*, p. 63.
112. *Sacred Books of the East*, Vol. XLIX, p. 166.
113. Rockhill, *op. cit.*, p. 63.
114. *Kalpa Sūtra*, 110.
115. *Sacred Books of the East*, Vol. XXII, p. 256; *Kalpa Sūtra* (Beṅgālī) by Basanta Kumāra Chaṭṭopādhyāya, p. 27.
116. *Hindū Sabhyatā*, p. 198.
117. *Āvaśyaka Cūrṇī*, Part 2, 164.
118. *Ibid.*, Part 1, p. 254.
119. *Bhagavatī*, 7-9-576.
120. *Buddhist India*, p. 3.
121. *Encyclopaedia of Buddhism*, p. 316.
122. *Therigāthā Aṭṭhakathā*, 139-43.
123. Rockhill, *Life of Buddha*, p. 63.
124. *Hindū Sabhyatā*, p. 183.
125. *Dialogues of Buddha*, Vol. 2, p. 78.
126. *Vāyu Purāṇa*, Chapter 99, śloka 319; *Matsya Purāṇa*, Chapter 271, Sl. 9.
127. *Dialogues of Buddha*, Vol. 2, p. 78.
128. *Dīgha Nikāya Aṭṭhakathā*, 1, 133.
129. Apte's *Sanskrit-English Dictionary*, Vol. 1, p. 580.
130. *Triśaṣṭi-śalākā-puruṣa-caritraṃ*, parva 10, sarga 6, śloka 309.
131. There is unanimity between the two names, Halla and Vihalla. The original text of the Nirayāvalīya has linked the whole episode with Vihalla. The Nirayāvalīya commentary,

the Bhagavatī commentary, *Bharateśvara-Bāhubali-vṛtti*, etc., make use of both the names. According to the Aṇuttarovavaiya, Vihalla and Vehāyasa were the sons of Celanā, and Halla the son of Dhariṇī. According to the *Nirayavalīya-vṛtti* and *Bhagavatī-vṛtti*, both Halla and Vihalla were born of Celanā. This is worthy of research.

132. It is said that the money value of the elephant and the necklace was as much as the value of Śreṇika's kingdom. (*Āvaśyaka Cūrṇī*, Second Half, p. 167).
133. *Nirayāvalīya Sutta* (with commentary), p. 6-1.
134. *Bhagavatī*, S.7. U. 9. Sūtra 301.
135. Kūlavālaka monk used to practise penances on the bank of a river. It was because of his penance that the flow of the river got a twist, from which he acquired his name. (*Uttarādhyayana Sūtra* with *Vṛtti* by Lakṣmī Vallabh, in Gujarātī) Ahmedabad, 1935, Part 1, p. 8.
136. *Ibid.*, p. 10.
137. *Ibid.*, p. 11.
138. *Bharateśvara Bāhubalī Vṛtti*, pp. 100-101.
139. Ācārya Bhikṣu, *Bhikṣu Grantha Ratnākara*, Vol. 2, p. 88.
140. *Buddhacaryā* (p. 484) states that costly and fragrant commodities were being unloaded near a mountain.
141. *Dīgha Nikāya Aṭṭhakathā*, (*Sumaṅgala-vilāsinī*), Vol. 2, p. 526. Also, B.C. Law, *Buddhaghoṣa*, p. 111 and *Hindū Sabhyatā*, p. 187.
142. *Dīgha Nikāya*, Parinivvāna Sutta, 2/3 (16).
143. *Ibid.*
144. *Dīgha Nikāya Aṭṭhakathā*, Vol. 2, p. 523.
145. *Hindū Sabhyatā*, p. 189.
146. *Nirayāvalīya Sutta* (ed. by P.L. Vaidya), p. 4.
147. *Uvavaī Sutta*, su. 7, p. 22.
148. *Ibid.*, Su. 33, p. 144.
149. *Āvaśyaka Cūrṇī*, Second half, p. 167.
150. Ācārya Buddhaghoṣa, *Sumaṅgala-vilāsinī*, Vol. 1, p. 137.
151. *Jātaka Aṭṭhakathā*, Vol. 4, p. 343; *Encyclopaedia of Buddhism*, p. 317.
152. *Ṭhāṇāga Sūtra Vṛtti*, Thā. 4, U. 3; *Āvaśyak Cūrṇī*, Second Half, pp. 176-77.
153. *Mahāvaṁsa*, 4/1.
154. *Dīgha Nikāya Aṭṭhakathā*, Vol. 1, pp. 237-38.
155. *Bhagavatī*, S.1. U.5. The names of hells given therein are Ratnaprabhā, Śarkarāprabhā, Bālukaprabhā, Paṅkaprabhā, Dhūmaprabhā, Tamaḥprabhā, Mahātamaḥ (Tamatamā) prabhā.
156. According to the *Jātaka Aṭṭhakathā* (vol. 5, pp. 266, 271) these names are Sañjīva, Kālasutta, Saṅghāta, Jalaraurava, Dhūmaraurava, Mahā-avīci, Tapana and Patāpana. The Divyāvadāna (67) has these names, except that it has Raurava in place of Jalaraurava and Mahāraurava in place of Dhūmaraurava. *Saṁyuta Nikāya* (6-1-10), *Aṅguttara Nikāya* (P.T.S. Vol. 5, p. 173) and *Sutta Nipāta, Mahāvagga, Kokalīya Sutta* (3/36) name ten hells as follows : Abbuda, Nirabbuda, Avaba, Aṭaṭa, Ahaha, Kumuda, Sogandhika, Uppala, Puṇḍarīka and Paduma. According to the Aṭṭhakathā, these are not the names of the hells, but the names of different time-spans one is to spend there. The *Āgamas* too have mention of diverse time-spans in hells. (*Vide Bhagavatī*, śataka 6, uddeśaka 7). Elsewhere in the Buddhist literature, we get a list of five hells only. In the Devadattasutta of the *Majjhima Nikāya* and in the *Jātakas*, one comes across the names of other hells also. For the hell named Lohakumbhī Niraya, *vide Jātaka Aṭṭhakathā*, Part 3, p. 22; Part 5, p. 269; and *Sutta Nipāta Aṭṭhakathā*, Part 1, p. 59.
157. *Dictionary of Pāli Proper Names*, Vol. 1, p. 35.
158. *Jātaka Aṭṭhakathā*, *Saṁkicca Jātaka*, No. 530.
159. *Cf. Nirayāvaliya*, Sūtra 23; *Nayadhamma-kahāo*, Śru. 1, adhyayana 1; *Aṅuttarovavaīya-dasāo*, 1/1.
160. This town should be located on the bank of the river Kṛṣṇā in the Deccan, near its confluence with the sea, for details, *vide Tīrthaṅkara Mahāvīra*, Part 2, pp. 641-43.

161. *Bhareteśvara Bāhuvalī Vṛtti,* p. 36.
162. As per Gilgit Manuscript (Part 3, 2, p. 22), Abhayarājakumāra was the son of Bimbīsara, born of a prostitute named Āmrapālī who hailed from Vaiśālī. In the original Pāli texts, the name of Bimbisāra's son from Āmrapālī is Vimala Koḍanna, who later became a Buddhist monk. (*Vide Theragāthā-Aṭṭhakathā*, 64).
163. *Theragāthā-Aṭṭhakathā*, 31-32.
164. *Majjhima Nikāya,* Abhayarājakumāra Sutta.
165. It is a pole in the threshing shed round which the bullocks move to separate the grains.
166. *Nayadhamma-kahāo,* 1/1.
167. *Bharateśvara Bāhuvalī Vṛtti,* p. 38.
168. *Triṣaṭi-śalākā-puruṣa-caritram*, parva 10, sarga 6, śloka 226-27, pp. 78-82.
169. On reaching Ujjain, Caṇḍa-pradyota realised that all this was a plot by Abhayakumāra of which he had been a victim. Out of sheer anger, he organised a counter-plot and took Abhayakumāra a prisoner. On regaining his freedom, Abhayakumāra took revenge on him, and made Caṇḍa-pradyota a captive. For details, *Triṣaṣṭi-śalākā-puruṣa-caritram,* parva 10, sarga 11, śloka 124-293; also, *Āvaśyaka Cūrṇī*, Second Half, pp. 159-163.
170. *Dhammapada-Aṭṭhakathā*, 13-4.
171. *Āvaśyaka Cūrṇī,* Second Second Half, p. 160.
172. Episode76.
173. 44-6-6.
174. According to the *Theragāthā Aṭṭhakathā* (1-58), Abhayarājkumāra had his spiritual eye opened when Buddha gave a sermon which became Tālacchigulupama Sutta.
175. *Dhammapada Aṭṭhakathā*, 13-4.
176. *Theragāthā,* 26.
177. *Theragāthā Aṭṭhakathā,* Part 1, pp. 83-84.
178. *Ibid*., 131-32.
179. *Dharmaratna-prakaraṇa,* Abhayarājakumāra Kathā, 1-130.
180. For details, vide "*Śreṇika Bimbisāra*" in this volume.
181. Hemacandra Yogaśāstra, with *Śvopajñavṛtti*, adhyayana, śloka 30, pp. 91-95.
182. For details, *vide "Ārdraka Muni"* in this volume.
183. An alternative view is that Abhayarājakumāra did not ask about "would-be liberated king," but about "duly crowned king." Vide Abhidhāna Rajendra, Vol. 3, p. 481.
184. *Bharateśvara Bāhubalī Vṛtti,* pp. 38-40.
185. Edited by Modi, p. 51.
186. For comparison, vide the account of Monk Skandaka elsewhere in this volume.
187. *Aṇuttarovavayiyadasā,* Varga 1, adhyayana 10.
188. Dalsukha Malvānīyā, *op. cit.*, p. 28.
189. Thera Apādāna Bhaddiyavaggo, Abhyayattheraapadānam.
190. Bhikṣu Jagadīśa Kāśyapa, *Khuddaka Nikāya,* Vol. 7, p. v.
191. *Avadāna*, 40.
192. *Ibid*., 37.
193. *Cf.* uddayana rāyā tāvasabhaṭṭo, *Āvaśyaka Cūrṇī*, First Half, p. 399.
194. *Vide* section on "Udayana" under the Monastic Order in this volume. For the Buddhist account, vide *Divyāvadāna, Rudrāyaṇavadāna*, 37.
195. *Divyavadāna*, edited by P.L. Vaidya, Intro.
196. *Ibid*., p. 17.
197. *Vide* subsection on "Ardrakakumāra" under section "Gośālaka" in this volume.
198. *Vide* section on "Bimbisāra" in this volume.
199. S.13, U.6.
200. *Uttarajjhayanāni*, 18/48.
201. *Bhagavatī*, S.13, U.6.
202. *Dhammapada-Aṭṭhakathā,* 2-1; *Triṣaṣṭi-śalākā-puruṣa-caritram*, parva 10, sarga 11, śloka 184-265.
203. *Kathāsaritsāgara*, 12/16/6.

204. *Triṣaṣṭi-śalākā-puruṣa-caritram*, parva 10, sarga 11, śloka 445-597; *Uttarājjhayanāni*, adhyayana 18, *Nemicandra vṛtti*. *Bharateśvara Bāhubalī*, Part 1, pp. 177-81.
205. *Triṣaṣṭi-śalākā-puruṣa-caritram*, parva 10, sarga 11, śloka 184-265.
206. *Ibid*., śloka 172-293.
207. *Uttarājjhayanāni*, adhyayana 9, *Nemicandra Vṛtti*.
208. 3-1-8, *Gopaka Moggalāna Sutta*.
209. *Cf. Bharateśvara Bāhubalī Vṛtti*, Part 1, p. 177.
210. *Triṣaṣṭi-śalākā-puruṣa-caritram*, 10/11/597.
211. *Bharateśvara Bhāhubalī Vṛtti*, Part 2, p. 323.
212. *Ibid*.
213. *Vide* section on "Mahākaccāyana" in this volume.
214. S. 12, U.2.
215. *Vide* section on "*Ajātaśatru Kūṇika*" in this volume.
216. *Vide* section on "*Jayantī*" in this volume.
217. Śrutaskandha 1, adhyayana 5.
218. In their early life, these three Śreṣṭhīs were the followers of heretical monks. Then they became Buddhists and erected guest houses for the monks, each in his own name. For details, vise *Dhammapada Aṭṭhakathā*, 2-1.
219. *Ibid*; also Nalinākṣa Datta, *Uttara Pradeśa me Buddha Dharma kā Vikāsa*, p. 114.
220. 34-3-3-4.
221. For details and also account of previous life, *Jātaka Aṭṭhakathā, Mataṅga Jātaka*, Sam. 497.
222. *Dhammapada Aṭṭhakathā*, 2-1.
    Cf. *tasmādimāṁ mūtrapurīṣapūrṇāṁ,*
    spṛṣṭuṁ hi yattāmapi notsaheyam.
    —*Divyāvadāna*, 36
223. Bodhirājakumāra was his son by Queen Vāsavadattā. For deails, *Majjhima Nikāya*, Bodhirājakumāra Sutta, 2/4/5; Also *Majjhima Nikāya* Aṭṭhakathā, 2/4/5.
224. *Kośala saṁyutta*, Yajña Sutta, 3-1-9.
225. *Dharmmapada Aṭṭhakathā*, 5-1; Also, *Buddhist Legends*, Vol. 2, p. 104 ff.
226. *Saṁyutta Nikāya*, 3-2-3.
227. *Majjhima Nikāya*, Aṅgulimāla Suttanta, 2/4/6.
228. *Majjhima Nikāya*, 2-2-9.
229. *Avadānakalpalatā*; Also, *Dictionary of Pāli Proper Names*, Vol. 2, p. 877, fn.
230. *Hindū Sabhyatā*, p. 194; *Buddhist India*, p. 11.
231. *Based on Dhammapada Aṭṭhakathā*, 4-3.
232. *Anāgatavaṁsa*; Also, *Dictionary of Pāli Proper Names*, Vol. 2, p. 174.
233. *Uvasagadasāo*, 9/10; also *Rayapaseṇīya Sutta*.
234. *Uvasagadasāo*, adhyayana, 1, 2, 3, 4, 5, etc.
235. *Dīgha Nikāya*, 2/10.
236. *Bhagavatī*, S.2, U.1.
237. *Cf.* so cedavo sāvao.
    Āvaśyaka Cūrṇī, Second Half, p. 164.
    cetakastu śrāvako.
    —*Triṣaṣṭi-śalākā-puruṣa-caritram*, 10-6-186.
238. *Hindū Sabhyatā*, p. 193.
239. Part 1, p. 336 (Bhāratīya Jñānapītha Edition, Kāśi).
240. *Tīrthaṅkara Mahāvīra*, Part 1, p. 96.
241. *Pāṇini Vyākaraṇa*, 6/2/34.
242. 3/23.
243. *Jinist Studies*, ed. by Muni Jina Vijayajī.
244. For illustration, Vide Narakeśarī, a fiction in Gujarātī by Jayabhikṣu, p. 234 fn.
245. Rockhill, *Life of Buddha*, p. 63.
246. *Bhāratīya Itihāsa, eka Dṛṣṭi*, p. 56.

15

LIBERATION

Bhagavān Mahāvīra entered into his liberation at Pāvā and Gautama Buddha entered into his liberation at Kuśinārā. As to the distance between the two places, we read, in part, as follows :

> *Pāvā-nagarato tīni gāvutāni kuśinārā-nagaram* which means that Pāvā was at a distance of three *gavyūtas* (about six miles) from Kuśinārā.[1]

We have it on the authority of Rāhul Sāṅkṛtyāyana, the Buddha, starting at midday from Pāvā, reached Kuśinārā in the evening. As he was ill and weak, so he stopped at several places to rest before he reached his destination. The distance between Kapilavastu (Lumbinī) and Kṣatriya-Kuṇḍapura is accepted to be about 250 miles.[2]

Thus, though born at a distance of 250 miles, the distance at the time of their death was no more than 6 miles. So it may be stated that the two who were not far apart from each other in their spiritual attainments came closer even in space at the time of their death.

The final (funeral) rites for both were performed by the Mallā *Kṣatriyas*. At the time of Mahāvīra's death, nine Mallās and nine Licchavīs were by his side. Eighteen kings who were the heads of their respective *gaṇas* at Kāśī and Kośala were at that time performing their *pauṣadha*. In the morning, they also joined the funeral procession. At the passing away of the Buddha, Ānanda came to Kuśinārā and broke the sad news to the Mallas who were assembled in the public hall. Ānanda did not consider Kuśinārā to be a suitable place for the death of the Buddha from which it should appear that the Mallas were perhaps more intimate with Mahāvīra than they were with the Buddha.

In the funeral ceremony of both, the Indras and their gods participated in a very large number, Mahāvīra's pyre was lit by Agnikumāra gods and it was cooled by Meghakumāra gods. The last mortal remains of both were carried away by the Indras of the upper and lower (subterranean) heavens. On both the occasions, the Indras and their gods were very much stricken with grief. There is, however, an important difference between the two, *viz.*, that whereas at the funeral of Mahāvīra, the leading-most role was played by the gods, human beings taking only a subsidiary role, at the funeral of the Buddha, human beings were the principal participants, and the gods only witnessed the occasion by remaining invisible in the sky. What the gods wanted about the Buddha's funeral and how they wanted it to be performed was communicated by the *arhat*-monks to the Mallas. The Buddhist account of (the participation by) the gods appears to be more realistic.

In their final years, both moved out from Rājagṛha. Mahāvīra chose Pāvā for his monsoon retreat and he passed away at this place in the last quarter of the new-moon night in the month of *Kārtika*. We have no record of any important event which might have occurred between Pāvā and Rājagṛha, nor any to indicate that Mahāvīra was taken ill before he passed away. As to the Buddha, we have a complete record of his wandering from Rājagṛha to Kuśinārā, and he is stated to have died for having taken a pig's meat. The date of his death has been accepted to be the full-moon night of the month of *Vaiśākha*. But according to the Sarvastivāda tradition, the Buddha (too) passed away on the full-moon night in the month of *Kārtika*.[3]

Before, their liberation, both delivered special sermons. Mahāvīra's sermon was a long one, but that of the Buddha was brief. There were many questions and answers on both the occasions. Many questions were asked by the disciples and all were duly answered by their respective masters. In both the traditions, however, some of the questions appear to be later interpolations and perhaps were not in the original. At a later period, these have been placed in the mouths of their respective leaders according to the needs of their followers. On the night during which he passed away, Mahāvīra initiated Hastipāla into monkhood with his own hands, and the Buddha did the same to Subhadra Parivrājaka.

On hearing the news about the passing the passing away of Mahāvīra, his very intimate disciple *Ganadhara* Gautama was very much afflicted with grief. The same thing happened to Ānanda who was a close and faithful associate of the Buddha, and Ānanda began to cry. Shortly after the outburst of this grief, *Gannadhara* Gautama attained his omniscience. Ānanda became an *Arhat* sometime after the passing away of the Buddha.

On their respective life-spans, Mahāvīra and the Buddha held widely different views. Mahāvīra said,

> "As to the possibility of increasing the life-span (of a *Tirthaṅkara*), well, this has never happened, nor can it ever happen."

But, according to the Buddha,

> "The *Tathāgata* is capable to live as long as a whole *kalpa* if he so chooses."

Kalpa Sūtta is the source book on the episode of Mahāvīra's liberation. Adopted from this source, it has been elaborated in the commentaries, *cūrṇīs* and biographies. *Kalpa Sūtra* is believed to have been composed by Bhadrabāhu who was the seventh Ācārya since Mahāvīra. Since it was first composed till the time of Devardhi Kṣamāśramaṇa when it was put into writing which event took place in c. 453 A.D., it appears that there had been a number of interpolations in the *Sūtra* which became an integral part of it. Bhadrabāhu's own time is believed to be 371-357 B.C.

The story of the liberation of the Buddha is contained in the *Mahāparinivvāna Sutta* of the *Dīgha Nikāya.* This Sutta includes sundry other discussions which one comes across at several places in other *Tripiṭakas*. From this it should appear that this *Sutta* was compiled on the basis of later gleanings. Of course, the *Dīgha Nikāya* is a part of the *Tripiṭakas,* but even Western Orientalists like Rhys Davids, E.J. Thomas and Wintenitz are of opinion that the *Mahāparinivvāna Sutta* must have been added at a somewhat later period.[4] This, however, should not be taken to mean that the *Mahāparinivvāna Sutta* is not very much posterior. The ideas, languages and style of the two are also expressive of their nearness in time. In the matter of rhetoric and exaggerations, there is much common ground between the two.

The account of Mahāvīra's liberation appears to be scrappy and somewhat disconnected, but no one gets the impression that some of the events have been later additions. Many of the events have been narrated in general terms as 'it so happened during that night'. The account of the Buddha's liberation is more consistent and more elaborate too.

The account of the liberation of Mahāvīra and the Buddha are given in this Chapter one after the other. Although the representation has had to be concise, care has, however, been taken to make it correspond to the original. *Kalpa Sūtra* is of course the principal work on Mahāvīra's liberation which has been used in the preparation of the present Chapter, but other sources utilised are the Bhagavatī, Jambū-dvīpa Paññatti, Saubhāgya-pancamyādi *Parva Kathā-Saṅgraha*, Mahāvīra Cariyam and many others. For the counter part of the Buddha story, the exclusive source used has been the *Mahāparinivvānna Sutta*. In both the cases, the original text of the main assertions has been given in the commentary.

LIBERATION OF MAHĀVĪRA

Starting from Rājagṛha, Mahāvīra came to Apāpā (Pāvāpurī). People assembled. In the course of his sermon, Mahāvīra said in part, as follows :

"In the presence of a *Tīrthaṅkara*, this land of Bhārata is like a heaven full of wealth and grains, dotted with villages and towns all over. In such a period (when a *Tīrthaṅkara* is alive), villages are prosperous as towns, towns as heavens, common folks as kings, and kings as Kuvera (the god of wealth) himself. In such a period, the Ācārya is like the Indra, the parents are like the gods, the mother-in-law is like one's own mother and father-in-law is like one's own father. In such a period, people know the distinction between the pious and the impious; they are polite, truthful, dedicated to the gods and subservient to their spiritual leaders and firm in right conduct. The wise people are honoured. Lineage, good conduct and learning are recognised. There are no disturbances and calamities. The monarchs are the followers of the Jina path.

"When, as now on, *Tīrthaṅkaras*, *Cakravartīs, Vāsudevas*, etc., will be no more, and *kevala* and *manaḥ-paryāya* knowledge will disappear from the land, the state of things in Bhāratavarṣa will steadily deteriorate. People will have more of anger and less of reason; standards will be badly shaken; arbitrariness will go up; piety will decline making room for impiety. Villages will wear the look of creamation grounds, towns will look haunted by spirits, honest people will be subdued like slaves and wicked people will be aggresive like monarchs. In the prevalent chaos, the 'logic of the fish' will be the order of the day in which the strong will torture upon the weak. The state of things in Bhāratavarṣa will be like a ship without a rudder. Thieves will commit more thefts, kings will levy more taxes and men and of the judiciary will accept more bribes. People will have a great attachment of wealth and grains.

"The preceptors' home (where scholars reside to learn) will lose their dignity. The teachers will not impart scriptural knowledge to the pupils. The students will not tender service unto the teachers. The earth will be full of insects and bacteria. The gods will disappear from the world. Sons will not pay attention to their parents. Daughters-in-law will lose their morals. Charity, conduct, penance and thought—all will sink to a low level. There will be splits and skirmishes within the spiritual orders. False weights and measures will be in use. *Mantras, tantras,* herbs, gems, flowers, fruits, substances, beauties, life-span, fortune, body-form and stature—all these will be very diminutive.

"Conditions will be extremely miserable in the sixth fraction of the time-cycle called non-bracing-non-bracing (*duḥṣama-duḥṣama*). Towards the end of the fifth fraction, called non-bracing (*duḥṣama*), there will be an Ācārya (monk) named Duḥprasaha, a nun named Phalguśrī, a *śrāvaka* named Nāgila and a *srāvikā* named Satyaśrī. Only these four will keep the (fourfold) order alive. The ruling monarch will be Bimalavāhana and Sumaka will be his minister. The people will have a height of 2 cubits (one yard) and they will have a life-span of 20 years. On the closing day of the fifth fraction of the time-cycle, the virtue of conduct will disintegrate in the morning, the virtue of administration will disintegrate at midday and fire will disintegrate in the afternoon.

"The fifth fraction of the time-cycle called *duḥṣama* will have a duration of 21,000 years and the sixth fraction called *duḥṣama-duḥṣama* will also have a similar duration. That will see the end of religion, society, and administration. The normal relations between parents and progeny will be gone. At the commencement of the sixth fraction, there will be cyclones and heavy showers causing a complete deluge.[5] Very few men and beasts will survive as seedings (when the cycle looks up). These will somehow keep themselves alive in the cravice and holes on the banks of the Gaṅgā and the Sindhu (which themselves will be no more wide than a chariot's route).[6] They will live on fish and meat.

"When the sixth fraction of the time-cycle will come to an end, the first fraction of the next half which is the up-phase of the time-cycle will commence. This period will bear resemblance with the sixth part of the prior half. The second fraction of the up-phase will resemble the fifth part of the previous down phase, and things beneficial will have their genesis. At the commencement of the second fraction, there will be a shower from a cloud named *Puṣkara-samvartaka* which will remove the heat from the earth. Then there will be milk showers which will help corn to sprout, and these will be followed by butter showers which will add alluvium to the earth. Then there will be nectarine showers which will help all types of flora to germinate. And the fifth and the last, there will be moisture-giving showers which will augment the moisture content of the earth. Each one of these showers will last for a whole week and they will be incessant.[7]

"The environment will again become more favourable. People will come out from the cravices and holes on the river banks and start living on the flat grounds. Gradually, they will wax in physical beauty, intellect and life-span. In the third fraction called unbracing-bracing (*duḥṣama-suṣamā*), villages, towns, etc., will come up. *Tīrthaṅkaras* will appear one after another. In the fourth fraction of the up-phase, people will be born as twins and die as twins. (In this system called *yaugalika*, children born as brother and sister live as man and wife). They will have big bodies and big spans of life. The *kalpa* trees will meet all their needs. The size of the body and the span of life will continue to increase in the fifth and the sixth fractions of the up-phase. And then a day will come when the up-phase of the time-cycle will come to its close. One down phase and one up phase together constitute one complete time cycle. Such time cycles have appeared in the past and they will continue to appear in the future. Those who make full propitiation of human life will break through the time cycles and attain liberation. Their soul will again its true self."[8]

Bhagavān Mahāvīra spent his last monsoon at Pāvāpuri. Hastipāla was the king of the place. Mahāvīra was encamped in his writers' building (*rajjuka/ sabhā),* which according to some was his customs office). The new-moon day of the month of *Kārtika* drew near. The last congregation met to attend the final sermon. Śakra the Indra of the gods, stood up and prayed. He was followed by King Hastipāla himself who stood up and prayed.

Now, *Bhagavān* Mahāvīra started his final sermon. He recited 55 *adhyayanas* on the whirl of the outcome of piety and another 55 on the whirl of the outcome of impiety.[9] At the present time, they exist as *Āgamas* called *Sukhavipāka* and *Duḥkha-vipāka.* Then he gave forth 36 *adhyayanas* of the *unasked vyākaraṇa* which have come down as an *Āgama* called *Uttarādhyayana.* While reciting the *adhyayana* named Pradhāna on Mother Marudevī, he became fixed in the *paryaṅka* posture.[10] Then gradually he became fixed in coarse *kāya-yoga* and stopped coarse *manaḥyoga* and coarse *vacana-yoga.* Then he changed over to fine *kāya-yoga* and cancelled coarse *kāya-yoga*, and also fine *manaḥ-yoga* and *vacana-yoga.* Then he attained the third step called *sukṣma-kriyā-apratipāti* of white (pure) meditation calles *śukla dhyāna.* Then he stopped even the fine *kāya-yoga* and reached the fourth step called *samucchinnakriyā-anivṛtti* of white meditation. Then he lived in the rock-like state (*śailaesī*) for as much time as is taken to utter *a, i, u, ṛ, l,* and having completely exhausted his non-terminable *karma,* Mahāvīra attained the state of perfection, enlightenment and liberation.[11]

It was the fourth month of the rainy season, the dark half of the month, the 15th day, the last full-moon night of the fortnight. Five years make one *yuga;* it was the second year of the *yuga* and it was named *Candra.* Twelve months make one year; it was the fourth month named *Prītivardhana.* There are two fortnights in a month; the fortnight was named *Nandīvardhana.* Fifteen days make a fortnight; it was the fifteenth day called *Agniveśya,* also called *Upaśama.* There are fifteen nights in a fortnight; it was the fifteenth night called *Devānandā* or *Nirati*. The lava at that time was *Ārca* the *prāṇa* was *Muhūrta,* the *stoka* was *Siddha,*[12] the *karaṇa* was *Nāga.*[13] There are 30 *muhūrtas* in one day-night; it was the twenty-ninth *muhūrta* named *Sarvārtha-siddhi.*[14] At that time, the asterism *Svāti* was in conjunction with the moon.

The final sermon of *Bhagavān* Mahāvīra lasted for 16 *praharas* (48 hours).[15] He was on a fast missing six meals.[16] There were many question and discussions. King Puṇyapāla enquired about the outcome of his eight dreams. On receiving the answer, he became indifferent to the world and became initiated as a monk.[17] King Hastipāla also received inspiration to be initiated as a monk.

On a point of enquiry, Indrabhūti Gautama asked,

> "*Bhante!* After your liberation, when will the fifth fraction of the time-cycle commence?"
>
> Mahāvīra—"Gautama! It will commence after the expiry of 3 years and eight and half months."

On further questions by Gautama, Mahāvīra gave out the names of the *Tīrthaṅkaras,* Vāsudevas, Baladevas, Patriarchs and other who would make their appearance in the next up-phase of the time-cycle.

Gaṇadhara Sudharman submitted thereafter as follows :

> "*Bhante!* When will the Sun Omniscience (*kaivalya-sūrya)* go out?"

Mahāvīra—"Twelve years after me, Gautama will attain perfection, and 20 years after me, you yourself will attain perfection. Sixty-four years after me, your disciple monk Jambū will attain perfection. In fact, he will be the last omniscient personality (of this phase). Jambū will be followed, in due order, by Prābhava, Sayyambhava, Yaśobhadra, Saṁbhūtivijaya, Bhadrabāhu and Sthūlabhadra, all of whom will be the masters of 14 *Pūrvas.* Among these, only Sayyambhava will be the author of Deśaveyaliya which he will write because of his *pūrva*-knowledge.[18]

As the final moments of Mahāvīra's liberation drew near, the seat of the Indra was shaken. With the family of his gods, he came to the spot. With tears in his eyes, he submitted,

> "*Bhante!* At the time of your entering into the womb, at your birth, initiation and at your attainment of omniscience, the asterism *Hastottarā* was in conjunction with the moon. At that time, an evil star named *Bhasma-graha* is about to come up. It will cast its bad influence on the star at your birth and stand in the way of the future progress of your monastic order. After 2000 years, when this evil star will be separated from the star at your birth, then the *śramaṇas,* the *nirgranthas* will be adored and honoured. So, till this evil star continues to haunt the star at your birth, I pray, you hold on your life-span in tact."

On this submission, the comments of *Bhagavān* Mahāvīra were as follows :

> "Śakra! Life-span can never be increased. It has never happened like that, nor will it ever happen like that. The non-bracing phase of the time-cycle will by itself be a handicap to the future progress of my order; but this is unavoidable."[19]

On the very day (when *Bhagavān* Mahāvīra was to enter into liberation), he sent his first *Gaṇadhara* Indrabhūti Gautama to a *Brāhmaṇa* named Devaśarmā in order to inspire him. The reason why Mahāvīra sent away his intimate disciple in that manner was that (being present on the spot), Gautama, who had enjoyed his close association for a long time would break down with grief at his death. Indrabhūti received the sad news of the liberation of *Bhagavān* Mahāvīra when he was at the house of the *Brāhmaṇa*, Devaśarmā. It came as a stroke of lightning on the devout heart of Indrabhūti. In a fit of soliloquy, he said,

'*Bhagavān*! What has thou done! On an occasion like this, I have been separated from thee. Is it possible that I would have acted like a child and tried to prevent your exit to the summum bonum. Did you conceive my affection for thee to be so very artificial? If perchance I had followed thee, would there have been so much shortage of space in the *Siddhaśilā*? Would I have been burden for thee? Henceforth, at whose lotus-like feet shall I bow in reverence? To whom shall I henceforth ask questions on life and liberation. Whom shall I henceforth address as '*Bhante*', and who will affectionately call me 'Goyama?'

Thus floating in the tormenting current of sentiments, Gautama somewhat controlled himself, and his thought-current was reversed :

'Well! Why am I blinded by affection? What is the attachment for one who is beyond all attachment-detachment (*vītarāga*)? This is no more than a one-sided affection in me for him. Enough with it. I give it up now. I am my own unity. I am shared by none. I belong to none; nothing (no one) here belongs to me. Attachment and malice are just perversion of the mind. Equanimity (balance) is the only strength and support for the soul'.

Thus passing through the deeper consciousness of the self, Indrabhūti Gautama attained omniscience right on the spot.[20]

During the night when *Bhagavān* Mahāvīra passed away, 9 Mallakīs, 9 Licchavīs and 18 *Gaṇa*-chiefs from Kāśī and Kośala were performing the vow of *pauṣadha*.[21]

To participate in the funeral rites of *Bhagavān* Mahāvīra, all the Indras of the gods and the *asuras* came down with their respective families of *devas* and *asuras*. All had tears in their eyes. All were overwhelmed with the feeling that they had been turned into orphans. At the order of the Śakra, the gods brought *gośīrṣa* sandal wood from Nandanavana. They brought water (milk) from the *Kṣīra-sāgara* (Ocean of Milk). With this water, Indra gave a bath to the body of Mahāvīra, applied perfumed pastes to it and covered it with divine cloth. Then the body was placed on a divine palanquin.

The palanquin was lifted up by the Indras. The gods showered divine flowers with shouts of 'victory'. On the way leading to the cremation ground, some gods and goddesses danced at the head of the palanquin, and some other gods worshiped the body with diamonds and gems. Overwhelmed with profound grief, the *śrāvakas* and the *śrāvakas* followed the palanquin. On arriving at the appropriate place, the planquin was placed on the ground. The Agnikumāra gods lit the pyre. The Vāyukumāra gods started the winds. Other gods emptied jars full of ghee and honey on the pyre. When the mortal remains of *Bhagavān* Mahāvīra were turned into ashes, the pyre was cooled by the Meghakumāra gods with water (milk) brought from *Kṣīrasāgara.* Śakrendra and Īśānendra respectively collected the right and left upper jaw-bones. Other gods collected teeth and other bones pieces. Human beings became happy to collect the ashes. In the end, at the place where the pyre was lit, the gods erected an altar of gems.[22]

During the night of the liberation of *Bhagavān* Mahāvīra, the surface of the earth was lit bright because of the coming of gods and goddesses.[23] Even men burnt lamps. Thus started the Festival of Light (*dīpāvalī*) on this earth.[24]

During the night of the liberation of *Bhagavān* Mahāvīra, the minutest of organisms called *kunthu* made it appearance on this earth. This was a symbolic indication that in future swarms of insects would be on the wax on this earth, and this would make restraint next to impossible. In anticipation of bad times ahead, many monks and nuns ended their lives by fasts unto death.[25]

LIBERATION OF GAUTAMA BUDDHA

Starting from Rājagṛha, the Buddha came to Vaiśālī. He spent there sometime and then came to Veluvagrāma (Beṇugrāma) to stay there during the monsoons. He asked the monks to find convenient places with friends and acquaintances around Vaiśālī to live there. This was the last monsoon sojourn for the Buddha.

During this sojourn, he fell victim to a mortal disease. The Buddha thought,

> 'It is not appropriate for me to die without bringing it to the notice of my attending monks and monks of my order beforehand'.

He held fast to the thread of life and recovered from the disease. On seeing the Leader fully recovered, Ānanda expressed a profound satisfaction and said,

> "*Bhante!* Because of your serious illness. I felt a blank within me. I had lost my sense of direction even. I had ceased to have a perception of religion."

Said the Buddha,

> "Ānanda! I have now become aged, old, worn out, exhausted, advanced

in age. I have touched 80. Like an old cart which can with difficulty be used with patches here and there, I am also somehow pulling on my body. But, you see, how can I live long in this state. So, Ānanda, henceforth live in the light of thyself, in the succour of thyself, with no other succour, in the light of religion, in the succour of religion, with nothing else to depend upon."

aṭṭadīpa viharatha aṭṭasaraṇā anannasaraṇā,
dhammadīva dhammasaraṇā anannasaraṇā.

One day, the Buddha was resting in a *caitya* named Cāpāla. The long-lived Ānanda sat beside him. To Ānanda *Bhagavān* Buddh said,

"Ānanda! I am in possession of four powers (*ṛddhipāda*). So if I desire, I can stay on for a full *kalpa.*"

But Ānanda missed even such a clear such a hint from the Buddha. He failed to request him to live on for a *kalpa* for the good of many, for the happiness of many. The Buddha repeated the same words for the second time and again for the third time. But Ānanda said nothing. The wicked Māra had full control of Ānanda's mind. Thereafter, to give a break to the talk, the Buddha said,

"Let us drop it, Ānanda. You will understand the implication tomorrow."

No sooner had Ānanda separated from the Buddha than Māra appeared before him and said,

"Bhante! You had said, in part, as follows : 'I shall not enter into liberation till that time when the monks and the nuns, the male followers and the female followers are not fixed in religion, are not versed in religion to be able to communicate it to others, till they are capable to prevent remorse; till the religion of the Buddha which is *brahmacarya* (non-sex) prospers, spreads and is not adopted by many. '*Bhante*! Now, all these have been fulfilled. So now, it is time for you to enter into liberation."

To this, the Buddha gave the following reply,

"Ye sinful! Be at peace. After three months from this day, I shall enter into liberation."

At the Cāpāla *caitya* on that day, the Buddha loosened his grip on the thread of life with conscience and feeling. There was a servere earth-quake at that time. The heavenly drums were beaten. Ānanda rushed to the Buddha and said,

> "*Bhante!* How very strange! How very wonderful! What's the cause for this severe earth-quake? What's the factor behind this all?"

The Buddha said,

> "There are eight causes for the earth-quake. One of these is that the *Tathāgata* gives up his hold on the thread of life. Just now, at the Cāpāla *caitya*, I have finished my elan vital. This is the reason for this earth-quake. This is the reason why the heavenly drums are beaten."

On hearing all this, Ānanda realised the situation. He said,

> "*Bhante!* Please live on for a *kalpa* for the good of many for the happiness of many."

The Buddha said,

> "Now make no such prayer to the *Tathāgata*. There is no more time for such prayers."

Still Ānanda repeated his prayer thrice. The Buddha said,

> "Why do you create an awkward situation for the *Tathāgata*? Drop this topic. Ānanda! If I do not live for a *kalpa*, you are person to blame for this. On many occasions did I mention to you the capability of the *Tathāgata* in this matter, but you held your tongue every time."

The Buddha rose and repaired to the summit-like shelter in Mahāvana. There he gave the following order to Ānanda :

> "Assemble at the *upasthāna* hall all the monks who may be living near Vaiśālī."

When the monks had assembled, the Buddha addressed them as follows :

> "Harken, of *Bhikṣus*! Any produced thing (*saṁskāra*) is liable to destruction. Be free from delusion and fulfil thy duty (*ādeya*). In the

very near future, after three months from this day, the *Tathāgata* is going to enter into liberation."

Bhagavān Buddha started from Vaiśālī to reach Kuśinārā. At the Ānanda caitya in Bhognagara, he said,

> "Bhikṣus! If you ever hear a monk saying, 'Ābus! I have heard this straight from the Buddha. This is *Dharma*. This is *Vinaya*. This is the counsel imparted by the Great Leader', then, I say, neither welcome the statement at once nor decry it. Check it from the *Sūtra,* and from the *Vinaya*. If you do not find it there, then take it for certain that the assertion has been ill-begotten by the said *Bhikṣu*. If, however, you find it in the *Sūtra,* and the *Vinaya*, then, take it to be the word of the *Tathāgata.*"

Starting from there, the Buddha reached Pāvā. He halted at the mango garden belonging to one Cuṇḍa, son of Karmāra. Cuṇḍa invited the Buddha with his monks for dinner at his residence. On the previous night, a special preparation was made from the dinner to be given next day. A huge quantity of meat from young pigs was cooked.[26] At the appointed hour, the Buddha came with his begging bowl and cloth the house of Cuṇḍa, the son of Karmāra and sat down to dinner. While dining, the Buddha said as follows to his host,

> "Don't give this rich meat to the monks. They wont's be able to digest it."

No sooner had he finished his dinner than the Buddha felt a serere pain in his abdomen. He vomited several times and this was full of blood.

Despite his being ill, the Buddha departed from Pāvā to reach Kuśinārā. Being tired, he sat on the road-side. As he became very thirsty, he asked Ānanda to fetch him some water from the river. Said Ānanda,

> "*Bhante!* Just now, 500 carts have passed through this river. This is a small stream and the water is already muddy. Just ahead of us, at a short distance from here, we shall come across the river Kakutthā. The water of that river is clean and tasteful. So, you may drink water there."

But the Buddha repeated his request for the second time and for the third time. So Ānanda was obliged to move out to fulfil his desire. To his surprise, he found that the water was calm and clean. He became very much delighted at the display of the great spiritual power of the Leader. He carried water in a bowl and offered it to the Buddha to drink.

As the Buddha sat resting, there came Pukkus, son of Malla, a disciple of Ālāra Kālām, who was passing by that way. He sat on one side and said,

> "*Bhante!* Initiated people (monks) move absorbed and carefree. Once it so happened that revered Ālāra Kālām was resting under a tree on the roadside. Five hundred carts passed from his hind. After some time, a member of the same *caravan* came to him and asked,
> "*Bhante!* Did you see the carts pass?"
> —"No, ābus, I did not see them."
> —"*Bhante!* Did you hear any sound?"
> —"No ābus, I did not heary any."
> —"*Bhante*! Were you asleep?"
> —"No, ābus, I was not.
> —"*Bhante*! There is dust deposited on your robe"
> —"Yes, it is there."

Then the man said,

> "How very strange! How very wonderful! The monks wander at ease, fully concentrated in self."

Said the Buddha,

> "Pukkus! Once I was encamped at Bhū-sāgar in Ātumā. At that time, there was a torrential shower. Thunders roared. At the fall of the lightning, two farmers and four bulls lost their lives. Just at that time, a man came to me and said, '*Bhante*! There were showers, there were thunders, and farmers and bulls have lost their lifes. *Bhante*! Did you realise all this?"

I said, "No ābus, I did not."
The man—"Where were you at that time?"

> —"Why? I was right here."
> —"*Bhante*! Did you hear the roar of thunder?"
> —"No, ābus, I did not."
> —"*Bhante*! Were you asleep at that time?"
> —"No, ābus, I was not."
> —"Were you in your full senses then?"
> —"Why? I was fully in my senses."
> "Pukkus! Then the man said, 'How strange! How Very wonderful! This is the real movement at ease."

On hearing this account, Pukkus, the son of Malla, was very much impressed. He said,

> "*Bhante*! This is even more strange than the passing of 500 or even 5000 carts. Whatever respect and devotion I had in Ālāra Kālām, I throw it to the winds, I wash it down in a quick-flowing river. From this day, please accept me as your worshipper who is come to take shelter with thee."

Pukkus presented to the Buddha two very costly and glittering shawls, one for the Lord himself and the other for Ānanda.

Pukkus, the son of Malla departed. Ānanda placed his own shawl also on the Buddha. A glow came out from the Buddha's body and outshone the brilliance of the shawls. On a point of enquiry from Ānanda, the Buddha said,

> "Such purification of pigment (of the skin) of the *Tathāgata* takes place on two occasions, *viz.*, once at the time of his enlightenment, and again at the time of his liberation. Tonight, in the last quarter, in the *śāla* forest of the Mallas at Kuśinārā, surrounded by *sāla* trees, the *Tathāgata* will enter into his liberation."

With his monks, the Buddha reached the bank of the river Kakutthā. He took his bath. He crossed through the river and came to a mango grove at the other bank. While taking rest there, the Buddha said to Ānanda,

> "Ānanda! If, in future, anyone blames Cuṇḍa, the son of Karmāra saying, 'Ābus Cuṇḍa! You have earned to gain, rather, you have suffered a severe loss; by eating the food served by you, the *Tathāgata* lost his life', then you remove this stigma from Cuṇḍa. You tell Cuṇḍa. 'You have earned a gain, a good gain; the *Tathāgata* entered into liberation by accepting food from thee'; and tell him further that two meals of the Buddha are of merit, *viz.,* one preceding his enlightenment and the other preceding his liberation."

Moving out from the mango grove on the bank of the river Kokutthā, *Bhagavān* Buddha took the road to Kuśinārā. Having crossed through the river Hiraṇyavatī, he reached the *sāla* forest at Kuśinārā named Upavattana which belonged to the Mallas. In a grove made by *śāla* trees, his cot was spread whereon he lay with his head towards the north.

At the time, the long-lived Upavana stood before the Buddha helping him with a fan. Suddenly the Buddha burst out,

"Get out, *bhikṣus*, get ye out from my presence."

At this Ānanda asked,

"*Bhagavān*! Why so?"

The Lord said,

"Ānanda! Gods from the ten heavens (*lokas*) have assembled to see the *Tathāgata* for the last time. All around this *sāla* forest, upto a distance of 12 *yojanas*, there is no vacant space even as much as to accomodate the tip of a hair. The gods are being irritated because of the obstruction caused by the monk with a fan in his hand."

Ānanda—"*Bhante*! In what state do you see the gods?" The Buddha—"Ānanda! Some are lamenting with their hairs dissheveled; some others are shouting holding each others hand; some are falling on the ground like trees hewn. They are all in grief saying, 'So soon the Sugata is entering into liberation; so soon the enlightened is going out of the world."

Ānanda—"*Bhante*! When you are alive, the monks, on completion of their monsoon sojourn, come from many directions to pay their homage and obeisance to you. We too benefit from their pious association. But, *Bhante*, in future, (after you enter into your liberation), what pious association shall we get, and to whom do we come to pay our homage and obeisance?"

The Buddha—"Ānanda! In future, four places will continue to provide the necessary inspiration to turn men away from the mundane life. They are :

1. the place where the *Tathāgata* has been born (Lumbinī),
2. the place where he has been enlightened (Bodhgayā),
3. the place where he started the Wheel of Religion (Sāranāth), and
4. the place where he enters into his liberation (Kuśinārā)."

— "*Bhante*! What should be our attitude to women-folks."
— "Not to look at them."
— "*Bhagavān*! In case one has already seen?"
— "Have no chat."
— "But, *Bhante*, where conversation is necessary?"
— "Then be fully alert, with your mind awakened."
— "*Bhante*! What funeral rites are to be performed for the *Tathāgata's* body?"
— "The same as are done to the body of a *Cakravartin*."
— *Bhante*! What are these performed for a *Cakravartin*?"
— "Ānanda! The body of a *Cakravartin* is to be wrapped with a new piece of cloth. Then it is wrapped with cotton, and with a new

piece of cloth again. Then the body is placed in an iron vat full of oil. Then a pyre is built with fragrant trees and the body of the *Cakravartin* is burnt on it. After the cremation, an altar is erected for the *Cakravartin* at a place where four roads meet."

The long-lived Ānanda went to his room and began to weep supporting himself against a poll. He said,

"Alas! How unfortunate am I! My Master is entering into liberation."

The Buddha enquired,

"Where is Ānanda?"
—"*Bhante*! He is weeping in his room."
—"Bring him hither."

Thereon the long-lived Ānanda came there. The Buddha spoke unto him as follows :

"Ānanda! Weep not. Lament not. I told you yesterday that the separation even of the dearest one is inevitable.
Ānanda! You have served the *Tathāgata* for a very long time. You are really meritorious. Now, you devote yourself to the attainment of liberation. Get rid of all fetters (*āśravas*)."

Ānanda—"*Bhante*! May ye not enter into liberation in this small township, in this branch township! There are many big cities,—Campā, Rājagṛha, Śrāvastī, Sāketa, Kośāmbī, Vārāṇasī. Choose anyone of these places for thy liberation. In these cities, there are many rich *Kṣatriyas*, many rich *Brāhmaṇas*, many other rich householders who hold thee in highest of esteems. They will worship the body of the *Tathāgata*."

The Buddha—"Ānanda! Don't ye say so. Kuśinārā has a very long history. At some remote past age, this city, then named Kuśāvatī, was the headquarter of *Cakravartin* Mahāsudarśana. You go to the city and tell the Mallas there that tonight, at the last quarter, the *Tathāgata* will enter into liberation. So came at once so that you may not repent later that you did not get a glimpse of him (when he was alive)."

Ānanda did as per the Buddha's wishes. The Mallas became sorry and grieved to get the news. All of them came to pay their homage and obeisance. Since time was very short, Ānanda took one family at a time to see the Buddha. In this manner, during the first quarter of the night, all the Mallas finished paying their homage and obeisance to the Buddha.

During the second quarter, Subhadra was initiated into monkhood (at the hand of the Buddha).

In giving out his Last Testament, the Buddha said,

1. "Ānanda! It is very likely that you will feel that the Leader is gone, that there are his words, but not the Leader himself. Ānanda! Take it in this manner that the religion I have propounded is your Leader after me, the Vinaya I have given is your Leader after me.
2. "Ānanda! Upto this time, when addressing one another, the monks have been using the word 'ābus'; but after I am gone, a monk junior to one is to be addressed as 'ābus', and a monk senior to one is to be addressed as '*Bhante*' or 'āyuṣmān'.
3. "Ānanda! After I am gone, if the *Saṅgha* so desires, it may drop the minor and ordinary rules for the monks.
4. "Ānanda! After I am gone, Monk Channa is to be made the *Brahmadaṇḍa*."

The addressing the assembled monks, the Buddha said,

> "If anyone from among you has any doubt about the Buddha, the *Dharma* and the *Saṅgha*, he may have his doubt clarified. Otherwise, he may later repent because he could have his doubt resolved."

The Buddha repeated the words for the second and for the third time, but the monks remained silent.

Said Ānanda,

> "*Bhante*! There is none among these 500 monks who has any shred of doubt. All have full faith in the Buddha, the *Dharma* and the *Saṅgha*."

Said the Buddha,

> hanta yani bhikṣave amantayami vo vayadhamma saṅkhara appamadena sampadeya ti
>
> "Hallow! *Bhikṣus*! I say so to you : Things done are transient; free from deceit, do your duties. These are the last words of the *Tathāgata* to you."

Bhagavān Buddha had his first bout of meditation. Having completed it, he had his second bout, then the third and the fourth. The one after the other, he attained Ākāśāntyāyatana (the first of the four formless *Brahmalokas*),

Vijñānāntyāyatana (the second), Akiñcanyāyatana (the third) and Naivasañjñāyatana (the fourth). Then he attained Saṁjñā-vedayita-nirodha (a form of trance). Ānanda said to Anuruddha,

> "Is *Bhagavān* liberated?"
> "No, not yet; he is in saṁjñā-vedayita-nirodha samāpatti."

Then the Buddha rose above saṁjñā-vedayita-nirodha and attained naivasaṁjñānasañjñāyatana. Then, one by one, having completed all the stages in the reverse order, he returned to the first meditation. Then again he moved up to come to the fourth, after having passed through the second and the third, and then he entered into his liberation. At the time the earth shook severely and the heavenly drums were beaten incessantly.

After the Buddha had passed away, Sahāmpati Brahmā, Śakra who is the Indra of the gods, long-lived Anuruddha and long-lived Ānanda offered, prayers to the departed Master.

At that time, the monks who had not yet transgressed attachment-detachment, began to lament and cry. They fell on the ground like hewn trees. Anuruddha tried to make them free from attachment.

The long-lived Ānanda came to Kuśinārā, met the Mallas at the public hall and said to them,

> "The *Bhagavān* has entered into liberation. He is no more."

The entire city of Kuśinārā had a shadow of gloom cast on it at this sad news.

The Mallas performed the liberation rites for six days. They made necessary preparations for the funeral. On the seventh day, eight Mallas lifted the body of the Buddha. They were followed by gods and men. The funeral procession stopped at a caitya name Mukuta-bandhana which was dedicated by the Mallas. Having received the Buddha's wishes from Ānanda, they arranged the funeral of a *Cakravartin* for him. Having completed the rites in due order, they placed the body on the pyre.

The Mallas wanted to lit the pyre, but they could not do so. Explaining the reason for this Anuruddha said,

> "Vāśiṣthas! You want to do something, and the gods want to do something else. It is the desire of the gods that the pyre be lit after the long-lived Mahākāśyapa has a chance to touch the Buddha's feet."
> —"*Bhante*! Where is the long-lived Mahākāśyapa at this moment?"

Anuruddha said,

> "With 500 monks following him, he is on the road between Pāvā and Kuśinārā."

On this the Mallas said,

> "We shall abide by the wishes of the gods."

The long-lived Mahākāśyapa arrived at last. He placed his rag on one shoulder, and then with folded hands, he thrice moved round the pyre. Then he removed the shroud a little and touched the Buddha's feet with his forehead. His 500 monks also did the same. No sooner were all these done than the pyre lit itself. After the body was consumed by the flames nothing remained, neither ashes nor charcoal. Just as butter or oil in a burning lamp simply ceases to exist, so did his skin, flesh, etc. Only the bones remained. When the body was thus consumed up, there appeared clouds in the sky, and these cooled the pyre.

The Mallas collected the bones and placed them in their public hall. For the safe-keeping of the last remains, a circle of guards was placed with javelins and another with bows and arrows. Dances and music were started in honour of the last remains.

Ajātaśatru, the King of Magadha sent a request to the Mallas which was as follows :

> "The *Bhagavān* was a *Kṣatriya* and I am also a *Kṣatriya*. So I should have a share of the bones on which I desire to raise an altar and offer worship."

Similar requests were sent by the Licchavīs of Vaiśālī, the Śākyas of Kapilavastu, the Buliyas of Allakappa, the Koliyas of Rāmagrāma, the *Brāhmaṇas* of Beṭhadvīpa and the Mallas of Pāvā. The Mallas of Kuśinārā made the following decision :

> "The *Bhagavān* entered into liberation at our place. So we wont's shares the bones with anyone."

The *Droṇa Brāhmaṇas* said to the Mallas :

> "This is not a fair decision. The *Bhagavān* was an embodiment of forgiveness, and we should also settle our affairs in the same spirit of

forgiveness. It is not good that we quarrel over the bones. If the bones are taken to eight places, then, there will be eight altars dedicated to him, and more people will get a chance to worship the Buddha."

The Mallas agreed. Then the *Droṇa Brāhmaṇas* divided the bones into eight shares and each was given to one people. The *Brāhmaṇas* kept for themselves the urn in which the bones were kept.

The Mauryas of Pippalīvana arrived and they collected whatever they could find from the remnants of the pyre and carried these with them. All erected altars on what they got.

On jaw-bone of the Buddha is worshipped in heaven and another in Gandhārpura, a third in Kaliṅgadeśa and the fourth in the domain of Nāgarāja (worlds of serpents). Forty hairs, porehairs, etc., were carried away by the gods, one each for each cakrāvalā.[27]

REFERENCES

1. *Dīgha Nikāya* Aṭṭhakathā (Sumaṅgala-vilāsinī).
2. Rāhula Sāṅkṛtyāyana, Introduction to the *Suyagdanga Sutta*, Page 1, Sūtragama Prakaśan Samiti, Gudgaon, 1961.
3. E.J. Thomas, *Life of Buddha*, p. 158.
4. Rhys Davids, *Dialogues of Buddha*, Vol. II, p. 72; E.J. Thomas, *op. cit.*, p. 156; Winternitz, *History of Indian Literature*, Vol. II, pp. 38-42.
5. *Bhagavatī*, S.7. U.6.
6. *Op. cit.*, S.7. U.6.
7. *Jambūdīva Paññatti Sutta*, Vakṣa 2, Kāl Adhikāra, According to this, after two showers lasting altogether for two weeks, there is a gap of one week. Again after the third and fourth shower, there is a gap of one week. Altogether, then, the showers inclusive of two gaps lasted for 49 days.
8. Nemicandra Sūri, *Mahāvīra Cariyam*.
9. *Samavāyāṅga Sutta*, Sama, 55; Kappa Sūtta Su. 147.
10. *Kappa Sutta*, Su. 147; *Uttarādhyayana Cūrṇī*, p. 283. The last Sutra in the Uttarādhyayana calls Mahāvīra 'Buddha'. *Cf.*
    i-i pāukare buddhe nāyaye parinivvuye
    Also *Kappa Sutta*, Kalpārtha Bodhinī, p. 123 for the posture in sitting. *Cf.*
    saṁpaliyaṅka-nisaṇṇe-samyak padmāsanenopaviṣṭa.
11. For complete details, *Kappa Sutta*, Su. 147.
12. According to the *Bhagavatī*, S. 6. U. 7,
    7 prāṇas make 1 stoka,
    7 stokas make 1 lava, and
    77 lavas make 1 muhūrta (48 minutes)
13. We have it in *Kalpārtha-bodhinī*, p. 112.
    śakunyādi-karaṇa-catuske tṛtīyamidaṃ
    amāvāsyottarārdhe avaśyaṁ bhavati etad.
14. For details about year, month, fortnight, day, night, *muhūrta*, etc., see *Kappa Sutta, Kalpārtha-bodhinī*, p. 113. The commentators have called these names of time-unit to be 'typically Jaina'.

15. *Saubhāgy-Pañcamyādi Parva-kathā Saṅgraha*, p. 100, *Vividha-tīrthakalpa*, p. 36.
16. *Kappa Sutta*, Su. 147; Nemicandra, *Mahāvīra Cariyaṃ*, p. 99.
17. *Saubhāgya-Pañcamyādi Parva-kathā Saṅgraha*, pp. 100-02.
18. *Ibid.*, p. 106.
19. We have the following in *Kappa Sutta, Kalpārtha-bodhinī*, p. 121.
jineśa 'tava janmarkṣa gantā bhasmaka durgrahaḥ,
bādhisyate sa varṣāṇāṁ sahasro dve tu śāsanam,
tasya saṅkrāmaṇāṁ yāvad bilambasva tataḥ prabho,
bhavat-prabhā-prabhāveṇa sa yathā bifalo bhavet,
Svāmi uce Śakra' kenāpi nāyuḥ sandhiyate kvacit,
duḥṣamabhāvato bādhā bhāvini mama śāsane.
20. *Kappa Sutta, Kalpārha-bodhinī*, p. 114.
21. *Kappa Sutta*, Su. 132.
22. *Triṣaṣṭi-salākā-puruṣa-caritraṃ*, Parva 10, Sarga 13.
23. *Kappa Sutta*, Su. 130-131.
24. *Saubhāgaya-Pañcamyādi Parva-kathā Saṅgraha*, p. 100-110.
25. *Kappa Sutta*, Su. 136-37.
26. In *Udana Attha-kathā*, 8/5, Buddhaghoṣa gives the following explanation of 'sukara-maddava'.
nāti-taruṇassa nātijiṇṇassa eka jeṭṭhaka-
sūkarassa pavatta mamasaṁ.
Some 'non-meat' explanations of the word have been given. But *Aṅguttara Nikāya* (*Pañcaka Nipāta*) gives support to Buddha's being a meat-eater. We have it that at the request of Grahapati Ugga, he took pig meat.
27. *Cf.*
ekāhi dana tidivehi pūjitā
ekā pana gandhārapure mahīyati
kāliṅgarañjo vijite punekaṁ
ekapana nāgarajā maheti
cattālīsa samā danta kesa-loma ca sabbaso
devā harisaṁ ekekaṁ cakkavāla paramparā tti.

16

WANDERINGS AND MONSOON CAMPS

Both the great men of their age bear a close resemblance in their wanderings as well as in their monsoon camps. Both walked through Magadha, Videha, Kāśī, Kośala, Vatsa, Aṅga, Vajjī, Malla and many other kingdoms. Rājagṛha, Mithilā, Vārāṇasī, Śrāvastī, Kauśāmbī, Campā, Vaiśālī and Pāvā,—these were the capitals of the aforesaid kingdoms. Both passed through these places many a time. Both spent a good number of their monsoons at these capital cities. According to the calculations given earlier in this book, both must have spent at least two monsoons together at Rājagṛha.

A complete account of Mahāvīra's monsoon camps is given in the *Kappa Sutta.*[1] Monsoon sojourns apart, the account of Mahāvīra's visit to other places is scattered throughout the *Āgamas* in the context of other events. A chronological account of the events of Mahāvīra's life is contained in the *niryukti, cūrṇī* and commentary of the Āvaśyaka, in the commentaries of the *Kappa Sutta,* and in the biographies of Mahāvīra written by Nemicandra, Guṇacandra and Hemacandra. But their is no separate account of his wanderings and monsoon camps either in the *Kappa Sutta* or in other Jaina literary literary works. Some recent scholars, notably Muni Kalyāṇavijayajī[2] and *Ācārya* Vijayendra Sūri[3] have sought to fill up this gap.

Mahāvīra's wanderings and Camps

Regarding the wanderings and monsoon camps of the Buddha, we do not have a chronological account in the main Buddhist *Piṭakas.* Effort has been made to record his monsoon camps at least after his enlightenment by the text of the *Aṅguttara Nikāya* Aṭṭhakathā,[4] Rhys Davids,[5] Rāhul Sāṅkṛtyāyana[6] and Bharat Singh Upādhyāya[7] have each sought to build up a complete account of the Buddha's wanderings and monsoon camps. Based on guess as these accounts are, they are likely to raise more controversy then they would solve. But in the absence of more authentic sources, we have to make use of them for whatever worth they may be. Given below are the two accounts, for Mahā-Sāṅkṛtyāyana respectively. It is expected that these accounts will provide a good comparative study. In preparing this comparative study, the author has kept in view considerations about correctness of dates given earlier in this book. For the sake of clarity and convenience to the readers, the lists of itineraries and monsoon camps have been provided on a comparative basis.

Mahāvīra's Wanderings and Camps
(as a monk)

B.C.	*Year (ordinal)*	*Wanderings*	*Camps*
569	1	Kudagrāma, Jñātakhaṇḍavana, Karmāragrāma, Kollāga Sanniveśa, Morāka Sanniveśa, Duijjantaka Āśrama, Aṣṭikagrāma.	Aṣṭikagrāma (Vardhamāna)
568	2	Morāka Sanniveśa, Vācālā, South Vācālā, Suvarṇa Vālukā (river), Rupya Vālukā (river), Kanakakhala Āśramapada, North Vācālā, Śvetāmbī, Surabhipura, the Gaṅgā, Thūṇāka Sanniveśa, Rājagṛha, Nālandā Sanniveśa	Nālandā Sanniveśā
567	3	Kollāga Sanniveśa, Suvarṇa-khala, Brāhmaṇagrāma, Campā	Campā
566	4	Kālāya Sanniveśa, Patta Kālāya, Kumāraka Sanniveśa, Coraka Sanniveśa, Pṛṣtha-Campā.	Pṛṣtha-Campā
565	5	Kayaṅgalā Sanniveśa, Śrāvastī, Halidduyaṁ, Jaṅgalā, Āvattā, Corāya Sanniveśa, Kālaṁkabukā Sanniveśa, Rāḍhadeśa (non-Āryan land), Pūrṇa-kalaśa (non-Āryan village), Malaya Pradeśa, Bhaddīyā.	Bhaddīyā
564	6	Kayalī Samāgama, Jambūsaṇḍa, Tambāya Sanniveśa, Kūpiya Sanniveśa, Vaiśālī, Grāmāka Sanniveśa, Śālīśīrṣa, Bhaddīyā.	-do-
563	7	Magadha, Ālaṁbhīyā.	Ālaṁbhiyā
562	8	Kundāla Sanniveśa Maddana Sanniveśa, Bahusālaga, Śālavana, Lohārgalā, Purimatāla, Śakatamukha park, Unnāga (Tunnāga), Gobhūmi, Rājagṛha.	Rājagṛha
561	9	Lāḍha, Vajrabhūmi, Suṁhabhūmi, non-Āryana lands.	Vajrabhūmi
560	10	Siddhārthapura, Kūmargrāma, Siddhārthapura, Vaiśālī, the Gandak (river), Vāṇijyagrāma, Śrāvastī.	Śrāvastī
559	11	Sānulaṭṭhiya Sanniveśa,	Vaiśālī

(Contd.,,,)

(Contd..)

1	2	3	4
		Dṛḍhabhūmi, Polāsa caitya, Vālukā, Subhoga, Succhetā, Malaya, Hatthisīsa, Tosali, Siddhārthapura, Vrajagāon, Ālaṁbhīyā, Seyaviā, Śrāvastī, Kośāmbī, Vārāṇasī, Rājagṛha, Mithilā, Vaiśālī (Kāma Mahāvena).	
558	12	Suṁsumārapura, Bhogapura, Nandigrāma, Meṇḍiyagrāmam, Kośāmbī, Sumaṅgala, Succhetā, Pālaka, Campā.	Campā
557	13	Jaṁbhīyagrāma, Meṇḍdhīya, Chammāṇi, Madhyama Apāpā, Jaṁbhiyagrāma, the Ṛju-vālukā (river as a Kevalin)	—
557	1	The Ṛju-vālukā, Pāvāpurī, Rājagṛha.	Rājagṛha
556	2	Rājagṛha, Brahmaṇakuṇḍa, Vaiśālī.	Vaiśālī
555	3	Vaiśālī, Kośāmbī, Śrāvastī Vāṇijyagrāma.	Vāṇijya-grāma
554	4	Vāṇijyagrāma, Rājagṛha	Rājgṛha
553	5	Rājagṛha, Campā, Vītabhaya, Vāṇijyagrāma.	Vāṇijya-grāma
552	6	Vāṇijyagrāma, Vārāṇasī, Ālaṁbhīyā, Rājagṛha.	Rājagṛha
551	7	Rājagṛha.	Rājagṛha
550	8	Rājagṛha, Ālaṁbhīyā, Kośāmbī, Vaiśālī.	Vaiśālī
549	9	Vaiśālī, Mithilā, Kākandī, Kāṁpilyapura, Polāsapura, Vāṇijyagrāma, Vaiśālī.	Vaiśālī
548	10	Vaiśālī, Rājagṛha.	Rājagṛha
547	11	Rājagṛha, Kṛtāṅgalā, Śrāvstī, Vāṇijyagrāma.	Vāṇijya-grāma
546	12	Vāṇijyagrāma, Brāhmaṇakuṇḍa, Kośāmbī, Rājagṛha.	Rājagṛha
545	13	Rājagṛha, Campā, Rājagṛha.	Rājagṛha
544	14	Rājagṛha, Kākindī, Mithilā, Campā.	Campā
543	15	Campā, Śrāvastī, Medhiyagrāma, Campā, Mithilā.	Mithilā
542	16	Mithilā, Hastināpura, Mocā City, Vāṇijyagrāma.	Vāṇijyagrāma
541	17	Vāṇijyagrāma, Rājagṛha.	Rājagṛha
540	18	Rājagṛha, Pṛṣṭha-Campā, Campā, Darśāṇapura, Vāṇijyagrāma.	Vāṇijya-grāma
539	19	Vāṇijyagrāma, Kāmpilya-pura, Vaiśālī.	Vaiśālī

(Contd,,,,)

(Contd..)

1	2	3	4
538	20	Vaiśālī, Vāṇijyagrāma, Vaiśālī.	Vaiśālī
537	21	Vaiśālī, Rājagṛha, Campā, Pṛṣṭha-Campā, Rājagṛha.	Rājagṛha
536	22	Rājagṛa, Nālandā.	Nālandā
535	23	Nālandā, Vāṇijyagrāma, Vaiśālī.	Vaiśālī
534	24	Vaiśālī, Sāketa, Vaiśālī.	Vaiśālī
533	25	Vaiśālī, Rājagṛha.	Rājagṛha
532	26	Rājagṛha, Nālandā.	Nālandā
531	27	Nālandā, Mithilā	Mithilā
530	28	Mithilā	Mithilā
529	29	Mithilā, Rājagṛha.	Rājagṛha
528	30	Rājagṛha, Apāpāpurī. (Liberation)	Apāpā-purī (Pāvā)
Buddha's Wanderings and Camps			
553	1	Kapilavastu, Anūpiyā (Malla) Rājagṛha, Uruvelā (According to the Mahāyāna tradition, Kapilavastu, Vaiśālī, Rājagṛha, Uruvelā).	Uruvelā (Senānīgrāma)
552	2	Uruvelā	Uruvelā
551	3	Uruvelā	Uruvelā
550	4	Uruvelā	Uruvelā
549	5	Uruvelā	Uruvelā
548	6	Uruvelā (After Enlightenment)	Uruvelā
547	1	Uruvelā, Gayā, Ṛṣipattana (Vārāṇasī)	Ṛṣipattana (Vārāṇasī)
546	2	Ṛṣipattana, Uruvelā, Gayā, Rājagṛha. (According to Bharat Singh Upādhyāya, Vaiśālī, Kapila-vastu, Anūpiyā, Rājagṛha).	Rājagṛha
545	3	Rājagṛha, Kapilavastu, Anūpiyā (Malla), Nalakalpana (Kośala) Rājagṛha. (According to Upādhyāya, Rājagṛha, Vaiśālī, Śrāvastī, Kitāgiri, Ālavī, Rājagṛha).	Rājagṛha
544	4	Rājagṛha, Vaiśālī, Śrāvastī, Rājagṛha (According to Upādhyāya).	Rājagṛha
543	5	Rājagṛha Kapilavastu, Vaiśālī.	Vaiśālī
542	6	Vaiśālī, Maṅkula Parvat.	Mankkula Parvat
541	7	Maṅkula Parvat, Rājagṛha, Śrāvastī, Trayastriṁśa.	Trayastriṁśa
540	8	Trastriṁśa, Saṁkāśyanagar, Śrāvastī, Rājagṛha, Vaiśālī, Suṁsumāragiri.	Suṁsumāragiri

(Contd.,,,)

(Contd..)

1	2	3	4
539	9	Suṁsumāragiri, Kośāmbī, Bālaka Loṇakāra, Prācīna Vamśadāva. (According to Upādhyāya, Kośāmbī, Kammāsadamma (Kuru).	Kośāmbī
538	10	Prācīna Vaṁśadāva, Pārileyaka, Śrāvastī.	Pārileyaka
537	11	Nālā (Ekanālā, according to Upādhyāya).	Nālā
536	12	Nālā, Nālandā, Pañcaśālā, Kammāsadamma (Kuru), Mathurā, Verañjā. (Śrāvastī, Verañjā, according to Upādhyāya).	Veranjā
535	13	Verañjā, Vārāṇasī, Vaiśālī Cāliya Paravat. (Verañjā, Mathurā, Veranjā, Koreyya, Saṅkassa, Kaṇṇakujja, Payāgapatitthana, Vārāṇasī, Vaiśālī, Śrāvastī, Cāliya Parvat, according to Upādhyāya).	Cāliya Parvat
534	14	Cāliya Parvat, Vaiśālī, Bhaddīyā, Āpaṇa (Aṅguttarāpa), Kuśinārā, Ātumā, Śrāvastī.	Śrāvastī
533	15	Śrāvastī, Manasākata (Kośala) Icchānaṅgala (Kośala), Opasāda, Khāṇumatta (Magadha), Campā, Kapilavastu.	Kapilavastu
532	16	Kapilavastu, Kētāgiri, Ālavī.	Ālavī
531	17	Ālavī, Rājagṛha (Ālavī, Śrāvastī, Ālavī, Rājagṛha, according to Upādhyāya).	Rājagṛha
530	18	Rājagṛha, Cāliya Parvat.	Cāliya Parvat
529	19	Cāliya Parvat, Campā, Kajagalā, Śilāvatī (Suhma), Setakaṇṇika (Suhma), Cāliya Parvat. (According to Upādhyāya, Cāliya Parvat, Ālavī, Cāliya Parvat).	-do-
528	20	Cāliya Parvat, Rājagṛha.	Rājagṛha
527	21	Rājagṛha, Śrāvastī, Kapilavastu, Sāmagāma, Pāvā, Vaiśālī. (According to Rāhula Sāmkṛtyāyana, he visited Sāmagāma and Pāvā only two years before liberation, and not at this date).	Śrāvastī

(Contd..)

1	2	3	4
526-503	22-45	Aṅga, Magadha, Kāśi, Kośala, Vijjī, Vaṁsa, Cedi, Pañcāla, Kuru, Videha, Śākya, Kiliya, Mallā and other republics and kingdoms.	
502	46	Śrāvstī, Rājagṛha, Vaiśālī, Pāvā and Kusinārā (Liberation)	Veluva (Vaiśālī)

REFERENCES

1. B.C. 122.
2. *Śramaṇa Bhagavān Mahāvīra.*
3. *Tīrthaṅkara Mahāvīra* (Part II).
4. 2-4-5.
5. Buddhism.
6. Buddhacaryā.
7. *Buddhakālīns Indian History*, Parishad Hindi Sāhitya Sammelan Prayāga, 1961.

17

THE NIGAṆṬHAS AND NIGAṆṬHA NĀTAPUTTA IN THE TRIPIṬAKAS

Compared to the Jaina *Āgamas* where Gautama Buddha has received very scant attention, the *Tripiṭakas* are over full with accounts about *Bhagavān* Mahāvīra. Therein he has been called Nigaṇṭha Nātaputta.[1] In general, the word '*nigaṇṭha*' stands for the Jaina monks. The word 'Nātaputta' has been used even in the Jaina *Āgamas* for Mahāvīra.[2] If we do not indulge into a speculation about the authenticity of the narrated events, then we can say without hesitation that they are very interesting, delightful and inspiring. They throw ample light on the mutual relation between the two orders, their doctrines and ideas.

There is no mention anywhere that Mahāvīra and Buddha had ever met each other. It is abundantly recorded that the two leaders had camped simultaneously in different parks of the same city. In the account of Gṛhapati Upāli and Asibandhakaputra Grāmaṇī, we come to know that both were in Nālandā at the same time; in the account of Siṁha Senāpati, we have it that both were at Vaiśālī. In the account of Abhayakumāra, it is mentioned that both were at Rājagṛha. The *Mahāsakuladāyī Suttanta* mentions seven spiritual leaders having camped in Rājagṛha during one rainy season. On the occasion of the display of "occult powers," they had assembled again at Rājagṛha.[3]

ODIUM THEOLOGICIUM

The idea and expression behind all the mentions in the *Tripiṭakas* narrate the superiority of Buddha over Mahāvīra. The best illustration of this communal narrowness are some of the episodes contained in the *Jātaka-Aṭṭhakathā*[4] and *Dhammapada-Aṭṭhakathā*.[5] One episode would at least appear at first sight to be exceedingly mean, though really it is not so. While, on the passing away of Mahāvīra, the bearer of the news, one *bhikṣu* Cuṇḍa, was being conducted to the presence of Buddha by Ānanda, the latter is recorded to have said, "*Ābusa* Cuṇḍa! This news will be worthy of presentation to the Lord when you meet him." (*atthi kho, idam, Ābusa cuṇḍa, kathāpābhatam bhagavantam dassanāya*). At first sight, it would appear that the news was heartily welcomed by Ānanda who, further, considered it to be worthy of presentation to the Lord. In one of my early articles, I have considered this observation threadbare.[6] Elsewhere too, on hearing of the death of Sāriputta, Ānanda is recorded to have made a similar observation.[7] From this it should appear that such was the vocabulary current in the Buddhist tradition even for a sad occasion; really it meant no insult.

In Pali literature, all references to Nigaṇṭha Nātaputta and the religion of the Nigaṇṭhas are in the nature of an attack. This does not mean that the ideas and the doctrines of the two sects were poles apart from each other. Often it is found that those who are nearest to each other are again most critical of each other. Differences from a distance are pardonable, but not those which are round the corner. This is purely mental factor. Even today, this is not rare. The diverse Jaina sects are more critical of one another than they are of the Buddhist or any other.

TOTALITY OF EPISODES

Only such episodes from the *Tripiṭakas* have been gleaned wherein Mahāvīra figures in some form. Even those passages have been collected wherein the members of the *Nigaṇṭha* order appear. Some of these have already been considered at various places in this book; but in the interest of totality or comprehensiveness, they have been brought in again in this Chapter. Dr. Hermann Jacobi has, in his Introduction to the *Jaina sūtras,* made a review of the references to Mahāvīra and the Nigaṇṭhas as they have figured in the *Tripiṭakas.* Such references are 11 in number. In Jacobi's view, that was the total number of references in the Pāli literature printed upto his time. In the present Chapter, more references have been added raising total to 51. Some of these additional references might not have been extent in Jacobi's time, but there were others which clearly escaped his notice. In the case of one text at least, while he has noticed some references, he has clearly missed a few others. Also the article by Dr. Malālsékhara entitled "Nigaṇṭha Nātaputta" is not comprehensive in this regard.[8]

In the present Chapter, especial care has been taken to see that not a single account about Nigaṇṭha Nātaputta and his order in the *Tripiṭakas* may escape attention. The *Aṭṭhakathās* and lesser texts have not been neglected, so that the present Chapter gives a complete view of the Nigaṇṭhas and Nigaṇṭha Nātaputta as they have appeared in the entire Buddhist literature and may be taken to be the most authentic. It is expected that it will be immensely valuable to the interested readers.

The discussion is a compact whole. But for the sake of convenience, it has been placed under three heads : *viz.*, episodes,(13) events(8) and references.(30) Separate comments have been added in each case.

EPISODES

1. Siṁha Senāpati

Siṁha Senāpati happened to be the general of the Licchavīs. He was a lay follower of Mahāvīra. Once when Mahāvīra and Buddha were encamped at different parks in the city of Vaiśālī, Siṁha wanted to pay Buddha a visit, but Nātaputta tried to dissuade him from it, because the Nigaṇthas held *kriyāvāda,* while Buddha taught *Akriyāvāda.* Siṁha tried to obtain the permission twice, and the third time he decided to go without permission. He came to Buddha, bowed and took a seat. Said he, "*Bhante!* I have heard that *Śramaṇa* Gautama believes in *Akriyāvāda* and guides his disciples into it.... I would like to know from you if anyone who depicts you like this gives a correct or a distorted description of your views?" To this, Buddha reacted,

> "Siṁha! There is reason why I am called *Akriyāvādī.* In my view, *Akriyā* covers the ill behaviour of the body, of the speach and of the mind. As I advise people to keep aside from these, I am called *Akriyāvādī*....But I am also called a *Kriyāvādī* because I advise people to indulge in *karma* which may lead to the purity of the body, of the speech and of the mind. I have also been described as *Ucchedavādī, Jugupsu, Vaināyika, Tapasvī, Apagarbha....* also *Assasanta* because I have acquired supreme bliss (consolation) and I speak of it and guide people into it."

When Siṁha expressed his decision to join Buddha's order, the account says, the Master advised him to consider the matter thoroughly before taking a step. He further advised him not to close his door to the *Nigaṇthas* for whom his house had so long been like a fueling station. This impressed Siṁha all the more. He joined the Buddhist order and invited Buddha to dinner with his monks. For the occasion, he arranged sumptuous meat dishes which the monks ate. As the feast was in progress, with Siṁha serving meat to the Lord with his own hands, the account says, the Nigaṇthas were heard shouting in the street, "Siṁha has got slaughtered Gautama." According to the account, this was lie, since Siṁha had taken necessary precaution beforehand.

At the end of the feast. Buddha permitted the use of meat unseen, unhead of and unsuspected, and departed.

Source—*Vinayapiṭaka Mahāvagga, Bhaivajya Khandhaka,* 6.4.8.

Comment

In the Jaina *Āgamas*, Siṁha Senāpati and men like him find no mention. Of course, it is neither strange nor improbable that some disciples of Mahāvīra would defect and join Buddha's order and vice versa; but had there been even a slightest hint about this episode in the Jaina *Āgamas,* it would have become historical. In the absence of it, the whole account becomes baseless motivated and concocted.

The Gujarātī writer Jaibhikṣu has, in his fiction entitled *Narakesarī,* identified Siṁha with King Ceṭaka, a close follower of Mahāvīra; but he has not cited the supporting material in favour of his conjecture.

A detailed account of Ceṭaka is not available in the Buddhist literature. The account of Siṁha apart, the only two places where Ceṭaka finds a mention are : *Aṅguttara Nikāya*[9] in the course of a discourse by Buddha on 'offer,' and in *Teragāthā*[10] wherein he has been mentioned as the uncle of a nun named Siṁha.

In the above account, Mahāvīra has been called a *Kriyāvādī.* In Mahāvīra's time, the word had a wide connotation. The Jaina tradition notes 363 varieties of *Kriyāvāda, Akriyāvāda, Ajñaravāda* and *Vinayavāda.*[11] These are exclusive of the views propounded by Mahāvīra. *Sūtrakṛtāṅga* describes Mahāvīra's *Kriyāvāda* in the following words : One who knows the soul, the universe, *Gati* and *Antargati,* permanent and transcient, life and death, the order of transmigration of the soul, the pain of living beings, influx and efflux of *karma,* experience with and exhaustion of *karma,* he alone is competent to discuss *kriyāvāda.*[12] He who knows these in the sense on practising these in trust sense is *Kriyāvādī.*[13]

Moreover, Mahāvīra was an *Anekāntavādī.* The gist of his doctrine was : *Āhaṁsu vijjacaraṇam Pamokkhaṁ.*[14] *i.e.*, the simultaneous existence of knowledge and action creates the possibility of *Mokṣa.*

In the episode quoted above, even Buddha spoke about the ill behaviour of the body, and sought to give an idea of *Kriyāvāda* and *Akriyāvāda* as he conceived these. The episode provides the basis of meat eating by the Buddhist monks, provided the meat is unseen, unheard of and unsuspected. Such meat was permitted by Buddha as edible for his monks. The Niganṭhas too have objected to the intake of intended meat. Event the account of *Ārdakakumāra*[15] decries the intake of intended meat.

2. Grahapati Upāli

The account starts with a meeting between Buddha and one Dīrgha Tapasvī, a monk in the order of Mahāvīra when both the leaders were camped at Nālandā. Buddha said,

> "How many kinds of acts *(karma), Tapassī,* effect and start demerit according to Nigaṇṭha Nātaputta?"

—"It is not his usage, Gautama, to employ the term *karma;* he speaks of inflictions or *daṇḍa."*

—"How many kinds of inflictions of *daṇḍa,* according to him, effect and start demerit?"

—"Three, Gautama, those of body, word and mind."

—"Which of these three does Nātaputta declare to be the most criminal in effecting and starting demerit?"

—"Those of body, the other two being less criminal."

—"You say, of the body; don't you?"

—"Yes, Sir, I said, of the body."

In this wise Buddha three times pinned the monk down to the issue.

At this point, *Dīgha Tapassī* said to Buddha, "And how many kinds of *daṇḍa,* according to you, Gautama, effect and start demerit?"

—"It is not the truth-finders usage, *Tapassī*, to employ the term *daṇḍa;* he speaks of *karma."*

—"How many kinds of *karma,* according to you, effect and start demrit?"

—"Three, *Tapassī,* those of body, word and mind."

—"Are these three distinct[8] each from the other two?"

—"Yes."

—"Which of these three you declare to be the most crominal, Gautama, in effecting and starting demerit?"

—"Those of mind, —the other two being less criminal."

—"Those of mind, you say. Is that right?"

—"Yes."

The Nigaṇṭha made Buddha repeat the same thrice, as he had done with him pinned him do to the issue and departed. As he was a little way off from the Nigaṇṭha camp, Mahāvīra enquired where he had been in the heat of the day, the *Dīgha Tapassī* narrated the whole account. To this Nātaputta gave his blessing and support saying,

> "Quite right, *Tapassī,* quite right. You answered Gautama like a well informed disciple who understands his Master's teachings. For, what show can the mind's *daṇḍa* make as compared with the stupendous *daṇḍa* of the body? Indeed, the *daṇḍa* of the body are the most criminal in effecting and starting demerit; those of word and mind being less criminal."

On hearing this, Gṛhapati Upāli, a lay disciple of Mahāvīra expressed a desire to go to Buddha and engage him in a discussion on the same topic. He assured Nātaputta that he would teach Buddha a right lesson. These are his words,

> "Just as an elephant at the age of sixty enters into a tank and plays the game called *Sandhovana,* in the same manner I will play *Sanadhovana* with Gautama. Please permit me to go and hold a discussion with Gautama."

Dīgha Tapassī dissented but Nātaputta apprehended no mishap and he permitted Upāli to go and hold a discussion with Gautama. Starting from there, Upāli came to the camp of Buddha. Being asked by him, Buddha reproduced the whole discussion he had with *Dīgha Tapassī* upon which Upāli said, —"*Tapassī*, Sir, was right, quite right, His answer was that of a well-informed disciple who understands his Master's teachings....."

Said Gautama Buddha, "If, Gṛhapati, you were to speak as one grounded in the Truth, we might have a talk about it.

Upāli agreed. Said Buddha, "Gṛhapati, take the case of a Niganṭha who, being sick and ill, very ill indeed, refuses cold water, and will only take warm water, so that he dies in the act of refusing to touch cold water. Where, according to Niganṭha Nātaputta, will he be reborn next?"

— "There is a heaven, Sir, called *Manaḥ-Sattva* and he will be reborn there, because he does in devotion to an idea."

—"*Gṛhapati*! Think carefully. Your present observation contradicts the previous one and your previous observation contradicts the presenet one. And yet you represented you could speak as one grounded in the Truth and able to discuss it."

Buddha raised the question of unintended slaughter by a Niganṭha rooted in the four vows while on movement, to which Upāli replied that it was not criminal if there was no intention behind to crime, but it was great crime if it was intentional. Asked Gautama Buddha,

> —"Where does Nātaputta classify intenion?"
> —"In *daṇḍa* of mind."

The discussion continued in similar line, in each case the *daṇḍa* of the mind taking precedence over the other two. A convinced Upāli said,

"I was pleased and won over by the very first of the Lord's illustrations. It was only because I wanted to listen to his nimble versatility in questioning that I thought I must maintain a hositle attitude. Wonderful, Sir, Wonderful. Just as a man might set upright again what has been cast down, etc., while life lasts."

Gṛhapati Upāli joined the order of Buddha, saluted him and departed. From that day, his door were shut for the Nigaṇṭhas. The rest of the account is still more derogatory. Upāli's conversion was reported to Nātaputta by *Dīgha Tapassī* at least three times before he was ready to accept it. Then he hurried to *Gṛhapati's* house to win him back. Needless to add, the reception was very cold. Upāli made it clear that the precepts of the Nigaṇṭhas were meant for the fools, not for a man like him. So, saying he sang in praise of Buddha when said Nātaputta, —"Pray, when, *Gṛhapati*, did you compose this eulogy of the recluse Gautama?" —"Like a vast heap of diverse flowers, Sir, from which a skilled garland-maker or his apprentice might have a garland manifold, —even so in the Lord there is full many a beauty, Yes, many hundreds of beauties to praise. Who will refuse praise where praise is due?"

Then and there, from the mouth of Nigaṇṭha Nātaputta, who could not bear to hear the Lord extolled,—there gushed hot blood.

Source : *Majjhima Nikāya, Upāli Suttānta,* 2.1.6

Comment

There is no mention anywhere in the Jaina *Āgamas* of there being a senior disciple of Mahāvīra named Upāli. It is nowhere in the Jaina tradition of a senior monk enquiring about the well being of a monk of anoter sect. It is also apparent from the conversation and address between *Dīgha Tapassī* and Buddha that Buddha was younger and Tapassī pretty old. This should lend support to Mahāvīra's being elder in age than Buddha.

In the discussion on *daṇḍa* and *karma,* the two words are synonyms.[16] As to *karma* of the mind, etc., there is no difference even in the Jaina tradition. It is not correct to describe Mahāvīra's views to be exclusively emphatic of the *karma* of the body. From the standpoint of virtue and vice, mind, word and body are equally important in the Jaina methodology. There are many accounts in Jaina tradition in which the *karma* of the mind have been highlighted. As examples may be cited the mental conflict in Rajarṣi Prasannacandra[17] the mental jealously of *Tāṇḍula Matsya*, the peeling of a *kacara* (a tiny fruit) by monk

Skandaka in his previous birth, etc.[18] The *Āgamas* go to the extent of saying that it is non-Āryan to say that difference in the number ofsense organs makes a difference in sin acquired from slaughter.[19] In his comment on the episode of Upāli, Dr. Jacobi has written, "Mahāvīra's description of the sin of the body as the most criminal is supported by the *Āgamas*. It is supported in *Sūtrakṛtāṅga* 2/4, 2/6."[20] This comment by Dr. Jacobi is not correct. What Mahāvīra said about the sin of the body in the sūtra under reference is limited by the context and what he rejected was the exclusive importance of the sin of the mind.[21] This episode describes the Niganṭha monks as discarding cold water and using warm water; this is very much consistent with the practice of the Nigantha monks.

3. Prince Abhaya

This is a story of Prince Abhaya who was a close disciple of Nātaputta. One day, so goes the account, Niganṭha Nātaputta asked him to go to Gautama and hold discussion with him. When the Prince asked what the line of discussion should be, Niganṭha Nātaputta said,

> "Go to him and ask this question—Would a Truth-finder say anything which would be displeasing and disagreeable to others? If he says yes, ask him how then he differs from the ordinary man—who does say what is displeasing and disagreeable to others. But if he says no, then you ask him how did he declare Devadatta to be a reprobate, a child of perdition, doomed to purgatory for ages and beyond all hope of redemption—words which angered and upset Davadatta. This two-edged question which you will put to him is more that he will be able either to spew out or to swallow down..."

The Prine invited the Lord with three others to a meal next day which the latter accepted by his usual silence. The meal over, the Prince started the discussion. To this, the Lord replied, "Prince! There can be no absolute answer to this."

On this the Prince narrated the background, whereupon the Lord said,

> "Prince! The Truth-finder never says anything which he knows to be false, untrue and unprofitable, and also displeasing and disagreeable to others never says anything which he knows to be a fact and true, but unprofitable, and also displeasing and disagreeable to others; but should

it be a fact and true and profitable, but also displeasing and disagreeable to others, then the Truth-finder knows the due reason to state it. He never says anything which he knows to be false, untrue and unprofitable, albeit pleasing and agreeable to others to hear; never says anything which he knows to be a fact and true but unprofitable, albeit pleasing and agreeable to others to hear; but if it be a fact and true and profitable, while pleasing and agreeable to others to hear, then the Truth-finder knows due reason when to state and why—out of pity for creatures."

To a further question by the Prince, *viz.*, when people came to the Truth-finder with their questions, did he reflect what their question would be and what his answer would be or did his answer came off-hand without reflection, the Lord said that just as the Prince himself who had a thorough knowledge about a chariot would answer any question about it offhand, and without reflection, so does the Truth-finder, adding, "Because, Prince, I have plumbed that particular constituent of the Doctrine and because my answer therefore comes to me offhand."

This was enough, and, the account says, the Prince became a disciple of Buddha.

Source : *Majjhima Nikāya, Abhaya Rājkumara Suttanta,* 2.1.8.

Comment

The same episode has been narrated in *Avadāna.*[21] Therein the *gāthā* on his earlier life states that he separated from Mahāvīra and became a follower of Buddha. Worthy of note is the wording of the prayer he offered to his new spiritual mentor : *Kittayitva jinavaram kittito homi savvada.*

4. Discussion on Karma

In the course of a lecture delivered to his monks at a place called Devadaha, Buddha reported the Nigaṇṭha view on *karma* in the following words : "Some *śramaṇas* and *brāhmaṇas* are of the view that whatever pleasure or pain, non-pleasure or non-pain one experiences is due to sin committed in the previous birth. When he is able to terminate his past *karma* through a rigorous penance and check their fresh influx, he is unfettered of *karma* bondage. With *karma* bondage unfettered, his suffering ends; with suffering ended, his pain is gone; with pain gone, all his troubles come to an end." Continued he,

"When I ask them, if I existed in the past, if I committed such and such sinful deed, if the suffering has end or is yet to end, etc., the Nigaṇṭhas look blank. They have no answer except repeating the familiar, *viz.*, that there Nigaṇṭha Nātaputta is all-knowing, all-seeing, having infinite *jñāna* and *darśana* are ever by his side.

Then he spoke about the Nigaṇṭha view of *Vedanīya Karma,* but here too, he said, they gave a wrong answer. For instance, "Oh *bhikṣu!* I asked the Nigaṇṭhas, when your endeavour is strong, do you experience a strong pain, and when it is not that strong, you experience not too strong a pain? They said, yes. I told them, because of their nescience, ignorance and illusion, their understanding was wrong. To this they gave no reply." Continued he,

"Then I asked, can a *karma* scheduled to be experienced in this life be transmitted to next life? They said, no.

"Can a *karma* scheduled to be experienced in the next life be brought backward to this life? They said, no.

"Can a *karma* giving pleasant experience be transformed into one giving unpleasant experience and vice versa? They said, no. In every case, they gave a negative reply."

He added, "People holding this sort of view are condemnable at ten places; people holding the view propagated by the Truth-finder are blessed at ten places for revealing the Truth." He gave the details of the ten places.

Source : *Majjhima Nikāya,* Devadana Suttānta 3.1.1.

Comment

In this episode, the description of omniscience and rigorous penance (see item 5 below) is similar to what is contained in *Cula-dukkha-khandhaka.* For all the questions, the Nigaṇṭhas have been made to give a negative reply. The position is that this may be correct for the *nikacita* state of *karma,* but not for many other states, like *udvartana, apāvartana, udirasaṅkramaṇ,* etc.

5. The Penance of the Nigaṇṭhas

This is what Buddha communicated to one of his followers named Mahānāma Śākya when he had come to see him at Nyagrodhāgrāma at Kapilavastu. Said he, "Once when I was on the Gṛdhrakūṭa hill at Rājagṛha, I saw quite a few Nigaṇṭha monks preparing for a rigorous penance on the Ṛṣigiri. When I asked them why they were going to torture themselves like that, they said that they had been advised to do so by their master who was all-knowing and all-seeing. This, they said, would end their past *karma,* and as they would not indulge in fresh *karma,* they would be free from all *karma* bondage in due course. They said that they were convinced of the truth underlying this view."

Continued he,

> "When I asked them if they at all existed in the past, if they had committed sin in the past, etc., they gave a negative reply and expressed their ignorance. Whereupon I said to them. It is for this reason that people with stained hands, people who are cruel and people who belong to low caste usually flock to the order of Nigaṇṭha Nātaputta."

"To my above assertions the Nigaṇṭhas replied : Ābusa Gautama! Happiness does not impart happiness; it is hardship that imparts happiness. For else, Śreṇika Bimbisāra, the ruler of Magadha, would be the happiest man."

Giving a twist to this, Buddha said, "I asked them if Bimbisāra could enjoy unobstructed happiness for a week, for six days, till for one day, without movement and in complete silence? When they said, no, I told them that I could do so. Then they admitted that I was the happiest man."

Mahānāma Śākya was happy to hear this and he welcomed the Lord's words.

Source : *Majjihma Nikāya,* Cule-dukkha-khandha Suttanta, 1.2.4.

Comment

Penance and omniscience highlighted here are perfectly in harmony with the Jaina view. The mode of discussion is, however, petty sectarian.

6. Asibandhaka-putra Grāmaṇī

Once when Buddha was at Nālandā, Asibhandhakaputra Grāmaṇī came to him. Buddha said,

> —"Grāmaṇī! What advise does your master, Nigaṇṭha Nātaputta, tender to his followers these days?"
>
> —"*Bhante!* He tells them that he who causes injury to others, tells a lie, commits theft, and acquires things not bestowed goes to hell; and the deeper down, the more intense his crime."
>
> —"But I think, according to your master, nobody ever goes to hell."
>
> —"*Bhante!* How is it so?"

Upon this, Buddha asked if in the course of a whole day, a man spent more time in causing injury, or in not causing injury, in committing theft or in non-theft, etc., to which Grāmaṇi's answer was that one spent more time in not causing injury, etc., than in causing them. Buddha said,

> "Grāmaṇi! Thus your master deviates from reality. The approach, I say, should be like this : a *śrāvaka* should ask himself if he had committed any crime. If he had, he must feel that it was wrong on his part. Then he must repent and decide not to indulge in it again. In doing all this, he saves himself from a lapse, you understand; and this applies to all the five lapse mentioned by your master. Such one acquires a right outlook. Such one free from all blemishes and weaknesses lives and moves in all directions. *Karma* putting him into a state of misery can stand no longer near him."

These words of the Truth-finder so impressed Grāmaṇī that he became his disciple then and there.

Source : *Saṁyutta Nikāya,* Śaṁkha sutta, 40.8.

Comment

In Āgama literature, we do not come across anyone of the name of Grāmaṇī. In the *Tripiṭakas,* the only other place in which he finds a mention is *Gramaṇī Saṁyutta.* Grāmaṇī means 'the leader of a village'"

The discussion centres on Four Vows. Buddha's refutation appears to be no more than jugglery of words. But in the same talk, Buddha himself considers non-injury, truth, etc., to be wholesome. In the *Pañca sīla* of the Buddhists, four items at least are identical with the four vows of the Niganṭhas.[22] Even amity, compassion, etc., mentioned by Buddha in this episode are in harmony with Patañjali's *Yogadarśana*[23] and the Jaina tradition.[24]

7. Famine in Nālandā

Once Nālandā was in the grip of a famine when Buddha was camped there with a large number of followers. Asked Niganṭha Nātaputta his follower Asibandhaka-putra Grāmaṇī to go to Buddha and enter into a discussion with him.

Said he,

> "Grāmaṇī! Go and ask *Śramaṇa* Gautama if he was bent on the

destruction of *kulas,* or at least on their misery by being at Nālandā with so many followers at a time when the area was in the grip of a severe famine. This two-edged question will be more than he will be able either to spew out or to swallow down."

Grāmaṇī did as he was asked to do. To his query, Buddha said, "Grāmaṇī! From now backwards, I can recall as much time as 91 *kalpas,* but I do not see a single *kula* which has been destroyed for making an offer from cooked food. A *kula* is destroyed not by my stay here, but for one or other of the following eight reasons : by the king, by thieves, by fire, by flood, when hoarded wealth is removed, when farm is not duly cultivated, by the birth of a worthless child and because of transience of every earthly object. If still someone says that I am bent on destroying the *kulas,* he will go to hell immediately on death."

Grāmaṇī was impressed. He joined the Buddha's order.

Source : *Saṁyukta Nikāya,* Kula Sutta, 40.1.9.

Comment

The *Āgamas* do not mention Nālandā ever being in the grip of a famine. The only thing that comes out of this story is that once Nātaputta and Buddha were in Nālandā at one and the same time.

8. Grahapti Chitra

One day when Nigaṇṭha Nātaputta was at Macchikasanda, Grahapati Chitra came to him. Nātaputta asked, "Grahapati! Can *Śramaṇa* Gautama restrain controversy and consideration and enter into an absolute *samādhi (avicāra-avitarka samādhi)?"*

—"*Bhante*! I do not accept this with devotion."

Nigaṇṭha Nātaputta praised his simplicity to the assembly. Asked Grahapati, "*Bhante!* According to you, which one is superior, knowledge or devotion?"

—"In my rating, knowledge is higher."

—"*Bhante!* When I so desire, I roam in first, second, third or fourth meditation. I stand in no need of knowing by devotion for a *Śramaṇa* or *brāhmaṇa."*

Said Mahāputta to the assembly, "How silly, crooked and cunning the Grahapati is."

The Grahapati burst out, "*Bhante*! Just now you extolled my simplicity and now you call me silly and cunning. You contradict yourself. *Bhante!* Ten questions are usually known in religion. If you know the answers, please come out."

So, saying, he produced the ten questions and departed.

Source : *Saṁyutta Nikāya,* Niganṭha Sutta, 39.8.

Comment

In Jaina Philosophy, *avitarka-avicāra samādhi* has been mentioned as a second step.[25] Citra Grahapati was a resident of Macchikāsanda and a cashier by profession.[26] He was thorough in his knowledge of religious themes. He had held discussions with many, such as Mahaka, Kāmabhū, Godatta,, Acela, Kāśyapa and many others.[27] Buddha considered him foremost in this respect.[28]

9. Hall of Curiosity Sutta

(This was a hall where people of different sects assembled and discussed their respective view-points). This is an account of a meeting between Buddha and Vatsa Gotra Parivrājaka. Vatsa Gotra said that once there was a discussion in the Hall of Curiosity that his own master Pūraṇa Kāśyapa could correctly say where a dead follower of his has been born. Other leaders, including Niganṭha Nātaputta, too, had this capacity. Then he added, people say that even *Śramaṇa* Gautama could say the whereabouts of his deceased followers. The leading disciples of these leaders were also endowed with the same faculty. But in the end, he added, they said some thing more about you, *viz.,* that you can say, so and so has uprooted his desires, so and so has cut his fetters, so and so has terminated his misery. So, I became anxious and curious to know about your way."

The rest of the account is irrelevant for our present purpose.

Comment

In the Jaina view, it is very commonplace to be able to tell the whereabout of departed soul. Mahāvīra was an omniscient personality. Even a lesser person who possessed upto extra-sensory knowledge could even do so.

Source : *Saṁyutta Nikāya,* Kutuhala Śala Sutta, 42.9.

10. Abhaya Licchavī

Once Abhaya Licchavī and another came to Ānanda at Vaiśālī and narrated the view of Nigaṇṭha Nātaputta on *karma nirjarā.*

"*Bhante!* What does the Lord say on this?"

Ānanda told him that his Lord has described at least three types of *nirjarā* and described them at length.

Source : *Aṅguttara Nikāya*, Tika Nipāta 74 (Hindi translation), pp. 227-28.

Comment

Abhaya Licchavī figures in another text, *Sālha Sutta,*[29] wherein Sālha who was accompanied by Abhaya in asking questions. Dr. Woodward[30] has identified Abhaya Licchavī with Prince Abhaya which is wrong. The former was a prince at Rājagṛha and the latter a resident of Vaiśālī. The discussion on penance is consistent with the Jaina view of penance. The word *'nirjarā'* has been very appropriately used.

11. Loka-finite or infinite

Two *brāhmins* came to Gautama Buddha presented the views of Pūraṇa Kāśyapa and Nigaṇṭha Nātaputta on *loka,* asking which one was correct and which one was wrong. Buddha did not discuss the correctness or otherwise of the two views, but stated his own.

Source : *Suttapiṭake, Aṅguttara Nikāya Pāli, Navaka Nipāto, Mahāvaggo, Lokāyatika Suttaṁ*, 9.4.7.

Comment

The rival viewpoints of Purāṇa Kāśyapa and Nigaṇṭha Nātaputta on *Loka* have been stated in identical terms. Then what is the point at issue? In both the views, the *loka* has been called infinite. According to its English translator, E.M. Herr, *Loka* is finite to Purāṇa Kāssapa but infinite to Nigaṇṭha Nātaputta.[31] The translator has done so on the basis of an alternate reading which the translator has given in the footnote, *loka* is *"anantaṁ"* to Pūraṇa Kāśyapa but *"antavantaṁ"* to Nigaṇṭha Nātaputta.[32] Well, this reading appears correct. For, according to Mahāvīra, *loka* is finite, but *aloka* is infinite.[33] In a further break up, Mahāvīra has called *loka* finite when viewed as an object and as space, but infinite when viewed as time and as a subjective factor.[34] It seems that the *brahmins* were concerned with *loka* as space which in the words of Mahāvīra was *sa-ante,* which comes near the reading in *Aṅguttara Nikāya.* The reason why Buddha evaded the question was that he had revealed this and eight other questions in *Majjhima Nikāya* and other texts.[35]

12. Jaina Śrāvaka Vappa

There is a preliminary discussion between the Jaina follower Vappa and the long-lived Mahāmaudgalyāyana on *karma* committed in a previous birth but its result not experienced then by one who is fully restrained and pious in this birth. The point at issue is, if he experiences the outcome in this birth. According to Vappa who is expressing the Jaina view, he does. The discussion is then referred to Buddha who had just arrived after evening meditation. Buddha broke up the issue under four heads, activity of the body, activity of words, activity of mind and removal of nesciences, and posed the question from a different angle and in each case, the answer of Vappa was now in the negative. He was convinced that Buddha was right and his own master was wrong. He became a follower of Buddha.

Source — *Suttapiṭake Aṅguttara, Nikāya Pāli,* Catukka-Nipāta Mahāvagga Vappasutta, 4.20.5, (from Hindi version), pp. 188-192.

Comment

Vappa was a Śākya king, Buddha's own uncle.[36] the Jaina sources, however, do not mention him. What Buddha told him was not contrary to the Jaina tradition, but he had confused him through his mode of presentation. Mrs. Rhys Davids has expressed the possibility of this Vappa being identical with "one of those five friends in whom the Śākyamuni sought fellow helpers.[37] But this is not correct. Both belonged to Kapilavastu, of course, but one was a *brahmin* of the Vāsiṣṭha line while the other was a Śākya *Kṣatriya*. The *brahmin* had been initiated much earlier. After Buddha's enlightenment, he and his friends attained the *arhat*-hood.[38]

Though he was Buddha's uncle, he was a follower of Mahāvīra, according to this account, which should easily establish Mahāvīra's seniority and the popularity of his religion. This may be the reason why Buddhism might have been influenced by Jainism.

13. Sakul Udāyi

Once Sakul Udāyi, the leader of the Parivrājakas, and Buddha were both camped at Rājagṛha. One day Buddha came to Udāyi and asked,

> "Udāyi! What are you talking about today?" Udāyi told him that when he was present at his camp and talking, his followers were all attention; but when he was out, they would indulge in all sorts of gossip. When Buddha expressed a desire to hear something from him, he said, "Only the other day, I met a leader who claims to be all-knowing and all-seeing. When I asked him about his genesis (prior birth), he looked blank." On this, Buddha enquired who this great leader was, and Udāyi reported that he was Nigaṇṭha Nātaputta.

Said Buddha,

> "Let him enter into a discussion with me and silence me, or I silence him. But let us drop this and let me tell you my view on this, etc."

Source : *Majjihma Nikāya,* Cūla-Sukula-Dāyī Suttānta, 2.3.9.

Comment

The episode contains a discussion on Omniscience.

EVENTS

14. News of Nātaputta's demise (1)

This is the repetition of the same episode as recounted in the introduction to this Chapter. Cuṇḍa's follower of Buddha, came with the news of the passing away of Nigaṇṭha Nātaputta. He reported it to Ānanda adding that a fight was going on in that camp among his followers. He was conducted to Buddha's presence to report the same to his spiritual leader.

Source : *Majjhima Nikāya, Samāgama Suttāta,* 3.1.4.

Comment

Vide Chapter on Chronology, discussion on the *nirvāṇa* of Mahāvīra.

15. News of Nātaputta's demise (2)

The same event is repeated in *Dīgha Nikāya,* Pāsādik Sutta 3/6. Comment as above.

16. A Discussion on Nātaputta's demise

In this account, when Nātaputta had passed away, Buddha had just arrived at Pāvā and camped at the newly constructed and elegant Assembly Hall of the Mallas. Cūṇḍa had reported about the severe in-fighting in the other camp. At Buddha's bidding, the discourse is beings given by Sāriputta. Buddha himself prostrated to have a rest. Sāriputta recounted the event and spoke in high praise of the teaching of Buddha.

Source : *Dīgha Nīkāya,* Saṅgiti-paryāya-Sutta, 3/18.

Comment

As Above.

17. Cause of the death of Niganṭha Nātaputta

The said Nātaputta was a resident of Nālandā. How did he die in Pāvā? Truth regarding Buddha's teaching was revealed to Gṛhapati Upāli. Be reproduced it in 10 verses when Nātaputta started vomiting blood. In that state he was carried to Pāvā. There he died.

Source : *Majjhima Nīkāya Aṭṭhakathā,*
Samāgama Sutta Vaṇṇanna, Part II, p. 34.

Comment

No such event has been noted anywhere in the Jaina texts. It does not even tally with the account of *Upāli Sutta on Majjhima Nikāya.* Hence, it is apparently a concoction of the *Aṭṭhakathā.* According to the Jaina account, starting from Rājagṛha Mahāvīra reached Pāvā where he camped for the monsoon months. There he passed away on the last day of the dark fortnight of the month of *Kārtika.* We do not find any account of his prolonged illness.

18. Display of Occult Powers

The story runs like this that once a merchant at Rājagṛha got a log of sandal wood which was curved into a bowl. He hanged it from a very tall poll and made an offer it to anyone who could pluck it down. The invitees, six spiritual leaders, which included Nigaṇṭha Nātaputta, assembled but failed. At last, one Piṇḍola Bhāradvāja, aco-disciple of Maudgalyāyana, went into the sky, pucked it from the poll, flew over Rājagṛha thrice and reached the ground. When Buddha came to know what one of his disciples had done, he openly chastised him, rejected the display of their occult powers by his disciples and prescribed that henceforth his *bhikṣus* would use only iron or earthen vessels.

Source : *Vinaya Piṭaka,* Cullavagga, 5.1.10.
also, *Dhammapada Aṭṭhakathā,* 4.2.

Comment

This is a fantastically exaggerated account. Even Buddha had disapproved the display of occult power. By what stretch of imagination would one say that Mahāvīra took part in the contest and failed? The Jaina tradition strictly prohibits the display of any power.[39] It appears that whenever the author of the *Tripiṭakas* wanted to insult the leaders of the other paths, he invariably indulged in this cheap device.

19. Six Buddhas

According to this account, six leaders who had declared themselves to be omniscient,—and this included Nigaṇṭha Nātaputta—while wandering, reached the city of Śrāvastī. Their respective disciples carried the news to the king. The king invited them all to the palace. They did not have the courage to face the king. But since their disciples would not be dissuaded, all of them reached the palace. The king offered them cushions to sit upon. But they preferred to squat on the bare ground. The reason why they did like this was that in taking the seat offered by the king, they would let their body be polluted by the king's power. The king's interpretation of this behaviour was that none of the six leaders possessed "white religion" (*śukla dharma).* The king asked if they were all Buddhas. They were afraid that if they answered in the affirmative, the king would put them to test, and if they failed, they would be punished and thrown out. So all of them said that they were not Buddhas. On this, the king dismissed them at once. As they stepped out of the palace, their disciples were waiting for them with great inquisitiveness. The leaders said,

> "Indeed we are Buddhas. But the king did not know the qualification of a Buddha. So, if our answer was in the affirmative, the king's mind

would have been overcast with doubt. So, we said that we were not Buddhas. For the rest, we are what we are. Our Buddhahood cannot be washed down."

Source : *Saṁyukta Nikāya Aṭṭhakathā,* 3.1.1.

Comment

This is nothing more than a false, concocted account.

20. Mṛgāra Śreṣṭhī

Mṛgāra Śreṣṭhī was a merchant at Śrāvastī. He celebrated the marriage of his sons with one Vaiśākhā, daughter of Dhanañjaya Śreṣṭhī. On this occassion, on the sixth day of the celebration, he invited the Niganṭha monks to his house to offer them food. All the Niganṭhas were assembled there. When Viśākhā was called upon to serve food, she had a severe reaction at the sight of the nudes. She declined at once to do anything with them and requested her father-in-law to turn them out of the house. The merchant begged to be forgiven and dismissed the monks with due respect. On another day, some Niganṭha monks came at the merchant's door to beg food, when Vaiśākhā dismissed them by saying that the merchant was eating cold (remnant from yesterday) food. So, the monks went away. The merchant heard these words and was aflame with anger. When he ordered his men to throw her out, she protested that that was not easy. She said that she could be rejected only after her guilt was established in the presence of elders from both sides who were present at her marriage. The elders assembled and Viśākhā's explanation on the allegations of the merchant was accepted by them. The merchant begged to be forgiven. Viśākhā was ready to do so and remain at the house on condition that Buddha and his *bhikṣus* were invited. The merchant agreed on condition that the invitees would be received by Viśākhā. This was done. Buddha arrived, but the merchant did not appear. Even at the dinner, he excused to be absent. At last, it was time to listen the words of Buddha. The merchant could no longer keep aside. As he started, the Niganṭha monks at the door urged him to listen from a distance and not to enter into the room where Buddha sat. But what a marvel, as Buddha began to speaks, the sins began to drop out from the merchants body and soon he was purified.

Source : *Dhammapada Aṭṭhakathā,* 4-4.

Comment

This appears to be an exaggerated concoction of the *Aṭṭhakathā* which does not figure anywhere in the Jaina *Āgamas* or in the original *Tripiṭakas.*

21. Garahadinna and Sirigutta

Two friends, Sirigutta and Garahadinna, lived at Śrāvastī. Sirigutta was a follower of Buddha while Garahadinna was a follower of the Nigaṇṭhas. They would often discuss their mutual faith and Garahadinna wanted to attract the other to his side. He would say, the Nigaṇṭhas were all-knowing and all-seeing, etc. So, one day Sirigutta invited 500 Nigaṇṭha monks to his house to test their omniscience. He had a deep ditch dug in his house which he covered with a deceptive net. Cushions were placed on the net. As the monks came and occupied the seats, they slipped down into the ditch.

This shocked his friend Garahadinna who was bent on taking revenge. After some time, he invited Buddha and his monks to his house and adopted the same device to trap them. But Buddha could foresee it. By dint of his spiritual power, he filled up the ditch with lotuses in full bloom so that he and his followers could comfortably take their seats. Then Buddha delivered his sermon which purified the two friends and many others.

Source : *Dhammapada Aṭṭhakathā,* 4-12.

Comment

This sort of partisan and sectarian stories were galore in both the Buddhist and Jaina traditions. In the Jaina tradition, there is the famous story of King Bimbisāra of Magadha and his consort Celanā. The former was a follower of Buddha and the latter of the Nigaṇṭhas. Once the Buddhist monks were invited to the palace. Celanā had their slippers collected, cut into fine pieces, boiled in butter milk and served to the monks who swallowed it with the greatest relish. To take revenge, the king one day saw a Nigaṇṭha monk in a temple settled in deep meditation. The king arranged to get a harlot and deposited her near the monk. Next morning, words went round that a Nigaṇṭha monk spent the night with a prostitute. People flocked in largest number. Even the king and the queen came. But all saw to their surprise that a monk was there alright, but he was a Buddhist monk. It seems that it was age when a race was going on for fabricating such stories to glorify one's own religion.

Even the *Questions of Milinda* (p. 350) has an exaggerated account of 84000 people been purified by Buddha's sermons in course of one day.

22. Pious outcome of Śramaṇahood

Once Buddha was camped at Rājagṛha when Ajātaśatru was the ruling monarch there. It was a moonlit night. The king was seated with his ministers. He expressed a desire that in such a beautiful night, it would be worthwhile to listen to the words of some advanced spiritual leader. All the ministers suggested one by one the names of the six enlightened persons of the age, including Niganṭha Nātaputta, but the king remained silent. The last name suggested was that of Buddha. This time, the king expressed a desire to go and see him. The king came to him, paid him homage, took a seat and said,

> "*Bhante!* People follow one craft or another and they become happy by earning a livelihood from it. Can we say the same about *Śramaṇa*-hood?"

On this, Buddha asked if the king had put the same question to other spiritual leaders and if so, to narrate what they had said to him. The king said that he had put the same question to Pūraṇa Kāśyapa, Gośālaka, Ajitakeśakambala and Prakrudha Kātyāyana and what they said in reply was all non-sense. Then, he said, he went to Niganṭha Nātaputta who spoke at length about his fourfold withdrawal, whereupon Buddha gave his solution in great detail. (See Chapter two above). The king was very much impressed by Buddha's words and he became his follower. The king confessed to him that he had been a patricide, but that he was penitent for this crime and that in future he would behave more carefully. Buddha forgave him and gave him his blessings. After the king had gone, Buddha told his monks that the king had committed a heinous crime, but for which he could have his spiritual eye opened on that very day.

Source : *Dīgha Nikāya,* Sāmaññjaphala Sutta, 1-2.

Comment

The fourfold withdrawal to which Buddha makes reference shows that he was acquainted with the fourfold path of *Pārśva* and he confused the views of Mahāvīra to be the same which is not correct. Besides, the four items described by him are a distortion. Buddha confused the four vows with the restraints prescribed by the Niganṭhas. We have a similar confusion about *catruyāma* in other Buddhist texts like *Cūlasakuladāyi* and *Grāmāṇī Saṁyutta.* It is not mentioned in the text under reference that Mahāvīra's name was suggested by any minister to king Ajātaśatru. It has, however, come down through the Mahāyāna tradition. In this account, all the other leaders have been called elderly and senior, from which it follows that Buddha was junior to all.

23. Buddha : Youngest among the spiritual leaders

Once when Buddha was camped in Jetavana at Śrāvastī, King Prasenajit of Kośala came to see him. Said the king, "Gautama! Do you with authority claim to have acquired unprecedented right enlightenment?" When Buddha replied in the affirmative, the king expressed surprise adding that when senior leaders like Pūraṇa Kāśyapa, Nigaṇṭha Nātaputta and others could not do so, he though young, could with authority claim to be rightly enlightened. Then Buddha spoke a few inspiring words at which the king was greatly impressed. He praised him and became one of his followers.

Source : *Saṁyukta Nikāya,* Dahara Sutta, 3-1-1.

Comment

This is the most glaring proof of Buddha's being the youngest among the contemporary spiritual leaders. While considering the contemporaneity of Mahāvīra and Buddha, Jacobi and other leaders have not touched this issue of seniority of Mahāvīra. Had it been readily available to them, they would have accepted Mahāvīra's seniority without dispute.

24. Sabhiya Parivrājaka

Once Buddha was camped in Rājagṛha. A friendly god gave some questions to Sabhiya Parivrājaka and asked him to become a *brahmacārī* (celibate) under one who could give satisfactory reply to those questions. In the morning, the Parivrājaka rose and went to all the spiritual leaders, including Nigaṇṭha Nātaputta, one after another; but none could give him a reply. They confused him instead with counter-questions. At last he came to Rājagṛha, in the presence of Buddha. The account says that the Parivrājaka produced his question, to which Buddha gave convincing answers, after which, needless to add, he became a follower of Buddha. Later, he joined the order as a monk, ended his sins and attained the rank of an *arhat.*

Source : *Suttanipāta, Mahāvagga,* Sabhiya Sutta.

Comment

This is another undoubted proof of Mahāvīra's seniority. Compared to Buddha, other spiritual leaders of the age have been described by *Sutta Nipāta* as *jiṇṇa* buddha, *mahāllakā, addhagata, vayo anupattā, thera, rattajñbhu, chira pavvajitā, i.e.*, worn, aged, elderly, long-lived, having attained age, senior, experienced and ever initated.[40]

Theregāthā Aṭṭhakatā and other texts contain details of Sabhiya Parivrājaka. A *subhaṭa* girl was placed for her instruction by her parents under a Parivrājaka. In course of time, the girl conceived. She was turned out of her parental home. She gave birth to a boy at a public place where four roads met. Since the boy was born in a *sabhā* or crowded place, he was named Sabhiya. These texts also contain account of his previous lives.[41]

25. Subhadra Parivrājaka

Subhadra Parivrājaka, a resident of Kuśinārā, had heard that Buddha was to pass away at that night. So he thought that he must see him and have his doubts clarified before it was too late. So he reached his camp. But since Buddha was tired, Ānanda would not admit him in the presence of the master. Subhadra insisted again and again. This reached the Buddha's ear. So he asked Ānanda to let him in. He asked if all the spiritual leaders of the age were correct in their stand, or not correct, or some were correct and others not. Said, Buddha, "Let up drop this and let me present my own stand." And then he spoke at length.

Source : *Dīgha Nikāya,* Mahāparinivvāṇa Sutta, 2.3.

Comment

As per this, Mahāvīra was alive at the time of Buddha's death, which is not correct.

26. Seven spiritual leaders at Rājagṛha

This is a account given by Śakula Udāyi to Gautama Buddha of the simultaneous presence of seven spiritual leaders at Rājagṛha during one monsoon and about the noisy debates in each camp as to which leader was really great. Some extolled Pūraṇa Kāśyapa, some Gośālaka, some Niganṭha Nātaputta and so on. Some, Udāyi reported, came out with the superiority of *Śramaṇa* Gautama.

Source : *Majjhima Nikāya,* Mahāsakuladavi Suttānta, 2.3.7.

Comment

The account highlights the simultaneous presence of the seven spiritual leaders at Rājagṛha during one monsoon.

27. Nigaṇṭha Uposatha

Once when Buddha was camped at Śrāvastī, Viśākhā, the mother of Mṛgāra, came to him pretty early in the morning. When Buddha asked about the purpose of her visit, she said that she had undergone *uposatha (*a vow with fast) and hence she had come on a visit. Buddha spoke at length about three types of *uposatha.* The first one, called *gopālauposatha,* was practised by the cowherds which according to him was without any great outcome or result. The second one he called *nigaṇṭha-uposatha,* practised by the *Nigaṇṭhas.* According to this, the monks would restrain their followers from committing *hiṁsā* (slaughter, injury) upto a hundred *yojanas* in each direction. They advise their followers to remove their clothes on the *uposatha* night, and not to think of their parents, wife, children, other near and dear ones temporarily as their own. This according to him was indulging in falsehood and hence virtually a puerile from of *uposatha.* The third which he considered to be correct he called the ārya *uposatha* which was the one prescribed by him to his followers and then he gave her the details about it. According to this, an *ārya* follower took shelter with *dharma, saṅgha* and Buddha and thought of and reviewed eightfold restraints in his life. The *uposatha* day was to be spent like that, according to him. This gave a great result. Then he gave an idea through comparisons as to how great it could be.

Source : *Aṅguttara Nikāya,* Tika Nipāta, 20.

Comment

Of the 12 vows of the Jainas, the eleventh one is *Pauṣadha,* of which a very distorted picture has been given here. In this, the follower takes a vow to desist from slaughter or injury upto a certain distance in each direction. It is not fair to say that he ceases from causing injury to some only and not to all. This vow is not a falsehood. The *pauṣadha* prescribes the life of a monk for a householder for one night when he takes out his clothes and ceases to think of his parents and near and dear ones as his own. Besides, he remains without food and water. But this is not basically different from what Buddha has prescribed, nor does it involve any form of theft, as suggested.

The Jaina text *Bhagavatī* (8/5/677) gives an exhaustive account of *Pauṣadha* on the basis of questions posed by the Parvrājakas to the Niganṭha monks, which were later represented by Gautama to Mahāvīra. The sole purpose of the Buddhist account appears to be to give a distorted version of the Jaina vow and enjoy a fun by laughing at it.

28. The place of the Niganṭhas in the Six Subcastes

The Buddha told Ānanda Rājagṛha that according to Pūraṇa Kāśyapa's classification, there were six subcastes as follows :

Black—Thieves, butchers, etc., who indulged in slaughter of others.
Blue—Beggars, *karmavādī, kriyāvādī,* etc.
Red—Niganṭha with a single piece of cloth.
Yellow—Niganṭha followers clad in white or nude.
White—Ājīvaka and their followers.
Pure white—Nanda, Vatsa, Kriṣa-sāṁkṛtya and Makhalī Gośāla.

Source : *Aṅguttara Nikāya,* 6.6.57.

Comment

Contrary to the authorship of these six subcastes to Pūraṇa Kāśyapa the text under reference, in others like *Dīgha Nikāya,* Sāmaññjaphala Sutta, *Saṁyukta Nikāya,* Khandhavagga, and *Majjhima Nikāya,* Khandaka Sutta, the authorship is attributed to Gośālaka. This is apparently a mistake. The Buddhist texts contain many other instances of false attribution[42] like this. For instance, *Saṁyutta Nikāya* attributes the *Ahetuvāda* of Gośālaka to Pūrāṇa Kāśyapa.[43] In *Jātaka Aṭṭhakathā,* the views of Pūraṇa Kāśyapa have been superimposed on Mahāvīra.[44] In *Saṁyukta Nikāya,* the entire viewpoint of Gosālaka has been placed under Prakrudha Kātyāyana.[45] In that text, the six subcastes have been attributed to the latter. The Tibetan edition of the *Tripiṭakas* attribute these to Ajit Keśakambala.[46] Buddhaghoṣa, the commentator of the *Tripiṭakas,* has, at many places, linked up the six subcastes with Gośālaka.[47] That the subcastes are due to Gośālaka can be established from the text of the Jaina *Āgama Bhagavatī.*[48] The most authoritative Buddhist text on this is *Sāmaññjaphala Sutta.*[49] According to this, too, the view is due to Gośālaka. The founders and followers of the Ājīvakas top the list. According to Dr. Basham, Pūraṇa Kāśyapa was the seniormost among the spiritual leaders of the age, while Gośālaka was young. When Pūraṇa Kāśyapa saw his view waning and that of Gośālaka waxing, he readily accepted the superiority of the latter.[50] If this view of Dr. Basham be accepted, then it tallies with the expression in the *Tripiṭakas* linking the six subcastes to Pūraṇa Kāśyapa. There are some differences in the meaning of the subcastes. According to one text, *Nigaṇṭha ekaśataka* have been placed under the third category of red. Dr. Herr's rendering of this is "Jaina and one with a loin (single) cloth."[51] The rendering by Dr. Basham[52], Dr. Hornell and Buddhaghoṣa[53] is "a Nirgranṭha in a single piece of cloth." The Buddhist Literature is galore with references to the clad Nigaṇṭhas.[54]

The reading for the third yellow subcaste is *gīhīodatavasanā acelaka-sabaka.* Dr. Basham's rendering of this is "the followers of the Acelakas—white clad disciples."[55] According to him, the word Acelaka stands for the Ājīvakas.[56] He is of the view that compared to the *bhikṣus* of all sects, even the Ājīvaka laymen have been considered superior.[57] In Buddhaghoṣa's view, the reading stands for the *nigaṇṭha śrāvakas.* His logic is that the *nigaṇṭha* householder *śrāvakas* make offer of food to the Ājīvaka monks and are hence superior to Nigaṇṭha monks.[58] Dr. Herri's translation of this reading is "white robbed householders and followers of naked ascetics."[59] Taking an overall views, it appears that *avadatavasana-gṛhī* and *acelaka śrāvaka* are two words. The word *gṛhī odāta vasanā* occurs in *Samāgama Sutta,*[60] *Pasādia Sutta*[61] and *Saṅgitī Paryāya Sutta,*[62] wherein *Nigaṇṭha Nātaputtasya sābakas* is the qualifying adjective. It follows easily that *avadata-vasana gṛhī* are the *śrāvakas* of Nigaṇṭha Nātaputta. It is difficult to say to which *śrāvaka* community the Buddhist text points. The Jaina texts are silent about "white clad householder *śrāvakas.*" Maybe, they are the *sthavir kalpī* monks. But more important had been the *Jina kalpa* monks. So, it is likely that these had been called the disciples of the Nigaṇṭha and the *Sthavira kalpī* monks had been called white clad household followers. Although according to Dr. Herr, *Acelaka Śrāvaka* means follower of *Acelaka,* but in this context, the word *Śrāvaka* should mean the follower of the *Acelaka* monks. The Buddhist tradition has used the word *Śrāvaka* to have been listed under subcaste five, it should be reasonable to classify the nude *bhikṣus* as the *Nigaṇṭha bhikṣus.*

According to Dr. Basham, "the white Ājīvikas and Ājīvinīs" fall under subcaste five.[63] Dr. Herr's translation is "Fakirs and their disciples."[64] Dr. Herr's translation appears to be more correct. The Jaina tradition has the concept of six *leṣyās* or tinges, *viz.,* black, blue, ash, red, pink and white. For details, *Uttarādhyayana Sūtra.*[65] The description of the tinges in the *Āgama* literature is well coordinated and exhaustive. Tinges differ from one another in colour smell, taste and touch. They may be subjective and objective. Details have been given of the quantum of tinges in the heavenly beings, human beings, subhuman beings and infernal beings. The first three tinges have been considered inauspicious and the last three auspicious. Such an exhaustive description is to be found nowhere else. According to the doctrine of tinges, the Vaimānika gods have, as per colour one or another of the first three tinges. According to a reference in the *Āgamas,* the Ājīvika *bhikṣu* may after death reach upto the twelfth heaven.[66] The implication is that they may have red, pink and white tinges. According to the Ājīvikas, the *niganṭhas* belong to the red and yellow groups. *Tejas* and *padma* are synonymous with *lohita* and *haridra.*[67]

According to Jacobi[68] and Basham,[69] Mahāvīra had based his doctrine of *leṣyā* on Gośālaka's theory of six subcastes. But the reverse may be equally possible. Dr. Basham's logic is that the doctrine of tinges is well coordinated and developed and hence it must have been based on the cruder and earlier view of Gośālaka. What, however, seems more probable is that many a doctrine from the *Pārśva* tradition later got incorporated in the Ājīvika, Buddhist and Jaina traditions. According to Buddha's classification, the six subcastes were as follows : black one to which belonged people of low castes, low habits and dark religion; black two with white *dharma,* black three with neither black nor white *dharma,* white one with black *dharma,* white two with white *dharma* and white three with neither black nor white.

Be it noted that Gosālaka's classification has relevance to present life only while those of Mahāvīra and Buddha to life hereafter. Wherefrom Buddha derived his classification is fairly clear. It was a part of the current gossip.

29. Saccak Niganṭhaputra

Saccaka Niganṭhaputra stands for the son of a mude monk.[70] (Here it should be taken as proper name). Saccaka was known to be a very powerful and well-versed monk who one day came to Buddha when he was camped at Vaiśālī. They hold a long discussion on sundry topics which impressed Saccaka. He said that he had held similar discussion with other leaders of the age, which included Niganṭha Nātaputra, but all of them appeared to be very confused. After this Saccaka departed.

Source : *Majjhima Nikāya,* Mahāsaccaka Suttānta, 1.4.6.

Comment

No such monk as Saccaka is known to the Jaina tradition. The account is exclusive to *Majjhima Nikāya* which further says that after he was defeated by Buddha, he invited the latter to a dinner. For the occasion, the Licchavīs had sent five hundred dishes. After the dinner was over, he prayed that the merit for this offer should go to the Licchavīs. Buddha said, "they will get as much as is due to the non-detached, and he should get as much as is due to the detached."[71]

Buddhaghoṣa writing in *Majjhima Nikāya Aṭṭhakathā* has written that there was a Nigaṇṭha and a Nigaṇṭhī who were immensely quarrelsome. They used to quarrel very often, but none could defeat the other. At last, the Licchavīs, caught hold of them and put them to wedlock. They had five children, four girl and the fifth one was Saccaka.[72] This Saccaka has been called by Buddha as *Agnivaiśyāyana* which was his line (*gotra*). Mahāvīra has also been referred to as *Agnivaiśyāyana* in the *Tripiṭakas.*[73] May be, at the time of the writing of the *Tripiṭakas,* this line was wrongly attributed to Mahāvīra. According to Jacobi, this confusion has resulted from the fact that Sudharmā was a *Agnivaiśyayāna.*[74] But, from the similarity of the two names, Nigaṇṭha Nātaputra and Nigaṇṭhaputra, it appears that this confusion is not with Sudharmā, but with Nigaṇṭhaputra. From the discussion he had with Buddha, it does not appear that Saccaka ever belonged to the Nigaṇṭha sect. Rather, in the text under reference, he has spoken ill of Mahāvīra. Had he been an important person in the Jaina tradition, he should have received attention at some place which he has not. Under the circumstances, the idea of Buddhaghoṣa is no more than a freak of imagination or a concocted legend.

30. Practice of Celibacy which is unpleasant to the Mind

This is from a discourse which Ānanda gave in an assembly of 500 Parivrājakas. According to him, there were four types of state of non-celibacy of which the first one he attributed to Nigaṇṭha Nātaputra. He said that this leader who claimed to be omniscient always enquired about the name and line of the persons he met and also about the name of the town and village he passed through. He often went to vacant homes to beg food and came back disappointed. And so on and so forth. In his list of this type of spiritual leaders, the fourth was Sañjaya Velaṭṭhiputra.

Source : *Majjhima Nikāya,* Sandaka Suttanta, 2.3.6.

Comment

According to Ānanda's description, all the spiritual leaders of the age were non-celibate with an unpleasant state of mind and were not even initiated. Nigaṇṭha Nātaputta was slightly better in this that he donned the robe of a monk. In any case, in Ānanda's admission, Mahāvīra was somewhat superior to the rest.

31. Gods of diverse views

One day when Buddha was at Rājagṛha, a few heretical gods who were the admirers of other spiritual leaders, including Niganṭha Nātaputta, came to Buddha and extolled their respective masters. Buddha gave them a hearing, but realised that it was Māra who was speaking through them. At last he said,

> "Just as among the bests are the Vipula mountain here at Rājagṛha, Kailāśa in the Himālayas,[75] the sun among the heavenly bodies moving through the sky, the ocean among the water reservoirs, and the moon among the planetary bodies, so is Buddha among all beings, including the *devas*, in the Universe."

Source : *Saṁyutta Nikāya,* Nanatitthiya Sutta, 2.3.10.

Comment

There are references in the *Āgamas* in which gods are found to be taking interest in the views and teachings of the spiritual leaders. The god who discussed with Kuṇḍakaulika who happened to be a follower of Mahāvīra appears to have been a admirer of Gośālaka. Śakaḍālaputra who was a follower of Gośālaka received a message from a god who was friendly to Mahāvīra.

32. Piṅgalakoccha Brahmin

Once when Buddha was at Śrāvastī, a Piṅgalakoccha *Brahmin* came to him and asked if the different spiritual leaders of the age were correct in their views, incorrect or partly correct and partly incorrect. Buddha did not evince interest in the question, but described at length his own views.

Source : *Majjhima Nikāya,* Cūla Sāropama Suttanta, 1.3.10.

Comment

It had always been the practice with Buddha to avoid questions and impose his own sermon.

33. Jaṭilasutta

Once when Buddha was at Śrāvastī, King Prasenajita came to him and took his seat. Just the seven Jaṭilas, seven Niganṭhas, seven nudes, seven clads in a single cloth and seven parivrājakas passed that way. The King enquired if anyone from among these was an *arhat* or on the road to *arhathood.* Buddha said, none. He added that only through a prolonged observation and association was it possible to know the conduct of a person. "Don't take any one at par on a short observation," he added.

Source : *Saṁyuktta Nikāya,* Jaṭilasutta, 3.2.1.

Comment

The account gives an idea of the statecraft of the time. It is strange that intelligence men used to roam about in the guise of monks.

34. Dhammika Upāsaka

Once when Buddha was at Śrāvastī, there came to him Dhammika *Upāsaka* with his five hundred *Upāsaka* followers and sang in praise of Buddha concluding, "In wisdom, no *vādī,* Nigaṇṭha or Ājīvaka is equal to you as one standing motionless is nowhere near a fast-moving man."

Source : *Sutta Nipāta, Culavagga,* Dhammika Sutta (Hindi), pp. 75.77.

Comment

While showering praise on Buddha, the Nigaṇṭhas have just been mentioned to cast slur on them. As per *Sutta Nipāta Aṭṭhakathā,* these five hundred *upāsakas* knew the art of flying and had conquered transmigration of soul.

35. Mahābodhikumāra

The ruling monarch at Vārāṇasī was Brahmadatta. In the same city lived a highly affluent *Brahmin.* A son was born to him and he was named Bodhikumāra. He grew into an accomplished young man. Later, he moved to the Himālayas and became a Parivrājaka monk. Many years after this he came back to his own city where at the insistence of the king he agreed to remain with the king in the palace garden. The king had five Ministers all of whom were corrupt people. They used to accepted money and sided with the criminal. Once an aggrived person came to the monk and insisted that justice be administered to him. When this was done, the king placed him charge of the judicial affairs of the state. This was too much for the Ministers to swallow. So they started poisoning the ears of the king. It was decided that the monk would be murdered by the Ministers as he would be coming to the palace to receive his food. The whole arrangement was complete. As the monk came, a dog whom the monk had fed on an earlier occasion sat across his path and began to bark wildly. This was a sufficient warning. The monk retraced his steps. He came back to his thatch in the garden and started preparing to depart. The king saw all this from his window. The king came to him at once and begged to be forgiven if he had caused him any annoyance. But the monk did not agree. The King's parting request was that he should come again to the city at his convenience, to which the monk agreed. The Ministers were now happy at their success. Once again they started their nefarious practices to the greatest unhappiness of the people. The Ministers then thought that the possibility of the monk ever coming back must be nipped in the bud. So, they reported to the King of an illicit connection existing between the monk and the queen. They suggested that the queen should be put to death on ground of adultery. The King agreed and the King's order was carried out. When this news spread into the city, the people in general and the four princes in particular became the enemies of the King and they thought of punishing the erring King. This news at last reached the ears of the monk in his cottage. He thought of saving the life of the King. He came to Vārāṇasī and defeated the five Ministers with arguments. The Ministers having been exposed, they were thrown out of the kingdom. The monk then spoke words of wisdom to the King and the four princes and departed.

The five Ministers were the five spiritual leaders of the age, including Niganṭha Nātaputta. The dog was Ānanda who had warned the monk.

Said Buddha in his sermon :

> "Not only in the present, but all along in the past, the truth-finder had demolished the views of others and established truth as discovered by himself."

Source : *Jātaka Aṭṭhakathā,* Mahābodhi Jātaka, 528 (Hindi), pp. 312-330.

Comment

Mahābodhi Jātaka and texts like that contain such stories as the present one to established the superiority of Buddha and to run down other leaders of the age.

36. A Peacock and a Crow

In the absence of a qualified person, the mediocre dominates. When a qualified person comes on the scene, the mediocre is coverted no more. Buddha narrated a story.

> "In olden times, during the reign of Brahmadatta at Vārāṇasī, *Bodhisattva* was born as a peacock. It grew up and lived to the delight

of everybody. Once a company of merchants sailed with merchandice and a direction-crow. They reached another kingdom named Bāberu where there was no bird. When the people saw the crow in a cage, they were surprised, delighted and bought it after much higgling for one hundred standard coins. The crow was reared up with the greatest care. After some time, the merchants came again, but this time with a peacock. The citizens at Bāberu saw the peacock and became mad after it. The new bird sang and danced to the delight of everybody. The bought it for one thousand standard coins. Compared to the crow, the peacock was more beautiful and received greater attention. The crow was henceforth virtually neglected. Needless to add, Oh *Bhikṣus*! at that time I was the peacock and Nigaṇṭha Nātaputta the crow."

Source : *Jātaka Aṭṭhakathā,* Bāberu Jātaka, 339 (Hindi), Part III, pp. 289-91.

Comment

The story is utterly mean and in bad taste. Although the *Jātakas* recognise that in the presence of a qualified person, the mediocre received no attention which is a truism, this story is not contained in the *Tripiṭakas.* Hence, it does not deserve any attention.

37. A discussion on meat eating

Once Siṅgha Senāpati invited Buddha to dinner when he served him meat. This attracted criticism in the Nigaṇṭha camp on the ground that this was intended meat. When the monks drew the attention of Buddha to this, he said the Nigaṇṭha Nātaputta is not only his critic now, he was also his critic in the previous birth too. Then he narrated a story.

"In a previous birth, when Brahmadatta was reigning at Vārāṇasī, *Bodhisattva* was born in a *Brahmin* family. When he came of age, he became a monk and discarded his home to take shelter in the Himālayan region. Once he came down in search of spicy food. A householder invited him and served meat which *Bodhisattva* ate. After *Bodhisattva* had dined, his host said that since he had prepared the meat for his sake, he must indeed share in the vice. So saying, he uttered a couplet. In another couplet, the *Bodhisattva* told him that even if he had served the meat of his wife or children, he would in no way be held responsible. Then he got up and departed. Needless to add, I was *Bodhisattva* and Nigaṇṭha Nātaputta was the householder."

Source : *Jātaka Aṭṭhakathā,* Telivad Jātaka, 246.

Comment

In *Vinaya Piṭaka* and *Aṅguttara Nikāya,* the critics of Buddha's eating intended meat have been said to be the Niganṭhas. The reference to a previous birth of Buddha and the inclusion of Niganṭtha Nātaputta in the *Aṭṭhakathā* appear to be the product of the fertile brain of the author of *Aṭṭhakathā*. Needless to add, such was the spirit of the age.

38. Four types of People

> "Monks! There are four types of people in the world, *viz.,* first, those who inflict hard penance on themselves, suffering on themselves; second, those who inflict hard penance on others, suffering on others; third, those who inflict hard penance and suffering on self and others; and fourth, those who impose hard penance and suffering neither on self nor on others. The last one can live on in perfect calm and quiet, being free from attachment, and be happy."

Then Buddha spoke at length on how one particular group of persons inflicted hard penance and suffering on themselves, how they begged, how they ate, how they lived and how they tonsured.

Source : *Aṅguttara Nikāya,* (Hindi), Part II, pp. 197-99.

Comment

The details given by Buddha of the first type of people tally with the description of the Niganṭha like as contained in *Daśavaikālika Sūtra* 95/1/27-43. Portions of this description may apply to the Ājīvikas and the followers of Pūraṇa Kāśyapa. Important in the description is the following line :

> "Not to take meat, not to eat fish, not to drink wine, not to take *meraya."*

This may be an evidence against meat eating by the Jaina monks.

39. Five faults of the Niganṭhas

> "Oh monks! Those Ājīvikas..........Niganṭhas.........senior monks... ....Jaṭilakas........Parivrājakas........Magandikas ....Daṇḍikas...... Ārudhakas.......*Gotamakas*......those who indulge in five crimes..... Which five?..........indulge in injury to living beings, in theft, in sex, in falsehood, in drink and intoxication, they are as if hurled into hell."

Source : *Aṅguttara Nikāya* (Hindi), Part II, p. 452.

Comment

The reference is to *Upasampadā Varga*. The same five have been mentioned for the Ājīvikas, the Jaṭilakas, the Parivrājakas, and others.

40. Clad Nigaṇṭhas

Once some Buddhist *Bhikṣus* saw some clad Nigaṇṭhas going. They said to one another. "These appear to be more civilised. At least they have covered the front portion. They have some sense of civilised life and social etiquette." Said one Nigaṇṭha in reply, "We don't bother about social etiquette and civilised life. We hold that even dust and dirt have life. We cover our bowls to keep them out. We cover ourselves." Then there ensued a long discussion between the monks of the two sects. After the *Bhikṣus* returned to Jetavana, Buddha said,

> "To be abashed when there is no ground for it, and no to be abashed when there is ground for it, this is a wrong outlook which leads to misery. To be afraid when there is no ground for it, and not to be afraid when there is ground for it, this is a wrong outlook which leads to misery."

Source : *Dhammapada Aṭṭhakathā*, 22.8.

Comment

Here is an account of Nigaṇṭhas who used clothes, but it is not clear what type of clothes they used and why? However, this much is established that the Buddhists knew of the *Sacelakas* and the *Acelakas*.

41. Murder of Maudgalyāyana

Knowing Maudgalyāyana to be a very resourceful person, monks of other sects hatched a conspiracy to have him killed. Some killers were hired for the purpose. They surrounded the monk in the Kālaśilā region. But the monk escaped through the key hole. The monk was encircled for the second time, but this time the monk decided to stay on. The killers pounced upon him, killed him and crushed his bones to dust and threw it behind some shrub. The soul of the monk came to the Truth-finder (Buddha) to pay his final homage. When the news reached King Ajātaśatru, he got all the monks and killers arrested, buried them waist and burnt them.

Source : *Dhammapada Aṭṭhakathā*, 10.7

Comment

This account is to be found in *Jātaka Aṭṭhakathā* as well as in *Dhammapada Aṭṭhakathā*. According to the former, the culprits were the Niganṭhas and according to the latter monks of other sects *(tairthikas).* Both appear to be false accounts to run others down. According to both Dr. Malālaśekhara[76] and Dr. Von West,[77] Ajātaśatru killed 500 Niganṭhas and so the Niganṭhas were not happy with him. But facts are just the reverse. Ajātaśatru has been neglected at many places by the Buddhists, while the Jaina tradition has held him in high esteem. (Vide Follower kings above), it does not seems possible that Ajātaśatru had killed 500 Niganthas.

42. Question of Milinda

In this account, the renounced King Milinda reviewed his army. Then he expressed a desire to hold discussion with some spiritual leader, when his ministers repeated the same six names, of which one was Niganṭha Nātaputta.

Source : *Questions of Minander,* Hindi translation by Bhikṣu Jagadīsa Kāśyapa, pp. 4-6.

Comment

Since Milinda lived at least six hundred years after the death of Buddha.[78] These six leaders could not have been present at that posterior date. According to *Bhikṣu* Jagadīsa Kāśyapa, perhaps their respective seats were named after the masters, like the seat of Śaṅkarācārya. But there is no solid ground for this surmise.

43. Niganṭhas in Laṅkā

This account about King Pāṇḍukābhaya of Laṅkā has a single line which may be of interest; "The king got erected apartments for the Niganṭha astrologers to the east of the cremation ground."

Source : *Mahāvaṁsa,* Book X, Śloka 77-79, 91-102.

Comment

If we are to believe this account, then the Niganṭhas had gone out of the country. Pāṇḍukābhaya was the king of Laṅkā at least 100 years before Asoka. Thus according to this account, before the emissaries of Asoka could reach Laṅkā, the Nigaṇṭhas were there. On this, we have nothing from the Jaina Sources, nor it is certain Nigaṇṭhas were monks or householders. The *Mahāvaṁsa Commentary* has described these *Nigaṇṭha* astrologers as "nagar *vārdhakī.*"

44. Pestilence in Vaiśālī

Once a pestilence had spread in Vaiśālī caused by a thousand sons of a Yakṣiṇī who hailed from the Himālayan region. People died like insects. They propitiate the devils, all stratagem was tried, but to no effect. Then the six leaders were brought in, but even they could do nothing. Then the souls of the victims of pestilence suggested that the Buddha should be brought from Rājagṛha to stop the devils. When this was done, the devils disappeared.

Souce : *Mahāvastu,* Tr. by J.J. Jones, Vol. I, pp. 208-209.

Comment

The story must have been prepared to extol the power and influence of Buddha. We have similar stories in the Jaina tradition. *Cf.* "Where the Jina dwells, there, upto a distance 25 *yojanas* in the four directions and 12½ *yojanas* above and the same distance below. There is no pestilence, draught, excessive rain, famine, etc."[79]

45. Ṇamo Buddhassa Ṇamo Arahantāṇam

In Rājagṛha, there lived two boys, one with a right outlook and the other with a wrong outlook. They were friends and used to play with a ball and a rod. While hitting the ball, the boy with right outlook would say, Ṇamo Buddhassa, and the boy with wrong outlook would say, Ṇamo Arahantāṇam. Needless to add, the victory was always with the former. This had its impact on the boy with a wrong outlook. He changed his core word.

One day he went with his father to the forest to collect fire wood. On their return journey, they stopped outside the city near a cremation ground to rest and relax. The bulls were unvoked. They slipped into the city. The father left the boy on the spot to look after the logs and went into the city in search of the bulls. By the time, he reached the city gate with the bulls, it was already closed. So the father and the boy were separated. At night, two spirits came to the cremation ground. One of them was with a right outlook and another with a wrong outlook. The latter wanted to do harm to the boy. As soon as he approached near him, the boy said, Ṇamo Buddhassa. The spirit refraced. Then the two spirits brought food from the kitchen of King Bimbisāra in a golden plate, appeared in the guise of his parents and fed the boy. But they forget to carry back the golden plate and restore it at its proper place. In the morning, the boy was arrested and brought before the king on a charge of theft from the royal kitchen. When the boy narrated the whole episode, the king in the company of the boy visited Buddha.

Source : *Dhammapada Aṭṭhakathā,* 21.5.

Comment

Ṇamo Buddhassa and Ṇamo Arahantaṇam are comparable core words of the two religions, and the use of the words by 'one with right outlook' and 'one with a wrong outlook' and to be found in both.

46. Offer to the Niganṭhas

Once Sāriputta asked his maternal uncle, a *Brahmin*, at Rājagṛha, if he indulged in any act earning merit. Said the *Brahmin*,

> "I make an offer worth a thousand coins per month to the Niganṭhas." Sāriputta conducted the *Brahmin* to Buddha where he was made to repeat the same words, when Buddha said to him, "If you continue to make an offer like this to the Niganṭhas for a thousand years, that will not equal to looking at my monks with a pleasant mind for a moment or making a spoonful of offer to them."

Source : *Dhammapada Aṭṭhakathā,* 8.5.

Comment

This is one more example of concocted stories in *Dhammapada Aṭṭhakathā*. This appears to have been the sole purpose. According to this story, Sāriputta's maternal uncle was a Niganṭha follower. In another story, we have seen that Buddha's own uncle had been described to be a Niganṭha follower. This establishes the fact that in many a family, both the religions were simultaneously observed. Both the religions have attached high value to making offers to their respective monks. But it is nowhere mentioned in the Jaina texts that any offer made to a Niganṭha monk earns one a seat in *Brahmaloka*.

47. Nālaka Parivrājaka

On a piece of information from a monk named Asita, Nālaka Parivrājaka came to Vārāṇasī came to Vārāṇasī, held discussions with all spiritual leaders, including Nigaṇṭha Nātaputta, one by one, but was not happy. At last, he had discussion with Buddha and he was satisfied.

Source : *Mahāvastu*, Tr. by J.J. Jones, Vol. III, pp. 379-88.

Comment

This story has come down from the Mahāyāna tradition. In the Hīnayāna tradition too, in *Sutta Nipāta, Nālaka Sutta,* 37, we have the same story, but other spiritual leaders have not been brought in.

48. With the Jina Śrāvakas

This is a story told by Buddha to his followers. When at Vaiśālī he went to a *Jina Śrāvaka* named Ārāḍhakālāma the core of whose teaching was, "Renounce, renounce," is *śrāvakas* would say, "we renounce, we renounce." He became a disciple unto him. Soon it was clear that Buddha knew no less than Ārāḍhakālāma. So, the latter made him his partner in the organisation. But, added Buddha, "I felt that this much knowledge was not adequate for the destruction of sin. I must search for more. So, I departed."

The same thing happened with another, Udraka Rāmiputra. Buddha departed from there too.

Source : *Mahāvastu*, Tr. by J.J. Jones, Vol. II, pp. 114-17.

Comment

This story too comes down from the Mahāyāna tradition. *Jina śrāvaka* here stands for a *nigaṇṭha* in the Pāli *Tripiṭakas. Mahāvastu* is written in Sanskrit. This is an admission of the fact that Buddha spent some time with the *Jina Śrāvakas* or *nigaṇṭhas* and learnt practices from them.

49. Bhadrā Kuṇḍalakeśā

This is the story of a girl at Rājagrha. She saw a thief being taken by hangmen to be hanged for committing theft. At the girl's insistence, the father of the girl bribed the hangmen and got the chief released. The girl married this man. After some time, at her husbands request, the girl, well dressed and with costly ornaments on, accompanied him to a hill to perform some *pūjā*. There the man expressed a desire to kill her and rob her. The girl reluctantly agreed, since there was no alternative; but she made a last request which was that he should embrace her to full length before he killed her. The man agreed. As the man held her in embrace, the girl gave him a mighty push so that he went deep down. the girl descended from there and became a nun in the Niganṭha order. She developed a habit of discussing with learned monks and defeating them. At last, the story concludes, she was defeated by Sāriputta and joined Buddha's order.

Source : *Dhammapada Aṭṭhakathā,* 8/3; *Therigāthā Aṭṭhakathā,* p. 99

She travelled to Magadha, Kośala, Kāśī, Vajjī, Aṅga and other places carrying the teachings of Buddha.[80] Buddha called her foremost among those with a sharp intellect.[81]

Comment

The narrative is interesting and full of events. Worthy of note is the fact that Buddha's foremost female disciple was initially in the Jaina order. The account contains words like 'tonsure' 'white clad *niganṭhas.*'

50. Astrologer Niganṭha

There lived an astrologer Niganṭha who had 500 followers. He lived on the bank of the Gaṅgā. In the course of a discussion, the question came up, what is luck. But no answer was forthcoming. So he came near the Bodhi tree where Buddha had just been enlightened. He put the question to him. Said Buddha,

> "One who has restraint, who praises hardship, is endowed with luck."

The Niganṭha was impressed. He became a follower of Buddha.

Source : S. Beal *Dhammapada,* translated from Chinese, pp. 103-104.

Comment

There is no mention of any such event in Jaina literature. This much is, however, established that before Buddha attained enlightenment, there were many senior

Jaina monks who were well advanced. Besides, it has been rare for many Jaina monks to defect from their order; but the Buddhist literature is full of such stories. These stories, however, serve one purpose which is to establish the greater antiquity of Jainism and seniority of Mahāvīra over Buddha.

51. A Nigaṇṭha in dust

In some northern province, there lived 500 *Brahmins*. They had heard of a Nigaṇṭha who lived on the bank of the Gaṅgā and who kept his body besmeared with dust. They set out to become his disciples. In the way, they became thirsty. Then a spirit gave them water and advised them not to go to the Nigaṇṭha but to Buddha. The *Brahmins* changed the course of their journey. They went to Buddha and became his *Śramaṇas*.

Source : Chinese *Dhammapada*, Tr. by S. Beal, p. 54.

REFERENCES

1. Sometimes Nigaṇṭha Nāthaputta and again Nigaṇṭha Nātaputa.
2. *Daśavaikālika Sūtra*, S. 6-20.
3. See items 2, 6, 1, 3, 13 and 17 below.
4. See items 34, 35 and 36 below.
5. See items 17, 18 and 40 below.
6. My article entitled "Pāli Vāṅmaya meṁ Bhagavān Mahāvīra" in *Bhikṣu Smṛti Grantha*, Śrī Jain Śvetāmbara Terāpanthī Mahāsabhā, Calcutta, 1960, Part 2, pp. 6-10.
7. *S.B.E.* Vol. XIV Introduction, p. XIV-XXIII.
8. *Dictionary of Pāli Proper Names*, Vol. II, pp. 61-65.
9. *The book of Gradual Sayings*, Vol. III, p. 38, Vol. IV, p. 69.
10. *Gāthā*, 77-81, Vol.
11. *Sūtrakṛtāṅga*, Sr. 1 Gāthā 1, Niryukti Gāthā 119-21.
12. *Ibid.*, 1.12.20-21.
13. *Ibid.*, 1.12.21.
14. *Ibid.*, 1.12.11.
15. Sthanāṅga, 5th 3/126; also *Āvaśyaka Sūtra*, Adhyayana, 4.
16. See above Chapter on "Follower King" item Śreṇika Bimbisāra.
17. Muni Dhanarājjī, *Bhāva Bhaskara Kāvyam*, Atmarama & Sons, Delhi.
18. *Ahiṁsa Paryavekṣaṇa*, p. 97.
19. *S.B.E.* Vol. XLV. Introduction, p. XVII.
20. See above "*Contemporary religious leaders*" item entitled Muni Ārdraka.
21. *Cf. Aṅguttara Nikāya*, Pañcaka Nipāta, 5/18.179.
22. *Samādhipāda*, 1.33.
23. *Śāntasudhārasa Bhavana* 13-16.
24. *Jaina Siddhānta Dīpikā*, 5/34.
25. *Dictioanry of Pāli Proper Names*, Vol. I, p. 865.
26. *Saṁyukta Nikāya*, Sāla Yatanavagga, Cittasamyutta.
27. *Aṅguttara Nikāya*, Etadaggavagga Sutta.
28. *Aṅguttara Nikāya, Chatukka Nipāta, Mahāvagga*, Sālha Sutta, 4.20.196.

29. *The Book of Gradual Sayings,* Vol. I, p. 200.
30. *Ibid.,* Vol. IV, pp. 287-88.
31. *Ibid.,* p. 288 fn.
32. *Bhagavatī Sūttra* 11-10-421.
33. *Ibid.,* 2-1-90.
34. *Majjhima Nikāya,* Chulamalukya, Sutta 63 : also *Dīgha Nikāya,* Poṭṭhapāda Sutta, 1.9.
35. *Aṅguttara Nikāya Aṭṭhakathā,* Part II, p. 559.
36. *The Book on Gradual Sayings,* Vol. II, Introduction, p. XIII.
37. *Vinaya Piṭaka, Mahāvagga Mahākhandhaka,* item on *Pañcavaggīya Bhikṣu.*
38. Vide *Preśnottara Tattvabodha, Gośālādhikāra* by Jayācārya, p. 190.
39. *S.B.E.* Vol. X, Part II, Introduction by Fausboll.
40. *Theragāthā Aṭṭhakathā,* 2,410.
41. *Saṁyutta Nikāya, Khandaka Saṁyutta, Majjhima Pannasaka, Upavagga, Mahālīsutta* 21-2-1-8, (Hindi), p. 352.
42. *Book of Kindred Sayings,* Vol. III, p. 61n.
43. Part III, p. 227.
44. 23-1-8.
45. A.L. Basham, *History and Doctrine of Ājīvikas,* p. 22.
46. *Sumaṅgalavilāsinī,* Part I, p. 162.
47. S. 15, Sūtra 550.
48. Dr. Basham, *op. cit.,* p. 23.
49. *Ibid.,* p. 90.
50. *The Book of Gradual Sayings,* Vol. III, p. 273.
51. *Ibid.,* p. 243.
52. *Encyclopaedia of Religion and Ethics.* Vol. I, p. 262.
53. *The Book of Kindred Sayings,* Vol. III, p. 17 fn.
54. E.W. Burlinghame, *Buddhist Legends,* Vol. III, p. 176.
55. *Op. cit.,* p. 139.
56. *Op. cit.,* p. 243.
57. *Op. cit.,* p. 243.
58. *Sumaṅgalavilāsinī,* Part I, p. 163. Basham, *op. cit.,* p. 139.
59. *The Book of Gradual Sayings,* Vol. III, p. 273.
60. *V. Majjhima Nikāya,* 3.1.5.
61. *Dīgha Nikāya,* 3/6.
62. *Ibid.,* 3/10.
63. *Op. cit.,* p. 243.
64. *Op. cit.,* p. 273.
65. *Adhyayana* 34/21-32.
66. See above discussion on Gośālaka : the proximity between the Jainas and the Ājīvikas.
67. Dr. Basham's translation of *haridra* as green is wrong.
68. *S.B.E.,* Vol. XIV, Introduction, p. XXX;
69. *Op. cit.,* p. 245.
70. *Ibid.*
71. *Majjhima Nikāya Aṭṭhakathā,* 1-450.
72. *Dīgha Nikāya,* Sāmaññjaphala Sutta.
73. *S.B.E.,* Vol. XLV, Introduction, p. XXI.
74. *Majjhima Nikāya Aṭṭhakathā.*
75. *Dictionary of Pāli Proper Names,* Part I, p. 35.
76. *Encyclopaedia of Buddhism,* p. 320.
77. *Questions of Milinda,* Hindi by *Bhikṣu* Jagadīśa Kaśyapa, p. 4.
78. Key to above, p. 6.
79. *Samavayāṅga Sūtra,* Sama. 34.
80. *Theragāthā,* 107-11.
81. *Aṅguttara Nikāya, Ekakkanipāta,* 14.

18

CODES AND BOOKS ON CONDUCT AND DISCIPLINE

Conduct and tradition aspects of the two religious may be a nice theme for comparative research. The subject is spread piecemeal in all the *Āgamas* and *Tripiṭakas,* but the main text of the Jainas on this subject is *Nisīha* and that of the Buddhists is *Vinaya Piṭaka.*

The Jaina *Āgamas* have been divided into four classes as *Aṅgas, Upāṅgas, Mūla Suttas* and *Cheda Suttas.* In the *Cheda* group, *Nisīha* is an important text. It has certain special characteristics of its own. Its study is permitted to a monk after three years of initiation provided he is serious. From the standpoint of age, a monk who is 16 is alone permitted to read it.[1] Till a monk becomes acquainted with the text of *Nisīha*, he cannot go to his own folks for begging,[2] nor is he considered fit to be a teacher.[3] To be the leadingmost among the monks, and to undertake solitary wanderings, the knowledge of *Nisīha* is very essential.[4] Unless a monk is versed in this text, he is not permitted to prescribe atonements to other monks. These should indicate the great importance of this particular text.

Authorship and Date of Composition

So, runs the traditional belief that all the *Āgamas* are the sacred words of *Bhagavān* Mahāvīra. The compilation of the *Aṅga* part of the *Āgamas* is attributed to Sudharmā Svāmī who was the fifth among the *Gaṇadharas* of Mahāvīra and immediate successor to his spiritual seat. *Āgamas* other than the *Aṅgas* have been the works by the senior and learned monks. But this does not mean that the latter works have moved apart in any way from the words of the Master. The ideas for all (*arthāgama*) are due to Mahāvīra, though the actual composition (*sutrāgama)* is due to some *Gaṇadhara* or senior monk. The monks who became the authors of the *Āgamas* were also the Masters of the *Pūrvas;* and the texts produced by them are as much revered as the texts produced by the *Gaṇadharas.* The next questions that arise are about the name of the author of *Nisīha*, and the date of its writing. As to its author, the commentaries, *cūrṇis,* and *niryuktis* have expressed diverse views. A second title of *Niśīha* is *Ācāra Prakalpa* or *Ācāraṅga (Ācāraṅga)*. In discussing this topic, the author of *Ācāraṅga cūrṇī* has interpreted the word *'sthavira'* to mean a *'Gaṇadhara.'*[5] *Ācāraya* Śīlāṅka's commentary on the word *'sthavira'* as it occurs in the *Ācāraṅga Niryukti (gāthā* 287) is *sthaviraih-śrutabṛddhai-ścaturdaśa-pūrva-vidviḥ.* This means that *sthaviras* are people who are advanced in *śruta* knowledge, and who are the masters of the 14 *Pūrvas.* The *cūrṇī* of *Pañcakalpa Vaṣyas* states as follows :

> "The author of this treatise on *ācāra* is Bhadrabāhu *Svāmī."*

According to some eulogistic *gāthās* on *Niśīha*, however, Viśākhācārya has been named as the author of this text.[6] It is, therefore, difficult to suggest a single name for the authorship of *Niśīha*. One reason for these different views on authorship may be the peculiar position of the text itself. From historical researches, it has become clear that in the beginning, the *Niśīha Sutta* was only a *cūlā* of the *Āyāraṅga Sutta,* and that the *Āyaraṅga* was the first of the 12 *Aṅgas* of which only upto the ninth *adhyayana* was written by a *Gaṇadhara.* Later, it was elaborated by senior monks, and these elaborations were added to the text in the form of first, second and third *cūlikās.* For the monks who violated the codes of conduct, a separate text on atonements was produced by the senior monks, and this was added as a *cūlā* to the *Ayāraṅga.* This was based on a section devoted to *Acāra-vastu* in the ninth-*Pūrva.* As this portion was related to the *Āyāraṅga,* it easily became its *cūlā.* It may be that this reflected in the second title of *Niśīha* which is *Ācāra.* For reason of secrecy, however, at a later period, the *cūlā* was again separated by the senior monks and then it was given the name *Niśīha*, and it became an important *Āgama* among the *Cheda Sūttas.* Difference about authorship is noticeable even in the *cūrṇīs* and commentaries, and it may be said that from a relative standpoint, both the claims may be taken as correct. This thus means that according to some Bhadrabāhu, and according to others Vaśākhācārya is the author of *Niśīha Sūttra.*

The date of compilation of *Niśīha* goes deep into antiqualty. According to Dalsukh Mālvaṇina, whoever may be its author, Bhadrabābhu or Viśākhācārya, it was written 150 and 175 years of the liberation of Mahāvīra.[7] Thus; it may be said that the ideas contained in this text are as old as 2500 years, and the written text itself is as old as 2300 years.

Intentions behind the word 'niśīha'

The Original word is *niśīha.* Some writers like the authors of the Digambara texts *Dhavalā, Jaya Dhavalā* and *Gommatasāra Ṭīkā,*—and this is supported by the Western scholars like Weber[8]—have read the word '*niśīha*' as a form of the Sanskrit word *niśīhiya, niśīhiya* or *nisehiya* from which they deduce that it is a text on 'don't do this, don't do that.'

According to the *Tattvārtha Bhāṣya, Niśītha* is the Sanskrit form of the word *nisiha;* and this is also the view taken by the writer of the *niryukti.* According to the author of the *Cūrṇī, niśītha* means 'lack of sun-shine' *(aprakāśa).* According to *Ācārya* Hemacandra, *niśītha* means mid-night. To quote his expression :

Niśīthastvardharātra[9]

Thus according to one school, the name of this *Sūtra* has a prohibitory significance, and according to another, it is something confidential which is not to be made public. Both the meanings are consistent with the subject-matter of the *Niśītha Sūtra.* It is confidential as its reading is not permitted in public as per the accepted tradition, and it is prohibitory since it contains a list of things not to be perpetrated. But strictly speaking, the truly prohibitory *Āgama* is *Ācārāṅga* which states very categorically, 'A monk should not do this."

In contrast, the literary form of the *Niśīha* is uniform from the beginning to the end which is that 'if a monk does this, he has to undergo such and such atonement.' From this angle, its leaning is more for secrecy than for prohibition. (For, it does not categorically prohibit anything). There are portions in the *Niśīha Sūtra* which deal with sexual desires which cannot be divulged in public (without being, liable to the charge of pornography).

The Original Text and its Elaboration

The original text of the *Niśīha Sūtra* is neither too elaborate nor too brief. It contains 20 Chapters called *uddeśakas.* Portions of the subject-matter in each *uddeśaka* are interconnected and portions are not so interconnected. The last *uddeśaka* throws light on the forms of atonement. Like other Jaina *Āgamas,* it is written in *Ardh-Māgadhī.* At many a place, the idea is very brief, and the reader has to look for help to understand its meaning. To cite one or two instances,

> "A monk who takes out the dirt of his eyes, of his ears, of his teeth and of his nails, cleans them, considers any other (monk) doing the same as good, has to undergo light atonement for a month (*laghumāsik).* A monk who removes and wipes out the sweat from his body, sweat from a particular part, removes and wipes out dirt, accumulated dirt, and

approves of any other doing the same has to undergo atonement for a month (*māsik*)."[10]

"A monk who brings food during a day and eats the food during a day has to undergo heavy atonement for four months."[11]

In texts like this, unless extra words are interpolated like 'beauty,' 'attachment' 'food brought during the first quarter and taken in the fourth quarter,' then the idea does not become clear. In 20 *uddeśakas* of this *Sūtra,* there are in all 1652 items of atonement.

As the expressions are brief, at a later period, *cūrṇīs, niryukits* and commentaries have been written by the *ācāryas.* All these taken together make a very large volume. But only the original *Niśīha* enjoys the *Āgamic* status (not *cūrṇīs,* etc.). Many commentators have astrayed from the text. This is the reason why no commentary is accepted as authoritative by all sects of the Jainas. For analysis and comments in this Chapter, only the text of *Niśīha Sūtra* is kept in view.

VINAYA PIṬAKA

Vinaya Piṭaka is one of the three *Piṭakas* which are the most authoritative texts of Buddhism. According to the traditional views, immediately after the liberation of the Buddha, the first Buddhist Council met under the Chairmanship of Mahākāssapa when the *Piṭaka* were codified. About the codification of the *Vinaya Piṭaka*, we have the following description in the *Pañcaśatikā Khandhaka* of *Cullavagga* which happens to be the concluding Chapter of *Vinaya Piṭaka* itself :

In addressing the monks, the long-lived Mahākāssapa said,

"Once I was in a forest between Pāvā and Kuśinārā with 500 monks. I was myself seated under a wayside tree when I saw an *ājīvaka* who was carrying some mandāra flowers and was on the road to Pāvā. I asked him,

Ābus! Do you know our leader?

The *Ājīvaka* said,

'Yes, *ābus,* I know him. He has entered into liberation a week ago. I am carrying these mandāra flowers there.'

"The very memory of *Śramaṇa* Gautama made some monks lament in grief, some fell down on the ground like trees hewn, some began to roll on the ground crying that the Lord has entered into liberation so early, and so on. But those monks who had conquered all attachments and become *vītarāgas* bore the loss with patience and memory, planted themselves in equanimity, and thought,

'Life is transient. Where can one meet him again'?

"At that time, one *parivrājaka* named Subhadra was seated there in that group. Said he,

'Monks! Don't be overwhelmed with grief. Don't lament for the loss. In a sense, his liberation is a boon to us. We were suppressed by him in many ways. He would tell us so often,—this is good for you, this is not good for you. Henceforth we shall do what we like, and we shall not do what we do not like. It will be good for us if we codify *dharma* and *vinaya.* Impiety is fast coming up and virtue is yielding ground; bad conduct is replacing good conduct. Impious people are becoming powerful and pious ones are becoming weak. People with good conduct are waning and people with bad conduct are flourishing like anything.'

"The monks said in one voice,

> '*Bhante!* You may kindly prepare a list of senior monks (who may undertake the work of codification).'

"Mahākāssapa agreed. Mahākāssapa prepared a list which had 499 names. The monks submitted again.

> '*Bhante!* Though long-lived Ānanda is not yet an *arhat,* yet he is a man who has conquered attachment, malice, affection, fear, indiscipline. Being a constant companion of the Buddha, he has acquired enough to *dharma* and *vinaya.* May his name be included in the list."

"Mahākāssapa included Ānanda in the list. In this manner, 500 monks were elected.

"In considering the venue where the Council should meet, the monks decided in favour of Rājagṛha which is a large city with considerable facility for loding for so many people. It was decided that a monsoon should be spent there in the codification of *dharma* and *vinaya.* It was also decided that other monks should not come to Rājagṛha during this period.

"The decision was placed before the assembly of monks and read out to all. The assembly gave its concent by remaining silent. Mahākāssapa repeated it for the second time and again for the third time. Then Mahākāssapa said,

> 'From the silence of the assembly, I take it that this assembly agrees

> that the monks named in the list are to spend the next monsoon at Rājagṛha, that they will codify *dharma* and *vinaya*, and that other monks will not visit Rājagṛha during this period.'

"As desired by the assembly, the senior monks arrived at Rājagṛha for the codification of *dharma* and *vinaya.* They recollected the words of the Master :

> 'First, rearrange properly what is dilapidated and broken,'

and they decided,

> 'In the first month, we shall do this, and then from the second month onward, we shall start codification.'

"Ānanda thought,

> 'When so many learned monks are participating in the Council, it is not worthwhile for me to be there.'

"He spent the greater part of the night in thinking like this. It was near dawn when he stretched his body with a view to have a nap. But before he could stretch his legs straight and place his head on the pillow, during this very brief span of time, he was suddenly liberated of all fetters and became on *arhat.* Thus the long-lived Ānanda took his seat in the Council only after he became an *arhat.*

"Addressing the Council, the long-lived Mahākāssapa said,

> *Ābuses!* May I have your attention. If you kindly permit me, I may ask Upāli about *Vinaya.'*

"Whereon said the long-lived Upāli,

> 'Harken ye all! If the Council permits, I may give answer to the questions put to me on *vinaya* by the long-lived Mahākāssapa.'

"(There was the tacit consent after which Mahākāssapa started) :

> '*Ābus!* Upāli! Where was the first *pārājikā* enunciated? (*Pārājikā* is explusion from the order in case of a servere crime).
> —'*Bhante!* At Rājagṛha.'

—'Against whom?'
—'Against Sudinna, son of Kālanda.'
—'What for?'
—'For indulging in sex behaviour.'

"After this, Mahākāssapa obtained all the details about the first explusion (*pārājikā),* its complete wording (*kathā*), its content (*nidāna),* its personalities (*pudgala),* its rules (*prajñapati),* its prescriptions (*anu-prajñapti),* its vice and atonement (*doṣa-daṇḍa)* and non-indulgence in it in future (*anāpatti).*

"(Mahākāssapa enquired about the second *pārājikā)"* :
'Upāli! Where was the second *pārājikā* enunciated?'
—*'Bhante!* At Rājagṛha.'
—'Against whom?'
—'Against Dhaniya, son of a potter.'
—'What for?'
—'For theft.'

"Mahākāssapa then enquired about its wording, contents, personalities, rules prescriptions, vice and atonement and non-indulgence in future.

"(Next he enquired about the third *pārājikā)"* :
'Upāli! Where was the third *pārājikā* enunciated'?
—*'Bhante!* At Vaiśālī.'
—'Against whom?'
—'Against several monks.'
—'What for'?
—'For committing murder.'

"Mahākāssapa then enquired about its wording, contents, personalities, rules prescriptions, vice and atonement, and non-indulgence in future.

"(And next he enquired about the fourth *pārājikā*)" :
'Upāli! Where was the fourth *pārājikā* enunciated'?
—'*Bhate!* At Vaiśālī.'
—'Against whom?'
—'Against monks living on the bank of the Vaggumudā.'
—'For the display of super-human powers.'

"Mahākāssapa then obtained its wording, contents, personalities, rules, prescriptions, vice and atonement, non-indulgence in future. In this manner,

Mahākāssapa asked questions on *vinaya* of monks and nuns, and Upāli gave answer to all of them."

Historical Perspective

Regarding the codification of ancient texts, tradition and history present these which are, in many cases, poles apart from one another. *Vinaya Piṭaka* is no exception to this. There are some scholars who go to the length of denying that there was any such thing as the first Buddhist Council. Thus, Oldenberg suggests that as the *Mahāparinivvāna Sutta* makes no mention about this first Council, it is no more than a historians' fancy.[12] Supporting this view, Frank writes,

> "The only material supporting the first Council are the 11th and the 12th Chapters of the *Cullavagga,* and this support has its root in tradition. Hence its value should not be over-estimated.[13] But Hermann Jacobi does not agree with this view. He is of opinion that if the *Mahāparinivvāna Sutta* makes no reference to the Council, it is because the Council had no relevance for the *Sutta.*[14] Some scholars are, however, of opinion that the two Chapters of the *Cullavagga* mentioned above must have once been parts of *Mahāparinivvāna Sutta,* but were at some later period included in the *Cullavagga.*[15] The real position appears to be that the literary style of, and the ideas contained in, the two Chapters are somewhat inconsistent and out of tune with the rest of the *Cullavagga,* but they bear a family affinity with the *Mahāparinivvāna Sutta.* In a text entitled *Saṁyukta Vastu,* the two accounts of the liberation of Gautama Buddha and the first Council are given together. This lends support to the contention of some scholars that these two Chapters were once parts of the *Mahāparinivvāna Sutta.* With so much support in its favour, the meeting of the first Buddhist Council cannot be ruled out altogether, though there is yet dearth of information about its deliberations. Besides, scholars hold different views about the material that was actually collected and codified at this Council. As G.C. Pande was opined, it would have been a sheer physical impossibility to compile the complete text either of the *Vinaya Piṭaka* or of the *Sutta Piṭaka* during that limited time.[16] The *Vinaya Piṭaka* mentions of the two Buddhist Councils, but not of the third which met sometime in the third century B.C., nor does it make mention of Emperor Asoka who ascended the throne in 269 B.C.[17] So, it may be said with a fair degree of certainity that the *Vinaya Piṭaka* must have been compiled before these two events. According to G.C. Pande, the *Vinaya Piṭaka* has reached the present

bulk only after passing through at least five enlargements from time to time.[18]

The date of the *Nisīha Sutta* has been accepted to be 150 to 175 years after the liberation of Mahāvīra which gives us 375 or 350 B.C. as a fairly certain date about its compilation. The approximate date of the compilation of the *Vinaya Piṭaka* may be around 300 B.C. So, it may be said that both the texts have come down to us from the fourth century B.C.

On the Language of the Texts

The Jaina *Āgamas* are written in *Ard-Māgadhī* and *Piṭakas* are written in *Pāli*. Both the languages have originally descended from *Māgadhī* which was the spoken language of some parts of the country at some period of time. In parts of Bihar, there is still a living dialect called '*magahī.*' The birth-place of Mahāvīra was Vaiśālī and that of the Buddha was Lumbinī, and the shortest distance between the two places has been accepted to be 250 miles. Even now the dialect of the two places have much similarity. The languages of Vaiśālī, however, came to be influenced by Maithilī and that of Lumbinī by Avadhī. The language of both the places is, however, known by a common name which is Bhojpurī. It may then be said that the contemporary Magadhī and Bhojpurī are considered by the scholars as the progency of what was once called Magadhī. It is also very likely that both Mahāvīra and Gautama Buddha spoke the same mother-tongue, Māgadhī. The Jaina canonists have called the language Māgadhī.[19] There may be several reasons why it is called Ardha-Māgadhī. It might have been the spoken language of some region in exactly the same form in which it has been used, or Māgadhī might have been mixed with some other languages (for which it was given the prefix ardha,[20] or it is quite likely that the canonists spoke diverse languages.

Both among the Jainas and the Buddhists, the canonical texts were preserved in memory for centuries. It is believed that the Buddhist texts lived in human memory for 24 generations and that the Jaina texts for 26, after which they were put to writing. During such a long period, the original texts must have been influenced by the spoken language of those in whose memory they lived, in consequence of which the language of the two sets of canonical texts have been somewhat different after they have been codified. Henceforth one became known as Pāli and the other as *Ardha-Māgdhī*. Since the two have been written different times, that may to some extent account for their linguistic difference. The words of the Buddha have also been called Pāli.[21] It is, therefore, very likely that the language in which the Buddhist texts have been written has been called by the same name. For the rest, in literary style and expression, the two texts, *Nisīha* and *Vinaya Piṭaka,* come so near to one another. The following, quoted from the two texts, will illustrate :

1. A monk who thinks that he has got a new pot, and so thinking, who rubs it with oil, ghee, butter and grease, once, and then often, repeatedly, and approves others doing the same, such a monk has to undergo light atonement for four months.

   A monk who thinks that he has got a new pot, and so thinking uses various dye powers like *lodraka, koṣṭaka, padma*, etc., paint them, and approves other monks doing the same, such a monk has to undergo light atonement for four months.

   A monk who thinks that he has got a new pot, and so thinking he washes it with live cold water, live hot water, washes again and again, and approves other monks doing the same, such a monk has to undergo light atonement for four months.[22]
2. A monk who accepts gold and silver, asks another to accept it, and makes use of the same gold or silver, such a monk has to undergo *nissaggiya pāticiya.*

   A monk who uses diverse coins has to undergo *Nisaggiya pāticiya.*[23]

A Review of Subject-matter

According to the *Āgamic* prescription, a monk is permitted to read the *Nisīha* at least three years after his initiation. Besides, *Nisīha* and other *Cheda Sūtras* are for the private use of the monks, and are not to be read in public, nor to be read by any householder for any spiritual purpose. As to the *Vinaya Piṭaka,* there is a similar prescription in the Buddhist tradition to the effect that it should be read by an initiated monk only.[24]

At first sight, such a restrictive prescription may appear to be the consequence of a narrow mentality and also unnecessary, but on a penetrating analysis one may see that there is a meaningful motive behind it. These texts deal primarily with atonements given to the monks and nuns of the order. Now, when there is an order, it should be conceivable that it shelters diverse sorts of people in it, and diverse situations also. *Bhagavān* Mahāvīra has himself said that as to conduct, if one monk is like the full moon, another may be no better than the moon on the first day of the fortnight.[25] The aim of the monastic order is to help the people within its fold to attain the topmost stage, but then it will be somewhat unnatural to conceive that all the people who are on the march are not at dissimilar levels. Though they started together, some of them may lag behind, some may falter and some may even drop down. Again, some of those who have dropped down may stand up and start moving again. Keeping these diverse situations in view, rules and regulations must exist for the order based on past experiences and anticipations about the future. Therefore, for an immature person, their reading may be positive harmful to the reader himself. Such a reader may read in the text a state of degeneration in the order which is no more than his own fancy. It is because of considerations like these, and not due to any narrowness of mind, that the reading of these texts is not permitted by lay men. The prescription is intended, not to hide the sin, but to prevent it from spreading.

Both *Nišīha* and *Vinaya Piṭaka* are exhaustive texts on the violation of the rules of *brahmacarya.* To lay readers, the text would appear vulgar, but in the field of research, both of them open new avenue of thinking for the scholar. Given below are extracts from the two texts on lapses from brahmacarya and atonements therefore.

Nišīha on Lapses from _Brahmacarya,_ etc.

1. A monk who indulges in *hasta-karma,* and approves of other monks doing the same has to undergo severe atonement for one month. (*Uddeśaka* 1.1).
2. A monk who strikes his penes with the finger, etc., and approves of other monks doing the same has to undergo severe atonement for a month. (1.2).
3. A monk who rubs his penes, and does so again and again, and approves of other monks doing the same has to undergo servere atonement for a month. (1.3).
4. A monk who rubs oil, etc., on the penes and approves it for others has to undergo severe atonement for a month. (1.4).
5. A monk who rubs paste, etc., on the penes and approves it for other has to undergo severe atonement of a month. (1.5).
6. A monk who washes his penes with cold or hot water and approves it for others has to undergo severe atonement for a month. (1.6).
7. A monk who uncovers the forepart of his penes and approves of others doing the same has to undergo severe atonement for a month. (1.7).
8. A monk who smells his own penes and approves of others doing the same has to undergo severe atonement for a month. (1.8).
9. A monk who places his penes into a hole and throws out semens and approves of others doing the same has to undergo severe atonement for a month. (1.9).

For a monk who desires to enjoy sexual pleasures with a grown up woman, the following atonements have been described :

1. A monk who desires to enjoy with a woman who is like his mother and approves the same for others has to undergo severe atonement for fourth months. (6.1).
2. A monk who places his finger, etc., in the uteras of a woman who is like his mother and approves of others doing the same has to undergo severe atonement for four months. (6.2).
3. A monk who has his penes rubbed by a woman who is like his mother and approves of others doing the same has to undergo severe atonement for four months. (6.4).
4. A monk who scribes a scroll conveying his love to a woman who is like his mother and approves of others doing the same has to undergo severe atonement for four months. (6.13).
5. A monk who offers an eighteen-stringed necklace, a nine-stringed necklace, a pearl necklace, a golden necklace, or any other, and ear-rings, etc., and approves of others doing the same has to undergo severe atonement for four months. (7.8 & 9).
6. A monk who gives instruction to a woman in sacred texts with a motive to have her and approves of others doing the same has to undergo severe atonement for four months. (7.88).
7. If a monk is wandering with a nun belonging to his own order or to another order, and if they are by chance separated so that the monk feels a pang and desires to meet her again, and if he approves of such behaviour in another monk, he has to undergo severe atonement for four months. (8.11).

In this manner, Chapters six, seven and eight of the *Niśīha* contain prescription of atonement for diverse sex lapses.

Vinaya Piṭaka on Lapses from *Brahmacarya*, etc.

The frank discussion of *Vinaya Piṭaka* which follows bears a close resemblance with the same in the *Niśīha* as given above :

1. While being tied to the monastic code of conduct, a monk who enjoys sex pleasures even with animals becomes a *parājika,* and makes himself unworthy of living with other monks.[26]
2. Throwing out semens consciously by a monk except in a dream is a lapse for which a monk is to be given atonement called *Saṅghādidesa.*[27]

3. If a monk with mental perversion touches the hand, hairs, or any other limb of a woman, the monk has to be given an atonement called *Saṅghādisesa.*[28]
4. If a monk with a mental perversion speaks indecent words to a woman about sex behaviour, then, the monk has to be given an atonement called *Saṅghādidesa.*[29]
5. If a monk with a mental perversion advises a woman that the highest service she can tender is to satisfy the sexual passions of such a devout person as himself, then, the monk has to be given an atonement called *Saṅghādidesa.*[30]
   The word *sanghādidesa* stands for a temporary expulsion from the order.
6. If a monk gives spiritual counsel to the nuns without the prior permission of the order, he is to undergo an atonement called *pācittiya.*[31]
7. Even when a monk is permitted to tender spiritual counsel to the nuns, he is not to do so after sun-set. If he does, he has to undergo an atonement called *pācittiya.*[32]
8. If under very special circumstances a monk goes to a nun to tender unto her spiritual counsel, then, he has to undergo an atonement called *pācittya.*[33]
9. If a monk sits alone with a nun who is also alone, then, he has to undergo an atonement called *pācittiya.*[34]
   (*Pācittiya* is a confession followed by an atonement as per prescription).

Nišīha Sutta has no separate prescription on *brahmacarya* for the monks and for the nuns. What is prescribed for the monks applies to the nuns. *Vinaya Piṭaka*, in contrast, has separate prescriptions for the two called *bhikkhupātimokkha* and *bhikkhuni-pātimokkha* respectively. Some of the prescriptions of *bhikkhuni-pātimokkha* are as follows :

1. A nun who uses an animal to satisfy her sex hunger is to be given a *pārājikā* (*i.e.*, she is to be expelled from the order).[35]
2. A nun who hides the lapses of a sister-nun who is fit for explusion is to be given a *pārājikā.*[36]
3. If out of passion a nun holds the hand of a man who is a victim of a similar passion, or enjoys holding the corner of his wrapper, or stands with him or talks with him, or reclines her body against him them, she is to be given *pārājikā.*[37]

If a nun indulges in misconduct, earns bad reputation, and is condemned, and if this nun becomes hostile to the order, hides the lapses of other nuns and remains in evil company, then, other nuns should speak to her as follows :

> "Sister! You indulge in misconduct, you have earned an ill-reputation, you are condemned by all. You are hostile to the order, you hide the lapses of other nuns and you indulge in evil ways. This order of nuns has conduct and Conscience as its ideals."

If inspite of this warning, the nun is not prepared to restrain and recuperate herself, then, the warning is to be repeated thrice. If still she be obstinate not to retrace she has to be expelled from the order.[38]

(A few more rulers regarding the nuns are quoted below) :

1. A nun who stands with a man in the darkness of the night where there is no lamp, and talks with him, she is to be given a *pācittiya.*
2. A nun who shaves hairs from the secret parts of her body is to be given a *pācittiya.*
3. A nun who indulges in unnatural acts has to be given a *pācittiya.*
4. If a nun while cleaning her uteras uses her two fingers in a manner exceeding the norm, then, she is to be given a *pācittiiya.*[39]

It may be asked why the writers of these whole texts incorporated material which would appear to be no better than pornography, and that to in such an elaborate and exposed manner. In considering this, we must admit that those people who had written these texts were very much above sex and hence they were free from hesitation in this matter. Now, in such a delicate matter as sex, only two types of men may be free from hesitation, *viz.,* first, moral wrecks and second truly saints. Surely, the writers of these texts belonged to the second category. Hesitation is a restrictive factor leading to incompleteness; but the writers of these texts who were naturally free were not liable to any such charge on account of hesitation.

There is a story in the *Purāṇas* (mythology). Three sages had once gone to the assembly of gods on some business. They were honourably seated on the right-hand side of Indra who is the king of gods, and so the whole assembly of gods was in front of the sages. Dances by heavenly nymphs started. At the sight of the beauty of the nymphs, the youngest monk shut his eyes and went into meditation. As the nymphs danced, they lost themselves in the dance and their divine garments were displaced. When the second monk saw this indecency on the part of the celestial damsels, he shut his eyes and went into meditation. The dance was still in progress, and in a short while, their garments dropped and the nymphs were completely naked. But the seniormost monk sat firm. On seeing this, Indra said,

"On Monk! How is it that you did not feel even the slightest hesitation to see the dance?"

The monk said,

"In the ups and downs of the dance, I did not find any difference. From the very first moment uptil now, I am in the same state of firmness."

On hearing this, Indra put a further question,

"But why did these two monks shut their eyes one after another?"

The senior monks said,

"They are still on the steps to *spiritual* perfection. When they will reach the top, they will have no more hesitation."

The same may be said about the contents of this Chapter. Common people wonder how the sages could write so succinctly. But the explanation is simple, *viz.*, that they did not have the least weakness in matters of sex so that they could write all this freely keeping in view the larger interest of the order. Most people in a country are good; but, at the same time, there are always some anti-social elements like thieves, looters etc. For the latter there are laws which state : for this type of theft, such is the penalty, for this type of misconduct, such is the penalty. The monks too have a society of their own. In this society, too, there may be some who are dishonest. Therefore, for the organisational code of the society of monks, for whom conduct is extremely valuable, the above rules are neither unnecessary nor unnatural.

Method of Atonement

Atonements and their diverse methods are based on psychological considerations in both the Jaina and the Buddhist orders. The Jaina order prescribes ten atonements as follows :

1. *Āloyanā (alocanā)* whose precise meaning has been as :

nibedanā tallakṣaṇaṁ śuddhiṁ yadarhatyaticāra jātaṁ tadālocana

When a fault has been committed, this atonement prescribes a free and frank confession by the monk to his *ācārya* without supressing anything. This washes clean his mental dirt.

2. *Padikkamaṇa (pratikramaṇa)* whose precise meaning has been given as

mithyā duṣkṛtaṁ

The monk desires himself that his fault may prove false, *i.e.*, may cease, This form of atonement is performed by the monk himself without the help of any other monk or *ācārya.*

3. *Tad-ubhayaṁ, i.e.*, a combination of confession and *pratikramaṇa.*
4. *Vivega* (*Viveka*) whose precise meaning has been given as *aśuddha bhaktyādi-tyāgaḥ.*
   (The monk resolves to give up all prohibited acts called *ādhākarma* like taking of impure prohibited food).
5. *Viusagga* (*Vyutsarga* or *Kāyotsarga*). This atonement is performed with the help of meditation. *Kāyotsarga* is a standing posture during the meditation during which the monk is supposed to lose his own body sense.
6. *Tavah (tapas)* whose precise meaning has been given as *nirvikṛtikādi.* (The monk is not to take milk, curd, etc., and to perform other penances).
7. *Cheya (cheda)* whose precise meaning has been given as *pravrajyā-parayāya hrasvīkaranam.*
   (This literally means shortening the stage of monkhood. By this compression, a monk who is junior in initiation may rise in seniority).
8. *Mūla* whose precise meaning has been given as *punardīkṣa* or reinitiation.
9. *Aṇavaṭṭhappā (anāvasthāpya)* whose precise meaning has been given as *kṛta-tapaso vratāropaṇam.*
   After a penance is performed, a concluding *vrata* or vow is to be added.
10. *Pārāñciya (pārāñcika)* whose precise meaning has been given as *liṅgādibhedam.*

In this form of atonement, a monk who has been expelled from the order discards the robes of a monk for some time during which period he decries himself in public, and thereafter he is taken back in the order.[40]

In the various commentaries of the *Niśīha,* diverse and elaborate interpretations have been made of the various atonements that have been prescribed. The *Niśīha Sūtra* prescribes atonements for a month and for four months. They are related to item 7 above entitled *cheda.* Thus in fulfilling atonement for a month, there is a compression of the state of monkhood by one month. *Cheda* atonement may be exchanged with the sixth item which is *tapaḥ.*

In that case, the monk instead of compressing the state of his monkhood, purifies himself by penance. Depending on the intensity of the lapse, a distinction has been drawn between light and heavy.

The *Vinaya Piṭaka* identifies eight lapses as follows :

1. 4 lapses of monk and 8 of a nun are *prājika.*
2. 13 lapses of a monk and 17 of a nun are *saṅghādidesa.*
3. 2 lapses of a monk are *aniyata.*
4. 30 lapses of a monk and 30 of a nun are *nissaggiya pācittiya.*
5. 92 lapses of a monk and 166 of a nun are *pācittiya.*
6. 4 lapses of a monk and 8 of a nun are *pāṭideśanīya.*
7. 75 lapses of a monk and 75 lapses of a nun are *sekhiya.*
8. 7 lapses of a monk and 7 lapses of a nun are *adhikaraṇa samatha.*

Atonement may be light or severe depending on the intensity of the crime.

In *pārājikā* atonement, the monk is expelled from the order for good.

In *saṅghādidesa,* a monk is separated from the order for a certain period of time.

In *aniyata,* the intensity of the crime is determined on the basis of some supporting proof, and then the monk is given an atonement on the basis of his fault.

In *nissaggiya pācittiya,* a monk confesses his lapse in the presence of the entire body of monks or in the presence of another monk, and expresses his resolve to be free from the lapse.

In *pācittiya,* a monk confesses and makes suitable atonement.

Seikhiya is an item of instruction which a monk is to fulfil. If he fails, he makes himself liable to atonement.

Adhikaraṇa samatha lays down the method of pacification where a quarrel has started. If this is not obeyed, then the monks makes himself liable to atonement.

The method in which the atonement is performed by a monk varies between one order and the other. In the Jaina order, the atonement is given by the *ācārya* or *guru*, The *ācārya* or *guru* is versatile with the *śruta* knowledge, and has many great qualities, like seriousness, etc. He is not entitled to disclose to anyone the atonement given to a monk. We have the following in the *Vyavahāra Sūtra* :

A monk at fault must confess to his *ācārya* or *upādhyāya* without reservation. If they are not near him (and hence are not available to him, then he must confess in the presence of some learned monk of the order. If, for some reason, that too is not possible, then, he should confess to a monk who is *pāraśvastha,* i.e., who puts on a monk's robe but who does not duly fulfil the code. If this also is not possible, then, he must confess to a lay follower who may have acquaintance with the life of monk and who may be conversant with the rules for atonement. If this is not possible, then, he should confess to a monk who is fixed in equanimity. And when none of these is possible, then, the monk goes to a solitary forest, turns to the east or to the north, bows to the Arihantas or the *Siddhas,* and keeping them as his witness, he announces his lapses, decries self and courts atonements as per his own idea.[41]

Unlike the Jaina method of atonement which is individual and private, in the Buddhist order atonement is given in public in the presence of other monks. The specific form of Buddhist atonement is given below :

On the fourteenth day of the dark half of the month and on the new-moon day, all the monks living at a place must assemble in the *uposatha* hall. As the Buddha named the whole order as his successor, the Buddhist order has no one who may be called an *ācārya*. So a senior monk presides over the meeting. Then the *pātimokkha* is read item by item. At the end of each item, the presiding monk asks,

> "In the matter just read, are all the monks pure (i.e., free from lapse)?"

If, on response to that, a monk stands up and desires to discuss his lapse relating to that item, then, the assembly considers his statement and purifies him. Then it is asked for the second time,

> "In this matter, are all the monks pure?"

And the same is repeated for the third time. In this manner, by repeating the same question thrice, it is publically ascertained that all are pure. In this manner, all the items are read one after another (to give the monks a chance to confess and to ascertain that all the monks are pure). The nuns of the order also read *bhikkhunī pātimokkha* in the same manner.[42]

On the question of Conduct (*Ācāra*)

The the code of conduct of the two orders becomes clear from the prescriptions of the *Nisītha* and the *Vinaya Piṭaka.* From a comparative study of the two, it appears that some of the prescriptions come very near to one another while some remains very far. Both the texts impose strict prohibition on violence, falsehood, theft, sex indulgence and accumulation of property. Atonements, both light and severe, have been prescribed if a monk indulges in anyone of these in one form or the other. But when everything is said, it must be admitted that regarding rules of conduct, the *Niśītha* prescriptions reach an extreme position, those in the *Vinaya Piṭaka* would appear to be somewhat crude, making concession or compromise with considerations of practical life. This is the fundamental difference between the two texts. The non-violence of a Jaina monk extends to earth, water, flora, air and fire as essential and unavoidable, and in case of a lapse, various monthly and four-monthly atonements have been laid down. The rules of the *Niśīha* make no concession to consideration of practical life; its exclusive emphasis is on the purity of doctrine. The position is reversed in the *Vinaya Piṭaka* wherein monastic order has been given precedence over doctrine.

According to the doctrine of the Jainas, water is life. So, a monk does not use water from river, tank or well, nor rain water. Only when it is boiled and made free from life, water becomes usable to a monk. In contrast, the *Vinaya Piṭaka* prescribes that water filtered through a piece of cloth may be used by a monk. If a monk does not filter it through cloth, he is required to undergo a *pācittiya*.[43] The Jaina monks are not allowed to take bath.[44] They do not take bath in part or of the whole body with even life-free (boiled) water. According to the *Vinaya Piṭaka,* a monk is not permitted bath before a fortnight. If he does, he has to undergo a *pācittiya*. Exception has been made for summer season, etc.[45] There are elaborate prescriptions as to how a monk is to take bath in rivers, tanks, etc. The point is that there is a gulf of difference between the Jaina and the Buddhists attitudes regarding life in earth, water, flora, etc.

Regarding cloth, the prescription of the *Niśītha Sūtra* is that if a monk accepts cloth made for him or bought for him, he must undergo light atonement for four months.[46] In contrast, the prescription of the *Vinaya Piṭaka* on this is as follows :

If a king, an official of the kingdom, or a householder sends a messenger with money to a monk and the said messenger tells the monk,

> "*Bhante*! This money has been sent for your robes. Please accept it."

The said monk should tell the messenger,

> "*Ābus!* I do not accept money for my robes."

If the said messenger offers the money to a householder and asks him to get the necessary robe for the monk, then, the monk is permitted to remind the householder thrice in the maximum about the same robe saying,

> "*Upāsaka!* I am in need of the robe."

If still the householder does not give the robe to him, he is permitted to go maximum three times and stand with a view to remind him about the robe. If, on this, the householder gives the robe, well and good. But if the monk goes beyond this prescription in order to recover the robe from the householder. Then, he has to undergo *nassaggiya pācittiya.* The monk should see the donor of money and tell him.

"Oh Long-lived man! Take care of your money lest it should be wasted."[47]

(On accumulation of store), the *Nisīha Sūtra* lays down : If a monk accumulates food, water, medicine, etc., even for a single night, he has to undergo severe atonement for four months.[48]

On this, the prescription of the *Vinaya Piṭaka* is :

Oh Monks! Ghee, butter, oil, honey and jaggery which are fit to be taken by the ailing monks may be kept for a maximum period of one week and put to use. If this period is exceeded, then, the monk has to undergo *nissagiya pācittiya.*[49]

In the Jaina order, monks are completely debarred from taking food at night.[50] According to the *Vinaya Piṭaka,* if a monk takes food in the afternoon (after mid-day), he has to undergo *pācittiya.*[51]

In the Jaina tradition, a monk receives food in his own begging bowl, brings it to his lodge and eats in some private place. In contrast, in the Buddhist tradition, a monk, when invited, goes to the residence of a householder to dine. A Chapter entitled *Sekhiya* in the *Vinaya Piṭaka*[52] lays down elaborately the careful way in which monks and nuns should go to a householder's residence to dine and take their seats. Even the instructions regarding dinning are interesting and are in good taste. In this matter, the resolves of the nuns are as follows :

1. I shall not open my mouth till the morsel is very near it.
2. While eating, I shall not put the whole palm in my mouth.
3. I shall not talk when I have food in my mouth.
4. I shall not make the food jump in my hand before I eat.
5. I shall not cut a morsel into pieces.
6. I shall not swell my cheeks while I eat.
7. I shall not throw my hands while eating.
8. I shall not spread crumbs on the floor.
9. I shall not lick my own tongue while eating.
10. I shall not make sound with my mouth while eating.[53]

Such resolves are also to be made by monks. The intake of garlic by the nuns is totally prohibited.[54]

On Initiation

There is a wide difference between the two traditions regarding the age at which a person may be taken as a monk into the order. In the Jaina tradition, one may be initiated when one is slightly above eight years of age.[55] If anyone is initiated before this age, he has to undergo atonement. According to the *Vinaya Piṭaka*, if a monk knowingly initiates another into monkhood before he is 20, then, the person so initiated is virtually uninitiated.[56]

Both Mahāvīra and the Buddha lived during the same age and in the same region. Both were sectarian leaders within the *śramaṇa* cult. But so much difference in their prescriptions regarding the age of initiation is really very surprising. The questions of initiation of a child into monkhood must have been a very burning topic of controversy in that age, and while on sect was in favour of initiating a child into monkhood, the other sect expressed itself to be against it. What is the reason for this?

Mahāvīra not only prescribed initiation in chidhood, he himself initiated Atimuktaka at a very young age. One day, *Gaṇadhara* Gautama was wandering in the city of Polāspur on a mission to beg food when suddenly a young boy named Atimuktaka caught his finger and said,

> "*Bhante!* Please come to my house to receive food."

The boy was not one who could be discouraged. Guatama came to his house and received food. After accepting food, as Gautama turned to go, the body followed behind him. When the two were on the road, Atimuktaka said,

> "*Bhante!* Where are you going?"
> —"I am going to *Bhagavān* Mahāvīra who is the fountainhead of peace."
> —"I am in need of peace myself. I must go to him."

Atimuktaka came to the garden where Mahāvīra was, and was duly initiated. One day, because of his immaturity as a child, Atimuktaka floated his begging bowl in a stream and enjoyed the fun of having floated a boat. The senior monks chastised him at once. But Mahāvīra prescribed atonement for him made him sin-free and said,

> "Atimuktaka looks like a young child, he will attain both supreme knowledge and liberation in this ver life."[57]

Mahāvīra has clearly stated that a boy who is slightly above eight may attain both supreme knowledge and liberation at that very age. But before this age, monkhood, knowledge and liberation,—all these are unattainable.[58] Prior permission of parents and elders is a must before initiation.

The history of, and intention behind, the rules of initiation in the Buddhist order are contained in the *Vinaya Piṭaka*. In the city of Rājagṛha, there were 17 boys who were friends. Upāli was their leader. One day, the parents of Upāli thought what career would be most suitable for him so that he might live happily after their death. The first idea that came to them was :

> "If he becomes a scribe, he will be happy for ever."

But before long, they thought,

> "In becoming a scribe, he will ache his fingers."

In this manner, they thought of various alternatives, but not one appeared to be wholly safe. In the end, they thought,

> "Only the monks who are the followers of Śākyaputra (Gautama Buddha) are happy. They get good food, they live in good houses. Upāli should be a monk in that order and live there so that he may be happy for ever."

Stated in one corner, Upāli heard the entire discussion between his parents. At once, he ran to his friends and said,

> "Come you all. Let us be initiated into monkhood by some monk of the order of Śākyaputra and be happy for ever."

All the boys agreed. When the parents saw that all wards cherished the same desire, they gave them permission to be initiated into monkhood. So, the boys came to some monks and were initiated as monks. During the day, they were happy, but at night, before day-break, they were very much distressed by hunger and cried bitterly,

> "Give us rice. Give us food to eat."

The elderly monks tried to pacify them saying,

> "*Ābuses!* Have patience. After day-break, eat *yabāgū,* rice or bread

whichever be available. If nothing is available, then, go out to beg and eat whatever you get."

The words of the senior monks were no sauce for the boys who were very hungry. They were restless and rolled on the bed.

(This happened everyday). One day, the Buddha came to know of it. He collected the monks around himself and said,

> "Monks! Men who are below 20 are unable to bear heat and cold, hunger and thirst, snake bite and scorpion bite, etc. They are unable to bear harsh words of their enemies, nor are they able to bear painful, severe, rough, harsh, adverse, unbearable and fatal diseases. Monks! Because of considerations such as these, I lay down that one should not be given *upasampadā* before 20."[59]

From that day, the minimum age for initiation into the Buddhist order became 20. But then occasions cropped up when it became necessary to accept a young boy below 20 into the order, so that the Buddha himself had to make concession. This was the creation of a new order of junior monks called sramaner. Once after an episode, the Buddha laid down the following rule :

> "A boy below 15 should not be made a sramaner. He who initiates one into the *śramaṇer* order before this age commits a crime named *dukkaṭa.*"[60]

There was a similar occasion, and concession was made for the second time. In consequence, a boy below 15 could henceforth be initiated as a *śramaṇer.*

Meanwhile, a complete family was wiped out during a pestilence, and only two very young boys survived. This family was very much devoted to Ānanda. So Ānanda took pity on the two orphans. He presented their case to the Buddha requesting him to give shelter to them in the order. Said the Buddha,

> "Ānanda! Are these boys able to fly crows?"
> —"*Bhante!* They are."

The Buddha collected all his monks round himself and said,

> "Monks! I permit a boy who is below 15 to be taken as *śramaṇer* provided he is able to fly crows."[61]

The story of Rāhula being made a *śramaṇer* is very interesting.[62] On this occasion, the Buddha gave the following rule,

"Monks! Without the permission of his parents, the son should not be initiated as a *śramaṇer*. If anyone does it, he commits a crime named *dukkaṭa*."[63]

The above accounts reveal the Jaina and the Buddhist views regarding initiation of young boys into monkhood. According to Mahāvīra, the minimum age for initiation is slightly more than 8 years. According to the Buddha, a boy (below 15) who was capable to fly crows could be given the status of *śramaṇer*. *Śramaṇer* in the Buddhist order is a step to full monkhood. On the whole, therefore, it may be said that young age has not been considered to be a disqualification for the purpose of spiritual practices in either order.

Position of Women in the two Orders

Mahāvīra's order was fourfold from the very start (which means that it included women with the same status as was given to men). According to the *Vinaya Piṭaka,* there was no provision for taking women as nuns in the Buddhist order. When and how women were accepted in the Buddhist order is, however, described in the said *Piṭaka* as follows :

Once the Buddha was lodged at the Nyagrodha guest house in Kapilvastu. His aunt *Prajāpati* came to him and said,

"Bhante! Please accept women in the order."

Said the Buddha,

"But I do not like the idea."

Gautamī repeated her request for a second and for a third time, without any favourable outcome.

After some time, when the Buddha was at Vaiśālī, Gautamī dressed herself like a nun, and, followed by many Śākya women, came to the guest house where the Buddha was. Ānanda saw her. A profound earnestness for joining the monastic order was revealed in all her limbs. Ānanda took pity on her. He came to the Buddha and said,

"Bhante! Please give a place to women in the order."

He repeated his request for three times, but the Buddha did not give his consent. At last, he said,

> "*Bhante!* Here is *Mahāprajāpati* Gautamī who did breast-feeding to the Lord at the premature demise of his mother. She must be accepted."

At this, the Buddha yielded. He accepted Ānanda's request. Certain rules were made for the nuns in the monastic order and Gautamī was accepted in it.[64]

REFERENCES

1. *Niśītha Cūrṇī,* Gāthā 6265; *Vyavahāra-Sūtra*, U. 10.20 and 21; *Vyavahāra Bhāṣya*, U.7. 202-03.
2. *Vyavahāra Sūtra*, U.6.2-3.
3. *Ibid.*, U.3.3.
4. *Ibid.*, U.3.1.
5. *Āyārāṅga Cūrṇī*, p. 336.
6. *Niśītha Sūtram*, Part IV, p. 395.
7. *Ibid.*, Part IV, p. 25.
8. "The name is explained strangely enough by Niśītha though the character of the contents would lead us to expect Niṣedha."
   —*Indian Antiquary*, Vol. 21, p. 97.
9. *Abhidhāna Cintāmaṇī Kośa* (Nāma-mālā, 2-59).
10. *Niśīha*, 3. 69-70.
11. *Ibid.*, 11-179.
12. Introduction to the *Vinaya Piṭaka*, XXIX, *Zeitschrift der Deutschen Morgenlandischen Gesellschaft*, 1898, pp. 613-94.
13. *Journal of the Pāli Text Society*, 1908, pp. 1-80.
14. *Zeitschrift der Deutschen Morgenlandischen Gesellschaft*, 1880, p. 184.
15. Finst & Obermiller, *Indian Historical Quarterly*, 1923; S.K. Dutt, *Early Buddhist Monachism*, p. 337.
16. G.C. Pande, *Studies in the Origin of Buddhism*, p. 10.
17. E.J. Thomas, *History of Buddhist Thought*, p. 10.
18. G.C. Pande, *Op. cit.*, p. 16.
19. *Samavāyāṅga*, p. 60.
20. The *Uvavai Sūtra* writes :
   .... savi ya nam addh-magaha bhasa tesiṁ sabbesiṁ ariyamanariyanaṁ appane sabhasae parinamenaṁ parinamai. According to the *Niśītha Cūrṇī*, magadadhavisayabhāsānivaddhaṁ addha-māgahaṁ aṭṭharasadesi bhāsānimayaṁ vā addhamāgahaṁ.
21. G.C. Pande, *Op. cit.*, p. 573.
22. *Niśīha Sūtra*, U. 14, 12-14.
23. *Vinaya Piṭaka, Pārājika Pāli*, 4-18, 125, 130.
24. *Vinaya Piṭaka, Pārājika Pāli*, Āmukha, by *Bhikṣu* Jagdīśa Kāśyapa, p. 6.
25. *Jñātā-dharma-kathāṅga Sūtra*, Adhyayana, 10.
26. *Vinaya Piṭaka*, Bhikkhupātimokkha, Pārājika, 1-1-21.
27. *Vinaya Piṭaka*, Bhikkupātimokkha, Saṅghādisesa, 2-1-3.
28. *Vinaya Piṭaka*, *Pārājika Pāli*, 2-2-37.
29. *Ibid.*, 2-3-51.

30. *Ibid.*, 2-4-58.
31. *Vinaya Piṭaka, Pācittīya*, 21.
32. *Ibid.*, 22.
33. *Ibid.*, 23.
34. *Ibid.*, 30.
35. *Vinaya Piṭaka, Bhikkhunī Pātimokkha*, Pārājika 1.
36. *Ibid.*, 6.
37. *Ibid.*, 8.
38. *Vinaya Piṭaka, Bhikkhunī Pātimokkha*, Saṅghādisesa, 12.
39. *Vinaya Piṭaka, Bhikkhunī Pātimokkha*, Pācittīya, 11, 2, 3 and 4 respectively.
40. *Ṭhaṇāṅga Sūtra*, 10.
41. *Vyavahāra Sūtra*, U.1, 34-39.
42. *Vinaya Piṭaka*, Nidāna.
43. *Vinaya Piṭaka, Bhikkhu Pātimokkha*, Pācittīya, 62.
44. *Daśaveyāliyan*, 6.61-64.
45. *Vinaya Piṭaka, Bhikkhu Pātimokkha*, Pācittīya, 57.
46. *Niśīha*, U.18, 35.
47. *Bhikkhu Pātimokkha*, Pācittīya, 10.
48. *Niśīha*, U.11, 179-83.
49. *Vinaya Piṭaka, Bhikkhu Pātimokkha,* Nissaggīya Pācittīya, 23.
50. *Daśaveyāliyan Adhyayana*, 4.
51. *Vinaya Piṭaka, Bhikkhu Pātimokkha*, Pācittīya, 37.
52. *Vinaya Pitaka, Bhikkhu Pātimokkha*, Sekhīya, 41-50.
54. *Vinaya Pitaka, Bhikkhunī Pātimokkha*, Pācittīya, 1.
55. *Vyavahāra Sūtra*, U.10, 24.
56. *Vinaya Piṭaka, Bhikkhu Pātimokkha*, Pācittīya, 65.
57. *Bhagavatī Sūtra*, S.5, U.4.
58. *Ibid.*, S.8, U.10.
59. *Vinaya Piṭaka, Mahāvagga*, Mahākhandhaka, 1-3-6.
60. *Ibid.*, 1-3-7.
61. *Ibid.*, 1-3-8.
62. See earlier Chapter on the Church and its expansion.
63. *Vinaya Piṭaka, Mahāvagga*, Mahākhandhaka, 1-3-11.
64. *Vinaya Piṭaka, Cullavagga*, Bhikkhunī Khandhaka, 10-1-4.

APPENDICES

APPENDIX–I

Nigaṇṭha and Nigaṇṭha Nāṭaputta in Tripiṭakas : Original Pāli

१

SINIHA SENĀPATI

तेन खो पन समयेन अभिञ्ञाता अभिञ्ञाता लिच्छवी सन्थागारे सन्निसिन्ना सन्निपतिता अनेकपरियायेन बुद्धस्स वण्णं भासन्ति, धम्मस्स वण्णं भासन्ति, सङ्घस्स वण्णं भासन्ति। तेन खो पन समयेन सीहो सेनापति निगण्ठसावको तस्सं परिसायं निसिन्नो होति। अय खो सीहस्स सेनापतिस्स एतदहोसि–"निस्संसयं खो सो भगवा अरहं सम्मासम्बुद्धो भविस्सति तथा हिमे अभिञ्ञाता अभिञ्ञाता लिच्छवी सन्थागारे सन्निसिन्ना सन्निपतिता अनेकपरियायेन बुद्धस्स वण्णं भासन्ति, धम्मस्स वण्णं भासन्ति, सङ्घस्स वण्णं भासन्ति। यन्नूनाहं तं भगवन्तं दस्सनाय उपसङ्कमेय्यं अरहन्तं सम्मासम्बुद्ध"ति। अथ खो सीहो सेनापति येन निगण्ठो नाटपुत्तो तेनुपसङ्कमि; उपसङ्कमित्वा निगण्ठं नाटपुत्तं एतदवोच–"इच्छामहं, भन्ते, समणं गोतमं दस्सनाय उपसङ्कमितुं"ति। "किं पन त्वं, सीह, किरियवादो समानो अकिरियवादं समणं गोतमं दस्सनाय उपसङ्कमिस्ससि? समणो हि, सीह, गोतमो अकिरियवादो, अकिरियाय धम्मं देसेति, तेन च सावके विनोती"ति। अथ खो सीहस्स सेनापतिस्स यो अहोसि गमियाभिसङ्खारो भगवन्तं दस्सनाय, सो पटिप्पस्सम्भि। दुतियं पि खो सम्बहुल अभिञ्ञाता अभिञ्ञाता लिच्छवी सन्थागारे सन्निसिन्ना सन्निपतिता अनेकपरियायेन बुद्धस्स वण्णं भासन्ति, धम्मस्स वण्णं भासन्ति, सङ्घस्स वण्णं भासन्ति। दुतियं पि खो सीहस्स सेनापतिस्स एतदहोसि–"निस्संसयं खो सो भगवा अरहं सम्मासम्बुद्धो भविस्सति, तथा हिमे अभिञ्ञाता अभिञ्ञाता लिच्छवी सन्थागारे सन्निसिन्ना सन्निपतिता अनेकपरियायेन बुद्धस्स वण्णं भासन्ति, धम्मस्स वण्णं भासन्ति, सङ्घस्स वण्णं भासन्ति। यन्नूनाहं तं भगवन्तं दस्सनाय उपसङ्कमेय्यं अरहन्तं सम्मासम्बुद्धं"ति। अथ खो सीहो सेनापति येन निगण्ठो नाटपुत्तो तेनुपसङ्कमि; उपसङ्कमित्वा निगण्ठं नाटपुत्तं एतदवोच–"इच्छामहं, भन्ते, समणं गोतमं दस्सनाय उपसङ्कमितुं"ति। "…..समणो हि, सीह, गोतमो अकिरियावादो अकिरियाय धम्मं देसेति, तेन च सावके विनेति"ति। दुतियं पि खो सीहस्स सेनापतिस्स यो अहोसि गमियाभि–सङ्खारो भगवन्तं दस्सनाय, सो पटिप्पस्सम्भि। ततियं पि खो...अभिञ्ञाता अभिञ्ञाता लिच्छवी सन्थागारे सन्निसिन्ना सन्निपतिता अनेकपरियायेन बुद्धस्स वण्णं भासन्ति, धस्सम्म वण्णं भासन्ति, सङ्घस्स वण्णं भासन्ति। ततियं पि खो सीहस्स सेनापतिस्स एतदहोसि...."निस्संसयं खो सो भगवा अरहं सम्मासम्बुद्धो भविस्सति, तथा हिमे

...अभिञ्ञाता अभिञ्ञाता लिच्छवी सन्थागारे सन्निसिन्ना सन्निपतिता अनेकपरियायेन बुद्धस्स वण्णं भासन्ति, धम्मस्स वण्णं भासन्ति, सङ्घस्स वण्णं भासन्ति। किं हिमे करिस्सन्ति निगण्ठा अपलोकिता वा अनपलोकिता वा? यन्नूनाहं अनपलोकेत्वा व निगण्ठे तं भगवन्तं दस्सनाय उपसङ्कमेय्यं अरहन्तं सम्मासम्बुद्ध"ति।

अथ खो सीहो सेनापति पञ्चमत्तेहि रथसतेहि दिवादिवस्स वेसालिया निय्यासि भगवन्तं दस्सनाय। यावतिका यानस्स भूमि, यानेन गन्त्वा याना पच्चोरोहित्वा पत्तिको व...येन भगवा तेनुपसङ्कमि; उपसङ्कमित्वा भगवन्तं अभिवादेत्वा एकमन्तं निसीदि। एकमन्तं निसिन्नो खो सीहो सेनापति भगवन्तं एतदवोच–"सुतं मेतं, भन्ते, 'अकिरियावादो समणो गोतमो अकिरियाय धम्मं देसेति, तेन च सावके विनेती'ति। ये ते, भन्ते, एवमाहंसु 'अकिरियवादो समणो गोतमो, अकिरियाय धम्मं देसेति, तेन च सावके विनेती'ति, कच्चि, ते, भन्ते, भगवतो वुत्तवादिनो, न च भगवन्तं अभूतेन अब्भाचिक्खन्ति, धम्मस्स च अनुधम्मं व्याकरोन्ति, न च कोचि सहधम्मिको वादानुवादो गारय्हं ठानं आगच्छति? अनब्भक्खातुकामा हि मयं, भन्ते भगवन्त"ति।

"अत्थि, सीह, परियायो, येन मं परियायेन सम्मा वदमानो वदेय्य–'अकिरियवादो समणो गोतमो, अकिरियाय धम्मं देसेति, तेन च सावके विनेती'ति। "अत्थि, सीह, परियायो, येन मं परियायेन सम्मा वदमानो वदेय्य–'किरियवादो समणो गोतमो किरियाय धम्मं देसेति, तेन च सावके विनेती'ति। "अत्थि, सीह, परियायो येन मं परियायेन सम्मा वदमानो वदेय्य–'उच्छेदवादो समणो गोतमो, उच्छेदाय धम्मं देसेति, तेन च सावके विनेती'ति। "अत्थि, सीह, परियायो, येन मं परियायेन सम्मा वदमानो वदेय्य–'जेगुच्छी समणो गोतमो, जेगुच्छिताय धम्मं देसेति, तेन च सावके विनेती'ति। "अत्थि, सीह, परियायो, येन मं परियायेन सम्मा वदमानो वदेय्य–'वेनयिको समणो गोतमो, विनयाय धम्मं देसेति, तेन च सावके विनेती'ति। "अत्थि, सीह, परियायो, येन मं परियायेन सम्मा वदमानो वदेय्ये–'तपस्सी समणो गोतमो, तपस्सिताय धम्मं देसेति, तेन च सावके विनेती'ति। "अत्थि, सीह, परियायो, येन च परियायेन सम्मा वदमानो वदेय्य–'अपगब्भो समणो गोतमो, अपगब्यताय धम्मं देसेति, तेन च सावके विनेती'ति। "अत्थि, सीह, परियायो, येन मं परियायेन सम्मा वदमानो वदेय्य–'अस्सत्थो समणो गोतमो, अस्सासाय धम्मं देसेति, तेन च सावके विनेती'ति।

"कतमो च, सीह, परियायो, येन मं परियायेन सम्मा वदमानो वदेय्य–अकिरियवादो समणो गोतमो, अकिरियाय धम्मं देसेति, तेन च सावके विनेती'ति? अहं हि, सीह, अकिरियं वदामि। कायदुच्चरितस्स वचीदुच्चरितस्स मनोदुच्चरितस्स; अनेकविहितानं...सम्मा वदमानो वदेय्य– 'अकिरियवादो समणो गोतमो, अकिरियाम धम्मं देसेति, तेन च सावके विनेती'ति।

"कतमो च, सीह, परियायो, येन मं परियायेन सम्मा वदमानो वदेय्य–'किरियवादो समणो गोतमो, ...।

"कतमो च, सीह, परियायो, येन मं परियायेन सम्मा वदमानो वदेय्य–'उच्छेदवादो, समणो गोतमो,.......।

"कतमो च, सीह, परियायो, येन मं परियायेन सम्मा वदमानो वदेय्य–'जेगुच्छी समणो गोतमो,.......।

"कतमो च, सीह, परियायो, येन मं परियायेन सम्मा वदमानो वदेय्य–'वेनयिको समणो गोतमो,.......।

"कतमो च, सीह, परियायो, येन मं परियायेन सम्मा वदमानो वदेय्य–''तपस्सी समणो गोतमो,.......।

"कतमो च, सीह, परियायो, येन मं परियायेन सम्मा वदमानो वदेय्य–''अपगब्भो समणो गोतमो,.......।

"कतमो च, सीह, परियायो, येन मं परियायेन सम्मा वदमानो वदेय्य–''अस्सात्सको समणो गातमो,.......।"

एवं वुत्तो सीहो सेनापति भगवन्तं एतदवोच–"अभिक्कन्तं, भन्ते,....पे०...उपासकं मं, भगवा धारेतु अज्जतग्गे पाणुपेतं सरणं गतं"ति। "अनुविच्चकारं खो, सीह, करोहि; अनुविच्चकारो तुम्हादिसानं भातमतुस्सानं साधु होती"ति। "इमिनापाहं, भन्ते, भगवतो मिय्योसोमत्ताय अत्तमन्नो अभिरद्धो, यं मं भगवा एवमाह–'अनुविच्चकारं खो, सीह, करोहि। अनुविच्चकारो तुम्हादिसानं ञातमनुस्सानं साधु होती'ति। मं हि भन्ते, अञ्ञतित्थिया सावकं लभित्वा केवलकप्पं वेसालि पटाकं परिहरेय्युं–'सीहो खो अम्हाकं सेनापति सावकत्तं उपगतो'ति। अथ च पन मं भगवा एवमाह–'अनुविच्चकारं खो, सीह, करोहि। अनुविच्चकारो तुम्हादिसानं ञातमनुस्सानं साधु होती'ति। एमाहं, भन्ते, दुतियं पि भगवन्तं सरणं गच्छामि धम्मं च भिक्खुसङ्घं च। उपासकं मं भगवा धारेतु अज्जतग्गे पाणुपेतं सरणं गतं"ति। "दीघरत्तं खो ते, सीह, निगण्ठानं ओपानभूतं कुलं, येन नेसं उपगतानं पिण्डकं दातब्बं मञ्ञेय्यासी"ति। "इमिनापाहं, भन्ते, भगवतो वचनेन भिय्योसोमत्ताय अत्तमनो अभिरद्धो, यं मं भगवा एवमाह–"दीघरत्तं खो ते, सीह, निगण्ठानं ओपानभूतं कुलं, येन नेसं उपगतानं पिण्डकं दातब्बं मञ्ञेय्यासी'ति। सुतं मेतं, भन्ते, 'समणो गोतमो एवमाह–मय्हमेव दानं दातब्बं, मय्हमेव सावकानं दानं दातब्बं, मय्हमेव दिन्नं महप्फलं, न अञ्ञेसं दिन्नं महप्फलं; मय्हमेव सावकानं दिन्नं महप्फलं, न अञ्ञेसं सावकानं दिन्नं महप्फलं'ति। अथ च पन मं भगवा निगण्ठेसु पि दाने समादपेति। अपि स, भन्ते, मयमेत्थ कालं जानिस्साम। एसाहं, भन्ते, ततियं पि भगवन्तं सरणं गच्छामि धम्मं च भिक्खुसङ्घं च। उपासकं मं, भन्ते, भगवा धारेतु अज्जतग्गे पाणुपेतं सरणं गतं"ति।

अथ खो भगवा सीहस्स सेनापतिस्स अनुपुब्बिं कथं कथेसि सेय्यथीदं–दानकथं..... अपरप्पच्चयो सत्थुसासने भगवन्तं एतदवोच–"अधिवासेतु मे, भन्ते, भगवा स्वातनाय भत्तं सद्धिं भिक्खुसङ्घेना"ति। अधिवासेसि भगवा तुण्हीभावेन। अथ खो सीहो सेनापति भगवतो अधिवासनं विदित्वा उट्ठायासना भगवन्तं अभिवादेत्वा पदक्खिणं कत्वा पक्कामि।

अथ खो सीहो सेनापति अञ्ञतरं पुरिसं आणापेसि–"गच्छ, भणे, पवत्तमंसं जानाही"ति। अथ खो सीहो सेनापति तस्सा रत्तिया अच्चयेन वणीत्तं खादनीयं भोजनीयं पटियादापेत्वा भगवतो

कालं आरोचापेसि–"कालो, भन्ते, निट्ठितं भत्तं"ति। अथ खो भगवा पुब्बण्हसमयं निवासेत्वा पत्तचीवरमादाय येन सीहस्स सेनापतिस्स निवेसनं तेनुपसङ्कमि, उपसङ्कमित्वा पञ्ञत्ते आसने निसीदि सद्धिं भिक्खुसङ्घेन।

तेन खो पन समयेन सम्बहुला निगण्ठा वेसालियं रथिकाय रथिकं सिङ्घाटकेन सिङ्घाटकं बाहा पग्गय्ह कन्दन्ति–"अज्ज सीहेन सेनापतिना थूलं पसु वधित्वा समणस्स गोतमस्स भत्तं कतं। तं समणो गोतमो जानं उद्दिस्सकतं मंसं परिभुञ्जति पटिच्चकम्मं"ति। अथ खो अञ्ञतरो पुरिसो येन सीहो सेनापति तेनुपसङ्कमि, उपसङ्कमित्वा सीहस्स सेनापतिस्स उपकण्णके आरोचेसि–यग्घे भन्ते, जानेय्यासि! एत्ते सम्बहुला निगण्ठा वेसालियं रथिकाय रथिकं सिङ्घाटकेन सिङ्घाटकं बाहा पग्गय्ह कन्दन्ति–'अज्ज साहेन सेनापतिना थूलं पसुं वधित्वा समणस्स गोतमस्स भत्तं कतं। तं समणो गोतमो जानं उद्दिस्सकतं मंसं परिभुञ्जति पटिच्चकम्मं"ति। अलं अय्यो, दीघरत्तं पि ते आयस्मन्तो अवण्णकामा बुद्धस्स, अवण्णकामा धम्मस्स, अवण्णकामा संघस्स। न च पन ते आयस्मन्तने जिरिदन्ति तं भगवन्तं असता तुच्छा मुसा अभूतेन अब्भाचिक्खिन्तं; न च भयं जीवितहेतु पि सञ्चिच्च पाणं जीविता वीरोपेथ्यामा"ति। अथ खो सीहो सेनापति नुद्धप्पमुखं भिक्खुसङ्घं पणीतेन खादनीयेन भोजनीयेन सहत्था...सन्तप्पेत्वा सम्पवारेत्वा-भगवन्तं भुत्ताविं ओनीतपत्तपाणिं एकमन्तं निसीदि। एकमन्तं निसिन्नं खो सीहं सेनापतिं भगवा धम्मिया कथाय सन्दस्सेत्वा समादपेत्वा समुत्तेजेत्वा सम्पहंसेत्वा उट्ठायासना पक्कामि ति। अथ खो भगवा एतस्मिं निदाने एतस्मिं पकरणे धम्मिं कथं कत्वा भिक्खू आमन्तेसि–"न, भिक्खवे, जानं उदिस्सकतं मंसं परिभुञ्जितब्बं। यो परिभुञ्जेय्य आपत्ति दुक्कटस्स। अनुजानामि, भिक्खवे, तिकोटिपरिसुद्धं मच्छमंसं–अदिट्ठं असुत्तं अपरिसंकितं"ति।[1]

एकं समयं भगवा वेसालियं विहरति महावने कूटागारसालायं। तेन खो पन समयेन सम्बहुला अभिञ्ञाता अभिञ्ञाता लिच्छवी०....।

एकमन्त निसिन्नं खो सीहं सेनापति भगवा धम्मिया कथाय सन्दरसेत्वा समादपेत्वा सम्पहंसेत्वा समुत्तेजेत्वा उट्ठायासना पक्कामी ति।[2]

२

GṚHAPATI UPĀLI

एवं मे सुतं। एकं समयं भगवा नालन्दायं विहरति पावारिकम्बवने। तेन खो पन समयेन निगण्ठो नातपुत्तो नालन्दायं पटिवसति महतिया निगण्ठपरिसाय सद्धिं। अथ खो दीघतपस्सी निगण्ठो नालन्दायं पिण्डाय चरित्वा पच्छाभत्तं पिण्डपातपटिक्कन्तो येन पावा रिकम्बवनं येन भगवा तेनुपसङ्कमि; उपसङ्कमित्वा भगवता सद्धिं सम्मोदि। सम्मोदनीयं कथं सारणीयं वीतिसारेत्वा एकमन्तं अट्ठासि। एकमन्तं ठितं खो दीघतपस्सिं निगण्ठं भगवा एतदवोच–"संविज्जन्ति खो, तपस्सी, आसनानि;

1. विनयपिटक, महावग्ग पालि, 6-19; 31-35, पृ० 248 से 252।
2. सुत्तपिटके अंगुत्तरनिकाय पालि, अट्ठकनिपात, महावग्गो, सीहसुत्तं, 8-2-2, पृ० 293 से 300।

सचे आकङ्खसि निसीदा"ति। एवं वुत्ते दीघतपस्सी निगण्ठो अञ्ञतरं नीचं आसनं गहेत्वा एकमन्तं निसीदि। एकमन्तं निसिन्नं खो दीघतपस्सिं निगण्ठं भगवा एतदवोच–"कति पन, तपस्सि, निगण्ठो नातपुत्तो कम्मानि पञ्ञापेति पापस्स कम्मस्स किरियाय पापस्स कम्मस्स पवत्तिया"ति?

"न खो, आवुसो गोतम, आचिण्णं निगण्ठस्स नातपुत्तस्स 'कम्मं, कम्मं'ति पञ्ञापेतुं; 'दण्डं, दण्डं'ति खो, आवुसो गोतम, आचिण्णं निगण्ठस्स नातपुत्तस्स पञ्ञापेतुं"ति।

"कति पन, तपस्सि, निगण्ठो नातपुत्तो दण्डानि।" पञ्ञापेति पापस्स किरियाय पापस्य कम्मस्स पवत्तिया"ति?

"तीणि खो, आवुसो गोतम, निगण्ठो नातपुत्तो दण्डानि पञ्ञापेति पापस्स कम्मस्स किरियाय पापस्स कम्मस्स पवत्तिया ति, सेय्यथीदं–कायदण्डं, वचीदण्डं, मनोदण्डं"ति।

"किं पन, तपस्सि, अञ्ञदेव कायदण्डं, अञ्ञं वचीदण्डं, अञ्ञं मनोदण्डं"ति?

"अञ्ञदेव, आवुसो गोतम, कायदण्डं, अञ्ञं वचीदण्डं, अञ्ञं मनोदण्डं"ति।

"इमेसं पन, तपस्सि, तिण्णं दण्डानं एवं पटिविभत्तानं एवं पटिविसिट्ठानं कतमं दण्डं निगण्ठो नातपुत्तो महासावज्जतरं पञ्ञापेति पापस्स०....पवत्तिया, यदि वा कायदण्डं, यदि वा वचीदण्डं, यदि वा मनोदण्डं"ति?

"इमेसं खो, आवुसो गोतम, तिण्णं दण्डानं एवं पटिविभत्तानं एवं पटिविसिट्ठानं कायदण्डं निगण्ठो०....पवत्तिया, नो तथा वचीदण्डं, नो तथा मनोदण्डं"ति।

"कायदण्डं ति, तपस्सि, वदेसि"?

"कायदण्डं ति, आवुसो गोतम, वदामि"।

"कायदण्डं ति, तपस्सि, वदेसि"?

"कायदण्डं ति, आवुसो गोतम, वदामि"।

"कायदण्डं ति, तपस्सि, वदेसि"?

"कायदण्डं ति, आवुसो गोतम, वदामी"ति।

इतिह भगवा दीघतपस्सिं निगण्ठं इमस्मिं कथावत्थुस्मिं यावततियकं पतिट्ठापेसि। एवं वुत्ते, दीघतपस्सी निगण्ठो भगवन्तं एतदवोच–"त्वं पनावुसो गोतम, कति दण्डानि पञ्ञापेसि पापस्स०. ...पवत्तिया"ति?

"न खो, तपस्सि, आचिण्णं तथागतस्स 'दण्डं, दण्डं'ति पञ्ञापेतुं; 'कम्मं, कम्मं'ति खो, तपस्सि, आचिण्णं तथागतस्स पञ्ञापेतुं"ति?

"त्वं पनावुसो गोतम, कति कम्मानि पञ्ञपेसि पापस्स०...पवत्तिया"ति?

"तीणि खो अहं, तपस्सि, कम्मानि पञ्ञपेमि पापस्स०...पवत्तिया, सेय्यथीदं–कायकम्मं वचीकम्मं, मनोकम्मं"ति।

"किं पनावुसो गोतम, अञ्ञदेव कायकम्मं, अञ्ञं वचीकम्मं, अञ्ञं मनोकम्मं"ति?

"अञ्ञदेव, तपस्सि, कायकम्मं, अञ्ञ वचीकम्मं, अञ्ञ मनोकम्मं"ति।

"इमेसं पनावुसो गोतम, तिण्णं कम्मानं एवं पटिविभत्तानं एवं पटिविसिट्ठानं कतमं कम्मं महासावज्जतरं पञ्ञपेसि पावस्स०...पवत्तिया, यदि वा कायकम्मं, यदि वा वचीकम्मं, यदि वा मनोकम्मं"ति?

"इमेसं खो अहं, तपस्सि तिण्णं कम्मानं एवं पटिविभत्तानं एवं पटिविसिट्ठानं मनोकम्मं महासावज्जतरं पञ्ञपेमि पापस्स०...पवत्तिया, नो तथा कायकम्मं, नो तथा वची कम्मं"ति।

"मनोकम्मं ति, आवुसो गोतम, वदेसि"?

"मनोकम्मं ति, तपस्सि वदामि"।

"मनोकम्मं ति, आवुसो गोतम, वेदसि"?

"मनोकम्मं ति, तपस्सि, वदामि"।

"मनोकम्मं ति, आवुसो गोतम, वदेसि"?

"मनोकम्मं ति, तपस्सि, वदामो"ति।

इतिह दीघतपस्सी निगण्ठो भगवन्तं इमस्मिं कथावत्थुस्मिं यावततियकं पतिट्ठापेत्वा उट्ठायासना येन निगण्ठो नातपुत्तो तेनुपसङ्कमि।

तेन खो पन समयेन निगण्ठो नातपुत्तो महतिया गिहिपरिसाय सद्धिं निसिन्नो होति बालकिनिया परिसाय उपालिपमुखाय। अद्दसा खो निगण्ठो नातपुत्तो दीघतपस्सिं निगण्ठं दूरतो व आगच्छन्तं; दिस्वान दीघतपस्मिं निगण्ठं एतदवोच–"हन्द, कुतो नु त्वं, तपस्सि, आगच्छसि दिवा दिवस्सा"ति?

"इतो हि खो अहं, भन्ते, आगच्छामि समणस्स गोतमस्स सन्तिका"ति।

"अहु पन ते, तपस्सि, समणेन गोतमेन सद्धिं कोचिदेव कथासल्लापो"ति?

"अहु खो मे, भन्ते, समणेन गोतमेन सद्धिं कोचिदेव कथासल्लापो"ति।

"यथा कथं पन ते, तपस्सि, अहु समणेन गोतमेन सद्धिं कोचिदेव कथासल्लापो"ति?

अथ खो दीघतपस्सी निगण्ठो यावतका अहोसि भगवता सद्धिं कथासल्लापो तं सब्बं निगण्ठस्स नातपुत्तस्स आरोचेसि। एवं वुत्ते, निगण्ठो नातपुत्तो दीघतपस्सिं निगण्ठं एतदवोच–"साधु साधु, तपस्सि! यथा तं सुतवता सावकेन सम्मदेव सत्थुसासनं आजानन्तेन एवमेवं दीघतपस्सिना निगण्ठेन समणस्स गोतमस्स व्याकतं। किं हि सोभति छवो मनोदण्डो इमस्स एवं ओलारिकस्स कायदण्डस्स उपनिधाय! अथ खो कायदण्डो व महासावज्जतरो पापस्स कम्मस्स किरियाय पापस्स कम्मस्स पवत्तिया, नो तथा वचीदण्डो, नो तथा मनोदण्डो"ति।

एवं वुत्ते, उपालि गहपति निगण्ठं नातपुत्तं एतदवोच–साधु, साधु, भन्ते दीघतपस्सि! यथा० ...तथा मनोदण्डो। हन्द चाहं, भन्ते, गच्छामि समणस्स गोतमस्स इमं पि कथावत्थुस्मिं वादं आरोपेस्सामि। सचे मे समणो गोतमो तथा पतिट्ठहिस्सति यथा भदन्तेन तपस्सिना पतिट्ठापितं;

सेय्यथापि नाम बलवा पुरिसो दीघलोमिकं एलकं लोमेसु गहेत्वा आकड्ढेव्य परिकड्ढेय सम्परिकड्ढेय्य, एवमेवाहं समणं गोतमं वादेन वादं आकड्ढिस्सामि परिकड्ढस्सामि सम्परिकड्ढिस्सामि। सेय्यथापि नाम बलवा सोण्डिकाकम्मकारो महन्तं सोण्डिकाकिलञ्ञं गम्भीरे उदकरदहे पक्खिपित्वा कण्णे गहेत्वा आकड्ढेय्य परिकड्ढेय्य सम्परिकड्ढेय्य, एवमेवाहं समणं गोतमं वादेन वादं आकड्ढिस्सामि परिकड्ढिस्सामि सम्परिकड्ढिस्सामि। सेय्यथापि नाम बलवा सोण्डिकाधुत्तो वालं कण्णे गहेत्वा ओधुनेय्य निद्धुनेय्य निप्फोटेय्य, एवमेवाहं समणं गोतमं वादेन बादं ओधुनिस्सामि निद्धुनिस्सामि निप्फोटेस्सामि। सेय्यथापि नाम कुञ्जरो सट्ठिहायनो गम्भीरं पोक्खरणिं ओगाहेत्वा साणधोविकं नाम कीलितजातं कीलति, एवमेवाहं समणं गोतमं साणधोविकं मञ्ञे कीलितजातं कीलिस्सामि। हन्द चाहं, भन्ते, गच्छामि समणस्स गोतमस्स इमस्मिं कथावत्थुस्मिं वादं आरोपेस्सामी"ति।

"गच्छ त्वं गहपति, समणस्स गोतमस्स इमस्मिं कथावत्थुस्मिं वादं आरोपेहि। अहं वा हि, गहपति, समणस्स, गोतमस्स वादं आरोपेय्य, दीघतपस्सी वा निगण्ठो, त्वं वा"ति।

एवं वुत्ते, दीघतपस्सी निगण्ठो निगण्ठं नातपुत्तं एतदवोच–"न खो मेतं, भन्ते, रुच्चत्ति यं उपालि गहपति समणस्स गोतमस्स वादं आरोपेय्य। समणो हि, भन्ते, गोतमो मायावी आवट्टनिं मायं जानाति याय अञ्ञतित्थियानं सावके अवाट्टेती"ति।

"अट्ठानं खो एतं, तपस्सि, अनवकासो यं उपालि गहपति समणस्स गोतमस्स सावकत्तं उपगच्छेय्य। ठानं च खो एतं विज्जति यं सण्णो गोतमो उपालिस्स गहपतिस्स सावकत्तं उपगच्छेय्य। गच्छ, त्वं, गहपति, समणस्स गोतमस्स इमस्मिं कथावत्थुस्मिं वादं आरोपेहि। अहं वा हि, गहपति, समणस्स गोतमस्स वादं आरोपेय्यं, दीघतपस्सी वा निगण्ठो, त्वं वा"ति।

दुतियं पि खो दीघतपस्सी...पे०...ततियं पि खो दीघतपस्सी निगण्ठो निगण्ठं नातपुत्तं एतदवोच–"न खो मेतं, भन्ते, रुच्चति यं उपालि गहपति समणस्स गोतमस्स वादं आरोपेय्य। समणो हि, भन्ते, गोतमो मायावी आवट्ठनिं मायं जानाति अञ्ञतित्थियानं सावके आवट्टेती"ति।

"अट्ठानं खो एतं, तपस्सि, ०..त्वं, वा"ति।

"एवं, भन्ते"ति खो उपालि गहपति निगण्ठस्स नातपुत्तस्स पटिस्सुत्वा उट्ठायासना निगण्ठं नातपुत्तं अभिवादेत्वा पदक्खिणं कत्वा येन पावारिकम्बवनं येन भगवा तेनुपसङ्कमि; उपसंकमित्वा भगवन्तं अभिवोदत्वा एकमन्तं निसीदि। एकमन्तं निसिन्नो खो उपालि गहपति भगवन्तं एतदवोच–"आगमा नु रिव्वध, भन्ते, दीघतपस्सी निगण्ठो"ति?

"आगमा रिव्वध, गहपति, दीघतपस्सी निगण्ठो"ति।

"अहु खो पन ते, भन्ते दीघतपस्सिना निगण्ठेन सद्धिं कोचिदेव कथासल्लापो"ति।

"अहु खो मे, गहपति, दीघपतस्सिना०...कथासल्लापो"ति।

"यथा कथं पन ते, भन्ते, अहु, दीघतपस्सिना०...कथासल्लापो"ति?

अथ खो भगवा यावतको अहोसि दीघतपस्सिना निगण्ठेन सद्धिं कथासल्लापो तं सब्बं उपालिस्स गहपतिस्स आरोचेसि।

एवं वुत्ते, उपालि गहपति भगवन्तं एतदवोच–"साधु साधु, भन्ते तपस्सी! यथा०... मनोदण्डो"ति।

"सचे खो त्वं, गहपति, सच्चे पतिट्ठाय मन्तेय्यासि सिया नो एत्थ कथासल्लापो"ति।

"सच्चे अहं, भन्ते, पतिट्ठाय मन्तेस्सामि; होतु नो एत्थ कथाल्लापो"ति।

"तं किं मञ्ञसि, गहपति, इधस्स निगण्ठो आबाधिको दुक्खितो बाल्हगिलानो सीतोदकपटिक्खित्तो उण्होदकपटिसेवी। सो सीतोदकं अलभमानो कालङ्करेय्य। इमस्स पन, गहपति, निगण्ठो नातपुत्तो कत्थूपपत्तिं पञ्ञापेती"ति?

"अत्थि, भन्ते, मनोसत्ता नाम देवा तत्थ सो उपपज्जति। "तं किस्स हेतु"? असु हि, भन्ते, मनोपटिबद्धो कालङ्करोती"ति।

"मनसि करोहि, गहपति, मनसि करित्वा खो, गहपति, व्याकरोहि। न खो ते सन्धियति पुरिमेन वा पच्छिमं, पच्छिमेन वा पुरिमं। भासिता खो पन ते, गहपति, ऐसा वाचा–"सच्चे अहं, भन्ते, पतिट्ठाय मन्तेस्सामि, होतु नो एत्थ कथासल्लापो"ति।

"किञ्चापि, भन्ते, भगवा एवमाह, अथ खो कायदण्डो व महासावज्जतरो पापस्स कम्मस्स किरियाय पापस्स कम्मस्स पवत्तिया, नो तथा वचीदण्डो, नो तथा मनोदण्डो"ति।

"तं किं मञ्ञसि, गहपति, इधस्स निगण्ठो नातपुत्तो चातुयामसंवरसंवुतो सब्बवारिवारितो सब्बवारियुतो सब्बवारिधुतो सब्बवारिफुटो। सो अभिक्कमन्तो पटिक्कमन्तो बहु खुद्दके पाणे सङ्घातं आपादेति। इमस्स पन, गहपति, निगण्ठो नातपुत्तो कं विपाकं पञ्ञापेती"ति।

"असञ्चेतनिकं, भन्ते, निगण्ठो नातपुत्तो नो महासावज्जं पञ्ञापेती"ति।

"सचे पन, गहपति, चेतेती"ति?

"महासावज्जं, भन्ते, होती"ति।

"चेतनं पन, गहपति निगण्ठो नातपुत्तो किस्मिं पञ्ञापेती"ति?

"मनोदण्डस्मिं, भन्ते"ति।

"मनसि करोहि, गहपति, ०....कथासल्लापो"ति।

"किञ्चापि, भन्ते, ०....मनोदण्डो"ति।

"तं किं मञ्ञसि, गहपति, अयं नालन्दा इद्धा चेव फीता च बहुजना आकिण्णमनुस्सा"ति?

"एवं भन्ते, अयं नालन्दा इद्धा चेव फीता च बहुजना आकिण्णमनुस्सा"ति।

"तं किं मञ्ञसि, गहपति, इध पुरिसो आगच्छेय्य उक्खित्तासिको। सो एवं वदेय्य–'अहं यावतिका इमिस्सा नालन्दाय पाणा ते एकेन खणेन एकेन मुहुत्तेन एकं मंसखलं एकं मंसपुञ्जं करिस्सामी'ति। तं किं मञ्ञसि, गहपति, पहोति नु खो सो पुरिसो यावतिका इमिस्सा नालन्दाय पाणा ते एकेन खणेन एकेन मुहुत्तेन एकं मंसखलं एकं मंसपुञ्जं कातुं"ति?

"दस पि, भन्ते, पुरिसा, वीसं पि, भन्ते, पुरिसा, तिंसं पि, भन्ते, पुरिसा, चत्तारीसं पि,

भन्ते, पुरिसा, पञ्ञास पि, भन्ते, पुरिसा, नप्पहोन्ति यावतिका इमिस्सा नालन्दाय पाणा ते एकेन खणेन एकेन मुहुत्तेन एकं मंसखलं एकं मंसपुञ्जं कातुं। किं हि सोभति एको छवो पुरिसो"ति!

"तं किं मञ्ञसि, गहपति, इध आगच्छेय्य समणो वा ब्राह्मणो वा इद्धिमा चेतोवसिप्पत्तो। सो एवं वदेय्य–'अहं इमं नालन्दं एकेन मनोपदोसेन भस्मं करिस्सामी'ति। तं किं मञ्ञसि, गहपति, पहोति नु खो सो समणो वा ब्राह्मणो वा इद्धिमा चेतोवसिप्पत्तो इमं नालन्दं एकेन मनोपदोसेन भस्मं कातुं"ति?

"दस पि, भन्ते, नालन्दा, वीसं पि नालन्दा, तिंस पि नालन्दा, चत्तारीसं पि नालन्दा, पञ्ञासं पि नालन्दा पहोति सो समणो वा ब्राह्मणो वा इद्धिमा चेतोवसिप्पत्तो एकेन मनोपदोसेन भस्मं कातुं। किं हि सोभति एका छवा नालन्दा"ति!

"मनसि करोहि, गहपति, ०...कथासल्लापो"ति।

"किञ्चापि, भन्ते, ०...मनोदण्डो"ति।

"तं किं मञ्ञसि, गहपति, सुतं ते दण्डकारञ्ञं कालिङ्गारञ्ञं मेज्झारञ्ञं मातङ्गारञ्ञं अरञ्ञं अरञ्ञभूतं"ति?

"एवं, भन्ते, सुतं मे दण्डकारञ्ञं०....अरञ्ञभूतं"ति।

"तं किं मञ्ञसि, गहपति, किन्ति ते सुतं केन तं दण्डकारञ्ञं०...अरञ्ञभूतं"ति।

"सुतं मेतं, भन्ते, इसीनं मनोपदोसेन तं दण्डकारञ्ञं०...अरञ्ञभूतं"ति।

"मनसि करोहि, गहपति, ०...कथासल्लापो"ति।

"पुरिमेनेवाहं, भन्ते, ओपम्मेन भगवतो अत्तमनो अत्तमनो अभिरद्धो। अपि चाहं इमानि भगवतो विचित्रानि पञ्हपटिभानानि सोतुकामो एवाहं भगवन्तं पच्चनीकं कातब्बं अमञ्ञिस्सं। अभिक्कन्तं, भन्ते, अभिक्कन्तं, भन्ते! सेय्यथापि, भन्ते, निक्कुज्जितं वा उक्कुज्जेय्य, पटिच्छन्नं वा विवरेय्य, मूल्हस्स वा मग्गं आचिक्खेय्य, अन्धकारे वा तेलपज्जोतं धारेय्य–चक्खुमन्तो रूपानि दक्खन्ती ति, एवमेवं भगवता अनेकपरियायेन धम्मो पकासितो। एसाहं, भन्ते, भगवन्तं सरणं गच्छामि धम्मं च भिक्खुसङ्घं च। उपासकं मं भगवा धारेतु अज्जतग्गे पाणुपेतं सरणं गतं"ति।

"अनुविच्चकारं खो, गहपति, करोहि, अनुविच्चकारो तुम्हादिसानं ञातमनुस्सानं साधु होती"ति।

"इमिनापाहं भन्ते, भगवतो भिय्योसो मत्ताय अत्तमनो अभिरद्धो यं मं भगवा एवमाह–'अनुविच्चकारं खो, गहपति, करोहि, अनुविच्चकारो तुम्हादिसानं ञातमनुस्सानं साधु होति'ति। मं हि, भन्ते, अञ्ञतित्थिया सावकं लभित्वा केवलकप्पं नालन्दं पटाकं परिहरेय्युं–'उपालि अम्हाकं गहपति सावकत्तं उपगतो'ति। अथ च पन मं भगवा एवमाह–'अनुविच्चकारं खो, ०...होती'ति। एसाहं, भन्ते, दुतियं पि भगवन्तं सरणं गच्छामि धम्मं च भिक्खुसङ्घं च। उपासकं मं भगवा धारेतु अज्जतग्गे पाणुपेतं सरणं गतं"ति।

"दीघरत्तं खो ते, गहपति, निगण्ठानं ओपानभूतं कुलं येन नेसं उपगतानं पिण्डकं दातब्बं मञ्ञेय्यास्सी"ति।

"इमिनापाहं, भन्ते, ०...एसाहं, भन्ते, ततियं पि०...सरणं गतं"ति।

अथ खो भगवा उपालिस्स गहपतिस्स अनुपुब्बिं कथं कथेसि, सेय्यथीदं–दानकथं सीलकथं सग्गकथं, कामानं आदीनवं ओकारं सङ्किलेसं, नेक्खम्मे आनिसंसं पकासेसि। यदा भगवा अञ्ञासि उपालिं गहपतिं कल्लचित्तं मुदुचित्तं विनीवरणचित्तं, उदग्गचित्तं, पसन्नचित्तं, अथ या बुद्धानं सामुक्कंसिका धम्मदेसना तं पकासेसि–दुक्खं, समुदयं, निरोधं, मग्गं। सेय्यथापि नाम सुद्धं वत्थं अपगतकालकं सम्मदेव रजनं पटिग्गण्हेय्य एवमेव, उपालिस्स गहपतिस्स तस्मिं एव आसने विरजं वीतमलं धम्मचक्खुं उदपादि–यं किञ्चि समुदयधम्मं सब्बं तं निरोधधम्मं' ति। अथ खो उपालि गहपति दिट्ठधम्मो पत्तधम्मो विदितधम्मो परियोगाल्हधम्मो निण्णविचिकिच्छो विगतकथङ्कथो वेसारज्जप्पत्तो अपरप्पच्चयो सत्थुसासने भगवन्तं एतदवोच–"हन्द च दानिमयं, भन्ते, गच्छाम बहुकिच्चा मयं बहुकरणीया"ति।

"यस्सदानि त्वं, गहपति, कालं मञ्ञसी"ति।

अथ खो उपालि गहपति भगवतो भासितं अभिनन्दित्वा अनुमोदित्वा उट्ठायासना भगवन्तं अभिवादेत्वा पदक्खिणं कत्वा येन सकं निवेसनं तेनुपसङ्कमि; उपसङ्कमित्वा दोवारिकं आमन्तेसि–"अज्जतग्गे, सम्म, दोवारिक, आवरामि द्वारं निगण्ठानं निगण्ठीनं, अनावटं द्वारं भगवतो भिक्खूनं भिक्खूनीनं उपासकानं उपासिकानं। सचे कोचि निगण्ठो आगच्छति तमेनं त्वं एवं वदेय्यासि–'तिट्ठ, भन्ते, मा पाविसि। अज्जतग्गे उपालि गहपति समणस्स गोतमस्स सावकत्तं उपगतो। आवटं द्वारं निगण्ठानं निगण्ठीनं, अनावटं द्वारं भगवतो भिक्खूनं भिक्खूनीनं उपासकानं उपासिकानं। सचे ते, भन्ते, पिण्डकेन अत्थो, एत्थेव तिट्ठ, एत्थेव ते आहरिस्सन्ती"ति।

"एवं, भन्ते"ति खो दोवारिको उपालिस्स गहपतिस्स पच्चस्सोसि।

अस्सोसि खो दीघतपस्सी निगण्ठो–"उपालि किर गहपति समणस्स गोतमस्स सावकत्तं उपगतो"ति। अथ खो दीघतपस्सी निगण्ठो येन निगण्ठो नातपुत्तो तेनुपसङ्कमि; उपसङ्कमित्वा निगण्ठं नातपुत्तं एतदवोच–"सुतं मेतं, भन्ते, उपालि किर गहपति समणस्स गोतमस्स सावकत्तं उपगतो"ति।

"अट्ठानं खो एतं, तपस्सि, अनवकासो यं उपालि गहपति समणस्स गोतमस्स सावकत्तं उपगच्छेय्य। ठानं च खो एतं विज्जति यं समणो गोतमो उपालिस्स गहपतिस्स सावकत्तं उपगच्छेय्या"ति।

दुतियं पि खो दीघतपस्सी निगण्ठो...पे०...ततीयं पि खो दीघतपस्सी निगण्ठो निगण्ठं नातपुत्तं एतदवोच–"सुतं मेतं, भन्ते, उपालिस्स गहपतिस्स सावकत्तं उपगच्छेय्या"ति।

"हन्दाहं, भन्ते, गच्छामि याव जानामि यदि वा उपालि गहपति समणस्स गोतमस्स सावकत्तं उपगतो यदि वा नो"ति।

"गच्छ त्वं, तपस्सि, जानाहि यदि वा०...नो"ति।

अथ खो दीघतपस्सी निगण्ठो येन उपालिस्स गहपतिस्स निवेसनं तेनुपसङ्कमि। अद्दसा खो दोवारिको दीघतपस्सिं निगण्ठं दूरतो व आगच्छन्तं। दिस्वान दीघतपस्सिं निगण्ठं एतदवोच–"तिट्ठ, भन्ते, मा पाविसि। अज्जतग्गे उपालि०.....आहारिस्सन्ती"ति।

"न मे आवुसो, पिण्डकेन अत्थो"ति वत्वा ततो पटिनिवत्तित्वा येन निगण्ठो नातपुत्तो तेनुपसङ्कमि; उपसङ्कमित्वा निगण्ठं नातपुत्तं नातपुत्तं एतदवोच–"सच्चं एव खो, भन्ते, यं उपालि गहपति समणस्स गोतमस्स सावकत्तं उपगतो। एतं खो ते अहं, भन्ते, नालत्थं न खो मे, भन्ते, रुच्चति यं उपालि गहपति समणस्स गोतमस्स वादं आरोपेय्य। समणो हि, भन्ते गोतमो मायावी आवट्टनिं मायं जानाति याय अञ्ञतित्थियानं सावके आवट्टेती ति। आवट्टो खो ते, भन्ते, उपालि गहपति समणेन गोतमेन आवट्टनिया मायाया"ति।

"अट्ठानं खो एतं, तपस्सि, ०...उपगच्छेय्या ति। हन्द चाहं, तपस्सि, गच्छामि याव चाहं सामं येव जानामि यदि वा उपालि गहपति समणस्स गोतमस्स सावकत्तं उपगतो यदि वा नो ति।

अथ खो निगण्ठो नातपुत्तो महतिया निगण्ठपरिसाय सद्धिं येन उपालिस्स गहपतिस्स निवेसनं तेनुपसङ्कमि। अद्दसा खो दोवारिको निगण्ठं नातपुत्तं दूरतो व आगच्छन्तं। दिस्वान निगण्ठं नातपुत्तं एतदवोच–"तिट्ठ, भन्ते, मा पाविसि। अज्जतग्गे उपालि०....आहरिस्सन्ती"ति।

"तेन हि, सम्म दोवारिक, येन उपालि गहपति तेनुपसङ्कम; उपसङ्कमित्वा उपालिं गहपतिं एवं वदेहि–निगण्ठो, भन्ते, नातपुत्तो महतिया निगण्ठपरिसाय सद्धिं बहिद्वारकोट्ठके ठितो; सो ते दस्सनकामो"ति।

"एवं, भन्ते"ति खो दोवारिको निगण्ठस्स नातपुत्तस्स पटिस्सुत्वा येन उपालि गहपति तेनुपसङ्कमि; उपसङ्कमित्वा उपालिं गहपतिं एतदवोच–"निगण्ठो, भन्ते, नातपुत्तो०....दस्सनकामो" ति।

"तेन हि, सम्म दोवारिक, मज्झिमाय द्वारसालाय आसनानि पञ्ञापेही"ति।

"एवं, भन्ते"ति खो दोवारिको उपालिस्स गहपतिस्स पटिस्सुत्वा मज्झिमाय द्वारसालाय आसनानि पञ्ञापेत्वा येन उपालि गहपति तेनुपसङ्कमि; उपसङ्कमित्वा उपालिं गहपतिं एतदवोच–"पञ्ञत्तानि खो, भन्ते, मज्झिमाय द्वारसालाय आसनानि। यस्सदानि कालं मञ्ञसी"ति।

अथ खो उपालि गहपति येन मज्झिमा द्वारसाला तेनुपसङ्कमि; उपसङ्कमित्वा यं तत्थ आसनं अग्गं च सेट्ठं च उत्तमं च पणीतं च तत्थ सामं निसीदित्वा दोवारिकं आमन्तेसि–"तेन हि, सम्म दोवारिक, येन निगण्ठो नातपुत्तो तेनुपसङ्कमि; उपसङ्कमित्वा निगण्ठं नातपुत्तं एवं वदेहि–'उपालि, भन्ते, गहपति एवमाह–पविस किर, भन्ते, सचे आकङ्खसी"ति।

"एवं, भन्ते"ति खो दोवारिको उपालिस्स गहपतिस्स पटिस्सुत्वा येन निगण्ठो नातपुत्तो० .....आकङ्खसी"ति।

अथ खो निगण्ठो नातपुत्तो महतिया निगण्ठपरिसाय सद्धिं येन मज्झिमा द्वारसाला तेनुपसङ्कमि। अथ खो उपालि गहपति–यं सुदं पुब्बे यतो पस्सति निगण्ठं नातपुत्तं नातपुत्तं दूरतो व आगच्छन्तं

दिस्वान ततो पुच्चुग्गन्त्वा यं तत्थ आसनं अग्गं च सेट्ठं च उत्तमं च पणीत च तं उत्तरासङ्गेन सम्मज्जित्वा परिग्गहेत्वा निसीदापेति सो–दानि यं तत्थ आसनं अग्गं च सेट्ठं च उत्तमं च पणीतं च तत्थ सामं निसीदित्वा निगण्ठं नातपुत्तं एतदवोच–"संविज्जति खो, भन्ते, आसनानि; सचे आकङ्खसि, निसीदा"ति। एवं वुत्ते, निगण्ठो नातपुत्ते उपालिं गहपतिं एतदवोच–"उम्मत्तोसि त्वं, गहपति, दत्तोसि त्वं, गहपति! 'गच्छामहं, भन्ते, समणस्स गोतमस्स वादं आरोपेस्सामी"ति गन्त्वा महतासि वादसङ्घाटेन पटिमुक्को आगतो। सेय्तथापि, गहपति, पुरिसो अण्डहारको गन्त्वा उब्भतेहि अण्डेहि आगच्छेय्य, सेय्यथा वा पन गहपति पुरिसो, अक्खिकहारको गन्त्वा उब्भतेहि आगच्छेय्य, एवमेव खो त्वं, गहपति, 'गच्छामहं, भन्ते, ०.....आगतो। आवट्टोसि खो त्वं, गहपति, समणेन गोतमेन आवट्टनिया मायाया"ति।

"भद्दिका, भन्ते आवट्टनी माया; कल्याणी, भन्ते, आवट्टनी माया; पिया मे, भन्ते, ञातिसालोहिता इमाय आवट्टनिया आवट्टेय्युं; पियानं पि मे अस्स ञातिसालोहितानं दीघरत्तं हिताय सुखाय; सब्बे चे पि भन्ते खत्तिया इमाय आवट्टनिया आवट्टेय्युं सब्बेसानं पिस्स खत्तियानं दीघरत्तं हिताय सुखाय; सब्बे चे पि भन्ते ब्राह्मणा....पे०....वेस्सा.....पे०....सुद्दा इमाय आवट्टनिया आवट्टेय्युं सब्बेसानं पिस्स सुद्दानं दीघरत्तं हिताय सुखाय; सदेवको चे पि, भन्ते लोको समारको सब्रह्मको सस्समणब्राह्मणी पजा सदेवमनुस्सा इमाय आवट्टनिया आवट्टेय्युं सदेवकस्त पिस्स लोकस्स समारकस्स सब्रह्मकस्स सस्समणब्राह्मणिया पजाय सदेवमनुस्साय दीघरत्तं हिताय सुखायाति। तेन हि, भन्ते, उपमं ते करिस्सामि। उपमाय पिधेकच्चे विञ्ञू पुरिसा भासितस्स अत्थं आजानन्ति।

भूतपुब्बं, भन्ते, अञ्ञतरस्स ब्राह्मणस्स जिण्णस्स वुड्ढस्स महल्लकस्स दहरा माणविका पजापती अहोसि अगब्भिनी उपविजञ्ञा। अथ खो, भन्ते, सा माणविका तं ब्राह्मणं एतदवोच–"गच्छ त्वं, ब्राह्मण, आपणा मक्कटच्छापकं किणित्वा आनेहि, यो मे कुमारकस्स कीलापनको भविस्सती' ति। एवं वुत्ते, भन्ते, सो ब्राह्मणो तं माणविकं एतदवोच–'आगमेहि ताव, भोति, याव विजायति। सचे त्वं, भोति कुमारकं विजायिस्सासि, तस्सा ते अहं आपणा मक्कटच्छापकं किणित्वा आनेस्सामि, यो ते कुमारकस्स कीलापनको भविस्सति। सचे पन त्वं, भोति, ०....भविस्सती' ति। दुतियं पि खो, भन्ते, सा माणविका....पे०....ततियं पि खो, भन्ते, सा माणविका तं ब्राह्मणं एतदवोच–'गच्छ त्वं, ब्राह्मण, आपणा मक्कटच्छापकं किणित्वा आनेहि, यो मे कुमारकस्स कीलापनको भविस्सती' ति। अथ खो, भन्ते सो ब्राह्मणो तस्सा माणविकाय सारत्तो पटिबद्धचित्तो आपणा मक्कटच्छापकं किणित्वा आनेत्वा तं माणविकं एतदवोच–'अयं ते, भोति, आपणा मक्कटच्छापको किणित्वा आनीतो, यो ते कुमारकस्स कीलापनको भविस्सती'ति। एवं वुत्ते, भन्ते, सा माणविका तं ब्राह्मणं एतदवोच–"गच्छ त्वं, ब्राह्मण, इम मक्कटच्छापकं आदाय येन रत्तपाणि रजतपुत्तो तेनुपसङ्कम; उपसङ्कमित्वा रत्तपाणिं रजकपुत्तं एवं वदेहि–इच्छामहं सम्म, रत्तपाणि, इमं मक्कटच्छापकं पीतावलेपनं नाम रङ्गजातं रजितं आकोटितपच्चाकोटितं उभतोभागविमट्ठं"ति।

"अथ खो, भन्ते, सो ब्राह्मणो तस्सा माणविकाय सारत्तो पटिबद्धचित्तो तं मक्कटच्छापकं आदाय येन रत्तपाणि रजकपुत्तो तेनुपसङ्कमि; उपसंकमित्वा रत्तपाणिं रजकपुत्तं एतदवोच–"इच्छामहं, रत्तपाणि, इमं०...उभतोभागविमट्ठं"ति। एवं वुत्ते, भन्ते, रत्तपाणि रजकपुत्तो तं ब्राह्मणं एतदवोच–'अयं

खो ते, भन्ते, मक्कटच्छापको रङ्गक्खमो हि खो, नो आकोटनक्खमो, नो विमज्जनक्खमो'ति। एवमेव खो, भन्ते, बालानं निगण्ठानं वादो रङ्गक्खमो हि खो बालानं नो पण्डितानं, नो अनुयोगक्खमो, नो विमज्जनक्खमो। अथ खो, भन्ते, सो ब्राह्मणो अपरेन समयेन नवं दुस्सयुगं आदाय येन रत्तपाणि रजकपुत्तो तेनुपसंकमि; उपसंकमित्वा रत्तपाणि रजकपुत्तं एतदवोच–'इच्छामहं सम्म, रत्तपाणि, इमं नवं दुस्सयुगं पीतावलेपनं० .... उमतोभागविमट्ठं"ति। एवं वुत्ते, भन्ते, रत्तपाणि रजकपुत्तो तं ब्राह्मणं एतदवोच–'इदं खो ते, भन्ते, नवं दुस्सयुगं रङ्गक्खमं चेव आकोटनक्खमं च विमज्जनक्खमं चा' ति। एवमेव खो, भन्ते, तस्स भगवती वादो अरहतो सम्मासम्बुद्धस्सं रङ्गक्खमो चेव पण्डितानं नो बालानं, अनुयोगक्खमो च विमज्जनक्खमो चा ति।

"सराजिका खो, गहपति, परिसा एवं जानाति–'उपालि गहपति निगण्ठस्स नातपुत्तस्स सावको"ति। कस्स तं, गहपति, सावकं धारेमा"ति?

एवं वुत्ते उपालि गहपति उट्ठायासना एकस उत्तरासङ्गं करित्वा येन भगवा तेनञ्जलिं पणामेत्वा निगट्ठं नातपुत्तं एतदवोच–"तेन हि, भन्ते, सुणोहि यस्साहं सावको ति–

"धीरस्स विगतमोहस्स, पभिन्नखीलस्स विजितविजयस्स।
अनीघस्स सुसमचित्तस्स, बुद्धसीलस्स साधुपञ्ञस्स।
वेसमन्तरस्स विमलस्स, भगवतो तस्स सावकोहमस्मि।।"

"कदा सञ्ञूल्हा पन ते, गहपति, इमे समणस्स गोतमस्स वण्णा"ति?

"सेय्यथापि, भन्ते, नानापुप्फानं महापुप्फरासि, तमेनं दक्खो मालाकारो वा मालाकारन्तेवासी वा विचित्तं मालं गन्थेय्य; एवमेव खो, भन्ते सो भगवा अनेकवण्णो अनेकसतवण्णो। को हि, भन्ते, वण्णारहस्स वण्णं न करिस्सती"ति?

"अथ खो निगण्ठस्स नातपुत्तस्स भगवतो सक्कारं असहमानस्स तत्थेव उण्हं लोहितं मुखतो उग्गच्छी"ति।[1]

३

ABHAYA RĀJAKUMĀRA

एवं मे सुतं। एकं समयं भगवा राजगहे विहरति वेलुवने कलन्दकनिवापे। अथ खो अभयो राजकुमारो येन निगण्ठो नातपुत्तो तेनुपसङ्कमि, उपसङ्कमित्वा निगण्ठ नातपुत्तं अभिवादेत्वा एकमन्तं निसीदि। एकमन्तं निसीन्नं खो अभयं राजकुमारो निगण्ठो नातपुत्तो एतदवोच–"एहि त्वं, राजकुमार, समणस्स गोतमस्स वादं आरोपेहि। एवं ते कल्याणो कित्तिसद्दो अब्भुगच्छिस्सत्ति–"अभयेन राजकुमारेन समणस्स गोतमस्स एवं महिद्धिकस्स एवं महानुभावस्स वादो अरोपितो"ति।

---

1. सुत्तपिटके, मज्झिमनिकाय पालि, मज्झिमपण्णासकं, उपालिसुत्तं, 6-1 से 21; पृ० 43 से 60।

"यथा कथं पनाहं, भन्ते, समणस्स गोतमस्स एवं महिद्धिकस्स एवं महानुभावस्स वादं आरोपेस्सामि"ति?

"एहि त्वं, राजकुमार, येन समणो गोतमो तेनुपसङ्कम; उपसङ्कमित्वा समणं गोतमं एवं वदेहि 'भासेय्य नु खो, भन्ते, तथागतो तं वाचं या सा वाचा परेसं अप्पिया अमनाया'ति? सचे ते समणो गोतमो एवं पुट्ठो एवं ब्याकरोति–'भासेय्य, राजकुमार, तथागतो तं वाचं या सा वाचा परेसं अप्पिया अमनापा' ति, तमेनं त्वं एवं वदेय्यासि–'अथ किं चरहि ते, भन्ते, पुथुज्जनेन नानाकरणं? पुथुज्जनो हि तं वाचं भासेय्य या सा वाचा परेसं अप्पिया अमनापा"ति। सचे पन ते समणो गोतमो एवं पुट्ठो एवं ब्याकरोति–'न, राजकुमार, तथागतो तं वाचं भासेय्य या सा वाचा परेसं अप्पिया अमनापा'ति, तमेनं त्वं एवं वदेय्यासि–'अथ किं चरहि ते, भन्ते, देवदत्तो ब्याकतो–आपायिको देवदत्तो, नेरयिको देवदत्तो, कप्पट्ठो देवदत्तो, अतेकिच्छो देवदत्तो ति? ताय च पन ते वाचाय देवदत्तो कुपितो अहोसि अनत्तमनो'ति। इमं खो ते, राजकुमार, समणो गोतमो उभतोकोटिकं पञ्हं पुट्ठो समानो नेव सक्खिति उग्गिलितुं न सक्खिति ओगिलितुं। सेय्यथापि नाम पुरिस्स अयोसिंघाटकं कण्ठे विलग्गं, सो नेव सक्कुणेय्य उग्गिलितुं न सक्कुणेय्य ओगिलितुं; एवमेव खो ते, राजकुमार समणो गोतमो इमं उभतोकोटिकं पञ्हं पुट्ठो समानो नेव सक्खिति उग्गिलितं न सक्खिति ओगिलितुं"ति।

"एवं, भन्ते"ति खो अभयो राजकुमारो निगण्ठस्स नातुपुत्तस्स पटिस्सुत्वा उट्ठायासना निगण्ठं नातपुत्तं अभिवादेत्वा पदक्खिणं कत्वा येन भगवा तेनपुसङ्कमि; उपसङ्कमित्वा भगवन्तं अभिवादेत्वा एकमन्तं निसीदि।

एकमन्तं निसिन्नस्स खो अभयस्स राजकुमारस्स सुरियं उल्लोकेत्वा एतदहोसि–"अकालो खो अज्ज भगवतो वादं आरोपेतुं। स्वे दानाहं सके निवेसने भगवती वादं आरोपेस्सामि"ति। भगवन्तं एतदवोच–"अधिवासेतु मे, भन्ते, भगवा स्वातनाय अत्तचतुत्थो भत्तं"ति। अधिवासेसि भगवा तुण्हीभावेन। अथ खो अभयो राजकुमारो भगवतो अधिवासनं विदित्वा उट्ठायासना भगवन्तं अभिवादेत्वा पदक्खिणं कत्वा पक्कामि। अथ खो भगवा तस्सा रत्तिया अच्चयेन पुब्बण्हसमयं निवासेत्वा पत्तचीवरमादाय येन अभयस्स राजकुमारस्स निवेसनं तेनुपसङ्कमि; उपसङ्कमित्वा पञ्ञत्ते आसने निसीदि। अथ खो अभयो राजकुमारो भगवन्तं पणीतेन खादनीयेन भोजनीयेन सहत्था सन्तप्पेसि सम्पवारेसि। अथ खो अभयो राजकुमारो भगवन्तं भुत्ताविं ओनीतपत्तपाणिं अञ्ञतरं नीचं आसनं गहेत्वा एकमन्तं निसीदि।

एकमन्तं निसिन्नो खो अभयो राजकुमारो भगवन्तं एतदवोच–"भासेय्य नु खो, भन्ते, तथागतो तं वाचं या सा वाचा परेसं अप्पिया अमनापा"ति?

"न ख्वेत्थ, राजकुमार, एकंसेना"ति।

"एत्थ, भन्ते, अनस्सुं निगण्ठा"ति।

"किं पन त्वं, राजकुमार, एवं वदेसि–"एत्थ, भन्ते, अनस्सु निगण्ठा"ति?

"इधाहं, भन्ते, येन निगण्ठो नातपुत्तो तेनुपसंकमि, उपसङ्कमित्वा निगण्ठं नातपुत्तं अभिवादेत्वा

एकमन्तं निसीदि। एकमन्तं निसिन्नं खो मं, भन्ते, निगण्ठो नातपुत्तो एतदवोच–"एहि त्वं, राजकुमार, समणस्स गोतमस्स वादं आरोपेहि। एवं ते कल्याणो कित्तिसद्दो अब्भुग्गाच्छस्सति–अभयेन राजकुमारेन समणस्स गोतमस्स एवं महिद्धिकस्स एवं महानुभावस्स वादो आरोपितो' ति। एवं वुत्ते, अहं, भन्ते, निगण्ठं नातपुत्तं एतदवोचं–'यथा कथं पनाहं, भन्ते, समणस्स गोतमस्स एवं महिद्धिकस्स एवं महानुभावस्स वादं आरोपेस्सामी'ति?

'एहि त्वं, राजकुमार, येन समणो गोतमो तेनुपसङ्कम' उपसङ्कमित्वा समणं गोतमं एवं वदेहि–भासेय्य नु खो, भन्ते, तथागतो तं वाचं या सा वाचा परेसं अप्पिया अमनापा ति? सचे ते समणो गोतमो एवं पुट्ठो एवं ब्याकरोति–भासेय्य, राजकुमार, तथागतो तं वाचं या सा वाचा परेसं अप्पिया अमनापा ति, तमेनं त्वं एवं वदेय्यासि–अथ किं चरहि ते, भन्ते, पुथुज्जनेन नानाकरणं? पुथुज्जनो पि हि तं वाचं भासेय्यं या सा वाचा परेसं अप्पिया अमनापा ति। सचे पन ते समणो गोतमो एवं पुट्ठो एवं ब्याकरोति–न, राजकुमार, तथागतो तं वाचं भासेय्य या सा वाचा परेसं अप्पिया अमनापा ति, तमेनं त्वं एवं वदेय्यासि–अथ किं चरहि ते, भन्ते, देवदत्तो ब्याकतो-आपायिको देवदत्तो, नेरयिको देवदत्तो, कप्पट्ठो देवदत्तो, अतेकिच्छो देवदत्तो ति? ताय च पन ते वाचाय देवदत्तो कुपितो अहोसि अनत्तमनो ति। इमं खो ते, राजकुमार, समणो गोतमो उभतोकोटिकं पञ्हं पुट्ठो समानो नेव सक्खिति उग्गिलितुं न सक्खिति ओगिलितुं। सेय्यथापि नाम पुरिसस्स अयोसिङ्घाटकं कण्ठे विलग्गं, सो नेव सक्कुणेय्य उग्गिलितुं न सक्कुणेय्य ओगिलितुं; एवमेव खो ते, राजकुमार, समणो गोतमो इमं उभतोकोटिकं पञ्हं पुट्ठो समानो नेव सक्खिति उग्गिलितुं न सक्खिति ओगिलितुं"ति।

Anukampāya appiyaṁ pi bhāseyya

तेन खो पन समयेन दहरो कुमरो मन्दो उत्तानसेय्यको अभयस्स राजकुमारस्स अङ्के निसिन्नो होति। अथ खो भगवा अभयं राजकुमारं एतदवोच–"तं किं मञ्ञसि, राजकुमार, सचायं कुमारो तुय्हं वा पमादमन्वाय धातिया वा पमादमन्वाय वा कट्ठं वा कठलं वा मुखे आहरेय्य, किन्ति नं करेय्यासी"ति?

"आहरेय्यस्साहं, भन्ते! सचे, भन्ते, न सक्कुणेय्यं आदिकेनेव आहतुं, वामेन हत्थेन सीसं परिग्गहेत्वा दक्खिणेन हत्थेन वङ्कङ्गुलिं करित्वा सलोहितं पि आहरेय्यं। तं किस्स हेतु? अत्थि मे, भन्ते, कुमारे अनुकम्पा"ति।

"एवमेव खो, राजकुमार, यं तथागतो वाचं जानाति अभूतं अतच्छं अनत्थसंहितं सा च परेसं अप्पिया अमनापा, न तं तथागतो वाचं भासति। यं पि तथागतो वाचं जानाति भूतं तच्छं अनत्थसंहितं सा च परेसं अप्पिया अमनापा, तं पि तथागतो वाचं न भासति। यं च खो तथागतो वाचं जानाति भूतं तच्छं अत्थसंहितं सा च परेसं अप्पिया अमनापा, तत्र कालञ्ञू तथागतो होति तस्सा वाचाय वेय्याकरणाय। यं तथागतो वाचं जानाति अभूतं अतच्छं अनत्थसंहितं सा च परेसं पिया मनापा, न तं तथागतो वाचं भासति। यं पि तथागतो वाचं जानाति भूतं तच्छं अनत्थसंहितं सा च परेसं पिया मनापा तं पि तथागतो वाचं न भासति। यं च तथागतो वाचं जानाति भूतं

तच्छं अत्थसंहितं सा च परेसं पिया मनापा, तत्र कालञ्ञू तथागतो होति तस्सा वाचाय वेय्याकरणाय। तं किस्स हेतु? अत्थि, राजकुमार, तथागतस्स सत्तेसु अनुकम्पा"ति।

Nanu thānasovetaṁ Tathāgataṁ patibhāti

"ये मे, भन्ते, खत्तियपण्डिता पि ब्राह्मणपण्डिता पि गहपति पण्डिता पि समणपण्डिता पि पञ्हं अभिसङ्खरित्वा तथागतं उपसङ्कमित्वा पुच्छन्ति, पुब्बेव नु खो, भन्ते, भगवतो चेतसो परिवितक्कितं होति 'ये मं उपसङ्कमित्वा एवं पुच्छिस्सन्ति तेसाहं एवं पुट्ठो एवं व्याकरिस्सामी' ति, उदाहु ठानसोवेतं तथागतं पटिभाती"ति?

"तेन हि, राजकुमार तञ्ञेवेत्थ पटिपुच्छिस्सामि, यथा ते खमेय्य तथा नं ब्याकरेय्यासि। तं किं मञ्ञसि, राजकुमार, कुसलो त्वं रथस्स अङ्गपच्चङ्गानं"ति?

"एवं, भन्ते, कुसलो अहं रथस्स अङ्गपच्चङ्गानं"ति।

"तं किं मञ्ञसि, राजकुमार, ये तं उपसङ्कमित्वा एवं पुच्छेय्युं–'किं नामिदं रथस्स अङ्गपच्चङ्ग"ति? पुब्बेव नु खो ते एतं चेतसो परिवितविकतं अस्स 'ये मं उपसङ्कमित्वा एवं पुच्छिस्सन्ति तेसाहं एवं पुट्ठो एवं व्याकरिस्सामी'ति, उदाहु ठानसोवेतं पटिभासेय्या"ति?

"अहं हि भन्ते, रथिको सञ्ञातो कुसलो रथस्स अङ्गपच्चङ्गानं! सब्बानि मे रथस्स अङ्गपच्चङ्गानि सुविदितानि। ठानसोवेतं मं पटिभासेय्या"ति।

"एवमेव खो, राजकुमार, ये ते खत्तियपण्डिता पि ब्राह्मणपण्डिता पि गहपतिपण्डिता पि समणपण्डिता पि पञ्हं अभिसङ्खरित्वा तथागतं उपसङ्कमित्वा पुच्छन्ति, ठानसोवेतं तथागतं पटिभाति तं किस्स हेतु? सा हि, राजकुमार, तथागतस्स धम्मधातु सुप्पटिविद्धा यस्सा घम्मधातुया सुप्पटिविद्धत्ता ठानसोवेतं तथागतं पटिभाती"ति।

"एवं वुत्ते, अभयो राजकुमारो भगवन्तं एतदवोच–अभिक्कन्तं, भन्ते, अभिक्कन्तं, भन्ते ....पे०....अज्जतग्गे पाणुपेतं सरणं गतं"ति।[1]

"पच्छिमे च भवे दानि गिरिब्बजपुरुत्तमे।
रञ्ञोहं बिम्बिसारस्स पुत्तो नामेन चामयो।।
"पापमित्तवसं गन्त्वा, निगण्ठेन विमोहितो।
पेसितो नाटपुत्तेन, बुद्धसेट्ठमुपेच्चहं।।
"पुच्छित्वा निपुणं पुञ्हं, सुत्वा व्याकरणुत्तमं।
पब्बजित्वान नचिरं, अरहत्तमपापुणिं।।
कित्तयित्वा जिनवरं, कित्तितो होमि सब्बदा।

---

1. सुत्तपिटके, मज्झिमनिकाय पालि, मज्झिमपण्णासकं, अभयराजकुमार सुत्तं 2-8-1 से 3, पृ० 67 से 71।

सुगन्धदेहवदनो, आसि मुखसमप्पितो।।
"तिक्खहासलहुपञ्ञो, महापञ्ञो तथेवहं।
विचित्तपटिमानो च, तस्स कम्मस्स वाहसा।।
"अमित्थवित्वा पदुमूलराहं, पसन्नचित्तो असमं सयम्भूं।
न गच्छि कप्पानि अपायभूमिं सतं सहस्सानि वलेन तस्स।।"[1]

४

KARMA-CARCĀ

Nigaṇṭhānaṁ dukhanijjarāvādo

एवं मे सुतं। एकं समयं भगवा सक्केसु विहरति देवदहं नाम सक्यानं निगमो। तत्र खो भगवा भिक्खू आमन्तेति–"भिक्खवो"ति। "भदन्ते"ति ते भिक्खू भगवतो पच्चस्सोसुं। भगवा एतदवोच–"सन्ति, भिक्खवे, एके समणब्राह्मणा एवंवादिनो एवंदिट्ठिनो–'यं किञ्चायं पुरिसपुग्गलो पटिसंवेदेति सुखं वा दुक्खं वा अदुक्खमसुखं वा, सब्बं तं पुब्बेकतहेतु। इति पुराणानं कम्मानं तपसा ब्यन्तीभावा, नवानं कम्मानं अकरणा, आयतिं अनवस्सवो; आयतिं अनवस्सवा कम्मक्खयो; कम्मक्खया दुक्खक्खयो; दुक्खक्खया वेदनाक्खयो; वेदनाक्खया सब्बं दुक्खं निज्जिण्णं भविस्सती' ति। एवंवादिनो, भिक्खवे, निगण्ठा। एवंवादाहं, भिक्खवे, निगण्ठे उपसङ्कमित्वा एवं वदामि–'सच्चं किर तुम्हे, आवुसो निगण्ठा, एवंवादिनो एवंदिट्ठिनो–यं किञ्चायं पुरिसपुग्गलो पटिसंवेदेति सुखं वा दुक्खं वा अदुक्खमसुखं वा, सब्बं तं पुब्बेकतहेतु...पे०...वेदनाक्खया सबबं दुक्खं निज्जिण्णं भविस्सती'ति? ते च मे, भिक्खवे, निगण्ठा एवं पुट्ठा 'आमा' ति पटिजानन्ति। त्याहं एवं वदामि–'किं पन तुम्हे, आवुसो निगण्ठा, जानाथ–अहुवम्हे व मयं पुब्बे, न नाहुवम्हा'ति?

'नो हिदं आवुसो'।

'किं पन तुम्हे, आवुसो निगण्ठा, जानाथ–अकरम्हे व मयं पुब्बे पापकम्मं, न नाकरम्हा'ति?

'नो हिदं, आवुसो'।

'किं पन तुम्हे, आवुसो निगण्ठा, जानाथ–एवरूपं वा एवरूपं वा पापकम्मं अकरम्हा'ति?

'नो हिदं, आवुसो'।

किं पन तुम्हे, आवुसो निगण्ठा, जानाथ–एत्तकं वा दुक्खं निज्जिण्णं, एत्तकं वा दुक्खं निज्जीरेतब्बं, एत्तकम्हि वा दुक्खे निज्जिण्णे सब्बं दुक्खं निज्जिण्णं भविस्सती'ति?

'नो हिदं, आवुसो'।

किं पन तुम्हे, आवुसो निगण्ठा, जानाथ–दिट्ठेव धम्मे अकुसलानं धम्मानं पहानं, कुसलानं धम्मानं उपसम्पदं ति?

1. सुत्तपिटके, खुद्दक निकाये थेरापदान पालि (2), भद्दियवग्गो, अभयत्थेरअपदानं, 55-7-216 से 221; पृ० 155।

'नो हिदं, आवुसो'।

'इति किर तुम्हे, आवुसो निगण्ठा, न जानाथ–अहुवम्हे व मयं पुब्बे न नाहुवम्हा ति, ०....कुसलानं धम्मानं उपसम्पदं। एवं सन्ते आयस्मन्तानं निगण्ठानं न कल्लमस्स वेय्याकरणाय–यं किञ्चायं पुरिसपुग्गलो पटिसंवेदेति सुखं वा दुक्खं वा अदुक्खमसुखं वा, सब्बं तं पुब्बेकतहेतु। इति पुराणानं कम्मानं तपसा ब्यन्तीभावा, नवानं कम्मानं अकरणा, आयतिं अनवस्सवो, आयतिं अनवस्सया कम्मक्खयो; कम्मक्खया दुक्खक्खयो; दुक्खक्खया वेदनाक्खयो; वेदनाक्खया सब्बं दुक्खं निज्जिण्णं भविस्सती' ति।०...।

"सेय्यथापि, आवुसो निगण्ठा, पुरिसो सल्लेन विद्धो अस्स सविसेन गाल्हूपलेपनेन; सो सल्लस्स पि वेधनहेतु दुक्खा तिब्बा कटुका वेदना वेदियेय्य। तस्स मित्तामच्चा ञातिसालोहिता भिसक्कं सल्लकत्तं उपट्ठापेय्युं। तस्स सो भिसक्को सल्लकत्तो सत्थेन वणमुखं परिकन्तेय्य; सो सत्थेन पि वणमुखस्स परिकन्तनहेतु दुक्खा तिब्बा कटुका वेदना वेदियेय्य। तस्स सो भिसक्को सल्लकत्तो एसनिया सल्लं एसेय्य; सो एसनिया पि सल्लस्स एसनाहेतु दुक्खा तिब्बा कटुका वेदना वेदियेय्य। तस्स सो भिसक्को सल्लकत्तो सल्लं अब्बुहेय्य; सो सल्लस्स पि अब्बुहनहेतु दुक्खा तिब्बा कटुका वेदना वेदियेय्य। तस्स सो भिसक्को सल्लकत्तो अगदङ्गारं वणमुखे ओदहेय्य; सो अगदङ्गारस्स पि वणमुखे ओदहनहेतु दुक्खा तिब्बा कटुका वेदना वेदियेय्य। सो अपरेन समयेन रूल्हेन वणेन सञ्छविना अरोगो अस्स सुखी सेरी सयंवसी येनकामङ्गमो। तस्स एवमस्स–अहं खो पुब्बे सल्लेन विद्धो अहोसिं सविसेन गाल्हूपलेपनेन। सोहं सल्लस्स पि वेधनहेतु दुक्खा तिब्बा कटुका वेदना वेदियिं। ०...। सोम्हि एतरहि रूल्हेन वणेन सञ्छविना अरोगो सुखी सेरी सयंवसी येनकामङ्गमो ति। एवमेव खो, आवुसो निगण्ठा, सचे तुम्हे जानेय्याथ–अहुवम्हे व मयं पुब्बे न नाहुवम्हा ति, ०...। यस्मा च खो तुम्हे, आवुसो निगण्ठा, न जानाथ–अहुवम्हे व मयं पुब्बे न नाहुवम्हा ति। ०...।

"एवं वुत्ते, भिक्खवे, ते निगण्ठा मं एतदवोचुं–'निगण्ठो, आवुसो, नाटपुत्तो सब्बञ्ञू सब्बदस्सावी, अपरिसेसं ञाणदस्सनं पटिजानाति, चरतो च मे तिट्ठतो च सुत्तस्स च जागरस्स च सततं समितं ञाणदस्सनं पच्चुपट्ठितं ति। सो एवमाह–अत्थि खो वो, आवुसो निगण्ठा, पुब्बे व पापकम्मं कतं, तं इमाय कटुकाय दुक्करकारिकाय निज्जीरेथ, यं पनेत्थ एतरहि कायेन संवुता वाचाय संवुता मनसा संवुता तं आयतिं पापकम्मस्स अकरणं। इति पुराणानं कम्मानं तपसा ब्यन्तीभावा, नवानं कम्मानं अकरणा, आयतिं अनवस्सवो; आयतिं अनवस्सवा कम्मखयो; कम्मक्खया दुक्खक्खयो; दुक्खक्खया वेदनाक्खयो; वेदनाक्खया सब्बं दुक्खं निज्जिण्णं भविस्सती ति। तं च पनम्हाकं रुच्चति चेव खमति च, तेन चम्हा अत्तमना'ति।

Afalo upakkamo afalaṁ padhānaṁ

"एवं वुत्ते अहं, भिक्खवे ते निगण्ठे एतदवोचं–'पञ्च खो इमे, आवुसो निगण्ठा, धम्मा दिट्ठेव धम्मे द्विधाविपाका। कतमे पञ्च? सद्धा, रुचि, अनुस्सवो, आकारपरिवितक्को, दिट्ठिनिज्झानक्खन्ति–इमे खो, आवुसो निगण्ठा, पञ्च धम्मा दिट्ठेव धम्मे द्विधाविपाका। तत्रायस्मन्तानं

निगण्ठानं का अतीतंसे सत्थरि सद्धा का रुचि को अनुस्सवो को आकारपरिवितक्को का दिट्ठिनिज्झानक्खन्ती' ति। एवंवादी खो अहं, भिक्खवे, निगण्ठेसु न कञ्चि सहधम्मिकं वादपटिहारं समनुपस्सामि।

"पुन च पराहं, भिक्खवे, ते निगण्ठे एवं वदामि–तं किं मञ्ञथ, आवुसो निगण्ठा, यस्मिं वो समये तिब्बो उपक्कमो होति तिब्बं पधानं, तिब्बा तस्मिं समये ओपक्कमिका दुक्खा तिब्बा कटुका वेदना वेदियेथ; यस्मिं पन वो समये न तिब्बा उपक्कमो होति न तिब्बं पधानं, न तिब्बा तस्मिं समये ओपक्कमिका दुक्खा तिब्बा कटुका वेदना वेदियेथा'ति?

'यस्मिं नो, आवुसो गोतम, समये तिब्बो उपक्कमो होति तिब्बं पधानं, तिब्बा तस्मिं समये ओपक्कमिका दुक्खा तिब्बा कटुका वेदना वेदियाम; यस्मिं पन नो समये न तिब्बो उपक्कमो होति न तिब्बं पधानं, न तिब्बा तस्मिं समये ओपक्कमिका दुक्खा तिब्बा कटुका वेदना वेदियामा'ति।

'इति किर, आवुसो निगण्ठा, यस्मिं वो समये तिब्बो उपक्कमो......वेदना वेदियेथ। एवं सन्ते आयस्मन्तानं निगण्ठानं न कल्लमस्स वेय्याकरणाय–यं किञ्चायं पुरिसपुग्गलो पटिसंवेदेति सुखं वा दुक्खं वा अदुक्खमसुखं वा, सब्बं तं पुब्बेकतहेतु...पे०...वेदनाक्खया सब्बं दुक्खं निज्जिणं भविस्सती ति। सचे, आवुसो निगण्ठा, यस्मिं वो समये तिब्बो उपक्कमो०.......भविस्सती ति। यस्मा च खो, आवुसो निगण्ठा, यस्मिं वो समये तिब्बो उपक्कमो०......वेदना वेदयमाना अविज्जा अञ्ञाणा सम्मोहा विपच्चेथ–यं किञ्चायं पुरिसपुग्गलो पटिसंवेदेति सुखं वा दुक्खं वा अदुक्खमसुखं वा सब्बं तं पुब्बेकतहेतु...पे०...वेदनाक्खया सब्बं दुक्खं निज्जिण्णं भविस्सती' ति। एवंवादी पि खो अहं, भिक्खवे, निगण्ठेसु न कञ्चि, सहधम्मिकं वादपटिहारं समनुपस्सामि।

"पुन च पराहं, भिक्खवे, ते निगण्ठे एवं वदामि–'तं किं मञ्ञथावुसो निगण्ठा, यमिदं कम्मं दिट्ठधम्मवेदनीयं तं उपक्कमेन वा पधानेन वा सम्परायवेदनीयं होतु ति लब्भमेतं"ति?

'नो हिदं, आवुसो'।

'यं पनिदं कम्मं सम्परायवेदनीयं तं उपक्कमेन वा पधानेन वा दिट्ठधम्मवेदनीयं होतू ति लब्भमेतं'ति?

'नो हिदं, आवुसो'।

'तं किं मञ्ञथावुसो निगण्ठा, यमिदं कम्मं सुखवेदनीयं तं उपक्कमेन वा पधानेन वा दुक्खवेदनीयं होतू ति लब्भमेतं'ति?

'नो हिदं, आवुसो'।

'यं पनिदं कम्मं दुक्खवेदनीयं तं उपक्कमेन वा पधानेन वा सुखवेदनीयं होतू ति लब्भमेतं' ति?

'नो हिदं, आवुसो'।

'तं किं मञ्ञथावुसो निगण्ठा, यमिदं कम्मं परिपक्कवेदनीयं तं उपक्कमेन वा पधानेन वा अपरिपक्कवेदनीयं होतू ति लब्भमेतं'ति।

'नो हिदं, आवुसो'।

'यं पनिदं कम्मं अपरिपक्कवेदनीयं तं उपक्कमेन वा पधानेन वा परिपक्कवेदनीयं होतू ति लब्भमेतं'ति?

'नो हिदं, आवुसो'।

'तं किं मञ्ञथावुसो निगण्ठा, यमिदं कम्मं बहुवेदनीयं तं उपक्कमेन वा पधानेन वा अप्पवेदनीयं होतू ति लब्भमेतं'ति?

'नो हिदं, आवुसो'।

'यं पनिदं कम्मं अप्पवेदनीयं तं उपक्कमेन वा पधानेन वा बहुवेदनीयं होतू ति लब्भमेतं' ति?

'नो हिदं, आवुसो'।

'तं किं मञ्ञथावुसो निगण्ठा, यमिदं कम्मं सवेदनीयं तं उपक्कमेन वा पधानेन वा अवेदनीयं होतू ति लब्भमेतं'ति।

'नो हिदं, आवुसो'।

'यं पनिदं कम्मं अवेदनीयं तं उपक्कमेन वा पधानेन वा सवेदनीयं होतू ति लब्भमेतं'ति?

'नो हिदं, आवुसो'।

'इति किर, आवुसो निगण्ठा, यमिदं कम्मं दिट्ठधम्मवेदनीयं तं उपक्कमेन वा पधानेन वा सम्परायवेदनीयं होतू ति अलब्भमेतं, यं पनिदं०........एवं सन्ते आयस्मन्तानं निगण्ठानं अफलो उपक्कमो होति, अफलं पधानं'।

"एवंवादी, भिक्खवे, निगण्ठा। एवंवादीनं, भिक्खवे, निगण्ठानं दस सहधम्मिका वादानुवादा गारय्हं ठानं आगच्छन्ति"।

"सचे, भिक्खवे, सत्ता पुब्बेकतहेतु सुखदुक्खं पटिसंवेदेन्ति; अद्धा, भिक्खवे, निगण्ठा पुब्बे दुक्कटकम्मकारिनो यं एतरहि एवरूपा दुक्खा तिब्बा कटुका वेदना वेदियन्ति। सचे, भिक्खवे, सत्ता इस्सरनिम्मानहेतु सुखदुक्खं पटिसंवेदेन्ति; अद्धा, भिक्खवे, निगण्ठा पापकेन इस्सरेन निम्मिता यं एतरहि एवरूपा दुक्खा तिब्बा कटुका वेदना वेदियन्ति। सचे, भिक्खवे, सत्ता सङ्गतिभावहेतु सुखदुक्खं पटिसंवेदेन्ति; अद्धा, भिक्खवे, निगण्ठा पापसङ्गतिका यं एतरहि एवरूपा दुक्खा तिब्बा कटुका वेदना वेदियन्ति। सचे, भिक्खवे, सत्ता अभिजातिहेतु सुखदुक्खं पटिसंवेदेन्ति; अद्धा, भिक्खवे, निगण्ठा पापाभिजातिका यं एतरहि एवरूपा दुक्खा तिब्बा कटुका वेदना वेदियन्ति। सचे, भिक्खवे, सत्ता दिट्ठधम्मूपक्कमहेतु सुखदुक्खं पटिसंवेदेन्ति; अद्धा, भिक्खवे, निगण्ठा एवरूपा दिट्ठधम्मूपक्कमा यं एतरहि एवरूपा दुक्खा तिब्बा कटुका वेदना वेदियन्ति।

"सचे, भिक्खवे, सत्ता पुब्बेकतहेतु सुखदुक्खं पटिसंवेदेन्ति, गारय्हा निगण्ठा; नो चे सत्ता पुब्बेकतहेतु सुखदुक्खं पटिसंवेदेन्ति, गारय्हा निगण्ठा। सचे, भिक्खवे, सत्ता इस्सरनिम्मानहेतु ०...एवंवादी, भिक्खवे, निगण्ठा। एवंवादीनं, भिक्खवे, निगण्ठानं इमे दस सहधम्मिका वादानुवादा गारय्हं ठानं आगच्छन्ति। एवं खो, भिक्खवे, अफलो उपक्कमो होति, अफलं पधानं।

Saphalo upakkamo saphalaṁ padhānaṁ

"कथं च, भिक्खवे, सफलो उपक्कमो होति, सफलं पधानं? इध, भिक्खवे, भिक्खु न हेव अनद्धभूतं अत्तानं दुक्खेन, अद्धभावेति, धम्मिकं च सुखं न परिच्चजति, तस्मिं च सुखे अनधिमुच्छितो होति। सो एवं पजानाति–इमस्स खो मे दुक्खनं निदानस्स सङ्खारं पदहतो सङ्खारप्पधाना विरागो होति, इम्मस्स पन मे दुक्खनिदानस्स अज्झुपेक्खतो उपेक्खं भावयतो विरागो होती" ति।०....

"सेय्यथापि, भिक्खवे, पुरिसो इत्थिया सारत्तो पटिबद्धचित्तो तिब्बच्छन्दो तिब्बापेक्खो। सो तं इत्थिं पस्सेय्य अञ्ञेन पुरिसेन सद्धिं सन्तिट्ठन्ति सल्लपन्तिं सञ्जग्घन्तिं संहसन्तिं। तं किं मञ्ञथ, भिक्खवे, अपि नु तस्स पुरिसस्स अमुं इत्थिं दिस्वा अञ्ञेन पुरिसेन सद्धिं सन्तिट्ठन्तिं सल्लपन्तिं सञ्जग्घन्तिं संहसन्तिं उप्पज्जेय्युं सोकपरिदेवदुक्खदोमनस्सूपायासा"ति?

"एवं भन्ते"।

"तं किस्स हेतु"?

"अमु हि, भन्ते, पुरिसो अमुस्सा इत्थिया सारत्तो०...।"

"अथ खो, भिक्खवे, तस्स पुरिसस्स एवमस्स–'अहं खो अमुस्सा इत्थिया सारत्तो०... यन्नूनाहं यो मे अमुस्सा इत्थिया छन्दरागो तं पजहेय्यं'ति। सो यो अमुस्सा इत्थिया छन्दरागो तं पजहेय्य। सो तं इत्थिं पस्सेय्य अपरेन समयेन अञ्ञेन पुरिसेन सद्धिं सन्तिट्ठन्तिं सल्लपन्तिं सञ्जग्घन्तिं संहसन्तिं। तं किं मञ्ञथ, भिक्खवे, अपि नु तस्स पुरिसस्स अमुं इत्थिं दिस्वा अञ्ञेन०....संहसन्तिं उप्पज्जेय्युं सोकपरिवदेवदुक्खदोमनस्सूपायासा"ति?

"नो हेतं, भन्ते"।

"तं किस्स हेतु"?

"अमु हि, भन्ते, पुरिसो अमुस्सा इत्थिया वीतरागो। तस्मा तं इत्थिं दिस्वा०.....।"

"एवमेव खो, भिक्खवे, भिक्खु न हेव अनद्धभूतं अत्तानं दुक्खेन अद्धभावेति। ०....।"

"पुन च परं, भिक्खवे, भिक्खु इति पटिसञ्चिक्खति–'यथासुखं खो मे विहरतो अकुसला धम्मा अभिवड्ढन्ति, कुसला धम्मा परिहायन्ति; दुक्खाय पन मे अत्तानं पदहतो अकुसला धम्मा परिहायन्ति, कुसला धम्मा अभिवड्ढन्ति। यन्नूनाहं दुक्खाय अत्तानं पदहेय्यं' ति। सो दुक्खाय अत्तानं पदहति। तस्स दुक्खाय अत्तानं पदहतो अकुसला धम्मा परिहायन्ति कुसला धम्मा अभिवड्ढन्ति। सो न अपरेन समयेन दुक्खाय अत्तानं पदहति। तं किस्स हेतु? यस्स हि सो, भिक्खवे, भिक्खु

अत्थाय दुक्खाय अत्तानं पदहेय्य स्वास्स अत्थो अभिनिप्फन्नो होति। तस्मा न अपरेन समयेन दुक्खाय अत्तानं पदहति। सेय्यथापि, भिक्खवे, उसुकारो तेजनं द्वीसु अलातेसु आतापेति परितापेति उजुं करोति कम्मनियं। यतो खो, भिक्खवे, उसुकारस्स तेजनं द्वीसु अलातेसु आतापितं होति ०....न सो तं अपरेन समयेन उसुकारो तेजनं द्वीसु अलातेसु आतापेति०....तं किस्स हेतु? यस्स हि सो, भिक्खवे, अत्थाय उसुकारो तेजनं द्वीसु अलातेसु आतापेय्य०.....स्वास्स अत्थो अभिनिप्फन्नो होति। तस्मा न अपरेन समयेन उसुकारोते जनं द्वीसु अलातेसु आतापेति०....एवमेव खो, भिक्खवे, भिक्खु इति पटिसञ्चिक्खति–'यथासुखं खो मे विहरतो अकुसला धम्मा अभिवड्ढन्ति०....स्वास्स अत्थो अभिनिप्फन्नो होति। तस्मा न अपरेन समयेन दुक्खाय अत्तानं पदहति। एवं पि, भिक्खवे, सफलो उपक्कमो होति, सफलं पधानं। ०....

"सचे, भिक्खवे, सत्ता पुब्बेकतहेतु सुखदुक्खं पटिसंवेदेन्ति; अद्धा, भिक्खवे, तथागतो पुब्बे सुकतमम्मकारी यं एतरहि एवरूपा अनासवा सुखा वेदना वेदेति। सचे, भिक्खवे, सत्ता इस्सरनिम्मानहेतु सुखदुक्खं पटिसंवेदेन्ति; अद्धा, भिक्खवे, तथागतो भद्दकेन इस्सरेन निम्मितो यं एतरहि एवरूपा अनासवा सुखा वेदना वेदेति। सचे, भिक्खवे, सत्ता सङ्गतिमावहेतु सुखदुक्खं पटिसंवेदेन्ति; अद्धा, भिक्खवे, तथागतो कल्याणसङ्गतिको यं एतरहि एवरूपा अनासवा सुखा वेदना वेदेति। सचे भिक्खवे, सत्ता अभिजातिहेतु सुखदुक्खं पटिसंवेदेन्ति; अद्धा, भिक्खवे, तथागतो कल्याणभिजातिको यं एतरहि एवरूपा अनासवा सुखा वेदना वेदेति। सचे, भिक्खवे, सत्ता दिट्ठधम्मूपक्कमहेतु सुखदुक्खं पटिसंवेदेन्ति; अद्धा, भिक्खवे, तथागतो कल्याणदिट्ठधम्मूपक्कमो यं एतरहि एवरूपा अनासवा सुखा वेदना वेदेति।

"सचे, भिक्खवे, सत्ता पुब्बेकतहेतु सुखदुक्खं पटिसंवेदेन्ति, पासंसो तथागतो; नो चे सत्ता पुब्बेकतहेतु सुखदुक्खं पटिसंवेदेन्ति, पासंसो तथागतो। सचे, भिक्खवे, सत्ता इस्सरनिम्मानहेतु सुखदुक्खं पटिसंवेदेन्ति, पासंसो तथागतो; नो चे सत्ता इस्सरनिम्मानहेतु सुखदुक्खं पटिसंवेदेन्ति, पासंसो तथागतो। सचे, भिक्खवे, सत्ता सङ्गतिभावहेतु सुखदुक्खं पटिसंवेदेन्ति, पासंसो तथागतो; नो चे सत्ता सङ्गतिभावहेतु सुखदुक्खं पटिसंवेदेन्ति, पासंसो तथागतो; सचे, भिक्खवे, सत्ता अभिजातिहेतु सुखदुक्खं पटिसंवेदेन्ति, पासंसो तथागतो; नो चे सत्ता अभिजातिहेतु सुखदुक्खं पटिसंवेदेन्ति, पासंसो तथागते। सचे, भिक्खवे, सत्ता दिट्ठधम्मूपक्कमहेतु सुखदुक्खं पटिसंवेदेन्ति, पासंसो तथागतो; नो चे सत्ता दिट्ठधम्मूपक्कमहेतु सुखदुक्खं पटिसंवेदेन्ति, पासंसो तथागतो। एवंवादी, भिक्खवे, तथागता। एवंवादीनं; भिक्खवे तथागतानं इमे दस सहधम्मिका पासंसट्ठाना आगच्छन्ती'ति।

इदमवोच भगवा। अत्तमना ते भिक्खू भगवतो भासितं अभिनन्दुं ति।[1]

---

1. सुत्तपिटके, मज्झिमनिकाय पालि, उपरिपण्णासकं, देवदह सुत्तं, 3-1-1 सं० 4, पृ० 1 से 20।

९

NIRGRANTHON KĀ TAPA

Appassāda kāma bahudukkha

एवं मे सुतं। एकं समयं भगवा सक्केसु विहरति कपिलवत्थुस्मिं निग्रोधारामे। अथ खो महानामो सक्को येन भगवा तेनुपसङ्कमि; उपसङ्कमित्वा भगवन्तं अभिवादेत्वा एकमन्तं निसीदि। ०....

"एकमिदाहं, महानाम, समयं राजगहे विहरामि गिज्झकूटे पब्बते। तेन खो पन समयेन सम्बहुला निगण्ठा इसिगिलिपस्से कालसिलायं उब्भट्ठका होन्ति आसनपटिक्खित्ता, ओपक्कमिका दुक्खा तिब्बा खरा कटुका वेदना वेदयन्ति। अथ ख्वाहं, महानाम, सायन्हसमयं पटिसल्लाना वुट्ठितो येन इसिगिलिपस्से कालसिला येन ते निगण्ठा तेनुपसङ्कमि; उपसङ्कमित्वा ते निगण्ठे एतदवोचं-'किन्नु तुम्हे, आवुसो, निगण्ठा अब्भट्ठका आसनपटिक्खित्ता, ओपक्कमिका दुक्खा तिब्बा खरा कटुका वेदना वेदयथा'ति? एवं वुत्ते, महानाम, ते निगण्ठा मं एतदवोचुं-'निगण्ठो आवुसो, नातपुत्तो सब्बञ्ञू सब्बदस्साबी अपरिसेसं ञाणदस्सनं पटिजानाति-चरतो च मे तिट्ठतो च सुत्तस्स च जागरस्स च सततं समितं ञाणदस्सनं पच्चुपट्ठितं ति। सो एवमाह-अत्थि खो वो, निगण्ठा, पुब्बे पापकम्मं कतं, तं इमाय कटुकाय दुक्करकारिकाय निज्जीरेथ; यं पनेत्थ एतरहि कायेन संवुतां वाचाय संवुता मनसा संवुता तं आयतिं पापस्स कम्मस्स अकरणं; इति पुराणानं कम्मानं तपसा ब्यन्तिभावा, नवानं कम्मानं अकरणा, आयतिं अनवस्सवो, आयतिं अनवस्सवा कम्मक्खयो, कम्मक्खया दुक्खक्खयो, दुक्खक्खयो वेदनाक्खयो, वेदनाक्खया सब्बं दुक्खं निज्जण्णं भविस्सती ति। तं च पनम्हाकं रुच्चति चेव खमति च, तेन चम्हं अत्तमना'ति।

"एवं वुत्ते, अहं, महानाम, ते निगण्ठे एतदवोचं-'किं पन तुम्हे, आवुसो निगण्ठा, जानाथ-अहुवम्हे व मयं पुब्बे न नाहुवम्हा'ति?

'नो हिदं, आवुसो'।

'किं पन तुम्हे, आवुसो निगण्ठा, जानाथ-अकरम्हे व मयं पुब्बे पापकम्म न नाकरम्हा'ति?

'नो हिदं, आवुसो'।

'किं पन तुम्हे, आवुसो निगण्ठा, जानाथ-एवरूपं वा एवरूपं वा पापकम्मं अकरम्हा'ति?

'नो हिदं, आवुसो'।

'किं पन तुम्हे, आवुसो निगण्ठा, जानाथ-एत्तकं वा दुक्खं निज्जण्णं, एत्तकं वा दुक्खं निज्जीरेतब्बं, एत्तकम्हि वा दुक्खे निज्जिणे सब्बं दुक्खं निज्जिणं भविस्सती'ति?

'नो हिदं, आवुसो'।

'किं पन तुम्हे, आवुसो निगण्ठा, जानाथ-दिट्ठेव धम्मे अकुसलानं धम्मानं पहानं, कुसलानं धम्मानं उपसम्पदं'ति?

'नो हिदं आवुसो'।

'इति किर तुम्हे, आवुसो निगण्ठा, न जानाथ–अहुवम्हे व मयं पुब्बे न नाहुवम्हा ति, न जानाथ–अकरम्हे व मयं पुब्बे पापकम्म न नाकरम्हा ति, न जानाथ–एवरूपं वा एवरूपं वा पापकम्मं अकरम्हा ति, न जानाथ–एत्तकं वा दुक्खं निज्जिण्णं, एत्तकं वा दुक्खं निज्जिरेतब्बं एतकम्हि वा दुक्खे निज्जिणे सब्बं दुक्खं निज्जिणं भविस्सती ति, न जानाथ–दिट्ठेव धम्मे अकुसलानं धम्मानं पहानं, कुसलानं धम्मानं उपसम्पदं। एवं सन्ते, आवुसो निगण्ठा, ये लोके लुद्दा लोहितपाणिनो कुरूरकम्मन्ता मनुस्सेसु पच्चाजाता ते निगण्ठेसु पब्बजन्ती'ति।

'न खो, आवुसो गोतम, सुखेन सुखं अधिगन्तब्बं, दुक्खेन खो सुखं अधिगन्तब्बं; सुखेन चावुसो गोतम, सुखं अधिगन्तब्बं अभविस्स, राजा मागधो सेनियो बिम्बिसारो सुखं अधिगच्छेय्य, राजा मागधो सेनियो बिम्बिसारो सुखविहारितरो आयस्मता गोतमेना'ति।

'अद्धायस्मन्तेहि निगण्ठेहि सहसा अप्पटिसङ्खा वाचा भासिता–न खो, आवुसो गोतम, सुखेन सुखं अधिगन्तब्बं, दुक्खेन खो सुखं अधिगन्तब्बं; दुखेन चावुसो गोतम, सुखं अधिगन्तब्बं अभविस्स, राजा मागधो सेनियो बिम्बिसारो सुखं अधिगच्छेय्य, राजा मागधो सेनियो बिम्बिसारो सुखविहारितरो आयस्मता गोतमेना ति। अदि च अहमेव तत्थ पटिपुच्छितब्बो–को नु खो आयस्मन्तानं सुखविहारितरो राजा वा मागधो सेनियो बिम्बिसारो आयस्मा वा गोतमो'ति?

'अद्धावुसो गोतमो, अम्हेहि सहसा अप्पटिसङ्खा वाचा भासिता न खो, आवुसो गोतमो, सुखेन सुखं अधिगन्तब्बं, दुक्खेन खो सुखं अधिगन्तब्बं; सुखेन चावुसो गोतम, सुखं अधिगन्तब्बं अभविस्स, राजा मागधो सेनियो बिम्बिसारो सुखं अधिगच्छेय्य, राजा मागधो सेनियो बिम्बिसारो सुखविहारितरो आयस्मता गोतमेना ति। अपि च तिट्ठतेतं, इदानि पि मयं आयस्मन्तं गोतमं पुच्छाय–को नु खो आयस्मन्तानं सुखविहारितरो राजा वा मागधो सेनियो बिम्बिसारो आयस्मा वा गोतमो'ति?

'तेन हावुसो निगण्ठा, तुम्हे व तथ्य पटिपुच्छिस्सामि, यथा वो खमेय्य तथा नं व्याकरेय्याथ। तं किं मञ्ञथावुसो निगण्ठा पहोति राजा मागधो सेनियो बिम्बिसारो, अनिञ्झमानो कायेन, अभासमानो वाचं, सत्त रत्तिन्दिवानि एकन्तसुखं पटिसंवेदी विहरितुं'ति?

'नो हिदं, आवुसो'।

'तं किं मञ्ञथावुसो निगण्ठा, पहोति राजा मागधो सेनियो बिम्बिसारो, अनिञ्झमानो कायेन, अभासमानो वाचं, छ रत्तिन्दिवानि....पे०....पञ्च रत्तिन्दिवानि....चत्तारि रत्तिन्दिवानि...तीणि रत्तिन्दिवानि. ...द्वे रत्तिन्दिवानि....एकं रत्तिन्दिवं एकन्तसुखं पटिसंवेदी विहरितुं'ति?

'नो हिदं, आवुसो'।

'अहं खो, आवुसो निगण्ठा, पहोमि अनिञ्झमानो कायेन, अभासमानो वाचं, एकं रत्तिन्दिवं एकन्तसुखं पटिसंवेदी विहरितुं। अहं खो, आवुसो निगण्ठा, पहोमि अनिञ्झमानो कायेन, अभासमानो वाचं, द्वे रत्तिन्दिवानि....तीणि रत्तिन्दिवानि....चत्तारि रत्तिन्दिवानि...पञ्च रत्तिन्दिवानि.....छ रत्तिन्दिवानि

....सत्त रत्तिन्दिवानि एकन्तसुखं पटिसंवेदी विहरितुं। तं किं मञ्ञथावुसो निगण्ठा, एवं सन्ते को सुखविहारितरो राजा वा मागधो सेनियो बिम्बिसारो अहं वा'ति?

'एवं सन्ते आयस्मा व गोतमो सुखविहारितरो रञ्ञा मागधेन सेनियेन बिम्बिसारेना' ति।

इदमवोच भगवा। अत्तमनो महानामो सक्को भगवतो भासितं अभिनन्दी ति।[1]

६

ASIBANDHAKAPUTRA GĀMAṆI

एकं समयं भगवा नालन्दायं विहरति पावारिकम्बवने। अथ खो असिबन्धकपुत्तो गामणि निगण्ठसावको येन भगवा तेनुपसङ्कमि; उपसङ्कमित्वा एकमन्तं निसीदि। एकमन्तं निसिन्नं खो असिबन्धकपुत्तं गामणिं भगवा एतदवोच-"कथं नु खो, गामणि, निगण्ठो नाटपुत्तो सावकानं धम्मं देसेती"ति?

"एवं खो, भन्ते, निगण्ठो नाटपुत्तो सावकानं धम्मं देसेति-'यो कोचि पाणं अतिपातेति सब्बो सो आपायिको नेरयिको, यो कोचि अदिन्नं आदियति सब्बो सो आपायिको नेरयिको, यो कोचि कामेसु मिच्छा चरति सब्बो सो आपायिको नेरयिको, यो कोचि मुसा भणति सब्बो सो आपायिको नेरयिको। यंबहुलं यंबहुलं विहरति तेन तेन नीयति' ति। एवं खो, भन्ते, निगण्ठो नाटपुत्तो सावकानं धम्मं देसेती"ति।

"यंबहुलं यंबहुलं च, गामणि, विहरति तेन तेन नीयति," एवं सन्ते न कोचि आपायिको नेरयिको, भविस्सति, यथा निगण्ठस्स नाटपुत्तस्स वचनं।

"तं किं मञ्ञसि, गामणि, यो सो पुरिसो पाणातिपाती रत्तिया वा दिवसस्स वा समयासमयं उपादाय, कतमो बहुतरो समयो यं वा सो पाणमतिपातेति यं वा सो पाणं नातिपातेती"ति?

"यो सो, भन्ते, पुरिसो पाणातिपाती रत्तिया वा दिवसस्स वा समयासमयं उपादाय, अप्पतरो सो समयो यं सो पाणमतिपातेति, अथ खो स्वेव बहुतरो समयो यं सो पाणं नातिपातेती"ति।

"यंबहुलं यंबहुलं च, गामणि, ०....। यो सो पुरिसो अदिन्नादायी रत्तिया वा दिवसस्स वा समयासमयं उपादाय, ०.....।

"यंबहुलं यंबहुलं च, ०.....गामणि,-यो सो पुरिसो कामेसुमिच्छाचारी रत्तिया वा दिवसस्स वा समयासमयं उपादाय, ०....।

"यंबहुलं यंबहुलं च, गामणि, ०...यो सो पुरिसो मुसावादो रत्तिया वा दिवसस्स वा समयासमयं उपादाय, ०....।

---

1. सुत्तपिटके मज्झिमनिकाय पालि, मूलपण्णासकं, चूलदुक्खक्खन्धसुत्तं, 14-2, 2; पृ० 126-131।

"इध, गामणि, एकच्चो सत्था एवंवादी होति एवंदिट्ठि–'यो कोचि पाणमतिपातेति सब्बो सो आपायिको नेरयिको, यो कोचि अदिन्नं आदियति सब्बो सो आपायिको नेरयिको, यो कोचि कामेसु मिच्छा चरति सब्बो सो आपायिको नेरयिको, यो कोचि मुसा भणति सब्बो सो आपायिको नेरयिको' ति। तस्मिं खो पन, गामणि, सत्थरि सावको अभिप्पसन्नो होति। तस्स एवं होती–'मय्हं खो सत्था एवंवादी एवंदिट्ठि–यो कोचि पाणमतिपातेति सब्बो सो आपायिको नेरयिको'ति। अत्थि खो पन मया पाणो अतिपातितो अहम्पम्हि आपायिको नेरयिको ति दिट्ठिं पटिलभति। तं, गामणि, वाचं अप्पहाय तं चित्तं अप्पहाय तं दिट्ठिं अप्पटिनिस्सज्जित्वा यथाभतं निक्खित्तो एवं निरये। मय्हं खो सत्था एवंवादी एवंदिट्ठि–यो कोचि अदिन्नं अदियति०....। मय्हं खो सत्था एवंवादी एवंदिट्ठि–यो कोचि कामेस मिच्छा चरति सब्बो०...। मय्हं खो सत्था एवंवादी एवंदिट्ठी–यो कोचि मुसा भणति०....।

"इध पन, गामणि, तथागतो लोके उपपज्जति अरहं सम्मासम्बुद्धो विज्जाचरणसम्पन्नो सुगतो लोकविदू अनुत्तरो पुरिसदम्मसारथि सत्था देवमनुस्सानं बुद्धो भगवा। सो अनेकपरियायेन पाणातिपातं गरहति विगरहति' 'पाणातिपाता विरमथा' ति चाह। अदिन्नादानं गरहति विगरहति 'अदिन्नादाना विरमथा' ति चाह। कामेसुमिच्छाचारं गरहति विगरहति 'कामेसुमिच्छाचारा विरमथा' ति चाह। मुसावादं गरहति विगरहति 'मुसावादा विरमथा' ति चाह। तस्मिं खो पन गामणि, सत्थरि सावको अभिप्पसन्नो होति। सो इति पटिसञ्चिक्खति–'भगवा खो अनेकपरियायेन पाणातिपातं गरहति विगरहति, पाणातिपाता विरमथा ति चाह। अत्थि खो पन मया पाणो अतिपातितो यावतको वा तावतको वा..., तं न सुट्ठु, तं न साधु। अहं चेव खो पन तप्पच्चया विप्पटिसारी अस्सं। न मेतं पापं कम्मं अकतं भविस्सती' ति। सो इति पटिसङ्खाय तं चेव पाणातिपातं पजहति। आयतिं च पाणातिपाता पटिविरतो होति। एवमेतस्स पापस्स कम्मस्स पहानं होति। एवमेतस्स पापस्स कम्मस्स समतिक्कमो होति।

'भगवा खो अनेकपरियायेन अदिन्नादान' ०....।

'भगवा खो पन अनेकपरियायेन कामेसुमिच्छाचारं' ०....।

'भगवा खो पन अनेकपरियायेन मुसावादं' ०....।

"सो पाणातिपातं पहाय पाणातिपाता पटिविरतो होति। अदिन्नादानं पहाय अदिन्नादाना पटिविरतो होती। कामेसुमिच्छाचारं पहाय कामेसुमिच्छाचारा पटिविरतो होति। मुसावादं पहाय मुसावादा पटिविरतो होति। पिसुणं वाचं पहाय पिसुणाय वाचाय पटिविरतो होति। फरुसं वाचं पहाय फरुसाय वाचाय पटिविरतो होति। सम्फप्पलापं पहाय सम्फप्पलापा पटिविरतो होति। अभिज्झं पहाय अनभिज्झालु होति। ब्यापादप्पदोसं पहाय अब्यापन्नचित्तो होति। मिच्छादिट्ठिं पहाय सम्मादिट्ठिको होति।

"स खो सो, गामणि, अरियसावको एवं विगताभिज्झो विगतब्यापादो असम्मूळ्हो सम्पजानो पटिस्सतो मेत्तासहगतेन चेतसा एकं दिसं फरित्वा विहरति, तथा दुतियं तथा ततियं, तथा चतुत्थं। इति उद्धमधो तिरिथं सब्बधि सब्बत्तताय सब्बावन्तं लोकं मेत्तासहगतेन चेतसा विपुलेन महग्गतेन

अप्पमाणेन अवेरेन अब्यापज्जेन फरित्वा विहरति। सेय्यथापि, गामणि, बलवा सङ्खधमो अप्पकसिरेनेव चतुद्दिसा विञ्ञापेय्य; एवमेव खो, गामाणि, एवं भाविताय मेत्ताय चेतोविमुत्तिया एवं बहुलीकताय यं पमाणकतं कम्मं, न तं तत्रावसिस्सति न तं तत्रावतिट्ठति।

"स खो सो, गामणि, अरियसावको एवं विगताभिज्झो विगतब्यापादो असम्मूल्हो सम्पजानो पटिस्सतो करुणासहगतेन चेतसा.... पे०..... मुदितासहगतेन चेतसा.... पे०..... उपेक्खासहगतेन चेतसा एकं दिसं फरित्वा विहरति, तथा दुतियं, तथा ततियं, तथा चतुत्थं। ०.....

एवं वुत्ते, असिबन्धकपुत्तो गामणि भगवन्तं एतदवोच–"अभिक्कन्तं भन्ते, अभिक्कन्तं, भन्ते ... पे०.... उपासकं मं भगवा धारेतु अज्जतग्गे पाणुपेतं सरणं गतं"ति।[1]

७

NĀLANDĀ MEN DURBHIKṢĀ

एकं समयं भगवा कोसलेसु चारिकं चरमानो महता भिक्खुसङ्घेन सद्धिं येन नालन्दा तदवसरि। तत्र सुदं भगवा नालन्दायं विहरति पावारिकम्बवने।

तेन खो पन समयेन नालन्दा दुब्भिक्खा होति द्वीहितिका सेतट्ठिका सलाकावुत्ता। तेन खो पन समयेन निगण्ठो नाटपुत्तो नालन्दायं पटिवसति महतिया निगण्ठपरिसाय सद्धिं। अथ खो असिबन्धकपुत्तो गामणि निगण्ठसावको येन निगण्ठो नाटपुत्तो नेतुपसङ्कमि; उपसङ्कमित्वा निगण्ठं नाटपुत्तं अभिवादेत्वा एकमन्तं निसीदि। एकमन्तं निसिन्नं खो असिबन्धकपुत्तं गामणि निगण्ठो नातपुत्तो एतदवोच–"एहि त्वं, गामणि समणस्स गोतमस्स वादं आरोपेहि। एवं ते कल्याणो कित्तिसद्दो अब्भुग्गच्छिस्सति–'असिबन्धकपुत्तेन गामणिना समणस्स गोतमस्स एवंमहिद्धिकस्स एवंमहानुभावस्स वादो आरोपितो"ति।

"कथं पनाहं, भन्ते, समणस्स गोतमस्स एवंमहिद्धिकस्स एवंमहानुभावस्स वादं आरोपेस्सामी"ति?

"एहि त्वं, गामणि, येन समणो गोतमो तेनुपसङ्कम; उपसङ्कमित्वा समणं गोतमं एवं वदेहि–'ननु, भन्ते भगवा अनेक परियायेन कुलानं अनुद्दयं वण्णेति, अनुरक्खं वण्णेति, अनुकम्पं वण्णेती' ति? सचे खो, गामणि, समणो गोतमो एवं पुट्ठो एवं व्याकरोति–'एवं गामणि, तथागतो अनेकपरियायेन कुलानं अनुद्दयं वण्णेति, अनुरक्खं वण्णेति, अनुकम्पं वण्णेती' ति, तमेनं त्वं एवं वदेय्यासि–'अथ किञ्चरहि, भन्ते, भगवा दुब्भिक्खे द्वीहितिके सेतट्ठिके सलाकावुत्ते महता भिक्खुसङ्घेन सद्धिं चारिकं चरति? उच्छेदाय भगवा कुलानं पटिपन्नो, अनयाय भगवा कुलानं पटिपन्नो, उपधाताय भगवा कुलानं पटिपन्नो'ति! इमं खो ते, गामणि, समणो गोतमो उभतोकोटिकं पञ्हं पुट्ठो नेव सक्खति उग्गिलितं नेव सक्खति ओगिलितु"ति। "एवं, भन्ते"ति

1. सुत्तपिटके, संयुत्तनिकाय पालि, सलायतनवग्गो, गामणिसंयुत्तं संखधमसुत्त, 42-8-8, पृ० 281-85।

खो असिबन्धकपुत्तो गामणि निगण्ठस्स नाटपुत्तस्स पटिस्सुत्वा उट्ठायासना निगण्ठं नाटपुत्तं अभिवादेत्वा पदक्खिणं कत्वा येन भगवा तेनुपसङ्कमि; उपसङ्कमित्वा भगवन्तं अभिवादेत्वा एकमन्तं निसीदि। एकमन्तं निसिन्नो खो असिबन्वकपुत्तो गामणि भगवन्तं एतदवोच–

"ननु, भन्ते, भगवा अनेकपरियायेन कुलानं अनुद्दयं वण्णेति, अनुरक्खं वण्णेति, अनुकम्पं वण्णेती"ति?

"एवं, गामणि, तथागतो अनेकपरियायेन कुलानं अनुद्दयं वण्णेति, अनुरक्खं वण्णेति, अनुकम्पं वण्णेती"ति।

"अथ किञ्चरहि, भन्ते, भगवा दुब्भिक्खे द्वीहितिके सेतट्ठिके सलाकावुत्ते महता भिक्खुसङ्घेन सद्धिं चारिकं चरति? उच्छेदाय भगवा कुलानं पटिपन्नो, अनयाय भगवा कुलानं पटिपन्नो, उपघाताय भगवा कुलानं पटिपन्नो"ति।

"इतो सो, गामणि, एकनवुतिकप्पे यमहं अनुस्सरामि, नाभिजानामि किञ्चि कुलं पक्कभिक्खानुप्पदानमत्तेन उपहतपूब्बं। अथ खो यानि तानि कुलानि अड्ढानि महद्धनानि महाभोगानि पहूतजातरूपरजतानि पहूतवित्तूपकरणानि पहूतधनधञ्ञानि, सब्बानि तानि दानसम्भूतानि चेव सच्चसम्भूतानि च सामञ्ञसम्भूतानि च। अट्ठ खो, गामणि, हेतू, अट्ठ पच्चया कुलानं उपघाताय। राजतो वा कुलानि उपघातं गच्छन्ति, चोरतो वा कुलानि उपघातं गच्छन्ति, अग्गितो वा कुलानि उपघातं गच्छन्ति, उदकतो वा कुलानि उपघातं गच्छन्ति, निहितं वा ठाना विगच्छति, दुप्पयुत्ता वा कम्मन्ता विपज्जन्ति, कुले वा कुलङ्गारो ति उप्पज्जति यो ते भोगे विकिरति विधामति विद्धंसेति, अनिच्चता येव अट्ठमी ति। इमे खो, गामणि, अट्ठ हेतु, अट्ठ पच्चया कुलानं उपधाताय। इमेसु खो, गामणि, अट्ठसु हेतूसु अट्ठसु पच्चयेसु संविज्जमानेसु यो मं एवं वदेय्य–'उच्छेदाय भगवा कुलानं पटिपन्नो, अनयाय भगवा कुलानं पटिपन्नो, उपघाताय भगवा कुलानं पटिपन्नो' ति, तं, गामणि, वाचं, अप्पहाय तं चित्तं अप्पहाय तं दिट्ठिं अप्पटिनिस्सज्जित्वा यथाभतं निक्खित्तो एवं निरये"ति। एवं वुत्ते, असिबन्धकपुत्तो गामणि भगवन्तं एतदवोच–"अभिक्कन्तं, भन्ते, अभिक्कन्तं, भन्ते...पे०....उपासकं मं भगवा धारेतु अज्जतग्गे पाणुपेतं सरणं गत"ति।[1]

८

CITRA GṚHAPATI

तेन खो पन समयेन निगण्ठो नाटपुत्तो मच्छिकासण्डं अनुप्पत्तो होति महतिया निगण्ठपरिसाय सद्धिं। अस्सोसि खो चित्तो गहपति–"निगण्ठो किर नाटपुत्तो मच्छिकासण्डं अनुप्पत्तो महतिया निगण्ठपरिसाय सद्धिं"ति। अथ खो चित्तो गहपति सम्बहुलेहि उपासकेहि सद्धिं येन निगण्ठो नाटपुत्तो तेनुपसङ्कमि; उपसङ्कमित्वा निगण्ठेन नाटपुत्तेन सद्धिं सम्मोदि। सम्मोदनीयं कथं सारणीयं वीतिसारेत्वा एकमन्तं निसीदि। एकमन्तं निसिन्नं खो चित्तं गहपतिं निगण्ठो नाटपुत्तो एतदवोच–सद्दहसि

1. सुत्तपिटके, संयुत्तनिकाय पालि, सलायतनवग्गो, गामणिसंयुत्तं, कुलसुत्त, 42-9-9, पृ० 285-87।

त्वं, गहपति, समणस्स गोतमस्स–अत्थि अवितक्को अविचारो समाधि, अत्थि वितक्कविचाराणं निरोधो"ति?

"न ख्वाहं, एत्थ, भन्ते, भगवतो सद्धाय गच्छामि। अत्थि अवितक्को अविचारो समाधि, अत्थि वितक्कविचारानं निरोघो"ति।

एवं वुत्ते, निगण्ठो नाटपुत्तो उल्लोकेत्वा एतदवोच–"इदं भवन्तो पस्सन्तु, याव उजुको चायं चित्तो गहपति, याव असठो चायं चित्तो गहपति, याव अमायावी चायं चित्तो गहपति, वातं वा सो जालेन बाधेतब्बं मञ्ञेय्य, यो वितक्कविचारे निरोधेतब्बं मञ्ञेय्य, सकमुट्ठिना वा सो गङ्गाय सोतं आवारेतब्बं मञ्ञेय्य, यो वितक्कविचारे निरोधेतब्ब मञ्ञेय्या"ति।

"तं किं मञ्ञसि, भन्ते, कतमं नु खो पणीततरं–ञाणं वा सद्धा वा"ति?

"सद्धाय खो, गहपति, ञाणं येन पणीततरं"ति।

"अहं खो, भन्ते, यावदेव आकङ्खामि, विविच्चेव कामेहि विविच्च अंकुसलेहि धम्मेहि सवितक्कं सविचारं विवेकजं पीतिसुखं पठमं झानं उपसम्पज्ज विहरामि। अहं खो, भन्ते, यावदेव आकङ्खामि, वितक्कविचारानं वूपसमा.....पे०....दुतिय झानं उपसम्पज्ज विहरामि। अहं खो, भन्ते, यावदेव आकङ्खामि, पीतिया न विरागा...पे०....ततियं झानं उपसम्पज्ज विहरामि। अहं खो, भन्ते, यावदेव आकङ्खामि, सुखस्स च पहाना....पे०....चतुत्थं झानं उपसम्पज्ज विहरामि। न सो ख्वाहं, भन्ते एवं जानन्तो एवं पस्सन्तो कस्स अञ्ञस्स समणस्स वा ब्राह्मणस्स वा सद्धाय गमिस्सामि। अत्थि अवितक्को अविचारो समाधि, अत्थि वितक्कविचारानं निरोधो"ति।

एवं वुत्ते, निगण्ठो नाटपुत्तो सकं परिसं अपलोकेत्वा एतदवोच–"इदं भवन्तो पस्सन्तु, याव अनुजुको चायं चित्तो गहपति, याव सठो चायं चित्तो गहपति, याव मायावी चायं चित्तो गहपती"ति।

इदानेव खो ते मयं, भन्ते, भासितं–'एवं आजाजानाम इदं भवन्तो पस्सन्तु, याव उजुको चायं चित्तो गहपति, याव असठो चायं चित्तो गहपति, याव अमायावी चायं चित्तो गहपती'ति। इदानेव च पन मयं, भन्ते, भासितं–'एवं आजानाम इदं भवन्तो पस्सन्तु, याव अनुजुको चायं चित्तो गहपति, याव सठो चायं चित्तो गहपति, याव मायावी चायं गहपती' ति। सचे ते, भन्ते, पुरिमं सच्चं, पच्छिमं ते मिच्छा। सचे पन ते, भन्ते, पुरिमं मिच्छा, पच्छिमं ते सच्चं। इमे खो पन, भन्ते, दस सहधम्मिका पञ्हा आगच्छन्ति। यदा नेसं अत्थं आजानेय्यासि, अथ मं पटिहरेय्यासि सद्धिं निगण्ठपरिसाय। एको पञ्हो एको उद्देसो एकं वेय्याकरणं। द्वे पञ्हा द्वे उद्देसा द्वे वेय्याकरणानि। तयो पञ्हा तयो उद्देसा तीणि वेय्याकरणानि। चत्तारो पञ्हा चत्तारो उद्देसा चत्तारि वेय्याकरणानि। पञ्च पञ्हा पञ्च उद्देसा पञ्च वेय्याकरणानि। छ पञ्हा छ उद्देसा छ वेय्याकरणानि। सत्त पञ्हा सत्त उद्देसा सत्त वेय्याकरणानि। अट्ठ पञ्हा अट्ठ उद्देसा अट्ठ वेय्याकरणानि। नव पञ्हा नव उद्देसा नव वेय्याकरणानि। दस पञ्हा दस उद्देसा दस वेय्याकरणानी" ति।

अथ खो चित्तो गहपति निगण्ठं नाटपुत्तं इमे दस सहधम्मिके पञ्हे आपुच्छित्वा उट्ठायासना पक्कामी ति।[1]

१

KUTUHALAŚĀLĀ SUTTA

अथ खो वच्छगोत्तो परिब्बाजको येन भगवा तेनुपसङ्कमि; उपसङ्कमित्वा भगवता सद्धिं सम्मोदि। सम्मोदनीयं कथं सारणीयं वीतिसारेत्वा एकमन्तं निसीदि। एकमन्तं निसिन्नो खो वच्छगोत्तो परिब्बाजको भगवन्तं एतदवोच–

"पुरिमानि भो गोतम, दिवसानि पुरिमतरानि सम्बहुलानं नानातित्थियानं समणब्राह्मणानं परिब्बाजकानं कुतूहलसालायं सन्निसिन्नानं सन्निपतितानं अयमन्तराकथा उदपादि–'अयं खो पूरणो कस्सपो सङ्घी चेव गणी च गणाचरियो च ञातो यसस्सी तित्थकरो साधुसम्मतो बहुजनस्स। सो पि सावकं अब्भतीतं कालङ्कतं उपपत्तीसु ब्याकरोति–'असु अमुत्र उपपन्नो, असु अमुत्र उपपन्नो' ति। यो पिस्स सावको उत्तमपुरिसो परमपुरिसो परमपत्तिपत्तो तं पि सावकं अब्भतीतं कालङ्कतं उपपत्तीसु ब्याकरोति–'असु अमुत्र उपपन्नो, असु अमुत्र उपपन्नो'ति।

"अयं पि खो मक्खलि गोसालो...पे०....अयं पि खो निगण्ठो नाटपुत्तो....अयं पि खो सञ्जयो बेलट्ठपुत्तो....अयं पि खो पकुधो कच्चानो....अयं पि खो अजितो केसकम्बलो सङ्घी चेव गणी च०....।

"अयं पि खो समणो गोतमो सङ्घी चेव गणी च गणाचरियो च ञातो यसस्सी तित्थकरो साधुसम्मतो बहुजनस्स। सो पि सावकं अब्भतीतं कालङ्कतं उपपत्तीसु ब्याकरोति–'असु अमुत्र उपपन्नो, असु अमुत्र उपपन्नो' ति। यो पिस्स सावको उत्तमपुरिसो परमपुरिसो परमपत्तिपत्तो तं च सावकं अब्भतीतं कालङ्कतं उपपत्तीसु न ब्याकरोति–'असु अमुत्र उपपन्नो, असु अमुत्र उपपन्नो'ति। अपि च खो नं एवं ब्याकरोति–अच्छेच्छि तण्हं, विवत्तयि संयोजनं, सम्मा मानाभिसमया अन्तमकासि दुक्खस्सा'ति। तस्स मय्हं, भो गोतम, अहु देव कङ्खा अहु विचिकिच्छा–'कथं नाम समणस्स गोतमस्स धम्मो अभिञ्ञेय्यो"ति?

"अलं हि ते, वच्छ, कङ्खितुं, अलं विचिकिच्छितुं कङ्खनीये च पन ते ठाने विचिकिच्छा उप्पन्ना। सउपादानस्स ख्वाहं, वच्छ, उपपत्तिं पञ्ञापेमि नो अनुपादानस्स। सेय्यथापि, वच्छ, अग्गि सउपादानो जलति, नो अनुपादानो; एवमेव ख्वाहं, वच्छ, सउपादानस्स उपपत्तिं पञ्ञापेमि, नो अनुपादानस्सा"ति।

"यस्मिं, भो गोतम, समये अच्चि वातेन खित्ता दूरं पि गच्छति, इमस्स पन भवं गोतमो किं उपादानस्मिं पञ्ञापेती"ति?

"यस्मिं खो, वच्छ, समये अच्चि वातेन खित्ता दूरं पि गच्छति, तमहं वातूपादानं पञ्ञापेमि। वातो हिस्स, वच्छ, तस्मिं समये उपादानं होती"ति।

1. सुत्तपिटके, संयुत्तनिकाय पालि, सलायतनवग्गो, चित्तसंयुत्तं, निगण्ठ नाटपुत्तसुत्तं, 41-8-8, पृ० 265-66।

"यस्मिं च पन, भो गोतम, समये इमं च कायं निक्खिपति सत्तो च अञ्ञतरं कायं अनुपपन्नो होति, इमस्स पन भवं गोतमो किं उपादानस्मिं पञ्ञापेती"ति?

"यस्मिं खो, वच्छ, समये इमं च कायं निक्खिपति सत्तो च अञ्ञतरं कायं अनुपपन्नो होति, तमहं तण्हूपादानं वदामि। तण्हा हिस्स, वच्छ, तस्मिं समये उपादानं होती"ति।[1]

१०
ABHAYALICCHAVI

एकं समयं आयस्मा आनन्दो वेसालियं विहरति महावने कूटागारसालायं। अथ खो अभयो च लिच्छवि पण्डितकुमारको च लिच्छवि येनायस्मा आनन्दो तेनुपसङ्कमिंसु; उपसङ्कमित्वा आयस्मन्तं आनन्दं अभिवादेत्वा एकमन्तं निसीदिंसु। एकमन्तं निसिन्नो खो अभयो लिच्छवि आयस्मन्तं आनन्दं एतदवोच–"निगण्ठो, भन्ते, नाटपुत्तो सब्बञ्ञू सब्बदस्सावी अपरिसेसं ञाणदस्सनं पटिजानाति–'चरतो च मे तिट्ठतो च सुत्तस्स च जागरस्स च सततं समितं ञाणदस्सनं पच्चुपट्ठितं' ति। सो पुराणानं कम्मानं तपसा ब्यन्तीभावं पञ्ञापेति नवानं कम्मानं अकरणा सेतुघातं। इति कम्मक्खया दुक्खक्खयो, दुक्खक्खया, वेदनाक्खयो, वेदनाक्खया सब्बं दुक्खं निज्जिण्णं भविस्सति–एवमेतिस्सा सन्दिट्ठिकाय निज्जराय विसुद्धिया समतिक्कमो होति। इध, भन्ते, भगवा किमाहा"ति?

"तिस्सो खो इमा, अभय, निज्जरा विसुद्धियो तेन भगवता जानता पस्सता अरहता सम्मासम्बुद्धेन सम्मदक्खाता सत्तानं विसुद्धिया सोकपरिदेवानं समतिक्कमाय दुक्खदोमनस्सानं अत्थङ्गमाय ञायस्य अधिगमाय निब्बानस्स सच्छिकिरियाय। कतमा तिस्सो? इध, अभय, भिक्खु सीलवा होति...पे०....समादाय सिक्खति सिक्खापदेसु। सो नवं च कम्मं न करोति, पुराणं च कम्मं फुस्स फुस्स ब्यन्तीकरोति। सन्दिट्ठिका निज्जरा अकालिका एहिपस्सिका ओपनेय्यिका पच्चत्तं वेदितब्बा विञ्ञूही ति।

"स खो सो, अभय, भिक्खु एवं सीलसम्पन्नो विविच्चेव कामेहि....पे०....चतुत्थं झानं उपसम्पज्ज विहरति। सो नवं च कम्मं न करोति, पुराणं च कम्मं फुस्स फुस्स ब्यन्तीकरोति। सन्दिट्ठिका निज्जरा अकालिका एहिपस्सिका ओपनेय्यिका पच्चत्तं वेदितब्बा विञ्ञुही ति।

"स खो सो, अभय, भिक्खु एवं समाधिसम्पन्नो आसवानं खया अनासवं चेतोविमुत्तिं पञ्ञाविमुत्तिं दिट्ठेव धम्मे सयं अभिञ्ञा सच्छिकत्वा उपसम्पज्ज विहरति। सो नवं च कम्मं न करोति, पुराणं च कम्मं फुस्स फुस्स ब्यन्तीकरोति। सन्दिट्ठिका निज्जरा अकालिका एहिपस्सिका ओपनेय्यिका पच्चत्तं वेदितब्बा विञ्ञूही ति। इमा खो, अभय, तिस्सो निज्जरा विसुद्धियो तेन भगवता जानता पस्सता अरहता सम्मासम्बुद्धेन सम्मदक्खाता सत्तानं विसुद्धिया सोकपरिदेवानं

---

1. सुत्तपिटके, संयुत्तनिकाय पालि, सलायतनवग्गो, अब्याकतसंयुत्तं, कुतूहलसालासुत्तं, 44-9-9; पृ० 341-42।

समतिक्कमाय दुक्खदोमनस्सानं अत्थङ्गमाय ञायस्स अधिगमाय निब्बानस्स सच्छिकिरियाया" ति।

एवं वुत्ते पण्डितकुमारको लिच्छवि अभयं लिच्छविं एतदवोच–"किं पन त्वं, सम्म अभय, आयस्मतो आनन्दस्स सुभासितं सुभासिततो नाब्भनुमोदसी"ति?

"क्याहं, सम्म पण्डितकुमारक आयस्मतो आनन्दस्स सुभासितं सुभासिततो नाब्भनुमोदिस्सामि! मुद्धा पि तस्स विपतेय्य यो आयस्मतो आनन्दस्स सुभासितं सुभासिततो नाब्भनुमोदेय्या"ति।[1]

११
LOKASĀNTA-ANANTA

1. अथ खो द्वे लोकायतिका ब्राह्मणा येन भगवा तेनुपसङ्कमिंसु; उपसङ्कमित्वा भगवता सद्धिं सम्मोदिंसु। सम्मोदनीयं कथं सारणीयं वीतिसारेत्वा एकमन्तं निसीदिंसु। एकमन्तं निसिन्ना खो ते ब्राह्मणा भगवन्तं एतदवोचुं–

2. "पूरणो, भो गोतम, कस्सपो सब्बञ्ञू सब्बदस्सावी अपरिसेसं ञाणदस्सनं पटिजानाति–'चरतो च मे तिट्ठतो च सुत्तस्स च जागरस्स च सततं समितं ञाणदस्सनं पच्चुपट्ठितं' ति। सो एवमाह–'अहं अनन्तेन ञाणेन अनन्तं लोकं जानं पस्सं विहरामी'ति। अयं पि, भो गोतम, निगण्ठो नाटपुत्तो सब्बञ्ञू सब्बदस्सावी अपरिसेसं ञाणदस्सनं पटिजानाति–'चरतो च मे तिट्ठतो च सुत्तस्स च जागरस्स च सततं समितं ञाणदस्सनं पच्चुपट्ठितं'ति। सो एवमाह–'अहं अनन्तेन ञाणेन अनन्तं लोकं जानं पस्सं विहरामी'ति। इमेसं, भो गोतम उभिन्नं ञाणवादानं उभिन्नं अञ्ञमञ्ञं विपच्चनीकवादानं को सच्चं आह को मुसा"ति?

3. "अलं, ब्राह्मणा! तिट्ठतेतं–'इमेसं उभिन्नं ञाणवादानं उभिन्न अञ्ञमञ्ञं विपच्चनीकवादानं को सच्चं आह को मुसा' ति। धम्मं वो, ब्राह्मणा, देसेस्सामि, तं सुणाथ, साधुकं मनसिकरोथ; भासिस्सामी"ति। "एवं, भो"ति खो ते ब्राह्मणा भगवतो पच्चस्सोसुं। भगवा एतदवोच[2].......।

१२
VAPPA-JAINA ŚRĀVAKA

एकं समयं भगवा सक्केसु विहरति कपिलवत्थुस्मिं निग्रोधारामे। अथ खो वप्पो सक्को निगण्ठसावको येनायस्मा महामोग्गल्लानो तेनुपसङ्कमि; उपसङ्कमित्वा आयस्मन्तं महामोग्गल्लानं अभिवादेत्वा एकमन्तं निसीदि। एकमन्तं निसिन्नं खो वप्पं सक्कं निगण्ठसावकं आयस्मा महामोग्गल्लानो एतदवोच–

---

1. सुत्तपिटके, अंगुत्तरनिकाय पालि, तिकनिपात, आनन्दवग्गो, निगण्ठसुत्तं, 3-8-4, पृ० 215।
2. सुत्तपिटके, अंगुत्तरनिकाय पालि, नवक-निपातो, महावग्गो, लोकायतिकसुत्तं, 9-4-7; पृ० 66-67।

"इधस्स, वप्प, कायेन संवुतो वाचाय संवुतो मनसा संवुतो अविज्जाविरागा विज्जुप्पादा। पस्ससि नो त्वं, वप्प, तं ठानं यतोनिदानं पुरिसं दुक्खवेदनिया आसवा अस्सवेय्युं अभिसम्परायं" ति?

"पस्सामहं, भन्ते, तं ठानं। इधस्स, भन्ते, पुब्बे पापकम्मं कतं अविपक्कविपाकं। ततोनिदानं पुरिसं दुक्खवेदनिया आसवा अस्सवेय्युं अभिसंपरायं"ति।

अयं चेव खो पन आयस्मतो महामोग्गल्लानस्स वप्पेन सक्केन निगण्ठसावकेन सद्धिं अन्तराकथा विप्पकता होति; अथ खो भगवा सायन्हसमयं पटिसल्लाना वुट्ठितो येन उपट्ठानसाला तेनुपसङ्कमि; उपसङ्कमित्वा पञ्ञत्ते आसने निसीदि। निसज्ज खो भगवा आयस्मन्तं महामोग्गल्लानं एतदवोच–

"काय नुत्थ, मोग्गल्लान, एतरहि कथाय सन्निसिन्ना; का च पन वो अन्तराकथा विप्पकता" ति?

इधाहं, भन्ते, वप्पं सक्कं निगण्ठसावकं एतदवोचं–'इधस्स, वप्प, कायेन०......अभिसंपरायं' ति? एवं वुत्ते, भन्ते, वप्पो सक्को निगण्ठसावको मं एतदवोच–'पस्सामहं, भन्ते०,......अभिसंपरायं' ति। अथ खो नो, भन्ते, वप्पेन सक्केन निगण्ठासावकेन सद्धिं अन्तराकथा विप्पकता; अथ भगवा अनुप्पत्तो"ति।

अथ खो भगवा वप्पं सक्कं निगण्ठसावकं एतदवोच–"सचे मे त्वं, वप्प अनुञ्ञेय्यं चेव अनुजानेय्यासि, पटिक्कोसितब्बं च पटिक्कोसेय्यासि, यस्स च मे भासितस्य अत्थं न जानेय्यासि ममेवेत्थ उत्तरि पटिपुच्छेय्यासि–'इदं, भन्ते, कथं, इमस्स को अत्थो' ति सिया नो एत्थ कथासल्लापो"ति।

अनुञ्ञेय्यं चेवाहं, भन्ते, भगवतो अनुजानिस्सामि, पटिक्कोसितब्बं च पटिक्कोसिस्सामि, यस्स चाहं भगवतो भासितस्स अत्थं न जानिस्सामि भगवन्तंयेवेत्थ उत्तरि पटिपुच्छिस्सामि–'इदं भन्ते, कथं, इमस्स को अत्थो' ति? होतु नो एत्थ कथासल्लापो"ति।

"तं किं मञ्ञसि, वप्प, ये कायसमारम्भपच्चया उप्पज्जन्ति आसवा विघातपरिलाहा, कायसमारम्भा पटिविरतस्स एवंस ते आसवा बिघातपरिलाहा न होन्ति। सो नवं च कम्मं न करोति, पुराणं च कम्मं फुस्स फुस्स ब्यन्तीकरोति, सन्दिट्ठिका निज्जरा अकालिका एहिपस्सिका ओपनेय्यिका पच्चत्तं वेदितब्बा विञ्ञूहि। पस्ससि नो त्वं, वप्प, तं ठानं यतोनिदानं पुरिसं दुक्खवेदनिया आसवा अस्सवेय्युं अभिसम्परायं"ति?

"नो हेतं भन्ते"।

"तं कि मञ्ञसि, वप्प, ये वचीसमारम्भपच्चया उप्पज्जन्ति आसवा०.......अभिसम्परायं"ति?

"नो हेतं, भन्ते"।

"तं किं मञ्ञसि, वप्प, ये मनोसमारम्भपच्चया उप्पज्जन्ति आसवा०......अभिसम्परायं"ति?

"नो हेतं, भन्ते"।

"तं किं मञ्ञसि, वप्प, ये अविज्जापच्चया उप्पज्जन्ति आसवा०.....अभिसम्परायं"ति?

"नो हेतं, भन्ते"।

"एवं सम्मा विमुत्तचित्तस्स खो, वप्प, भिक्खुनो छ सततविहारा अधिगता होन्ति। सो चक्खुना रूपं दिस्वा नेव सुमनो होति न दुम्मनो; उपेक्खको विहरति सतो सम्पजानो। सोतेन सद्दं सुत्वा...पे०....धानेन गन्धं धायित्वा....पे०...जिव्हाय रसं सायित्वा....पे०.....कायेन फोट्ठब्बं फुसित्वा....पे०....मनसा धम्मं विञ्ञाय नेव सुमनो होति न दुम्मनो; उपेक्खको विहरति सतो सम्पजानो। सो कायपरियन्तिकं वेदनं वेदियमानो 'कायपरियन्तिकं वेदनं वेदियामी' ति पजानाति; जीवितपरियन्तिकं वेदनं वेदियमानो 'जीवितपरियन्तिकं वेदनं वेदियामी' ति पजानाति, 'कायस्स भेदा उद्धं जीवितपरियादाना इधेव सब्बवेदयित्मनि अनभिनन्दितानि सीती भविस्सन्ती' ति पजानाति।

सेय्यथापि, वप्प, थूणं पटिच्च छाया पञ्ञायति। अथ पुरिसो आगच्छेय्य कुदालपिटकं आदाय। सो तं थूणं मूले छिन्देय्य; मूले छिन्दित्वा पलिखणेय्य; पलिखणित्वा मूलानि उद्धरेय्य, अन्तमसो उसीरनालिमत्तानि' पि। सो तं थूणं खण्डाखण्डिकं छिन्देय्य। खण्डाखण्डिकं छेत्वा फालेय्य फालेत्वा सकलिकं सकलिकं करेय्य। सकलिकं सकलिकं कत्वा वातातपे विसोसेय्य। वाततपे विसोसेत्वा अग्गिना डहेय्य। अग्गिना डहेत्वा मसिं करेय्य। मसिं करित्वा महावाते वा ओफुणेय्य नदिया वा सीधसोताय पवहेम्य। एवं हिस्स, वप्प, या थूणं पटिच्च छाया सा उच्छिन्नमूला तालावत्थुकता अनभावङ्कता आयतिं अनुप्पादधम्मा।

"एवमेव खो, वप्प, एवं सम्मा विमुत्तचित्तस्स भिक्खुनो छ सतत विहारा० .....पजानाति"।

एवं वुत्ते वप्पो सक्को निगण्ठसावको भगवन्तं एतदवोच–"सेय्यथापि, भन्ते, पुरिसो उदयत्थिको अस्सपणियं पोसेय्य। सो उदयं चेव नाधिगच्छैय्य, उत्तरिं च किलमथस्स विघातस्स भागी अस्स। एवमेव खो अहं, भन्ते, उदयत्थिको वाले निगण्ठे पयिरुपासिं। स्वाहं उदयं चेव नाधिगच्छिं, उत्तरिं च किलमथस्स विघातस्स भागी अहोसिं। एसाहं, भन्ते, अंज्जतग्गे यो मे बालेसु निगण्ठेसु पसादो तं महावाते वा ओफुणामि नदिया वा सीघसोताय पवाहेमि। अभिक्कन्तं, भन्ते...पे०... उपासकं मं, भन्ते, भगवा धारेतु अज्जतग्गे पाणुपेतं सरणं गतं"ति।[1]

१३

SAKULA UDĀYĪ

Satatam samitam sabbaññjutā

"एवं मे सुतं। एकं समयं भगवा राजगहे विहरति वेलुवने कलन्दकनिवापे। तेन खो पन समयेन सकुलुदायी परिब्बाजको मोरनिवापे परिब्बाजकारामे पटिवसति महतिया परिब्बाजकपरिसाय सद्धिं। अथ खो भगवा पुब्बण्हसमयं०....पच्छा पि सवनाय। यदाहं, भन्ते, इमं परिसं अनुपसङ्कन्तो होमि अथायं परिसा अनेकविहितं तिरच्छानकथं कथेन्ती निसिन्ना होति; यदा च खो अहं, भन्ते,

1. सुत्तपिटके, अंगुत्तरनिकाय पालि, चतुक्कमिपात, महावग्गो, वप्पसुत्तं, 4-20-5; पृ० 210-213।

इमं परिसं उपसङ्कन्तो होमि अथायं परिसा ममञ्ञेव मुखं उल्लोकेन्ती निसिन्ना होति–'यं नो समणो उदायी धम्मं भासिस्सति तं सोस्सामा' ति; यदा पन, भन्ते भगवा इमं परिसं उपसङ्कन्तो होति अथाहं चेव अयं च परिसा भगवतो मुखं उल्लोकेन्ता निसिन्ना होम–'यं नो भगवा धम्मं भासिस्सति तं सोस्सामा'ति।

"तेनहुदायि, तं एवेत्थ पटिभातु यथा मं पटिभासेय्यासि"।

"पुरिमानि, भन्ते, दिवसानि पुरिमतरानि सब्बञ्ञू सब्बदस्सावी अपरिसेसं ञाणदस्सनं पटिजानमानो चरतो च मे तिट्ठतो च सुत्तस्स च जागरस्स च सततं समितं ञाणदस्सनं पच्चुपट्ठितं ति। सो मया पुब्बन्तं आरब्भ पञ्हं पुट्ठो समानो अञ्ञेनञ्ञं पटिचरि, बहिद्धा कथं अपनामेसि, कोपं च दोसं च अप्पच्चयं च पात्वाकासि। तस्म मय्हं, भन्ते, भगवन्तं येव आरब्भ सति उदपादि–'अहो नून भगवा, अहो नून सुगतो! यो इमेसं धम्मानं सुकुसलो"ति।

"को पन सो, उदायि सब्बञ्ञू सब्बदस्सावी०....पात्वाकासी"ति?

"निगण्ठो, भन्ते, नातपुत्तो"ति।

Pubbantā parantapañhavissajjane Samattho

यो खो, उदायि, अनेकविहितं पुब्बेनिवासं अनुस्सरेय्य, सेय्यथीदं–एकं पि जाति द्वे पि जातियो...पे०....इति साकारं सउद्देसं अनेकविहितं पुब्बेनिवासं अनुस्सरेय्य, सो वा मं पुब्बतं आरब्भ पञ्हं पुच्छेय्यं; सो वा मे पुब्बन्तं आरब्भ पञ्हस्स वेय्याकरणेन चित्तं आराधेय्य, तस्स वाहं पुब्बन्तं आरब्भ पञ्हस्स वेय्याकरणेन चित्तं आराधेय्यं।

"यो खो, उदायि, दिब्बेन चक्खुना विसुद्धेनं अतिक्कन्त-मानुसकेन सत्ते पस्सेय्य चवमाने उपपज्जमाने हीने पणीते सुवण्णे दुब्बण्णे, सुगते दुग्गते यथाकम्मूपगे सत्ते पजानेय्य, सो वा मं अपरन्तं आरब्भ०......वाहं अपरन्तं आरब्भ०.....मे अपरन्तं आरब्भ....०वाहं अपरन्तं आरब्भ०. ....आराधेय्यं।

"अपि च, उदायि, तिट्ठतु पुब्बन्तो, तिट्ठतु अपरन्तो। धम्मं ते देसेस्सामि–इमस्मिं सति इदं होति, इमस्सुप्पादा इदं उप्पज्जति; इमस्मिं असति इदं न होति, इमस्स निरोधा इदं निरुज्झती"ति।[1] ०......

1. सुत्तपिटके, मज्झिमनिकाय पालि, मज्झिमपण्णासकं, चूलसकुलुदायिसुत्तं, 29-1-2; पृ० 255-57।

१४
NIRVĀṆA-SAṀVĀDA–1

Nātaputte Kālaṅkate bhinnā nigaṇṭha

एवं मे सुतं। एकं समयं भगवा सक्केसु विहरति सामगामे। तेन खो पन समयेन निगण्ठो नातपुत्तो पावायं अधुनाकालङ्कतो होति। तस्स कालङ्किरियाय भिन्ना निगण्ठा द्वेधिकजाता भण्डनजाता कलहजाता विवादापन्ना अञ्ञमञ्ञं मुखसत्तीहि वितुदन्ता विहरन्ति–"न त्वं इमं धम्मविनयं आजानासि, अहं इमं धम्मविनयं आजानामि। किं त्वं इमं धम्मविनयं आजानिस्ससि! मिच्छापटिपन्नो त्वमसि, अहमस्मि सम्मापटिपन्नो। सहितं मे, असहितं ते।। पुरेवचनीयं पच्छा अवच, पच्छावचनीयं पुरे अवच। अधिचिण्णं ते विपरावत्तं। आरोपितो ते वादो। निग्गहितोसि, चर वादप्पमोक्खाय; निब्बेठेहि वा सचे पहोसी"ति। वधो येव खो मञ्ञे निगण्ठेसु नात्तपुत्तियेसु वत्तति। ये पि निगण्ठस्स नातपुत्तस्स सावका गिही ओदातवसना ते पि निगण्ठेसु नातपुत्तिगेमु निब्बिन्नरूपा विरत्तरूपा पटिवानरूपा यथा तं दुरक्खाते धम्मविनये दुप्पवेदिते अनिय्यानिके अनुपसमसंवत्तनिके असम्मासम्बुद्धप्पवेदिते भिन्नरूपे अप्पटिसरणे।

अथ खो चुन्दो समणुद्देसो पावायं वस्सं वुत्थो येन सामगामो येनायस्मा आनन्दो तेनुपसङ्कमि; उपसङ्कमित्वा आयस्मन्तं आनन्दं अभिवादेत्वा एकमन्तं निसीदि। एकमन्तं निसिन्नो खो चुन्दो समणुद्देसो आयस्मन्तं आनन्दं एतदवोच–"निगण्ठो, भन्ते, नातपुत्तो पावायं अधुनाकालङ्कतो। तस्स कालंङ्किरियाय भिन्ना निगण्ठा द्वेधिकजाता .....पे०....भिन्नथूपे अप्पटिसरणे"ति। एवं वुत्ते, आयस्मा आनन्दो चुन्दं समणुद्देसं एतदवोच–"अत्थि खो इदं, आवुसो चुन्दं, कथापाभतं भगवन्तं दस्सनाय। आयाम, आवुसो चुन्द, येन भगवा तेनुपसङ्कमिस्साम; उपसङ्कमित्वा एतमत्थं भगवतो आरोचेस्सामा"ति। "एवं, भन्ते"ति खो चुन्दो समणुद्देसो आयस्मतो आनन्दस्स पच्चस्सोसि।

अथ खो आयस्मा च माननदो चुन्दो च समणुद्देसो येन भगवा तेनुपसङ्कमिंसु; उपसङ्कमित्वा भगवन्तं अभिवादेत्वा एकमन्तं निसिदिंसु। एकमन्तं निसिन्नो खो आयस्मा आनन्दो भगवन्तो एतदवोच–"अयं, भन्ते, चुन्दो समणुद्देसो एवमाह–'निगण्ठो, भन्ते, नातपुत्तो पावायं अधुनाकालङ्कतो। तस्स कालङ्किरियाय भिन्ना निगण्ठा द्वेधिकजाता.....पे०....भिन्नथूपे अप्पटिसरणे"ति। तस्स मय्हं, भन्ते एवं होति–'माहेव भगवतो अच्चयेन सङ्घे विवादो उप्पज्जि; स्वास्स विवादो बहुजनाहिताय बहुजनासुखाय बहुनो जनस्स अनत्थाय अहिताय दुक्खाय देवमनुस्सानं"ति।[1]

---

1. सुत्तपिटके, मज्झिमनिकाय पालि, उपरिपण्णासकं, सामगामसुत्तं 3-4-1; पृ० 37-38।

१५
NIRVĀṆA-SAṀVĀDA–2

Nigaṇṭho Nātaputto Kālaṅkato

एवं मे सुतं। एकं समयं भगवा सक्केसु विहरती वेधञ्ञा नाम सक्या तेसं अम्बवने पासादे। तेन खो पन समयेन निगण्ठो नाटपुत्तो पावायं अधुनाकालङ्कतो होति। तस्स कालङ्किरियाय भिन्ना निगण्ठा द्वेधिकजाता भण्डनजाता कलहजाता विवादापन्ना अञ्ञमञ्ञं मुखसत्तीहि वितुदन्ता विहरन्ति–"न त्वं इम धम्मविनयं आजानासि, अहं इमं धम्मविनयं आजानामि। किं त्वं इम धम्मविनयं आजानिस्ससि? मिच्छापटिपन्नो त्वमसि, अहमस्मि सम्मापटिपन्नो। सहितं मे, असहितं ते। पुरेवचनीयं पच्छा अवच, पच्छावचनीयं पुरे अवच। अधिचिण्णं ते विपरावत्तं। आरोपितो ते वादो। निग्गहितो त्वमसि। चर वादप्पमोक्खाय। निब्बेठेहि ना सचे पहोसी"ति। वधो एव खो मञ्ञे निगण्ठेसु नाटपुत्तियेसु वत्तति। ये पि निगण्ठस्स नाटपुत्तस्स सावका गिही ओदातवसना ते पि निगण्ठेसु नाटपुत्तिसेयु निब्बिन्नरूपा विरत्तरूपा पटिवानरूपा–यथा तं दुरक्खाते धम्मविनये दुप्पवेदिते अनिय्यानिके अनुपसमसंवत्तनिके असम्मासम्बुद्धाप्पवेदिते भिन्नथूपे अप्पटिसरणे।

अथ खो चुन्दो समणुद्देसो पावायं वस्सुंवुट्ठो येन सामगामो येनायस्मा आनन्दो तेनुपसङ्कमि; उपसङ्कमित्वा आयस्मन्तं आनन्दं अभिवादेत्वा एकमन्तं निसीदि। एकमन्तं निसिन्नो खो चुन्दो समणुद्देसो आयस्मन्तं आनन्दं एतदवोच–"निगण्ठो, भन्ते, नाटपुत्तो पावायं अधुनाकालङ्कतो। तस्स कालङ्किरियाय भिन्ना निगण्ठा द्वेधिकजाता....पे०....भिन्नथूपे अप्पटिसरणे"ति।

एवं वुत्ते, आयस्मा आनन्दो चुन्दं समणुद्देसं एतदवोच–"अत्थि खो इदं, आवुसो चुन्द, कथापाभतं भगवन्तं दस्सनाय। आयामावुसो चुन्द, येन भगवा तेनुपसङ्कमिस्साम; उपसङ्कमित्वा एतमत्थं भगवतो आरोचेस्सामा"ति। "एवं, भन्ते"ति खो चुन्दो समणुद्देसो आयस्मतो आनन्दस्स पच्चस्सोसि।

अथ खो आयस्मा च आनन्दो चुन्दो च समणुद्देसो येन भगवा तेनुपसङ्कमिंसु; उपसङ्कमित्वा भगवन्तं अभिवादेत्वा एकमन्तं निसीदिंसु। एकमन्तं निसिन्नो खो आयस्मा आनन्दो भगवन्तं एतदवोच–"अयं, भन्ते, चुन्दो समणुद्देसो एवमाह–निगण्ठो, भन्ते, नाटपुत्तो पावायं अधुनाकालङ्कतो। तस्स कालङ्किरियाय भिन्ना निगण्ठा....पे०......भिन्नथूपे अप्पटिसरणे"ति।[1]

---

1. सुत्तपिटके, दीघनिकाय पालि, पाथिकवग्गो, पासादिक सुत्तं, 3-6-1; पृ० 91-92।

१६
NIRVĀṆA-CARCĀ

Sāriputto anuññjñāto dhammiyā Kathāya

एवं मे सुतं। एकं समयं भगवा मल्लेसु चारिकं चरमानो महता भिक्खुसङ्घेन सद्धिं पञ्चमत्तेहि भिक्खुसतेहि येन पावा नाम मल्लानं नगरं तदवसरि। तत्र सुदं भगवा पावायं विहरति चुन्दस्स कम्मारपुत्तस्स अम्बवने।

तेन खो पन समयेन पावेय्यकानं उब्भतकं नाम नवं सन्थागारं अचिरकारितं होति अनज्झावुत्थं समणेन वा ब्राह्मणेन वा केनचि वा मनुस्सभूतेन। अस्सोसुं खो पावेय्यका मल्ला–"भगवा किर मल्लेसु चारिकं चरमानो महता भिक्खुसङ्घेन सद्धिं पञ्चमत्तेहि भिक्खुसतेहि पावं अनुप्पत्तो पावायं विहरति चुन्दस्स कम्मारपुत्तस्स अम्बवने"ति। अथ खो पावेय्यका मल्ला येन भगवा तेनुपसङ्कमिंसु, उपसङ्कमित्वा भगवन्तं अभिवादेत्वा एकमन्तं निसीदिंसु। एकमन्तं निसिन्ना खो पावेय्यका मल्ला भगवन्तं एतदवोचुं–"इध, भन्ते, पावेय्यकानं मल्लानं उब्भतकं नाम नतं सन्थागारं अचिरकारितं होति अनज्झावुत्थं समणेन वा ब्राह्मणेन वा केनचि वा मनुस्सभूतेन। तं च, खो, भन्ते, भगवा पठमं परिभुञ्जतु। भगवता पठमं परिभुत्तं पच्छा पावेय्यका मल्ला परिभुञ्जस्सन्ति। तदस्स पावेय्यकानं मल्लानं दीघरत्तं हिताय सुखाया"ति। अधिवासेसि खो भगवा तुण्हीभावेन।

अथ खो पावेय्यका मल्ला भगवतो अधिवासनं विदित्वा उट्ठायासना भगवन्तं अभिवोदत्वा पदक्खिणं कत्वा येन सन्थागारं तेनुपसङ्कमिंसु, उपसंकमित्वा सब्बसन्थरिं सन्थागारं सन्थरित्वा भगवतो आसनानि पञ्ञापेत्वा उदकमणिकं पतिट्ठपेत्वा तेलप्पदीपं आरोपेत्वा येन भगवा तेनुपसङ्कमिंसु; उपसङ्कमित्वा भगवन्तं अभिवादेत्वा एकमन्तं अट्ठंसु। एकमन्तं ठिता खो ते पावेय्का मलया भगवन्तं एतदवोचुं–"सब्बसन्थरिसन्थतं, भन्ते, सन्थागारं। भगवतो आसनानि पञ्ञत्तानि, उदकमणिको पतिट्ठापितो, तेलपदीपो आरोपितो। यस्स दानि, भन्ते, भगवा कालं मञ्ञती"ति।

अथ खो भगवा निवासेत्वा पत्तचीवरमादाय सद्धिं भिक्खुसङ्घेन येन सन्थागारं तेनुपसङ्कमि; उपसङ्कमित्वा पादे पक्खालेत्वा सन्थागारं पविसित्वा मज्झिमं थम्भं निस्साय पुरत्थाभिमुखो निसीदि०। ....। अथ खो भगवा पावेय्यके मल्ले बहुदेव रत्तिं धम्मिया कथाय सन्दस्सेत्वा समादपेत्वा समुत्तेजेत्वा सम्पहंसेत्वा उय्योजेसि–"अभिक्कन्ता खो, वासेट्ठा, रति। यस्स दानि तुम्हे कालं मञ्ञथा"ति। "एवं, भन्ते"ति खो पावेय्यका मल्ला भगवतो पटिस्सुत्वा उट्ठापासना भगवन्तं अभिवादेत्वा पदक्खिणं कत्वा पक्कमिंसु।

अथ खो भगवा अचिरपक्कन्तेसु पावेय्यकेसु मल्लेसु तुण्हीभूतं तुण्हीभूतं भिक्खुसङ्घ अनुविलोकेत्वा आयस्मन्तं सारिपुत्तं आमन्तेसि–"विगतथिनमिद्धो खो, सारिपुत्त, भिक्खुसङ्घो। पटिभातु तं, सारिपुत्त, भिक्खुनं धम्मी कथा। पिट्ठि मे आगिलापति। तमहं आयमिस्सामी"ति। "एवं, भन्ते"ति खो आयस्मा सारिपुत्तो भगवतो पच्चस्सोसि। अथ खो भगवा चतुग्गुणं सङ्घाटिं

पञ्ञापेत्वा दक्खिणेन पस्सेन सीहसेय्यं कप्पेसि, पादे पादं अच्चाधाय, सतो सम्पजानो, उट्ठानसञ्ञं मनसि करित्वा।

Nigaṇṭha bhinna bhaṇḍanajāta

तेन खो पन समयेन निगण्ठो नाटपुत्तो पावायं अधुनाकालङ्कतो होति। तस्स कालङ्किरियाय भिन्ना निगण्ठा द्वेधिकजाता भण्डनजाता कलहजाता विवादापन्ना अञ्ञमञ्ञं मुखसत्तीहि वितुदन्ता विहरन्ति–"न त्वं इमं धम्मविनयं आजानासि, अहं इमं धम्मविनयं आजानामि। किं त्वं इमं धम्मविनयं आजानिस्ससि! मिच्छापटिपन्नो त्वमसि, अहमसि सम्मापटिपन्नो। सहितं मे, असिहतं ते। पुरेवचनीयं पच्छा अवच, पच्छावचनीयं पुरे अवच। अधिचिण्णं ते विपरवत्तं आरोपितो ते वादो। निग्गहितो त्वमसि। चर वादप्पमोक्खाय। निब्बेठेहि वा सचे पहोसि"ति। वधो येव खो मञ्ञे निगण्ठेसु नाटपुत्तियेसु वत्तति। ये पि निगण्ठस्स नाटपुत्तस्स सावका गिही ओदातवसना ते पि निगण्ठेसु नाटपुत्तियेसु निब्बिन्नरूपा विरत्तरूपा पटिवानरूपा–यथा तं दुरक्खाते धम्मविनये दुप्पवेदिते अनिय्यानिके अनुपसमसंवत्तनिके असम्मासम्बुद्धप्पवेदिते भिन्नथूपे अप्पटिसरणे।

अथ खो आयस्मा सारिपत्तो भिक्खू आमन्तेसि–"निगण्ठो, आवुसो, नाटपुत्तो पावायं अधुनाकालङ्कतो। तस्स कालङ्किरियाय भिन्ना निगण्ठा द्वेधिकजाता....पे०.....भिन्नथूपे अप्पटिसरणे"।

"एवञ्हेतं, आवुसो, होति दुरक्खाते धम्मविनये दुप्पवेदिते अनिय्यानिके अनुपसमसंवत्तनिके असम्मासम्बुद्धप्पवेदिते। अयं खो पनावुसो, अम्हाकं भगवता धम्मो स्वाक्खातो सुप्पवेदितो निय्यानिको उपसमसंवत्तनिको सम्मासम्बुद्धप्पवेदितो, तत्थ सब्बेहेव सङ्गायितब्बं, न विवदितब्बं, यथयिदं ब्रह्मचरियं अद्धनियं अस्स चिरट्ठितिकं, तदस्स बहुजनहिताय बहुजनसुखाय लोकानुकम्पाय अत्थाय हिताय सुखाय देवमनुस्सानं। कतमो चावुसो, अम्हाकं भगवता धम्मो स्वाक्खातो सप्पवेदितो निय्यानिको उपसमसंवत्तनिको सम्मासम्बुद्धप्पवेदितो, यत्थ सब्बेहेव सङ्गायितब्बं, न विवदितब्बं, यथयिदं ब्रह्मचरियं अद्धनियं अस्स चिरट्ठितिकं, तदस्स बहुजनहिताय बहुजनसुखाय लोकानुकम्पाय हिताय सुखाय देवमनुस्सानं?..........."[1]

१७

NIGAṆṬHA NĀTAPUTTA KĪ MṚTYU KĀ KĀRAṆA

ननु अयं नातपुत्तो नालन्दावासिको। सो कस्मा पावायां कालकतो? ति। सो किर उपालिना गाहापतिना पटिबिद्धसच्चेन दसहि गाथाहि भाषिते बुद्ध गुणे सुत्वा उण्हं लोहितं छड्डेसि। अथ नं अफासुकं गहेत्वा पावां अगमंसु। सो तत्थ कालं अकासि।[2]

---

1. सुत्तपिटके, दीघनिकाय पालि, पाथिकवग्गो, संगीतिसुत्तं, 3-10-1, 2, 3; पृ० 166-168।
2. मज्झिमनिकाय अट्ठकथा, सामगामसुत्त वण्णना (आई०बी० होर्नर द्वारा सम्पादित), खण्ड-4, पृ० 34।

१८
DIVYAŚAKTI PRAKARŚAṆE

तेन खो पन समयेन राजगहकस्स सेट्ठिस्स महग्घस्स चन्दनस्स चन्दनगण्ठि उप्पन्ना होति। अथ खो राजगहकस्स सेट्ठिस्स एतदहोसि–"यन्नूनाहं इमाय चन्दनगण्ठिया पत्तं लेखापेय्यं। लेखं च मे परिभोगं भविस्सति, पत्तं च दानं दस्सामी"ति। अथ खो राजगहको सेट्ठि ताय चन्दनगण्ठिया पत्तं लिखापेत्वा सिक्काय उड्डित्वा वेलग्गे आलगेत्वा वेलुपरम्पराय बन्धित्वा एमवाह–"यो समणो वा ब्राह्मणो वा अरहा चेव इद्धिमा च दिन्नञ्ञेव पत्तं ओहरतू"ति। अथ खो पूरणो कस्सपो येन राजगहको सेट्ठि तेनुपसङ्कमि; उपसङ्कमित्वा राजगहकं सेट्ठिं एतदवोच–"अहं हि, गहपति, अरहा चेव इद्धिमा च, देहि मे पत्तं"ति। "सचे, भन्ते, आयस्मा अरहा चेव इद्धिमा च दिन्नञ्ञेव पत्तं ओहरतू"ति। अथ खो मक्खलि गोसालो.....अजितो केसकम्बलो..... पकुधो कच्चायनो....सञ्जयो वेलट्ठपुत्तो....निगण्ठो नातपुत्तो येन राजगहको सेट्ठि तेनुपसङ्कमि, उपसङ्कमित्वा राजगहकं सेट्ठिं एतदवोच–"अहं हि, गहपति, अरहा चेव इद्धिमा च, देहि मे पत्तं"ति। "सचे, भन्ते, आयस्मा अरहा चेव इद्धिमा च, दिन्नञ्ञेव पत्तं ओहरतू"ति।

तेन खो पन समयेन आयस्मा च महामोग्गल्लानो आयस्मा च पिण्डोलभारद्वाजो पुब्बण्हसमयं निवासेत्वा पत्तचीवरमादाय राजगहं पिण्डाय पविसिंसु। अथ खो आयस्मा पिण्डोलभारद्वाजो आयस्मन्तं महामोग्गल्लानं एतदवोच–"आयस्मा खो महामोग्गल्लानो अरहा चेव इद्धिमा च। गच्छावुसो, मोगल्लान, एतं पत्तं ओहर। तुय्हेसो पत्तो"ति। "आयस्मा पि खो पिण्डोलभारद्वाजो अरहा चेव इद्धिमा च। गच्छावुसो, भारद्वाज, एतं पत्तं ओहर। तुय्हेसो पत्तो"ति। अथ खो आयस्मा पिण्डोलभारद्वाजो वेहासं अब्भुग्गन्त्वा तं पत्तं गहेत्वा निक्खत्तं राजगहं अनुपरियायि।

तेन खो पन समयेन राजगहको सेट्ठि सपुत्तदारो सके निवेसने ठितो होति पञ्जलिको नमस्समानो–इधेव, भन्ते, अय्यो भारद्वाजो अम्हाकं निवेसने पतिट्ठातू ति। अथ खो आयस्मा पिण्डोलभारद्वाजो राजगहकस्स सेट्ठिस्स निवेसने पतिट्ठासि। अथ खो राजगहको सेट्ठि आयस्मतो पिण्डोलभारद्वाजस्स हत्थतो पत्तं गहेत्वा महग्घस्स खादनीयस्स पूरेत्वा आयस्मतो पिण्डोलभारद्वाजस्स अदासि। अथ खो आयस्मा पिण्डोलभारद्वाजो तं पत्तं गहेत्वा आरामं अगमासि। अस्सोसुं खो मनुस्सा–अय्येन किर पिण्डोलभारद्वाजेन राजगहकस्स सेट्ठिस्स पत्तो ओहारितो ति। ते च मनुस्सा उच्चासद्दा महासद्दा आयस्मन्तं पिण्डोलभारद्वाजं पिट्ठितो पिट्ठितो अनुबन्धिसु।

अस्सेसि खो भगवा उच्चासद्दं, महासद्दं; सुत्वान आयस्मन्तं आनन्दं आमन्तेसि–"किं नु खो सो, आनन्द, उच्चासद्दो महासद्दो"ति? "आयस्मता, भन्ते, पिण्डोलभारद्वाजेन राजगहकस्स सेट्ठिस्स पत्तो ओहारितो। अस्सोसुं खो, भन्ते, मनुस्सा–अय्येन किर पिण्डोलभारद्वाजेन राजगहकस्स सेट्ठिस्स पत्तो ओहारितो ति। ते च, भन्ते, मनुस्सा उच्चासद्दा महासद्दा आयस्मन्तं पिण्डोलभारद्वाजं पिट्ठितो पिट्ठितो अनुबन्धा। सो एसो, भन्ते, भगवा उच्चासद्दो महासदो"ति। अथ खो भगवा एतस्मिं निदाने एतस्मिं पकरणे भिक्खुसङ्घं सन्निपातापेत्वा आयस्मन्तं पिण्डोलभारद्वाजं

पटिपुच्छि–"सच्चं किर तया, भारद्वाज, राजगहकस्स सेट्ठिस पत्तो ओहारितो"ति? "सच्चं भगवा"ति। विगरहि बुद्धो भगवा–"अननुच्छविकं, भारद्वाज, अननुलोमिकं अप्पतिरूपं अस्सामणकं अकप्पियं अकरणीयं। कथं हि नाम त्वं, भारद्वाज, छवस्स दारुपतस्स कारणा गिहीनं उत्तरिमनुस्सधम्मं इद्धिपाटिहारियं दस्सेस्ससि। सेय्यथापि, भारद्वाज, मातुगामो छवस्स मासकरूपस्स कारणा कोपिनं दस्सेति, एवमेव खो तया, भारद्वाज, छवस्स दारुपत्तस्स कारणा गिहीनं उत्तरिमनुस्सधम्मं इद्धिपाटिहारियं दस्सितं। नेतं, भारद्वाज, अप्पसन्नानं वा पसादाय, पसन्नानं वा मिय्योभावाय। अथ ख्वेतं, भारद्वाज, अप्पसन्नानं। चेव अप्पसादाय पसन्नानं च एकच्चानं अञ्ञथत्ताया"ति। अथ खो भगवा पिण्डोलभारद्वाजं अनेकपरियायेन विगरहित्वा, दुब्भरताय दुप्पोसताय महिच्छताय असन्तुट्ठिताय सङ्गणिकाय कोसज्जस्स अवण्णं भासित्वा अनेकपरियायेन सुभरताय सुपोसताय अप्पिच्छस्स सन्तुट्ठस्स सल्लेखस्स धुतस्स पासादिकस्स अपचयस्स विरियारम्भस्स वण्णं भासित्वा, भिक्खूनं तदनुच्छविकं तदनुलोमिकं धम्मिं कथं कत्वा भिक्खू आमन्तेति–

"न भिक्खवे, गिहीनं उत्तरिमनुस्सधम्मं इद्धिपाटिहारियं दस्सेतब्बं। यो दस्सेय्य, आपत्ति दुक्कटस्स। भिन्दथेतं भिक्खवे, दारुपत्तं, सकलिकं सकलिकं कत्वा, भिक्खूनं अञ्जनुपपिसनं देथ। न च, भिक्खवे, दारुपत्तो धारेतब्बो। यो धारेय्य, आपत्ति दुक्कटस्सा"ति।

..."न, भिक्खवे, सोवण्णमयो पत्तो धारेतब्बो....पे०....न रूपियमयो पत्तो धारेतब्बो...न मणिमयो पत्तो धारेतब्बो....न वेलुरियमयो पत्तो धारेतब्बो......न फलिकमयो पत्तो धारेतब्बो... ..त कंसमयो पत्तो धारेतब्बो,......न काचमयो पत्तो धारेतब्बो......न तिपुमयो पत्तो धारेतब्बो.. ...न सीसमयो पत्तो धारेतब्बो......न तम्बलोहमयो पत्तो धारेब्बो। यो धारेय्य, आपत्ति दुक्कटस्स। अनुजानामि, भिक्खवे, द्वे पत्ते–अयोपत्तं, मत्तिकापत्तं"ति।[1]

२२

ŚRĀMAṆYA PHALA

Añjñjatithiyā

एवं मे सुतं। एकं समयं भगवा राजगहे विहरति जीवकस्स कोमारभच्चस्स अम्बवने महता भिक्खुसङ्घेन सद्धिं अड्ढतेलसेहि भिक्खुसतेहि। तेन खो पन समयेन राजा मागधो अजातसत्तु वेदेहिपुत्तो तदहुपोसथे पन्नरसे कोमुदिया चातुमासिनिया पुण्णाय पुण्णमाय रत्तिया राजामच्चपरिवुतो उपरिपासादवरगतो निसिन्नो होति। अथ खो राजा मागधो अजातसत्तु वेदेहिपुत्तो तदहुपोसथे उदानं उदानेसि–"रमणीया वत भो दोसिना रत्ति, अभिरूपा वत भो दोसिना रत्ति, दस्सनीया वत भो दोसिना रत्ति, पासादिका वत भो दोसिना रत्ति, लक्खञ्ञा वत भो दोसिना रत्ति! कं नु ख्वज्ज, समणं वा ब्राह्मणं वा पयिरुपासेय्याम, यं नो पयिरुपासतो चित्तं पसीदेय्या"ति?

एवं वुत्ते, अञ्ञतरो राजामच्चो राजानं मागधं अजातसत्तुं वेदेहिपुत्तं एतदवोच–"अयं, देव,

1. विनयपिटके, चुल्लवग्ग पालि, खुद्दकवत्थुक्खन्धकं, पिण्डोलभारद्वाजपत्तंवत्थु, 5-5-10; पृ० 199-201।

पूरणो कस्सपो सङ्घी चेव गणी च गणाचरियो च, ञातो, यसस्सी, तित्थकरो, साधुसम्मतो बहुजनस्स, रत्तञ्ञू, चिरपब्बजितो, अद्धगतो, वयोअनुप्पत्तो। तं देवो पूरणं कस्सपं पयिरुपासतु। अप्पेव नाम देवस्स पूरणं कस्सपं पयिरुपासतो चित्तं पसीदेय्या"ति। एवं वुत्ते, राजा मागधो अजातसत्तु वेदेहिपुत्तो तुण्ही अहोसि।

अञ्ञतरो पि खो राजामच्ची राजानं मागधं अजातसत्तुं वेदेहिपुत्तं एतदवोच–"अयं, देव, मक्खलि गोसाली सङ्घी०.....।"

अञ्ञतरो पि खो राजामच्ची राजानं मागधं अजातसत्तुं वेदेहिपुत्तं एतदवोच–"अयं, देव, अजितो केसकम्बलो सङ्घी०......।"

अञ्ञतरो पि खो राजामच्ची राजानं मागधं अजातसत्तुं वेदेहिपुत्तं एतदवोच–"अयं, देव, पकुधो कच्चायनो सङ्घी०.....।"

अञ्ञतरो पि खो राजामच्ची राजानं मागधं अजातसत्तुं वेदेहिपुत्तं एतदवोच–"अयं, देव, सञ्जयो बेलट्ठपुत्तो सङ्घी०......।"

अञ्ञतरो पि खो राजामच्चो राजानं मागधं अजातसत्तुं वेदेहिपुत्तं एतदवोच–"अयं, देव, निगण्ठो नाटपुत्तो सङ्घी चेव गणी च गणाचरियो च, ञातो, यसस्सी, तित्थकरो, साधु सम्मतो बहुजनस्स, रत्तञ्ञू, चिरपब्बजितो, अद्धगतो वयोअनुप्पत्तो। तं देवो निगण्ठं नातपुत्तं पयिरुपासतु। अप्पेव नाम देवस्स निगण्ठं नाटपुत्तं पयिरुपासतो चित्तं पसीदेय्या"ति। एवं वुत्ते, राजा मागधो अजातसत्तु वेदेहिपुत्तो तुण्ही अहोसि।

Rājā Jīvakambavane bhagavantaṁ upasaṅkami

तेन खो पन समयेन जीवको कोमारभच्चो रञ्ञो मागधस्स अजातसत्तुस्स वेदेहिपुत्तस्स अविदूरे तुण्हीभूतो निसिन्नो होति। अथ खो राजा मागधो अजातसत्तु वेदेहिपुत्तो जीवकं कोमारभच्चं एतदवोच–"त्वं पन, सम्म जीवक, किं तुण्ही"ति?

"अयं, देव, भगवा अरहं सम्मासम्बुद्धो अम्हाकं अम्बवने विहरति महता भिक्खुसङ्घेन सद्धिं अड्ढतेलसेहि भिक्खुसतेहि। तं खो पन भगवन्तं एव कल्याणो कित्तिसद्धो अब्भुग्गतो–'इति पि सो भगवा, अरहं, सम्मासम्बुद्धो, विज्जाचरणसम्पन्नो, सुगतो, लोकविदू, अनुत्तरो, पुरिसदम्मसारथि, सत्था देवमनुस्सानं, बुद्धो, भगवा'ति। तं देवो भगवन्तं पयिरुपासतु। अप्पेव नाम देवस्स भगवन्तं परिरुपासतो चित्तं पसीदेय्या"ति।

"तेन हि, सम्म जीवक, हत्थियानानि कप्पापेही"ति। "एवं, देवा"ति खो जीवको कोमारभच्चो रञ्ञो मागधस्स अजातसत्तुस्स वेदेहिपुत्तस्स पटिस्सुणित्वा पञ्चमत्तानि हत्थिनिकासतानि कप्पापेत्वा रञ्ञो च आरोहणीयं नागं, रञ्ञो मागधस्स अजातसत्तुस्स वेदेहिपुत्तस्स पटिवेदेसि–"कप्पितानि खो ते, देव, हत्थियानानि। यस्सदानि कालं मञ्ञसी"ति।

अथ खो राजा मागधो अजातसत्तु वेदेहिपुत्तो पञ्चसु हत्थिनिकासतेसु पच्चेका इत्थोयो

आरोपेत्वा, आरोहणीयं नागं अभिरुहित्वा, उक्कासु धारियमानासु, राजगहम्हा निय्यासि महच्चा राजानुभावेन; येन जीवकस्स कोमारभच्चस्स अम्बवनं तेन पाय्यासि।

अथ खो रञ्ञो मागधस्स अजातसत्तुस्स वेदेहिपुत्तस्स अविदूरे अम्बवनस्स अहुदेव भयं, अहु छम्भितत्तं, अहु लोमहंसो। अथ खो राजा मागधो अजातसत्तु, वेदेहिपुत्तो भीतो संविग्गो लोमहट्ठजातो जीवकं कोमारभच्चं एतदवोच–"कच्चि मं, सम्म जीवकं, न वञ्चेसि? कच्चि मं, सम्म जीवक, न पलम्भेसि? कच्चि मं, सम्म जीवक, न पच्चत्थिकानं देसि? कथं हि नाम ताव महतो भिक्खुसङ्घस्स अड्ढतेलसानं भिक्खुसतानं नेव खिपितसद्दो भविस्सति न उक्कासितसद्दो निग्घोसो" ति!

"मा भायि, महाराज; मा भायि, महाराज। न ते, देव, वञ्चेमि। न तं, देव, पलम्भामि। न तं, देव, पच्चत्थिकानं देमि। अभिक्कम, महाराज, अभिक्कम, महाराज। एते मण्डलमाले झायन्ती"ति।

अथ खो राजा मगधो अजातसत्तु वेदेहिपुत्तो यावतिका नामस्स भूमि नागेन गन्त्वा, नागा पच्चोरोहित्वा, पत्तिको व येन मण्डलमालस्स द्वारं तेनुपसङ्कमि, उपसङ्कमित्वा जीवकं कोमारभच्चं एतदवोच–"कहं पन, सम्म जीवक, भगवा" ति?

"एसो, महाराज, भगवा; एसो, महाराज, भगवा मज्झिमं थम्भं निस्साय पुरत्थाभिमुखो निसिन्नो, पुरक्खतो भिक्खुसङ्घस्सा"ति।

अथ खो राजा मागधो अजातसत्तु वेदेहिपुत्तो येन भगवा तेनुपसङ्कमि; उपसङ्कमित्वा एकमन्तं अट्ठासि। एकमन्तं ठितो खो राजा मागधो अजातसत्तु वेदेहिपुत्तो तुण्हीभूतं भिक्खुसङ्घं अनुविलोकेत्वा रहदमिव विप्पसन्नं, उदानं उदानेसि–"इमिना मे उपसमेन उदयभद्दो कुमारो समन्नागतो होतु येनेतरहि उपसमेन भिक्खुसङ्घो समन्नागतो"ति।

"अगमा खो त्वं, महाराज, यथापेमं"ति।

"पियो मे, भन्ते, उदयभद्दो कुमारो। इमिना मे, भन्ते, उपसमेन उदयभद्दो कुमारो समन्नागतो होतु येनेतरहि उपसमेन भिक्खुसङ्घो समन्नागतो"ति।

अथ खो राजा मागधो अजातसत्तु वेदेहिपुत्तो भगवन्तं अभिवादेत्वा, भिक्खुसङ्घस्स अञ्जलिं पणामेत्वा, एकमन्तं निसीदि। एकमन्त निसिन्नो खो राजा मागधो अजातसत्तु वेदेहिपुत्तो भगवन्तं एतदवोच–"पुच्छेय्यामहं, भन्ते, भगवन्तं किञ्चिदेव देसं, सचे मे भगवा ओकासं करोति पञ्हस्स वेय्याकरणाया"ति।

"पुच्छ, महाराज, यदाकङ्खसी"ति।

Sāmaññaphalapucchā

"यथा नु खो इमानि, भन्ते, पुथुसिप्पायतनानि, सेय्यथिदं–हंत्थारोहा अस्सारोहा रथिका धनुग्गहा चेलका चलका पिण्डदायका ऊग्गा राजपुत्ता पक्खन्दिनो महानागा सूरा चम्मयोधिनो

दासिकपुत्ता आलारिका कप्पका न्हापका सूदा मालाकारा रजका पेसकार, नलकारा कुम्भकारा गणका मुद्दिका, यानि वा पनञ्ञानि पि एवंगतानि पुथुसिप्पायतनानि, ते दिट्ठेव धम्मे सन्दिट्ठिकं सिप्पफलं उपजीवन्ति; ते तेन अत्तानं सुखेन्ति पीणेन्ति, मातापितरो सुखेन्ति पीणेन्ति, पुत्तदारं सुखेन्ति पीणेन्ति, मित्तामच्चे सुखेन्ति पीणेन्ति, समणब्राह्मणेसु उद्धग्गिकं दक्खिणं पतिट्ठपेन्ति सोवग्गिकं सुखविपाकं सग्गसंवत्तनिकं। सक्का नु खो, भन्ते, एवमेव दिट्ठेव धम्मे सन्दिट्ठिकं सामञ्ञफलं पञ्ञपेतु"ति?

Cchātitthiyavāda

"अभिजानासि नो त्वं, महाराज, इमं पञ्हं अञ्ञे समणब्राह्मणे पुच्छिता" ति?

"अभिजानामहं, भन्ते, इमं पञ्हं अञ्ञे समणब्राह्मणे पुच्छिता"ति।

"यथा कथं पन ते, महाराज, ब्याकरिंसु, सचे ते अगरु भासस्सू"ति।

"न खो मे, भन्ते, गरु, यत्थस्स भगवा निसिन्नो, भगवन्तरूपो वा"ति।

"तेन हि, महाराज, भासस्सू"ति।

Pūraṇakassapavādo

"एकमिदाहं, भन्ते, समयं येन पूरणो कस्सपो तेनुपसङ्कमिं; उपसङ्कमित्वा पूरणेन कस्सपेन सद्धिं सम्मोदिं। सम्मोदनीयं कथं सारणीयं वीतिसारेत्वा एकमन्तं निसीदिं। एकमन्तं निसिन्नो खो अहं, भन्ते पूरणं कस्सपं एतदवोचं–'यथा नु खो इमानि, भो कस्सप, पुथुसिप्पायतनानि, ०.......।

"एवं वुत्ते, भन्ते, पूरणो कस्सपो मं एतदवोच–'करोतो खो, महाराज, कारयतो छिन्दतो छेदापयतो पचतो पाचापयतो०........।

इत्थं खो मे, भन्ते, पूरणो कस्सपो सन्दिट्ठिकं सामञ्ञफलं पुट्ठो समानो अकिरियं ब्याकासि। सेय्यथापि भन्ते, अम्बं वा पुट्ठो लबुजं ब्याकरेय्य, लबुजं वा पुट्ठो अम्बं ब्याकरेय्य; एवमेव खो मे, भन्ते, पूरणो कस्सपो सन्दिट्ठिकं सामञ्ञफलं पुट्ठो समानो अकिरियं ब्याकासि। तस्स मय्हं, भन्ते, एतदहोसि–'कथं हि नाम मादिसो समणं वा ब्राह्मणं वा विजिते वसन्तं अपसादेतब्बं मञ्ञेय्या' ति। सो खो अहं, भन्ते, पूरणस्स कस्सपस्स भासितं नेव अभिनन्दिं नप्पटिक्कोसिं। अनभिनन्दित्वा अप्पटिकोसित्वा अनत्तमनो, अनत्तमनवाचं अनिच्छारेत्वा, तमेव वाचं अनुग्गण्हन्तो अनिकुज्जन्तो उट्ठायासना पक्कमिं।"

Makkhaligosālavādo

"एकमिदाहं, भन्ते, समयं येन मक्खलि गोसालो०.......।

Ajitakesakambalavādo

"एकमिदाहं, भन्ते, समयं येन अजितो केसकम्बलो०.......।

Pakudhakaccāyanavādo

"एकमिदाहं, भन्ते, समयं येन पकुधो कच्चायनो०........।

Nigaṇṭhanātaputtavādo

"एकमिदाहं, भन्ते, समयं येन निगण्ठो नाटपुत्तो तेनुपसङ्कमिं; उपसङ्कमित्वा निगण्ठेन नाटपुत्तेन सद्धिं सम्मोदिं। सम्मोदनीयं कथं सारणीयं वीतिसारेत्वा एकमन्तं निसीदिं। एकमन्तं निसिन्नो खो अहं, भन्ते, निगण्ठं नाटपुत्तं एतदवोचं–'यथा नु खो इमानि, भो अग्गिवेस्सन, पुथुसिप्पायतनानि....पे०....सक्का नु खो, भो अग्गिवेस्सन, एवमेव दिट्ठेव धम्मे सन्दिट्ठिकं सामञ्ञफलं पञ्ञपेतुं"ति?

"एवं वुत्ते, भन्ते, निगण्ठो नाटपुत्तो मं एतदवोच–'इध, महाराज, निगण्ठो चातुयामसंवरसंवुतो होति। कथं च, महाराज, निगण्ठो चातुयामसंवरसंवुतो होति? इध, महाराज, निगण्ठो सब्बवारिवारितो च होति, सब्बवारियुत्तो च, सब्बवारिधुतो च, सब्बवारिफुटो च। एवं खो, महाराज, निगण्ठो चातुयामसंवरसंवुतो होति। यतो खो, महाराज, निगण्ठो एवं चातुयामसंवरसंवुतो होति; अयं वुच्चति, महाराज, निगण्ठो गतत्तो च यतत्तो च ठितत्तो चा' ति।"

"इत्थं खो मे, भन्ते, निगण्ठो नाटपुत्तो सन्दिट्ठिकं सामञ्ञफलं पुट्ठो समानो चातुयामसंवरं ब्याकासि। सेय्यथापि, भन्ते, अम्बं वा पुट्ठो लबुजं ब्याकरेय्य, लबुजं वा पुट्ठो अम्बं ब्याकरेय्य; एवमेव खो मे, भन्ते, निगण्ठो नाटपुत्तो सन्दिट्ठिकं सामञ्ञफलं पुट्ठो समानो चातुयामसंवरं ब्याकासि। तस्स मय्हं, भन्ते, एतदहोसि–'कथं हि नाम मादिसो समणं वा ब्राह्मणं वा विजिते वसन्तं अपसादेतब्बं मञ्ञेय्या' ति। सो खो अहं, भन्ते, निगण्ठस्स नाटपुत्तस्स भासितं नेव अभिनन्दिं नप्पटिक्कोसिं। अनभिनन्दित्वा अप्पटिक्कोसित्वा अनत्तमनो, अनत्तमनवाचं अनिच्छारेत्वा, तमेव वाचं अनुग्गण्हन्तो अनिक्कुज्जन्तो, उट्ठायासना पक्कमिं।

Sañjjayabelaṭṭhaputtavādo

"एकमिदाहं, भन्ते, समयं येन सञ्चयो बेलट्ठपुत्तो०......।

Buddhavādo

Pathamasanditthisamañjñjaphala

"सोहं, भन्ते, भगवन्तं पि पुच्छामि–'यथा नु खो इमानि, भन्ते, पुथुसिप्पायतनानि०...।

Ajattu upāsakattapātī vadna

एवं वुत्ते, राजा मागधो अजातसत्तु वेदेहिपुत्तो भगवन्तं एतदवोच–"अभिक्कन्तं, भन्ते,

अभिक्कन्तं, भन्ते। सेय्यथापि, भन्ते, निक्कुज्जितं वा उक्कुज्जेय्य, पटिच्छन्नं वा विवरेय्य, मूल्हस्स वा मग्गं आचिक्खेय्य, अन्धकारे वा तेलपज्जोतं धारेय्य चक्खुमन्तो रूपानि दक्खन्ती ति; एवमेवं, भन्ते, भगवता अनेकपरियायेन धम्मो पकासितो। एसाहं, भन्ते, भगवन्तं सरणं गच्छामि धम्मं च भिक्खुसङ्घं च। उपासकं मं भगवा धारेतु अज्जतग्गे पाणुपेतं सरणं गतं। अच्चयो मं, भन्ते, अच्चगमा यथाबालं यथामूल्हं यथाअकुसलं, योहं पितरं धम्मिकं धम्मराजानं इस्सरियकारणा जीविता वोरोपेसिं। तस्स मे, भन्ते, भगवा अच्चयं अच्चयतो पटिग्गण्हातु आयतिं संवराया"ति।

"तग्घ त्वं, महाराज, अच्चयो अच्चगमा यथाबालं यथामूल्हं यथाअकुसलं, ये त्वं पितरं धम्मिकं धम्मराजानं जीविता वोरोपेसि। यतो च खो त्वं, महाराज, अच्चयं अच्चयतो दिस्वा यथाधम्मं पटिकरोसि, तं ते मयं पटिग्गण्हाम। बुद्धिहेसा, महाराज, अरियस्स विनये यो अच्चयं अच्चयतो दिस्वा यथाधम्मं पटिकरोति, आयतिं संवरं आपज्जती"ति।

एवं वुत्ते, राजा मागधो अजातसत्तु वेदेहिपुत्तो भगवन्तं एतदवोच–"हन्द च दानि मयं, भन्ते, गच्छाम। बहुकिच्चा मयं बहुकरणीया"ति।

"यस्सदानि, त्वं, महाराज, कालं मञ्ञसी"ति।

अथ खो राजा मागधो अजातसत्तु वेदेहिपुत्तो भगवतो भासितं अभिनन्दित्वा अनुमोदित्वा उट्ठायासना भगवन्तं अभिवादेत्वा पदक्खिणं कत्वा पक्कामि।

अथ खो भगवा अचिरपक्कन्तस्स रञ्ञो मागधस्स अजातसत्तुस्स वेदेहिपुत्तस्स भिक्खू आमन्तेसि–"खतायं, भिक्खवे, राजा। उपहतायं, भिक्खवे, राजा। सचायं, भिक्खवे, राजा पितरं धम्मिकं धम्मराजानं जीविता न वोरोप्रेस्सथ, इमस्मिं येव आसने विरजं वीतमलं धम्मचक्खुं उप्पज्जिस्सथा"ति। इदमवोच भगवा। अत्तमना ते भिक्खू भगवतो भासितं अभिनन्दुं ति।[1]

२३

BUDDHA : DHARMĀCĀRYON MEN KAMṢTHA

एवं मे सुतं। एकं समयं भगवा सावत्थियं विहरति जेतवने अनाथपिण्डिकस्स आरामे। अथ खो राजा पसेनदि कोसलो येन भगवा तेनुपसङ्कमि; उपसङ्कमित्वा भगवता सद्धिं सम्मोदि। सम्मोदनीयं कथं सारणीयं वीतिसारेत्वा एकमन्तं निसीदि। एकमन्तं निसिन्नो खो राजा पसेनदि कोसलो भगवन्तं एतदवोच–"भवं पि नो गोतमो अनुत्तरं सम्मासम्बोधिं अभिसम्बुद्धो ति पटिजानाती"ति?

यं हि तं, महाराज, सम्मा वदमानो वदेय्य 'अनुत्तरं सम्मासम्बोधिं अभिसम्बुद्धो' ति, ममेव तं सम्मा वदमानो वदेय्य! अहं हि, महाराज, अनुत्तरं सम्मासम्बोधिं अभिसम्बुद्धो"ति।

"ये पि ते, भो गोतम, समणब्राह्मणा सङ्घिनो गणिनो गणाचरिया ञाता यसस्सिनो तित्थकरा

1. सुत्तपिटके, दीघनिकाय पालि, सीलक्खन्धवग्गो, सामञ्ञफलसुत्तं, 1-2-1 से 6 ; पृ० 41 से 75।

साधुसम्मता बहुजनस्स, सेय्यथीदं–पूरणो कस्सपो, मक्खलि गोसालो, निगण्ठो नाटपुत्तो, सञ्जयो वेलट्ठपुत्तो, पकुधो कच्चायनो, अजितो केसकम्बलो; ते पि मया 'अनुत्तरं सम्मासम्बोधिं अभिसम्बुद्धो ति पटिजानाथा' ति पुट्ठा समाना अनुत्तरं सम्मासम्बोधिं अभिसम्बुद्धो ति न पटिजानन्ति; किं पन भवं गोतमो दहरो चेव जातिया नवो च पब्बज्जाया"ति?

"चत्तारो खो मे, महाराज, दहरा ति न उञ्ञातब्बा, दहरा ति न परिभोतब्बा। कतमे चत्तारो? खत्तियो खो, महाराज, दहरो ति न उञ्ञातब्बो, दहरो ति न परिभोतब्बो। उरगो खो महाराज, दहरो ति न उञ्ञातब्बो, दहरो ति न परिभोतब्बो। अग्गि खो, महाराज, दहरो ति न उञ्ञातब्बो, दहरो ति न परिभोतब्बो। भिक्खु, खो, महाराज, दहरो ति न उञ्ञातब्बो, दहरो ति न परिभोतब्बो। इमे खो, महाराज, चत्तारो दहरा ति न उञ्ञातब्बा, दहरा ति न परिभोतब्बा"ति।

इदमवोच भगवा। इदं वत्वान सुगतो अथापरं एतदवोच सत्था–

"खत्तियं जातिसम्पन्नं, अभिजातं यसस्सिनं।
दहरो ति नावजानेय्य, न नं पिरभवे नरो।।
"ठानं हि सो मनुजिन्दो, रज्जं लद्धान खत्तियो।
सो कुद्धो राजदण्डेन, तस्मिं पक्कमते भुसं।
तस्मा तं परिवज्जेय्य, रक्खं जीवितमत्तनो।।
"गामे वा यदि वा रञ्ञे, यत्थ पस्से भुजङ्गमं।
दहरो ति नावजानेय्य, न नं परिभवे नरो।।
"उच्चावचेहि वण्णेहि, उरगो चरति तेजसी।
सो आसज्ज डंसे बालं, नरं नारिं च एकदा।
तस्मा तं परिवज्जेय्य, रक्खं जीवितमत्तनो।।
"पहूतभक्खं जालिनं, पावकं कण्हवत्तनिं।
दहरो ति नावजानेय्य, न नं परिभवे नरो।।
"लद्धा हि सो उपादानं, महा हुत्वान पावको।
सो आसज्ज डहे बालं, नरं नारिं च एकदा।
तस्मा तं परिवज्जेय्य, रक्खं जीवितमत्तनो।।
"वनं यदग्गि डहति, पावको कण्हवत्तनी।
जायन्ति तत्थ पारोहा, अहोरत्तानमच्चये।।
"यञ्च खो सीलसम्पन्नो, भिक्खु डहति तेजसा।
न तस्स पुत्ता पसवो, दायादा विन्दरे धनं।
अनपच्चा अदायादा, तालावत्थू भवन्ति ते।।

"तस्मा हि पण्डितो पोसो, सम्पस्सं अत्थमत्तनो।
भुजङ्गमं पावकं च, खत्तियं च यसस्सिनं।
भिक्खुं च सीलसम्पन्नं, सम्मदेव समाचरे"ति।।

एवं वुत्ते, राजा पसेनदि कोसलो भगवन्तं एतदवोच–"अभिक्कन्तं, भन्ते अभिक्कन्तं, भन्ते! सेय्यथापि भन्ते, निक्कुज्जितं वा उक्कुज्जेय्य पटिच्छन्नं वा विवरेय्य मूळ्हस्स वा मग्गं आचिक्खेय्य अन्धकारे वा तेलपज्जोतं धारेय्य–चक्खुमन्तो रूपानि दक्खन्ती ति; एवमेवं भगवता अनेकपरियायेन धम्मो पकासितो। एसाहं, भन्ते, भगवन्तं सरणं गच्छामि धम्मं च भिक्खुसङ्घं च। उपासकं मं, भन्ते, भगवा धारेतु अज्जतग्गे पाणुपेतं सरणं गतं"ति।[1]

२४

SABHIYA PARIVRĀJAKA

एवं मे सुतं। एकं समयं भगवा राजगहे विहरति वेलुवने कलन्दकनिवापे। तेन खो पन समयेन सभियस्स परिब्बाजकस्स पुराणसालोहिताय देवताय पञ्हा उद्दिट्ठा होन्ति–"यो ते, सभिय, समणो वा ब्राह्मणो वा इमे पञ्हे पुट्ठो ब्याकरोति तस्स सन्तिके ब्रह्मचरियं चरेय्यासी"ति।

अथ खो सभियो परिब्बाजको तस्सा देवताय सन्तिके ने पञ्हे उग्गहेत्वा ये ते समणब्राह्मणा सङ्घिनो गणिनो गणाचरिया ञाता यसस्सिनो तित्थकरा साधुसम्मता बहुजनस्स, सेय्यथीदं–पूरणो कस्सपो मक्खलिगोसालो अजितो केसकम्बलो पकुधो कच्चानो सञ्चयो बेलट्ठपुत्तो निगण्ठो नाटपुत्तो, ते उपसङ्कमित्वा ते पञ्हे पुच्छति। ते सभियेन परिब्बाजकेन पञ्हे पुट्ठा न सम्पायन्ति; असम्पायन्ता कोपं च दोसं च अप्पच्चयं च पातुकरोन्ति। अपि च सभियंयेव परिब्बाजकं पटिपुच्छन्ति।

अथ खो सभियस्स परिब्बाजकस्स एतदहोसि–"ये खो ते भोन्तो समणब्राह्मणा सङ्घिनो गणिनो गणाचिरया ञाता यसस्सिनो तित्थकरा साधुसम्मता बहुजनस्स, सेय्यथीदं–पूरणो कस्सपो ....पे०.....निगण्ठो नाटपुत्तो, ते मया पञ्हे पुट्ठा न सम्पायन्ति, असम्पायन्ता कोपं च दोसं च अप्पच्चयं च पातुकरोन्ति; अपि च मञ्ञेवेत्थ पटिपुच्छन्ति। यन्नूनाहं हीनायावत्तित्वा कामे परिभुञ्जेय्यं"ति।

अथ खो सभियस्स परिब्बाजकस्स एतदहोसि–"अयं पि खो समणो गोतमो सङ्घी चेव गणी च गणाचिरयो च ञातो यसस्सी तित्थकरो साधुसम्मतो बहुजनस्स; यन्नूनाहं समणं गोतमं उपसङ्कमित्वा इमे पञ्हे पुच्छेय्यं"ति।

अथ खो सभियस्स परिब्बाजकस्स एतदहोसि–"ये पि खो ते भोन्तो समणब्राह्मणा जिण्णा वुड्ढा महल्लका अद्धगता वयोअनुप्पत्ता थेरा रत्तञ्ञू चिरपब्बजिता सङ्घिनो गणिनो गणाचिरया ञाता यसस्सिनो तित्थकरा साधुसम्मता बहुजनस्स सेय्यथीदं–पूरणो कस्सपो...पे०....निगण्ठो नाटपुत्तो, ते पि मया पञ्हे पुट्ठा न सम्पायन्ति, असम्पायन्ता कोपं च दोसं च अप्पच्चयं च पातुकरोन्ति,

1. सुत्तपिटके, संयुत्तनिकाय पालि, सगाथवग्गो, कोसलसंयुत्तं, दहरसुत्त, 3-1-1 से 4; पृ० 67-69।

अपि च मञ्ञेवेत्थ पटिपुच्छन्ति; किं पन मे समणो गोतमो इमे पञ्हे पुट्ठो ब्याकरिस्सति! समणो हि गोतमो दहरो चेव जातिया नवो च पब्बज्जाया"ति।

अथ खो सभियस्स परिब्बाजकस्स एतदहोसि–"समणो खो दहरो ति न उञ्ञातब्बो न परिभोतब्बो। दहरो पि चेस समणो गोतमो महिद्धिको होति महानुभावो, यन्नूनाहं समणं गोतमं उपसङ्कमित्वा इमे पञ्हे पुच्छेय्यं"ति।

अथ खो सभियो परिब्बाजको येन राजगहं तेन चारिकं पक्कामि। अनुपुब्बेन चारिकं चरमानो येन राजगहं वेलुवनं कलन्दकनिवापो, येन भगवा तेनुपसङ्कमि; उपसङ्कमित्वा भगवता सद्धिं सम्मोदि। सम्मोदनीयं कथं साराणीयं वीतिसारेत्वा एकमन्तं निसीदि। एकमन्तं निसिन्नो खो सभियो परिब्बाजको भगवन्तं गाथाय अज्झभासि–

"कङ्खी वेचिकिच्छी आगमं, (इति सभियो)
पञ्हे पुच्छितुं अभिकङ्खमानो।
तेसन्तकरो भवाहि पञ्हे मे पुट्ठो,
अनुपुब्बं अनुधम्मं ब्याकरोहि मे"।।
"दूरतो आगतोसि सभिय, (इति भगवा)
पञ्हे पुच्छितुं अभिकङ्खमानो।
तेसन्तकरो भवामि पञ्हे ते पुट्ठो,
अनुपुब्बं अनुधम्मं ब्याकरोमि"ते।।
"पुच्छ मं सभिय पञ्हं,
यं किञ्चि मनसिच्छसि।
तस्स तस्सेव पञ्हस्स,
अहं अन्तं करोमि ते"ति।।

अथ खो सभियस्स परिब्बाजकस्स एतदहोसि–"अच्छरियं वत, भो, अब्भुतं वत, भो! यं वताहं अञ्ञेसु समणब्राह्मणेसु ओकासकम्ममत्तं पि नालत्थं तं मे इदं समणेन गोतमेन ओकासकम्मं कतं"ति। अत्तमनो पमुदितो उदग्गो पीतिसोमनस्सजातो भगवन्तं पञ्हं अपुच्छि–

"किं पत्तिनमाहु भिक्खुनं, (इति सभियो) ०......" (112)

अथ खो सभियो परिब्बाजको भगवतो भासितं अभिनन्दित्वा अनुमोदित्वा अत्तमनो पमुदितो उदग्गो पीतिसोमनस्सजातो उट्ठायासना एकंसं उत्तरासङ्गं करित्वा येन भगवा तेनञ्जलिं पणामेत्वा भगवन्तं सम्मुखा सारुप्पाहि गाथाहि अभित्थवि–

"यानि च तीणि यानि च सट्ठि, ०......" (137)

अथ खो सभियो परिब्बाजको भगवतो पादेसु सिरसा निपतित्वा भगवन्तं एतदवोच–"अभिक्कन्तं,

भन्ते....पे०....एसाहं भगवन्तं सरणं गच्छामि धम्मं च भिक्खुसङ्घं च; लभेय्याहं, भन्ते, भगवतो सन्तिके पब्बज्जं, लभेय्यं उपसम्पदं"ति।

"यो खो, सभिय, अञ्ञतित्थियपुब्बो इमस्मिं धम्मविनये आकङ्खति पब्बज्जं आकङ्खति उपसम्पदं, सो चत्तारो मासे परिवसति; चतुन्नं मासानं अच्चयेन आरद्धचित्ता भिक्खू पब्बाजेन्ति उपसम्पादेन्ति भिक्खुभावाय। अपि च मेत्थ पुग्गलवेमत्तता विदिता"ति।।

"सचे, भन्ते, अञ्ञतित्थियपुब्बा इमस्मिं धम्मविनये आकङ्खन्ता पब्बज्जं आकङ्खन्ता उपसम्पदं चत्तारो मासे परिवसन्ति, चतुन्नं मासानं अच्चयेन आरद्धचित्ता भिक्खू पब्बाजेन्ति उपसम्पादेन्ति भिक्खुभावाय, अहं चत्तारि वस्सानि परिवसिस्सामि; चतुन्नं वस्सानं अच्चयेन आरद्धचित्ता भिक्खू पब्बाजेन्तु उपसम्पादेन्तु भिक्खूभावाय।"ति। असत्थ खो सभियो परिब्बाजको भगवतो सन्तिके पब्बज्जं अलत्थ उपसम्पदं....पे०.....अञ्ञतरो खो पनायस्मा सभियो अरहतं अहोसी ति।[1]

२५

SUBHADRAPARIVRĀJAKA

तेन खो पन समयेन सुभद्दो नाम परिब्बाजको कुसिनारायं पटिवसति। अस्सोसि खो सुभद्दो परिब्बाजको-"अज्ज किर रत्तिया पच्छिमे यामे समणस्स गोतमस्स परिनिब्बानं भविस्सती"ति। अथ खो सुभद्दस्स परिब्बाजकस्स एतदहोसि-"सुतं खो पन मेतं परिब्बाजकानं वुड्ढानं महल्लकानं आचरियपाचरियानं भासमानानं-'कदाचि करहचि तथागता लोके उप्पज्जन्ति अरहन्तो सम्मासम्बुद्धा' ति। अज्जेव रत्तिया पच्छिमे यामे समणस्स गोतमस्स परिनिब्बानं भविस्सति। अत्थि च मे अयं कङ्खाधम्मो उप्पन्नो-'एवं पसन्नो अहं समणे गोतमे। पहोति मे समणो गोतमो तथा धम्म देसेतुं यथाहं इमं कङ्खाधम्मं पजहेय्यं' ति। अथ खो सुभद्दो परिब्बाजको येन उपवत्तनं मल्लानं सालवनं येनायस्मा आनन्दो तेनुपसङ्कमि; उपसङ्कमित्वा आयस्मन्तं आनन्दं एतदवोच-'सुतं मेतं.....०। साधाहं, भो आनन्द, लभेय्यं समणं गोतमं दस्सनाया"ति। एवं वुत्ते, आयस्मा आनन्दो सुभद्दो परिब्बाजकं एतदवोच-"अलं आवुसो सुभद्द, मा तथागतं विहेठेसि। किलन्तो भगवा"ति। दुतियं पि खो सुभद्दो परिब्बाजको....पे०....ततियं पि खो सुभद्दो परिब्बाजको आयस्मन्तं आनन्दं एतदवोच० .....।

अस्सोसि खो भगवा आयस्मतो आनन्दस्स सुभद्देन परिब्बाजकेन सद्धिं इमं कथासल्लापं। अथ खो भगवा आयस्मन्तं आनन्दं आमन्तेसि-"अलं, आनन्द, मा सुभद्दं वारेसि। लभतं, आनन्द, सुभद्दो तथागतं दस्सनाय। यं किञ्चि मं सुभद्दो पुच्छिसति सब्बं तं अञ्ञापेक्खो व पुच्छस्सति, नो विहेस्सापेक्खो। यं चस्साहं पुट्ठो ब्याकरिस्सामि, तं खिप्पमेव न आजानिस्सती"ति। अथ खो आयस्मा आनन्दो सुभद्दं परिब्बाजकं एतदवोच-"गच्छावुसो सुभद्द, करोति ते भगवा ओकासं"ति। अथ खो सुभद्दो परिब्बाजको येन भगवा तेनुपसङ्कमि; उपसङ्कमित्वा भगवता सद्धिं सम्मोदि।

1. सुत्तपिटके, खुद्दकनिकाये, सुत्तनिपात पालि, महावग्गो, सभियसुत्तं, 3-6; पृ० 344-53।

सम्मोदनीयं कथं सारणीयं वीतिसारेत्वा एकमन्तं निसीदि। एकमन्तं निसिन्नो खो सुभद्दो परिब्बाजको भगवन्तं एतदवोच–"येमे, भो गोतम समणब्राह्मणा सङ्घिनो गणिनो गणाचिरया ञाता यसस्सिनो तित्थकरा साधुसम्मता बहुजनस्स, सेय्यथिदं–पूरणो कस्सपो, मक्खलि गोसालो, अजितो केसकम्बलो, पकुधो कच्चायनो, सञ्जयो बेलट्ठपुत्तो, निगण्ठो नाटपुत्तो, सब्बेते सकाय पटिञ्ञाय अब्भञ्ञिंसु, सब्बेव न अब्भञ्ञिंसु उदाहु एकच्चे अब्भञ्ञिसु एकच्चे न अब्भञ्ञिसु"ति?

"अलं, सुभद्द, तिट्ठतेतं–सब्बेते सकाय पटिञ्ञाय अब्भञ्ञिसु, सब्बंव न अब्भञ्ञिंसु, उदाहु एकच्चे अब्भञ्ञिसु एकच्चे न अब्भञ्ञिसू ति। धम्मं ते, सुभद्द, देसेस्सामि, तं सुणाहि, साधुकं मनसिकरोहि, भासिस्सामी"ति।

"एवं, भन्ते"ति खो सुभद्दो परिब्बाजको भगवतो पच्चस्सोसि। भगवा एतदवोच–

"यस्मिं खो, सुभद्द धम्मविनये अरियो अट्ठङ्गिको मग्गो न उपलब्भति, समणो पि तत्थ न उपलब्भति। दुतियो पि तत्थ समणो न उपलब्भति। ततियो पि तत्थ समणो न उपलब्भति। चतुत्थो पि तत्थ समणो न उपलब्भति। यस्मिं च खो, सुभद्द, धम्मविनये अरियो अट्ठङ्गिको मग्गो उपलब्भति, समणो पि तत्थ उपलब्भति। दुतियो पि तत्थ समणो उपलब्भति। ततियो पि तत्थ समणो उपलब्भति। चतुत्थो पि तत्थ समणो उपलब्भति। इमस्मिं खो, सुभद्द, धम्मविनये अरियो अट्ठङ्गिको मग्गो उपलब्भति। इधेव, सुभद्द, समणो, इध दुतियो समणो, इध ततियो समणो, इध चतुत्थो समणो। सुञ्ञा परप्पवादा समणेभि अञ्ञेहि। इमे च, सुभद्द, भिक्खू सम्मा विहरेय्युं, असुञ्ञो लोको अरहन्तेहि अस्सा"ति।

एकूनतिंसो वयसा सुभद्द,
यं पब्बजिं किंकुसलानुएसी।
बस्सानि पञ्ञास समाधिकानि,
यतो अहं पब्बजितो सुभद्द।
ञायस्स धम्मस्स पदेसवत्ती,
इतो बहिद्धा समणो पि नत्थि।।

....एवं वुत्ते, सुभद्दो परिब्बाजको भगवन्तं एतदवोच–"अभिक्कन्तं, भन्ते, अभिक्कन्तं, भन्ते! सेय्यथापि, भन्ते, निक्कुज्जितं वा उक्कुज्जेय्य, पटिच्छन्नं वा विवरेय्य, मूल्हस्स वा मग्गं आचिक्खेय्य, अन्धकारे वा तेलपज्जोतं धारेय्य, चक्खुमन्तो रूपानि दक्खन्ती ति; एवमेवं भगवता अनेकपरियायेन धम्मो पकासितो। एसाहं, भन्ते, भगवन्तं सरणं गच्छामि धम्मं च भिक्खु सङ्घं च। लभेय्याहं, भन्ते, भगवतो सन्तिके पब्बज्जं लभेय्यं उपसम्पदं"ति।[1].......

---

1. सुत्तपिटके, दीघनिकाय पालि, महावग्गो, महापरिनिब्बान सुत्त, सुभद्दपरिब्बाजकवत्थु, 3-23-85-88; पृ० 115-17।

२६

RĀJAGṚHA MEN SĀTON DHARMANĀYAKA

Gaṇācariyesu Ko Sāvakasavakato

एवं मे सुतं। एकं समयं भगवा राजगहे विहरति वेलुवने कलन्दकनिवापे। तेन खो पन समयेन सम्बहुला अभिञ्ञाता अभिञ्ञाता परिब्बाजका मोरनिवापे पिरब्बाजकारामे पटिवसन्ति, सेय्यथीदं–अन्नभारो वरधरो सकुलुदायी च परिब्बाजको अञ्ञे च अभिञ्ञाता अभिञ्ञाता परिब्बाजका। अथ खो भगवा पुब्बण्हसमयं निवासेत्वा पत्तचीवरमादाय राजगहं पिण्डाय पाविसि। अथ खो भगवतो एतदहोसि–"अतिप्पगो खो ताव राजगहे पिण्डाय चरितुं। यन्नूनाहं येन मोरनिवापो परिब्बाजकारामो येन सकुलुदायो परिब्बाजको तेनुपसङ्कमेय्यं"ति। अथ खो भगवा येन मोरनिवापो परिब्बाजकारामो तेनुपसङ्कमि। तेन खो पन समयेन सकुलुदायी परिब्बाजको महतिया परिब्बाजकपरिसाय सद्धिं निसिन्नो होति उन्नादिनिया उच्चासद्दमहासद्दाय अनेकविहितं तिरच्छानकथं कथेन्तिया, सेय्यथीदं–राजकथं०....इतिभवाभवकथं इति वा। अद्दसा खो सकुलुदायी परिब्बाजको भगवन्तं दूरतो व आगच्छन्तं। दिस्वान सकं परिसं सण्ठपेसि–"अप्पसद्दा भोन्तो होन्तु; मा भोन्तो सद्दमकत्थ। अयं समणो गोतमो आगच्छति; अप्पसद्दकामो खो पन सो आयस्मा अप्पसद्दस्स वण्णवादी। अप्पेव नाम अप्पसद्दं परिसं विदित्वा उपसङ्कमितब्बं मञ्ञेय्या"ति। अथ खो ते परिब्बाजका तुण्ही अहेसुं। अथ खो भगवा येन सकुलुदायी परिब्बाजको तेनुपसङ्कमि। अथ खो सकुलुदायी परिब्बाजको भगवन्तं एतदवोच–"एतु खो, भन्ते, भगवा। स्वागतं, भन्ते, भगवतो। चिरस्सं खो, भन्ते, भगवा इमं परियायमकासि यदिदं इधागमनाय। निसीदतु, भन्ते, भगवा; इदमासनं पञ्ञत्तं"ति। निसीदि भगवा पञ्ञत्ते आसने। सकुलुदायी पि खो परिब्बाजको अञ्ञतरं नीचं आसनं गहेत्वा एकमन्तं निसीदि। एकमन्तं निसिन्नं खो सकुलुदायि परिब्बाजकं भगवा एतदवोच–

"कायनुत्थ, उदायि, एतरहि कथाय सन्निसिन्ना, का च पन वो अन्तराकथा विप्पकता"ति?

"तिट्ठतेसा, भन्ते, कथा याय मयं एतरहि कथाय सन्निसिन्ना। नेसा, भन्ते, कथा भगवतो दुल्लभा भविस्सति पच्छा पि सवनाय। पुरिमानि, भन्ते, दिवसानि पुरिमतरानि नानातित्थियानं समणब्राह्मणानं कुतूहलसालायं सन्निसिन्नानं सन्निपतितानं अयमन्तराकथा उदपादि–'लाभा वत, भो, अङ्गमगधानं, सुलद्धलाभा वत, भो, अङ्गमगधानं! तत्रिमे समणब्राह्मणा सङ्घिनो गणिनो गणाचरिया ञाता यसस्सिनो तित्थकरा साधुसम्मता बहुजनस्स राजगहं वस्सावासं ओसटा। अयं पि खो पूरणो कस्सपो सङ्घी चेव गणी च गणाचरियो च ञातो यसस्सी तित्थकरो साधुसम्मतो बहुजनस्स; सो पि राजगहं वस्सावासं ओसटो। अयं पि खो मक्खलि गोसालो....पे०....अजितो केसकम्बलो. ...पकुधो कच्चायनो......सञ्जयो बेलट्ठपुत्तो.......निगण्ठो नातपुत्तो सङ्घी चेव०.....वस्सावासं ओसटो। अयं पि खो समणो गोतमो सङ्घी चेव०.....वस्सावासं ओसटो। को नु खो इमेसं भवतं समणब्राह्मणानं सङ्घीनं गणीनं गणाचरियानं ञातानं यसस्सीनं तित्थकरानं साधुसम्मतानं बहुजनस्स

सावकानं सक्कतो गरुकतो मानिसो पूजितो, कं च पन सावका सक्कत्वा गरुं कत्वा उपनिस्साय विहरन्ती"ति?

"तत्रेकच्चे एवमाहंसु–'अयं खो पूरणो कस्सपो सङ्घी चेव०....बहुजनस्स; सो च खो सावकानं न सक्कतो न गरुकतो न मानितो न पूजितो, न च पन पूरणं कस्सपं सावका सक्कत्वा गरुं कत्वा उपनिस्साय विहरन्ति। भूतपुब्बं पूरणो कस्सपो अनेकसताय परिसाय धम्मं देसेति। तत्रञ्ञतरो पूरणस्स कस्सपस्स सावको सद्दमकासि–मा भोन्तो पूरणं कस्सपं एतमत्थं पुच्छित्थ; नेसो एतं जानाति; मयमेतं जानाम, अम्हे एतमत्थं पुच्छथ; मयमेतं भवन्तानं ब्याकरिस्सामा ति। भूतपुब्बं पूरणो कस्सपो बाहा पग्गय्ह कन्दन्तो न लभति–अध्यसद्दा भोन्तो होन्तु, मा भोन्तो सद्दमकत्थ। नेते, भवन्ते, पुच्छन्ति, अम्हे एते पुच्छन्ति; मयमेतेसं ब्याकरिस्सामा ति। बहु खो पन पूरणस्स कस्सपस्स सावका वादं आरोपेत्वा अपक्कन्ता–न त्वं इमं धम्मविनयं आजानासि, अहं इमं धम्मविनयं आजानामि, किं त्वं इमं धम्मविनयं आजानिस्ससि, मिच्छा पटिपन्नो त्वमसि, अहमस्मि सम्मापटिपन्नो, सहितं मे, असहितं ते, पुरेवचनीयं पच्छा अवच, पच्छावचनीयं पुरे अवच, अधिचिण्णं ते विपरावत्तं, आरोपितो ते वादो, निग्गहितोसि, चर वादप्पमोक्खाय निब्बेठेहि वा सचे पहोसी ति। इति पूरणो कस्सपो सावकानं च सक्कतो०.....उपनिस्साय विहरन्ति। अक्कुट्ठो च पन पूरणो कस्सपो धम्मक्कोसेना'ति।

"एकच्चे एवमाहंसु–'अयं पि खो मक्खलि गोसालो.....पे०.....अजितो केसकम्बलो.... .पकुधो कच्चायनो.....सञ्जयो बेलट्ठपुत्तो....निगण्ठो नातपुत्तो सङ्घी चेव०.....धम्मक्कोसेना' ति।

"एकच्चे एवमाहंसु–'अयं पि खो समणो गोतमो सङ्घी चेव०....सावकानं सक्कतो गरुकतो मानितो। पूजितो, समणं च पन गोतमं सावका सक्कत्वा गरुं कत्वा उपनिस्साय विहरन्ति। भूतपुब्बं समणो गोतमो अनेकसताय परिसाय धम्मं देसेति। तत्रञ्ञतरो समणस्स गोतमस्स सावको उक्कासि। तमेनाञ्ञतरो ब्रह्मचारी जन्नुकेन घट्टेसि–अप्पसद्दो आयस्मा होतु, मायस्मा सद्दमकासि, सत्था नो भगवा धम्मं देसेती' ति। यस्मिं समये समणो गोतमो अनेकसताय परिसाय धम्मं देसेति, नेव तस्मिं समये समणस्स गोतमस्स सावकानं खिपितसद्दो वा होति उक्कासितसद्दो वा। तमेनं महाजनकायो पच्चासीसमानरूपो पच्चुपट्ठितो होति–यं नो भगवा धम्मं भासिस्सति तं नो सोस्सामा ति। सेय्यथापि नाम पुरिसो चातुम्महापथे खुद्दमधुं अनेलकं पीलेय्य। तमेनं महाजनकायो पच्चासीसमानरूपो पच्चुपट्ठितो अस्स। एवमेव यस्मिं समये समणो गोतमो अनेकसताय परिसाय धम्मं देसेति, नेव तस्मिं समये समणस्स गोतमस्स सावकानं खिपितसद्दो वा होति उक्कासितसद्दो वा। तमेनं महाजनकायो पच्चासीसमानरूपो पच्चुपट्ठितो होति–यं नो भगवा धम्मं भासिस्सति तं नो सोस्सामा ति। ये पि समणस्स गोतमस्स सावका सब्रह्मचारीहि सम्पयोजेत्वा सिक्खं पच्चक्खाय हीनायावत्तन्ति ते पि सत्थु चेव वण्णवादिनो होन्ति, धम्मस्स च वण्णवादिनो होन्ति, सङ्घस्स च वण्णवादिनो होन्ति, अत्तगरहिनो येव होन्ति अनञ्ञगरहिनो, मयमेवम्हा अलक्खिका मयं अप्पपुञ्ञा ते मयं एवं स्वाक्खाते धम्मविनये पब्बजित्वा नासक्खिम्हा यावजीवं परिपुण्णं परिसुद्धं ब्रह्मचरियं चरितुं ति।

ते आरामिकभूता वा उपासकभूता वा पञ्चसिक्खापदे समादाय वत्तन्ति। इति समणो गोतमो सावकानं सक्कतो०.....विहरन्ती"ति।[1]

२७

NIGAṆṬHA UPOSATHA

एवं मे सुतं। एकं समयं भगवा सावत्थियं विहरति पुब्बारामे मिगारमातुपासादे। अथ खो विसाखा मिगारमाता तदहुपोसथे येन भगवा तेनुपसङ्कमि; उपसङ्कमित्वा भगवन्तं अभिवादेत्वा एकमन्तं निसीदि। एकमन्तं निसिन्नं खो विसाखं मिगारमातरं भगवा एतदवोच–"हन्द कुतो नु त्वं, विसाखे, आगच्छसि दिवा दिवस्सा"ति?

"उपोसथाह, भन्ते, अज्ज उपवसामी"ति।

"तयो खोमे, विसाखे, उपोसथा। कतमे तयो? गोपालकुपोसथो, निगण्ठुपोसथो, अरियुपोसथो। कथं च, विसाखे, गोपालकुपोसथो होति? सेय्यथापि, विसाखे, गोपालको सायन्हसमये सामिकानं गावो निय्यातेत्वा इति पटिसञ्चिक्खति–'अज्ज खो गावो अमुकस्मिं च अमुकस्मिं च पदेसे चरिंसु, अमुकस्मिं च अमुकस्मिं च पदेसे पानीयानि पिविंसु; स्वे दानि गावो अमुकस्मिं च अमुकस्मिं च पदेसे चरिस्सन्ति, अमुकस्मिं च अमुकस्मिं च पदेसे पानीयानि पिविस्सन्ती' ति; एवमेव खो, विसाखे, इधेकच्चो उपोसथिको इति पटिसञ्चिक्खति–'अहं ख्वज्ज इदं चिदं च खादनीयं खादिं, इदं चिदं च भोजनीयं भुञ्जिं; स्वे दानाहं इदं चिदं च खादनीयं खादिस्सामि, इदं चिदं च भोजनीयं भुञ्जिस्सामी' ति। सो तेन अभिज्झासहगतेन चेतसा दिवसं अतिनामेति। एवं विसाखे, गोपालकुपोसथो होति। एवं उपवुत्थो खो, विसाखे, गोपालकुपोसथो न महप्फलो होति न महानिसंसो न महाजुतिको न महाविप्फारो।

"कथं च, विसाखे, निगण्ठुपोसथो होति? अत्थि, विसाखे, निगण्ठा नाम समणजातिका। ते सावकं एवं समादपेन्ति–'एहि त्वं' अम्भो पुरिस, ये पुरत्थिमाय दिसाय पाणा परं योजनसतं तेसु दण्डं निक्खिपाहि; ये पच्छिमाय दिसाय पाणा परं योजनसतं तेसु दण्डं निक्खिपाहि; ये उत्तराय दिसाय पाणा परं योजनसतं तेसु दण्डं निक्खिपाहि; ये दक्खिणाय दिसाय पाणा परं योजनसतं तेसु दण्डं निक्खिपाही' ति। इति एकच्चानं पाणानं अनुद्दयाय अनुकम्पाय समादपेन्ति, एकच्चानं पाणानं नानुद्दयाय नानुकम्पाय समादपेन्ति। ते तदहुपोसथे सावकं एवं समादपेन्ति–'एहि त्वं, अम्भो, पुरिस, सब्बचेलानि निक्खिपित्वा एवं वदेहि–नाहं क्वचनि कस्सचि किञ्चनतस्मिं, न च मम क्वचनि कत्थचि किञ्चनतत्थी ति। जानन्ति खो पनस्स मातापितरो–'अयं अम्हाकं पुत्तो' ति; सो पि जानाति–'इमे मय्हं मातापितरो'ति। जानन्ति खो पनस्स पुत्तदारो–'अयं मय्हं भत्ता' ति; सो पि जानाति–'अयं मय्हं पुत्तदारो'ति। जानन्ति खो पनस्स दासकम्मकरपोरिसा–'अयं अम्हाकं अय्यो' ति; सो पि जानाति–'इमे मय्हं दासकम्मकरपोरिसा'ति। इति यस्मिं समये सच्चे

1. सुत्तपिटके, मज्झिमनिकाय पालि, मज्झिमपण्णासकं, महासकुलुदायिसुत्तं, 27-1; पृ० 224-228।

समादपेतब्बा मुसावादे तस्मिं समये समादपेन्ति। इदं तस्स मुसावादस्मिं वदामि। सो तस्सा रत्तिया अच्चयेन भोगे अदिन्नं येव परिभुञ्जति। इदं तस्स अदिन्नादानस्मिं वदामि। एवं खो, विसाखे, निगण्ठुपोसथो होति। एवं उपवुत्थो खो, विसाखे, निगण्ठुसोपथो न महप्फलो होति न महानिसंसो न महाजुतिको न महाविप्फरो।

"कथं च, विसाखे, अरियुपोसथो होति? उपक्किलिट्ठस्स, विसाखे, चित्तस्स उपक्कमेन परियोदपना होति। कथं च, विसाखे, उपक्किलिट्ठस्स चित्तस्स उपक्कमेन परियोदपना होति? इध, विसाखे, अरियसावको तथागतं अनुस्सरति–'इति पि सो भगवा अरहं सम्मासम्बुद्धो विज्जाचरणसम्पन्नो सुगतो लोकविदू अनुत्तरो पुरिसदम्मसारथि सत्था देवमनुस्सानं बुद्धो भगवा' ति। तस्स तथागतं अनुस्सरतो चित्तं पसीदति, पामोज्जं उप्पज्जति। ये चित्तस्स उपक्किलेसा ते पहीयन्ति, सेय्यथापि, विसाखे, उपक्किलिट्ठस्स सीसस्स उपक्कमेन परियोदपना होति।[1].......

२८

CHA ABHIJĀTIYON MEN NIRGRANTHA

एकं समयं भगवा राजगहे विहरति गिज्झकूटे पब्बते। अथ खो आयस्मा आनन्दो येन भगवा तेनुपसङ्कमि; उपसङ्कमित्वा भगवन्तं अभिवादेत्वा एकमन्तं निसीदि। एकमन्तं निसिन्नो खो आयस्मा आनन्दो भगवन्तं एतदवोच–"पूरणेन, भन्ते, कस्सपेन छलभिजातियो पञ्ञत्ता–तण्हाभिजाति पञ्ञत्ता, नीलाभिजाति पञ्ञत्ता, लोहिताभिजाति पञ्ञत्ता, हलिद्दाभिजाति पञ्ञत्ता, सुक्काभिजाति पञ्ञत्ता, परमसुक्काभिजाति पञ्ञत्ता।"

"तत्रिदं, भन्ते, पूरणेन कस्सपेन तण्हाभिजाति पञ्ञत्ता, ओरब्भिका सूकरिका साकुणिका मागविका लुद्दा मच्छघातका चोरा चोरघातका बन्धनागारिका ये वा पनञ्ञे पि केचि कुरूरकम्मन्ता।

"तत्रिदं, भन्ते, पूरणेन कस्सपेन नीलाभिजाति पञ्ञत्ता, भिक्खू कण्टकवुत्तिका ये वा पनञ्ञे पि केचि कम्मवादा किरियवादा।

"तत्रिदं, भन्ते, पूरणेन कस्मपेन लोहिताभिजाति पञ्ञत्ता, निगण्ठा एकसाटका।

"तत्रिदं, भन्ते, पूरणेन कस्सपेन हलिद्दाभिजाति पञ्ञत्ता, गिही ओदातवसना अचेलकसावका।

"तत्रिदं भन्ते, पूरणेन कस्सपेन सुक्काभिजाति पञ्ञत्ता, आजीवका आजीवकिनियो।"[2]

२९

SACCAKA NIGANṬHAPUTRA

Saccakassa pañjho

एव मे सुतं। एकं समयं भगवा वेसालियं विहरति महावने कूटागारसालायं। तेन खो पन

1. सुत्तपिटके, अंगुत्तरनिकाय पालि, तिकनिपात, महावग्गो, उपोसथसुत्तं, 3-7-10; पृ० 190-91।
2. सुत्तपिटके, अंगुत्तनिकाय पालि, छक्क-निपाता, महावग्गो, छलभिजातिसुत्तं, 6-6-3; पृ० 93-94।

समयेन भगवा पुब्बण्हसमयं सुनिवत्थो होति पत्तचीवरमादाय वेसालिं पिण्डाय पविसितुकामो। अथ खो सच्चको निगण्ठपुत्तो जङ्घाविहारं अनुचङ्कममानो येन अनुविचरमानो महावनं कूटागारसाला तेनुपसङ्कमि। अद्दसा खो आयस्मा आनन्दो सच्चकं निगण्ठपुत्तं दूरतो व आगच्छन्तं। दिस्वान भगवन्तं एतदवोच–"अयं, भन्ते, सच्चको निगण्ठपुत्तो आगच्छति भस्सप्पवादको पण्डितवादो साधुसम्मतो बहुजनस्स। एसो खो, भन्ते, अवण्णकामो बुद्धस्स, अवण्णकामो धम्मस्स, अवण्णकामो सङ्घस्स। साधु, भन्ते, भगवा मुहुत्तं निसीदतु अनुकम्पं उपादाया"ति। निसीदि भगवा पञ्ञत्ते आसने। अथ खो सच्चको निगण्ठपुत्तो येन भगवा तेनुपसङ्कमि; उपसङ्कमित्वा भगवता सद्धिं सम्मोदि, सम्मोदनीयं कथं सारणीयं वीतिसारेत्वा एकमन्तं निसीदि। एकमन्तं निसिन्नो खो सच्चको निगण्ठपुत्तो भगवन्तं एतदवोच–०.....

Saccakassa Bhagavatī Saddhā

एवं वुत्ते, सच्चको निगण्ठपुत्तो भगवन्तं एतदवोच–"अच्छरियं, भो गोतम, अब्भुतं, भो गोतम! यावञ्चिदं भोतो गोतमस्स एवं आसज्ज आसज्ज वुच्चमानस्स, उपनीतेहि वचनप्पथेहि समुदाचरियमानस्स, छविवण्णो चेव परियोदायसि, मुखवण्णो च विप्पसीदति, यथा तं अरहतो सम्मासम्बुद्धस्स। अभिजानामहं, भो गोतम, पूरणं कस्सपं वादेन वादं समारभिता। सो पि मया वादेन वादं समारद्धो अञ्ञेनञ्ञं पटिचरि, बहिद्धा कथं अपनामेसि, कोपं च दोसं च अप्पच्चयं च पात्वाकासि। भोतो पन गोतमस्स एवं०....अरहतो सम्मासम्बुद्धस्स। अभिजानामहं, भो गोतम, मक्खलिं गोसालं....पे०....अजितं केसकम्बलं.....पकुधं कच्चायनं....सञ्जयं बेलट्ठपुत्तं.....निगण्ठं नाटपुत्तं वादेन वादं समारभिता। सो पि मया वादेन०.....अप्पच्चयं च पात्वाकासि। भोतो पन गोतमस्स एवं०....बहुकिच्चा मयं, बहुकरणीया"ति।

"यस्स दानि त्वं, अग्गिवेस्सन, कालं मञ्ञसी"ति।

अथ खो सच्चको निगण्ठपुत्तो भगवतो भासितं अभिनन्दित्वा अनुमोदित्वा उट्ठायासन पक्कामी ति।[1]

३०

ANĀŚVĀSIKA BRAHMACARYAVĀSA

Cattāro abhramacaryavāsa

एवं मे सुतं। एकं समयं भगवा कोसम्बियं विहरति घोसितारामे। तेन खो पन समयेन सन्दको परिब्बाजको पिलक्खगुहायं पटिवसति महतिया परिब्बाजकपरिसाय सद्धिं पञ्चमत्तेहि परिब्बाजकसतेहि। अथ खो आयस्मा आनन्दो सायण्हसमयं पटिसल्लाना वुट्ठितो भिक्खू आमन्तेसि–"आयामावुसो, येन देवकतसोब्भो तेनुपसङ्कमिस्साम गुहादस्सनाया"ति। "एवमावुसो"ति

1. सुत्तपिटके, मज्झिमनिकाय पालि, मूलपण्णासकं, महासच्चकसुत्तं, 36-1-1 से 36-5-35; पृ० 291-309।

खो ते भिक्खू आयस्मतो आनन्दस्स पच्चस्सोसुं। अथ खो आयस्मा आनन्दो सम्बहुलेहि भिक्खूहि सद्धिं येन देवकतसोब्भो तेनुपसङ्कमि। तेन खो पन समयेन सन्दको परिब्बाजको महतिया परिब्बाजकपरिसाय सद्धिं निसिन्नो होति उन्नादिनिया उच्चासद्दमहासद्दाय अनेकविहितं तिरच्छानकथं कथेन्तिया, सेय्यथीदं–राजकथं चोरकथं महामत्तकथं सेनाकथं भयकथं युद्धकथं अन्नकथं पानकथं वत्थकथं सयनकथं मालाकथं गन्धकथं ञातिकथं यानकथं गामकथं निगमकथं नगरकथं जनपदकथं इत्थिकथं सूरकथं विसिखाकथं कुम्भाट्ठानकथं पुब्बपेतकथं नानत्तकथं लोकक्खायिकं समुद्दक्खायिकं इतिभवाभवकथं इति वा। अद्दसा खो सन्दको परिब्बाजको आयस्मन्तं आनन्दं दूरतो व आगच्छन्तं। दिस्वान सकं परिसं सण्ठपेसि–"अप्पसद्दा भोन्तो होन्तु, मा भोन्तो सद्दमकत्थ; अयं समणस्स गोतमस्स सावको आगच्छति समणो आनन्दो। यावता–खो पन समणस्स गोतमस्स सावका कोसम्बियं पटिवसन्ति, अयं तेसं अञ्ञतरो समणो आनन्दो। अप्पसद्दकामा खो पन ते आयस्मन्तो अप्पसद्दविनीता अप्पसद्दस्स वण्णवादिनो; अप्पेव नाम अप्पसद्दं परिसं विदित्वा उपसङ्कमितब्बं मञ्ञेय्या"ति। अथ खो ते परिब्बाजका तुण्ही अहेसुं।

अथ खो आयस्मा आनन्दो येन सन्दको परिब्बाजको तेनुपसङ्कमि। अथ खो सन्दको परिब्बाजको आयस्मन्तं आनन्दं एतदवोच–"एतु खो भवं आनन्दो, स्वागतं भोतो आनन्दस्स। चिरस्सं खो भवं आनन्दो इमं परियायमकासि यदिदं इधागमनाय। निसीदतु भवं आनन्दो, इदमासनं पञ्ञत्त"ति। निसीदि खो आयस्मा आनन्दो पञ्ञत्ते आसने। सन्दको पि खो परिब्बाजको अञ्ञतरं नीचं आसनं गहेत्वा एकमन्तं निसीदि। एकमन्तं निसिन्नं खो सन्दकं परिब्बाजकं आयस्मा आनन्दो एतदवोच–"कायनुत्थ, सन्दक, एतरहि कथाय सन्निसिन्ना, का च पन वो अन्तराकथा विप्पकथा"ति?

तिट्ठतेसा, भो आनन्द, कथा याय मयं एतरहि कथाय सन्निसिन्ना। नेसा भोतो आनन्दस्स कथा दुल्लभा भविस्सति पच्छा पि सवनाय। साधु वत भवन्तं येन आनन्दं पटिभातु सके आचरियके धम्मिकथा"ति।

"तेन हि, सन्दक; सुणाहि, साधुकं मनसि करोहि; भासिस्सामी"ति।

"एवं भो"ति खो सन्दको परिब्बाजको आयस्मतो आनन्दस्स पच्चस्सोसि। आयस्मा आनन्दो एतदवोच–"चत्तारोमे, सन्दक, तेन भगवता जानता पस्सता अरहता सम्मासम्बुद्धेन अब्रह्मचरियवासा अक्खाता चत्तारि च अनस्सासिकानि ब्रह्मचरियानि अक्खातानि, यत्थ विञ्ञू पुरिसो ससक्कं ब्रह्मचरियं न वसेय्य, वसन्तो च नाराधेय्य ञायं धम्मं कुसलं"ति।

कतमे पन ते, भो आनन्द, तेन भगवता जानता पस्सता अरहता सम्मासम्बुद्धेन चत्तारो अब्रह्मचरियवासा, अक्खाता, यत्थ विञ्ञू०.....कुसलं"ति।

"इध, सन्दक, एकच्चो सत्था एवंवादी होति एवंदिट्ठी–'नत्थि दिन्नं, नत्थि यिट्ठं, नत्थि हुतं, ०.....।

"पुन च परं, सन्दक, इधेकच्चो सत्था एवंवादी होति एवंदिट्ठी–'करोता कारयतो०.....।

"पुन च परं, सन्दक, इधेकच्चो सत्था एवंवादी होति एवंदिट्ठी–'नत्थि होतु, नत्थि पच्चयो०.

....।

"पुन च परं, सन्दक, इधेकच्चो सत्था एवंवादी होति एवंदिट्ठी–सत्तिमे काया अकटा अकटविधा०....।

"इमे खो ते सन्दक, तेन भगवता जानता पस्सता अरहता सम्मासम्बुद्धेन चत्तारो अब्रह्मचरियवासा अक्खाता यत्थ०....कुसलं"ति।

Cattāri Anassāsikāni Brahmacariyāni

"अच्छरियं, भो आनन्द, अब्भुतं, भो आनन्द! यावञ्चिदं तेन भगवता०....अब्रह्मचरियवासा व समाना 'अब्रह्मचरियवासा' ति अक्खाता यत्थ०.....कुसलं ति। कतमानि पन तानि, भो आनन्द, तेन भगवता जानता पस्सता अरहता सम्मासम्बुद्धेन चत्तारि अनस्सासिकानि ब्रह्मचरियानि अक्खातानि यत्थ०....कुसलं" ति?

"इध, सन्दक, एकच्चो सत्था सब्बञ्ञू सब्बदस्सावी अपरिसेसं ञाणदस्सनं पटिजानाति–'चरतो च मे तिट्ठतो च सुत्तस्स च जागरस्स च सततं समितं ञाणदस्सनं पच्चुपट्ठितं' ति। सो सुञ्ञं पि अगारं पविसति, पिण्डं पि न लभति, कुक्कुरो पि डसति, चण्डेन पि हत्थिना समागच्छति, चण्डेन पि अस्सेन समागच्छति, चण्डेन पि गोणेन समागच्छति, इत्थिया पि पुरिसस्स पि नामं पि गोत्तं पि पुच्छति, गामस्स पि निगमस्स पि नामं पि मग्गं पि पुच्छति; सो 'किमिदं' ति पुट्ठो समानो 'सुञ्ञं मे अगारं पविसितब्बं अहोसि', तेन पाविसिं; 'पिण्डं मे अलद्धब्बं अहोसि', तेन नालत्थं; कुक्कुरेन डंसितब्बं अहोसि, तेनम्हि दट्ठो; चण्डेन हत्थिना समागन्तब्बं अहोसि, तेन समागमिं; चण्डेन अस्सेन समागन्तब्बं अहोसि, तेन समागमिं; चण्डेन गोणेन समागन्तब्बं अहोसि; तेन समागमिं; इत्थिया पि पुरिसस्स पि नामं पि गोत्तं पि पुच्छितब्बं अहोसि, तेन पुच्छिं; गामस्स पि निगमस्स पि नामं पि मग्गं पि पुच्छितब्बं अहोसि, तेन पुच्छिं ति। तत्र, सन्दक, विञ्ञू पुरिसो इति पटिसञ्चिक्खति–अयं खो भवं सत्था सब्बञ्ञू सब्बदस्सावी अपरिसेसं ञाणदस्सनं पटिजानाति.......... पे०........ गामस्स पि निगमस्स पि नामं पि मग्गं पि पुच्छितब्बं अहोसि, तेन पुच्छिं ति। सो 'अनस्सासिकं इदं ब्रह्मचरियं' ति–इति विदित्वा तस्मा ब्रह्मचरिया निब्बिज्ज पक्कमति। इदं खो, सन्दक, तेन भगवता जानता पस्सता अरहता सम्मासम्बुद्धेन पठमं अनस्सासिकं ब्रह्मचरियं अक्खातं यत्थ विञ्ञू०....कुसलं।

०........"इमानि खो, सन्दक, तेन भगवता जानता पस्सता अरहता सम्मासम्बुद्धेन चत्तारि अनस्सासिकानि ब्रह्मचरियानि अक्खातानि यत्थ विञ्ञू०.....कुसलं"ति।[1]

---

1. सुत्तपिटके, मज्झिमनिकाय पालि, मज्झिमपण्णासकं, सन्दक सुत्तं, 26-1-2; पृ० 217-220।

३१
VIBHINNA MATON MEN DEVA

एवं मे सुतं। एकं समयं भगवा राजगहे विहरति वेलुवने कलन्दकनिवापे। अथ खो सम्बहुला नानातित्थियसावका देवपुत्ता असमो च सहलि च नीको च आकोटको च वेगब्भरि च माणवगारियो च अभिक्कन्ताय रत्तिया अभिक्ककन्तवण्णा केवलकप्पं वेलुवनं ओभासेत्वा येन भगवा तेनुपङ्कमिंसु; उपसङ्कमित्वा भगवन्तं अभिवादेत्वा एकमन्तं अट्ठंसु। एकमन्तं ठितो खो असमो देवपुत्तो पूरणं कस्सपं आरब्भ भगवतो सन्तिके इमं गाथं अभासि–

"इध छिन्दितमारिते, हतजानीसु कस्सपो।
न पापं समनुपस्सति, पुञ्ञं वा पन अत्तनो।
स वे विस्सासमाचिक्खि, सत्था अरहति माननं"ति।।

अथ खो सहलि देवपुत्तो मक्खलिं गोसालं आरब्भ भगवतो सन्तिके इमं गाथं अमासि–

"तपोजिगुच्छाय सुसंवुतत्तो,
वाचं पहाय कलहं जनेन।
समो सवज्जा विरतो सच्चवादी,
न हि नून तादिसं करोति पापं"ति।।

अथ खो नीको देवपुत्तो निगण्ठं नाटपुत्तं आरब्भ भगवतो सन्तिके इमं गाथं अभासि–

"जेगुच्छी निपको भिक्खु, चातुयामसुसंवुतो।
दिट्ठं सुतं च आचिक्खं, न हि नून किब्बिसी सिया"ति।।

अथ खो आकोटको देवपुत्तो नानातित्थिये आरब्भ भगवतो सन्तिके इमं गाथं अभासि–

"पकुधको कातियानो निगण्ठो,
ये चापिमे मक्खलिपूरणासे।
गणस्स सत्थारो साभञ्ञप्पत्ता,
न हि नून ते सप्पुरिसेहि दूरे"ति।।

अथ खो बेगब्भरि देवपुत्तो आकोटकं देवपुत्तं गाथाय पच्चभासि–

"सहाचरितेन छवो सिगालो,
न कोत्थुको सीहसमो कदाचि।
नग्गो मुसावादी गणस्स सत्था,
सङ्कस्सराचारो न सतं सरिक्खो"ति।

अथ खो मारो पापिमा वेगब्भरिं देवपुत्तं अन्वाविसित्वा भगवतो सन्तिके इमं गाथं अभासि–

"तपोजिगुच्छाय आयुत्ता, पालयं पविवेकियं।
रूपे च ये निविट्ठासे, देवलोकाभिनन्दिनो।
ते वे सम्मानुसासन्ति, परलोकाय मातिया"ति।

अथ खो भगवा, 'मारो अयं पापिमा' इति विदित्वा, मारं पापिमन्तं गाथाय पच्चभासि–

"ये केचि रूपा इध वा हुरं वा,
ये चन्तलिक्खस्मिं पभासवण्णा।
सब्बे व ते ते नमुचिप्पसत्था,
आमिसं व मच्छानं वधाय खित्ता"ति।।[1]

३२
PIṄGALA KOCCHA BRĀHMAṆA

Pañjca sārtthika Puggala

एवं मे सुतं। एकं समयं भगवा सावत्थियं विहरति जेतवने अनाथपिण्डिकस्स आरामे। अथ खो पिङ्गलकोच्छो ब्राह्मणो येन भगवा तेनुपसङ्कमि; उपसङ्कमित्वा भगवता सद्धिं सम्मोदि। सम्मोदनीयं कथं सारणीयं वीतिसारेत्वा एकमन्तं निसीदि। एकमन्तं निसिन्नो खो पिङ्गलकोच्छो ब्राह्मणो भगवन्तं एतदवोच–"येमे, भो गोतम, समणब्राह्मणा सङ्घिनो गणिनो गणाचिरया ञाता यसस्सिनो तित्थकरा साधुसम्मता, बहुजनस्स, सेय्यथीद–पूरणो कस्सपो, मक्खलि गोसालो, अजितो केसकम्बलो, पकुधो कच्चायनो, सञ्चयो बेलट्ठपुत्तो, निगण्ठो नाटपुत्तो, सब्बेते सकाय पटिञ्ञाय अब्भञ्ञंसु सब्बे व नाब्भञ्ञंसु, उदाहु एकच्चे अब्भञ्ञंसु एकच्चे नाब्भञ्ञंसू"ति?

"अलं, ब्राह्मण, तिट्ठतेतं–सब्बेते सकाय पटिञ्ञाय अब्भञ्ञंसु सब्बे व नाब्भञ्ञंसु, उदाहु एकच्चे अब्भञ्ञंसु एकच्चे नाब्भञ्ञंसू ति। धम्मं ते, ब्राह्मण देसेस्सामि, तं सुणाहि, साधुकं मनसि करोहि; भासिस्सामी"ति।

"एवं, भो" ति खो पिङ्गलकोच्छो ब्राह्मणो भगवतो पच्चस्सोसि। भगवा एतदवोच[2]–०.....

३३
JAṬILA SUTTA

एकं समयं भगवा सावत्थियं विहरति पुब्बारामे मिगारमातुपासादे। तेन खो पन समयेन भगवा सायन्हसमयं पटिसल्लाना वुट्ठितो बहिद्वारकोट्ठके निसिन्नो होति। अथ खो राजा पसेनदि कोसलो येन भगवा तेनुपसङ्कमि; उपसङ्कमित्वा भगवन्तं अभिवादेत्वा एकमन्तं निसीदि।

तेन खो पन समयेन सत्त च जटिला सत्त च निगण्ठा सत्त च अचेलका सत्त च एकसाटका सत्त च परिब्बाजका परूळ्हकच्छनखलोमा खारिविविधमादाय भगवतो अविदूरे अतिक्कमन्ति। अथ

---

1. सुत्तपिटके, संयुत्तनिकाय पालि, सगाथवग्गो, देवपुत्तसंयुत्तं, नानातित्थियसावकसुत्तं, 2-30-44-45; पृ० 64-65।
2. सुत्तपिटके, मज्झिमनिकाय पालि, मूलपण्णासकं, चूळसारोपमसुत्तं, 3-1-1; पृ० 248।

खो राजा पसेनदि कोसलो उट्ठायासना एकंसं उत्तरासङ्गं करित्वा दक्खिणजाणुमण्डलं पठवियं निहन्त्वा येन ते सत्त च जटिला सत्त च निगण्ठा०......। तेनञ्जलिं पणामेत्वा तिक्खतुं नामं सावेसि–"राजाहं, भन्ते, पसेनदि कोसलो....पे०.....राजाहं, भन्ते, पसेनदि कोसलो"ति।

अथ खो राजा पसेनदि कोसलो अचिरपक्कन्तेसु तेसु सत्तसु च जटिलेसु सत्तसु च निगण्ठेसु ०.......। येन भगवा तेनुपसङ्कमि; उपसङ्कमित्वा०.....एतदवोच–"ये ते, भन्ते, लोके अरहन्तो वा अरहत्तमग्गं वा समापन्ना एते तेसं अञ्ञतरा"ति।

"दुज्जानं खो एतं, महाराज, तया गिहिना कामभोगिना पुत्तसम्बाधसयनं अज्झासन्तेन कासिकचन्दनं पच्चनुभोन्तेन मालागन्धविलेपनं धारयन्तेन जातरूपरजतं सादियन्तेन–'इमे वा अरहन्तो, इमे वा अरहत्तमग्गं समापन्ना' ति।

"संवासेन खो, महाराज, सीलं वेदितब्बं। तं च खो दीघेन अद्धुना, न इत्तरं; मनसिकरोता, नो अमनसिकरोता; पञ्ञवता, नो दुप्पञ्ञेन। संवोहारेन खो, ०....। अपादासु खो, ०....साकच्छाय खो, ०.....।

"अच्छरियं, भन्ते, अब्भुतं भन्ते! यावसुभासितमिदं, भन्ते, भगवता–'दुज्जानं खो एतं, ०....।

"एते, भन्ते, मम पुरिसा चरा ओचरका जनपदं ओचरित्वा आगच्छन्ति। तेहि पठमं ओचिण्णं अहं पच्छा ओसापयिस्सामि। इदानि ते, भन्ते, तं रजोजल्लं पवाहेत्वा सुन्हाता सुविलित्ता कप्पितकेसमस्सू ओदातवत्था पञ्चहि कामगुणेहि समप्पिता समङ्गीभूता परिचारेस्सन्ती"ति।

अथ खो भगवा एतमत्थं विदित्वा तायं बेलायं इमा गाथायो अभासि–

"न वण्णरूपेन नरो सुजानो,
न विस्ससे इत्तरदस्सनेन।
सुसञ्ञतानं हि वियञ्ञनेन,
असञ्ञता लोकमिमं चरन्ति।।"
"पतिरूपको मत्तिकाकुण्डलो व,
लोहड्ढमासो व सुवण्णछन्नो।
चरन्ति लोके परिवारछन्ना,
अन्तो असुद्धा बहि सोभमाना"ति।[1]

३४

DHAMMIKA SUTTA

एवं मे सुतं। एकं समयं भगवा सावत्थियं विहरति जेतवने अनाथपिण्डिकस्स आरामे। अथ खो धम्मिको उपासको पञ्चहि उपासकसतेहि सद्धिं येन भगवा तेनुपसङ्कमि; उपसङ्कमित्वा भगवन्तं अभिवादेत्वा एकमन्तं निसीदि। एकमन्तं निसिन्नो खो धम्मिको उपासको भगवन्तं गाथाहि

1. सुत्तपिटके, संयुत्तनिकाय पालि, सगाथवग्गो, कोसलसंयुत्त, सत्तजटिलसुत्तं, 3-11-27 से 30; पृ० 76-78।

अज्झभासि–

"पुच्छामि तं गोतम भूरिपञ्ञ,
कथङ्करो सावको साधु होति।
यो वा अगारा अनगारमेति,
अगारिनो वा पनुपासकासे।।"
०..."ये केचिमे तित्थिया वादसीला,
आजीवका वा यदि वा निगण्ठा।
पञ्ञाय तं नातितरन्ति सब्बे,
ठितो वजन्तं विय सीघगामिं।।"[1]

Mahābodhi Kumāra

किं नु दण्डं किं अजिनं किं छत्तं किं उपाहनं
किं अंकुसं च पत्तं च संघाटिं चापि ब्राह्मण
तरमाणरूपो गण्हासि किं नु पत्थयसे दिसं।।1।।
द्वादसेतानि वस्सानि वुसितानि तवन्तिके,
नाभिजानामि सोनेन पिंगलेन अभिनिकूजितं।।2।।
स्वायं दित्तो व नदति सुक्कदाठं विदंसयं
तव सुत्वा समरिस्स वीतसद्धस्स मम पति।।3।।
अहु एस कतो दोसो, यथा भाससि ब्राह्मण,
एस भिय्यो पसीदामि, वस ब्राह्मण मा गम।।4।।
सब्बसेतो पुरे आसि, ततोपि सबलो अहु।
सब्बलोहितको दानि, कालो पक्कितुं मम।।5।।
अब्भन्तरं पुरे आसि ततो मज्झे ततो बहि।
पुरा निद्धमना होति सयं एव चजं अहं।।6।।
वीतसद्धं न सेवेय्य उदमानं व अनोदकं।
सचे पि नं अनुखणे वारि कद्दमगन्धिकं।।7।।
पसन्नं एव सेवेय्य, अपसन्नं विवज्जये।
पसन्नं पयिरुपासेय्य, रहदं व उदकत्थिको।।8।।

1. सुत्तपिटके, खुद्दकनिकाये, सुत्तनिपात पालि, चूलवग्गो, धम्मिकसुत्तं, 2-14-156 से 161; पृ० 323-324।

भजे भजन्तं पुरिसं अभजन्तं न भाजये,
असप्पुरिसधम्मोसो यो भजन्तं न भाजति।।9।।
यो भजन्तं न भजति सेवमानं न सेवति।
स बे मनुस्सपापिट्ठो मिगो साखस्सितो यथा।।10।।
अच्चाभिक्खणसंसग्गा असमोसरणेन च।
एतेन मित्ता जीरन्ति अकाले याचनाय च।।11।।
तस्मा नाभिक्खण गच्छे न च गच्छे चिराचिरं।
कालेन याचं याचेय्य एवं मित्ता न जीररे।। 12।।
अतिचिरंनिवासेन पियो भवति अप्पियो।
आमंत खो तं गच्छाम पुरा ते होम अप्पिया।। 13।।
एवं चे याचमानानं अञ्जलिं नावबुज्झसि।
परिवारकानं सत्तानं वचनं न करोसि नो।
एवं तं अभियाचाम, पुन कयिरासि परियायं।। 14।।
एवञ्चे नो विहरतं अन्तरायो न हेस्सति
तुय्हं चापि महाराज मय्हं च रट्ठवडढन।
अप्पेव नाम पस्सेम अहोरत्तानमच्चये।। 15।।
उदीरणा चे संगत्या भावायमनुवक्तति
अकामा अकरणीयं वा करणीयं वापि कुब्बति।
अकामकरणीयस्मिं कुविध पापेन लिप्पति।। 16।।
सो चे अत्थो च धम्मो च कल्याणो न पापको।
भोतो चे वचनं सच्चं सुहतो वानरो मया।। 17।।
अत्तनो चेहि वादस्स अपराधं विजानिय।
न मं त्वं गरहेय्यासि, भोतो वादोहि तादिसो।। 18।।
इस्सरो सब्बलोकस्स सचे कप्पेति जीवितं
इद्धिव्यसनभावञ्च कम्मं कल्याणपापकं।
निद्देसकारी पुरिसो इस्सरो तेन लिप्पति।। 19।।
स चे अत्थो च धम्मो च कल्याणो न च पापको।
भोतो चे वचनं सच्चं सुहतो वानरो मया।। 20।।

अत्तनो चे हि वादस्स अपराधं विजानिय।
न मं त्वं गरहेय्यासि, भोतो वादो हि तादिसो।। 21।।
सचे पुब्बेकतहेतु सुखदुक्खं निगच्छति,
पोराणकं कतं पापं तं एसो मुच्चते इणं,
पोराणकं इणमोक्खो, क्विध पापेन लिप्पति।। 22।।
सोचे अत्थो च धम्मो च कल्याणो न च पापको।
भोतो च वचनं सच्चं सुहतो वानरो मया।। 23।।
अत्तनो चे हि वादस्स अपराधं विजानिय।
न मं त्वं गरहेय्यासि, भोतो वादो हि तादिसो।। 24।।
चतुन्नं एव उपादाय रूपं सम्भोति पाणिनं
यतो च रूपं सम्भोति तत्थेव अनुपगच्छति।। 25।।
इधेव जीवति जीवो पेच्च पेच्च विनस्सति,
उच्छिज्जति अयं लोको ये बाला ये च पण्डिता।
उच्छिज्जमाने लोकस्मिं क्विध पापेन लिप्पति।। 26।।
सोचे अत्थो च धम्मो च कल्याणो न च पापको।
भोतो चे वचनं सच्चं सुहतो वानरो मया।। 27।।
अत्तनो चे हि वादस्स अपराधं विजानिय।
न मं त्वं गरहेय्यासि, भोतो वादो हि तादिसो।। 28।।
आहु खत्तविधा लोके बाला पण्डितमानिनो।
मातरं पितरं हञ्ञे अथो जेट्ठं पि भातरं।
हनेय्य पुत्ते च दारे च अथो चे तादिसो सिया।। 29।।
यस्स रुक्खस्स छायाय निसीदेय्य सयेय्य वा।
न तस्स साखं भञ्जेय्य, मित्तदूभी हि पापको।। 30।।
अथ अत्थे समुप्पन्ने समूलं अपि अब्बहे।
अत्थो मे सम्बलेनति सुहतो वानरो मया।। 31।।
सोचे अत्थो च धम्मो च कल्याणो न च पापको।
भोतो चे वचनं सच्चं सुहतो वानरो मया।। 32।।
अत्तनो चे हि वादस्स अपराधं विजानिय।
न मं त्वं गरहेय्यासि, भोतो वादो हि तादिसो।। 33।।

अहेतुवादो पुरिसो पुरिसो यो च इस्सरकुत्तिको
पुब्बेकती च उच्छेदी यो च खत्तविधो नरो,
एते असप्पुरिसा लोके बाला पण्डितमानिनो,
करेय्य तादिसो पापं अथो अञ्ञं पि कारये,
असप्पुरिससंसग्गो दुक्खन्तो कतुकुद्रयो।। 34-35।।

उरब्भरूपेन वाकासु पुब्बे
असंकितो अजयूथं उपेति,
हन्त्वा उराणिं अजियं अजं च
चित्रासयित्वा येन कामं पलेति।। 36।।

तथाविधेके समणब्राह्मणासे
छदनं कत्वा वञ्चयन्ती मनुस्से
अनासका थण्डिलसेय्यका च
रजोजल्लं उक्कुटिकप्पधानं
परियायभत्तं च अपानकत्तं
पापाचरा अरहन्तो वदाना।। 37।।

एते असप्पुरिसा लोके बाला पण्डितमानिनो,
करेय्य तादिसो पापं अथो अञ्ञंपि कारये,
असप्पुरिससंसग्गो दुक्खन्तो कदुकुद्रयो।। 38।।
याहु नत्थि विरियं ति हेतुञ्च अपवदन्ति
[ये] परकारं अत्तकारञ्च
ये तुच्छं समवण्णयुं,
एते असप्पुरिसा लोके बाला पण्डितमानिनो,
करेय्य तादिसो पापं अथो अञ्ञंपि कारये,
असप्पुरिससंसग्गो दुक्खन्तो कदुकुद्रयो।। 39-40।।
सचे हि विरियं नास्स कम्मं कल्याणपापकं।
न भरे वडढकिं राजा न पि यन्तानि कारये।। 41।।
यस्मा च विरियं अत्थि कम्मं कल्याणपापकं
तस्मा यन्तानि कारेन्ति राजा भरति वडढकिं।। 42।।

यदि वस्ससतं देवो न वस्से न हिमं पते।
उच्छिजेय्य अयं लोको विनस्सेय्य अयं पजा।। 43।।
यस्मा च वस्सती देवो हिमं चानुफुसीयति।
तस्मा सस्सानि पच्चन्ति रट्ठं च पल्लते चिरं।। 44।।
गवं चे तरमानानं जिम्हं गच्छति पुंगवो
सब्बा ता जिम्हं गच्छन्ति नेत्ते जिम्हगते सति।। 45।।
एवमेवं मनुस्सेसु यो होति सेट्ठसम्मतो
सो चे अधम्मं चरति पगेव इतरा पजा
सब्बं रट्ठं दुक्खं सेति राजा चे होति अधम्मको।। 46।।
गवं चे तरमानानं उजुं गच्छति पुंगवो।
सब्बा ता उजुं गच्छन्ति नेत्ते उजुगते सति।। 47।।
एवमेव मनुस्सेसु यो होति सेट्ठसम्मतो
सो चेपि धम्मं चरति पगेव इतरा पजा,
सब्बं रट्ठं सुखं सेति राजा चे होति धम्मिको।। 48।
महारुक्खस्स फलिनो आमं छिदन्ति यो फलं।
रसं चस्स न जानाति बीजं चस्स विनस्सति।। 49।।
महारुक्खूपमं रट्ठं अधम्मेन यो पसासति।
रसं चस्स न जानाति रट्ठं चस्स विनस्सति।। 50।।
महारुक्खस्स फलिनो पक्कं छिन्दति यो फलं।
रसं चस्स विजानाति बीजं चस्स न नस्सति।। 51।।
महारुक्खूपमं रट्ठं धम्मेन यो पसासति।
रसं चस्स विजानाति रट्ठं चस्स न नस्सति।। 52।।
यो च राजा जनपदं अधम्मेन पसासति।
सब्बोसधीहि सो राजा विरुद्धो होति खत्तियो।। 53।।
तत्थेव नेगमे हिंसं ये युत्ता कयविक्कये।
ओजदानबलीकरे स कोसेन विरुज्झति।। 54।।
पहारवरखेतञ्ञु संगामे कतनिस्समे।
उस्सिते हिंसयं राजा स बलेन विरुज्झति।। 55।।
तत्थेव इसयो हिंसं सञ्ञते ब्रह्मचारयो।
अधम्मचारी खत्तियो सो सग्गेन विरुज्झति।। 56।।

यो च राजा अधमट्ठो भरियं हन्ति अदूसिकं
लुद्दं पसवते ठानं पुत्तेहि च विरुज्झति।। 57।।
धम्मं चरे जनपदे नेगमेसु बलेसु च।
इसयो च न हिंसेय्य पुत्तदारे समं चरे।। 58।।
स तादिसो भूमिपति रट्ठपालो अकोधनो।
सामन्ते सम्पकम्पेति इन्दो व असुराधिपो।। 59।।[1]

३६
MAYŪRA AURA KĀKA

अदस्सनेन मोरस्स, सिखिनो मञ्जुभाणिनो।
काकं तत्थ अपूजेसुं, मंसेन च फलेन च।।
यदा च सरसम्पन्नो, मोरो बावेरुमागमा।
अथ लाभो च सक्कारो, वायसस्स अहायथ।।
याव नुप्पज्जती बुद्धो, धम्मराजा पभङ्करो।
ताव अञ्ञे अपूजेसुं, पुथू समणब्राह्मणे।।
यदा च सरसम्पन्नो, बुद्धो धम्मं अदेसयि।
अथ लाभो च सक्कारो, तित्थियानं अहायथा ति।।[2]

३७
MĀṀSĀHĀRA CARCĀ

हन्त्वा छेत्वा वधित्वा च, देति दानं असञ्ञतो।
एदिसं भत्तं भुञ्जमानो, स पापमुपलिम्पति।।
पुत्तदारं पि चे हन्त्वा, देति दानं असञ्ञतो।
भुञ्जमानो पि सप्पञ्ञो, न पापमुपलिम्पती ति।।[3]

---

1. जातक, पंचम खण्ड, महाबोधि जातक, पृ० 317-327।
2. सुत्तपिटके, खुद्दकनिकाये, जातकपालि, 'पठमो भागो', चतुक्कनिपातो, बावेरु जातक, 4-339-153 से 156; पृ० 104।
3. सुत्तपिटके, खुद्दकनिकाये, जातकपालि 'पठमो भागो', दुकनिपातो, तेलोवाद जातक, 2-246, 192-193; पृ० 64।

३८
CĀRA PRAKĀRA KE LOGA

"चत्तारोमे, भिक्खवे, पुग्गला सन्तो संविज्जमाना लोकस्मिं। कतमे चत्तारो? इध भिक्खवे, एकच्चो पुग्गलो अत्तन्तपो होति अत्तपरितापरितापनानुयोगमनुयुत्तो। इध, पन, भिक्खवे, एकच्चो पुग्गलो परन्तपो होति परपरितापनानुयोगमनुयुत्तो। इध पन, भिक्खवे, एकच्चो पुग्गलो अत्तन्तपो च होति अत्तपरितापनानुयोगमनुयुत्तो, परन्तपो च परपरितापनानुयोगमनुयुत्तो। इध पन, भिक्खवे, एकच्चो पुग्गलो नेवत्तन्तपो होति नात्तपरितापनानुयोगमनुयुत्तो न परन्तपो न परपरितापनानुयोगमनुयुत्तो। सो नेव अत्तन्तपो न परन्तपो दिट्ठेव धम्मे निच्छातो निब्बुतो सीतीभूतो सुखप्पटिसंवेदी ब्रह्मभूतेन अत्तना विहरति।

"कथं च, भिक्खवे, पुग्गलो अत्तन्तपो होति अत्तपरितापनानुयोगमनुयुत्तो? इध, भिक्खवे, एकच्चो अचेलको होति मुत्ताचारो हत्थापलेखनो नएहिभद्दन्तिको नतिट्ठभद्दन्तिको नाभिहटं न उद्दिस्सकतं न निमन्तनं सादियति। सो न कुम्भिमुखा पटिग्गण्हाति, न कलोपिमुखा पटिग्गण्हाति, न एलकमन्तरं न दण्डमन्तरं न मुसलमन्तरं न द्विन्नं भुञ्जमानानं न गब्भिनिया न पायमानाय न पुरिसन्तरगताय न सङ्कित्तीसु न यत्थ सा उपट्ठितो होति न यत्थ मक्खिका सण्डसण्डचारिनी न मच्छं न मंसं न सुरं न मेरयं न थुसोदकं पिबति। सो एकागारिको वा होति एकालोपिको द्वागारिको वा होति द्वालोपिको...पे०...सत्तागारिको वा होति सत्तालोपिको; एकिस्सा पि दत्तिया यापेति द्वीहि पि दत्तीहि यापेति...पे०....सत्तहि पि दत्तीहि यापेति; एकाहिकं पि आहारं आहारेति द्वाहिकं पि आहारं आहारेति...पे०....सत्ताहिकं पि आहारं आहारेति। इति एवरूपं अड्ढमासिकं पि परियायभत्तभोजनानुयोगमनुयुत्तो विहरति। सो साकभक्खो पि होति सामाकभक्खो पि होति नीवारभक्खो पि होति दद्दुलभक्खो पि होति हटभक्खो पि होति कणभक्खो पि होति आचामभक्खो पि होति पिञ्ञाकभक्खो पि होति तिणभक्खो पि होति गोमयभक्खो पि होति; वनमूलफलाहारो पि यापेति पवत्तफलभोजी। सो साणानि पि धारेति मसाणानि पि धारेति छवदुस्सानि पि धारेति पंसुकूलानि पि धारेति तिरीटानि पि धारेति अजिनं पि धारेति अजिनक्खिपं पि धारेति कुसचीरं पि धारेति वाकचीरं पि धारेति फलकचीरं पि धारेति केसकम्बलं पि धारेति बालकम्बलं पि धारेति उलूकपक्खं पि धारेति; केसमस्सुलोचको पि होति केसमस्सुलोचनानुयोगमनुयुत्तो; उब्भट्ठको पि होति आसनप्पटिक्खित्तो; उक्कुटिको पि होति उक्कुटिकप्पधानमनुयुत्तो कण्टकापस्सयिको पि होति कण्टकापस्सये सेय्यं कप्पेति; सायततियकं पि उदकोरोहनानुयोगमनुयुत्तो विहरति। इति एवरूपं अनेकविहितं कायस्स आतापनपरितापनानुयोगमनुयुत्तो विहरति। एवं खो, भिक्खवे, पुग्गलो अत्तन्तपो होति अत्तपरितापनानुयोगमनुयुत्तो।[1]

---

1. सुत्तपिटके, अंगुत्तरनिकाय पालि, चतुक्कनिपातो, महावग्गो, अत्तन्तपसुत्तं, 4-20-8; पृ० 219-20।

३९
NIRGRAṆTHON KE PĀÑCA DOṢA

"पञ्चहि, भिक्खवे, धम्मेहि समन्नागतो आजीवको यथाभतं निक्खित्तो एवं निरये। कतमेहि पञ्चहि? पाणातिपाती होति, अदिन्नादायी होति, अब्रह्मचारी होति, मुसावादी होति, सुरामेरयमज्जपमादट्ठायी होति। इमेहि खो, भिक्खवे, पञ्चहि धम्मेहि समन्नागतो आजीवको यथाभतं निक्खित्तो एवं निरये"ति।

"पञ्चहि, भिक्खवे, धम्मेहि समन्नागतो निगण्ठो....मुण्डसावको....जटिलको....परिब्बाजको ....मागण्डिको.....तेदिण्डिको.....आरुद्धको....गोतमको.....देवधम्मिको यथाभतं निक्खित्तो एवं निरये। कतमेहि पञ्चहि? पाणातिपाती होति, अदिन्नादायी होति.....पे०.....सुरामेरयमज्जपमादट्ठायी होती। इमेहि खो, भिक्खवे, पञ्चेहि धम्मेहि समन्नागतो देवधम्मिको यथाभतं निक्खित्तो एवं निरये"ति।[1]

४२
MILINDA PRAŚNA

अतीते किर कस्सपस्स भगवतो सासने वत्तमाने गङ्गाय समीपे एकस्मिं आवासे महाभिक्खुसङ्घो पटिवसति। तत्थ वत्तसीलसम्पन्ना भिक्खू पातो 'व उट्ठाय यट्ठिसमज्जनियो आदाय बुद्ध-गुणे आवज्जन्ता अङ्गणं सम्मज्जित्वा क्कवरब्यूहं करोन्ति।।

अथे' को भिक्खु एकं सामणेरं, 'एहि सामणेर, इमं कचवरं छड्डेही'-ति आह। सो असुणन्तो विय गच्छति। सो दुतियम्पि ततियम्पि आमन्तियमानो असुणन्तो विय गच्छते 'व। ततो सो भिक्खु दुब्बचो वता' यं सामणेरोति कुद्धो सम्मज्जनिदण्डेन पहारं अदासि। ततो सो रोदन्तो भयेन कचवरं छड्डेन्तो इमिना' हं कचवरछड्डनपुञ्ञकम्मेन यावा 'हं निब्बानं पापुणामि एत्थ 'न्तरे निब्बत्तनिब्बतट्ठाने मज्झन्तिकसुरियो विय महेसक्खी महातेजो भवेय्यं' ति पठमपत्थनं पट्ठपेसि।।

कचवरं छड्डेत्वा नहान 'त्थाय गङ्गातित्थं गतो गङ्गाय ऊमिवेगं गगरायमानं दिस्वा,-'यावा' हं निब्बानं पापुणामि एत्थ 'न्तरे निब्बत्तनिब्बत्तट्ठाने अयं ऊमिवेगो विय ठानुप्पत्तिकपटिभानो भवेय्यं अक्खयपटिभानो 'ति दुतियम्पि पत्थनं पट्ठपेसी।।

सो पि भिक्खु सम्मज्जनिसालाय सम्मज्जनिं ठपेत्वा नहान 'त्थाय गङ्गातित्थं गच्छन्तो सामणेरस्स पत्थनं सुत्वा-एस मया पयोजितो ति ताव एवं पत्थेसि। मय्हं किं न समिज्झिस्सती' ति चिन्तेत्वा-यावा 'हं निब्बाणं पापुणामि एत्थन्तरे निब्बत्तनिब्बत्तट्ठाने अयं गङ्गाऊमिबेगो विय अक्खयपटिभानो भवेय्यं, इमिना पुच्छितपुच्छितं सब्बं पञ्हपटिभानं विजटेतुं निब्बेठेतुं समत्थो भवेय्यं' ति पत्थनं पट्ठपेसि।।

ते उभो पि देवेसु च मनुस्सेसु च संसरन्ता एकं बुद्धन्तरं खेपेसुं। अथ अम्हाकं भगवता

---

1. सुत्तपिटके, अंगुत्तरनिकाय पालि, पंचकनिपातो, सिक्खापदयेय्यालं, आजीवकसुत्तं, 5-28-8-17।

पि यथा मोग्गलिपुत्ततिस्सत्थेरो दिस्सति, एवमे'ते पि दिस्सन्ति, मम परिनिब्बानतो पञ्चवस्ससते अतिक्कन्ते एते उप्पज्जिस्सन्ति। यं मया सुखुमं कत्वा देसितं धम्मविनयं, तं एते पञ्हपुच्छनं ओपम्मयुत्तिवसेन निज्जटं निग्गुम्बं कत्वा विभजिस्सन्ती' ति निद्दिट्ठा।।

तेसु सामणेरो जम्बुदीपे सागलनगरे मिलिन्दो नाम राजा अहोसि, पण्डितो व्यत्तो मेधावी पटिबलो अतीता'नागतपच्चुप्पन्नानं समन्तयोगविधानक्रियानं करणकाले निसम्मकारी होति। बहूनि च'स्स सत्थानि उग्गहितानि होन्ति; सेय्यथी'दं, सुति सम्मुति संख्या योगो नीति विसेसिका गणिका गन्धब्बा तिकिच्छा धनुब्बेदा पुराणा इतिहासा जोतिसा माया हेतु मन्तना युद्धा छन्दसा मुद्दा वचनेन एकूनवीसति। वितण्डवादी दुरासदो दुप्पसहो पुथुतित्थकरानं अग्गम'क्खायति। सकल-जम्बुदीपे मिलिन्देन रञ्ञा समो कोचि ना' होसि, यदि' दं थामेन जवेन सूरेन पञ्ञाय अड्ढो महद्धनो महाभोगो अनन्तबलवाहनो।।

अथे'कदिवसं मिलिन्दो राजा अनन्तबलवाहनं चतुरङ्गिनिं बलग्गसेनाव्यूहं। दस्सनकम्यताय नगरा निक्खमित्वा बहिनगरे सेनागणनं कारेत्वा सो राजा भस्सप्पवादको लोकायत वितण्डजन-सल्लापप्पवत्तकोतूहलो सुरियं ओलोकेत्वा अमच्चे आमन्तेसि, बहु ताव दिवसा' वसेसो; किं करिस्साम इदाने'व नगरं पविसित्वा? अत्थि को पि पण्डितो समणो वा ब्राह्मणो वा सङ्घी गणी गणाचरियो, अपि अरहन्तं सम्मासम्बुद्धं पटिजानमानो, यो मया सद्धिं सल्लपितुं सक्कोति कङ्खं पटिविनोदेतुं' ति।।

एवं वुत्ते पञ्चसतायोनका राजानं मिलिन्दं एतदवोचु-अत्थि महाराज छ सत्थारोपूरणो कस्सपो, मक्खलि गोसालो, निगन्थो नातपुत्तो, सञ्जयो बेलट्ठपुत्तो, अजितो केसकम्बली पकुधो कच्चायनो। ते सङ्घिनो गणिनो गणाचरियका ञाता यसस्सिनो तित्थकरा, साधुसम्मता बहुजनस्स, गच्छ त्वं महाराज ते पञ्हं पुच्छस्सु, कङ्खं पटिविनोदयिस्सू'ति।।'

1. मिलिन्दपञ्हो, बाहिर कथा, पृ० 2-5।

APPENDIX - II

Glossary of Jaina Technical Terms

Abhigama : Knowledge; Five duties to be observed by the votary, when he enters into the monks' residence. These duties are : (i) renunciation of animate materials (ii) limitation of inanimate materials (iii) folding of hands on seeing a monk (iv) concentration of mind and (v) wrapping of scarf round the face.

Abhigraha : Specific secret mental resolve .

Abhijati : Effect.

Abhīkṣṇa Jnānopayoga : Perpetual pursuit of knowledge.

Acelaka : Devoid of clothes; Naked; Few clothes.

Acitta : In-animate matter, non-sterilised.

Acyuta : Twelfth heaven; *See* Deva

Adhyavasāya : Thought, mental effort.

Aghātī-karma : Non-destructive karmas. The karmas, which do not destroy the inherent attributes of knowledge etc. of the soul, are called non-destructive karmas. There are four such karmas : (i) feeling producing (ii) life-span (iii) physique-making and (iv) status-determining. *See* 'Ghati-karma.'

Agurulaghu: Neither heavy nor light, Neither greatness nor smallness.

Akalpanīya : Prohibited, Faulty.

Akevalī : A state before acquiring omniscience; Non-omniscient.

Akṣiṇa-mahānasa Labdhi : A supernatural or divine power acquired through specific austerities. The foods prepared could be served for hundreds or thousands of people until the austerite does not eat.

Amarśauṣadha Labdhi : A supernatural power acquired though observance of specific austerity. Just as all the diseases are pacified by the bath in elixir, all the diseases are destroyed only by the touch of this type of austerite; Supernatural power of tactile medication.

Anagāra Dharma : The monastic religion; Observance of vows without any transgression or exception.

Anaśana : Life-long renunciation of four-fold food; Fasting.

Anga : Primary canon, *See* 'Dvādaśāngī'.

Anīka : Army and Army commander; They have to fight in the form of dancers and musicians during war.

Antarāya Karma : Obstructive karma; A karma which obstructs the gains etc. on its fruition.

Aṇuvrata : The partial renunciation of violence, falsity, stealing, non-celibacy or sex and possessions as per capacity. This is the conduct of householder votaries. Minor vows.

Apaścima : Māraṇāntika Sanlekhanā : A fast unto death devoid of attachment with body after subsiding the passions at the time of death.

Apavartana : Attenuation; Loss in fruitioning power of duration and intensity of karmas.

Apratikarma : Absence of physical activities like raising up, sitting, sleeping and walking etc. during fasting. This occurs during the tree-like steadfast fasting.

Arhat : *See* Arihanta.

Arihanta : A person, victor of the enemies of attachment and aversion and enriched with specific grandeur; A paragon of the Jainas; Venerable; Enlightened.

Arthāgama : The scriptures in the form of meaning.

Asankhya-pradeśī : Innumerable-pointed; The point (pradeśa) is defined as the indivisible part of an entity. The entity is called innumerable-pointed which has innumerable number of points. Every living being is innumerable-pointed.

Aticāra : Transgression, Infraction. It is to partially violate the vow or arrange factors for violation of a vow.

Atiśaya : Excellence; Excessively extra-ordinary specificity of the qualities found in human beings in a normal way.

Atthama Tapa : An austerity of fasting of three days, Telā.

Auddeśika : Particularised; Food, clothes or residence specially meant for offering to the wandering monks, striver monks, passionless monk and others.

Autpātiki Buddhi : Inborn intellect; An intellect grasping the matters unseen, unheard and un-analysed and materialising it.

Avadhijnāna : Clairvoyance; Knowledge of perceptible substances through the soul without the help of senses and mind; Limiting knowledge.

Avasarpiṇī kāla : Devolution cycle of time; The division of time cycle where the bone-joints and configurations of the living beings gradually get weakened, the life-span and size decrease, and there is a gradual loss of rise, activity, valour, potency, self-exertion and prowess. During this period, the colour, smell, taste and touch also get dull. The auspicious volitions go on decreasing and inauspicious volitions go on increasing. There are six spokes of this devolution epoch :

1. Extreme Plentitude. 2. Plentitude. 3. Plentitude-cum-penury. 4. Penury-cum-plentitude. 5. Penury. 6. Extreme penury.

Ava-svāpini : Deep sleep.

Āgāradharma : Acceptance of vows with exceptions, Householders' religion.

Āgāra-dharma-praiṇdhi : Prominently managing the external dress and ornaments.

Ākāśātipātī : Divine power of (i) getting rains of desired materials like silver etc. or undesired entities or (ii) moving in sky by learnings or smearing of feet.

Ārā : Section; Spoke of time.

Ārta-dhyāna : To be anxious about the separation of the desired and non-separation of the undesired; A kind of meditation; Sorrowful meditation.

Ārogya : Heaven of the Buddhas.

Āśatanā : Disrespect; To level false charges on teachers; To dishonour them or feel superior to them.

Āsrava : Door of influx of karmas; Influx; The karma-attracting volitions of the self.

Ātāpanā An austerity of putting the body in distress by heat and cold etc.

Ātma-rakṣaka : Body-guards of Indra. They have to be ever-ready for the protection of Indra.

Āyambila vardhamāna Tapa : An austerity, in which a kneaded or parched grain (or its powder) is eaten once a day by steeping it in water, is called 'Āyambila' (tasteless food). The gradually increasing level of this austerity is called by this name. In this austerity, there is one fasting after an Āyambila, one fasting after two Āyambila, one fasting after three Āyambila .... fasting after 100 Āyambilas. This austerity takes a time of 20 years, 9 months and 20 days.

Bādara Kāya-yoga : Gross physical activity.

Bādara Mana-yoga : Gross mental activity.

Bādara Vacana-yoga : Gross vocal activity.

Bāla Maraṇa : Fools' death; Death under non-restrained or ignorant state.

Bāla-tapasvī : An ignorant austerite; Undertaking austerities with ignorance.

Baladeva : The elder step-brother of Vāsudeva. There are nine Baladevas born in each of the evolution and devolution epoch. Their mothers see four dreams. After the death of Vāsudeva, they get initiated and undertake hard austerities, for spiritual progress. Some of them get liberation while others take rebirth in heavens.

Bandha : Bondage; Karmic bonding, Intimate contact of karmic mattergies with the soul.

Belā : Two day fasting.

Bhadra Pratimā : A kind of austerity with meditation; Undertaking meditation for four Praharas each facing in eastern, western, southern and northern direction.

Bhakta-pratyākhyāna : Life-long renunciation of three or four kinds of food under inflictions or without inflictions.

Bhāva : Mode; Thoughts.

Bhava-siddhika : Liberatable beings; Living beings having a capacity for liberation.

Bhāvitātmā : Purified soul; Purified soul engaged in restraint; Monastic mental resolves.

Bhavya : Liberatable beings; *See* Bhavasiddhika.

Bhikṣu-pratimā : The practice of austerity by the monks with specific mental resolve; There are twelve monastic mental resolves. The first mental resolve has a period of one month. The second mental resolve has a period of two months; The third has a period of three months; the fourth has a period of four months, the fifth one has a period of five months; the sixth one has a period of six months and the seventh one has a period of seven months. The period of the eighth, ninth and tenth mental resovles has a duration of one week each. The eleventh mental resolve has a period of one fortnight. The twelfth mental resolve has a period of one night.

There is one delivery of food-intake in the first resolve. The second, third, fourth, fifth, sixth and seventh resolves have two, three, four, five, six and seven deliveries respectively. The eighth, ninth and tenth resovles have alternative four-fold food renunciation and intake of Āyambila on completion. The eleventh resolve has 3-day fasting with four-fold food renunciation as an essentiality. The 4-day fasting is essential in the twelfth mental resolve. Please, see the description of 8th, 9th, 10th, 11th and 12th mental resolve under the descriptions of first seven-day, second seven-day, third seven-day, single day and single night mental resolves respecitively. While undertaking and observing these mental resolves, the monk renounces the total attachment with the body and he is always engrossed in the attachment with his soul alone. He endures all the sufferings and afflictions due of gods, humans and animals with equanimous attitude while alleviating his dejected mentality.

Bhũta : One-sensed beings-trees etc.; A synonym of 'Jīva'.

Bhuvanapati : Mansional gods; *See* 'Deva'.

Brahmaloka : Fifth heaven, *See* 'Deva'.

Caccara : Chowk; A place where more than four roads meet or cross together.

Cakra-ratna : Gem-wheel. The first jewel out of fourteen jewels of cakravartī. It has a golden edge. Its spokes are made of red gem (Lohitākṣa). Its centre is made up of diamond gem. It is complete in all respects and it is also divine. The army of cakravartī follows the direction in which this gem-wheel moves. The distance of Yojana is the distance it moves in one day. Due to the effect of this wheel, many kings surrender the cakravartī without fighting while some others surrender him after fighting.

Cakravartī : Most praiseworthy and excellent man of his era. He bears a gem-wheel. There are 63 torch-bearers in every evolution and devolution epoch—24 Ford-builders, 12 Cakravarties, 9 Vāsudevas, nine Baladevas, and nine anti-Vāsudevas. The Cakravarti is the soverign ruler of the six sections of Bharata region. There are fourteen jewels of a Cakravartī : (i) wheel (ii) umbrella (iii) royal staff (iv) sword (v) gems (vi) leathers (vii) Kakiṇī gem (viii) army commander (ix) house lords (x) carpenters (xi) royal priest (xii) women (xiii) horses (xiv) elephants.

Carama : Ultimate, Last

Cāraṇa-ṛddhi-dhara : Proficient in the prodigy of sky-movement; *See* Janghācāraṇa, Vidyācāraṇa.

Cāritra : The best practices performed with the objective of the purification of the soul.

Caturdaśa-pūrva : The fourteen pre-canons (Pūrvas). They are included in the twelfth primary canon of Dṛstivāda (Discourses on Doctrines). The fourteen pre-canons are as below.

(1) The Pre-canon on Origination; (2) The Pe-canon on the Top Tenets; (3) The Discourses on Potency; (4) The Discourses of Relativism; (5) The Discourses on knowledge; (6) The Discourses on Truth; (7) The Discourses on Soul; (8) The Discourses on Karma; (9) The Discourses on Renunciation; (10) The Discourses on Learnings; (11) The Discourses on Welfare and Auspicious Events; (12) The Science of Vitality or Health; (13) The Pre-canon on performing Arts and Crafts; (14) The Essence of the Universe.

Caturgati : Four destinities; Wandering of soul in four destinities or four kinds of birth-states like infernal, peripatetics, astral and celestials.

Cāturyāma : Four Major vows; The five major vows are included in the four major vows during the periods of 22 ford-builders excluding the first and the last out of 24 ones.

Caubīsī : The twenty-four ford-builders in the evolution or devolution epochs.

Caudaha Ratna : *See* Cakravartī.

Caudaha Vidyā : Fourteen kinds of learnings : (1) six Vedangas (components) : (1) phonetics (2) rituals and conduct (3) grammar (4) metrology, (5) astrology (6) etymological commentaries. (7-10) Four vedas : Rg, Yajur, Sāma and Athārva (11) Mimāṁsā (12) Nyāya (13) Religions (14). Legends (Purāṇas).

Chadmastha : Non-omniscient; The term 'Chadma' is the fruition of destructive karmas. The soul under this kind of state is called 'chadmastha'. The Jīva is called chadmastha until he acquires the omniscience.

Chattham Tapa : Austerity of two-day fasting (Belā).

Darśana : Intuition; Conation; Grasping of general attributes of a general-cum-specific entity overlooking the specific attributes.

Daśama Tapa : An austerity of 4-day fasting.

Deíavratī : Partial observer of vow (not total).

Deva : Special-bed-born living beings; Gods; Celestials; There are four kinds of celestial :

1. Mansional gods; 2. Peripatetic gods; 3. Astral gods; 4. Empyrean gods.

1. *Mausional gods* : The thickness of Ratnaprapha hell has 12 layers. The first two are empty. The rest ten have residents. The ten kinds of mansional gods-fiendish youths, serpentine youths, vulturine youths, lightning youths, oceanic youths, directional youths, areal youths, electric youths reside there. They have bright shine like a child. That is why, the term 'youth' (Kumāra) is used with their names. Their residences are called 'Mansions' (Bhuvana). It is due to this that these gods are called mansional gods.
2. *Peripatetic gods* : There are eight kinds of peripatetic gods—Kinnara, Kimpuruṣa, Rākṣasa, Bhūta and Piśāca, Mohoraga, Gandharva etc.
3. *Astral gods* : There are five classes of astral gods : moon, sun, planets, asterisms and stars.
4. *Empyrean gods* : There are two kinds of empyrean gods : (i) Born-in Kalpas (ii) Born-in beyond-Kalpas. The 'Kalpa' term means permissible conduct, empyrean-size earth, a system-having the categories or greats of Indra, Indra-equivalents etc. There are twelve kinds of Kalpa : (i) Saudharma, (ii) Īsanā (iii) Sanatkumāra (iv) Māhendra (v) Arahma (vi) Lāntaka (vii) Śukra (viii) Sahasrāra (ix) Ānata (x) Prāṇata (xi) Āraṇa (xii) Acyuta. The Kalpas of Saudharma and Īśāna are situated parallely in the south and north of Meru at a height of 1½ Rajju above it. The Kalpas of Sanatkumāra and Māhendra are also situated parallel on the upper side of Saudharam and Iśana Kalpa, Brahma, Lāntaka, Śukra and Sahasrāra are also above them one over the other. The Kalpas of Ānata and Prāṇata are both parallel. The Kalpas of Āraṇa and Acyuta are also parallel to them but above them. The life-span of Kalpa empyreans are as below :

Kalpa	Min-Life-span	Max life-span
1.	1P	2 Sāgaras
2.	1P	> 2 Sāgaras
3.	2 Sāgaras	7 Sāgaras
4.	2 Sāgaras	> 7 Sāgaras
5.	7 Sāgaras	10 Sāgaras
6.	10 Sāgaras	14 Sāgaras
7.	14 Sāgaras	17 Sāgaras
8.	17 Sāgaras	18 Sāgaras
9.	18 Sāgaras	19 Sāgaras
10.	19 Sāgaras	20 Sāgaras
11.	20 Sāgaras	21 Sāgaras
12.	21 Sāgaras	21 Sāgaras

The term' Beyond-Kalpas' (Kalpātita) means the heavens where there is no difference of senior or junior. All are Indras (Ahamindras-I am Indra). They are divided into two categories. (i) Graiveyaka (neck of the Jaina universe) and (ii) Anuttara (Incomparable).

According to Jaina canons, the shape of the universe is like a man with spanned feet. The Graiveyakas are positioned near its neck. That is why, they are so-called. There are nine of them : (i) Bhadra (virtuos), (ii) Subhadra (Pious) (3) Sujāta (well-bred), (iv) Saumanasa (Mind-pleasing), (v) Priya-darśana (lovely-sight) (vi) Sudarśana (well-sighted) (vii) Amogha (Unfailing), (viii) Su-prati-buddha (well-enlightened) and (ix) Vanśidhara (Flutist). They have three triads each of which has three heavens.

The Anuttara (incomparable) heavens are the best of all the empyrean planes. They are five in number : (1) Vijaya (Victory), (2) Vaijayanta (Banner) (3) Jayanta (Moon), (4) Aparājita (Invincible) and (5) Sarvārtha-siddhi (All-accomplished). The four of them are in four directions and the fifth-Sarvārthasiddhi is in the center of them.

The graded heavens are 12 and non-graded heavens are 14. Thus, their total number is 26. All of them have a gradual increase in seven characteristics and gradual decrease in four characteristics.

The seven characteristics are as below :

1. Life-span.
2. *All the four kinds of powers* : (i) Infliction of pain when angry, (ii) infliction of pleasure when kind, (iii) prodigies of miniaturisation etc., and (iv) get others work forcefully are gradually increasing. But they do not utilise them because of the retardation of passions. The magnanimity, impartiality and seriousness is also gradually increasing these.
3. *Happiness* : The pleasure due to experience of desired sensual objects.
4. *Brilliance* : The great shine of body, dress and ornaments.
5. *Purity of Aureoles* : Piety in volitions.
6. *Capacity of Senses* : The power of grasping the desired sense-objects like beauty and sounds from a distance.
7. *Clairvoyance* : The range of power of knowing through right and wrong clairvoyance.

The following are the four characteristics which gradually decrease :

1. *Motion* : Power of movement and movement in practice from one place to another place.
2. *Occupancy of Body* : Height of the body.
3. *Family* : The family of gods and goddesses and empyrean planes.
4. *Pride* : The pride of residence, family, power, sensualism, splendour and life-span.

Devādhideva : The highest of the deities; *See* Arihanta

Dig-virati Vrata : Vow of limitation of directional movement; This is the sixth vow of a Jaina votary. Under this vow, the votary limits the movements in all the ten directions.

Dik-kumariyān : Goddesses engaged in the delivery of the ford-builders. There are 56 of these goddesses. Their residences are also different. There are eight residences in lower world, eight in the upper world on Meru mountain, eight on eastern Rucakādri, eight on southern Rucakādri, eight on western Rucakādri, eight on Northern Rucakādri, four on Intermediate Rucaka mountain and four on Rucaka island.

Disācara : Degraded or derailed disciple.

Dravya-liṅgī : Having physical or outer signs; only external garb.

Duṣama-suṣama : The fourth spoke of the devolution epoch which has more penury than plentitude; Penury-cum-plentitude.

Dvādaśa Pratimā : Twelve Mental Resolves; *See* Bhikṣu-pratimā.

Dvādaśāṅgī : Twelve-limbed Jaina scripture; The term 'Anga' (limb) is defined as the collection of the sermons of the ford-builders by the chief disciples in the form of scriputral texts. They are twelve in number. This total collection in known as twelve-limbed or 'Dvādaśāṅgī'. Just as there are twelve main parts—2 feet, 2 thighs, 2 breasts, two sides, 2 arms, 1 neck and 1 head—in the body of human beings, there are tweve limbs of the scripture-man. Their names are :

1. *Āyaro* : (Monastic Conduct).
2. *Sūyagadānga* : (Limb of Tenets).
3. *Thāṇanga* : (Numerated Stationings).
4. *Samavāyānga* : (Numerated Categories).
5. *Viyaha-paṇṇatti* : (Enunciation of Explanations).
6. *Nāyā-dhamma-Kahānga* : (Religious Stories of Jnātṛs).
7. *Uvāsaga-dasānga* : (Decad of Votaries).
8. *Antagada-dasānga* : (Decad of Worldly Terminators)
9. *Aṇuttarova-vāiya dasānga* : (Decad of Anuttara-borns).
10. *Panhāvagaraṇa* : (Interpretation of Prognositics).
11. *Vipāka-suttānga* : (Doctrine of Fruition).
12. *Ditthi-vāya* : (Discourses on Doctrines).

Dvimāsikī to Sapta-māsikī Pratimā : The mental resolves of the monk in which he accepts the foods in the form of two, three, four, five, six and seven deliveries of foods upto two to seven months as the case may be.

Dvitīya-sapta-ahorātrika-pratimā : A specific mental resolve in which a monk undertakes alternate fasting with renunciation of four-fold food. The monk undertakes physical detachment postures like sitting on hands-on-knees (utkatuka), sleeping like bent-stick (Laganda-śāyī), lying like a straight staff (Dandāyata) outside the village etc.

Eka Ahotātra Pratimā : It is the practice of posture of detachment with body (kāyotsargā) with hung arms outside the village when he is undertaking four-fold food-renunciation for three-days.

Eka-rātri-pratimā : It is to undertake the posture of detachment with body, with hanging arms, unblinking eyes, sight on single object and standing in Jina-posture—(standing even with a distance of four Angulas between the feet) and bent body outside the village for a night while undertaking four-day fasting with four-fold food-renunciation.

This mental resolve can be undertaken only when permitted by the preceptor with purified soul possessed of specific bone-joints, patience and prowess.

Ekā-daśāṅgī : Eleven primary canons; They do not include Dṛṣtivāda (Discourses on Doctrines); *See* Dvādaśāṅgī.

Ekā-satikā : A single untailored cloth which was used by the votaries for curbing the violence to living beings, during speaking.

Ekavalā Tapa : It is a kind of austerity based on a specific immaginary figure. It is run on the basis of a diagram (*See* the figure 1). It takes 1 year, 2 months and 2 days for a single step. There are a total of four steps. Thus, the whole austerity takes a period of 4 years, 8 months and 8 days. The renunciation of denatured foods is not necessary in the first breaking up of the austerity. But there is renunciation of denatured foods in the breaking up of fasting in the second step. There is renunciation of smearing in the third step and breaking up of fasting but Āyambila in the fourth step.

Gaccha : Group of monks.

Gaṇa : Group of multitude; Group of dissciples of two Ācāryas.

Gaṇadhara : Chief disciples of the ford-builders possessing a number of attributes like super-knowledge and intuition. They compile the sermons of the ford-builders in the form of texts.

Gaṇipitaka : The tewlve-fold scripture is a treasure of the Ācārya. Hence, it is also called as Basket of the Ācārya.

Gāthāpati : Lord of house; Lord of a great and rich family. A person who has both the professions—agriculture and trade.

Ghāti-karma : According to Jainism, the cause of worldly cycle is the karmas. When there are vibrations in the space-points of soul due to wrongness, non-abstinence, non-vigilance, passions and activity, the infinite-times-infinite karma-convertible mattergies associate with the space points occuring in the specific areas of the soul like the water and milk. These mattergies are called 'karmas'. The karmas are divided mainly in two classes : (i) Destructive and (ii) Non-destructive. The karmas which destroy the inherent attributes of knowledge etc. of the soul, are called 'destructive karmas'. There are four of them : (i) Knowledge-obscuring (ii) Intuition or conation-obscuring (iii) Deluding, and (iv) Obstructive.

Gotra-karma : Status-determining karma; A karma whose fruition leads one to be designated as high and low. The high-status determining karma is earned by not being proud of caste, family, power, beauty/personality, austerity, scriptural knowledge, gains and splendour etc. The pride about them earns low status, determining karma.

Graiveyakas : Empyrean planes above the heavens. They are nine in number.

Guṇaratna (Rayaṇa) Samvatsara Tapa : It is a specific austerity resulting in a large amount of karmic shedding or an asuterity in which the yearly time is spent with the enrichment of the quality of karmic shedding. This austerity lasts for more than a year. That is why, it is called a year-round austerity. In undertaking this austerity,

(i) There is alternate fasting in the first month.

(ii) There are two-day fastings in the second month.

Similarly, there is sixteen day fasting in the sixteenth month.

During the period of austerity, there is endurance of heat in the sun in the day with a posture of sitting-on-hands-on-knee (utkatukāsana). In the night, there is nakedness with heroic posture (virāsana). This austerity takes 13 months and seven days. There are 76 days of breaking the fast. (*See* the figure 3 in the end.)

Guṇavarta : Supplementary vows of votary; The three vows-sixth, seventh and eighth-of votary are called supplementary vows, Reinforcing vows, *See* Bāraha-vrata.

Guru - laghu : Heavy-cum light; Smallness and greatness.

Guru Cāturmāsika Prāyaścitta. A kind of expiation, in which there is suspension of monkhood for four months.

Guru Māsika Prāyaścitta : A kind of expiation in which there is suspension of monkhood for a month.

Gyāraha-Pratimā : Eleven mental resolves; The mental secret resolves of the votaries are called mental resolves. The votary moves towards spiritualism through their observance. They are given below :

(i) *Mental Resolve of Faith* **:** Period of observance : 1 month; To have predilection in religion; to alleviate related flaws while having pure faith.

(ii) *Mental Resolve of Vows* **:** Period of observance : 2 months; Acceptance of the vows of five minor vows and three suplementary vows (Guṇavratas), undertaking of fasts.

(iii) *Mental Resolve of Equanimity* **:** Period of observance : 3 months; Acceptance of the vows of equanimity and limitation of movement in directions.

(iv) *Mental Resolve of Fasting* **:** Period of observance : 4 months; Undertaking fastings on eighth, fourteenth, dark and bright fifteenth days of the month.

(v) *Mental Resolve of Posture of Physical Detachment* **:** Period of observance: 5 months; Undertaking the posture of physical detachment in the night, not to eat in night. Not to pass *dhoti* between the legs and tuck it in the waist; To be celibate in the day and limitation of sex in the night.

(vi) *Mental Resolve of Celibacy* **:** Period of observance : 6 months; Observance of total celibacy.

(vii) *Mental Resolve of Renunciation of Animate Things* **:** Period of observance: 7 months; Renunciation of animate food.

(viii) *Mental Resolve of Renunciation of Domestic Violence or Sinful Activities*: Period of observance : 8 months; Not to undertake any sinful activities or got done by others.

(ix) *Mental Resolve of Renunciation of Service by Others* : Period of observance : 9 months; Not to get the sinful activities done through servants and other persons.

(x) *Mental Resolve of Renunciation of the Particularised* : Period of observance : 10 months; Renunciation of particularised foods; During this stage, the votary tonsures his hairs by razor or keeps the hair-crest- or top-knot. He does not say anything except, "I know or I do not know" on being asked about the household problems.

(xi) *Mental Resolve of Remaining Monk-like* : Period of observance : 11 months; During this period, the votary tonsures his head by razor or hand-plucks the hairs. He accepts the garb of a monk, conduct of a monk and accessories of a monk. The attachment with his family members, however, remains. Hence, he goes to persons of his family for alms-begging.

Hallā : A specific insect having a shape similar to the grass of Govalika creeper.

Iccha-parimāṇa Vrata : The fourth vow of the votary, in which he limits the possessions; Vow of limiting possessions.

Īryā samiti : Carefulness in walking (*See*, Samiti)

Jallauṣdha Labdhi : A supernatural power acquired through specific austerity. Due to this prodigy, all the diseases of patients are alleviated by the dirt of ear, nose and body of the austerite.

Jambūdvīpa : There are innumerable island-continents and occans in the middle universe. Every island-continent is surrounded by the ocean and each ocean is surrounded by the island-continent. Jambūdvīpa is in the centre of all of them. It is 1 lac Yojana wide from east to west and south to north. There are seven regions located in it : (i) Bharata (ii) Haimavata (iii) Hari (iv) Videha (v) Ramyak (vi) Hairaṇyavata and (vii) Airāvata. The Bharata region is in the south, Airāvata region is in the north, and the Videha (Mahā-videha) region is in the east and west.

Janghācāraṇa Labdhi : The supernatural power or prodigy of sky-movement through patting of thighs. The prodigy can be acquired by the monk practising the austerity of 3-day fasting (Telā). By patting the thighs, the monk can fly away upto the thirteenth continent of Rucakavara in a single flight in oblique direction. While returning, he can have his first pace at the eighth continent of of Nadiśvara and, then, reach the same place in Jambūdvipa wherefrom he started in his second pace. If the sky-movement refers to upper direction, he can reach the Pānduka Forest of Meru mountain in a single leap, and while returning, he can reach the place wherefrom he started by placing one foot at Nadana forest.

Jātismaraṇa jnāna : The knowledge of earlier birth. Due to this knowledge, a man can know from one to nine earlier births. According to an opinion, one can know about 900 earlier births.

Jina : The soul-victor of the enemies of attachment and aversion. The terms 'Arhat', Tīrthankara' etc. are its synonyms.

Jina-kalpika : Jina-modelled; To engage one-self in practising the best of the conduct after dissociating from the monk-group. This conduct is as difficult as that of the ford-builders. That is why, it is called 'Jina-modelled'. The practitioner does not make any effort to pacify the disease. He is not distrubed from the natural pains due to cold and heat etc. He does not change his line of action due to the inflictions by the deities, human beings and animals. He accepts alms with secret mental resolve. He is always absorbed in meditation and posture of physical detachment. The practice of this conduct could be undertaken by a person who is enriched with specific knowledge and bone-joints.

Jīna-mārga : The path or religion propounded by the Jinas.

Jītācāra : Traditional conduct.

Jīva : Five-sensed living being.

Jnāna : Knowledge; To grasp only the specific attributes or entities irrespective of their general attributes.

Jnānāvaraṇīya Karma : Knowledge-obsuring karma; A karma which covers the attribute of knowledge of the soul.

Jṛmbhaka : They are self-willed or unrestrained gods. They are always delightful, sportive, sexy and ill-conducting. They defame the person on whom they get angry. They glorify the person who keeps them satisfied. They have ten classes:

1. Food supplier; 2. Drinks suppliers; 3. Dress/fabric supplier.; 4. Residence supplier.; 5. Bedding suppliers; 6. Flower suppliers; 7. Fruit suppliers; 8. Flower and fruit suppliers; 9. Learnings teachers; 10. Non-manifest gods.

These gods function to reduce or increase the quantities of food etc., to increase or decrease any entity and to make a thing tasteful or tasteless. They reside in large Vaitādhya, Citra, Vicitra, Yamaka, Samaka and Kancana mountains. Their life span is one Palyopama years. They circle around Jambūdvīpa three times a day on the commands of the guardian gods. They also protect and preserve the grains, water, clothes, metals like gold etc., residences, flowers and fruits, learnings and many other common materials. They are peripatetic gods.

Jyotiṣka : The Astral gods; *See* Deva.

Kalpa : Prescibed conduct, sanctions, rules.

Kalpa-Vṛkṣa : Wish-fulfilling tress; The specific trees through which the supplies of the means of foods and drinks, residence and accessories, light and fire, sports and recreations are easily satisfied. There are ten kinds of wish-fulfilling tress.

Kanakāvali Tapa : A specific austerity based on a specific imaginary figure of ornament made of golden gems. It is run on the basis of the diagram (*See* the figure 2 at the end of this appendix). It takes 1 year, 5 months and 12 days for a single step. It has also four steps. The renunciation of denatured food is not essential in the breaking of fast in the first step. However, it is essential in the second step. The renunciation of smearing food in the third step and there is Āyambila in the fourth step.

Karaṇa : Volitions; Activities related with self-done, got-done and approval-based functions.

Karma : The specific aggregates of mattergy transformed into karmas and attracted by the good and bad propensities of the living beings; Karma; Deeds; Actions.

Kārmikī Buddhi : The intellect developed through the regular practice and thoughts; Experience-based intellect.

Khādima : Edible materials like dry fruits and sweets.

Kilviṣika : The gods who belong to the inferior class; Sinful gods.

Kṣira-Samudra : This is the fifth ocean surrounding Jambūdvīpa. It is this ocean where the hand-plucked hairs of the ford-builders were cast of by the Indra; Milky ocean.

Kutnkāpaṇa : Universal supermarket; A place where all kinds of materials including living and non-living ones are available. In this shop, rich person is charged rupees one thousand and the cakravarti etc. are changed a lac of rupees for a thing for which a common man is charged only five rupees.

The shop-keeper used to accomplish some peripatetic god. The same god managed for every material of the shop. However, some other people say that these shops were without owner or keeper. The peripatetic gods only were running them and were accepting the price of the materials sold.

Labdhi : Supernatural power; Prodigy; Superattainment; Specific powers acquired through the purificatory processes of the soul.

Labdhi-dhara : Endowed with specific supernatural power.

Laghu-caturmāsika Prayaścitta : A kind of expiation, through which the flaws are purified through the austerities etc.

Laghu-sinha-niṣkrīdita Tapa : A kind of austerity; Minor austerity of lion-like pastime : Just as a lion looks behind while moving forward, similarly, this austerity involves gradual increase and decrease in the austerity (of fasting) in a serial order. It has two varieties : (i) Minor and (ii) Major. In the minor austerity, there is a maximum of 9-day penance and, then, gradual decrease of the period of penance. The period for the whole undertaking is 6 months and seven days. There are also four traditions of this austerity which can be judged from the diagram later (*See* Figure 5).

Lāntaka : The sixth heaven; *See* 'Deva'.

Leśyā : The volitions of the soul occurring due to the mattergies of yoga-variforms; Aureole; Colouration.

Loka : The place of existence of the realities of (i) medium of motion (ii) medium of rest (iii) extensive space (iv) time (v) mattergy and (vi) the living being.

Lokāntika : There are five layers of the fifth heaven. These layers are equivalent to the storeys of the houses. There are eight black rows in four normal and four intermediate directions in the mobile channel in southern direction near the third layer named Ariṣta (Unhurt). There are nine empyrean planes of initiation-promoter gods. The eight planes are there in the eight rows and the ninth one is in the centre of them. Their names are as below.

(i) Arci (Flame) (ii) Arcimāla (Group of flames) (iii) Vairocana (Creator) (iv) Prabhankara (Lustre) (v) Candrābha (Moon-shine) (vi) Sūryābha (like sunshine) (vii) Śukrābha (like venus-shine) (viii) Superatiṣthā (well-located) (ix) Riṣtābha (wine-like shine- central plane).

The gods are called 'lokāntika' as they live in the end of the fifth heaven—Brahmaloka. They are normally free from sensualism. Hence, they have been called as 'deital miraculous monks' (Devarṣi). As per ancient tradition, they encourage the ford-builders for initiation.

Lokapāla : Guardians gods of boundary. Every Indra has four guardians goods each. They are highly prodigied. They are lords of many gods and goddesses.

Mahābhadra Pratimā : A kind of austerity preceeded with meditation; To undertake physical detachment posture (Kāyotsarga) for a day facing each of the four directions.

Mahākalpa : A specific time built; Bhagavati Sūtra describes the value of Mahākalpa in the following way : "The river Gangā is 500 Y long, 1//2 Y wide and 500 D deep. Seven such Gangās make a Mahāgangā, seven Mahagangas make a Sādīna Gangā, seven Sādīna Gangās make a Mṛtyu-gangā; seven Mṛtyu-gangās make a Lohita gangā (Red Gangā); seven Lohita Gangās make a Avanti-Gangās and seven Avanti-gangās make a Pramā-vanti Gangā. Thus, there are 1,17,649 Gangā rivers.

The sand-particles of these rivers have two varieties : (i) fine and (ii) gross. The fine particles are not desirable here. Out of the gross sand-particles, one particle is taken out every hundred years. Thus, the time required for emptying the sand-particles of these Gangās is called the time-unit of Mānāsa-sara. The three lac Mānāsa-sāras make a period of Mahākalpa. 24 lac Mahākalpas make a unit of Mahāmānasa. The unit of Mānasa-sāra has three varieties. Maximal, medial and manimal Majhhima-Nikāya sandak suttanta 2.3.6 has given the value of 84000 Mahakalpas in a little different way. Accordingly, there are 80 Antar-kaplas (interrupted Kalpas in a Mahākalpas.)

Mahānirgrantha : Ford-builder; Tīrthankara.

Mahā-pratimā Tapa : An austerity of great mental resolve; *See* 'Eka-rātri-pratimā'.

Mahā-sinha-niṣkrīdita Tapa : A kind of Austerity; A major austerity of lion-like pastime; Just as a lion looks behind while moving forward and, similary, this austerity involves gradual increase and decrease in austerity (of fasting) in serial order. This austerity has two varieties : (i) Major, and (ii) Minor. In the proposed austerity, there is a maximum of 16-day austerity of increasing fasts followed by 16-day decreasing fasting. It takes 1 year, 6 months and 18 days for the complete austerity. There are four traditions of this austerity. The order of this austerity runs as per the diagram (*See* Figure 4).

Mahā-videha kṣetra : A region in Jambūdvīpa; *See* 'Jambūdvīpa'.

Mahāvrata : Major vows; Finer vows; life-long physical, vocal and mental renunciation of violence, non-truth, stealth, non-celibacy and attachmental possession. The total renunciation of all these five sins leads them to be called as major vows or 'Mahāvratas'. This is the good conduct for those moving towards spiritual practices after renouncing the householder-ship.

Manah-paryaya Jnāna : Telepathy; Mind-reading knowledge; The knowledge of mental states according to mind variforms.

Mandalika Rājā : The ruler of a mandala or territory.

Mankha : Alms-beggars eking out their livelihood through paintings.

Manthū : Powder of dried plums etc.,

Mānuṣottara Parvata : Name of a mountain in Jaina Universe beyond which human beings can not go. There is Lavaṇa ocean surrounding Jambūdvīpa. Dhātaki Khanda Dvīpa surrounds this ocean which is sorrounded by Kālopdadhi ocean. There is Puṣkara Dvīpa surrounding Kāloadhi ocean. The Māunuṣottara mountain is in the centre of Puṣkara Dvīpa. It divides this dvīpa in two parts. This mountain forms the boundary of human universe and time-zone. No person except the monks with supernatural power of moving through the touch of things or specific learnings can go beyond this mountain.

Mārga : Path; The path of liberation in the form of right knowledge etc.

Māsiki Bhikṣu Pratimā : The mental resolve of taking one delivery of food and one delivery of water daily for a month,

Mati-jnāna : Sensory knowledge; a knowledge occurring through the instrumentality of senses and mind.

Meru-parvata ki cūlikā : Summit of Meru mountain; There is Meru mountain in the centre of Jambūdvīpa which is 1 lac Yojanas high and has a golden shine. There is 40 Y summit on this mountain. There are four forests also on this mountain : (i) Bhadraśāla (ii) Nandana (iii) Saumanasa, and (iv) Pānduka. The Bhadraśāla forest surrounds the mountain equiel to the surface of the earth. The Nandana forest is 500 Y high above it where even the gods go for their pastimes. There is the Saumanasa forest 62,500 Y above this forest. And there is the Pānduka forest spread around the summit. There are four golden rocks in this forest where the birth celebrations of the ford-builders are held.

Mithyātāva : Wrong faith; Reverse belief about the reality or knowledge.

Mokṣa : Liberation; Salvation; The positioning of soul in its own nature after the total destruction of all the karmas.

Mūlaguṇa : Basic attributes; The vows which are like the root of the tree of conduct. There are five minor vows for the votary and there are five major vows for the monks.

Nāgendra : The Lord of serpentine youths of the mansional gods.

Nairaujika Bhava : Mode of infernals.

Ṇamotthuṇam: The Prākṛta eulogy of the Enlightened and the salvated ones.

Nandiśvara Dvīpa : The eighth island-continent from Jambūdvīpa.

Naraka : Hells; Those places in the Jaina lower world where the inimense sinners are born to bear the fruits of their sins. They are seven in number :

1. *Ṛatna-Prabhā* : (gem-shine, Full with terrible black gems).
2. *Śarkarā-prābha* : (stone-shine, full with stones edged with bears and spears).
3. *Bālukā-prabhā* : (sand-shine, highly hot sand hotter than the sand of the oven of the grain-parcher).
4. *Panka-prabhā* : (mud-shine, full of mud like that of blood, flesh and pus).
5. *Dhūmra-prabhā* : (smoke-shine, full of sour smoke like that of smokes form burning chillies and mustards).
6. *Tamah-prabhā* : (darkness-shine, full of deep darkness).
7. *Mahātamah-prabhā* : (Deep-darkness shine, full of deepest darkness.)

Nidāna : A mental thorn of future desires; *See*, Nidāna íalya under 'śalya'.

Nikācita : Incapacitation; It is a state of incapacitation of factors leading to the fruition of karmas as per their duration of bonds.

Ninhava : Concealment, Denial of doctrines of the ford-builders.

Nirgrantha Pravacana : Jaīna scriptures sermonised by the ford-builders.

Nirjarā : Karmic shedding; The purity of the soul due to the shedding of karma through austerity.

Nirhārima : Taking-out of dead-body from the hermitage; *See* 'Pādopagamana'.

Nitya-pinda : Intake of food daily from one house.

Padānusāri Labdhi : A supernatural power acquired by observance of specific austerity; Syllable-based prodigy; Accordingly, one knows the text in full on listening or knowing any one syllable of the text from the beginning, middle or end.

Pādopagamana : Fasting under tree—like-steadfast state; A kind of fasting in which the monk stays steadfast like a tree and does neither help himself nor seeks help from others and renounces all kinds of efforts and activities. It is essential that all the four kinds of food is renounced. It has two varieties:

1. *Nirhārima* : (Taken-out after death). The dead body of the monk who died in the hermitage under the vow of tree-like steadfast fasting, is taken out of it for ritualisation. The term ' Nirhāra' means to 'take out' the abandoned body in this way.
2. *Anirhārima* : (Lonely death). The abandonment of body under tree-like steadfast fasting in a lonely place like forest is not taken out to other places for ritualisation. This type of body-abandonment is called 'lonely death'.

Palyopama : A pit- 1Y deep, 1Y long and 1Y wide· is densely filled with hairs of beings born-in-pairs in uttarakuru and having a life of 1-7 days and cutting each of them into innumerable parts. It should be so packed that no fire could burn it, no water could enter in and it should not show any flexibility even when all the army of a universal monarch passes over it. One hair-piece should be taken out form the pit after each hundred years. The time taken to remove all the hair-pieces in this way and, thus, emptying the pit, is the Palyopama time (in years).

Pānca Divya/Āścarya : Five splendours manifesting at the time of food-intake by the omniscients :

1. Rains of variety of gems.
2. Divine clothes.
3. Sacred fragrant water.
4. Shower of fragrant flowers.
5. Divine sounds or drum beating by the gods.

Panca-muṣtika luncana : Plucking of hairs by dividing the head in five portions.

Pandita-maraṇa : Prudents' death; Death under meditation while observing vows in full.

Pāpa : Inauspicious karmic mattergy; Sin; The causes of sin are also called 'sin' formally.

Pāriṇāmikī Buddhi : The intellect devolped due to long experience.

Parīṣaha : Afflictions; Variety of physical troubles during the ascetic life.

Pārívanātha-santānīya : Belonging to Pārśvanātha tradition.

Pārśvastha : Slack monks; Those monks who have only the garb of monk but who do not observe the conduct properly.

Paryāya : Mode; The changing nature of the substances.

Pauṣadha (Povāsa) : 1-day fasting; Renunciation of the four-fold food and sinful activities for a day and night.

Prajnapti ādi Vidyā : There are sixteen goddesses of learning as below :

1. Prajnapti 2. Rohiṇī 3. Vajra-śṛnkhalā 4. Kuliśānkaśā 5. Cakreśvarī 6. Naradattā 7. Kāli 8. Mahākali 9. Gaurī 10. Gāndhārī 11. Sarvāstra-mahājālā 12. Mānavī 13. Vairotyā 14. Acchuptā 15. Mānasī 16. Mahāmānasika.

Prāṇa : 2-4-sensed living beings; A synonym for the living beings in general; vitality.

Prāṇata : The tenth Kalpa or heaven; *See* 'Deva'.

Prītidāṇa : Awarding the person conveying good news.

Prathama-sapta-Ahorātra Pratimā : Alternate fasting for seven days with renouncing of four-fold foods : undertaking of physical detachmental posture like squatting, one-sided sleeping or supine-sleeping

Prati-codanā : Contrary preceptual injunction

Prati-sāraṇā : Remembrance of contrary doctrines.

Pratyākhyāna : Renunciation; Abandonment.

Pratyupadhāra : Disrespect.

Pravacana-prabhāvanā : Glorification of the religious order through many ways.

Pravṛtta-Parihāra : Entry into the interior of the body.

Pravṛtti-vāduka : Specific messenger to receive and acquire new (of the group).

Pravartinī : The chief nun promoting the other nuns to undertake selfless service and other religious activities as directed by the head of the group.

Pravṛtta-Parihāra : Entry into the interior of the body.

Pravṛtti-vāduka : Specific messenger to receive and acquire new (of the group).

Prayaścitta : Expiation; Atonement, To repent internally for purification of flaws occuring during spiritual practices. It is undertaken ten-foldly :

1. *Ālocanā* : Confession; To request the senior monk or preceptor about the defects/flaws during the spiritual practices.
2. *Pratikramaṇa* : Penitential retreat; Expression by the aspirant 'Let my sins be annulled' while undertaking sel-expiation for the transgressions or offences.
3. *Tadubhaya—Both of (1) and (2)* : Confession and penitential retreat.
4. *Viveka* : Discrimination; Renunciation of foods after learning about its particularisation.
5. *Kāyotsarga* : Physical detachmental posture; Renunciation of attachment with the body with due concentration.
6. *Tapa* : Austerity; Penances; External austerities like fasting etc.
7. *Cheda* : Reducing the standing of the monk. According to this expiation, the junior monks become senior to the transgressor monk during that period of reduction in rank.
8. *Mūla* : Re-initiation.

9. *Anavasthapya* : Temporary expulsion; Re-initiation after specific austerities.
10. *Pārancika* : Re-initiation after reproach; Self-condemination in public after changing the garb of monkhood for a specific time after expulsion form the group.

Prītidāna : Awarding the person conveying good news.

Puṇya : Auspicious karmic mattergy; Sacred; The causes of earning sacredness are also formally called 'Sacred'.

Rajoharaṇa : Whisk-brooms of Jina monks; An accessary of Jaina monks which is used for cleaning the ground etc.

Rāṣtriya : The officer, who is appointed to administer the province or nation.

Rju-Prājna : Simple and intelligent.

Rju-jada : Simple and ignorant; Simple but unable to understand the meanings of scriptures.

Rucakavara Dvīpa : The thirteenth island-continent from Jambūdvīpa.

Sāgaropama, Sāgara : A larger unit of time. It is equal to 10 crore r̄ crore = 10^{15} Palyopama years.

Sahasrapāka Taila : A thousand-times digested oil made from many medicinal substance or the oil whose preparation has cost 1000 gold coins.

Sahasrāra Kalpa : Eighth heaven; Thousand-faceted kalpas; *See*, 'Deva'.

Śaileśī Avasthā : Rock-like steadfast state; The state of the monk in the fourteenth spiritual stage—when there is cessation of mental, vocal and bodily activities—is called the rocklike-steadfast state : This state is the highest state of meditation which causes Meru—like steadiness and non-trembling.

Srīdevī : Name of the chief queen of Cakravartī. She is 4 Angulas lesser in height than Cakravartī. She is always ever-young. The diseases are pacified by her touch only. She does not have any issue.

Śalya : Stings or thorns (which cause pains). It has three varieties :
1. *Deceit* : Having a volition of deception. To confess a transgression deceitfully or request it to the teacher in a different way; Charging others falsely.
2. *Future Desires* : To think about acquiring the splendour of kings, gods etc. in the next birth due to spiritual practices like austerities, celibacy etc. on seeing their grandeur.
3. *Wrong-faith* : To have faith in perversity.

Samācārī : Essential monastic conduct.

Samādhi-danā : Provision of mental equanimity; Affording mental health by serving the minister, preceptor, seniors, novices, ailing and austerite monks.

Samādhi-maraṇa : Death under meditation; Death under detachmental volition while observing the scriptutral conduct.

Sāmānika : Co-chiefs; Indra-equivalents; These gods have the same life-span etc. as the Indra. But they are not Indras. These gods are like ministers, parents, and teachers etc. for the Indra.

Samavasaraṇa : The place of Holy assembly where the ford-builders sermonise; Assembly of the ford-builder.

Samaya : The smallest unit of time.

Samāyika Cāritra : Total abstinence from sinful activites; Conduct of equanimity.

Sambhinna-śrotṛ-labdhi : A supernatural power of all-sensing through one sense; A specific divine power acquired by specific austerity. Due to this power, one could grasp objects of all the five senses simultaneously through one sense only. The sounds of conch and drum etc. in the army of Cakravartī can be separately identified through this power.

Samiti : Carefulness; Propensities favouring restraint; There are five carefulnesses : (1-5) Carefulness in walking, speaking, examining the purity of foods, picking and placing and excretions.

1. *Īryā (Walking)* : Walking with forward looking a couple of paces ahead for success in observance of right knowledge, faith, conduct and self-study and excluding sensuals.
2. *Bhāṣā (Speaking)* : Speaking sinless, beneficial, limited and doubtless speech avoiding the defects of language.
3. *Eṣaṇā (Examination of purity of foods)* : Search for the general essentials like foods and drinks etc. and supporting essentials like bed, blankets while avoiding the defects of various types.
4. *Ādāna-nikṣepaṇa (Picking and Placing)* : To pick and place clothes, vessels etc. carefully.
5. *Excretion (utsarga)* : Excretion of urine, feces, spittings, and phelgm etc. on inanimated and pre-observed ground.

Samucchinna-kriyā-nivṛtti : Cessation of subtle activity; The fourth variety of pure meditation; Where all the activities are stopped. *See* 'Sukla dhyāna'.

Samvara : Stoppage; Control of volitions of the soul causing influx of the karmas.

Samyak-darśana : Right faith; Righteousness.

Samyak-dṛṣṭi : Right-faithed; Right visioned; A person having accurate faith in spiritual entities.

Samyaktva : Righteousness; Accurate belief in realities.

Samyaktvī : Right-faithed; Enriched with right faith/righteouness.

Sanhanana : Bone-joints; Tight bonding of bones of the body; Physical strength.

Sacelaka : Having clothes; Having costly clothes.

Sanjnī-garbha : The place of birth of the human beings; A specific term of Ājīvika sect.

Sankramaṇa : Transition; Mutual change of homologous karmic species.

Sangha : Gathering of monk-groups; The group of disciples of more than two heads of monk.

Sanlekhanā : Austerity of leaning and thinning the passions etc. with austerity and physical and mental concentration.

Sanniveśa : Suburb

Sansthāna : Configuration; A specific shape.

Santhārā : Renunciation of foods etc. at the last stage of life.

Sanyūthā Nikāya : The group of infinite living beings. A specific term of Ājīvikas.

Sa-pratikarma : Activities during fasting; Activities of walking, sleeping, sitting and standing etc. during fasting. These activities are there during the fasting by gradual rejection of foods.

Sapta-saptamikā Pratimā : Seven-septadic mental resolves; This mental resolve lasts for 49 days. There are septads of seven day each. In the first septad, there is intake of one delivery of each of food and drink which gradually increases upto seven deliveries of each of them. This auterity involves posture of physical detachment alongwith the deliveries.

Sarvārtha-siddha : Last of the Anuttara empyrean abodes; All-accomplished empyreans; Penultimate liberated; *See* 'Deva'.

Sarvato-bhadra Pratimā : All-welfare mental resolve; Two methods of this resolve are found in literature. According to one method, there is undertaking of posture of detachment with body for one day (24 hrs) each facing in each of the ten directions. It is mentioned that Bhagvan Mahāvīra followed this method only. According to the second method, there are two varieties of this mental resolve : (i) Minor (ii) Major.

1. *Minor Savato-bhadra Pratimā* : The 'Sarvatobhadra' is the method of placing the numbers in a square in such a way that addition of horizontal and vertical direction is the same as shown in the figure. This austerity of mental resolve, in the first stage, begins, with a fast which gradually increases upto 5-day fasting. In the second stage, the middle number is taken as the number of days of fasting and the fastings are, then, completed in full five sections. Similar order of fasting continues next time. As per one system, the total period of this mental resolve is 3 months and 10 days (100 days). There are four systems of this austerity. Their order is as given in the diagram below in Table 1.
2. *Major Sarvato-bhadra Pratimā* : This austerity starts with fasting of a day and it goes on increasing gradually upto 7-day fasting. The order of increase in fasting is as per the minor type. The only difference is that there is the longest fasting period of 5 days while in this case, it is 7 days. The period of this austerity is 1 yr., 1 month and 10 days (i.e. 405 days). There are four

1	2	3	4	5
3	4	5	1	2
5	1	2	3	4
2	3	4	5	1
4	5	1	2	3

Table 1 :
Minor Sarvatobhadra Pratima

1	2	3	4	5	6	7
4	5	6	7	1	2	3
7	1	2	3	4	5	6
3	4	5	6	7	1	2
6	7	1	2	3	4	5
2	3	4	5	6	7	1
5	6	7	1	2	3	4

Table 2 :
Major Sarvatobhadra Pratima

systems of this austerity which follow the diagram as shown below in Table 2.

Sarvauṣadha Labdhi : A supernatural power of meditation through all parts of the body; A supernatural power acquired by a specific austerity. The rain water, river water and air, if touched by the body of this austerite, become eliminators of disease and curer of poisons. If any material mixed with poison is there in his utensils or mouth, it becomes depoisoned. Even the memory of this austerite depoisons the most poisonous substance. His body-parts like nails, hairs and teeth etc. also serve as divine medicine.

Śatapāka Taila : A hundered-times digested oil made from many medicinal substances or the oil which has been prepared by spending 100 gold coins.

Ṣat-Āvaśyaka : Six essential duties; Six dis-passionation devices; The essential duty (Āvaśyaka) is defined as those duties to be performed by the living being or soul for acquiring right faith, knowledge and conduct. There are six essential duties :

1. *Eqanimity (Sāmāyika)* : To live with equanimity; To have equanimous behaviour with all.
2. *Eulogy of Twenty-four (Catur-vinśati-stava)* : Eulogisation of qualities of the ford-builders with devotion.
3. *Veneration (Vandanā)* : The three-fold auspicious activity through which the venerable and respectable persons are offered devotion and regards.
4. *Penitential Retreat (Pratikarmaṇa)* : To move towards sacred activities after having gone in reverse direction non-vigilarntly. Thus, gradual movement towards auspicious activities after abandoning the inauspicious activities. It is the confession of one's own offences in brief.
5. *Postures of Abandonment of Bodily Attachment. (Kāyotsarga)* : To abandon attachment with the body with due concentration.
6. *Renunciation (Pratyākhyāna)* : Renunciation of specific item for a specific period.

Sattva : Living beings of earth, water, air and fire class; A synonym of Jīva or the living being.

Saudharma : Righteous; The first heaven; *See* 'Deva'.

Sāvadya : Sinful

Śayyātara : Owner of monk residence.

Śeṣa-kāla : Time after the Rainy residence of the monks.

Siddhi: Accomplishment; Salvation; The state acquired by the destruction of all the karmas.

Śikṣā vrata : Educative vows : The educative vows are defined as those vows which are repetitively practiced and, therefore, practice-prominent.

Śleṣmauṣadha Labdhi : A supernatural power of medication by phelgm; A divine power acquired by specific austerity. Accordingly, the rubbing of a small amount of phelgm of the austerite could completely remove the leprosy of the person.

Snātaka : Bodhi-sattva.

Śruta-bhakti : Scriptutral devotion; Devotional hymn of scriputres; The constant promotion of scriptural knowledge with devotion and removal of dis-interest about it.

Śruta-jnāna: Vocable knowledge; Scriptural knowledge; A sensory knowledge capable of making others understand through of physical vocables like words, gestures, symbols etc.

Sthāvara : Non-mobile beings; One-sensed beings; Living beings incapable of movements for beneficial propensities and aviodance of non-beneficial propensities.

Sthavira : Senior monks; Stabilisers of lax monks in their spiritual practices. There are three kinds of senior monks : (i) senior-by-initiation (ii) senior-by birth and (iii) senior-by-scriputral knowledge.

1. *Senior-by-inititaion (Pravrjyā-sthavira)* : The monks whose initiation period has been twenty years or more.
2. *Senior-by-birth (Jāti-sthavira)* : The monks who are aged sixty years or more.
3. *Senior-by-scriptural knowledge (Śruta-sthavira)* : The monks who have mastered over the primary texts of Sthānānga (Numerated Stationings), Samvāyānga (Numerated Categories) and others.

Sthavira-kalpika: Commune-dweller monks; Spiritual practice while living in the group of monks; Promotion of Jina scripures and austerities; Improving the qualities of knowledge, faith and conduct in the monk-disciples; Reside in one place only due to weakened body and old age avoiding defects of foods and supporting accessories there.

Sthiti-patita : A 10-day birth (of a son) ceremony as per family tradition.

Śukla-dhyanā : White, pure or absolute meditation; Pure reflective meditation; It has four varieties :

1. *Pṛthaktva-vitarka-savicāra* : (Meditation on differential conceptual thinking with shifting).
2. *Ekatva-vitarka-savicāra* : (Meditation on mono-aspectal conceptual thinking with shifting).
3. *Sūkṣma-kriyā-apratipāti* : (infallible subtle activity).
4. *Samucchinna-kriyā-nivṛtti* : (Cessation of subtle activity).

Sūkịma-Kriyā-apratipāti : State of infallible subtle activites; The third stage of pure meditation where other kinds of activites are stopped except the subtle involuntary activities like respiration etc.; *See* 'Śukla-dhyāna'.

Suṣama : Plentitude; The second spoke of the devolution epoch where there is some lesser plentitude than the first spoke.

Suṣama-Duṣama : Plentitude-cum-penury; The third spoke of devolution epoch (or the fourth spoke of the devolution epoch) where there is some penury also alongwith plentitude.

Sūtra : Scriptures; Aphorism.

Sūtrāgama : Basic scriptures.

Svādima : Relishable edibles; Mouth-purifying materials like betel-nuts, cardamums etc.

Tāla-puta viṣa : Name of a poison effecting death in a time of clapping the hands.

Tamah-prabhā : Name of a hell (smoke-shine); *See* 'Naraka'.

Tattva : Meaning; Essence; Reality; Real

Tejo-leśyā : Red Aureole; A supernatural power of destruction associated with heat. This power can be acquired through specific austerity. One should undertake two-day fastings for six-months. During breaking of fast, the aspirant should eat a handful of fried cake of black gram (urda) and a handful of water. He should practise endurance of intense heat in the sun with face upward in the place set for this austerity. After this practice, one acquires the power of destruction associated with heat. It is called 'brief' when it not practised. It is called 'detailed or extended' when it is practiced. The person with this supernatural powei achieves capability to destroy, kill, root out and inflame the sixteen countries of (1) Anga (2) Banga (3) Magadha (4) Malaya (5) Mālava, (6) Accha (7) Vatsa (8) Kautsa (9) Pātha (10) Lata (11) Vajra (12) Mauli (13) Kāśī (14) Kośala (15) Avādha (16) Sambhuttara and others. The power which is used to counter this power is called 'cold supernatural power of Red aureole.'

Tīrtha : A ford through which the worldly ocean can be crossed; The four-fold order of right sages, nuns, votary and votaress; The sermons of ford-builders and their chief-disciples are also called as ford. The ford-builders sermonise only after acquiring omniscience. It is on the basis of their sermons that people become sages, nuns, votary and votaress.

Tīrthankara : The attained person enforcing the religious fords; Ford-builders.

Tīrthānkara Gotra-Nama-Karma : The physique-making karma of Ford-buildership; A physique-making karma whose fruition leads one to be born as ford-builder.

Tiryak Gati : The sub-human destinity.

Trāyastrinśa : Empyreans serving as ministers or guides to the Indras.

Tridandī Tāpasa : Three-staffed specific Ascetics; An ascetic penalised by three kinds of violence of mind, speach and body.

Tṛtiya-sapta-ahorātra-pratimā : Alternate seven-day fasting with renunciation of four-fold foods by a monk, and to undertake detachmental postures of cow-milking, heroic or mango-like curved type outside the village etc.

Udīraṇa : Pre-maturation, Fruition of karmas prior to regular duration.

Udvartanā : Delayed fruition of karmas; The increase in fruitional power of the duration and intensity of karmas.

Upānga : Subsidiary/secondary canons; Canonical sub-limbs; The post-canonical scriputre composed by scripture-ominiscient or pre-canonist Ācārya to elaborate the contents of primary canons. There are twelve of these secondary texts :

(i) Uvavāī (ii) Raya-paseṇiya (iii) Jivābhigama (iv) Paṇṇavaṇā (v) Sūriya-paṇṇattī (vi) Jambūdiva-paṇṇattī (vii) Canda-paṇṇattī (viii) Nirayā-valiā (ix) Kalpāvatansikā (x) Pupphiyā (xi) Pupphacūliya (xii) Vanhi-dasā.

Upayoga : Functional consciousness; Applied consciousness-knowledgc and conation/ Intuition. There are five knowledges :

(i) Sensory (ii) Vocable (iii) Clairvoyance (iv) Telepathy or mind-reading and (v) ominiscience/absolute.

There are four kinds of conations:

(i) ocular (ii) Non-ocular (iii) Clarivoyant (iv) Absolute.

Utsarpiṇī : Evolution epoch; It is that division of time where the living beings have gradually increasing in auspicious bone-joints and configurations. The life-span and size gradually increase. There is gradual increase in rise, activities, valour, potency, self-exertion and prowess. During this period, the colour, smell, taste, and touch of mattergies also get auspicious. The most inauspicious volitions become gradually less inauspicious, auspicious, better and best auspicious.

During the devolution period, there is the worst state in the end of the epoch while there is the best state during the evolution period in the end.

Utsūtra-prarūpaṇā : Enuncation against the rule or actuality.

Uttara Guṇa : Subsidiary/ secondary qualities; Propensities to protect primary qualities. They are purity of foods, carefulness, reflections, austerities, mental resolves, secret resolves etc. for monks and direction-binding vow etc. for the votary.

Uttarāsanga : Scarf.

Vaimānika : Empyrean gods; *See* 'Deva'.

Vainayikī Buddhi : Reverential intellect; Intellect acquired through the service or teachings of the teachers.

Vaiśravaṇa : God of wealth; Kubera.

Vaiyāvṛtti : Selfless service; Service of ministers, preceptors, novice, ailing austerite and senior monks and co-religious persons, family, group and four-fold order of the religion through foods etc.

Vajra-madhya-candra Pratimā : A one-month long mental resolve with the thounderbolt-like fasting order. It starts with the first day of dark fortnight and has the food-intake of deliveries according to the rise and fall of the phases of moon for a month. At the beginning, there is a food-intake of 15 deliveries gradually decreasing upto one delivery on the fifteenth dark day. It is, then, followed by two deliveries on the first day of bright fortnight with a gradual increase upto 15 deliveries on fourteenth day. There is fasting on bright fifteenth day.

Vakra-Jada : Crooked-cum-foolish; A person who disregards the real spiritual knowledge despite teachings and showing his foolishness as a form of skill-fulness through his outwitting due to crookedness.

Varṣī-dāna : Year-long daily donation by the ford-builders.

Vāsudeva : A category of Torch-bearers; Those persons appear on earth as Vāsudeva who take birth on the basis of their future desires in earlier birth in heavens or hells. There are nine Vāsudevas each in evolution and devolution epochs. When they are concieved, their mothers have seven dreams. Their colour of the body is black. They are rulers of three sections of Bharata region. They acquire this position by killing their enemies-anti-Vāsudevas. They have seven gems :

1. Sudarśana cakra (Handsome discus).
2. Amogha khadga (Unfailing sword).
3. Kaumodikī gadā (Moonlight-like mace).
4. Amogha vāṇa (Unfailing arrow).
5. Garuda-dhvaja ratha (Eagle-flagged-chariot).
6. Puṣpa-mālā (Flower garland).
7. Kaustubha mani (Kaustubha gem).

Vibhanga Jnāna : Wrong clairvoyance; The clairvoyance is defined as the knowledge of mattergic objects by the soul without the assistance of senses and mind. The knowledge of the wrong-faithed one is called wrong clairvoyance.

Vidyācāraṇa Labdhi : A supernatural power of desired movement through learnings or magic. This power is acquired by the monk undertaking the austerity of 3-day fasting. One can reach the eighth Nandiívara Dvīpa in two-fold sky-movement with a small support as per scriptural prescriptions. One can move upto Mānuṣottara mountain in the first step, and one can reach the starting point in a single step while returning. Similarly, one can reach Meru in two steps of flight while moving in upper direction and reach the starting point in a single step while returning.

Vijaya Anuttara Vimāna : Beyond-kalpa Anuttara plane-named Vijaya; *See* 'Deva'.

Vikurvaṇa Labdhi : Supernatural power of protection; A specific divine power acquired through a specific austerity. Due to this, many kinds of form can be created. The body may be made as fine as a thread which could pass through the hole of a needle. The body can be made so high that even the Meru mountain may look upto his knees. The body can be made lighter than air and heavier than diamond. There could be walking on water like that on earth and dive in the earth like water. One can pass through the mountain without hindrance like passage through the hole and there can be invisiblisation like air everywhere. One can fill the universe with many kinds of form, one can subjugate even the cruel animals.

Vipruṣauīadha Labdhi : A supernatural power of medication by excretions; A divine power acquired by a specific austerity. The drops of feces and urinary excretions serve as divine medicines for the patients.

Vītarāgatā Virādhaka : Non-practitioner in toto; A person not practicing the accepted vows in toto; Dying even before undertaking atonement of his evil deeds or sins.

Vyantara : Peripatetic gods; Forest-residing gods; *See* 'Deva'.

Yaugalika : Born-in-pairs; The period of civilisation prior to the human civilisation when the human beings were born in pairs. All their necessities were satisfied through the wish-fulfilling trees.

Yava-madhya Candra Pratimā : A one-month long mental resolve; This resolve is completed by taking deliveries of food in increasing and decreasing order like the shape of the barely grain according to loss or gain in the phases of the moon and starting with the bright first day of the month. For example, one has an intake of one delivery on the bright first day, two deliveries on the second day and so on upto 15 deliveries on the fifteenth bright day. Now, one has 14 deliveries on the dark first day and so on gradually decreasing upto one delivery on the dark fourteenth day and, have fasting on the dark fifteenth day of the month.

Yoga : Propensities/activities of mind, speech and body.

Yojana : A unit of distance equal to 4 Kroras ~8 miles ~13.28 km. When Cakravarti Bharata started for his victory mission, the gem-wheel was moving ahead of his army. The Yojana was designated as a distance travelled by the gem-wheel on the first day.

चित्र 1

एकावली तप

की परिभाषा से संबंधित

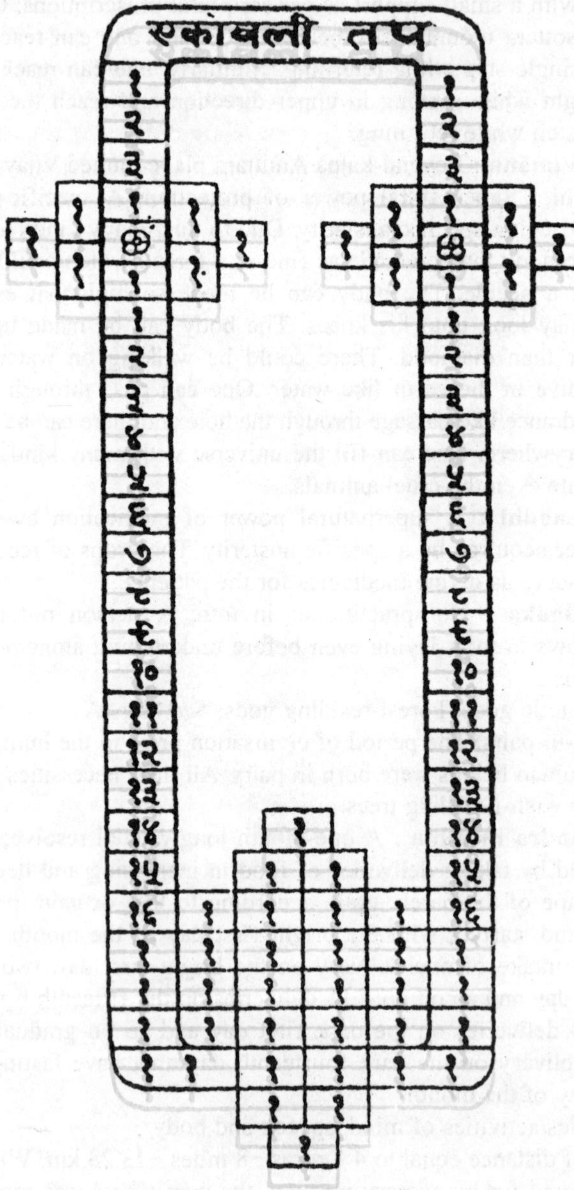

चित्र 2

कनकावली तप

की परिभाषा से संबंधित

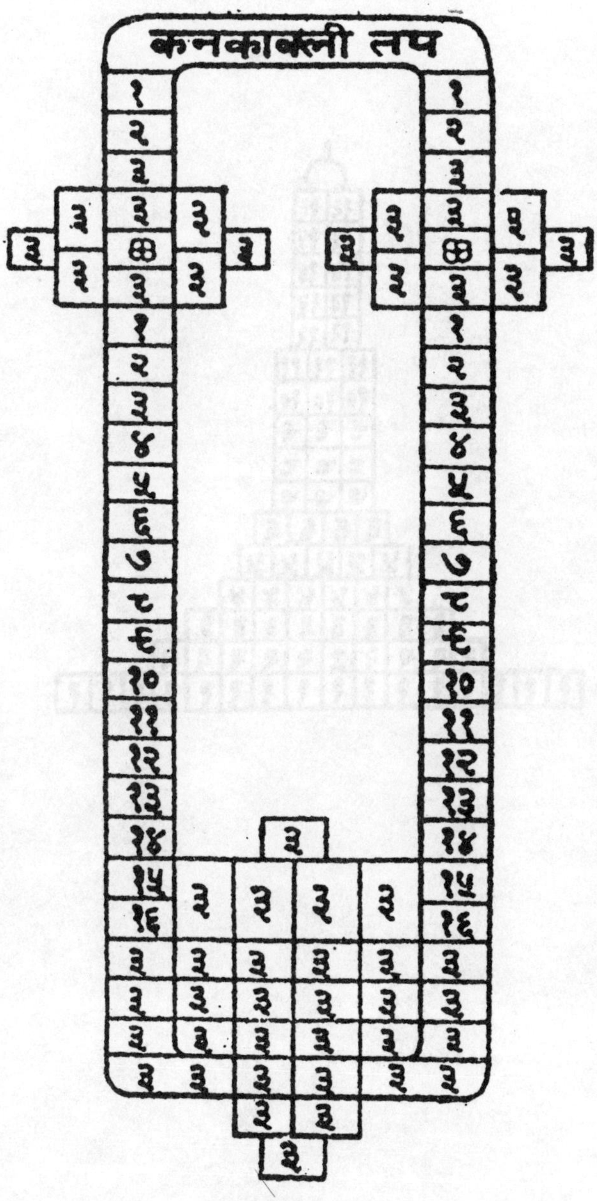

चित्र 3

गुणरत्न (रयण) संवत्सर तप

की परिभाषा से संबंधित

चित्र 4

महासिंह निष्क्रीड़ित तप

की परिभाषा से संबंधित

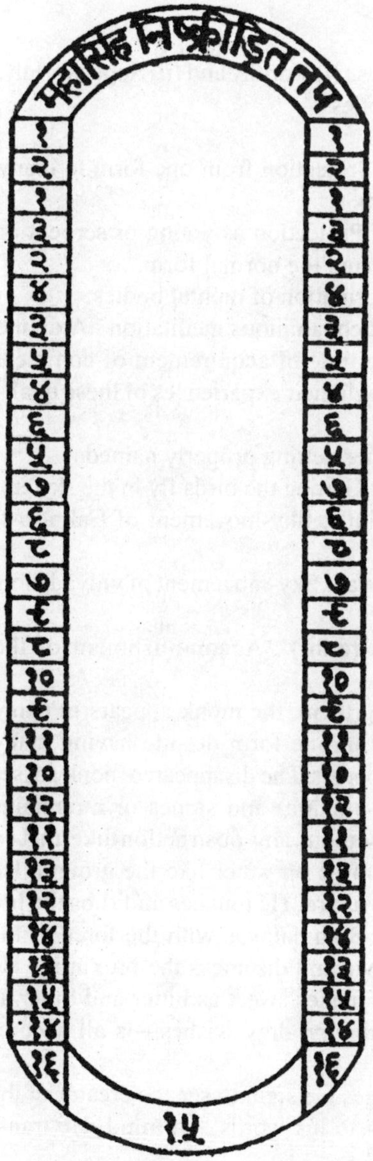

चित्र 5

लघुसिंह निष्क्रीड़ित तप

की परिभाषा से संबंधित

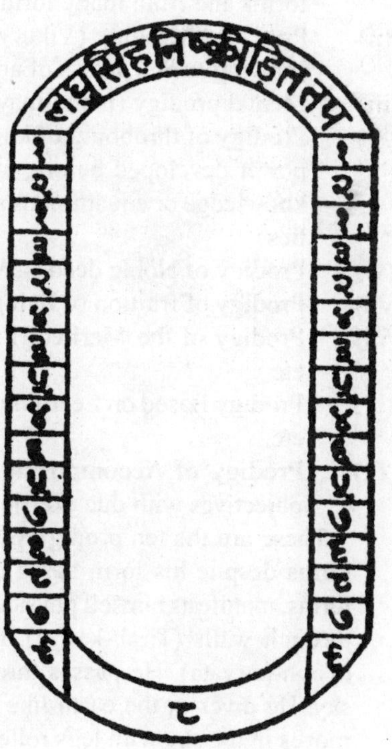

APPENDIX - III

Glossary of Buddhist Technical Terms

Abhijāti: Birth.

Abhijnā : Divine power; Basically, it has two varieties : (i) worldly and (ii) Superworldly.

The worldly divine powers have five varieties :

I. *Varied-prodigy (Ṛddhi-vidha):*

(i) Prodigy of forms—Adhiṣṭhāna ṛddhi : Protection from one form to many forms and from many forms to one form.

(ii) Protection prodigy (Vikurvana ṛddhi) : Protection as young or serpent or showing varied arrays of army after leaving the normal form.

(iii) Mental prodigy (mano-maya ṛddhi) : Formation of mental bodies.

(iv-v) Prodigy of throbbing of knowledge and equanimous meditation : A divine power developed before, after or at the time of acquirement of complete knowledge or equanimous state or through their experiences of these qualities.

(vi) Prodigy of Noble deeds : Wandering after getting properly named.

(vii) Prodigy of fruition or flying (vipakāja): Getting the birds fly in the sky etc.

(viii) Prodigy of the Merited (Punyavān ṛddhi) : Sky-movement of Cakravartī etc.

(ix) Prodigy Based on Learnings (Vidyā-maya) : Sky-movement of vidyādharas etc.

(x) Prodigy of Accomplishment (Siddha-ṛddhi) : Accomplishment of the objectives with due exertion.

These are the ten prodigies. On acquiring them, the monk appears in many forms despite his form being one, appears in one form despite having many forms, manifests himself physically and disappears. The disappeared monk passes through walls (Tirah-kadya), fences (Tira-prakāra) and stones or mountains (Tirah-parvata). He passes through them without any obstruction like that in sky. He dives in the earth like water. He moves on water like the ground. He moves in the sky with legs rolled round like a bird. He touches and rubs the hot sun and moon by hand. He subjugates the Brahmalokas with the force of his physical strength. He proximates the distance and distances the proximity. He makes little as more and more as little. He makes sweet as bitter and bitter as sweet. In short, whatever the monk with this prodigy wishes—is all accomplished.

The endowment of these prodigies enlarges the sight to see the creator of the universe-Brahma. It qualifies him to listen to his words and mind. He transforms the body into mind and mind into the body.

2. *Prodigy of Perceptible Divine Hearing (Divya-śrotra-dhātu)* : The monk endowed with this pure and supernatural power of divine hearing can listen to the near and distant sounds or words like the gods. The monk possessed of this prodigy can identify the sounds like 'this is the sound of conch or kettle-drum' out of many kind of sounds, being created even in Brahmaloka.
3. *Prodigy of Mind-reading (Metoparya Jnāna)* : The monk endowed with this prodigy knows the minds of others. He knows one as having attachmental mind when he has this type of mind. He knows others' mind in the same way as it exists at the moment such as detached mind, mind with aversion, mind devoid of aversion, deluded, mind, undeluded mind, distracted mind, abridged mind, intelligent mind, mind devoid of intelligence, inferior mind, superior mind and absorbed mind (concentrated mind), non-concentrated mind, detached and non-liberated mind.
4. *Prodigy of Memory of Earlier Births (Pūrva-nivāsa-anusmṛti-jnāna)* : The monk endowed with this prodigy remembers many kinds of earlier births. He can remember one, two, hundred, thousand, hundred thousand etc. births. He can remember many periods of duration of dissolution, creation and destruction-cum-origination of the universe. He remembers that at that time, he was in a particular place, state of birth, species, destinity and state of knowledge. I was in a specific state of birth. I had this name, lineage, lifespan, food and experience of pleasure and pain. I was born in a specific place after death from there where I had this name ..... etc. After death there, I am born here in this Kṣatriya or Brahmin family. The heretics remember their earlier births unto 40 Kalpas (a unit of time equivalent to 20 Antar-Kalpas). The natural votary remembers earlier births upto 100 or 1000 Kalpas, the great/senior votaries remember earlier births upto 80 lacs of Kalpas, the topmost votaries remember the earlier births upto innumerable lacs of Kalpa years the self-enlightened one remembers the earlier births upto two innumerable lacs of Kalpa year and the Buddha remembers the earlier births upto a period without measure.
5. *Prodigy of Departure and Arrival (Cyutotpādana Jnāna)* : A monk endowed with the superhuman divine sight can know and see the different living beings while dying, taking birth, in good state and in bad state. He can also know the living beings with good or bad colours, acquiring good or bad rebirth, and achieving the birth state according to his own karmas. The living beings behaved badly with body, speech and mind. They condemned the noble people. They had wrong-faith. They acted as wrong-faithed. Now, they have acquired the infernal destinity and misfortune after their death. Some others behaved well bodily, vocally and mentally. Some praised the noble people. They had right faith. They acted as right-faithed. They have now acquired good destinity and heavens. Thus, he knows ail ... through his divine eye.
6. *Prodigy of Destruction of Causes of Karmic Influx (Āsrava kṣaya)* : The monk endowed with this prodigy wanders in the world with self-realisation after knowing the self in this same birth by acquiring influx-less supreme mind and wisdom.

Adhikaraṇa Samaya: The violation of conduct for pacifying the quarrels is also a default.

Adhiṣthāna Pāramitā: Perfection in resolve; Steadiness; Remaining totally steady in one's resolve like a mountain which does not tremble and waver, and which remains steady in its own place/position.

Adhvanika: Permanent.

Agniśālā : Water-healing room.

Akuśala Karma : Sinful activities; Activities always resulting in bad effects.

Anagāmī: Not taking birth again; The yoga-practicing mendicant becomes as not taking birth again after totally destroying the desire for lust for sensuals and doing undesirable for others.

Anāśvāsika: Mentally non-satisfying.

Anavasrava/Anāsrava : Non-influx of karma; Devoid of karmic fruition.

Aniyata: Unspecified; Uncertain; A mendicant proposes for one of the three defaults of Pārājika, Sanghādidesa, and Pācittiya before a believer votaress in solitude. When the incident is presented before the monk-assembly, the default of the mendicant is decided on the basis of the statement of the votaress, the mendicant is awarded expiation. As the offence is not pre-decided, this is called unspecified or uncertain.

Anuprajnapti: Address.

Anuśāsanīya prātihārya: Discipline Keeping; The mendicant has the discipline : "Think thus, do not think thus; Think thus in your mind, do not think thus in your mind; Do not do this, leave it, accept it."

Anuśrava : Scriptural tradition.

Anuśrāvaṇa : Post-promulgation query; After disciplinary promulgation, one asks the mendicant group :'Whosoever accepts the order, please keep silence; whosoever do not accept, please express their mind.'

Apāyika : Moving to the evil destinity/state.

Arhat :The mendicant alleviates the attachment in perceptibles, non-perceptibles, pride, arrogance and ignorance (ne-science) and becomes the Enlightened or Venerable (Arhat) one. All his bad karmas get off and all his influxes are destroyed. After death, his worldly cycle is totally terminated. The causes of his worldly life are removed and his worldly pains are permanently over. This is the state of the liberated while living and supreme position.

Aṣtangika Mārga : The eight-fold noble path :
(i) Right vision, (ii) Right resolve, (iii) Right speech, (iv) Right action, (v) Right livelihood, (vi) Right conduct, (vii) Right memory, and (viii) Right meditation.

Aupapātika : The infernal and celestial beings.

Avici Naraka : The lowest of all the eight hells (of Buddhists) where there is fierce fire always burning in the area of 100 Yojanas.

Avicīrṇa : Not performed.

Avitarka-vicāra- samādhi : The mendicant acquires the state of uni-channeled thought on scriptural knowledge who finds flaws in scriptures and does not find flaws in shifting process and, therefore, crosses the first stage of meditation with a desire to leave even that knowledge. Out of the four meditations, the concentration on first, second and third meditation is known as this form of concentration.

Avyākṛta : Indescribalde.

Ācāryaka : The religion.

Ādeíanā Prātihārya : Miracle of sermons; Accordingly, one can express the resolves of the minds of others after knowing it through one's own mind.

Ājāniya: Belonging to excellent/noble caste.

Ākāśānantyāyatana: The third out of the four form-less Brahmalokas ?

Āknicanyāyatana : The fourth out of the four formless Brahmoloka ?

Ānantarya Karma : Sinful karmas; Post-actions-fruition karma; There are five such karmas — (i) Murder of mother, (ii) Murder of father, (iii) Murder of Arhat, (iv) Causing blood flow from the body of the Buddha, (v) Creation of dissension in the group. These five sins are called 'Post-action fruition karmas'. By performing these acts, the human being does never get liberation after destroying the causes influx in the same birth. The result of these sins follows them.

Ānupūrvī Kathā: Story narrated in succession. Accordingly, the stories related with donation, good conduct (sila) and heavens are narrated. The bad affects of sensualism are described and the importance of renunciation of sufferings and detachment is illustrated.

Āpatti : Penalty of offences.

Ārya-satyā: Noble Truth : (i) Suffering, (ii) Cause of suffering, (3) Alleviation of suffering, and (iv) Methods of alleviation of suffering.

Āsrava : Karmic influx; Mental impurities; There are four kinds of mental impurities : (i) Desire, (ii) Birth, (iii) Vision, and (iv) Ne-science.

Āssa-santa: Assuring.

Bala: Virtues; Capacities. There are five virtues : (i) Faith, (ii) Potency, (iii) Recall or memory, (iv) Mental concentration, (v) Supreme wisdom.

Bhakta-ccheda : Non-availability of Food.

Bhavāgra : End point or pinnacle of the world; The practitioner of meditation and yoga enters the subtle world from the gross would due to his meditation. He moves into this world with such a speed that he reaches a point where the world ends. This point is known as the pinnacle of the world.

Bhinna-stūpa : Foundation-less structure.

Bodhi-manda : The compound of Buddha temple in Buddha-Gayā.

Bodhisattva : An individual who accumulates such a knowledge and sacredness through his efforts during many earlier births that he may become Buddha any time in future.

Bodhi-vṛkṣa : The Tree of Enlightenment.

Bodhyanga (Seven) : Factors of Enlightenment : There are seven factors : (i) Memory, (ii) Potency, exertion or internal energy, (iii) Affection or delight, (iv) Mental concentration, (v) Dis-interestedness, and (vi) Pacification of body and mind (Praśrabdhi).

Brahmacarya vāsa :Initiation; Celibacy.

Brahmacarya-phala : Effect of Celibacy : The Religion of Buddha.

Brahma-danda : Supreme punishment; The mendicant, who is awarded supreme punishment, may speak to other mendicants at his will, but they can neither speak to him nor address or exert control over him.

Brahma-loka : World of Brahma; The best among all the seventeen worlds of gods.

Their residents are called Brahmas.

Brahma-vihāra : Supreme wanderings/Reflections; The reflection on four virtues : (i) Friendship, (ii) Compassion, (iii) Delightness, and (iv) Dis-interested-ness.

Buddha Kolāhala : Proclamation about the birth of the omniscient Buddha, thousand years before his birth. The guardian gods wander with proclamation, "Thousand years from now, the Buddha will take birth in this world."

Buddha-bija : The future Buddha.

Buddhāntara : Interval between the liberation of one Buddha and appearance of another Buddha.

Buddhaśrī: Excellence of Buddha.

Caitya-garbha: The main sanctuary of the temple.

Cakra-ratna : Gem-wheel; The first gem of Cakravartī out of the seven ones. It has 1000 spokes, the centre or nave of the wheel is ring-shaped. It is completely symmetrical and divine. The army of Cakravartī moves in the direction of its movement. The army stops wherever this wheel stops. Due to the effect of this wheel, the kings become sub-ordinates of Cakravartī without any fight and he instructs them about the five good conducts (Panca-sāla).

Cakravāla : Circular system of universe; There are innumerable circular systems in this universe. A circular system is like a world in itself whose length and width is 12,03,450 Yojanas and whose circumference is 36,10,350 Yojanas. The thickness of each circle is 2,40,000 Yojanas and it is surrounded by a layer of 4,80,000 Yojanas of deep water. There is an air-layer of 9,60,000 Yojanas thickness Surrounding this water. In the center of each circle, there is a Sinerū mountain whose height is 1,68,000 Yojanas. Half of its height is under sea and half is on the surface. There are seven series of mountain surrounding the Sinerū mountain (I) Yugandhara, (2) Isadhara, (3) Karavikā. (4) Sudassana, (5) Semidhara. (6) Vinataka, and (7) Assa-kaṇṇa. The lord of gods (Mahāraja devas) and their attendant yakṣas (demons) reside over these mountains. There is Himavān mountain in the circle which is 100 Yojanas high and which has 84000 peaks. The circular rock is surrounding the whole circular system.

Every circular system has one sun and moon with a width of 49 and 50 Yojanas respectively. Every circular system has palaces for Trāyastīna gods, asura gods and Avici-inferals.

There are four great islands or continents named Jambudvīpa, upper-goyāna, eastern Videha and Uttarakuru. Each continent is surrounded by 500 small islands. There is the Lokantarika Niraya (intra-mundane hell). The light of the suns brightens only one circular system. However, the radiance of Buddha can brighten all the circular systems.

Cakravartī: Wheel-turning monarch; Universal monarch; A great person possessed of seven gems — (i) wheel, (ii) elephant, (iii) horses, (iv) Jewels, (v) wife, (vi) Lord of businessman or citizens, and (vii) gem-leader (according to Majjhima Nikāya etc.) or son-(according to Dīgha-Nikāya etc.) and four prodigies—(i) supreme beauty, (ii) long-life, (iii) Diseaseless-ness (Nirātan-katā) and (iv) dearness to all Brahmanas and businessmen or citizens.

Cāra dvīpa : Four islands: Four islands in the four directions of Sumeru mountain. There is Pūrva Videha in the east, Upper-goyāna in the east, Uttarakuru in the north and Jambūdvīpa in the south.

Cāra-Ṛddhipāda : Four methods of acquiring accomplishment of concentration :

1. Concentration acquired through good karmas (chanda).
2. Concentration acquired by potency or inner energy.
3. Concentration acquired by meditation (mental).
4. Concentration acquired by mental deliberations.

Cārikā : Wandering for teaching the religion. It has two varieties : (i) Immediate (tvarita) and (ii) Normal. The accidental wandering to enlighten a distant votary is the immediate wandering. In contrast, the normal wandering is to walk daily for a Yojana or half-a-Yojana in order of villages or towns with intake of foods and for the purpose of the beneficiation of the public.

Catu-madhura snāna : Bath in four-pleasant things :Butterfat, Butter, honey and sugar.

Cātūrdvīpika : Simultaneously raining cloud on all the four-continental earth.

Cātūr-mahā-rātrika devatā : (i) Dhṛtasāṣra/(ii) Virūdha (iii) Virūpakaṣa and (iv) Vaisravaṇa are called the four catur-maharajika gods. Their one day is equal to 50 years of human beings. The thirty such days make up a month and 12 months make up a year. Their life-span is 500 such years. (App 90 lac of years).

Catūryāma : The four-fold doctrine of Mahāvira :

1. The knotless restrains the use of (unsterilied) water.
2. The knotless instructs to restrain all the kinds of sin.
3. The knotless becomes sin-free by restraining himself from all the sins.
4. The knotless is always engaged in restraining himself from all kinds of sin.

According to Dīgha-nikaya Sīhanada sutta, the four-fold doctrine is as follows :

1. Not to do violence to the living beings, not to get it done, nor to approve it (Non-violence).
2. Not to steal, not to get it done, nor to approve it (non-stealing).
3. Not to speak false, not to get false spoken, nor to approve false speaking (truth).
4. Not to involve in five-fold sensual gratification, not to get others involved in them and not to approve them.

Chanda: Attachment.

Cīvara : Reddish dress of mendicants which is prepared by jointing many pieces of cloth. According to Vinaya (Text of Monastic Conduct), the mendicants are prescribed to have three reddish dresses :

1. *Antara-vāsaka* (cloth to be wrapped below the waist). It is wrapped like a lungi.
2. *Uttarāsangu (upper garment)* : A 5 H long and 4 H wide(1 h = 1.5 ft) cloth used for wrapping the upper part of the body like a cover.
3. *Sanghātī (Folded cloth on shoulders)* : A cloth whose length and width is similar to the upper garment but it is doubly stitched. It is kept on shoulders with folds. It is used to cover the head and body during cold or other occasions.

Dākṣiṇeya : Presentable; Present or gift is the donation capable of awarding the otherworld (heavens). The person capable of receiving presents is called presentable.

Dāna-Pārmitā : Perfection or fullness in donations; Offer of desired materials to the beggars or mendicants without caring for wealth, riches, sons, wives or body etc. just like the water-pitcher which becomes empty by turning it down.

Daśa-bala: Ten virtues:

(i) To know as proper what is proper and improper what is improper.

(ii) To know the position and causes of fruition of karmas done in present, past and future.

(iii) To know properly the superb intelligence (gāminī pratipadā).

(iv) To know the universe and manifold elemental universes properly.

(v) To know the living beings with different thoughts properly.

(vi) To know the weakness and strength of senses of other living beings.

(vii) To know the raise, cleansing, defilements of attachment, concentration, meditation and liberation properly.

(viii) To know the things about the earlier births properly.

(ix) To see the living beings taking birth, dying and going to the heavens through the pure and divine eyes.

(x) Realisation of supreme wisdom and liberation of influx-less mind due to destruction of influx.

Daśa-sahasra-Brahmānda : Ten thousand circular systems of the world which are Buddha areas in the form of his birth.

Deśanā : Acceptance of one's own guilt or fault; Teachings.

Dhāraṇā : Holding; To say after looking the public or monks on listening to the sermons, "I hold that the public accepts what I have said; That is why, it is silent."

Dharma: Religion; Teachings of Buddha on religion and philosophy to different people at different places, and under different circumstances. It is also called as 'Sūtra'.

Dharma vinaya : Opinion.

Dharma-cakra-pravartana : Enforcement of the wheel of teaching the religion. The first teaching of religion to the five mendicants is know as 'Dharma-cakra-pravartana Sūtra'.

Dharma-cakṣu : Knowledge of religion.

Dharma-dhātu: Object of mind.

Dharma-kathika : Teacher of Dharma.

Dharma-paryāya : Teachings of religion.

Dharmatā: Specificity.

Dhūtavādī : Detachment or renunciation-based life-style. The term 'Dhuta' means the one who has combed the defilements. It also means the religion of carding off the defilements. A person who combs his defilements off by the mental or other components and teaches others to do the same, is called 'cleansed' or 'follower of cleansing'. There are 13 components of cleansing (Dhūtangas or Resolves of cleansing) :

(i) Resolve for wearing reddish clothes made of rags found on sands, rubbish, crematorium and sandy rods.

(ii) Resolve for wearing three reddish clothes, shoulder-cloth, upper garment, and waist-wrapping garment.

(iii) Resolve to subsist on begging.

(iv) Resolve for begging without gap of houses; Begging round from houses from one center to the other corner without gap.

(v) Resolve for single-dieting.
(vi) Resolve for taking foods only from a single container despite having many containers having foods but refusing to take from them.
(vii) Resolve for no-food after taking it once like the khalu bird.
(viii) Resolve for residing in the forest.
(ix) Resolve for living under the tree.
(x) Resolve for living under open space.
(xi) Resolve for living in the crematorium.
(xii) Resolve for sitting and sleeping on particularised bed, "it is for you" The resolve is in the form of as it is.
(xiii) Resolve for taking rest or sleep without lying.

Dhyāna (Cāra) : Four-fold meditation; In the first meditation, there are five components— (i) discursion, (2) thought, (3) affection, (4) happiness, and (5) concentration. The deep engagement of mind in the object is called discursion. This is the propensity of not allowing the object out of mind. The term 'affection' means mental pleasure. One gets delight by subduing the five hindrances (Nīvaraṇas) of desire, sinful activity, somnambulism, arrogance and disgust. The delightness creates affection. The term 'happiness' means physical joy. The affection causes the body to be pacified which gives pleasure. The concentration means 'samādhi'. Thus, the affectionate pleasure due to desirelessness, bereft of sinful Karmas, discursion, and thought leads to the first stage of meditation.

In the second meditation, there is no discursion and thought. In their absence, one gets concentration and vigilance. In this stage, faith gets stronger and the affection, pleasure and concentràtion become prominent.

In the third meditation, there is no component of affection even. There is prominence of concentration and pleasure. The thought of pleasure does not create deviations in mind. However, there is specific attribute of forbearance and concentration during this meditation.

In the fourth meditation, there is even no fourth component of pleasure. There are two propensities of disinterestedness and memory developing in this meditation alongwith concentration. There is the forsaking of physical pleasure of pain in this stage and there is bereavement of attachment and aversion. During this best meditation, the mind becomes totally cleansed and pure due to the forsaking of pleasure and pain and mental satisfaction and dis-satisfaction.

Dīgha-bhāṇaka: Ancient teachers learning Dīgha-nikāya by rote.

Divya Cakṣu : Divine sight; Engagement of one's mind to learn about the birth and death of the living beings by acquiring concentrated, pure and steady mind.

Droṇa : A measure for measuring the grains in olden times. This is bigger than Nāli :

4 Prasthas = 1 Kudava

4 Kudava = 1 Droṇa

1 Prastha is nearly equal to 0.25 Seer, hence 1 Droṇa is app. equal to 4 Seers or is 3.20 kg [*Abhidhāna Cintamaṇi Kośa* 3.50].

Dukkata kā doṣa : Offence of sin.

Gamika : Departing mendicant.

Ghatikāra : Mahābrahmā; God of Creation.

Ījjhāna: Burrnese year : Mynmar year.

Indra-kīla : A colossal iron-pillar or rock near the entry gate of the city to check the attack of the enemy.

Jambūdvīpa : An island 10,000 Yojanas wide, whose 4000 Yojana area is filled with water and is called as ocean. The human beings reside in an area of 3000 Yojanas.

The rest of the 3000 Yojana area consists of the Himavan mountain (Himālaya) which is 500 Yojanas high adorned with 84,000 peaks and which has 500 rivers flowing around it.

Janghā-vihāra: Walking.

Jantā-ghara: Bath-room.

Jāti-sangraha : Collection of relatives and followers for their enlightenment.

Jnāna-darśana : Realisation of realities.

Jnapti: Information; To inform the group of mendicants in proper order : "If the groups feels proper, it should follow it."

Kalpa : A Time unit of innumerable years. There are four kinds of Kalpa :

1. *Samvarta Kalpa* : Kalpa of world-dissolution.
2. *Samarta-sthāyī Kalpa*: Kalpa of duration of dissolution.
3. *Vivarta kalpa* : Kalpa of creation.
4. *Vivarta-sthāyī-kalpa* : Kalpa of duration of world creation.

In the *Samvarta Kalpa*, there is dissolution of the creation and there is the birth of the creation in the Vivarta Kalpa. They are gradually occurring in the world. The life-span of celestials are measured in Kalpas. The Kalpa-unit has a higher value than the time to take out all the mustard seeds densely filled in a 1 Y^3-pit at the rate of one seed per 100 years.

Kalpika-kutiyā : Store house, Store.

Kārṣapaṇa : A capper coin of that period; (app. 10 gms of today).

Karuṇā: Compassion; The attitude of compassion towards all the living beings of the world.

Kathā-vastu: Discussion, Dispute.

Kāya-smṛti : Recollection of respirations of body; The mendicant sits in a forest, under a tree or an empty house. He undertakes postures and keeps his body straight. He inhales with recollection, he exhales also with recollection. He experiences while inhaling and exhaling long breath. When he inhales and exhales short breath, he also experiences it. The mendicant, then, practices the process of inhaling and exhaling while experiencing the position of his whole body. He practices the inhaling and exhaling after suspending or retaining the breath for some time. This practice leads him to be vigilant, alert and restrained. Thus, while wandering, his greedy attitudes are destroyed. The mind is instilled inside and becomes concentrated and absorbed.

Kleśa: Defilements of mind.

Kriyāvādī: Actionist; One who sermonises actions only.

Kṣānti-pāramitā : Perfection of forbearance; Just as the earth endures all the materials-pure and impure—thrown over it, does not show anger but always has delightful mind; similarly, the mendicant should always bear the respect and disrespect equally and acquire the highest stage of forbearance.

Kṣīnāsrava : A state of Arhat-hood; Destroyed-desires.

Kuśala Dharma : Pious activities; Ten auspicious moral latencies or pre-dispositions which are always there at every moment during the observance of good activities.

Kutūhalaśālā : Hall of religious discussion; A place where followers of different religions discuss their religion and the audience listens to them curiously.

Loka-dhātu : The Realm of universe.

Madhyama Pratipadā :Middle path; A path between the extreme sensualism and extreme detachment.

Mahā-abhijnā-cārikā : Nun with great divine powers; *See* 'Abhijnā'.

Mahābhi-niṣkramaṇa : Great going out after leaving home by Bodhisattva for initiation.

Mahāgocara : Resident of densely populated area near a pleasant garden.

Mahā-brahmā : Gods having a life-span of one innumerable Kalpas residing in the world of Brahma; *See* 'Brahmaloka'.

Maitrī: Friendship towards all.

Maitrī-ceto-vimukti : Reflective release of friendship-ful mind in the form of, "May all the living beings live without enmity and violence. May all the living beings enjoy their lives with happiness."

Maitri-pāramitā : Perfection of friendship; Just as the water cools every body-sinner and the sacred and cleanses the defilements of both, similarly, the perfection of friendship means to expand this attitude with equanimous views towards all-the well-wishers as well as bad wishers.

Maitri-sahagata citta : Mind associated with the attitude of friendship.

Māṇavaka : Son of Brāhmana.

Manomaya Loka : The world of gods; Mental world.

Māra : The term has many meanings : (i) Death in general, (ii) Suffering or defilement which leads man to take birth in deathful world. (iii) Name of the son of the Vaśavarti god who presumed himself as the ruler of the world of desires. Whosoever undertook the spiritual practices on leaving sensualism, was taken as his enemy. He tried to deviate him from his path.

Miuditā: Satisfaction; Delight.

Naigama : An official post like the wealthy person of the city, but a little higher in Status.

Nairyāṇika : One who ferries over the sufferings.

Naiṣkarmya Pāramitā : Perfection or fullness in desirelessness; Just as a prisoner does neither have any attachment with the prison even after long stay there, nor he is ever eager to reside there, similarly, this fullness means to take all types of birth as prison and to wish for getting away from them.

Naiva-sanjanā-sanjnāyatana : The fourth non-perceptible world of Brahma out of Four : Non-perception-cum-non-non-perception .

Nāli : A measure of measuring grain in ancient times. It was app. equal to 1.5 Seers or 1.25 kg (as per '*Buddha-kalina Bharatiya Bhūgola*', p. 552).

Nidāna : Cause; Desire for future.

Nirmāṇarati devatā : Gods with power of multiplication; These gods change their forms on their own will. They feel joy in this action. Their one day is equal to 800 years of human world. Thirty days are equal to one month and twelve months make a year. Their life-span is eight thousand such divine years.

Nissaggiya Pācittiya : A kind of expiation; Requital of offence occurs when the mendicant leaves the order after accepting the offence before the group, single monk or many monks.

Pānca Mahātyāga : Five-great renunciations : (i) wealth, (ii) body, (iii) life, (iv) offspring, and (v) wife.

Pānca Mahāvilokana : Five objects of great thinking; While residing in the Tusita world, Bodhisattva thinks about his (i) time, (ii) island, (iii) country, (iv) family, (v) mother, and (vi) life-span related with his birth.

Panca-śila : Five good conducts :

(i) Abstinence from violence or killing.
(ii) Abstinence from taking not-given (non-stealing).
(iii) Abstinence from non-celibacy (celibacy).
(iv) Abstinence from false speech (truth).
(v) Abstinence from taking intoxicating materials.

Pānṣukūlika : Resolver of wearing reddish clothes made of rags.

Pārājika : Expiation of expulsion; When there is a grave default, the mendicant is expelled from the order.

Paramārtha-pāramita : Completely resolute in meditational practices; Not to deviate from practice even at the death-point. There are ten perfections of such practices.

Pāramitā : Perfection; Sitting with resolve for practices where the care for body is completely renounced. There are ten such resolves.

Paranirmita-vaśavartī devatā : Goods controlled by others; Their abodes are ruled by the Māra-evil destroyer. Their one day is equal to 1600 human-years. Thirty such days make a month and twelve months make a year. Their life-span is 16000 such divine years.

Pariveṇa: Hall of studies; A hall where the monks gather and study. This place is surrounded by walls and there is an open courtyard.

Pati-bhāna : Explanation of variegated questions.

Pāti-desanīya : Forgiveness for defaults; The defaulter monk requests the order of monks : " I have done an improper and condemnable offence. I beseech pardon for this".

Pinda-pāta : Food-in-alms; The mendicant stands at the door of a householder with his begging bowl. He stands pacified with his eyes down there. A member of the family drops the alms in his bowl and bows before him. The mendicant moves ahead with blessings to him. When the begging bowl is full, he returns to his monastery. The food served to the mendicant with invitation is also included in the term.

Pinda-pātika : A mendicant having black-bee-like alms or food collecting.

Prajnā : Supreme wisdom of emptiness ; Destruction of ne-science.

Prajnā Pāramitā : Perfection of supreme wisdom; Just as the mendicant subsists on alms and does not leave any one of excellent, medium or low families during his alms-begging, similarly, he should acquire the highest wisdom through questionings from wise men.

Prajnapti : Enunciations; Prescription, religious code.

Prātihārya: Miracles.

Pratimokṣa: Monastic Rules of conduct; The Vinaya Pitaka (Basket of Mendicants, Code of Conduct) has two independent chapters — one on the conduct of male mendicants and the other on the conduct of nuns. They contain 227 and 311 rules respectively. All the mendicants and nuns gather in the vow-observance hall on the dark fourteenth and bright fifteenth day and recite and repeat these rules.

Pratipāda: Path; Knowledge.

Prati-samvit-prāpta : Acquirement of distinct knowledge is called 'Prati-sambhidā'. There are four such distinct knowledges :

(i) *Distinctive knowledge of objects (Artha-prati-samhhidā)* : The five points-cause—based effect, Nirvana (Nirukti), meanings of what has been said, fruition and action—are called 'objects' (artha). The distinctive knowledge of these objects is called 'Distinctive knowledge of objects.'

(ii) *Distinctive knowledge of Buddha Sermons (Dharma)* : There are five Dharmas (1 -2) Cause and (resulting in) effect, (3) the sermonised noble path, (4) good actions, and (5) bad actions. The deep looking into these Dharmas is called the Distinctive knowledge of 'Dharma'.

(iii) *Distinctive knowledge of Etymology (Nirukti)* : The distinctive knowledge through Magadhi— the basic language of all the living beings about the derivative nature of the objects and sermons and their behaviours, statements about them and ascertaining their true nature is called Distinctive knowledge of etymology or derivation. The person proficient in this kind of knowledge knows the meanings of the words like 'touch' experience (vedana, pain) etc. They do not have any nature.

(iv) *Distinctive knowledge of explanations (pratibhāga)* : The support of the knowledge looking into the knowledge of all the objects is the knowledge itself or the objects and duties conveyed by it is called the Distinctive knowledge of explanations.

Pratītya-samutpāda : Relative causality; Origination of an entity after destruction of another one. The material causes of aggregates are : (i) Form, (ii) Feeling, (iii) Instincts (iv) Pre-disposition, and (v) Intellect or cognition.

Pratyanta: Boundary.

Pratyaya : Cause (Primary and secondary); Permissible articles of mendicants. There are four such articles : (i) Reddish dress, (ii) Food-in-alms, (iii) Beds and seats, and (iv) Medicines for curing ailment.

Pratyeka-buddha: Self-enlightened; A person who self-realises the essence of religion. He does not need any teacher for learning the religion.

Pṛthak-Jana: Common man who has not acquired the state of noblehood. There are eight noble states of noble-hood of the path of liberations :

(1-2) Path of resolute movement (srotāpanna) and its effect.

(3-4) Path of ultimate arrival (saṛkdāgāmī) and its effect.

(5-6) Path of non-arrival (anāgāmī) and its effect.

(7-8) Path of enlightened-hood (Arhat) and its effect.

Pudgala : Individual; Living being.

Pūrvalakṣaṇa: Pre-signals; Presentation of an oldman, diseased man, dead corpse and initiated saint by the Sahampati Brahma to promote initiation of the Bodhisattva while going to see the garden before renouncing the house.

Ṛddhi-prātihārya : Miraculous deeds due to yogic power; Accordingly, the mendicant can transform himself into many forms, and many forms into one form. He can manifest himself and he can also disappear. He can cross through the walls, stone-rocks and mountains like that in the sky without any strike. He can dive in earth like in water. He can move on water like that on the earth. He can fly in the sky with rolled legs like the birds. He can touch the mighty sun and moon and rub them with his hands. He can go to the Brahmaloka associated with his body.

Sa-brahmacārī: Fellow disciple; Sramaṇa initiated in the same order.

Samādhi : Rightful concentration of mental activities on a single substratum; Purification of mind.

Sahampati Brahmā : The great Brahma (a god) on whose request, Buddha preached his religion. On many occasions, he secret-visited Buddha. He was the mendicant named Sahaka during the time of Kasyapa Buddha. He was born as Mahabrahma in the world of Brahma as a result of his observance of five qualities (indriyas) of faith, potency, memory, meditation and wisdom.

Śaikṣya: Novice; Learner; The novice learner is defined as that who has acquired four paths (out of five except the Arhat one), and three effects (out of four, fruition, exertion, similar to cause and control). He has to learn about others. The mendicants who have acquired the Arhat-hood, are called Non-novices.

Sakṛdāgāmī: Coming only once in future. The mendicant, in his first stage, moves on to the path of liberation after winning over the five obstructions of lust for senses and thoughts of evil on others. At this stage, the main activity is to destroy karmic influx. If he does not acquire Arhat-hood in this birth, he may acquire it in the next birth by taking birth once again.

Sallekha-vṛtti : Propensity of renunciation; An austerity; The person is said to have the best renunciation tendency who observes all the conducts even at the time of his imminent death without doing and getting the splendours, attendants and state of activities on the basis of his qualities of few desires and overlooking the enunciations of Bhagavan Buddha.

The term 'nimitta' means a servant who takes care of residence, beds and seats. When the householders ask, "What is being done? Who is getting it done", one should say, 'no body' or say anything like this.

The term 'avabhasa' means 'splendour'. It is illustrated like, "O worshippers, where do you live ?"

"We live in a palace".

"O worshippers, the mendicants should not need the palaces". The statement like this or similar should be made.

The term 'parikatha' means the state of affairs. It is illustrated by stating like "There is difficulty of residence for the mendicants" or any other statement with reference to specific states.

Samādhi-bhāvanā : A reflection which leads to Buddhahood in the same birth.

Sambodhi: Buddha-hood.

Samgati : Destiny, Future eventuality.

Samyak-sambuddha-pravedita : Perceived by the Buddha.

Sāndṛṣtika: Symbolic; Worth looking into; The term 'sandṛṣti' means to see. The term here, thus, means worth looking into. The extraordinary religion, while being observed checks the cycle of birth and death. That is why, it is called "worth looking into".

Sanghādi-sesa : Short-period expulsion of the defaulter mendicant for purification of his default.

Sanghāta: Net, Web.

Sanjnā: Preliminary knowledge; Instinct. The knowledge like 'this is this object' after the contact of sense and the object is called instinct or sanjna.

Sanjna-vedayita-nirodha : A kind of samādhi where there is non-existence of knowledge and experiencing. The mendicant under this samādhi does not feel, 'I will acquire the state of suppression of knowledge and experiencing,' " I am acquiring this state of samādhi," "I have acquired this state of samādhi". The mind of aspirant gets accustomed in such a way that he acquires this state of samādhi. In this samādhi, there is, first, the suppression of speech, followed by body and mind.

Sannipāta :Gathering, Assembly.

Sansthāgāra : Meeting Hall.

Santuṣita : Son of gods in the Tusita world.

Sarvārthāka Mahāmātya : Private secretary.

Satya-pāramita : Perfection of truth; Just as the star of Venus does not deviate from its path in any season, similarly, this perfection means not to deviate from the path of truth despite hundreds of troubles and allurements of riches etc.

Saundika Karmakara: Brewer, Distiller.

Sekhiya : Commandments whose violation is a fault.

Śiksāpada : Monastic rules.

Śīla : Good conduct; Abstinence from fully prohibited activities like violence etc.; Purity of body.

Śīla-pāramitā : Perfection in good-conduct; Just as the camari (deer or cow) protects her tail disregarding even her life, similarly, the mendicant should always be resolute for the protection of his good conduct even at the cost of his life.

Smṛti-samprajanya : Consciousness and experience.

Sramaṇa Pariṣkāra : Four kinds of things acceptable by the mendicant :

(i) Reddish clothes made of rags,
(ii) Food-in-alms,
(iii) Seats, beds and residence, and
(iv) Medicines for ailments.

Śrāmaṇera : Wearing of reddish clothes after getting initiated. Under this condition, the Buddhist scripture is taught. The aspirant has to live with the initiator and to undertake ten vows of good conduct : abstinence from violence, stealing, illicit sex; false speech, intoxication materials, evening meals, amorous disposition, cosmetisation, high seat and gold and silver.

Srotā-patti : Coming into the stream of liberation; To be on the path of liberation where from there is no possibility of downfall. The mendicant is called to be on the path of liberation when he crosses over the three obstacles of disgust, existencial attitude and faith in wrong conduct. The mendicant on the path of liberation attains liberation in a maximum of seven rebirths.

Sthavira : Senior monk; One becomes sthavira after ten years of initiation and becomes 'Mahāsthavira' after twenty years of initiation.

Styāna-gṛddha : Somnambulist; Laziness of body and mind.

Su-ākhyāta: Well-narrated; Well-said.

Su-nirmita : Son of the gods of Nirmāṇa-rati heavenly world.

Su-pravedita: Well-realised; Well-proclaimed.

Su-yāma : Son of the gods of Yama heavenly world.

Thallaccaya : Big offence.

Tina Vidyā : Three learnings : The following are the three learnings:

(i) Memory of earlier birth.
(ii) Knowledge about birth and death.
(iii) Knowledge of destruction of mental defilements.

Trāyastrinśa devatā : These are the empyrean gods whose lord is Śakra. Their one day is equal to 50 years of human world. Thirty such days make up a month, 12 such months make up a year. Their life-span is 1000 such years (~1,80 Inc years.)

Tuṣita devatā : The Bodhi-saṭṭvas live in the palaces of Tuṣita (satisfied) gods. They take birth in the world after completing their life-span there. They, then, get Nirvaṇa after acquiring enlightenment. Their one day is equal to 400 years of human beings. Thirty days make up a month, twelve months make up a year. Their lifespan is 4000 such divine years.

Udāna : Breathing upwards; Words from the mouth of the mendicants out of delightful mood.

Unnīsa-vidyāyen : Nineteen learnings : (i) Scripture, (ii) Smṛtis-books on canonical code of law, (iii) Sānkhya, (iv) Yoga, (v) Nyāya (logic based), (vi) Vaiśeṣika (Specificists), (vii) Mathematics, (viii) Music, (ix) Vaidyaka : Science of life-span, (x) Four Vedas, (xi) All Legendary, Books, (xii) History, (xiii) Astrology, (xiv) Incantationolgoy, (xv) Logic, (xvi) Mystical formulary of worship (tantra), (xvii) Military science, (xviii) Meterology, and (xix) Palmistry.

Upa-pāramitā : Secondary Perfections : Renunciation of external materials with great resolution in the objective. There are ten secondary perfections.

Upaśama-samvartanika : Propitiator of peace.

Upa-sampadā : Ritual of initiation; A person desirous of monkhood is ritually initiated after he has learnt and understood the religion. When the monk assembly is there, the novice presents himself before it, and he is examined by the assembly. When he passes the test, he is taken into the group of monks, and he is, then, called 'Bhikṣu' (mendicant). He has to observe 227 rules under the laws of Buddhist monastic conduct. A person can be initiated only after he is twenty years old.

Upasthāka : Accompanying attendant.

Upasthiāna-śālā: Meeting Hall.

Upekṣā : Dis-interested-ness towards the world.

Upekṣā pāramitā : Perfection in Disinterested-ness; Just as the earth overlooks on the good or bad materials thrown over it without any pleasure or pain, similarly, the perfection-in-disinterestedness means to be equanimous in the state of pains and pleasures and to move towards the highest state of indifference.

Uposatha : Vows; A votary Or worshipper, with clean dress, goes to the Buddhist monastery. We kneels down before the mendicant and requests him, "O venerable, I speech you to award me eight vows of good conduct with three refuges (of Buddha, Religion and order)". The votary repeats his request thrice. The mendicant awards him one vow each time and stops for a moment; the votary respects the vow every time. The votary, then, resides in the monastery for the whole day, observes all the eight vows of good conduct and spends his day in pious thoughts. Many votaries observe these vows for the whole life. The eight vows of good conduct are as below :

1. I will live by renouncing the violence or destruction of vitalities.
2. I will live by renouncing the things not-given (or stealing).
3. I will live by renouncing the sensual desires.
4. I will live by renouncing the falsity.
5. I will live by renouncing the use of intoxicating materials.
6. I will live by renouncing the foods in the evening.
7. I will live by renouncing the use of dance, songs, instrumental music, amorous pastimes, garlands, cosmetics, smearing pastes, and beautification of body.
8. I will live by renouncing the high seat and decorated bed.

Uposathā- gāra : Hall for observing vows.

Uttara-kuru : An island among the four islands.

Uttara-manuṣya-dharma : Divine powers.

Vārṣika Śātika : A loin or waist-wrapping cloth used during the rainy season because of non-drying of clothes in this season.

Vaśavartī : Son of gods born in the palace of Paranirmita Vaśavartī gods.

Vidarśanā/Vipaṇyanā : Insight introspection; Knowledge of wisdom or truth which accrues due to the realisation of momentariness, sufferability and non-soulness of entities.

Vihāra : Monastery; Hermitage.

Vijnanānantyāyatana : Thought on infiniteness of cognition/perception; The second of four formless abodes of Brahmaloka.

Vimukti : Liberation.

Vināya : Scripture on monastic rules, A text in which the monastic rules for monks and nuns are detailed. (Vinaya-pitaka).

Vīrya Pāramitā : Perfection of potency or exertion; Just as the lion is always vigilant, active and mentally resolute while sitting, standing or walking, similarly, the mendicant should acquire the highest potency by being active in all the birth-stales.

Viśvakarmā : God of Architecture; A god resident of Trāvatinśa heaven who is the architect among the gods. He is present before the Buddha for architectural work on the command of Íakra at different times.

Vyākaraṇa: Forecast, Grammar; Explanation.

Vyāpādā: Mischief; Treachery.

Yāma-devatā : Tutelary deity of village; There is one day of 200 years of human world. Thirty such days make a month, and 12 such months make a year. The lifespan of these tutelary gods is 2000 such divine years.

Yaṣti : A measure of length :
20 Yaṣtis = I Vṛṣabha.
80 Vṛṣabha = 1 Gāvuta.
4 Gāvuta = 1 Yojana I 8 miles.

Yojana : 2 miles : 3.32 kms.

BIBLIOGRAPHY

Agama Literature

Aṇuttarovavāiyadasāṅga-sūtra : (Jaina Āgama) Ed. Modi S.C., Publishers—Gurjara Grantharatna Karyalaya, Ahmedabad. 1932.

Aṇuttarovavāiyadasāṅg-sūtra : With Vṛtti of Sūri, Abhayadeva, Ātmānanda Jain Sabhā, Bhavanagar, 1921.

Antakṛddaśāṅga-sūtra : (Jaina Āgama) Ed. Modi S.C., Publishers—Gurjara Grantharatna Karyālaya, Ahmedabad, 1932.

Antakṛddaśāṅga-sūtra : Together with Vṛtti of Sūri Abhayadeva, Publishers—Jain-dharma-prasāraka Sabhā, Bhavanagar, 1933.

Ācārāṅga-cūrṇī : Gaṇe Jinadāsa, Publishers—Ṛsabhadeva Kesarīmala Saṁsthā, Ratlam, 1941.

Ācārāṅga sūtra : (Jaina Āgama) together with Vṛtti of Ācārya Śīlaṅka, Publishers—Agamodaya Samiti, Surat, 1935.

Ācārāṅga sūtra : (Hindi Translation) Translated by Muni Saubhāgyamala, Ed. Nalavāyā Vasantī Lāla, Publisher—Jaina, Sāhitya Samiti, Ujjain, 1950.

Ādi Purāṇa : Ācārya Jinasena, Ed. Pandita Pannā Lāla Jaina, Publishers—Bhāratīya Jñānapīṭha, Kāsī, 1963.

Āvaśyaka cūrṇī (Vol. II) : Gaṇi Jinadāsa, Publishers—Ṛsabhadeva Kesarīmala Institute, Ratlam, 1928.

Āvaśyaka Niryukti : Ācārya Bhadrabāhu, along with Malayagirī Vṛtti, Publishers—Āgamodaya Samiti, Bombay, 1928.

Āvaśyaka Niryukti : Ācārya Bhodrabāhu, along with Haribhadrīya Vṛtti, Publishers —Āgamodaya Samiti, Bombay, 1961.

Āvaśyaka Niryukti Dīpikā (Vol. III) : Māṇikya-śekhara, Surat, 1939.

Uttara Purāṇa : Ācārya Guṇabhadra, Publishers—Bhāratīya Jñānapīta, Kāśī, 1954.

Uttarādhyayana sūtra : (Jaina Āgama) Ed. & Pub. Vādekara (Prof.) R.D., N.B. Vaidya, Poona, 1954.

Uttarādhyayana sūtra : (Hindi Tr.), Mahārāja Ātmārāmajī, Pub. Jaina Śāstramāla, Lahore.

Uttarādhyayana sūtra : Alongwith Nemicandra's Vṛtti, Bombay, 1937.

Uttarādhayana sūtra : Comm, of Bhāvaviyayajī, Pub. Ātmānanda Jaina Sabā, Bhāvanagar.

Uttarādhyaya sūtra : (Vol. IV) : Comm. of Lakṣmī Vallabha, Tr. Pt. Hīrālāla Hamsarāja, Pub. Manivāe Rājakarariā, Ahmedabad, 1935.

Upadeśa Prāsāla (Four Volumes) : Sūri Lakṣmīvijaya, Pub. Jaina Dharma Prasāraka Sabhā, Bhavanagar, 1914-1923.

Upadeśamālā : Gaṇi Dharmadāsa, Comm. of Gaṇi Rāmavijaya, Pub. Hīrā Lāla Hamsarāja, Jamanagar, 1934.

Upāsakadasāṅga sūtra : (Jaina Āgama) Ed. & Tr. into English Gore N.A., Pub. Oriental Book Agency, Poona, 1953.

Uvavī sutta : Hindi Tr., Tr. by Muni Umeśacandrajī, Pub. Akhila Bhāratīya Sādhumāgrī Jaina Sanskṛti Rakṣaka Saṅgha, Sailana (M.P.), 1963.

Ṛṣi-maṇḍala-Vṛtti: Sūri Dharmaghoṣa (with Tr. in Gujarātī by Śāstrī Hariśaṅkara Kālidāsa and Skt. Commentry by Gaṇi Śubhavardhana), Publisher—Śrī Jaina Vidyāsāta, Dosīvādānī Pola, Ahmedabad, 1901.

Aupapātika (uvavāī) sūtra : (Jaina Āgama) with Vṛtti of Sūri Abhayadeva, Pub. Devacanda Lālabhāī Pusta Koddhara Fund, Surat.

Kalpa sūtra : (Jaina Āgama), Pub. Sārābhāī Maṇilāla Navāba, Ahmedabad, 1941.

Kalpa sūtra : (Bengali Tr.) Tr. by Basantakumāra Cattopādhyāya, Pub. Calcutta University, Calcutta.

Kalpa sūtra : Kalpadruma-kālikā Vṛtti (Hindi Tr.), Pub. Kota Chābādā's Jain Śve. Saṅgha, 1933.

Kalpa sūtra : Kalpalatā Commentry, Pub. Velajī Śivajī Company, Dāna Baṇḍāra, Bombay, 1918.

Kalpa sūtra : Kalpārthabodhinī, Ed., Gaṇi Buddhisāgara, Pub. Jainadatta Sūri Jñāna Bhaṇḍāra, Bombay, 1942.

Kalpasūtrārtha Prabodhinī : Sūri Rajendra, Pub. Rajendra Pravacana Kāryalaya, Khudālā, 1933.

Kalpa sūtra Bālavabodha : Buddhavijaya.

Kahāvalī : Bhadreśvara, Ed. Dr. U.P. Shah, Pub. Gayakwad Oriental Series, Baroda.

Gommata-sāra : Nemicandra Siddhānta Cakravartī, Vṛtti by Paṇḍita Manohara Lāla resident of Pāḍhama. 1913.

Caupanna Mahāpurisa Cariyam : Śīlācārya.

Citra Kalpa sūtra : Ed. Navba Sarabhāī Manilāla, Ahmedabad, 1941.

Jambudvīpa Pannatti sūtra : (Jaina Āgama) with Vṛtti of Gaṇi Śānticandra, (Vol. I, II), Pub. Devacanda Lālabhāī Pustakoddhāra Fund, Surat. 1920.

Jayadhavatā Vṛtti : (Kasāyapāhuḍa) Vīrasenācārya, Ed., Siddhānta-śāstrī Pt. Mūlacanda, Siddhānta-śāstrī, Pt. Kailaśacandra, Pra. Bhā. Di. Jain Saṅgha, Mathura, 1961.

Jñātādharma Kathāṅga sūtra : (Jaina Āgama) Along with Vṛtti of Sūri Abhayadeva, Ed. Sūri Ācārya Candrasāgara, Pub., Siddhacakra Sāhitya Pracāraka Samiti, Surat, 1951.

Jñātādharmakathāṅga sūtra : (With Hindi Tr.) Ed., Bhārilla, Pt. Śobhācandra, Śrī Trilokaratna Sthā. Jain Dhārmika Parīkṣā Board, Pāthadhī, Ahmedabad, 1964.

Tattvārtha Bhāṣya : Umāsvāti, Pub., Rāyacanda Jaina Śāstramālā, Hīrābāgha, Bombay, 1906.

Tapaccha Paṭṭāvali : Gaṇi Dharmasāgara, Ed. Pt. Kalyāṇa Vijayajī, Bhavanagar, 1940.

Titthogālī Painnaya : (Jain work) Unpublished manuscript.

Tiloyapaññatti : Ācārya Yativṛṣabha, Ed., Hīralāla Jain & A.N. Upādhye, Pub., Jaina Saṁskṛti Saṁrakṣaka Saṅgha, Solapur, 1951.

Trilokasāra : Siddhāntacakravartī Ācārya Nemīcandra, Tr., Pt. Ṭoḍarmalajī, Pub., Hindī Jaina Sāhitya Prasāraka Kāryālaya, Bombay, 1911.

Triṣaṣṭi-śalākāpuruṣā-caritram : (Gujarāti Tr., IV Volumes), Ācārya Hemacandra, Pub., Jaina Dharma Prasārakasabhā, Bhavanagar.

Darśanasāra : Devasenācārya, Ed., Pt. Nāthurāma Premī, Pub., Jaina Grantharatnākara Kāryālaya, Bombay, 1920.

Daśavaikālika sūtra : Vacana Pramuka Ācārya Śrī (Tulasī, Pub., Jaina Śve. Terāpanthī, Mahāsabhā, Calcutta, 1963.

Daśavaikālika Cūrṇī : Agastya Siniha, Pub., Prākṛta Text Society, Ahmedabad.

Daśavaikālika Cūrṇī : Mahattara Gaṇi Śri Jinodāsa, Pub., Devacanda Lālabhāī Javerī, Surat, 1933.

Daśāśrutaskandha : Ed. & Pub., Ātmārāmajī Mahāraja, Pub., Jaina Śāstramālā, Lahore, 1936.

Dharmaratna Prakaraṇa : Śrī Śānti Sūri, Pub., Ātmānanda Jaina Sabhā, Bhavanagar, 1925.

Nirayāvaliyāo : (Jain Āgama), Ed., A.S. Gopānī, B.J. Cokasi, Pub., Śambhubhāī Jamasī Sahu, Pub., Gurjara Grantha-ratna Kāryālaya, Ahmedabad, 1927.

Nirayāvaliyāo : Candra Sūri, alongwith Sanskrit Commentry, Pub., Āgamodaya Samiti, Surat, 1921.

Nirayāvalikā : (Alongwith Sundara Bodhi Commentry & (Hindi-Gurjara Tr.) Mahārāja Ghasī Lālajī, Pub., A.B. Śve. Sehā Jaina Śāstroddhāra Samiti, Rajkot, Saurāṣṭra, 1960.

Niśitha Sūtra : (Alongwith Sabhāṣya Cūrṇī, Ed., Upādhyāya Kavi Śrī Amara Muni, Muni Śrī Kanhaiyālāla 'Kamala', Pub., Sanmati Jñānapīṭha, Agra, 1960.

Pañcakalpa-bhāṣya : Gaṇi Saṅghadāsa.

Pañca Vastuka : Ācārya Haribhadra Sūrī, Pub., Devacanda Lālabhāī Jaina Pustakoddhāra Fund, Surat, 1927.

Pariśiṣṭa Parna : Ācārya hemacandra, Ed. Setha Hargobindadāsa, Pub., Jain Dharma Pracāraka Sabhā, Bhavanagara, 1957.

Pariṣiṣta Parṇa : Ācārya Hemacandra, Ed., Dr. Herman Jacobi, Pub., Asiatic Society of Bengal, Calcutta, 1932.

Bhagavatī Sūtra : (Jain Āgama) Alongwith Vṛtti of Abhayadeva Sūri, Pub., Ṛṣabhadevajī, Kesarīmalajī Jain Śvetāmbara Saṁsthā, Ratlam, 1937.

Bhagavatī Sūtra : (Alongwith Gujarātī Tr.) Ed. & Tr., Paṇḍita Becaradāsa Dośī, Bhagavānadāsa Harakhacanda Dośī, Jināgama Prakāśaka Sabhā, Ahmedabad, 1922-31, 63.

Bharateśvara Bāhubalī Vṛtti : (Two Volumes) Śubhaśīla Gaṇi, Pub., Devacanda Lāla Bhāī Jain, Pustakodhāra Fund, Surat, 1932.

Bhāva Saṅgaraha : Ācārya Devasena, Ed., Pannālāla Sonī, Pub., Maṇikyacandra Digambara Jain Granthamālā Samiti, Hindi Grantha Ratnākara Office, Bombay. 1921.

Mahāvīra Cariyam : Guṇacandra, Pub., Devacanda Lālabhāī Jain Pustakodhāra Fund, Surat.

Mahāvīra Cariyam : Nemīcandra, Pub., Atmārama Sabhā, Bhavanagar, 1926.

Mahāvīra Svāmī No Saṁyama Dharma : (Sūtrakṛtāṅga no Chāyānuvāda) Tr. Gopāladāsa Jīvābhāi Paṭela, Pub., Navajīvana Kāryālaya, Ahmedabad, 1935.

Vaṅgacūliyā : (Jaina Painnā Grantha) Yaśobhadra, Pub., Maḍayatta, Falaudi, Maravada, 1923.

Vicāra Śreṇī : Ācārya Merutuṅga, Pub., Jaina Sāhitya Saṁśodhaka (Magazine), Poona, May, 1925.

Vividha Tirthakalpa : Ācārya Jinaprabhā Sūri, Ed., Jinavijaya Muni, Pub., Bhāratīya Vidyāpītha, Siṅghī Jain Granthamālā, Serial No. 10, Śantiniketana, Bangal, 1934.

Viśeṣovaṣyaka Bhāṣya : (Saṭīka) Jinabhadra Gaṇi Kṣamāśramaṇa, Vṛtti by Koṭyācārya, Pub., Ṛṣabhadeva & Kesarīmala Śve. Institute, Ratlam, 1936-37.

Viśeṣāvaṣyaka Bhāṣya : (Saṭīka Gujarātī Anuvāda) Tr., Cunnīlāla Hukumacanda, Pub., Āgamodaya Samiti, Bombay, 1923.

Vyavahāra Sūtra Sabhāṣya (Jain Āgama) Alongwith Malayagiri Vṛtti, Ed., Muni Māṇeka, Pub., Vakīla Trikamalāla Agaracanda, Ahmedabad, 1928.

Ṣaṭkhaṇḍāgama : (Dhavala Ṭīkā), Ācārya Vīrasena, Ed., Hīralāla Jain, Pub., Seṭha Sitāvarāya Lakhamīcanda, Amaravati (Brara), 1941-57.

Samavāyāṅga Sūtra : (Jain Āgama) Alongwith Vṛtti of Abhayadeva Sūri, Ed., Master Nagīnadāsa Nemacanda, Pub., Seṭha Māṇekalāla Cunnilāla, Kāntilāla, Cunnilāla, Ahmedabad, 1938.

Sūtrakṛtāṅga Sūtra : (Jain Āgama) Along with Vṛtti of Śīlāṅkācārya, Ed., Paṇyāsapravara Śrīcandasāgara Gaṇi, Pub., Śrī Gauḍīrī Pārśvanātha Jain Derāsara Peḍhī, Bombay, 1949.

Sūtrakṛtāṅga Sūtra : (Alongwith Commentry & Hindi Tr.) Tr., Pt. Ambikādatta Ojhā, Vyākaraṇācārya, Pub., Śrī Mahāvīra Jain Jñānodaya Society, Rajkot, 1938.

Sūtrakṛtāṅga Sūtra : (Hindi Tr.) Tr. Rāhula Saṅkṛtyāyana, Pub., Sūtrāgama Prakāśana Samiti, Gurgaon (Cantt.), Haryana, 1961.

Sena Praśna : Praśna Ratnākarābhidhā : Śrīsena Praśna) collected by Śrī Śubhavijaya Gaṇi, Pub., Devacanda Lālabhāī Jain Pustakoddhāra Fund, Bombay, 1918.

Saubhāgyapañcamyādi Parvakathā Saṅgraha : Kṣmākalyāṇakopādhyāya, Pub., Hindi Jaināgama Prakāśaka Samiti Kāryālaya, Kota, 1933.

Sthānāṅga Sūtra : (Jaina Āgama) along with Vṛtti of Abhayadeva Sūri, Pub., Āgamodaya Samiti, Surat, 1920.

Sthānāṅga-samavāyāṅga : (Gujarātī Tr.) Tr. Dalaksukha Mālavariyā, Pub., Gujarāta Vidyāpīṭha, Ahmedabad, 1955.

Harivaṁśa Purāṇa : Jinasena Sūri, Ed. Pt. Pannālāla Jain, Pub., Bhāratīya Jñanapīṭha, Kāśī, 1963.

Antagaddasao. Tr. by L.D. Barnett, London, 1907.

Avasyaka Erzeulang (German Translation of Āvaśyaka kathā): Tr. by Ernst Leumann, Leipzig, 1897.

Gaina Sūtras, Part I (Ācārāṅga Sūtra & Kalpa Sūtra) : Tr. by Dr. Hermann Jacobi, Pub. Sacred Books of the East Series, Vol. XXII, Oxford. 1884.

Gaina Sūtras, Part II (Sūtrakūṛtāṅga Sūtra & Uttarādhyayana Sūtra) : Tr. by Dr. Hermann Jacobi, Sacred Books of the East Series, Vol. XLV, Oxford, 1899.

Triṣaṣṭi-śalākā-puruṣācaritra (4 volumes): Tr. by H.M. Johnson, Pub. by Gaekvad Oriental Series, Baroda, 1930.

Uvasagdasao (2 Parts) : Tr. 4 Ed. by A.F. Rudolf Hoernle Pub., Bibliotheca Indica, Calcutta, 1888-1890.

Tripiṭaka Literature

Aṅguttara Nikāya : (Hindi Tr., Volumes I & II) Tr. Bhadanta Ānanda Kauśalyāyana, Pub., Māhābodhi Sabhā, Calcutta, 1957-1963.

Aṅguttaronikāya Aṭṭhakathā : (Manoratha Pūraṇī) Ācārya Buddraghoṣa Ed., Harmana Kopa, Pub., For Pāli Text Society by Lyujhāka & Co., London, 1924, 1956.

Aṅgūttara Nikāya Pāli : (Tripiṭaka, IV Volumes) : Ed, Bhikṣu Jagadīśa Kāsya, Pub., Pāli Prakāśana Maṇḍala, Navanālanda Mahāvihāra Nālandā, Bihar, 1960.

Anāgata-vaṁśa : Ed., Menayefa, pub., Journal of Pāli Text Society, 1886.

Apadāna Pāli: (From Khuddaka Nikāya, Vol. VI & VII), (Tripiṭaka), (Vol. II) : Ed., Bhikṣu Jagadīśa Kāśyapa, Pub., Pāli Prakāśana Maṇdala, Navanālandā Mahāvihāra, Nālandā, Bihar, 1959.

Avadāna Kalpalatā : (Bandha Sanskrit Text) (Vol. II), Kṣemendra, Ed., Śaratcandradāsa & Pt. Harimohana Vidyābhūsaṇa, Pub., Bibliotheka Indica, Calcutta, 1888.

Avadāna Śatakam : (Baudha Sanskrit Granthāvali-19), Ed., Dr. P.L. Vaidya, Pub., Mithilā Vidyāpīṭha, Darbhanga, 1958.

Itivuṭṭaka Pāli : Ed., Bhikṣu Jagadīśakāsyapa, Pub., Pāli Prakāśana Maṇḍala, Navanālanda Mahāvihāra, Nalanda, 1959.

Itivuttaka : (Hindi Tr.,) Bhikṣu Dharmarakṣita, Pub., Mahābodhi Sabhā Sāranātha, 1955.

Udāna Aṭṭhakathā : (Paramatthadīpanī) Ācārya Dhammapāla, Pub., Pāli Text Society, London, 1926.

Udāna Pāli : Ed., Bhikṣu Jagadīśa Kāśyapa, Pub., Pāli Prakāśana Maṇḍala, Navanālandā Mahāvihāra, Nalanda, Bihar, 1959.

Udāna : (Hindi Tr.) Tr., Bhikṣu Jagadīśa Kāśyapa, Pub., Mahābodhi Sabhā, Sāranātha, 1938.

Gilgit Manuscripts (Vinayavastu) : (Baudha Sanskrit Text). (Vol. III), Ed., Dr. Nalinākṣadatta, Prof. D.M. Bhaṭṭācārya and Vidyāvāridhi Pt. Śivanātha Śarmā, Śrīnagara, Kashmir,1942.

Jātaka Aṭṭhakathā Pāli : (Vol. I) Ācārya Buddhaghoṣa, Ed., Bhikṣu Dharmarakṣita, Pub., Bhāratī Jñānapīṭha, Banaras, 1951.

Jātaka-aṭṭhakathā : (Vol. VII) Ācārya Buddhaghoṣa, Ed., V. Fausaboll, London, 1877-1897.

Jātaka : (Aṭṭhakathā, Hindi Tr.) Volumes I to VI), Tr., Bhadanta Ānanda Kośalyāyana, Pub., Hindi Sāhitya Sammelana, Prayaga, 1956.

Jātaka Pāli : (Tripiṭaka) Ed., Bhikṣu Jagdīśa Kāśyapa, Pub., Pāli Prakāśana Maṇḍala, Navanālandā Mahāvihāra, Nālandā, Bihar, 1959.

Theragāthā Pāli : (Paramatthadīpanā) (Vol. II) Ācārya Dhammapāla, Ed., F.L. Woodward, Pub., For Pāli Text Society By Lywzaka & Co., London, 1959.

Theragāthā Pāli : (Tripiṭaka) (Khuddaka Nikāya, Vol. II), Bhikṣu Jagadīśa Kāśyapa, Pub., Pāli Prakāśana Maṇḍala, Navanālandā Mahāvihāra, Nalanda, Bihar, 1959.

Theragātha : (Hindi Tr.) Tr. Bhikṣu Dharmaratna, Pub., Mahābodhi Sabhā, Sāranātha, Benaras, 1959.

Therīgāthā Aṭṭhakathā : (Paramatthadīpanī) Ācārya Dhammapāla, Ed., E. Müllar, Pub., Pāli Text Society, London, 1893.

Therīgāthā Pāli : (Tripiṭaka) (Khuddaka Nikāya, Vol. II), Ed., Bhikṣu Jagadīśa Kāsyapa, Pub., Pāli Prakāśana, Navanālandā Mahāvihāra, Nalanda, Bihar, 1959.

Therigāthā : (Hindi Tr.) Tr., Bharat Singh Upādhyāya, Pub., Sastā Sāhitya Maṇḍala Prakāśana, Delhi, 1950.

Divyavadāna : (Baudhā Sanskrit Granthāvali-20) Ed., Dr. P.L. Vaidya, Pub., Mithila Vidyāpīṭha, Darbhanga, 1960.

Dīghanikāya Aṭṭhakathā : (Sumaṅgalavilāsinī) (Vol. III), Ācārya Buddhaghoṣa, Pub., Pāli Text Society, London, 1886-1932.

Dīgha Nikāya Pāli : (Tripiṭaka) (Vol. III) Ed., Bhikṣu Jagadīśa Kāśyapa, Pub., Pāli Prakāśana Maṇḍala, Navanālandā Mahāvihāra, Bihar, 1958.

Dīgha Nikāya : (Hindi Tr.) Tr. Rāhula Sāṅkṛtyāyana, Pub., Mahābodhi Sabhā, Sāranātha, Benāras, 1936.

Dīpavaṁsa : (Cīlonī Pāli Text) Ed. & Tr. Oldenberg, Pub., Williams and Norget, London, 1879.

Dhammapada Aṭṭhakathā : (Vol. V) Ācārya Buddhaghoṣa, Ed. H.C. Norman, Pub. Pāli Text Society, London, 1906-1915.

Dhammapada Pāli : (Ed., Bhikṣu Jagadīśa Kāśyapa, Pub., Pāli Prakāśana Maṇḍala, Navanālandā Mahāvihāra, Nalanda, Bihar, 1959.

Dhammapada : (Stories & Hindi Tr.) (II Edition) Tr., Tripiṭakācārya, Bhikṣu Dharmarakṣita, Master Khelāḍīlāla & Sons, Sanskrit Book Depot, Kacoḍī Galī, Vāranasī-1, 1959.

Peṭāvatthu Aṭṭhakathā : Ed., E. Hardy, Pub., Pāli Text Society, London, 1901.

Buddhacarita : (Along with Hindi Tr.) (II Volumes) Aśvaghoṣa, Ed. and Tr., Sūryanārāyaṇa Chaudharī, Pub., Sanskrit Bhavana, Kaṭhautiya, Distt. Purniya, Bihar, 1943-1953.

Bhagavān Buddhanā Pacāsa Dharma Saṁvādo (Majjhim Nikāya) : (Gujarati) Tr., Dharmānanda Kauśāmbī, Pub., Gujarāta Vidyā Pīṭha, Ahmedabad, 1951.

Mañjuśrī Mūlakalpa : (Baudha Sanskrit Text) Ed., T. Gaṇapati Śāstrī, Pub., Trivendram Sanskrit Series, Trivendram, 1927.

Majjhima Nikāya Aṭṭhakathā : (Papañcasadanī) (V Volumes) Ācārya Buddhaghoṣa, Ed., I. B. Harner, Pub., For Pāli Text Society By Oxford University Press, 1922-1938.

Majjhima Nikāya Pāli : (Tripiṭaka) (III Volumes) Ed., Bhiskṣu Jagadīśa Kāśyapa, Pub., Pāli Prakāśana Maṇḍala, Navanālandā Mahāvihāra, Bihar, 1958.

Majjhima Nikāya : (Hindi Tr.) Tr. Rāhula Saṅkṛtyāyana, Pub., Mahābodhi Sabhā, Sāranātha, Benaras, 1933.

Mahāyāna Sūtra Saṅgraha : (Baudha Sanskrit Granthāvali-17) Ed. Dr. P.L. Vaidya, Pub., Mithilā Vidyāpīṭha, Darbhanga, 1961.

Mahāvaṁsa : (Silonī Pāli Text) Ed., Gaigar, Pub., Pāli Text Society, London, 1912.

Mahāvaṁsa : (Hindi Tr.) Tr. Bhadanta Ānanda Kauśalyāyana, Pub., Hindi Sāhitya Sammelana, Prayāga, 1956.

Mahāvastu : (Baudha Sanskrit Text) (III Vol.) Ed. Senārta, Peris, 1882-1897.

Milinda Pañho : (Pāli) Ed., R.D. Vaḍekara, Pub., Bombay University, Bombay, 1940.

Milinda Praśna : (Hindi Tr.) Tr. Bhadanta Ānanda Kauślyāyana, Pub.

Vinayapiṭaka Aṭṭhakathā : (Samantapāsādikā) (VII Vol.) Ācārya Buddhaghoṣa, Ed., J. Takakusu, Makoṭo Nagai, Pub., Pāli Text Society, London, 1947.

Vinayapiṭaka Aṭṭhakathā : (Samantapāsādikā) (II Vol.) Pub., & Ed., Dr. Nathamala Ṭāṇṭiyā, Ed., Bīrbala Śarmā, Pub., Navanālandā Mahāvīhara, Nalanda, Bihar, 1965.

Vinayapiṭaka Pāli : (Tripiṭaka) (V Vol.) Ed., Bhikṣu Jagadīśa Kāśyapa, Pub., Pāli Prakāśana Maṇḍala, Navanālandā Mahāvihāra, Nalanda, Bihar, 1956.

Vinayapiṭaka : Tr., Rāhula Sāṅkṛtyāyana, Pub., Mahābodhi Sabhā, Sāranātha, Benaras, 1935.

Lalitavistara : (Baudha Sanskrit Granthāvali-1) Ed. Dr. P.L. Vaidya, Pub., Mithilā Vidyāpīṭha, Darbhanga, 1958.

Saṁyuttanikāya Aṭṭhakathā : (Ācārya Buddhaghoṣa) Ed. F.L. Woodward, Pub., Pāli Text Society, London, 1929-1937.

Saṁyuttanikāya Pāli : (Tripiṭaka, IV Volumes), Ed., Bhikṣu Jagadīśa Kāśyapa, Pub., Pāli Prakāśana Maṇḍala, Navanālandā Mahāvihāra, Nalanda, Bihar, 1959.

Saṁyuttanikāya : (Hindi Tr.) (Vol. I, II) Tr., Bhikṣu Jagadīśa Kāśyapa, Tripiṭakācārya Bhikṣu Dharma Rakṣita, Pub., Mahābodhi Sabhā, Saranatha, Benaras, 1954.

Saddharmapuṇḍarīka Sūtraṃ : (Baudha Sanskrit Granthāvali-6), Ed., Dr. P.L. Vaidya, Pub., Mithilā Vidyāpīṭha, Darbhanga, 1961.

Suttanipāta Aṭṭhakathā : (Paramatthajotikā) (Vol. II) Ācārya Buddhaghoṣa, Pub., Pāli Text Society, London, 1961-1918.

Suttanipāta Pāli : (Tripiṭaka, Khuddakanikāya, Vol. I) Ed., Bhkṣu Jagadīśa Kāśyapa, Pub., Pāli Prakāśana Maṇḍala, Navanālandā Mahāvihāra, Nalanda, Bihar, 1959.

Suttanipāta : (Hindi Tr.) Tr., Bhikṣu Dharmaratna, Pub., Mahābodhi Sabhā, Saranatha, Benaras, 1960.

The Book of Discipline (Eng. Tr. of Vinaya Piṭaka) (5 Vols.) : Tr. by I.B. Horner, Pub., for Pāli Text Society by Luzac & Co., London (Second edition), 1949-52.

The Book of Gradual Sayings (Eng. Tr. of Aṅguttara Nikāya) (Vols. I, II & V) Tr. by F.L. Woodward (Vols. III- IV), Tr. by E.M. Hare, Pub., for Pali Text Society by Luzac & Co., London (Second edition), 1951-55.

The Book of Kindred Sayings (Eng. Tr. of Saṁyutta Nikāya) (Vols. I & II) Tr. by Mrs. Rhys Davids; (Vols. III, IV & V), Tr., by F.L. Woodward, Pub., for Pāli Text Society by Luzac & Co., London (Second edition), 1950-56.

Buddhism in Translation : (Eng. Tr. of selected chapters of Buddhist scriptures), Tr., by Henry Clarke Warren, Ed., by Charles Rockwel Leumann, Pub., Harward Oriental Series, Cambridge Mass, Harward University, 1953.

Buddhist Legends : (Eng. Tr. of Dhammapada-Aṭṭahakathā) (3 Vols.), Tr, by E.W. Burlinghame, Pub., Hardward Oriental Series, Cambridge Massachusetts Hardward University, 1921.

Buddhist Mahāyāna Texts : (Eng. Tr. of Amitayrudhyana Sutra & other Mahāyāna Sūtras), Tr. by F. Max Müller & J. Takakusu, Pub., Sacred Books of the East Series, Vol. XLX, Part II, Oxford, 1894.

Buddhist Suttas : (Eng. Tr. of seven important Buddhist suttas), Tr. by T.W. Rhys Davids, Pub. Sacred Books of the East Series, Vol, XI, Oxford, 1900.

Dhammapada (Eng. Tr.) Tr. by F. Max Müller, Sacred Books of the East Series, Vol. X, Part I, Oxford, 1881.

Dhammapada : (With Accompanying Narratives) (Tran. from the Chinese), Tr. by Samual Beal, Pub., Susil Gupta (India) Ltd., Calcutta-12, (Second edition), 1952.

Dialogues of the Buddha : (Eng. Tr. of Dīgha Nikāya (3 Vols), Tr. by T.T. Rhys Davids & C.A.F. Rhys Davids, Pub., *Sacred Books of the Buddhists Series*, Vol. II to IV, Oxford, London, 1899-1921.

Dipavaṁsa : (Eng. Tr. with Pāli Text), Ed. & Tr. by H. Oldenberg, London & Edinburgh, 1879.

Further Dialogues of the Buddha : (Eng. Tr. of Majjhimanikāya) (2 Vols.), Tr. by Lord Chalmers, Pub., Sacred Books of the Buddhists Series, Vol. V, VI, London, 1926-1927.

Jātaka : (Eng. Trans.) (7 Vols) Tr. under the Editorship of E.B. Cowell, Cambridge, 1895-913.

Mahāvaṁśa : (Eng. Trans.) Tr. by W. Geger, assised by Mabel Haynes Bode, Pub. Pāli Text Society, London, 1912.

Mahāvastu : (Eng. Trans.) (3 Vols.) Tr. by J.J. Jones, Pub. Sacred Books of the Buddhists Series, Vol. XXVII, Luzac & Co., London, 1952-1956.

Psalms of Brethern : (Eng. Trans. of Therigāthā) Tr. by Mrs. Rhys Davids, London, 1913.

Psalms of Sisters : (Eng. Trans. of Therigāthā) Tr. by Mrs. Rhys Davids, London, 1909.

The Questions of King Milinda : (Eng. Tr. of Milindapañho) Tr. by T.W. Rhys Davids, Pub. Sacred Books of the East Series, Vol. XXXV, XXXVI, Oxford, 1890-94.

Sutta Nipāta : (Eng. Trans.) Tr. by V. Fausboll, Pub. Sacred Books of the East Series, Vol. X, Part II, Oxford, 1890.

Verses of Uplift : (Eng. Tr. of Udana) Tr. by F.L. Woodward, Pub. Sacred Books of the Buddhists Series, London, 1935.

Vinaya Texts : (Eng. Tr. of Vinaya Piṭaka) (3 Vols.) Tr. by T.W. Rhys Davids and H. Oldenberg, Pub. Sacred Books of the East Series, Vols. XIII, XVII & XX, Oxford, 1881-1885.

Other Literatures

Ajātaśatru : (21st Ed.) Jaiśaṅkara Prasāda, Pub., Bhāratī Bhaṇḍāra, Leader Press, Allahabad, 1965.

Anuttaropapātika Daśā : Eka Adhyayana : Pt. Becaradāsa Dośī, Ed., Vijayamuni Śāstrī, Pub., Sanmati Jñānapīṭha, Agra.

Abhidhāna Cintāmaṇī Nāmamālā : (Alongwith Svopajñavṛtti) Ācārya Hemacandra, Ed., Vijayadharma Sūri, Pub., Yaśovijaya Jain Granthamālā, Benaras and Bhavanagar, 1915.

Abhidhāna Rājendra : (7 Volumes) Ācārya Vijaya Rājendra Sūri, Ratlam, 1913-34.

Asoka : Yadunandana Kapūra, Agra, 1962.

Asoka Ke Dharmalekha : (Text & Tr.) Janārdana Bhaṭṭa, Allahabad.

Asoka Ke Dharmalekha : Ed., Janārdana Bhaṭṭa, Pub., Publication Division, Ministry of Information and Broadcasting, Old Secretariate, Delhi, 1957.

Aṣṭādhyāyī : Pāṇinī.

Ahiṁsā Paryāvekṣaṇa : Muni Śrī Nāgarājajī, Pub., Sahityaniketana, Delhi, 1961.

Āgamayuga Kā Jaina Darśana : Dalasukha Mālavāṇīya, Pub., Sanmati Jñānapīṭha, Agra, 1956.

Ācārya Buddhaghoṣa : Bhikṣu Dharmarakṣita, Pub., Mahābodhi Sabhā, Saranatha, Varanasi, 1956.

Ādarśa Budha Mahitaeṅ : Kumārī Vidyāvatī "Malavikā", Pub., Bhāratiya Mahābodhi Sabhā, Saranatha, Benaras, 1956.

Ārya Saṁskṛti Ke Mūlādhāra : Ācārya Baladeva Upādhyāya, Pub., Śāradā Mandira, Benaras, 1947.

Uttaraparadeśa men Baudha Dharma kā Vikāsa : Dr. Nalinākṣadatta and Kṛṣṇadatta Vājapeyī, Pub., Publication Bureau of the Govt. of Uttarapradeśa, Luckhnow, 1956.

Uttara Hindustāna men Jaina Dharma : (Gujarāti Translation) Author & Tr.,

Cimanlāla Jecanda Śāha, Pub., Longmans Green & Co., London, 1937.

Kathā Saritsāgara : Somadeva, Tr., Kedāranātha Śarmā 'Sārasvata' Pub., Bihar Rāṣṭrabhāṣā Pariṣad, Patna, 1960.

Gupta Sāmrājya kā Itihāsa : Upādhyāya Dr. Vasudeva, Pub., Indian Press Ltd., Allahabad, 1952.

Cāra Tīrthaṅkara : Pt. Sukhalālajī, Pub., Jain Saṁskṛti Saṁśodhana Maṇḍala, Benaras, 1954.

Jain Sāhitya aura Itihāsa : Premī Nāthurāma, Pub., Hindī Grantha-ratnākara Kāryālaya, Bombay, 1958.

Jain Siddhānta Dīpikā : Ācārya Śrī Tulasī, Pub., Ādarśa Sāhitya Saṅgha, Churu, 1952.

Jaināgama Śabada Saṅgraha : (Gujarātī) Śatāvadhānī Pt. Muni Śrī Ratnacandrajī, Pub., Saṅghavī Gulāb Canda Jasarāja, Śrī Līmadī (Kathiawada), 1926.

Tattvasamuccaya : Dr. Hīrālāla Jain, Pub., Bharata Jain Mahāmaṇḍala, Vardha, 1952.

Tīrthaṅkara Mahāvīra : (Vol. II) Ācārya Vijayendra Sūri, Pub., Kaśīānātha Sarāfa, Yaśodharma Mandira, Bombay, 1960.

Tīrthaṅkara Vardhamāna : Śrīcanda Rāmpuriyā, Pub., Hamīramala Pūnamacanda Rāmapuriyā, Calcutta, 1953.

Darśana aura Cintana : Pt. Sukhalālajī, Pub., Pt. Sukhalālajī Sammāna Samiti, Ahmedabad, 1957.

Darśana Didarśana : (III Edition) Rāhula Sāṅkṛtyāyana, Pub., Kitāba Mahal, Allahabada, 1961.

Dharma aura Darśana : Dr. Baladeva Upādhyāya, M.A., Sāhityācarya, Pub., Śāradā Mandira, Banaras, 1945.

Narakesarī : (Gujarātī) Jayabhikkhu, Pub., Jīvanamaṇī Sadvacanamālā Trust Ahmedabad, 1962.

Pāiasaddamahaṇṇavo : Pt. Haragovindadāsa Trivikramacanda Śeṭha, Ed. Dr. Vāsudevaśaraṇa Agravāla, Pt., Dalasukhabhāī Mālavāniyā, Pub., Prākṛta Grantha Pariṣad, Varanasi, 5, 1963.

Pāṇinikālīna Bhāratavarṣa : Dr. Vāsudeva Śaraṇa Agravāla, Pub., Motilal Banarasidasa, Benaras, 1956.

Pātañjala Yogadarśana : (III Edition) Maharṣi Patañjali, Pub., Gītā Press, Gorakhpur, 1956.

Pārśvanātha kā Caturyāma Dharma : Dharmānanda Kośāmbī, Tr., Śrīpāda Jośī, Pub., Hemacandra Modī Pustakamālā Trust, Bombay, 1957.

Pāli Sāhitya kā Itihāsa : (II Edition) Bharat Singh Upādhyāya, Pub., Hindi Sāhitya Sammelan, Prayag, 1963.

Praśnottara Tattvabodha : Śrīmajjayācārya, Pub., Osvāla Press, Calcutta.

Praśnopaniṣad : (VI Edition) Śāṅkarabhāṣya, Pub., Gītā Press, Gorakhpur, 1953.

Prākṛta Bhāṣāon kā Vyākaraṇa : Dr. Richard Pischal, Tr. Dr. Hemacandra Joshi, Pub., Bihāra Rāṣṭra Bhāṣa Pariṣad, Patna, 1960.

Prākṛta Sāhitya kā Itihāsa : Dr. Jagadīśacandra Jain, Pub., Chowkhambā Vidyā Bhavana, Vārāṇasī, 1961.

Prācīna Bhārata : Gaṅgā Prasāda Mehta.

Prācīna Bhārata : C.M. Śrīnivāsacārī Rāmasvāmī Āyaṅgara, Allahabad, 1950.

Prācīna Bhārata Kā Itihāsa : (III Edition) Dr. Ramāsaṅkara Tripāṭhī, Pub., Motilal Banarsidass, Delhi, 1962.

Prācīna Bhāratavarṣa : Dr. Tribhuvanadāsa Leharacanda Sāha, Pub., Śaśikānta & Co., Baroda, 1935-36.

Buddha aura Baudha Sādhaka : Bharata Singh Upādhyāya, Pub., Sastā Sāhitya Maṇḍala Prakāśana, Delhi, 1950.

Buddhakālīna Bhāratīya Bhūgola : Dr. Bharata Singh Upādhyāya, Pub., Hindi Sāhitya Sammelana, Prayag, 1962.

Buddha Carita : Dharmānanda Kośāmbī, Pub., Navajīvana Kāryālaya, Ahmedabad, 1937.

Buddha Caryā : Rāhula Sāṅkṛtyāyana, Pub., Śivadāsa Gupta Sevā Upavana, Kāśī, 1932.

Buddhapūrva Bhārata kā Itihāsa : Dr. Śyāmabihārī Miśra & Śukarājabihārī Miśra, Pub., Hindi Sāhitya Sammelana, Prayag.

Buddhalīlā : (IV Edition) Dharmānanda Kośāmbī, Pub., Gujarāta Vidyāpīṭha, Ahmedabada, 1956.

Bṛhatkathākośa : Ācārya Hariṣeṇa, Ed., Dr. A.N. Upādhye, Pub., Siṅghī Jain Granthamālā, Bombay, 1943.

Bṛhatkathāmañjarī : Kṣemendra.

Baudhakālīna Bhārata : Janārdana Bhaṭṭa, Pub., Sāhitya Ratnamālā Kāryālaya, Kāśī, 1926.

Baudha Dharma ke 2500 Varṣa : (Annual Issue of 'Ājakala') Publications Division, Old Secretariat, Delhi, 1960.

Baudha Dharma ke Vikāsa Kā Itihāsa : Dr. Govindacandra Pandeya, Pub., Hindi Samiti Information Division, U.P., Luckhnow, 1963.

Baudha Dharma Darśana : Ācārya Narendradeva, Pub., Bihāra Rāṣṭra Bhāṣā Pariṣad, Patnā, 1956.

Baudha Parva : (Marāṭhī work).

Baudha Saṅghano Paricaya : Dharmānanda Kośāmbī, Pub., Gujarāti Purātattva Mandira, Ahmedabad, 1925.

Baudha Sāhitya kī Sāṁskṛtika Jhalaka : Parśurāma Caturvedi, Pub., Sāhitya Bhavana (Pvt.) Ltd., Allahabad, 1958.

Brahmāṇḍapurāṇa : Pub., Nandalāla Mora, Clive Row, Calcutta.

Bhagavāna Buddha : Dharmānanda Kośāmbī, Pub., Sāhitya Academy, Rājakamala Publications, Bombay, 1956.

Bhagavān Pārśvanātha kī Paramparā kā Itihāsa : Muni Śrī Jñānasundarajī, Pub., Ratna Prabhākara Jñāna Puṣpamālā, 1943.

Bhagavāna Mahāvīra aura Mahātmā Buddha : Kāmata Prasāda Jain, Pub., Mūlacanda Kiśanadāsa Paḍiyā, Jain Vijaya Printing Press, Surat, 1926.

Bhārata-mukti : (Hindi Poem) Poet Ācārya Śrī Tulasī, Ed., Muni Śrī Sāgaramalajī Śramaṇa, Muni Śrī Mahendra Kumārajī I, Pub., Atmārāma & Sons, Delhi, 1963.

Bhāgavata Purāṇa : Pub., Gītā Press, Gorakhpur.

Bhārata kā Bṛhad Itihāsa : (IV Edition) Śrī Netra Pānde.

Bhārata ke Prācīna Rājavaṁśa : Mahāmahopādhyāya Pt. Viśveśvaranātha Rau, Pt. Nāthūrāma 'Premī,' Hindi Grantha Ratnākara Kāryālaya, Bombay, 1927.

Bhāratīya Itihāsa Eka Dṛṣṭi : Dr. Jyotiprasāda Jain, Pub., Bhāratīya Jñānpīṭha, Banaras, 1957.

Bhāratīya Itihāsa kī Bhūmikā : Dr. Rājabalī Pāṇḍe, Pub., Malhotra Brothers, Delhi, 1949.

Bhāratīya Prācīna Lipimālā : Rāyabahādur Paṇḍita Gaurīśaṅkar Hīrācand Ojhā, Pub., Rajpūtānā Museum, Ajmer, 1918.

Bhāratīya Saṁskṛti aura Usakā Itihāsa : Dr. Satyāketu Vidyālaṅkāra.

Bhāva Bhāskara Kāvyam : Muni Śrī Dhanarājajī Pub., Atmārāma & Sons, Delhi, 1961.

Bharamavidhaṁsanam : Jayācārya, Pub., Osvāla Press, Calcutta, 1923.

Matsya Purāṇa : Pub., Nandalāla Mora, 5 Clive Ro, Calcutta, 1958.

Mahābhāṣya : Maharṣi Patañjalī, Ed., Bhārgava Śāstrī, Pub., Nirṇayasāgara Press, Bombay, 1951.

Mahāvīra Kathā : (Gujarāti) Gopāladāsa Jivābhāī Paṭel, Pub., Gujarāta Vidyāpīṭha, Ahmedabad, 1941.

Mṛcchakaṭika : Śūdraka, Ed. Goḍabole, Pub. Bombay Sanskrit Series, No. 52, Bombay, 1896.

Vāyu Purāṇa : Pub., Mansukharāya Mora, 5 Clive Row, Calcutta, 1959.

Viṣṇu Purāna : Pub. Gītā Press, Gorakhpur.

Vīranirvāṇa Saṁvat aura Jain Kālagaṇanā : Muni Kalayāṇavijayajī, Pub., Śāstra Samiti, Jalaur (Marwar), 1920.

Vaijayantikoṣa : Ed. Gustaf Opert (?), Madras, 1893.

Vaiśālī : Vijayendra Sūrī, Pub., Yaśodharma Mundira, Bombay, 1958.

Śāntasudhārasa Bhāvanā : Ācārya Vinayavijayajī, Pub., Jain Dharma Prasāraka Sabhā, Bhāvanagar, 1937.

Śramaṇa Bhagavān Mahāvīra : Muni Kalyāṇavijayajī, Pub., Śāstra Saṅgraha Samiti, Jalaur (Marwar), 1941.

Svapnavāsavadatta : (Sanskrit Drama) Bhāsa, Ed., T. Gaṇapati Śāstrī, Trivendram, 1913.

Hindu Sabhyatā : Dr. Rādhākumuda Mukarjī, Tr. Dr. Vāsudeva Śaraṇa Agravāla, Pub., Rajkamal Publication, Bombay, 1955.

Ancient Coins & Measures of Ceylon : Rhys Davids.

Age of Nandas and Mauryas : Ed. K.A. Nīkaṇṭha Śāstri, Pub., Motilal Banarsidass, Benaras, 1952.

The Age of Imperial Unity : (*The History and Culture of Indian People*, Vol. II) Ed. Radhakumud Mukherjee, Pub., Bhāratīya Vidyā Bhavan, Bombay, 1960.

An Advanced History of India : R.C. Majumdar, H.C. Ray Chaudhuri, K.K. Dutta, Pub., Macmillan & Co., London, 2nd Edition, 1950.

Ancient India : E.J. Rapson, 1922.

Ancient Indian Historical Tradition : E.J. Pargiter, Pub., Motilal Banarsidass, Delhi. (New Edition), 1962.

Archaeological Survey of Western India : Bühler.

Asoka : D.R. Bhandarkar, Pub. S. Chand & Co., Delhi, 1923.

Asoka : Vincent A. Smith, Ed. Sir William Wilson Hunter, Pub., S. Chand & Co., Delhi, (Inidan reprint of Second Edition), 1959.

Buddha : *His Life, His Teachings, His Order* : Manmath Nath Shastri, Pub., Society for the Resuscitation of Indian Literature, Calcutta (Second edition), 1910.

Buddhism : T.W. Rhys Davids, Pub., Home University Library, London, 1912.

Buddhist India : T.W. Rhys Davids, Pub., T. Fisher Unwin, London, 1903.

The Cambridge History of India : Ed. E.J. Rapson, Pub., Cambridge University Press, 1921, Indian Reprint, Pub., S. Chand & Co., Delhi, 1955.

Chandragupta Maurya and His Times : Dr. Radha Kumud Mukharjee, Pub. Rajkamal Publications, Bombay, 1952.

Chronological Problems : Dr. Shantilal Shah, Pub., The Author, Bonn, Germany, 1934.

Chronology of Ancient India : Dr. Sita Nath Pradhan, Calcutta, 1927.

Corporate Life in Ancient India : Dr. R.C. Majumdar, Calcutta, 1918.

Corpus Inscriptionum Indicarum : (Vol. III) I. F. Fleet, Calcutta, 1888.

Der Buddhismus : Prof. Kern Pub., O. Schulge, Leipzig, 1883.

Dictionary of Pāli Proper Names : (2 Vols.) Dr. G.P. Malala Sekera, Pub., Pāli Text Society, London, 1960.

Early Buddhist Monarchism : S.K. Dutta.

Early History of India : Dr. Vincent A. Smith, Oxford, 4th Edition, 1924.

Encyclopaedia of Buddhism : Dr. G.P. Malala Sekera, Pub., Govt. of Ceylon, 1963.

Encyclopaedia of Religion and Ethics : Ed. Hasting, Edinburgh, 1908-1926.
Epitome of Jainism : Purana Chandra Nahar and Krishna Chandra Ghosh, Pub. Gulab Kumari Library, Calcutta, 1919.
Gautam the Man : Mrs. Rhys Davids, Pub., Luzac & Co., London.
Grammatik Der Prakrit Sprachan : Richard Pischel, Strassburg, 1900.
Hindu Polity : Dr. K.P. Jayaswal, Pub. Bangalore Printing and Publishing Co., Bangalore, 1955.
Hindus : Ward.
The History and Doctrines of the Ajivakas : Dr. A.L. Basham, Pub., Luzac & Co., London. 1957.
History of Buddhism in India : Tarnath, Tr. into German by A. Schiefner, St. Petersburg, 1869.
History of Buddhist Thought : Edward J. Thomas, London, 1933.
Indiche Paeleographic Bühler.
Indological Studies : B.C. Law, Vol. I & II, Pub., Indian Research Institute, Calcutta, 1950-52; Vol. III, Pub., Ganga Nath Jha Research Institute, Allahabad, 1954.
Inscriptions of Aśoka : Hultsch.
The Jinist Studies : Dr. Otto Stein, Ed. Jina Vijaya Muni with the Co-operation of Dr. A.S. Gopani, Pub., Jain Sāhitya Saṁśodhaka Pratiṣṭhāna, Ahmedabad, 1948.
Life and Work of Buddhaghosha : B.C. Law, Pub., Thacker Spink & Co., Calcutta & Simla, 1923.
Life of Buddha & Early History of His Order : (Described from Tibetan Works) Tr. W. Woodvillae Rockhill, Pub., Trubner's Oriental Series, London, 1907.
Life of Buddha : E.J. Thomas, Pub., Routledge & Kegen Paul Private Ltd., London, 1956.
Life or Legend of Gautama : P. Bigandet, 4th Edition, 1911.
Miscellaneous Essays : C.T. Colebrooke, London, 1873.
Outline of Jain Philosophy : J.L. Jaini, Pub., Cambridge Univeristy Press, 1916.
Oxford History of India : V.A. Smith, Oxford.
The Political History of Ancient India : H.C. Raichudhuri, Pub., Calcutta University, 6th Edition, 1953.
The Practical Sanskrit English Dictionary : (3 Vols.) Prin. V.S. Apte, Ed. P.K. Gode & C.G. Curve, Pub., Prasad Prakashan, Poona, 1957.
Praśnopaniṣad : Tr. F. Max Müller, Pub., Sacred Books of the East Series, Vol. XV, Oxford.
Pre-Buddhistic Indian Philosophy : B.M. Barua, Calcutta.
The Pūraṇa Text of the Dynasties of the Kali-Age : F.E. Pargiter, Oxford University Press, 1913.

The Religion of India : E.W. Hopkins, Pub., Grinn & Co., Boston, U.S.A. 1895 (*Hand Books on the History of Religions,* Vol. I, Ed. Morris Jestrow).
Śākya : Mrs. Rhys Davids.
Studies in Jainism : Dr. Hermann Jacobi, Ed. Jina Vijaya Muni, Pub. Jain Sāhitya Saṁśodhaka Kāryālaya, Ahmedabad, 1946.
Studies in the Origins of Buddhism : G.C. Pande.
Studies in Mañjuśrīmūlakalpa : Dr. K.P. Jayaswal.
Synchronismes Chinois : Tchang.

Journal, Magazines, Commemoration Volumes etc.

Anekānta : (Bi-monthly), Pub., Vīrasena Maṇḍala, Delhi.
Ācārya Śrī Tulsī Abhinandana Grantha : Pub., Ācārya Śrī Tulsī Dhavala Samāroha Samiti, Delhi, 1962.
Jain Bhāratī : (Weekly) Pub., Jain Śvetāmbara, Terāpanthī Mahāsabhā, Calcutta.
Jain Satyaprakāśa : Magazine.
Prabuddha Karnāṭaka : (Kannaḍa Tri-monthly).
Bhāratiya Vidyā : (Research Journal) Pub., Bhāratiya Vidyā Bhavana, Bombay.
Bhikṣu Smṛti Grantha : Pub., Jain Śvetāmbara Terāpanthī, Mahāsabhā, Calcutta, 1962.
Vīra : (Fortnighty) Pub., Akhila Bhāratīya Digambara Jain Pariṣad, Delhi.
Śramaṇa : (Monthly) Pub., Pārśvanātha Vidyāśrama, Varanasi.
Hindustāna : (Daily), Delhi.
B.C. Law Commemoration Volume, Calcutta. 1945.
Indian Antiquary, Bombay.
Indian Epheminis.
Indian Historical Quarterly, Calcutta.
Journal of Asiatic Society, Baptist Mission, Calcutta.
Journal of Bihar & Orissa Research Society, Patna, Bihar.
Journal of Pāli Text Society, London.
Journal of Royal Asiatic Society, Bengal.
Journal of Royal Asiatic Society, Great Britain : Pub., Trubner & Co., London.
Mahāvīra Commomeration Volume : (Vol. I) Pub., Mahāvīra Jaina Society, Agra, 1948-49.
Leitschrift der Dautschen Morgenlaudischan Gesellschaft.

LITERARY GEMS BY THE SAME AUTHOR

Hindi

Āgama aura Tripiṭaka : Eka Anuśīlana. Volumes I & II.

Matimādhurya.
Ahiṁsā Viveka.
Nayā Yuga : Nayā Darśana.
Naitika Vijñāna.
Ahiṁsā Paryāvekṣaṇa.
Jaināgama : Digdarśana.
Jaina Darśana aura Ādhunika Vijñāna.
Aṇuvrata Jīvana-darśana.
Ahiṁsā ke Āñcala men.
Ācārya Bhikṣu aura Mahātmā Gāndhī.
Aṇu se pūrṇa kī Ora.
Aṇuvrat Vicāra.
Navīna Samāja Vyavasthā men Dāna aura Dayā.
Ācārya Tulsī : Eka Adhyayana.
Prerṇā Dīpa.
Sarvadharma Sadbhāva.
Terāpantha Digdarśana.
Aṇuvrata Krānti ke Baḍhate Carṇa.
Aṇuvrat-āndolana aura Vidyārthī-varga.
Aṇuvrata Digdarśana.
Aṇuvrata Āndolana.
Aṇuvrata Dṛṣṭi.
Yugapravartaka Bhagvān Mahāvīra.
Yugadharma Terāpantha.
Bāla-dīkṣā : Eka Vivecana.
Maryādā Mahotsava : Itihāsa aura Paricaya.
Mahāvīra aura Buddha kī Samasāmayikata
Mañjila kī Ora.
Terāpantha Śāsana-praṇālī.
Satya Mañjila : Samīkṣā Rāha.
Mana ke Dvandva : Śabdon kī Kārā.
Yathārtha ke Paripārśva men.

Saṁskṛta

Bhikṣu Caritram.
Mātherāna Suṣamā.
Bhakteruktayaḥ.
Āśu Kāvyāni.
Nīti Nīlotpalāni.
Lalitāṅga Caritram.

English

Āgama aura Tripiṭaka : Eka Anuśīlana-Vol. I.
New Age : A New Outlook.
Aṇuvrata Ideology.
Light of Inspiration.
Jain Philosophy & Modern Science.
Studies of Aṇuvrata Movement.
Pity and Charity in the New Pattern of Society.
A Pen-Sketch of Ācārya Tulasī.
Glimps of Aṇuvrata.
Glimps of Terāpantha.
Contemporaniety and Chronology of Mahāvīra and Buddha.
Theory of Relativity and Syādvāda.
King Bimbisāra and King Ajātaśatru in the age of Mahāvīra & Buddha.

INDEX